The User's Guide to College Writing

Reading, Analyzing, and Writing

Second Edition

Nancy M. Kreml
Diane Rose Carr
Douglas Capps
Janice Jake
Sharon May

Midlands Technical College

PEARSON

Longman

New York   San Francisco   Boston
London   Toronto   Sydney   Tokyo   Singapore   Madrid
Mexico City   Munich   Paris   Cape Town   Hong Kong   Montreal

VICE PRESIDENT/EDITOR-IN-CHIEF	Joseph P. Terry
SENIOR ACQUISITIONS EDITOR	Steven Rigolosi
DEVELOPMENT EDITOR	Anne Brunell Ehrenworth
SENIOR SUPPLEMENTS EDITOR	Donna Campion
MEDIA SUPPLEMENTS EDITOR	Nancy Garcia
SENIOR MARKETING MANAGER	Melanie Craig
PRODUCTION MANAGER	Eric Jorgensen
PROJECT COORDINATION, TEXT DESIGN, AND ELECTRONIC PAGE MAKEUP	Pre-Press Company, Inc.
COVER DESIGN MANAGER	Nancy Danahy
COVER ILLUSTRATION/PHOTO:	Vasily Kandinsky (1866–1944/Russian), *Variierte Rechtecke* 1929, india ink and paper. © Christie's Images/Superstock
MANUFACTURING BUYER	Lucy Hebard
PRINTER AND BINDER	RR Donnelley & Sons Company
COVER PRINTER	Coral Graphic Services

For permission to use copyrighted material, grateful acknowledgment is made to the copyright holders on pp. 565–567, which are hereby made part of this copyright page.

Library of Congress Cataloging-in-Publication Data

The user's guide to college writing : reading, analyzing, and writing / Nancy M. Kreml . . . [et al.].— 2nd ed.
    p. cm.
  Includes bibliographical references and index.
  ISBN 0-321-10388-2
    1. English language—Rhetoric. 2. Report writing. I. Kreml, Nancy M.

PE1408.U68 2003
808'.042—dc21   2003043860

Please visit us at **http://www.ablongman.com**

1 2 3 4 5 6 7 8 9 10—DOH—06 05 04 03

Detailed Contents

6   Prewriting: Freewriting, Listing, Mapping, Questioning   99

7   Organizing the Material: Planning, Outlining, and Thinking About Audience   116

A brief overview of contents appears on the inside front cover.

A list of proofreading symbols appears on the inside back cover.

Rhetorical Contents

Definition

Poetry

Fiction

Preface

We first wrote *The User's Guide to College Writing* because we could not find a text that suited our needs. The five authors of this book have taught composition for a number of years. Most recently, we worked together in a large writing program that included a committee appointed to train adjunct faculty and to identify materials considered appropriate for our students. For many years, we struggled to find a rhetoric that addressed the needs of our students—a reader that was appropriate for adult learners in a composition course and a handbook that did not confuse students. We finally decided to write our own. Teachers and students who used our book responded with enthusiasm and with suggestions of their own, which we have incorporated in this edition. We hope that this book will help you fill those gaps you also may have identified and that it will help your students become successful academic writers.

Although the five of us do not subscribe to the same philosophical, theoretical, or pedagogical base, we all teach the same students. In writing *The User's Guide to College Writing: Reading, Analyzing, and Writing*, we have been governed by what we have found to be effective in teaching our students. This book represents the synthesis of what we've learned over the years about explaining the process and strategies of reading and writing to our students. Happily, the majority of these students succeeded in subsequent courses throughout their academic career, so we want to share the materials we've developed with our colleagues across the country.

NEW TO THIS EDITION

- Two new chapters on writing in the modes of exposition and argumentation
- A new chapter on writing about literature
- A new chapter on research, with guidance on writing papers using both MLA and APA documentation styles
- Additional assignments geared toward collaborative writing, as well as examples and guidelines for working in groups
- New material on writing for evaluation, designed to assist students in preparing portfolios, taking timed writing tests, and writing essay exams
- New readings that explore universal themes

FEATURES OF THE BOOK

Several key features distinguish *The User's Guide to College Writing: Reading, Analyzing, and Writing.*

Emphasis on Academic Writing and Reading

Some writing textbooks focus only on personal writing tasks, and many of these include readings that are used only as springboards for personal essays. These texts also tend to include writing assignments that do not appeal to adult learners and do not provide students with the thinking, reading, and writing skills necessary to succeed in subsequent college courses. We believe that the best way to prepare students for academic writing is to give them academic writing tasks designed for their reading and thinking levels and to move them from less difficult to more difficult academic writing tasks through the course of the academic term.

This is not to say that we do not value personal writing, but we have developed academic assignments that require students to both respond to the reading and incorporate their own ideas, opinions, experiences, and observations. With the skills related to personal writing and academic writing, students should be prepared to handle any writing task they encounter.

Flexible Options

We recognize that different instructors will use a variety of means for reaching the range of student needs that they encounter. We have organized the chapters in Part Two around the steps in the process of reading and writing, but in each chapter, we have incorporated much more than any writer could use in one paper. We provide various approaches and alternatives to each step to allow flexibility for instructors. We have also included separate chapters on approaches that may be used at the instructor's discretion: writing using research, writing about literature, writing in the traditional modes. In addition, we have threaded some necessary instruction throughout the book: using computers for writing and reading, expanding instruction for ESL students, and adapting assignments for collaborative work in groups or pairs. This material is indicated with

Collaboration

special icons. Instructors can choose to teach any or all of these options, allowing the book to be customized to the needs of any particular classroom.

In-depth Discussion of Each Step in the Writing Process

The User's Guide to College Writing: Reading, Analyzing, and Writing is written for students who do not have an innate sense of written English and therefore need very specific, concrete tools to work with. We have found that many of our inexperienced writers do not have the skills or confidence that would allow them to become creative and inspired writers. We believe that *The User's Guide* can teach these students the reading, writing, and thinking skills to help them become productive and successful.

One Central Reading in Part Two

Instead of introducing a new reading for each step in the process, which is the common organizing method for current rhetoric/readers, Part Two, "Using Essential Strategies for Writing Essays," focuses on one reading: Mark Mathabane's "My Father's Tribal Rule." This method allows students to see the entire process as it relates to one reading, making it easier to understand how the steps are related and how one moves from step to step. Also, using one reading keeps constant the skill level introduced in each chapter in Part Two.

Flexibility in Selecting Readings for Assignments

Because so many examples and so much instructional material is devoted to the reading used in Part Two, some instructors may prefer to use a different reading when assigning students writing tasks related to a reading. To that end, we have included in Part Five, "Essays and Readings," a wide range of readings appropriate for a variety of reading levels and writing assignments. Any of these readings can be assigned instead of Mathabane's "My Father's Tribal Rule." This flexibility helps instructors ensure that the student is working independently and not relying too heavily on material included in the textbook.

Unique Chapters

This book includes chapters that explain the critical thinking steps in writing that are often omitted in basic and freshman composition rhetorics. For example, "Analyzing the Assignment for an Essay," Chapter 5, and "Evaluating Your Prewriting," Chapter 7, explore two thinking steps that students rarely find explained in their textbooks. While we recognize that there are many ways to complete these activities successfully, we describe some of the techniques that our students have found helpful as they've begun their development as critical thinkers and writers.

We've also separated the revision and editing steps from the proofreading and formatting steps. Students often try to do all three activities as one step, and we find that they do little actual deep revision for content and organization.

Plentiful Examples of Student Writing

The User's Guide includes many examples of work in progress by student writers, giving realistic models to the students who will use the book. These examples include journal entries, reading responses, answers to questions, and many drafts of essays as they move through the writing process—from the very rough, early attempts to the finished final product. In addition, Chapter 20 includes several complete student essays written in response to the readings.

A Handbook that Emphasizes Error Correction

The handbook in this text is unique. We do not attempt to provide instruction and exercises on every point of grammar. Instead, we focus on the major errors that interfere with communication and often mark students as illiterate in college and in the workplace. In addition, instead of simply stating grammar rules, we have provided an explanation of each rule so that students can find and correct errors in their writing.

We also recognize that students who successfully complete their first composition have not completely mastered or internalized the skills of editing and proofreading. In fact, as students are given more difficult tasks and critical thinking assignments in subsequent courses, they often make many more grammar and usage errors because they are struggling to articulate more complex ideas. For these reasons, we have included instruction on keeping an editing log. By using this log, students learn their weaknesses in grammar and usage and have a means of reminding themselves of what they need to check when finishing a draft for submission and evaluation.

English as a Second Language Features

We have included instruction for students for whom English is a second language and have marked these sections with a special ESL icon. We have found that the same techniques for helping ESL students learn grammar and usage also work very well with those native English speakers who are not accustomed to communicating in standard written English. Therefore, we encourage you to consider using some of these techniques with all students, not just those traditionally considered ESL. Moreover, students who speak English as a second language can also assist in explaining complicated grammar and usage rules and applying those rules to writing. This peer assistance improves the confidence of ESL students, while improving the editing and proofreading skills of native speakers. In addition, these interactions provide ESL students opportunities for learning American idioms for both spoken and written English.

ESL

Integrated Coverage of Personal Writing and Collaboration

Rather than having separate chapters on word processing, writing personal essays, and collaboration, we have included relevant instruction on these skills where they best fit into the writing process. Chapter 2 gives an overview of these strategies, and icons throughout the text draw students' and instructors' attention to the relevant sections. We have also created boxes for computer tips as well as summary boxes for steps in the writing process. Each chapter begins with a list of the steps discussed in the previous chapter as well as those addressed in that chapter. This is designed to assist students in using the text as a reference book.

Plentiful Exercises

The User's Guide offers a wealth of exercises geared toward both individual and group work. These exercises appear throughout the book and are designed as material for discussion and in-class practices. They are designed to lead to a discussion of the options available to readers and writers, as well as a discussion of the ways to evaluate the effectiveness of a piece of writing. Finally, the exercises encourage students to apply these exercises to their own writing.

ORGANIZATION: HOW TO USE THIS BOOK

Consider this book a well-stocked filing cabinet of materials for teaching students to write academic discourse. In your filing cabinet, you might file all of your handouts on prewriting together, your notes on drafting behind that, and your materials on revision next, but you probably don't teach your class from the front of your file drawer to the back. Instead, you choose a few materials that will expose your students to a skill and have them practice using it before you move on to the next skill.

Use this book the same way. In each chapter explanations, examples, and activities related to the same skill are grouped together so they are easy to find. You and your students should pick and choose activities that are helpful, but you shouldn't feel obligated to use all of them.

Also, you should feel free to revisit chapters throughout the course as needed. After all, learning to write is not a linear process; it's more like learning to shoot a lay-up. To shoot a lay-up, a basketball player must learn several skills: dribbling toward the basket, shifting the ball to the shooting hand, jumping off the appropriate foot, and shooting the ball. However, the player doesn't practice each skill until he or she has it down perfectly and then go on to the next skill. Instead, the player understands how each skill is to be acquired, practices each skill to get the feel of it, and spends most of the time practicing the skills together. The player may return to an individual skill and practice it again, but he or she will always have to return to the entire sequence of skills.

Classroom Flexibility

Not all students need every chapter of this book. Some students already know how to respond to a writing prompt. Other students wrestle with this skill and need to spend substantial time learning to analyze an assignment. Still other students are competent with some assignments but need to practice responding to different types of prompts. Depending on the needs of your students, you have many choices:

- Assign exercises, activities, and explanations for class work and discussion;
- Assign exercises, activities, and explanations for students to read independently and then ask questions in class;
- Assign exercises, activities, and explanations to individual students who need additional work in specific areas;
- Omit those parts of the book in which your students are proficient.

Encourage your students to use this book as a tool and a resource. Like a handbook, *The User's Guide* can provide help in specific areas while students are writing on their own. In fact, this book is written with the assumption that no one class and no one student will use all of it. Instead, users of this text should use the parts that are helpful, skipping around as needed.

We have organized the book by parts of the reading and writing process. We do not imply that this organization is the only way, or even the best way, to teach writing. We know that writing programs are different and that the students they serve are different. Therefore, we invite you to use the material provided in any order you determine to be best for your students and your program.

SUPPLEMENTS

Instructor's Manual and Companion Website

An instructor's manual is available to accompany *The User's Guide to College Writing*. This instructor's manual includes

- Sample course plans
- A variety of student worksheets
- Tips for working with ESL students
- Suggestions for teaching each chapter
- Suggestions for teaching each reading
- Answers to exercises

For a copy, please ask your Longman sales representative for ISBN 0-321-10390-4. For additional exercises and Internet-based activities, visit *The User's Guide to College Writing* online at http://www.ablongman.com/kreml.

The Longman Ancillary Package

In addition to the preceding book-specific supplements, many other supplements are available for both instructors and students. All of these supplements are available either free or at greatly reduced prices.

For Additional Reading and Reference

The Dictionary Deal. Two dictionaries can be shrinkwrapped with this text at a nominal fee. *The New American Webster Handy College Dictionary* is a paperback reference text with more than 100,000 entries. *Merriam Webster's Collegiate Dictionary*, tenth edition, is a hardback reference with a citation file of more than 14.5 million examples of English words drawn from actual use.

For more information on how to shrinkwrap a dictionary with your text, please contact your Longman sales representative.

Penguin Quality Paperback Titles.   A series of Penguin paperbacks is available at a significant discount when shrinkwrapped with this text. Some titles available are Toni Morrison's *Beloved*, Julia Alvarez's *How the Garcia Girls Lost Their Accents*, Mark Twain's *Huckleberry Finn, Narrative of the Life of Frederick Douglass*, Harriet Beecher Stowe's *Uncle Tom's Cabin*, Dr. Martin Luther King, Jr.'s *Why We Can't Wait*, and plays by Shakespeare, Miller, and Albee. For a complete list of titles or more information, please contact your Longman sales consultant.

100 Things to Write About.   This 100-page book contains 100 individual assignments for writing on a variety of topics and in a wide range of formats, from expressive to analytical. Ask your Longman sales representative for a sample copy. 0-673-98239-4

Newsweek Alliance.   Instructors may choose to shrinkwrap a 12-week subscription to *Newsweek* with any Longman text. The price of the subscription is 59 cents per issue (a total of $7.08 for the subscription). Available with the subscription is a free "Interactive Guide to *Newsweek*"—a workbook for students who are using the text. In addition, *Newsweek* provides a wide variety of instructor supplements free to teachers, including maps, Skills Builders, and weekly quizzes. For more information on the *Newsweek* program, please contact your Longman sales representative.

Electronic and Online Offerings

The Longman Writer's Warehouse.   This innovative and exciting online supplement, written by developmental English instructors, is the perfect accompaniment to any developmental writing course and covers every part of the writing process. Also included are journaling capabilities, multimedia activities, diagnostic tests, an interactive handbook, and a complete instructor's manual. The Writer's Warehouse requires no space on your school's server; rather, students complete and store their work on the Longman server, and can access it, revise it, and continue working at any time. For more details about how to shrinkwrap a free subscription to The Writer's Warehouse with this text, please consult your Longman sales representative. For a free guided tour of the site, visit http://longmanwriterswarehouse.com.

The Writer's ToolKit Plus.   This CD-ROM offers a wealth of tutorial, exercise, and reference material for writers. It is compatible with either a PC or Macintosh platform, and it is flexible enough to be used either occasionally for practice or regularly in class lab sessions. For information on how to bundle this CD-ROM with your text, please contact your Longman sales representative.

Research Navigator, by H. Eric Branscomb and Doug Gotthoffer.   A guide to online research. Featuring the Longman Internet Guide and access to the Research Navigator Database, this guide gives students and instructors instant access to thousands of academic journals and periodicals any time from any computer with an Internet connection. With helpful tips on the writing process, online research, and finding and citing valid sources, starting the research process has never been easier! Free when packaged with this textbook. Please consult your Longman sales representative.

The Longman Electronic Newsletter.   Twice a month during the spring and fall, instructors who have subscribed receive a free copy of the Longman Developmental English Newsletter in their e-mailbox. Written by experienced classroom instructors, the newsletter offers teaching tips, classroom activities, book reviews, and more. To subscribe, visit the Longman Basic Skills Website at http://www.ablongman.com/basicskills, or send an e-mail to BasicSkills@ablongman.com.

For Instructors

Electronic Test Bank for Writing.   This electronic test bank features more than 5,000 questions in all areas of writing, from grammar to paragraphing, through essay writing, research, and documentation. With this easy-to-use CD-ROM, instructors simply choose questions from the electronic test bank, then print out the completed test for distribution. CD-ROM: 0-321-08117-X. Print version: 0-321-08486-1.

Competency Profile Test Bank, Second Edition.   This series of 60 objective tests covers ten general areas of English competency, including fragments, comma splices and run-ons, pronouns, commas, and capitalization. Each test is available in remedial, standard, and advanced versions. Available as reproducible sheets or in computerized versions. Free to instructors. ISBN: 0-321-02224-6.

Diagnostic and Editing Tests and Exercises, Sixth Edition.   This collection of diagnostic tests helps instructors assess students' competence in Standard Written English for purpose of placement or to gauge progress. Available as reproducible sheets or in computerized versions and free to instructors. Paper: 0-321-19647-3. CD-ROM: 0-321-19645-7.

ESL Worksheets, Third Edition.   These reproducible worksheets provide ESL students with extra practice in areas they find the most troublesome. A diagnostic test and posttest are provided, along with answer keys and suggested topics for writing. Free to adopters. 0-321-07765-2

Longman Editing Exercises.   Fifty-four pages of paragraph editing exercises give students extra practice using grammar skills in the context of longer passages. Free when packaged with any Longman title. 0-205-31792-8. Answer key: 0-205-31797-9.

80 Practices.   A collection of reproducible, ten-item exercises that provide additional practices for specific grammatical usage problems, such as comma splices, capitalization, and pronouns. Includes an answer key and free to adopters. 0-673-53422-7

CLAST Test Package, Fourth Edition.   These two 40-item objective tests evaluate students' readiness for the CLAST exams. Strategies for teaching CLAST preparedness are included. Free with any Longman English title. Reproducible sheets: 0-321-01950-4.

TASP Test Package, Third Edition.   These 12 practice pretests and posttests assess the same reading and writing skills covered in the TASP examination. Free with any Longman English title. Reproducible sheets: 0-321-01959-8.

Teaching Online: Internet Research, Conversation, and Composition, **Second Edition.**   Ideal for instructors who have never surfed the Net, this easy-to-follow guide offers basic definitions, numerous examples, and step-by-step information about finding and using Internet sources. Free to adopters. 0-321-01957-1

Using Portfolios.   This supplement offers teachers a brief introduction to teaching with portfolios in composition courses. This essential guide addresses the pedagogical and evaluative use of portfolios, and offers practical suggestions for implementing a portfolio evaluation system in a writing class. 0-321-08412-8

The Longman Instructor's Planner.   This all-in-one resource for instructors includes monthly and weekly planning sheets, to-do lists, student contact forms, attendance rosters, a grade book, an address/phone book, and a mini-almanac. Ask your Longman sales representative for a free copy. 0-321-09247-3

For Students

Researching Online, **Fifth Edition.**   A perfect companion for a new age, this indispensable new supplement helps students navigate the Internet. Adapted from *Teaching Online,* the instructor's Internet guide, *Researching Online* speaks directly to students, giving them detailed, step-by-step instructions for performing electronic searches. Available free when shrinkwrapped with this text. 0-321-09277-5

A Guide for Peer Response, **Second Edition.**   This guide offers students forms for peer critiques, including general guidelines and specific forms for different stages in the writing process. Also appropriate for freshman-level course. Free to adopters. 0-321-01948-2

Ten Practices of Highly Successful Students. This popular supplement helps students learn crucial study skills, offering concise tips for a successful career in college. Topics include time management, test-taking, reading critically, stress, and motivation. 0-205-30769-8

The Longman Writer's Journal. This journal for writers, free with any Longman English text, offers students a place to think, write, and react. For an examination copy, contact your Longman sales consultant. 0-321-08639-2

The Longman Researcher's Journal. This journal for writers and researchers, free with this text, helps students plan, schedule, write, and revise their research project. An all-in-one resource for first-time researchers, the journal guides students gently through the research process. 0-321-09530-8

The Longman Writer's Portfolio. This unique supplement provides students with a space to plan, think about, and present their work. The portfolio includes an assessing/organizing area (including a grammar diagnostic test, a spelling quiz, and project planning worksheets), a before and during writing area (including peer review sheets, editing checklists, writing self-evaluations, and a personal editing profile), and an after-writing area (including a progress chart, a final table of contents, and a final assessment). Ask your Longman sales representative for ISBN 0-321-10765-9.

[FOR FLORIDA ADOPTIONS] *Thinking Through the Test,* **by D. J. Henry.** This special workbook, prepared specially for students in Florida, offers ample skill and practice exercises to help students prep for the Florida State Exit Exam. To shrinkwrap this workbook free with your textbook, please contact your Longman sales representative. Available in two versions: with answers and without answers. Also available: two laminated grids (one for reading, one for writing) that can serve as handy references for students preparing for the Florida State Exit Exam.

[FOR NEW YORK ADOPTIONS] Preparing for the CUNY-ACT Reading and Writing Test, edited by Patricia Licklider. This booklet, prepared by reading and writing faculty from across the CUNY system, is designed to help students prepare for the CUNY-ACT exit test. It includes test-taking tips, reading passages, typical exam questions, and sample writing prompts to help students become familiar with each portion of the test.

[FOR TEXAS ADOPTIONS] *The Longman TASP Study Guide,* **by Jeanette Harris.** Created specifically for students in Texas, this study guide includes straightforward explanations and numerous practice exercises to help students prepare for the reading and writing sections of the Texas Academic Skills Program Test. To shrinkwrap this workbook with your textbook, please contact your Longman sales representative.

ACKNOWLEDGMENTS

Many thanks to the reviewers who provided us with valuable feedback: Kay Berg, Sinclair Community College; Gary Cale, Jackson Community College; Dawn Leonard, Charleston Southern University; Carol Luvert, Hawkeye Community College; Bethany Reid, Everett Community College.

Every published book reflects the work of hundreds of people, many of whom the authors never have the opportunity to thank in person. We'd like to thank all those who contributed to make this textbook a reality. In particular, we would like to thank Steven Rigolosi, our Acquisitions Editor at Longman, for sharing our vision; Anne Brunell Ehrenworth, our Developmental Editor, for guiding us through the publication process; Gordon Laws, Project Manager, and Deborah Prato at Pre-Press Company, Inc., for their careful editing and suggestions for improving this edition; Eric Jorgensen, Production Manager; and Nancy Danahy for the cover design. We would also like to thank all of the book representatives who have worked with Longman and Pearson over the years for convincing us to write and then revise this book.

Our thanks also go to Mark and Gail Mathabane for not only providing us with the central reading for this text but also their visits to Columbia, South Carolina, to discuss Mark's writing and experiences with our students and the community. *The State Newspaper* graciously allowed us to use local writers' editorials as teaching materials for the English 100 program as well as in both editions of this text.

We are most indebted to the students at Midlands Technical College in Columbia, South Carolina, particularly those in English 100, who not only taught us what they need to know about composition but also demanded that we find new ways to explain the writing process. A special thanks to the students who allowed us to print examples from their writing assignments for their basic composition course: Keenan Johnson, J. P. Myers, Meg Christmas, Larry Evans, Rodell S. Johnson, Benjamin W. Munden, Sr., Lois Johnson, Jane Smith, and Marilyn Mallory.

We would also like to thank the faculty and staff at MTC for their support throughout the process of writing both editions. The former English Department Chair, Dianne Luce, supported and encouraged our work. The English and Developmental Studies Departments, particularly the English 100 Committee, provided us with the opportunituy to develop our teaching philosophy and pedagogy: Barbara Armbruster, Laurie Berry, Alice Davis, Jackie Frederick, Stan Frick, Keith Higginbotham, Glenn James, Cindy Rogers, and Linda Smith. We would also like to thank Dr. Jean Mahaffey, former Vice President for Education and faculty member of the English Department, and Dr. Ron Drayton, current Vice President for Arts and Sciences, for creating a work environment in which experimentation is valued and for supporting the work of the English 100 Committee.

We are also indebted to some very special people who have been at various times MTC employees and MTC students: Muffy Allison, Monica Boucher-Romano, Nicole Oliver, Penny Osborne, Connor Stewart, Gregory Taylor, and

Phillip Whitehead. We would also like to thank MTC employee Lisa Cheeks. Without their work to support our many professional projects, we could not have found the time or energy to complete either edition of the textbook. Thanks for all of the researching, copying, running errands, and just being there over the years.

Our families have tolerated our work on both editions over the course of many years. Not only have they supported us emotionally by listening to our joys and frustrations, they spent a weekend together at the beach so we could begin writing the manuscript. Thanks to Raedonna Blair, Curtis Carr, Lena Jake, Bruce Martin, Miles Martin, Caroline Ochola, Eunita Ochola, Maureen Ochola, Daniel Posselt, and Theo Posselt for tolerating our many hours at the computer, on the phone, and in meetings. Extra thanks to Bill Kreml for proofreading the manuscript, and to Lisa Jackson for not only proofreading and insightful suggestions but for her good humor and willingness to host our work sessions. Thanks to the late Mary Mace for letting us use the beach house. A special thanks to Pigwig Jackson, who is a much better writer than any of us will ever be. We would also like to pay tribute to our four-legged family members: the late Carl, Clint, Cujo, the late Eunice, Fernie, Heddy, Jake, Nugget, Sherman, the late Sidney, Sos, and Zena, who all assisted in the writing of an edition of the textbook—often by sleeping on or chewing on the manuscript or by typing on the computer.

We need to thank those who sacrificed their offices in Columbia, South Carolina, which provided us with work space as we waited for appointments: Dr. Gerald Fishman and Dr. Robert Sexton. We would also like to thank the owners and employees of numerous restaurants in Columbia, South Carolina, who fortunately did not charge us rent as we worked through and sat for long hours after the wonderful meals they served at Applebee's, Basil Pot, Beulah's, Blue Marlin, California Dreaming, Dixie Seafood, Fatz, Keg o' Nails, New Orleans Restaurant, Rising High Bakery, Rosewood Market, Ruby Tuesdays, and Tiffany's Bakery.

PART ONE

Introduction

1 The Circle of Reading, Writing, and Critical Thinking

Most of the assignments you get in college will require you to read and to write. You'll be required to read textbooks and write answers to exam questions about them; you'll write **summaries** and **critiques** of articles and chapters in books; and you'll write research papers. You'll be using reading and writing skills in your personal life and work life, too: replying to letters and memos, reading reports and summarizing them, and looking up technical information and writing explanations that inexperienced people can understand. All these different occasions for using reading and writing together may seem to be reason enough to prepare to use the two skills together. In addition, if you look more closely at how your mind works when you're reading and writing, you'll see that the two skills are very closely related and that using both gives you a little more mental power than using each separately.

HOW WRITING IMPROVES READING

Reading is not just the passive act of photocopying the words from the text onto your mind. It's an active process, one that involves using knowledge you already have to help you understand new concepts and, even more, to decide whether those new ideas are worthwhile. Part of learning to read this way is knowing that you must be a reader who is active—willing to work hard and to consider new ideas.

One of the best ways to develop reading skills and attitudes is through writing. Private or **personal writing**, or notes for yourself, can help you *prepare* to read by thinking and then writing about a topic: taking notes, jotting down questions, describing reactions, and making comparisons can help you *while* you read. Writing can also help you *after* you read. It is a way of reviewing and seeing how the ideas in a reading are related to each other and to your own ideas. Later chapters in this book give specific techniques for doing all these things.

However, it is another type of writing—**essay** writing—that will help you to become a wiser reader. When you write an essay about a reading, you will not focus only on your first thoughts and responses to the reading. You'll need to examine your responses carefully and consider exactly how they fit with the reading. You'll then return to the reading to be sure that you've reported the author's ideas accurately and clearly.

HOW READING IMPROVES WRITING

One of the biggest problems for any writer is finding material to write about. All of us have spent some time looking at a blank sheet of paper, trying to come up with something to say, or, finally, writing some words just to fill up the page. Another problem that writers face is remembering that they are writing to readers. It's hard to imagine how your reader might respond to what you've written if you have no idea who your reader is. The most obvious way that reading will improve your writing is by giving you something to say and by helping you understand or imagine possible readers.

When you write in response to something you've read, you have a clear starting place. You know you're writing to a specific person, and you know the idea that you want that person to understand—you have a clear **audience** and a clear **purpose**. But sometimes when you are writing for school assignments you may lose sight of your audience. Reading can help you to be aware of who your possible readers might be. For example, if you've read one or more essays explaining why distributing birth control in high schools is a bad idea, you have a much more specific idea of how to reply to those writers when you decide to write your own essay in favor of this practice. You know their real reasons for believing as they do, and you know the kinds of experiences they have had. You can much more easily decide which reasons you need to discuss and what kinds of examples the readers will understand. So reading can help you find material to write about, and it can help form a clear picture of the audience you expect to have as readers.

HOW READING AND WRITING IMPROVE THINKING

But reading and writing actually affect each other in much stronger ways. You really learn to write better by reading, and you learn to read better by writing—and both skills work together to improve your ability to think. Look at how you learn other skills: if you want to learn to drive a car, for example, you first watch someone else drive and then try to drive yourself. If you try to learn how to dance, you learn partly by watching other people dance. And if you want to learn to write, you will read others' writing. Sometimes you are able to learn a dance step just by imitation and can't explain exactly how you make the movements that you make—your body has started to "think" as a dancer's does. Learning to write is a similar process. You learn many complicated kinds of words and sentences by observing the ways that other writers put words together. Gradually your understanding of the words changes your ideas, and you become a better thinker.

Now that you're in college, one skill you will be learning by observing and practicing is how to use many new languages: the languages of technical fields, like engineering or computers; the language of specific courses, like history or psychology; and even the language of academic books and papers. It's not just a matter of memorizing a list of vocabulary words, like *archetypal, persist, multitude*. You must also learn to follow long and complicated sentences and paragraphs. You probably will not hear a sentence such as the following in conversation, but it's not unusual in a history book.

Having seen that the archetypal patterns persist throughout a multitude of cultures, we can assume that the term "universal" has some validity.

You'll acquire the ability to read a sentence like this just as you learned to drive or dance. You'll encounter sentences that use these words and follow these rules, and, as you did when you learned to dance or drive, you'll try out parts of the sentences yourself, without necessarily thinking about the fact that you are imitating something. You may also look critically at the sentence you create by imitation and decide that it's not as clear as it should be, and then you may search for other, clearer ways to express your own ideas.

A common type of academic assignment that requires you to go back and forth between reading and writing is the research paper. When you read a passage written by another writer, you can understand it on many different levels. If you simply skim over it, you may be able to remember the general idea. If you underline passages and key words, you will have a much deeper understanding. But if you understand the author's ideas well enough to restate them in your own words, you have truly taken in the ideas and made them a part of your own thinking process. If the material you work with is difficult, you will be extending your thinking processes to fit the demands of the writer's thought.

As you read and write in each subject, you'll begin to learn the language of that field. You'll also learn about bigger things than sentences. If you're assigned to write a research paper for a psychology class, probably the first thing you'll want to do is see an example of a paper written for that class so you can get an idea of the kind of writing you'll need to do. You may look at papers written by other students as well as professional papers. As you read these examples, you will notice the kinds of language the writers use—for example, you'll see terms such as *dependent variable*, which you may have thought you understood when you read the text. Now that you need to make the idea of *dependent variables* a part of your own paper and must organize your ideas around that central idea, you will have to thoroughly understand what it means. You'll have to look up the words and if necessary talk with your instructor until you have a very clear idea of the meaning of the term. When you try to write your own research paper, you'll go back to your examples and read them again. Then you'll examine your own writing and probably revise it to be more like your model.

As you write this paper, you'll also be using other sources. For example, you may find that one writer says the following.

Hypnotherapy may become the triggering mechanism for recovery of repressed memories of physical and mental abuse.

You work with reading and understanding this idea and finally restate it in your own words.

A person might forget painful childhood experiences but remember them later if hypnotized by a psychologist.

This has given you a new idea. You've also gained a clear understanding of the meaning of important words (*hypnotherapy, triggering mechanism, repressed memories*), and you've also seen how those words are used in a sentence. You continue to do research and find that another writer says this.

Current schema often present the phenomenon of repressed memory as pseudomemory, since reconstructive distortions are frequently the product of patients' response to therapists' own unconscious suggestions.

You are now familiar with the term *repressed memory*, so, with help from a dictionary and your psychology textbook, you work with the rest of this sentence until you can restate it in your own words.

Some theories say that people believe they remember things that did really happen or that happened in a different way. Because they trust and want to please the psychologist, they make up these false memories without realizing that they are doing it.

Now you have another idea, as well as additional vocabulary: *schema, phenomenon, reconstructive distortions*. You also have two different ideas to compare. When you begin to write your paper, you can say something like this.

Psychologists disagree about the recovery of repressed memories. Some believe there are actual memories of real abuse, but others think that patients unconsciously create memories as a result of suggestions from others.

You may go on from here to find some ways to decide which of these ideas you want to accept. You may do this by reading more or talking with your instructor and other students. You may think about your own ideas—maybe you decide that repressed memories are not the same for everyone. Depending on your assignment, you may or may not include your own conclusions in your psychology research paper. However, once you've thought about an idea deeply enough to be able to put it in your own words, you probably won't just drop it. The combination of reading and writing has stretched your mind, and it probably won't shrink back again any time soon.

An important thing is happening as you go through this process: you're learning to think about psychology. You learn some of this thinking by listening to the instructor and participating in class discussions, but a good bit of the change in your ability to think results from reading and writing, especially as you work with both processes together. Your ideas become increasingly more complex, and soon you will be able to recognize errors and problems in some of the things you read. At this point, you will finally be able to develop and express your opinions about them. A closer look at these related skills may help you see what you will be learning as you use this book.

WHAT IS READING?

As you begin your life as a college student, you will want to learn how to be successful. You will quickly find out that success depends on writing and reading and on making sure your skills will take you where you want to go. What are the biggest problems in writing and reading for college students? When college professors are asked this question, many will answer that the biggest problem is that students just don't do the reading—at all. When students are asked why they don't complete reading assignments, many have two answers: one is that they can't understand the readings, and the second is that the readings are boring.

Let's start with the idea that those two answers are really the same. Of course, reading may be boring if you already know all the facts and ideas in the reading. But you probably won't be taking many courses that you've already mastered. The chances are great that the reading doesn't interest you because you don't yet know enough about the subject to really be reading the material. You can't really read a book or essay or story unless you can be involved in the subject. A book is not a funnel that lets the author pour knowledge into your brain. It's more like a slot machine, where you get something back only when you put something in. When you read, you get back a lot more than you put in. The best part about reading is that it's not a game of chance.

For example, suppose a student in Wisconsin reads a story about violence in Northern Ireland, a story about a prisoner who becomes friendly with the men who guard him. If this student knows nothing at all about Ireland and does nothing but read the story, it will probably seem distant, confusing, and pointless. But if that same student has read the newspapers even a little, she may have learned something about the long history of conflict there. She may have had a history class in which she learned that Ireland was once a separate country. She may remember some Irish music or think about her Irish friends. But even if Ireland doesn't ring any bells at all for her, she may be able to think of a time when she found something good in people who were supposed to be her enemies. If she can bring any of this experience to the story, she'll be able to understand it much more and will find it much more interesting. Because she can invest some of her own knowledge and ideas, she will be able to get more meaning and ideas from the reading in return.

The Four Levels of Reading

In this book, we'll be looking at four different levels of reading. At all these levels, you'll be using what you already know to help you understand something new.

The Levels of Reading
Breaking the code
Understanding the idea
Reacting emotionally
Thinking critically

Breaking the Code   Many people still think of reading as matching letters to sounds and figuring out how to pronounce a word. For example, when you see the word *symbiotic*, you recognize that the letter *y* in this word must be pronounced like the letter *i*. But decoding the pronunciation is only one step in reading. Think about how that works: you can match the sound to the letter only if you already know the sound, and you can identify the word on paper only if you know the spoken word or have some way of learning it. So there's more to reading than pronouncing words.

Understanding the Idea   If you find a sentence with the word *symbiotic* in it, you may need to look it up in the dictionary. There you will find that *symbiosis* is the relationship between two very different organisms that live very closely together and benefit each other. You think about animals and plants you know and then remember learning about birds that live with crocodiles and clean the crocodiles' teeth. The bird benefits by getting food, and the crocodile benefits by getting clean teeth. That makes the word understandable, but you didn't figure it out by learning how to decode the letters. You used the knowledge you already had and put it together in a new way to get a new understanding.

This same process is even more important when we read more than just one word. Suppose you see the following sentence.

The police and the drug dealers developed a symbiotic relationship in that town.

Now you know what *symbiosis* means, so you think of what you know about word endings, and you decide that *symbiotic* is a form of *symbiosis*. But police and drug dealers couldn't really live together in the way that birds and crocodiles do. So you need a more complicated way of understanding this. You have learned what the word means; you already have some knowledge about police and criminals; and you know that sometimes language is used to make comparisons. You now understand the sentence to mean that the police and the drug dealers in that town help each other out. You don't know the specific details because that information must come from additional reading.

Reacting Emotionally   After you understand an idea, you don't just accept it and file it away; you react to it in some way. Your first reaction may be emotional: you may feel angry to think that police and criminals could work together. You may feel indignant, because you may have worked in law enforcement and you may think police are often misjudged. You may laugh, because you've seen cases where police have accepted bribes. Notice that your emotional reaction depends also on what you already know of the world, and emotional reactions can be very different for different people.

Remember that boredom is a form of emotional response. When your main reaction to something you have read is that it's boring, you're not really thinking about the ideas in the reading but about your feelings. It's fine to have that feeling, but you can't stop with your feelings. You must move on to thinking about what you read, no matter how you feel.

Thinking Critically   To come to any agreed-on understanding of the preceding sentence, you will need to read critically. This does not mean necessarily finding fault with everything you read. **Critical reading** involves specific types of thinking.

- Thinking about what you read, not just reacting emotionally.
- Thinking about what the author wants you to see and making judgments about that.
- Thinking about why you react the way you do to what the author says.

To be able to think critically, you will need to ask questions about what you've read. Look again at the sentence *The police and the drug dealers developed a symbiotic relationship in that town.* Here are a few ways to think critically about it.

What town was this?

How did the police and criminals benefit each other?

What facts prove that this took place?

Does this seem similar to things that happen here?

What facts do I know that contradict or support this?

What difference does this make?

The answers to these questions will help you as a reader decide whether to accept the statement or not. Without the answers, you may finally have to decide that the sentence is just an idea and won't really be able to say whether it's accurate or not.

If you apply this critical reading process to much of the written material you encounter, you will see how necessary critical reading is for people who live in a complex and diverse society. This book will ask you to develop your ability to read critically.

EXERCISE 1.1 After reading each of the following numbered sentences, indicate what kind of reading is being used in each of the lettered responses—breaking the code, understanding the idea, reacting emotionally, or thinking critically.

1. Capital punishment represents the final stage in the dehumanization process.

   A. To *dehumanize* means to take away the human qualities of something. Therefore, this sentence says that people are made into something less than human when they are legally executed for a crime.

   B. People who oppose capital punishment make me sick.

   C. In what way are criminals dehumanized? What are the other stages? Can a human being really be something not human?

2. Bilingual education will undermine the unity of our country.

   A. In what way will the unity of the country be affected by the language people speak? Is there any evidence for this? Are there many countries in which more than one language is spoken? Is unity more important than the other benefits of teaching children in two languages?

   B. *Bilingual* means speaking two languages. I've heard of programs where children of immigrants are taught math and science classes in Spanish. Maybe that's what this sentence is about.

   C. I'm not an immigrant, and I don't have children. This topic is boring.

EXERCISE 1.2 Using a dictionary if necessary and your own experience if possible, explain what the following sentences mean. Then give an example of an emotional and a critical response to each.

   A. The digital revolution will soon make VCRs obsolete.

   B. Smokers' rights are abrogated by the passage of no-smoking bills in some states.

   C. All students must attend an orientation seminar.

The Purposes of Reading

You read for many different purposes. When you read a love letter or an angry editorial, you're mainly reading for the emotional content, but when you read a recipe or a course description, you're looking for information. Other reading that you do requires a more thoughtful reaction that will require you to invest more effort. As a student reading a textbook for your psychology course, your main purpose may be to make a good grade in the course. As a citizen and a consumer, you'll be confronted by advertising asking you to choose products and politicians. In all of these roles, you'll need strong critical reading skills to make intelligent choices.

There will be many purposes for your reading. These are likely to be the most common ones.

▪ *Personal reading:* You will read a wide variety of things as a part of your personal life. You may read for information to help you decide which car to buy, or you may read horror novels for entertainment. You determine your own purpose in your personal reading. When you read for personal reasons, you may decide not to read something that's difficult or uninteresting unless it's something you really need to know.

▪ *Academic reading:* When you are reading in college, you will not have a choice about whether you want to read something or not. Your professors will expect you to learn the material, and often that will mean reading chapters or whole books that may be very difficult for you. The purpose of these assignments is partly to give you an understanding of the specific material in the course and partly to improve your thinking skills. You should expect to follow certain steps with academic reading: (1) reread the material several times, (2) mark the book and make notes, (3) use a dictionary, and (4) think about what you have read. In Chapter 4, we will show you some specific techniques. The goals of academic reading usually involve the following.

Gathering facts and ideas about a topic

Thinking critically about these facts and ideas

Relating facts and ideas to other readings, lectures, and discussions

▪ *Professional reading:* Reading at work is often very similar to academic reading. You must read certain things because you need the information or because you must make a judgment about ideas presented by the writer. You may see the purpose more clearly, but sometimes reports written by other workers or customers may be difficult to read because they're not written as clearly as much professional writing. You will find that the same critical reading skills you used in academic reading will be necessary when you read for work.

Improving Your Reading

Whether you read for personal, academic, or professional reasons, it is definitely possible to improve your reading skills. The following list shows you several ways to work to become a better reader. The most important is simply that *you must read*.

Ways to Improve Your Reading
Be willing to work
Be willing to see new ideas
Read methodically
Read widely
Prepare to read by increasing your knowledge of the world

Be Willing to Work   The most important step in improving your reading is motivation. You must realize, however, that reading is not just a matter of skimming across the pages of a book. You must be willing to work and to invest both time and energy: using dictionaries, taking notes, reading and rereading difficult passages, answering questions.

Be Willing to See New Ideas   Another important part of improving your reading is letting go of the fear of new things and being willing to try hard to use your mind in new ways. Thinking involves examining ideas, not just memorizing. You must be willing to take time to understand ideas even if they challenge the way you see the world. You don't have to give up your own beliefs, but you must be willing to hear ideas in addition to those that are comfortable to you.

Read Methodically Learn to use the best techniques for reading carefully and working with what you read. You may have learned some of these in other courses, or they may be new to you, but if you practice them with your academic reading, they will help you understand complex and difficult material.

Read Widely Form an ongoing habit of reading, like the habit of brushing your teeth or exercising. You have seen how much reading depends on the knowledge and experience you already have. Many of the techniques offered by this book will show you how to use your knowledge and experience even more deeply. One of the best ways to increase your knowledge of the world and your experience in life is to read widely. You should take every opportunity to increase your general and personal reading as well as the reading you do for school. Eventually you will see how much that increased knowledge of the world will pay off. One of your goals as a college student should be to increase your reading by some or all of these experiences.
Here are some ways to read more widely.

- Read a newspaper every day.
- Read magazines.
- Subscribe to newspapers or magazines, or read them in the library.
- Join a book club.
- Talk with friends about books.
- Print and read articles from the Internet.
- Choose a subject and learn all you can about it.
- Trade books and magazines with friends.
- Visit bookstores and used bookstores.
- Look for books at garage sales.
- Ask teachers for old books and magazines.

Prepare to Read by Increasing Your Knowledge of the World We've seen how you use the knowledge you already have to understand new ideas in your reading. This means that one way to become a better reader is to have more knowledge. All of us gain some knowledge just by living in the world. By making the choice to go to college, you will be increasing your knowledge through all of your courses. You will also be increasing your knowledge through other activities: reading outside the classroom; talking with classmates, neighbors, friends, and coworkers; watching informative programs on television; and visiting museums, zoos, churches, and different kinds of stores. Anything you learn or experience will give you a little more material to use when you come to the next difficult reading.

These are some ways to increase your knowledge and experience.

- Read widely.
- Watch informative programs on television.
- Watch news programs regularly.
- Read the newspaper.
- Get to know new people and talk with them.
- Go to new parts of town.
- Visit museums, zoos, churches, and different kinds of stores.
- Ask questions.

WHAT IS WRITING?

Differences Between Speaking and Writing

Writing is one way to use language, but it is not the first way we learned to express ourselves. We first learned to communicate by speaking and listening and only later by writing and reading. Why is speaking so easy for us, yet writing often so difficult? Even though both involve communicating through language, there are several significant differences between speaking and writing.

First, most of us are more accustomed to spoken language. While some forms of speaking, such as speaking in front of a group, may be less comfortable, most of us are at ease speaking with other people on a casual basis. We have also learned quite naturally how to change our speech depending on whom we are talking to. For example, we probably don't talk the same way to our friends as we do to our employers. While we need to make the same adjustments when we write, we don't have as much practice. Furthermore, the standards of correctness in written language—punctuation, paragraphing, and so forth—tend to be less familiar to us than those we have to consider when we speak.

Second, we are more motivated to speak than to write. Whether we are ordering a meal, purchasing a product, or telephoning a friend, we find it essential to speak. However, it has often been possible to get by without writing very often or very much (though e-mail is making the written word more important for many people). If we want to participate in the events going on around us in our society—which is based on spoken words (think of television and radio)—we have to communicate, and the easiest means of communication is often speaking.

Third, we have the sense that what we write is permanent. Our writing (mistakes and all) is recorded where it can be read again and again. What we speak, however, seems temporary and easily corrected if it doesn't come out the way we want it to.

Finally, the biggest difference between speaking and writing is the relationship with an audience. For a writer, audience refers to the intended readers of the writing. For a speaker, *audience* refers to the listeners who are physically present.

Importance of Audience

When you see your audience or listen to their reactions, you can adjust what you say to them. If they don't understand, you can explain further. If they are getting bored, you can try to make it more interesting. If they are offended by what you are saying, you can change your tactics or your tone. When you are writing and the audience is not present, you have to guess how they will react.

Identifying your audience and thinking about their needs help determine the content of your writing. For instance, if you are writing an **argumentative essay** about censoring sex and violence on television, the wording and specific issues you discuss will depend on characteristics of your audience—their gender, age, education, and occupations. If your reader is a priest, you might focus more on religious matters, but if your reader is a politician, you might center the discussion around legal issues. What you say and how you say it is determined to a large extent by your audience.

In some situations, you may not know who your audience is. If you are writing a letter to your school paper about the student council, your specific audience might be the members of the student council. If the letter appears in the school paper, friends and others familiar with the issue might read it, but so might students, faculty, staff, and parents you don't know. You would need to consider whether they will be familiar with the issue you're addressing and how much background information they will need to understand why you are writing the letter, what your concerns are, and what you are trying to accomplish. When your audience consists of people you don't know, you must provide enough information to ensure that they can understand you.

THE FIVE LEVELS OF WRITING

The Five Levels of Writing
Personal
Colloquial
Informal
Formal
Academic

Your audience helps you to decide what kind of language you want to use as well as what information you need to give. You need to think about what kind of writing is appropriate for your reader. One way to think about choosing the language for your audience is to think about the *level* of writing, just as you think about the type of clothing to wear for a particular occasion. If you're going out with friends, you'll probably wear casual clothes, like nice jeans and a t-shirt, but if you're going to a wedding, you'll probably wear very formal, elegant clothes. You'll make similar choices about your writing, which generally falls under one of the following categories.

Personal Writing Personal writing is intended only for you. It does not have to be correct or organized so that anyone but you can follow it. Here are some typical examples.

grocery list

class notes

journal

brainstorming or prewriting for future writing

EXAMPLE: Mom and Dad's party—2 pm—Jan. 12—Clubhouse

Colloquial Writing **Colloquial communication** is intended for an audience you know well and who does not expect you to be formal or correct. Because your message will be specific to that audience, you may use abbreviations and references known only by that audience.

advertisements

note or letter to friend

EXAMPLE: Mom and Dad's 50th is coming up on January 12. We're throwing a party for them at 2:00 at the clubhouse. Y'all come.

Jimmy, BB, and Allie

Informal Writing **Informal communication** is intended to be read by an audience, usually peers, who will expect a standard form and some amount of correctness but not formal language.

signs

interoffice memo

newsletter

EXAMPLE: Come help us celebrate our parents' 50th wedding anniversary at 2 p.m. on January 12 at the Forest Lake Country Club.

James, Bruce, and Alice Kelly

Computer Tip

Remember that using e-mail doesn't change the fact that you must write differently for different audiences. Before you click on "Send," read even a short note once with your reader in mind. Think about the words you've chosen and the information you've included: Is this right for your reader? Is it clear?

Formal Writing   **Formal communication** is intended to be read by an audience who will expect a standard form and error-free grammar and spelling. This audience may be readers you don't know well or who are above you in some chain of command (teachers, employers, etc.).

> research papers
>
> job résumés
>
> cover letters
>
> formal invitations

EXAMPLE: James, Bruce, and Alice Kelly
cordially invite you to a reception honoring
Mr. and Mrs. Walter B. Kelly
on the joyous occasion of their fiftieth wedding anniversary
at two o'clock on Saturday, January 12, 2002
at the Forest Lake Country Club

EXERCISE 1.3	**Write a paragraph describing a trip you have taken, using each level of writing.**

Academic Writing   The writing you do in your college classes—**academic writing**, as it is called—will require a type of wording, structure, and adherence to certain rules not required by other forms of writing. A library research paper will require you to use quotes, provide citations, supply a works cited list, and conform to the rules of a formal style guide, such as that issued by the Modern Language Association (MLA) or the American Psychological Association (APA). In later chapters, we will discuss the special rules of academic writing—not only in your English class but in any class, from history to psychology to business—that require you to write college-level essays.

When you write in an academic setting, you must be particularly mindful of your audience. You may consider your instructor to be an immediate audience completely familiar with the topic you're discussing, but this can be a dangerous assumption. Listen closely to an instructor's directions when an assignment is given because he or she may identify the audience. However, don't make the mistake of assuming that your instructor knows everything about the subject or reading you are discussing. When you make this assumption, you may leave out important information and create an essay that is vague and too general.

If you are discussing a short story, you can't just say that the main character's actions reveal his lack of self-respect. Even though your instructor will have read the story many times, he or she may not be sure which actions you are referring to, may not understand how these actions reveal the main character's lack of self-respect, or may not even agree with you that these actions show a lack of self-respect. Even when writing for your instructors, assume that they need to be reminded of the issues in the reading you are examining.

One way to define your readers is to assume that they have never read the story or essay you are discussing. Using this strategy will ensure that all readers will understand what you are saying.

Remember that academic writing is an exercise in communication, not merely a performance on which you will be graded. You will want to write to be understood, not just to impress your instructor or earn a high grade.

The Importance of Purpose

Another element that determines the form and wording of your writing is your reason for writing it. The wording and structure of a piece of writing—a note to a coworker, a cover letter for a job application, a letter of complaint to a business, a proposal for funding a new project in your job, an essay for a college class—change when your reason for writing changes. Often audience and purpose go hand in hand, as we see in the following exercise.

EXERCISE 1.4

Read the following account of an automobile accident.

On Monday, September 9, I was driving to work in my 1997 Nissan Sentra, headed north on Devine Street. I was checking my hair in the rearview mirror and turning up the radio because my favorite song was playing. When I looked back at the road, I noticed the car in front of me stopping quickly. I put on my brakes and stopped just before rear-ending the other car. I then felt a bump as the car behind me ran into my car. I got out of the car, but the car that hit me—a large green sedan—drove away. Four other cars were stopped behind it, and the drivers of those cars told me that they had hit each other. A woman walking her dog said she got the license number of the car that left and wrote it down for me.

Now write the story as you would tell it to each of the following audiences.

A. The judge in traffic court

B. Your best friend

C. Your younger brother, who is a reckless driver

D. Classmates in a college class in criminal justice studying evidence

What differences do you notice between each story? Why did you make those choices? What purposes were you trying to achieve in each account?

The Purposes of Writing

You can look at the purposes of writing in several ways. You can think in general terms about the kind of reaction you want your audience to have, or you can think about the specific kind of task you want to accomplish. Is it part of your personal life, your school or academic life, or your work? Let's look at four purposes of writing and how they are combined.

> **The Purposes of Writing**
>
> *To think* (you will create and organize ideas)
>
> *To inform* (your reader will understand)
>
> *To persuade* (your reader will agree)
>
> *To entertain* (your reader will enjoy)

■ *To think on paper and organize thoughts:* You may write things down to help you remember them, or to learn new material, or to help you think through a problem or issue. Usually the personal writing you do for this purpose—notes, outlines, freewriting, journals, memos to yourself—will be meaningful and useful to you rather than to another audience.

■ *To inform:* When you write to inform, you want your audience to understand a concept, procedure, or fact. You may write to teach your audience (such as writing instructions for a friend who will be taking care of your pets while you are on vacation), to demonstrate your knowledge (such as writing an exam), or to explain how to use a piece of equipment at work.

■ *To persuade:* When you write to **persuade**, you want to convince your audience to act or believe in a certain way: you want them to agree with you. You may write a personal letter urging a friend to move to a new house, or you may write an evaluation of an employee, asking for a higher salary for that person. In college, you may write an essay arguing that one view of history is more valid than another.

■ *To entertain:* You may write to entertain your audience, to make them laugh, to tell them a story. You want your audience to enjoy what you have written. A letter to a friend may describe in an amusing way your problems learning to use a computer.

Often you will use the last three purposes in the same piece of writing. For instance, if you are writing to persuade your audience to vote for a particular issue or candidate, you may have to inform your audience about the issue or the candidate. You may include a paragraph with a suspenseful story to illustrate the need for better safety procedures at work.

EXERCISE 1.5 | Write a paragraph on the city or town where you live, using each of the following purposes.

    A. Persuade a business to relocate

    B. Explain the history of the area for a history or sociology class

    C. Make notes on areas where you might want to consider buying a new house

    D. Tell a friend about holiday decorations in your neighborhood

Improving Your Writing

Sometimes people get the idea that they are born bad writers, almost as if writing ability is purely genetic, like red hair. But the truth is that writing ability can be greatly improved, especially the writing you do for academic or professional purposes. Writing is a skill that you learn, and you *can* learn to become a better writer. Here are some helpful principles to remember.

How to Improve Your Writing
Be willing to work
Be willing to wrestle with your writing
Use other people's writing as models
Accept constructive criticism
Write often

■ *Be willing to work:* Writing is hard work. To improve your writing, you will need to make a commitment of time and energy. You can't just copy papers over to make them neater—you must put forth the effort to make serious changes. Remember that all good writing has been revised many times.

■ *Be willing to wrestle with your writing:* Don't give up when the writing doesn't come easily. You can think of each writing task as a problem to be solved. If you stop before finding a solution, then you haven't completed the task.

■ *Use other people's writing as models:* When you find techniques that work for other writers, try using them yourself. For example, if you find the details in George Orwell's "A Hanging" (pp. 48–51) very effective, you may want to try to include more details in your own writing.

■ *Accept constructive criticism:* Listen to your instructors, tutors, and classmates when they offer suggestions. They aren't making a final judgment on whether your writing is good or bad but are giving you helpful steps to follow. Respond with your mind, not your feelings, and act on their suggestions.

■ *Write often:* As with any skill, the more you practice it, the better you become. If you've ever played sports, you know the importance of consistently practicing. Not every day will be a good day, but your overall performance will improve.

How to Write More Often

Keep a journal. Record not just what happens to you (like in a diary), but what you think about it. Write down reactions to what you have read or heard on the news or seen in a movie or talked with a friend about. You may want to keep a specific kind of journal—a dream journal, a gardening journal, a travel journal—to record one specific activity you enjoy.

Write thank you notes. Be as specific as you can in describing what the other person has done that you appreciate.

continued on next page

continued from previous page

Write an e-mail to someone. Remember your audience when you write.

Write a love letter. Try to find new ways to describe your feelings.

Write what you would like to say to someone you are upset with. (You don't have to show it to anyone.)

Write a letter to a politician or a letter to the editor. Discuss an issue that is important to you.

Write some instructions for a friend. Describe how to do something you do particularly well.

Make a list. Keep track of books you're read or movies you've seen.

Write down some of your childhood memories. Include stories told by other family members.

Write a letter to someone you have a problem with. Try to resolve the problem.

Write to learn for an exam. Outline your notes.

Write your own questions for an exam.

READING, WRITING, THINKING, AND THIS BOOK

This book is based on the idea that your success in college and in the work you choose to do will partly depend on your ability to continue to improve your reading, writing, and thinking skills. This book also assumes that focusing on reading and writing together to write essays is one of the most efficient ways to use both skills to improve your ability to think. As you work in each chapter, you'll see that we frequently ask you to use reading as a way to improve your writing and to use writing as a way to help your reading. You will not use all the options we offer, but you will find some that will help you to become a better reader and writer. We hope that this process will also help you see your ideas more clearly—and that you will be proud of the essays you will be writing.

2 Essential Tools for College Writers: The Skills for Success

Reading, writing, and **critical thinking** will probably continue to be essential skills for you as a worker and as a citizen for the rest of your life. During the time that you're in college, however, you will need to focus on some very specific skills that you'll need to develop in order to succeed in many of your courses. You must learn to write **essays**, a format for writing that underlies many types of writing required in college. In many essays, you will respond to one or more readings, but sometimes you will write more generally, drawing mainly on your experience of the world. In other assignments, you will need to locate information and ideas from other sources, so your essays will include research, and you will have to learn to use the computer efficiently as a writer and researcher. If you're learning English as a new language, you also may need to learn some ways of approaching academic writing that may be different from your former practices.

Each of these skills will be discussed throughout the book at specific points where they are especially appropriate to the reading-writing-thinking process. In this chapter, you will see icons (see the bottom of page 25, for example) that highlight certain skills. A list of pages where each skill is discussed is also provided. You can also use the table of contents and the index to help you locate the information you need.

THE ESSAY: A FORMAT COMBINING READING, WRITING, AND CRITICAL THINKING

Reading, writing, and critical thinking come together in the basic form of academic writing: the essay. Your college essay assignments will require you to demonstrate your understanding of readings and to report what you understand. Sometimes your essays will focus on your response to one reading, but in others, you may use a variety of readings to **support** larger ideas. In later courses, your instructors may call these essays by many names—research papers, critical papers, reports, analyses, critiques—but no matter what the name, you will still use the basic principles of the essay: relating your reading to your own writing.

Before you go on to learn all the various kinds of **academic** and business writing you may encounter in your life, you must first master the format of the essays. All other longer papers are variations on this basic format, which consists of three parts.

- The **introduction** gives your reader an idea of what the essay will be about.
- The **body** is always divided into several parts, and each part supports the main idea in some way and develops each part completely.
- The **conclusion** returns to the main idea to show the reader how the parts of the body support the main idea.

Almost any complete piece of writing will have these three parts, whether it's a business proposal, a chemistry lab report, or a psychology research paper. In short essays (like those you'll write for the assignments in this book), each part may be just one paragraph, but in longer papers, a part may be several paragraphs or even several pages.

When you write for a specific situation, whether it's a college course or a business transaction, each of these three parts will be subdivided into other parts. Part of learning to write an essay will involve learning how to subdivide your writing. This course is intended to teach you to relate your reading to your writing and thinking, so the required parts will reflect that relationship. Let's now look again at the parts of the essay with the subdivisions added (a

Parts of an Essay Based on a Reading and Critical Thinking

Introduction (pp. 149–165)

The introduction prepares the reader for the ideas developed in the essay and provides some background necessary to understand the context for these ideas.

- The **lead-in** involves the reader in the topic.
- The **author** and the **title of the reading** identifies the reading that the (student) writer is responding to.
- The **main idea of the reading** explains the main points of the reading.
- The (student's) **writer's thesis** tells your main idea, and it may include a plan of development to indicate how the thesis will be developed in the body.

Body (pp. 170–176)

The body consists of several paragraphs divided according to different reasons that support the thesis or different ways that the thesis is *true*.

- Each body paragraph contains the following features.

    A **topic sentence** that gives the main idea of the paragraph. The topic sentence can also clarify how the paragraph develops the thesis.

continued on next page

> *continued from previous page*
>
> **Examples and ideas from the reading** that make the author's ideas clear.
>
> **Examples and ideas from the student writer** that make clear the student writer's support for the main idea of each paragraph.
>
> A **concluding sentence** that reminds the reader how the support relates to the main idea of the paragraph.
>
> ### Conclusion (pp. 184–185)
>
> The conclusion is a return to the main idea and reminds the reader how the body supports the thesis.
>
> ■ The conclusion always restates the (student's) **writer's thesis.**
>
> ■ If the essay is in response to a reading, the conclusion reconnects with the relevant main idea(s) of the reading.
>
> ■ The main ideas of the body paragraphs are listed.
>
> ■ The conclusion usually ends on a final thought, such as a general observation, a recommendation, or a warning.

complete explanation of how to develop each part is found on the pages in parentheses).

Chapters 8, 9, and 10 present a complete explanation of how to write all the parts of an essay. Here is an essay written in response to George Orwell's "A Hanging" (pp. 48–51). The major parts of the essay are labeled on the left side, and the parts of each paragraph are labeled on the right. You can see that the writer has many options about where to put a certain part of an essay. For example, in the first body paragraph, the discussion of material from the reading comes first, followed by the student's own example and explanation. These parts are in a different order in the second body paragraph, where the student's own material comes before the ideas from the reading.

Obeying Orders

INTRODUCTION

1   Most people go through their lives following orders, without questioning whether they should obey so readily. The military is based upon the assumption that all orders will be carried out without question. Laws and regulations work only when we expect people to obey them without question. Safety of children often depends on their following adults' orders and rules without question. Even at work, we have agreed to follow the company's orders just to carry out our jobs. Although people do follow most of the orders given on a daily basis, some situations force a person to question whether or not an order

lead-in

INTRODUCTION —

should be followed. One such situation is depicted in George Orwell's "A Hanging," in which Orwell and fellow British police officers in Burma execute a man. ⎤ author, title of reading

In the essay, Orwell makes an argument against capital punishment. But the essay can also be read to show us why we should not always follow orders. ⎤ main idea of reading

When an order conflicts with our morals or risks the lives of other people, it should not be carried out. ⎤ THESIS

BODY PARAGRAPHS —

2 Whenever we must decide whether to follow an order, we should first ask ourselves if following the order will risk the ⎤ topic sentence

safety of others. Orwell was a police officer and was expected to enforce British law in colonial Burma. In this job, he should have expected to see people die. However, faced with an execution Orwell discovers that he believes it is wrong to take another person's life: "Until that moment I had never realized what it means to destroy a healthy, conscious man. When I saw the prisoner step aside to avoid the puddle I saw the mystery, the unspeakable wrongness, of cutting a life short when it is in full tide" (49). ⎤ examples and ideas from reading

By coming face to face with the condemned man, Orwell realizes that killing another human is wrong. Even when we do not know the persons involved, we should not follow orders if there is a possibility that someone may get hurt. I encountered such a situation last week when an angry customer called to complain about her toaster exploding. I reported her story to my supervisor because I thought the Quality Management staff should be made aware of the possible safety problem. My supervisor ordered me to send the customer a new toaster, but not to send a copy of the complaint to Quality Management. He was concerned that it would create needless work and worry since this complaint was the first report of any problems with this model of toaster. Even though I disagreed with my supervisor, I did what he said at the time. However, I feel guilty when I think that a faulty toaster produced by my company may cause families to lose their homes and maybe ⎤ examples and ideas from student writer

even their lives. I now have to make a choice—follow my boss' orders or follow my own morals. ⎤ concluding sentence

BODY PARAGRAPHS —

3 It seems obvious that one should follow one's own morals if they conflict with an order. However, acting on this belief ⎤ topic sentence

is difficult. I may have to risk my job to let Quality Management know about the complaint. The company may even decide not to investigate the safety of the toaster. Then, I may ⎤ examples and ideas from student writer

BODY PARAGRAPHS

have to choose to inform the public, and such action may prevent me from getting another job. These are the same decisions Orwell faces as a young man. He realizes that capital punishment is wrong, but as an individual member of the police force, he does not try to prevent the execution and does not refuse to participate. He goes along with the crowd because he feels outnumbered, and he may have even been afraid he will be punished if he refuses to participate. But those are excuses we use to justify our actions. Instead of justifying, Orwell should have stated how he felt and refused to participate even at his own risk. In fact, had he stated his feelings aloud, others might have joined him. It is evident from everyone's behavior that Orwell was not alone in his doubt. Something in the other people's behavior led Orwell to believe they shared his feelings. He claims that the others wanted to get the execution finished as quickly as possible, as if to rid themselves of an unpleasant task. When the man was crying "Ram!" everyone, including Orwell, had "the same thought": "oh, kill him quickly, get it over, stop that abominable noise" (50). Here it is evident that continuing to hear the man cry might push them to the breaking point. When the execution was over and "the dead man was a hundred yards away," they drank and laughed about other executions where the condemned did not cooperate (51). These references to other executions show that they are trying to eliminate their guilt by convincing themselves that their actions are routine and therefore acceptable. When you have to convince yourself that following an order is the right thing to do, it is obvious that the order conflicts with your own values and morals.

examples and ideas from reading

concluding sentence

CONCLUSION

4   While most people agree that protecting others from harm and obeying one's own morals is more important than blindly following orders, Orwell's and my experiences show that it is difficult to do what is right when everyone else obeys the order. However, following an order just because everyone else does is not acceptable, and an individual must stand up for what he believes to be right. When we see immoral or harmful behavior, it is our duty to make it known because facing the risk of punishment is better than having to live with the guilt.

summary of ideas

return to thesis

As you become more experienced in writing essays, you will learn to write many variations on this basic pattern. For example, you'll learn to decide when you must clearly state your thesis in the introduction and when you can save it for the conclusion, or when you can imply the topic sentence of a paragraph or introduce it in between two examples. Many instructors will want you to feel confident that you can write an essay with all these parts clearly stated before you try your hand at the variations. Also, you'll find that you may use any number of body paragraphs. The examples in this book usually contain from two to four body paragraphs because short essays are easier to control than long ones. In later courses, you'll need to write much longer essays, and you may find that you will need more than one paragraph for the introduction and the conclusion.

However, some essential aspects of the essay will be the same, no matter how long the essay is or how many variations you use. Essays always focus on one central point, they always use supporting ideas to develop that point, and they always have some ways of developing those ideas, whether they are examples, quotations, facts, summaries, explanations, or comparisons.

RESEARCH IN ACADEMIC WRITING

Writing in college may mean that you must not only respond to something you read, but also that you must locate additional material at some point in your essay. Instructors in writing and other college courses may assign many different types of research, and they may use different names for the kinds of papers they assign. Be sure that you understand what kind of research your instructor wants you to do and what format you should use. These are the main types of research assignments.

- *Research papers* are papers based almost totally on outside sources. They are usually fairly long, but are basically organized like an essay.
- *Essays with research* are papers based primarily on the student's own ideas, supported by research.
- *Summaries* give the main ideas of one or more sources. Sometimes they provide information concisely so others can evaluate if they wish to read the original.
- *Critiques* include a basic summary of a source, but they also include an evaluation of the source in terms of the goals of the work, accuracy of information, credibility of the author, and appropriateness of the source for the writer's purpose (as in a recommendation or a comparison).
- *Annotated bibliographies* have **citations** for sources followed by brief summaries or critiques. An annotated bibliography may stand alone or be part of a paper.

Different types of assignments will require you to do research at one or more distinct points in the writing process. For this reason, you will find information on different stages of research at several points in this book. Look

For Information on Research

Locating Material and Using the Library: pp. 328–333

Evaluating Sources: pp. 329–330

Taking Notes: pp. 101–106, 333

Organizing the Paper: pp. 116–147, 204–209, 282–302, 302–309, 350

Writing with Sources: pp. 155–157, 172–174, 335–337, 340–342

Documenting Sources: pp. 335–344

| Research |

for the **Research** symbol in the margin. Here's a brief list of the main sections on research.

Avoiding Plagiarism

When you research a topic, or when you write in response to another writer, you will need to be careful to avoid plagiarism. **Plagiarism** is using someone else's ideas, facts, or words as if they were your own. In colleges, universities, and schools in the United States, it is very important to make a clear distinction between your own work and someone else's. If you use ideas, facts, or words from another writer and don't explain clearly who wrote them, your instructor may believe that you are cheating and give you a low grade or make you rewrite the paper. In some cases, you could face even greater punishment, such as failing the course or being asked to leave the college. You may have heard of people being sued over the rights to song lyrics or movie ideas. Plagiarism can lead to a lawsuit.

Some students believe that if they can find papers on the Internet that were written by other students and turn them in as their own work, the instructor will never find out. This is a big mistake. Instructors quickly learn your individual writing style and will recognize any changes. Also, a paper someone else wrote for another class is not likely to fit your assignment. Furthermore, your instructor may ask you to supply notes and **drafts**, which you won't have. And remember, instructors know how to use the Internet, too, and they can locate any paper you can—and often more easily. Of course, the most important reason for doing your own work is that you will need the reading and writing skills taught in the course to succeed in other courses and, later, your job. You must *practice* those skills to be able to improve your ability.

Other students don't mean to be dishonest, but they aren't sure how to inform the reader that they are using another writer's work. This book will show you easy ways to do that; it is called **documentation**. When you use accepted ways of documenting sources, the reader can easily see which ideas, facts, and words are your own and which belong to another writer.

Documenting Your Sources

This book shows you how to use MLA style to document your sources. What does this mean? *Style* in this sense refers to how you format your essay and how you show where you found your material. In the text of the essay it must be clear where the information comes from. Also, the list of references (the *Works Cited* list) gives specific publication information about your sources in a particular format. You must follow a certain order and certain rules of punctuation and capitalization. **MLA** is the abbreviation for Modern Language Association, which is the professional organization for scholars who research and write about literature and language. Most English instructors will expect you to learn this style first, so this book presents the basics of MLA. Once you learn MLA, you will understand how documentation works and why it is important.

If you write a paper for another type of course, you may be asked to use a very different style. Psychology and other social sciences use **APA** (American Psychological Association) style, and some sciences use CSE (Council of Science Editors). These formats usually include the same information as MLA but in a different order or with different punctuation. You should ask the instructor of the course which style you should use. This book also includes information on using APA style because almost every college student will write papers in social science classes.

Libraries and writing centers usually have many different books explaining each style in detail, and there are also excellent Websites on each. The information you get from a Website has the advantage of being more current, since these styles often change as methods of research and writing change. Increased access to the Internet and word-processing programs have caused great changes in MLA and other styles recently.

Like other aspects of research, documentation will be introduced in this book at the points where you might be likely to use it. The boxes that follow list where you can find information about using MLA and APA styles.

Details of Using MLA Style

Parenthetical Documentation: pp. 335–337

Citations: pp. 337–339

Sample MLA Style Paper: pp. 350–352

Writing in Response to Literature: pp. 310–327

Details of Using APA Style

Parenthetical Documentation: pp. 340–342
Citations: pp. 342–344
Sample APA Style Paper: pp. 352–354

THE ESSAY: WRITING A PERSONAL ESSAY

Not every essay you write will respond to something written by another author. Sometimes you will write an essay relying only on your own thoughts and experiences. The format of the essay and the process of writing it are pretty much the same whether you respond directly to another writer or develop your ideas entirely on your own. The following box lists the parts of an essay when no outside reading is used.

Parts of a Personal Essay

Introduction (pp. 165–168)

The introduction prepares the reader for the ideas developed in the essay and provides some background necessary to understand the context for these ideas.

■ The **lead-in** involves the reader in the topic.

■ The lead-in also provide all of the **background information** necessary to understand the basic starting point of the essay. This background functions similarly to the summary of a reading.

■ The (student's) **writer's thesis** tells your main idea and may include a plan of development to indicate how the thesis will be developed in the body.

Body (pp. 179–183)

The body consists of several paragraphs divided according to different reasons that support the thesis or different ways that the thesis is *true*.

■ Each body paragraph contains the following features.

   A **topic sentence** that gives the main idea of the paragraph. The topic sentence can also clarify how the paragraph develops the thesis.

   Examples and ideas from the writer that clearly support the main idea of each paragraph

   A **concluding sentence** that reminds the reader how the support relates to the main idea of the paragraph

continued on next page

continued from previous page

Conclusion (pp. 191–194)

The conclusion is a return to the main idea and reminds the reader how the body supports the thesis.

- The conclusion always restates the **writer's thesis.**
- The conclusion reconnects with the relevant main idea(s) of the body paragraphs.
- The conclusion usually ends on a final thought, such as a general observation, a recommendation, or a warning.

In the sample essay that follows, each of these divisions and subdivisions is labeled. Notice how the entire essay continues to focus on one central idea.

There's No Such Thing as "Just Following Orders"

INTRODUCTION

1   I have what I call a "button board." It is like a bulletin board, but it only contains buttons. In the middle of my board are my two favorites: "Question Authority" and "No B.S. Please." The two are closely related in my mind. One is an obvious reminder that just because something or someone is an authority, they should not be automatically accepted. The second explains why authorities sometimes cannot be trusted. Sometimes following orders involves just following unreasonable and arbitrary rules. Of course, sometimes, following orders prevents chaos. But I believe that there are certain situations when people should not follow orders. I can imagine at least three situations in which not following orders or not obeying an authority is preferable to following orders. The most obvious situation is one in which someone tells you to do something that is clearly against your morals. Another situation is one in which the orders or instructions you are given seem to be harmful to the larger society around us. A different kind of situation is when a person just has to stand up for common sense and reasonable behavior, even if following orders does not do anyone specific harm or damage.

lead-in

discussion of ideas

THESIS

BODY PARAGRAPH

2   We are all familiar with what is referred to as "the Holocaust" in Nazi Germany during World War II. This must be for many people the epitome of what happens when many people

BODY PARAGRAPH

follow orders that were immoral, and it was definitely one time when those immoral orders should not have been followed. Of course, authority there was fragmented. Not every "undesirable" was arrested and sent to concentration camps in one moment—some people just vanished. Although Adolf Hitler was elected as Chancellor of Germany, the population did not have a referendum and vote "yes" or "no" on a proposition like: "arrest, steal from, put into concentration camps, starve, work until exhaustion, physically abuse, and then kill all undesirable people." No, the people just did their little parts in obeying orders, like just identifying suspicious individuals, just driving the transport trains, just guarding the individuals, just collecting property, just making an inventory of individuals, just taking "abandoned" property, etc. The list could be very long, but each little act followed an immoral order, in the long run, although only a few people actually pulled triggers, pushed buttons, or turned knobs that delivered physical pain and death. And of course, everyone could rationalize their little part by saying that this was a wartime situation and different rules applied and that after the war everything would be better and you could afford to have scruples then. But even war is no excuse for following immoral orders.

topic sentence

ideas and examples

concluding sentence

BODY PARAGRAPH

3   Usually obeying an authority in a situation like the Holocaust also involves fear. The individuals who obey authority are afraid of what might happen to other people they care for like family members. It doesn't take a holocaust to make that fear real. For example, people who work for a business or company that does harm to other individuals or the public in general might be afraid to disobey because they will lose their jobs and their families will suffer—but they need to learn to look beyond that fear and see the great harm they are causing by following orders that are not always as clearly immoral as the Holocaust. People who have worked for companies that fail to advance people of different races, ethnic backgrounds, or members of one sex may complain about the company's policies, but they do not refuse to work—and they should. The personnel managers continue to hire, fire, and promote those people their bosses tell them to, even if they may disagree about who is really more qualified for a particular position. Similarly, people who work for companies that pollute or

topic sentence

BODY PARAGRAPH

wastefully use more resources than they are entitled to may keep their jobs because they fear to lose the money and benefits provided to themselves and their family members. For example, a public facility may refuse to let a non-profit organization reserve its space in advance because it wants to hold it in reserve for potentially paying companies. That is, the administrator is reinterpreting her position as caretaker of public facilities; she wants to generate funds by using those public facilities. In this case, the person making reservations may be told to tell a middle-school enrichment program for at-risk students that the facilities are unavailable because an insurance company has inquired—just inquired—about using the facilities to host a management training seminar. But the facilities were built with public monies allocated for the public use, and were not intended as a money-making resource for the public. Should the reservation assistant follow orders and tell the at-risk program coordinator to call back later? Or should she make a reservation for 50 seventh graders who need positive experiences with public facilities, who need to learn that official programs do not mean detention or summer school? This is definitely a time to disobey orders. The effect of this bad order was not as drastically harmful as the effect of the Holocaust, but ultimately society would have benefited if this bureaucrat had put morals before profit.

ideas and examples

concluding sentence

BODY PARAGRAPH

4   Some orders may not violate moral principles, but go against common sense. These orders, too, should be disobeyed. Once I had a job searching for information on-line and in a special library for a project on allocation of public funds according to demographic factors—people's different backgrounds and socioeconomic status. It was just a summer job, but I enjoyed it. I made folders of related information, and I got to decide how to organize the information and what supporting documentation and photocopies to include for support. I compared expenditures per student in Minnesota to expenditures per student in my own state. But there was one drawback. The project administrator kept calling meetings. He would call them whenever he wanted to communicate with us. (Of course, he could have used the Internet for most of them!) He would call them without any notice. He would call them at 9:00 a.m. for 11:00 a.m. There was no crisis. He just called

topic sentence

ideas and examples

BODY PARAGRAPH

meetings. I wrote a letter asking for at least 24-hours notice for meetings that did not have at least that much notice. I said I could not guarantee that I would attend meetings if I did not have at least that much notice. And I got fired. Is this really an example of not following orders? In a way, no. But, in another way, yes. If something does not make sense, just "because someone says to" is not enough reason to do it. People should not follow orders that are motivated only by an individual's ego. People should follow orders that are reasonable. If people get into a habit of not questioning orders and people who give orders become complacent about having to justify their orders—even to employees, the world could become a dangerous place.

ideas and examples

concluding sentence

CONCLUSION

5   Should we follows orders? Yes, if they make sense and do no harm, or less harm than not following them. Sometimes, in a moment of crisis, following orders of an authority figure, such as a park ranger or medical professional, is the right thing to do. In such moments, the person giving the orders clearly has the other person's best interests in mind. But in most other situations, it is always a good idea to question authority and to evaluate the reasons underlying any order. Even getting used to "just following orders" without thinking is dangerous in a free society. It is also true that sometimes there may be great pressures on people to try to survive, but surviving at the expense of ethical and moral behavior, maybe even at the expense of other people's chances for advancement, health, or even lives only makes us part of the immoral and unethical behavior. Even if we are only a small part of a larger organization, we are still responsible for what we agree to do. If more people would question authority and refuse to mindlessly follow orders, the world would be a better place. Not only would there be less B.S., but there might even be less corruption, discrimination, and other unethical and immoral behavior.

return to main idea

The chapters that cover developing an essay will show you steps that respond to readings, but many of the steps are the same when you develop a personal essay based only on your own ideas, observations, or experiences. You'll find the **Tips** symbol in the margin to help you recognize sections that will be especially useful when writing this kind of essay. Here's a brief list of pages you'll use if you are *not* writing in response to a reading.

TIPS

CYBER COLLEGE: WRITING, READING, THINKING— AND COMPUTERS

Computers provide a way to improve your work efficiently without recopying your paper between drafts. This is important when you revise or edit your drafts. You may improve the parts you are working on, but you are very likely to introduce new errors if you are just copying what is correct. (Try it. Copy this entire paragraph in a hurry and see if you are accurate or if you have made some mistakes.) Another reason computers are good writing tools is that you can rearrange either large parts of your writing or individual sentences many times to discover which order is best. There are many other reasons to use a computer when writing. You can probably add to this list.

- Word-processed papers can be saved and reprinted.
- Word-processed papers can become parts of larger projects.
- Group work is easier if everyone has an electronic version of their contributions and the parts can be merged together to create a larger uniform document.
- More individual help in revising and editing is available on computers. These computer program aids include **spell checks**, **grammar checks**, style checks, and format checks. Grammar and spelling tutorials are also available as computer software.
- Keeping an **Editing Log** (see pp. 245–247) is easier with a computer.
- If you are unable to come to class, you can e-mail your paper to your instructor (and not lose points because the paper is late).
- An instructor can e-mail comments back to you, so it's not necessary to go to the instructor's office.
- Employers assume more and more that all employees will have some kinds of word-processing skills.

The Computer Skills You'll Need

Using computers can improve the quality of the work you do. You should start using them for writing essays and doing other assignments as soon as possible. Even if it seems that doing the first draft takes more time on the computer, in the long run you will save time, and your work will improve. The more you use a computer, the quicker your skills will improve. Here are the essential skills you should try to master as soon as you come to college.

Keyboarding—learning to type by touch

Word processing—learning a recently published and commonly used program such as Word for Windows or WordPerfect

Sending e-mail—sending and receiving messages and attachments

Finding information on the Web—using **search engines** and databases

Downloading files—moving information from the Internet to your own computer

Chatrooms, discussion Webs/boards, listservs—using the Internet for conversations, especially about classes

Evaluating Internet material—learning to distinguish good information from bad

Computer Tips

Although using a computer to write papers has many advantages, there are also some potential problems you should try to avoid. Follow these tips to use computers more efficiently in your own work.

Saving Your Work   It is very important to save your work. After all, one of the main reasons you are word-processing your work is so you won't have to re-type all of your papers. If you are working on your own computer, you can save your files on the hard drive. However, because you may be working on your paper in more than one location, you will want to save it in a way that is accessible when you are not at home.

- **Always save your work on a disk**. Do not use public hard drives, such as the hard drives on computers in a writing center or a learning center. Lab assistants and tutors periodically clean all documents off the hard drives, so your paper may be deleted as a matter of lab policy. You may also be unable to get to the computer you saved your document on. If the computers are not networked, you will not be able to retrieve your document unless you work on the same computer.

- **Give obvious names to your files**. *Paper2*, *Essay3* or *Paper2-rev1* is easy to remember. You may find it helpful to add the date to the name—for example, *P1-2-18-02*.

- **Make backup copies of your files**. You may lose a disk, or the disk may become damaged or corrupted.

- **Save your revised work with a new name** (using *Save as*). You will need to keep older drafts. If you save a file with the same name, the most recent version will replace the older draft and the older draft will be lost. If you had some good ideas, notes, or prewriting that might be useful in a later revision, you should save the new draft under a different name. Your instructor may also require you to show rough drafts as part of the assignment in order for you to get full credit.

- **Label the disk you are working on** so you do not bring the wrong disk to class or the computer lab.

- **Beware of viruses**. Learn how use virus checkers, and do not use pirated software. Be careful when you copy material from the Internet. You may also get viruses from using public labs.

- **Learn to send files as attachments**. If you do not have a disk with you and you are working on a public computer, you can send yourself the file as an e-mail attachment.

- **Learn to save files in different formats**. If you are working on different computers, or if you are working on a group project, you need to save backup copies of your work as .rtf (rich text format) files and .txt (text) files. Do not assume that others have the same word-processing program or that they have a version that is compatible with your computer.

Spell Checking Your Work   Learn to use the spell checker in your word-processor program, but check each word that is highlighted/underlined by the spell checker.

- When in doubt, you should use a dictionary. That way you can check to see if the underlined word is a real word that is not in the spell checker's list or if the suggested correction is what you want to say.

- Most names are not part of the dictionary of spell checkers. Last names like *Mathabane* will be underlined, even if they are correct.

- Spell checkers just check the word against a list. They do not check to see if the word makes sense in that context. For example, *bought* and *brought* are both verbs, but they have different meanings. Some "unrecognized" misspellings can change the meaning of a sentence: *They voted to except him* and *They voted to accept him* have different meanings.

- Spell checkers usually count repeated words as mistakes. However, read the sentence below. Sometimes a word needs to be repeated because it serves different functions, as in *That that that I deleted should have been left in.*

■ Because most people are not efficient and accurate keyboarders, they make more spelling mistakes. They may type *van* for *can* or *nut* for *but*. Read your paper aloud to catch this type of typographical error that spell checkers miss.

Grammar Checking Your Work   Most grammar checkers are not very accurate. They are no substitute for a good tutor or instructor. They will not do your important jobs of editing and proofreading your paper.

■ While grammar checkers can help you see if a sentence is very long, this does not necessarily mean all long sentences should be changed. Some long sentences are effective. For example, you may need a long, balanced list of equally important points.

■ Grammar checkers may not allow you to have compound words like *student work assistants*. They may also suggest that you add an *-s* to a present tense verb following an irregular plural noun: *The electronic media support this type of regulation.*

■ Grammar checkers may make automatic corrections unless you have turned off that option. They may change a specific unusual detail into a more common phrase that is not correct in the context. The grammar checker will automatically change *doe snot* to *does not*, even if you were discussing a deer with a runny nose.

Formatting Your Paper   Learn to use the tool bars to format your paper according to your instructor's specifications.

■ Be sure to leave one-inch margins on all sides, insert page numbers (with your name), and double-space the body of the paper. Center headings, and include identification information on the first page or the title page (if you have a separate one). Indent using the Tab key, and only use the **Enter (Return)** key if you want to start a new paragraph. See the sample paper in Chapter 13.

■ Ask your instructor what **format** you should follow for the *Works Cited* or *References* section. Usually you will need to have a **hanging indent**. Only use a hard return (the **Enter** key) between separate works. Do not line up the indented lines using the **Tab** key.

E-mailing Your Document   You should become familiar with how your instructor wants you to send electronic versions of your paper. Sending a file as an attachment will save most of the formatting. Also, you can probably cut and paste a file inside a regular e-mail message, although most of the formatting will be lost.

Tips for Using a Computer Effectively

- Always save your document on a disk.
- Keep backup copies.
- Learn to "Save as" with a new name.
- Watch out for viruses.
- Check the spell checker.
- Don't rely on grammar checkers.
- Be careful when formatting your paper.
- Learn to e-mail your work.
- Learn to send attachments with your e-mail.
- Learn to save your work in different formats.

EVALUATION: ESSAY EXAMS, THE WRITING PROCESS, AND PORTFOLIOS

Evaluation is another way of talking about grading. Your instructor may also refer to evaluation as assessment. In a writing class, you may be evaluated in different ways.

In some courses, you will need to write **essay exams**. You should prepare for these exams in much the same way you would prepare for an exam in a content subject, such as history. You should also practice timed writing in examlike conditions. Finally, before you write the exam, you should learn how you will be evaluated and practice applying the instructor's evaluation criteria to your own work.

Because revising and editing are such important parts of **the writing process**, you may be evaluated on how well you can show improvement between early drafts and final drafts in your writing. You may also be asked to critically evaluate your writing yourself. That is, you may need to explain how your writing satisfies the requirements for a course or measures up to the standards of a course. You may need to demonstrate that you understand the steps an independent writer follows.

You may also be evaluated holistically on the major work you produce for a course. This means you will prepare a **portfolio** of your course work, arranged and organized according to your instructor's specific instructions. Portfolios often include self-assessment, especially assessment focused on the notions of the writing process and developing the skills necessary to be an independent writer in college. You may be asked to introduce your portfolio with a cover letter that discusses the strengths and weaknesses of your writing at the beginning of the course and the strengths and weaknesses of your writing at the end of the course. More information on writing for evaluation is given in Chapter 14.

ENGLISH AS A SECOND LANGUAGE (ESL) AND THIS BOOK

If you have learned English as a second language, many of the sections of this book should be especially helpful to you. Your fellow students whose native language is English are actually learning a new language, too: they are learning to read and write Academic English instead of the more informal English they often use when speaking. They will need to develop proficiency in Academic English and distinguish it from the writing style they use in e-mails or informal letters. In many parts of the book, you'll find that the information and explanations you need as an ESL student are included as parts of the chapters intended for all students. To find those sections easily, look for the **ESL** symbol in the margin. For easy reference, here are some sections you should find useful.

ESL

> ### *Useful Pages for Solving ESL Problems*
>
> Reading: pp. 65–66, 75–76, 81–82
>
> Analyzing the Assignment: pp. 78–82, 91–92
>
> Prewriting: pp. 105–106
>
> Organizing: pp. 125, 141–142
>
> Writing: pp. 156–158, 171, 184–185
>
> Revising: pp. 199–202, 230
>
> Editing: pp. 235–268
>
> Modes of Developing an Essay (Expository and Argumentative Essays): pp. 282–309
>
> Research: pp. 328–356
>
> Documentation of Sources (MLA and APA): pp. 335–339, 340–344
>
> Writing about Literature: 310–327
>
> Evaluation (Essay Exams and Portfolios): 270–281
>
> Handbook (Grammar and Mechanics): 358–418

Reading and Vocabulary

Learning new vocabulary is a big task when learning a new language. When you first began to study English, you may have memorized lists of words. You may still want to work on memory, but as much as possible you should now try to learn to understand words from their **context**, which is exactly what native speakers must also do (see p. 65). Be sure that you have two dictionaries. Don't rely on your ESL dictionary only. You should also use a college-level dictionary for native speakers. You may find useful explanations in either dictionary, but be sure to look for the appropriate meaning for the sentence (see p. 66).

Keeping Lists

Keeping a small notebook with you at all times and jotting down new words is one additional way to increase your knowledge of English. You may encounter words in your textbooks for many subjects, in advertisements, in newspapers, and in many other places. Write down the word and your best guess at the meaning, and then check the meaning in a dictionary when you have time.

Words alone, however, may not be enough. You also need to know how words are used. In English and in other languages, certain words are customarily used together. For example, take the word *bill*, meaning money owed for services or goods. You might hear American English speakers say, "Pay the bill," but you would not hear them say, "Pay for the bill," "Cash the bill," or "Spend the bill," although the dictionary meanings of some of these words may seem to be very close to the meaning of *pay*. These common combinations of words are called **collocations**, and you may want to keep a vocabulary list that includes the phrase where you found the word. You can ask instructors, tutors, and other students for other possible collocations for your words, so leave room to add to your list.

Some combinations of words have meanings that are entirely different from the meaning of the individual words. These are called **idioms**, and you may want to keep a special section of your notebook for these expressions. Idioms are more common in spoken language and slang, but you will find idioms even in academic writing, and certain subjects (like computer science) may have their own idioms. For example, when someone says she "crashed her hard drive," she means that the main part of her computer doesn't work, but she does not mean that it is physically broken. If your college has a writing center, it may have a dictionary of idioms, but you may still want to keep your own list.

Steps in the Reading and Writing Process

You may find that the many steps outlined in this book are helpful, or you may not understand why you need to do so many different things before, during, and after you read an article or write an essay, especially if you are accustomed to reading difficult material and writing academic essays about it. The explanations in the chapters should help you understand how the steps lead to the kind of reading and writing expected in colleges in the United States. If you try the steps, you may find them helpful, but if you've already developed the skills of reading, writing, and critical thinking, you may need to spend your time working with vocabulary and editing.

You may find that the kind of reading and writing expected in this course is very similar to the kind you've done in other classes, but you should not be surprised if your instructor asks for something different from what you've done before. Look at the examples in the chapters related to your assignments, especially the explanations with the **ESL** icon, and ask your instructor if you still don't understand what the terms mean. Check the Glossary for more explanations of the terms in this book.

Look especially at the sections on stating the **thesis** sentence (pp. 157–161). This is a very important element in academic writing in the United States. You may not feel it is important to plainly state the central idea of your essay, but your instructors will probably prefer that you clearly state the main idea. Also, look at sections on support (pp. 170–171), which tell you the kinds of facts, examples, and explanations expected in this kind of writing.

It is also important to understand plagiarism (pp. 26–27). When writing for other readers—especially academic writing—instructors, employers, and others who are evaluating your writing will insist that every word or idea that you did not think of yourself must be documented (pp. 334–344). Some instructors may mistakenly believe that you are trying to cheat if you do not identify and document sources. Employers or clients may think you are stealing ideas or specific phrasing from others. This means that you must always identify very explicitly where you found the words or ideas (also called *sources*).

Group Work

One common activity in different stages of reading and writing is group work. You may be familiar with this way of learning, or maybe you think only the instructor can help you to improve your writing. Many instructors, however, want you to learn to understand different points of view about articles that you read. They want you to learn to write for many different audiences, so they will ask you to discuss your reactions to articles written by your fellow students as well as by professional writers. They may also ask you to check each other's writing for errors in grammar, spelling, and punctuation—called **editing**. If this kind of classwork is new to you, you should read the sections on **peer editing** (pp. 247–248). You may find that working with other students is very helpful because often they will see problems in your writing that you may not recognize.

Collaboration You also may find that looking for other students' problems helps you learn to find your own. Look for the **Collaboration** symbol to find these activities.

USING THE SKILLS OF COLLEGE READING, WRITING, AND THINKING

In the rest of this book, you will find much more material on writing essays, using sources, using the computer, and using the English language. This book will help you to improve in those areas and to find specific remedies for problems you encounter in your writing assignments. Talk with your instructor, tutors, and fellow students to find the sections that will help you the most. Read the sections carefully, try the exercises, and review when you go on to use the skill in your reading and writing. This book will work for you if *you* will work.

3 Five Readings for Analysis

The five essays in this chapter will be used as examples throughout the rest of the book. You may want to read them as you come to them in the following chapters, or you may want to read them early in the course so that you can understand the references as you encounter them.

Measuring Success

by Renee Loth

Renee Loth is an award-winning veteran journalist and editor. She frequently comments on politics and the media. Loth, writing in the Boston Globe Magazine *in 1997, questions our definitions of success. Is success only financial, or can it mean other things?*

1 Back when I was a callow college student, I devised a neat grid system for what I hoped would be my life's achievements. I could count my life a good one, I thought, if I could attain both success and happiness. So I set about analyzing the component parts of each: Happiness I subdivided into sections labeled health and love; success, I determined, was composed of wealth and fame.

2   Once I actually entered the world of work, however, I learned that success is not so easy to define. For one thing, when I made my simple calculation, I never took into account the joy of creation; the approbation of one's peers; the energy of collaboration; or the sheer satisfaction of a job well done. These are real qualities of success that live outside of wealth or fame. Also, I found that definitions of success are mutable, shifting along with our changing values. If we stick with our chosen fields long enough, we sometimes have an opportunity to meet our heroes, people we thought wildly successful when we were young. A musician friend told me that he spent most of his youth wanting to play like the greats, until he started getting to know some of them. To his surprise, many turned out to be embittered, dulled by drink or boredom, unable to hold together a marriage, or wantonly jealous of others. That's when he realized he wanted to play like himself.

3   Success is defined differently by different people. For some, it is symbolized by the number of buttons on the office phone. For others, it is having only one button and a secretary to field the calls. Some think the more nights and weekends they spend at the office, the more successful they must be. For others, success is directly proportional to time off.

4   And what about those qualities I did include in my handy grid system? Wealth—beyond what is needed to provide for oneself and one's family, with a little left over for airfare to someplace subtropical in January—turned out to be superfluous. And the little experience I had with fame turned out to be downright scary.

5   Several years ago, I had occasion to appear on a dull but respected national evening television news show. My performance lasted exactly six minutes, and my name flashed only twice. But when I got home from the live broadcast, my answering machine had maxed out on messages.

6   I heard from a woman I had last seen in Brownie Scouts. I heard from former boyfriends, conspiracy theorists, and celebrity agents. I even got an obscene phone call—what kind of pervert watches PBS?—from someone who might have been an old friend pulling my leg. At least, I hope so.

7   For weeks afterward, I received tons of what an optimist might call fan mail. One fellow insisted that if I froze a particular frame of a political campaign ad I had been discussing, I could see the face of Bill Clinton in the American flag. Somebody sent me a chapter of a novel in progress with a main character disturbingly like me. Several people sent me chain letters.

8   I was relieved when the fickle finger of fame moved on to someone else.

9   When I was young and romanticizing about success, I liked a particular Joni Mitchell lyric: "My struggle for higher achievement and my search for love don't seem to cease." Ah, but the trouble with struggling and searching is that it keeps us in a permanent state of wanting—always reaching for more. The drive to succeed keeps us focused on the future, to the detriment of life in the moment. And the moment is all we ever really have.

10   When I look back at my simplistic little value system, I am a bit chagrined at how absolute I thought life was. But I am also happy to report that the achievements that have come my way are the ones that count. After twenty years of supercharged ambition, I have stumbled upon this bit of wisdom. Who needs wealth and fame? Two out of four ain't bad.

My Father's Tribal Rule

by Mark Mathabane

Mark Mathabane grew up in South Africa and experienced the hardships of the years of apartheid. A college scholarship brought him to the United States. This selection is taken from his autobiography, Kaffir Boy, *published in 1986. Math-*

abane now lives in Oregon. His latest work of nonfiction is Miriam's Song: A Memoir. *Mathabane's recent novel,* Ubuntu, *is a thriller set in apartheid South Africa.*

1 One night our dingy shack, which had been leaning precipitously on the edge of a *donga*[1] collapsed. Luckily no one was hurt, but we were forced to move to another one, similarly built. This new shack, like the old one, had two rooms and measured something like fifteen by fifteen feet, and over-looked the same unlit, unpaved, potholed street. It had an interior flaked with old whitewash, a leaky roof of rusted zinc propped up by a thin wall of crumbling adobe, two tiny windows made of cardboard and pieces of glass, a creaky, termite-eaten door too low for a person of average height to pass through without bending double, and a floor made of patches of cement and earth. It was similar to the dozen or so shacks strewn irregularly, like lumps on a leper, upon the cracked greenless piece of ground named yard number thirty-five.

2 In this new shack my brother, George, was weaned. It was amusing to wit-ness my mother do it. The first day she began the process she secretly smeared her breasts with red pepper and then invited my brother to suckle. Unsuspecting, George energetically attacked my mother's breast only to let go of it instantly and start hollering because of the hot pepper. This continued throughout the day whenever he wanted to suckle. Finally, after a few days, he began to dread the sight of my mother's breast, and each time she teased him with it he would turn his face. He was now weaned. My father bought a small white chicken, my mother brewed beer, a few relatives were invited, and a small celebration was held to mark George's passage from infancy to child-hood. He was almost two years old. He now had to sleep with Florah and me in the kitchen.

3 Soon after George was weaned my father began teaching him, as he had been teaching me, tribal ways of life. My father belonged to a loosely knit group of black families in the neighborhood to whom tribal traditions were a way of life, and who sought to bring up their offspring according to its laws. He believed that feeding us a steady diet of tribal beliefs, values, and rituals was one way of ensuring our normal growth, so that in the event of our re-turning to the tribal reserve, something he insistently believed would happen soon, we would blend in perfectly. This diet he administered religiously, seem-ingly bent on moulding George and me in his image. At first I had tried to re-sist the diet, but my father's severe looks frightened me.

4 A short, gaunt figure, with a smooth, tight, black-as-coal skin, large prominent jaws, thin, uneven lips whose sole function seemed to be the pro-duction of sneers, a broad nose with slightly flaring nostrils, small, bloodshot eyes which never cried, small, close-set ears, and a wide, prominent fore-head—such were my father's fearsome features.

5 Born and bred in a tribal reserve and nearly twice my mother's age, my fa-ther existed under the illusion, formed as much by a strange innate pride as

---

[1]*donga*: ravine

by a blindness to everything but his own will, that someday all white people would disappear from South Africa, and black people would revert to their old ways of living. To prepare for this eventuality, he ruled the house strictly according to tribal law, tolerating no deviance, particularly from his children. At the same time that he was force-feeding us tribalism we were learning other ways of life, modern ways, from mingling with children whose parents had shed their tribal cloth and embraced Western culture.

6   My father's tribal rule had as its fulcrum the constant performing of rituals spanning the range of day-to-day living. There were rituals to protect the house from evildoers, to ward off starvation, to prevent us from becoming sick, to safeguard his job, to keep the police away, to bring us good luck, to make him earn more money and many others which my young mind could not understand. Somehow they did not make sense to me; they simply awed, confused and embarrassed me, and the only reason I participated in them night after night was because my father made certain that I did, by using, among other things, the whip, and the threat of the retributive powers of my ancestral spirits, whose favor the rituals were designed to curry. Along with the rituals, there were also tribal laws governing manners.

7   One day I intentionally broke one of these laws: I talked while eating.

8   "That's never done in my house," my father screamed at me as he rose from the table where he had been sitting alone, presiding over our meal. I was eating *pap 'n vleis*[2] out of the same bowl with George and Florah. We were sitting on the floor, about the brazier, and my mother was in the bedroom doing something.

9   "You don't have two mouths to afford you such luxury!" he fumed, advancing threateningly toward me, a cold sneer on his thin-lipped, cankerous mouth. He seemed ten feet tall.

10   Terrified, I deserted the *pap 'n vleis* and fled to Mother.

11   "Bring him back here, woman!" my father called through the door as he unbuckled his rawhide belt. "He needs to be taught how to eat properly."

12   I began bawling, sensing I was about to be whipped.

13   My mother led me into the kitchen and pleaded for me. "He won't do it again. He's only a child, and you know how forgetful children are." At this point George and Florah stopped eating and watched with petrified eyes. "Don't give me that," snarled my father. "He's old enough to remember how to eat properly." He tore me away from my mother and lashed me. She tried to intervene, but my father shoved her aside and promised her the same. I never finished my meal; sobbing, I slunk off to bed, my limbs afire with pain where the rawhide had raised welts. The next day, as I nursed my wounds, while my father was at work, I told my mother that I hated him and promised her I would kill him when I grew up.

14   "Don't say that!" my mother reprimanded me.

15   "I will," I said stoutly, "if he won't leave me alone."

16   "He's your father, you know."

---

[2]*pap 'n vleis*: porridge with meat

17   "He's not my father."

18   "Shut that bad mouth of yours!" My mother threatened to smack me.

19   "Why does he beat me, then?" I protested. "Other fathers don't beat their children." My friends always boasted that their fathers never laid a hand on them.

20   "He's trying to discipline you. He wants you to grow up to be like him."

21   "What! Me! Never!" I shook with indignation. "I'm never going to be like him! Why should I?"

22   "Well, in the tribes sons grow up to be like their fathers."

23   "But we're not living in the tribes."

24   "But we're still of the tribes."

25   "I'm not," I said. Trying to focus the conversation on rituals, my nemesis, I said, after a thoughtful pause, "Is that why Papa insists that we do rituals?"

26   "Yes."

27   "But other people don't."

28   "Everybody does rituals, Mr. Mathabane," my mother said. "You just don't notice it because they do theirs differently. Even white people do rituals."

29   "Why do people do rituals, Mama?"

30   "People do rituals because they were born in the tribes. And in the tribes rituals are done every day. They are a way of life."

31   "But we don't live in the tribes," I countered. "Papa should stop doing rituals."

32   My mother laughed. "Well, it's not as simple as that. Your father grew up in the tribes, as you know. He didn't come to the city until he was quite old. It's hard to stop doing things when you're old. I, too, do rituals because I was raised in the tribes. Their meaning, child, will become clear as you grow up. Have patience."

33   But I had no patience with rituals, and I continued hating them.

34   Participation in my father's rituals sometimes led to the most appalling scenes, which invariably made me the laughingstock of my friends, who thought that my father, in his ritual garb, was the most hilarious thing they had ever seen since natives in Tarzan movies. Whenever they laughed at me I would feel embarrassed and would cry. I began seeking ways of distancing myself from my father's rituals. I found one: I decided I would no longer, in the presence of my friends, speak Venda, my father's tribal language. I began speaking Zulu, Sotho, and Tsonga, the languages of my friends. It worked. I was no longer an object of mockery. My masquerade continued until my father got wind of it.

35   "My boy," he began. "Who is ruler of this house?"

36   "You are, Papa," I said with a trembling voice.

37   "Whose son are you?"

38   "Yours and Mama's."

39   "Whose?"

40   "Yours."

41   "That's better. Now tell me, which language do I speak?"

42   "Venda."

43   "Which does your mama speak?"

44   "Venda."

45   "Which should you speak?"

46   "Venda."

47   "Then why do I hear you're speaking other tongues; are you a prophet?"

48   Before I could reply he grabbed me and lashed me thoroughly. Afterward he threatened to cut out my tongue if he ever again heard I wasn't speaking Venda. As further punishment, he increased the number of rituals I had to participate in. I hated him more for it.

Getting Off the Welfare Carousel

by Teresa McCrary

Teresa McCrary, as a single parent, relied on government subsidies while attending college. This essay was originally published in Newsweek *in 1993.*

1   I am a welfare mom, and I have one thing to say: stop picking on us! There are 5 million families on welfare in the United States, most of them single women with kids. Is this really such a major financial burden? I believe we're targeted because we're an easy mark. Because we have no money, there are no lobbyists working on our behalf either in Washington, D.C., or in local legislatures. I want to tell you who we are and why we stay home with our children.

2   The stereotypical welfare mom has 10 kids, including a pregnant teenage daughter, all taking advantage of the dole. I have never personally known such a woman. Most of the mothers I know are women who forgo the usual round of job searches and day care so they can mind their homes and children in a loving and responsible way. We may not have paying jobs, but any mother, married or single, working or retired, will tell you that motherhood is a career in itself.

3   Yet we are constantly told we should go out and get real jobs. Yes, most of us are unemployed: do we really have a choice? Last time I looked, the unemployment rate was more than 6 percent. If the unemployed can't find work, where are we moms supposed to look? The only jobs open to us are maid work, fast-food service and other low-paying drudgery with no benefits. How are we expected to support our children? Minimum wage will not pay for housing costs, health care, child care, transportation and work clothes that an untrained, uneducated woman needs to support even one child.

4   Many of us take money under the table for odd jobs, and cash from generous friends and relatives to help support our families. We don't report this money to the Aid to Families with Dependent Children, because we can't afford to. Any cash we get, even birthday money from grandparents, is deducted from the already minuscule benefits. We're allowed between $1,000 and

$3,000 in assets including savings and property, automobiles and home furnishings. We are told that if we have more than that amount, we should be able to sell some things and live for a year from the proceeds. Can you imagine living on $3,000 a year?

5   As for child support, unless the money sent to the state by the father is greater than AFDC benefits, the family receives only $50 monthly. We are told that the state intends to prosecute "deadbeat dads" for back support. Seldom do news stories mention that, in the case of welfare families, the state keeps collected back support. Although this reduces the tax burden, none of the money goes to the children. Outsiders are led to believe that the children will benefit, and they do not. No wonder some welfare moms—and their children's fathers—believe it's not worth the effort to try to get the dads to pay up. If we could have depended on these men in the first place, we would not be on welfare.

6   So what about family values? Those of us who do not have a man in our lives do the emotional job of both mother and father. My daughter says she should give me a Father's Day card, because I am just as much a father to her as a mother. On top of these two careers, we are told we should work.

7   We could hold down a minimum-wage job, unarguably the hardest work for the least amount of money, if we could find an employer willing to hire us full time (most low-wage jobs are part time). Unable to afford child care, we'd have latch-key children whose only good meal of the day would be school lunch. The whole paycheck would go to housing and job expenses. When we got home exhausted, we'd clean house, help with homework, listen to how the kids' day went—feeling relieved if none of them had been teased for their garage-sale clothes. We'd pray that nobody got sick, because we couldn't afford a day off work or doctor fees (welfare pays very little, but it has the important benefit of health care). We'd worry about getting laid off at any moment—in tough times, minimum wage jobs are the first to go.

8   These fears cause stress that may result in child abuse. Many times we feel, no matter how hard we try, that in some way our children are being neglected if we are holding down a job. So we stay home. We've learned that we can depend only on ourselves. We don't enjoy living at the poverty level, but we can't see a minimum-wage job as the answer.

9   I believe that we single mothers must become self-sufficient through education and training. And that means both money and patience on the taxpayers' part. I, and the other welfare moms I know at school, maintain a 3.0 grade average or better. Are we exceptions to the rule? Maybe not; perhaps people in my circumstances are more motivated to make better lives for themselves. Fighting the low self-esteem brought on by divorce and poverty, we have taken the difficult step, usually without a support system, of going back to school. By carefully scheduling classes and studying late at night, I have been able to care for my kids while learning TV and radio production.

10   College may be out of reach for many. By raising tuition and entrance requirements, most colleges and universities are barring us from their campuses. Even President Clinton's proposed two-year training program may not help

much. Vocational or technical schools mean training for low-paying jobs. Still, we'll be told to find work or lose our benefits.

11   If the government keeps decreasing or eliminating the programs we and the children depend upon for survival, here's what will happen: in a few years, instead of 5 million single women and their children on welfare, there will be 5 million single women and their children on the streets. I don't know how many starving millions the United Nations is trying to help in Somalia. But if people keep picking on us, the United Nations will have to help the United States feed *us.*

A Hanging

by George Orwell

George Orwell is the pen name of Eric Arthur Blair, who worked during the early 1930s to enforce the laws of the British Empire in Burma before becoming a writer in England. His novels 1984 *and* Animal Farm *satirize political oppression. This essay was originally published in* Shooting an Elephant and Other Essays *(1946).*

1   It was in Burma, a sodden morning of the rains. A sickly light, like yellow tin-foil, was slanting over the high walls into the jail yard. We were waiting outside the condemned cells, a row of sheds fronted with double bars, like small animal cages. Each cell measured about ten feet by ten and was quite bare within except for a plank bed and a pot of drinking water. In some of them brown silent men were squatting at the inner bars, with their blankets draped round them. These were the condemned men, due to be hanged within the next week or two.

2   One prisoner had been brought out of his cell. He was a Hindu, a puny wisp of a man, with a shaven head and vague liquid eyes. He had a thick, sprouting moustache, absurdly too big for his body, rather like the moustache of a comic man on the films. Six tall Indian warders were guarding him and getting him ready for the gallows. Two of them stood by with rifles with fixed bayonets, while the others handcuffed him, passed a chain through his hand-cuffs and fixed it to their belts, and lashed his arms tight to his sides. They crowded very close about him with their hands always on him in a careful, ca-ressing grip, as though all the while feeling him to make sure he was there. It was like men handling a fish which is still alive and may jump back into the water. But he stood quite unresisting, yielding his arms limply to the ropes, as though he hardly noticed what was happening.

3   Eight o'clock struck and a bugle call, desolately thin in the wet air, floated from the distant barracks. The superintendent of the jail, who was standing apart from the rest of us, moodily prodding the gravel with his stick, raised his head at the sound. He was an army doctor, with a grey

toothbrush moustache and a gruff voice. "For God's sake hurry up, Francis," he said irritably.

4 "The man ought to have been dead by this time. Aren't you ready yet?"

5 Francis, the head jailer, a fat Dravidian[1] in a white drill suit and gold spectacles, waved his black hand. "Yes sir, yes sir," he bubbled. "All iss satisfactorily prepared. The hangman iss waiting. We shall proceed."

6 "Well, quick march, then. The prisoners can't get their breakfast till this job's over."

7 We set out for the gallows. Two warders marched on either side of the prisoner, with their files at the slope; two others marched close against him, gripping him by arm and shoulder, as though at once pushing and supporting him. The rest of us, magistrates and the like, followed behind. Suddenly, when we had gone ten yards, the procession stopped short without any order or warning.

8 A dreadful thing had happened—a dog, come goodness knows whence, had appeared in the yard. It came bounding among us with a loud volley of barks, and leapt round us wagging its whole body, wild with glee at finding so many human beings together. It was a large woolly dog, half Airedale, half pariah. For a moment it pranced round us and then, before anyone could stop it, it had made a dash for the prisoner, and jumping up tried to lick his face. Everyone stood aghast, too taken aback even to grab at the dog.

9 "Who let that bloody brute in here?" said the superintendent angrily. "Catch it, someone!"

10 A warder, detached from the escort, charged clumsily after the dog, but it danced and gambolled just out of his reach, taking everything as part of the game. A young Eurasian jailer picked up a handful of gravel and tried to stone the dog away, but it dodged the stones and came after us again. Its yaps echoed from the jail walls. The prisoner, in the grasp of the two warders, looked on incuriously, as though this was another formality of the hanging. It was several minutes before someone managed to catch the dog. Then we put my handkerchief through its collar and moved off once more, with the dog still straining and whimpering.

11 It was about forty yards to the gallows. I watched the bare brown back of the prisoner marching in front of me. He walked clumsily with his bound arms, but quite steadily, with that bobbing gait of the Indian who never straightens his knees. At each step his muscles slid neatly into place, the lock of hair on his scalp danced up and down, his feet printed themselves on the wet gravel. And once, in spite of the men who gripped him by each shoulder, he stepped slightly aside to avoid a puddle on the path.

12 It is curious, but till that moment I had never realised what it means to destroy a healthy, conscious man. When I saw the prisoner step aside to avoid the puddle, I saw the mystery, the unspeakable wrongness, of cutting a life short when it is in full tide. This man was not dying, he was alive just as we were alive. All the organs of his body were working—bowels digesting food, skin renewing itself, nails growing, tissues forming—all toiling away in

---

[1]*Dravidian*: ethnic group from South Asia

solemn foolery. His nails would still be growing when he stood on the drop, when he was falling through the air with a tenth of a second to live. His eyes saw the yellow gravel and the grey walls, and his brain still remembered, foresaw, reasoned—reasoned even about puddles. He and we were a party of men walking together, seeing, hearing, feeling, understanding the same world; and in two minutes with a sudden snap, one of us would be gone—one mind less, one world less.

13   The gallows stood in a small yard, separate from the main grounds of the prison, and overgrown with tall prickly weeds. It was a brick erection like three sides of a shed, with planking on top, and above that two beams and a crossbar with the rope dangling. The hangman, a grey-haired convict in the white uniform of the prison was waiting beside his machine. He greeted us with a servile crouch as we entered. At a word from Francis the two warders, gripping the prisoner more closely than ever, half led, half pushed him to the gallows and helped him clumsily up the ladder. Then the hangman climbed up and fixed the rope round the prisoner's neck.

14   We stood waiting, five yards away. The warders had formed in a rough circle round the gallows. And then, when the noose was fixed the prisoner began crying out on his god. It was a high, reiterated cry of "Ram![2] Ram! Ram! Ram!," not urgent and fearful like a prayer or a cry for help, but steady, rhythmical, almost like the tolling of a bell. The dog answered the sound with a whine. The hangman, standing on the gallows, produced a small cotton bag like a flour bag and drew it down over the prisoner's face. But the sound, muffled by the cloth, still persisted, over and over again: "Ram! Ram! Ram! Ram!"

15   The hangman climbed down and stood ready, holding the lever. Minutes seemed to pass. The steady, muffled crying from the prisoner went on and on, "Ram! Ram! Ram!" never faltering for an instant. The superintendent, his head on his chest, was slowly poking the ground with his stick; perhaps he was counting the cries, allowing the prisoner a fixed number—fifty, perhaps, or a hundred. Everyone had changed colour. The Indians had gone grey like bad coffee, and one or two of the bayonets were wavering. We looked at the lashed, hooded man on the drop, and listened to his cries—each cry another second of life; the same thought was in all our minds: oh, kill him quickly, get it over, stop that abominable noise!

16   Suddenly the superintendent made up his mind. Throwing up his head he made a swift motion with his stick. "Chalo!" he shouted almost fiercely.

17   There was a clanking noise, and then dead silence. The prisoner had vanished, and the rope was twisting on itself. I let go of the dog, and it galloped immediately to the back of the gallows; but when it got there it stopped short, barked, and then retreated into a corner of the yard, where it stood among the weeds, looking timorously out at us. We went round the gallows to inspect the prisoner's body. He was dangling with his toes pointed straight downwards, very slowly revolving, as dead as a stone.

---

[2]*Ram*: name of deity worshipped in South Asia

18   The superintendent reached out with his stick and poked the bare body; it oscillated, slightly. *"He's* all right," said the superintendent. He backed out from under the gallows, and blew out a deep breath. The moody look had gone out of his face quite suddenly. He glanced at his wristwatch. "Eight minutes past eight. Well, that's all for this morning, thank God."

19   The warders unfixed bayonets and marched away. The dog, sobered and conscious of having misbehaved itself, slipped after them. We walked out of the gallows yard, past the condemned cells with their waiting prisoners, into the big central yard of the prison. The convicts, under the command of warders armed with lathis,[3] were already receiving their breakfast. They squatted in long rows, each man holding a tin pannikin, while two warders with buckets marched round ladling out rice; it seemed quite a homely, jolly scene, after the hanging. An enormous relief had come upon us now that the job was done. One felt an impulse to sing, to break into a run, to snigger. All at once everyone began chattering gaily.

20   The Eurasian boy walking beside me nodded towards the way we had come, with a knowing smile: "DO you know, sir, our friend (he meant the dead man), when he heard his appeal had been dismissed, he pissed on the floor of his cell. From fright—Kindly take one of my cigarettes, sir. Do you not admire my new silver case, sir? From the boxwallah,[4] two rupees eight annas. Classy European style."

21   Several people laughed—at what, nobody seemed certain.

22   Francis was walking by the superintendent, talking garrulously: "Well, sir, all hass passed off with the utmost satisfactoriness. It wass all finished—flick! like that. It iss not always so—oah, no! I have known cases where the doctor wass obliged to go beneath the gallows and pull the prisoner's legs to ensure decease. Most disagreeable!"

23   "Wriggling about, eh? That's bad," said the superintendent.

24   "Ach, sir, it iss worse when they become refractory! One man, I recall, clung to the bars of hiss cage when we went to take him out. You will scarcely credit, sir, that it took six warders to dislodge him, three pulling at each leg. We reasoned with him. 'My dear fellow,' we said, 'think of all the pain and trouble you are causing to us!' But no, he would not listen! Ach, he wass very troublesome!"

25   I found that I was laughing quite loudly. Everyone was laughing. Even the superintendent grinned in a tolerant way. "You'd better all come out and have a drink," he said quite genially. "I've got a bottle of whisky in the car. We could do with it."

26   We went through the big double gates of the prison, into the road. "Pulling at his legs!" exclaimed a Burmese magistrate suddenly, and burst into a loud chuckling. We all began laughing again. At that moment Francis's anecdote seemed extraordinarily funny. We all had a drink together, native and European alike, quite amicably. The dead man was a hundred yards away.

---

[3]*lathis*: heavy wood and metal sticks
[4]*boxwallah*: peddler

The Story of an Hour

by Kate Chopin

Kate Chopin (1851–1904) grew up in St. Louis, moved to Louisiana with her husband, and returned to St. Louis after his death. Her novel, The Awakening, *is about a sensual, independent-minded woman, and is regarded as an early feminist work. "The Story of an Hour" (1894) presents a very short time in a woman's life, although it reveals much about her life. This surprising short story suggests that people are not always aware of their inner feelings.*

1 Knowing that Mrs. Mallard was afflicted with heart trouble, great care was taken to break to her as gently as possible the news of her husband's death.

2 It was her sister Josephine who told her, in broken sentences, veiled hints that revealed in half concealing. Her husband's friend Richards was there, too, near her. It was he who had been in the newspaper office when intelligence of the railroad disaster was received, with Brently Mallard's name leading the list of "killed." He had only taken the time to assure himself of its truth by a second telegram, and had hastened to forestall any less careful, less tender friend in bearing the sad message.

3 She did not hear the story as many women have heard the same, with a paralyzed inability to accept its significance. She wept at once, with sudden, wild abandonment, in her sister's arms. When the storm of grief had spent itself she went away to her room alone. She would have no one follow her.

4 There stood, facing the open window, a comfortable, roomy armchair. Into this she sank, pressed down by a physical exhaustion that haunted her body and seemed to reach into her soul.

5 She could see in the open square before her house the tops of trees that were all aquiver with the new spring life. The delicious breath of rain was in the air. In the street below a peddler was crying his wares. The notes of a distant song which some one was singing reached her faintly, and countless sparrows were twittering in the eaves.

6 There were patches of blue sky showing here and there through the clouds that had met and piled one above the other in the west facing her window.

7 She sat with her head thrown back upon the cushion of the chair, quite motionless, except when a sob came up into her throat and shook her, as a child who has cried itself to sleep continues to sob in its dreams.

8 She was young, with a fair, calm face, whose lines bespoke repression and even a certain strength. But now there was a dull stare in her eyes, whose gaze was fixed away off yonder on one of those patches of blue sky. It was not a glance of reflection, but rather indicated a suspension of intelligent thought.

9 There was something coming to her and she was waiting for it, fearfully. What was it? She did not know; it was too subtle and elusive to name. But she felt it, creeping out of the sky, reaching toward her through the sounds, the scents, the color that filled the air.

10   Now her bosom rose and fell tumultuously. She was beginning to recognize this thing that was approaching to possess her, and she was striving to beat it back with her will—as powerless as her two white slender hands would have been.

11   When she abandoned herself a little whispered word escaped her slightly parted lips. She said it over and over under her breath: "Free, free, free!" The vacant stare and the look of terror that had followed it went from her eyes. They stayed keen and bright. Her pulses beat fast, and the coursing blood warmed and relaxed every inch of her body.

12   She did not stop to ask if it were not a monstrous joy that held her. A clear and exalted perception enabled her to dismiss the suggestion as trivial.

13   She knew that she would weep again when she saw the kind, tender hands folded in death; the face that had never looked save with love upon her, fixed and gray and dead. But she saw beyond that bitter moment a long procession of years to come that would belong to her absolutely. And she opened and spread her arms out to them in welcome.

14   There would be no one to live for during those coming years; she would live for herself. There would be no powerful will bending her in that blind persistence with which men and women believe they have a right to impose a private will upon a fellow creature. A kind intention or a cruel intention made the act seem no less a crime as she looked upon it in that brief moment of illumination.

15   And yet she had loved him—sometimes. Often she had not. What did it matter! What could love, the solved mystery, count for in face of this possession of self-assertion which she suddenly recognized as the strongest impulse of her being.

16   "Free! Body and soul free!" she kept whispering.

17   Josephine was kneeling before the closed door with her lips to the keyhole, imploring for admission. "Louise, open the door! I beg; open the door—you will make yourself ill. What are you doing, Louise? For heaven's sake open the door."

18   "Go away. I am not making myself ill." No; she was drinking in a very elixir of life through that open window.

19   Her fancy was running riot along those days ahead of her. Spring days, and summer days, and all sorts of days that would be her own. She breathed a quick prayer that life might be long. It was only yesterday she had thought with a shudder that life might be long.

20   She arose at length and opened the door to her sister's importunities. There was a feverish triumph in her eyes, and she carried herself unwittingly like a goddess of Victory. She clasped her sister's waist, and together they descended the stairs. Richards stood waiting for them at the bottom.

21   Some one was opening the front door with a latchkey. It was Brently Mallard who entered, a little travel-stained, composedly carrying his gripsack and umbrella. He had been far from the scene of the accident, and did not even know there had been one. He stood amazed at Josephine's piercing cry; at Richards' quick motion to screen him from the view of his wife.

22   But Richards was too late.

23   When the doctors came they said she had died of heart disease—of joy that kills.

PART TWO

Using Essential Strategies for Writing Essays

4 Reading in College:
Surveying, Annotating, Reviewing, Evaluating

What You Need to Do First

- Prepare to read by thinking, talking, and writing about the topic
- Preview what you'll read to get the main idea
- While you read, keep your mind focused by writing and thinking
- Look back over the reading to be sure you understand it
- Evaluate the reading to determine its value
- Learn from the reading to improve your own writing

The Reading Process

Prepare to read.

Survey before reading.

Read actively.

Review after reading.

Evaluate what you've read.

Model on the reading

When you read an advertisement, you're not supposed to think about it—you're just supposed to let it slide into your mind. But when you read more serious material, you can't just let the words slide in—especially not if you must prepare a written response. If you have acquired the habit of easy reading that just flows through your mind, you'll need to find some ways of stopping and looking carefully at what you're reading and what you think about it. The ideas in this chapter will help you pay attention to different parts of a reading. If reading is usually slow and painful for you, you'll also find the techniques discussed here to be helpful. These techniques will not help you read faster, but they will help you understand what you've read. Reading carefully usually requires six steps.

STEP 1. PREPARE TO READ: OPEN UP THE TOPIC

The process of reading actually begins before you read, when you make your mind ready to receive an author's ideas. You may prepare simply by thinking about ideas or experiences you've had and comparing them with those suggested by the title or introduction to a reading. You can help your mind focus on the topic of the reading by writing about it or talking it over with friends and classmates.

Freewriting About the Topic: Sometimes your instructor will ask you to think or write about a topic before assigning a reading. Usually this kind of writing is not intended to be evaluated, so you should write quickly, without worrying about making sense or being correct; this writing is a way of getting your mind "geared up" for the reading. In Chapter 6, you'll learn more about this kind of writing, called **freewriting**. For example, to prepare for reading the essay your instructor might ask you to write about the following.

If you had all the money you wanted, what else would you need to be happy?

You might think about this briefly, and then begin writing something like this.

> In a way I think success means money. I always dream about having a lot of money and buying a car, a house, fabulous clothes, going on trips. Not worrying about the bills. I've had to work at so many boring jobs and I still don't really have what I want. So if I can get a degree and get a job I think I'll feel good. But really when I think about success I guess I know that's just the beginning. Success is when people look up to you and talk about how good you're doing—like in my family they always talk about my cousin who owns her own business. But then sometimes I think she's not really as happy as my sister who's a nurse, because my sister really helps people and also doesn't have to worry about whether she'll do OK next year—she knows she'll always have a job. I guess success would be when you do something you feel really good about. And right now I'm not quite sure what that will be for me. Maybe I'd be a success if I went into computers or quit college and became a musician, or maybe I'd think I was successful if I just had a happy family.

Once you've written something like this, and you've developed some of your own ideas, you don't need to do anything else for now. This writing has served its purpose by getting you ready to read. Be sure to keep this writing, though, because it might be very useful if you have additional writing assignments related to this reading.

What if your instructor doesn't assign a prereading topic? You can create your own. You might want to look at the title and main idea of an essay (see Step 2, following) and ask yourself what experiences you've had that relate to the ideas, or ask yourself what you already know about the topic (or what you guess will be the topic).

EXERCISE 4.1	Prepare to read "My Father's Tribal Rule" by Mark Mathabane (pp. 42–46). Before you read, think about the following **prompt**.

Can you recall any conflicts between parents and children in your family or among your family members?

Now write a page or two about family conflicts that will make you ready to think about ideas or events in the reading. Don't worry at this point about organization or editing because you're using this writing to prepare you to understand the reading.

Talking about the Topic: You may also prepare yourself to read about a topic by discussing the concept with friends or classmates. Often they have ideas that you have not thought about, and talking to them helps you clarify your own ideas. You'll find some guidelines for working with peers on pp. 247–248. If you discover that you disagree with others in your group, remember that at this point you are not trying to decide who is right and who is wrong. What matters is that you have prepared your mind to think about the topic that the reading will address. For example, suppose you discuss this topic in a group.

What is your idea of a successful person?

You will probably find that some people think that money is important, some argue for love or family, some for being a good person, some for being happy, and so on. You will not be able to change each other's minds, but when you go on to read Loth's essay on success, it will be easier to understand if you have already experienced how much difference there is in people's ideas of success.

EXERCISE 4.2	Prepare to read "My Father's Tribal Rule" by Mark Mathabane (pp. 42–46). Before you read, discuss the following **prompt** with a small group of classmates:
Collaboration	*Should parents try to force their children to follow the parents' customs, even if the children live in a different culture?*
	Remember that you are just exploring the general theme at this point, not trying to resolve questions, but be ready to share your group's ideas with the rest of the class.

STEP 2. SURVEY BEFORE READING: GET THE BIG PICTURE

When you're trying to understand a reading, it's helpful to make a **survey** of the central topic of the reading. It's like trying to put together a jigsaw puzzle: you know it's much easier to figure out where the pieces go when you can see the picture on the box. The same is true in reading. You will have a clearer understanding of specific details, words, sentences, and even paragraphs when you have some general idea about the reading. To see the overall pattern in written material, try some of these hints.

1. *Read any introductory material.* The notes that are sometimes included before a reading are put there to help you understand the material. Read the introductory notes on page 41. What do you learn? Why might this be important? You might make these observations.

   The notes talk about other definitions of success, and they also explain that the author once defined success as financial success, but now has changed her mind. [This gives you an idea of what to expect.] The notes also say she was recently a college student and that this article was written for the *Boston Globe Magazine* in 1997. [Now you know that it was written for American readers in the recent past. She will probably expect her readers to know and understand the life of a young American in the late 1990s.]

2. *Look at the important parts: title, first and last paragraphs, and subtitles* (if there are any). Read these important parts for a general idea of the topic. Here is one essay with everything but those parts erased. Look over these parts.

TITLE —⎡

Measuring Success

FIRST
PARAGRAPH —⎡

Back when I was a callow college student, I devised a neat grid system for what I hoped would be my life's achievements. I could count my life a good one, I thought, if I could attain both success and happiness. So I set about analyzing the component parts of each: Happiness I subdivided into sections labeled health and love; success, I determined, was composed of wealth and fame.

LAST
PARAGRAPH —⎡

When I look back at my simplistic little value system, I am a bit chagrined at how absolute I thought life was. But I am also happy to report that the achievements that have come my way are the ones that count. After 20 years of supercharged ambition, I have stumbled upon this bit of wisdom. Who needs wealth and fame? Two out of four ain't bad.

3. *Make some guesses about the main ideas of the reading.* What can you conclude about the reading from the title and first and last paragraphs above? Here are some guesses you might make.

Title: Suggests that success can be measured.

First paragraph: Describes the author's original definition of happiness as health and love, and success as fame and money; says that these definitions come from the time when she was in college.

Last paragraph: Says that she has changed her ideas about success. I guess that there's a reason why she changed, maybe something that happened. She says that she doesn't have wealth and fame, but does have "two out of four." Looking back at the introduction, she talks about four things: money, fame, health, and love. If she doesn't have money and fame, that leaves two, so I guess that this means she does have health and love. Because she also says "the achievements that have come my way are the ones that count." This means the reading will probably show how "health" and "love" are more valuable than "money" and "fame." As I read, I will look for evidence that "money" and "fame" have become less important.

4. *Ask questions before and during reading.* Questions will help you to keep your mind focused on your reading. Look for the answers to specific questions as you read. The questions you ask before you read might come from the parts you observed in your survey and the

guesses you made. You noticed that the author had different ideas when she was a student (mentioned in the first paragraph) from those she has now (mentioned in the last paragraph). This might lead you to some questions about the change:

What caused the change?

What does she mean by *happiness* and *success?*

Is it true that she doesn't have any wealth or fame?

What does she count as health and love?

You should continue to ask questions while you're reading because not all of the ideas will be present in the parts you've surveyed.

5. *Connect your guesses with your experience:* Recall any thinking or writing about your own ideas or experiences you may have done before writing. If you didn't do any writing, you may want to do some after you have made some guesses and asked some questions. You may also want to add to what you have written. If you wrote before reading, you may now want to add a more specific response to the topic as you see it now:

I think there are other things besides money that matter but I don't know how much I'd like life without money. I guess it depends on how much. I sure want to have enough to live on and not worry all the time about bills and getting evicted and things like that.

Once again, keep any writing you do at this point. You may use it later when writing or revising a paper about these readings.

| EXERCISE 4.3 | Survey "My Father's Tribal Rule" by Mark Mathabane (pp. 42–46). When experienced readers survey a reading, they often do it mentally, but since you may be practicing a new skill, you should write down any responses to the following that you can clearly express: |

1. *Read any introductory material:* Look over notes at the beginning or end of the reading. Could it be important to know in what year this was written, or where the author lived?

2. *Look at the important parts.* Check the title, the first and last paragraphs, and subtitles. Does the title hint where the author grew up? Is the last paragraph different from the first paragraph?

3. *Make some guesses about the main ideas of the reading.* Is Mathabane probably writing about his own experience? At what age? What aspects of his life—school, family, work, sports—are involved?

4. *Ask questions before and during the reading.* Try making your guesses into questions. What question could you ask about the title?

5. *Connect your guesses with your experience.* Before writing, you might have thought or written about conflicts you have had with your family. Does the title of the reading suggest that the author might have had a conflict with his father? Was it similar to yours or different?

| EXERCISE 4.4 | In a group, compare your answers to the assignment in Exercise 4.3. If different group members have different ideas about the probable topics in the reading, try to see what led to those thoughts. What hints did group members use to reach their conclusions? |

Collaboration

STEP 3. READ ACTIVELY

Even a reading that seems to make a simple point or tell a clear story may have some complex and interesting ideas. You may miss those ideas if you read too quickly and superficially. To help you look closely for the ideas that are suggested as well as the ones that are openly stated, and to keep your mind focused, you'll need to put your mark on the reading—to read actively. You can do this several ways, as listed in the following box.

How to Read Actively

In your own book or on a photocopy of the reading:

Underline or highlight words, phrases, sentences.

Ask new questions as you go.

Write notes in the margin.

Circle words you don't know.

You must be able to write on the reading to read it well, so make a photocopy if you don't want to write in your book. Also, have both a highlighter and pen and pencil handy. It will be much easier to keep your mind on the reading if you physically mark it as you read.

Because these marks will also be useful to you when you return to the reading while you're writing, you should be sure that you'll still be able to read your signs later on. Don't underline, circle, or highlight everything, because then nothing will stand out. If you don't want to write in the book you're using, you can photocopy the section you're reading. We have included on the opposite page an example of an essay (pp. 62) that has been **annotated**.

Measuring Success   *Renee Loth*

1   Back when I was a callow college student, I devised a neat grid system for what I *2 out of 4!* hoped would be my life's achievements. I could count my life a good one, I thought, if I could attain both success and happiness. So I set about analyzing the component parts of each: Happiness I subdivided into sections labeled health and love; success, I determined, was composed of wealth and fame.

2   Once I actually entered the world of work, however, I learned that success is not so easy to define. For one thing, when I made my simple calculation, I never took into account the joy of creation; the approbation of one's peers; the energy of collaboration; or the sheer satisfaction of a job well done. These are real qualities of success that live outside of wealth or fame. Also, I found that definitions of success are mutable, shifting along with our changing values. If we stick with our chosen fields long enough, we sometimes have an opportunity to meet our heroes, people we thought wildly successful when we were young. A musician friend told me that he spent most of his youth wanting to play like the greats, until he started getting to know some of them. To his surprise, many turned out to be embittered, dulled by drink or boredom, unable *caused her to change?* to hold together a marriage, or wantonly jealous of others. That's when he realized he wanted to play like himself.

3   Success is defined differently by different people. For some, it is symbolized by the number of buttons on the office phone. For others, it is having only one button and a secretary to field the calls. Some think the more nights and weekends they spend at the office, the more successful they must be. For others, success is directly proportional to time off.

connect to ideas of success? new definition

4   And what about those qualities I did include in my handy grid system? Wealth—beyond what is needed to provide for oneself and one's family, with a little *me too* left over for airfare to someplace subtropical in January—turned out to be superfluous. And the little experience I had with fame turned out to be downright scary.

5   Several years ago, I had occasion to appear on a dull but respected national evening television news show. My performance lasted exactly six minutes, and my *made her change?* name flashed only twice. But when I got home from the live broadcast, my answering machine had maxed out on messages.

6   I heard from a woman I had last seen in Brownie Scouts. I heard from former boyfriends, conspiracy theorists, and celebrity agents. I even got an obscene phone call—what kind of pervert watches PBS?—from someone who might have been an old friend pulling my leg. At least, I hope so.

not same as love

7   For weeks afterward, I received tons of what an optimist might call fan mail. One fellow insisted that if I froze a particular frame of a political campaign ad I had been discussing, I could see the face of Bill Clinton in the American flag. Somebody *why? b/c* sent me a chapter of a novel in progress with a main character disturbingly like me. *tells why* Several people sent me chain letters. *she changed*

8   I was relieved when the fickle finger of fame moved on to someone else.

9   When I was young and romanticizing about success, I liked a particular Joni Mitchell lyric: "My struggle for higher achievement and my search for love don't seem to cease." Ah, but the trouble with struggling and searching is that it keeps us in a permanent state of wanting—always reaching for more. The drive to succeed *can't ever* keeps us focused on the future, to the detriment of life in the moment. And the *reach success-* moment is all we ever really have. *new definition*

10   When I look back at my simplistic little value system, I am a bit chagrined at how absolute I thought life was. But I am also happy to report that the achievements that have come my way are the ones that count. After twenty years of supercharged ambition, I have stumbled upon this bit of wisdom. Who needs wealth and fame? Two out of four ain't bad.

what 2? health + love, not wealth + fame

Here are some approaches for annotating readings. Read these explanations to understand how the annotations work.

1. *Answers and new questions.* Look again at the questions you asked and the guesses you made about "Measuring Success." Since one of your guesses was that something might have made the writer change, underline or put a note beside paragraph 2 describing what she heard from her friend about his disappointment when he met his heroes. Note also her experience with fame that "turned out to be downright scary" in paragraph 4 (with details in paragraphs 5 through 7).

   Look for the answers you can't find. The authors refers to "two out of four" components of success that she does have, but she does not tell us much about those in the body of the essay. You'll thus want to write a question to help you remember that this problem is still not solved.

2. *Surprises.* Look for unexpected ideas. If you didn't guess that the writer would discuss the idea that success can never really be reached, underline that point in paragraph 9, and perhaps write a question beside it.

3. *Connections.* Look for ideas that do—and do not—connect with each other. Some ideas will be clearly connected: in the last paragraph, Loth mentions looking back at her "simplistic little value system" and "two out of four" achievements. These are linked to the definition she gave in paragraph 1. So draw a line or make a note to show the connection. Other times, ideas will not seem to fit with anything else: in paragraph 9, she discusses the idea that we never really achieve satisfaction but are "always reaching for more." Since she has not mentioned this idea anywhere else, you now have a new question: How is this related to her main idea? In paragraph 2 she also brings up a new idea: being yourself rather than imitating other people. You might question why she never discusses this idea again.

4. *Contradictions.* Look for points that seem to contradict other points. Loth says that happiness is love, but then in paragraph 7 she discusses hearing from old boyfriends as a problem that made her realize that fame is not so wonderful. You might ask how these ideas are different.

5. *Repetitions.* Loth repeats certain words over and over: *success* or *succeed* (title, paragraphs 1, 2, 3, 9), *define* or *definition* (2, 3), *fame* (1, 2, 4, 8). Think about the effects she achieves by doing this.

6. *Sentences or words that look different on the page.* Paragraph 9 is a single sentence; Loth's other paragraphs all have several sentences. You might ask why she chooses to write a paragraph with only one sentence.

7. *Solutions to problems.* Sometimes you find the solution to the problems that arise as you read. You asked why paragraph 8 is a single sentence. Looking back, you may realize that she's pointing out one of her changed feelings: her bad experiences with fame made her dislike it, which is the opposite of what she predicted when she was a college student (paragraph 1). Make a note in the margin.

8. *Connections with your own ideas and experience.* In the survey stage, you wrote about money and success (pp. 59–60). You see that Loth's new idea of having enough money rather than extreme wealth—"what is needed to provide for oneself and one's family, with a little left over for airfare to someplace subtropical in January" (paragraph 4)—is very much like yours. Make a note of the similarity.

9. *New words.* Circle words and phrases you don't understand. In Loth's essay these may include *callow, grid, approbation, mutable, embittered, wantonly, superfluous, maxed out on, theorists, fickle, detriment, chagrined.* Think also about familiar words used in a new way—the word *absolute,* for example. Usually you have seen it used with an *-ly* to mean *very,* as in "That was *absolutely* fabulous!" If you don't know the word *simplistic,* think about the word *simple,* which you know means *easy, uncomplicated,* or *plain.*

EXERCISE 4.5

Read "My Father's Tribal Rule" (pp. 42–46) actively. Using a copy that you are able to write on, mark the important points in this reading with a highlighter or pen as you read. Remember, don't underline or highlight every sentence. Also, be sure to write notes about questions, answers, or observations. You may not find all the following categories in any one reading, but many of them will probably be there.

1. *Answers:* Look for answers to the guesses you made and the questions you asked.

2. *Surprises:* Look for anything that seems different from what you expect.

3. *Connections:* Look for ideas that connect with each other and also for those that don't seem related at all.

4. *Contradictions:* Look for points that seem to contradict each other.

5. *Repetitions:* Make a list of or number the important words that are repeated.

6. *Sentences or words that look different on the page:* Note sentences or paragraphs that seem to stand out.

7. *Solutions to new problems:* Make a note in the margin of problems that you find as you read, and note any answers you discover.

8. *Connections with your own ideas and experience:* Look back at ideas you noted before you read. Do you see any connections (even contrasts) with ideas and events you described or explained?

9. *New words:* Circle words and phrases you don't know and familiar words used in a new way.

EXERCISE 4.6

Work with a partner and compare your questions about the reading from Exercise 4.5. Did you learn anything from your partner's questions? IMPORTANT: Don't try to answer each other's questions yet; just be sure you've thought of

Collaboration | all the questions you might want to ask, and add any questions you added from your partner's reading. You can do the same with vocabulary that you each noticed—add to each other's lists, but don't try to define the words yet.

STEP 4. REVIEW

Review Tools
Check vocabulary
Answer questions
Map the reading
Restate the main idea
Reread

Unless you take the final step of reviewing what you've just read, you may not be aware of any parts you don't understand. Some of the work of active reading can be completed here, and you can use it to help you put all the parts together and make sense of the reading as a whole. So begin by looking back at the guesses you made and the questions you asked before you read, and look also at the words you circled, the points you underlined or highlighted, and the notes you wrote as you read, using these review tools.

Check Vocabulary

When you find words you don't recognize in a reading, you should mark them rather than stopping to look them up or figure them out, because stopping in the middle of reading may confuse you. Look back at the words you circled. You don't have to look up every word in the dictionary, but plan to look up the most unfamiliar words. Make sure you understand all the words you've marked. The following box gives you some ways of doing this.

How to Check Vocabulary

Context: Guess the meaning of a word by understanding the rest of the sentence or paragraph.

Notes: Check the definitions at the bottom of the page (footnotes) or the end of the reading (endnotes).

Dictionary: Make sure you know how to use the dictionary. If more than one meaning for a word is given, be sure that you select the one that makes sense in the context of the sentence you are reading.

Sometimes you can use just one of these tools, but often you'll have to use a combination. Let's try using some of them with "Measuring Success" (pp. 41–42).

Context   Some of the words you circle may make sense as you continue to read. In paragraph 2, *mutable* is explained as "shifting along with our changing values." In paragraph 10, Loth refers to her value system as *simplistic* and *little.* You may thus guess that *simplistic* seems related to *simple,* and means *very simple* or *overly simple.*

Notes   Though this essay has no footnotes or endnotes, others do; always check for them.

Dictionary   If you marked *callow* in paragraph 1, you may find that the dictionary offers two meanings for the word: (1) young, inexperienced and (2) unfeathered. Since it makes no sense to speak of a college student as being featherless, you assume that *callow* in this sentence means *inexperienced*. In paragraph 2 if you marked *wantonly*, you won't find it in the dictionary. You will find the word *wanton*, a word that has at least ten meanings, many of them including words you also don't know. The first meaning is the most common: "Done maliciously or unjustifiably." If you don't know those words either, you might want to give up, but try one more time—you'll find that *maliciously* refers you to *malice*, which finally has a meaning you understand: "a desire to inflict harm on others." Place part of that definition in the sentence and it seems to make sense: these successful people may desire to hurt other people that make them jealous. Similar processes help you with the other words you've marked as unknown.

Let's now look at *absolute* in paragraph 10. The first meaning—"complete; perfect"—seems to work, implying that life is not as perfect as Loth thought it was going to be, that her original ideas were too easy.

Answer Your Own Questions

Think back to the questions you had when you first surveyed "Measuring Success," and look back at the questions you asked as you annotated. Try to answer them. Here are some possible answers:

What caused the change?   In paragraph 2, she discusses seeing other things she hadn't considered; in paragraphs 2 and 3, she describes her friend's experience with people he thought successful and other definitions of success; finally in paragraphs 4 through 8 she gives details about how unhappy she was when she finally achieved her goal of fame. I'd say that she was changed by her own success and what she saw and heard from other people.

What does she mean by happiness and success?   She gives some examples of success. Her own fame on the evening news, the success of friends. She describes some definitions that she learned later: creativity, approval, working with others, doing something well, having enough money to live on. She never really discusses happiness.

Is it true that she doesn't have any wealth or fame?   Eventually she does have some fame, but she doesn't like it. She isn't poor, and she says she realizes that being really rich isn't important, but she never says why.

What does she count as health and love? She never says what she thinks about health and love.

Try also to answer any questions that you may have written in the margins as you read.

Why doesn't she say anything about health and love? This is still a problem because she doesn't write about these, and she doesn't really ever tell very much about what wealth is. What she says about fame is mainly that she didn't want it after all. She never did really tell what she means, but she's told a lot about how she changed her mind. So the idea of changing her mind must be very important.

Why does she say that we are "always wanting more," and why does she bring up the idea that being yourself is more important than being well known? She also doesn't go into detail about these. Maybe they are more examples of possible things a person could think, and they might even be some things that made her realize that her early ideas were wrong. She brings up a lot of different ideas. Maybe her point is that defining success is very complicated.

What's different about her old boyfriends who call when she's been on TV (an experience she seems to describe as unpleasant) and love, which she still suggests is important? Since she never goes into detail about her idea of love, she must not intend that as the main point she's making, but since she thinks that an old friend may have made an obscene call as a bad joke, she clearly is showing that people who only pay attention when you're famous aren't necessarily kind to you. This must be part of what she learned about the idea of success being more complicated than she thought it was when she was young.

Restate the Main Idea in Your Own Words

Restating the main idea of a reading in your own words is a good way to see the point that the author is making. The author's thoughts can become a part of your own thinking when you translate them into your own words. If you can't restate the main idea, you may not yet completely understand the reading. If that's the case, go back to Steps 2 and 3, or discuss the reading with your instructor. You might go through the following stages as you develop your statement of the main idea of "Measuring Success."

1. Write the idea in one sentence, answering this question: *What does the author want me to know after reading this?*

The author wants me to know that success isn't really just wealth and fame, because fame can be a problem.

2. Check this statement of the main idea against the notes and answers you've written. *Is everything in the reading related to this statement?*

My statement of Loth's main idea leaves out the points about always wanting more and about different definitions of success and about changing our views of success over time.

3. If your first attempt doesn't seem to be a statement that really fits the whole reading, look back at the reading and your notes. Try a revised statement that does cover the whole reading: *What does the author want me to know after reading this?*

The author wants me to know that young people often think things like success can be defined very simply as fame and wealth but when they get older they learn that it's more complicated than that.

4. Look again at the reading and your notes. *Is everything in the reading related to this statement of the main idea?*

This seems to cover it all.

Reread the Material

At this point, try one more reading of the material. Read this time at a rate that's comfortable for you. If you find new questions or ideas, stop and work with them, but be sure to return after that to one complete, smooth rereading. This will help you see how the details and different parts of the reading all work to support the main idea.

EXERCISE 4.7   **Review "My Father's Tribal Rule" (pp. 42–46). Once you've read the material carefully, you are ready to review it. Use these five review tools.**

1. *Check vocabulary:* Look back at the unfamiliar words you circled. This reading included some words and phrases from other languages. Did you check footnotes to find the meaning?

2. *Answer your own questions:* Try to answer the questions you had when you first surveyed the reading as well as questions that occurred to you later.

3. *Restate the main idea in your own words:* Write the idea in one sentence, answering this question: *What does the author want me to know after reading this?* Check this statement of the main idea against the notes and answers you've made. *Is everything in the reading related to this idea?* If your first attempt doesn't fit the whole reading, look back at the reading and your notes. Try a revised statement that does cover the whole reading: *What does the au-*

thor want me to know after reading this? Check again with the reading and your notes. *Is everything in the reading related to this idea?*

4. *Reread the material:* Finish your review by going through the entire reading again at a comfortable pace. You may find that you see some details or events in a different way when you reread. Add any new observations to your annotations.

EXERCISE 4.8

Collaboration

Working with a partner, review your answers to Exercise 4.7.

a. Did each of you answer your own questions? Can you suggest other answers, or are those the best?

b. Did each of you find a good definition for the vocabulary words you selected? Do these definitions make sense in the sentences where the words are used?

c. Do you agree with each other's statement of the main idea? Why or why not?

STEP 5. EVALUATE

Research

When you read an assignment from a textbook, you may feel that you don't need to question it, but you should form the habit of evaluating everything you read, whether it's from a textbook, a magazine, or the Internet. Just because something is published does not mean that it is true, especially on the Internet. Here are some questions you should ask about any reading. Even though you will not always be able to answer every question in complete detail, those you can answer will help you be fairly sure of a reading's validity. The questions you can't answer give you questions to keep in your mind about that source.

How to Evaluate a Reading

Whose words: Is the author expressing his own opinion, or telling you what someone else says about the ideas in the reading?

Tone: What's the author's attitude toward what is written? Does she want you to take it seriously and literally, or is she saying the opposite of what she means, or is she exaggerating? Why? What does she really mean, and how do you know that?

Bias: Does the author have any reason to gain by persuading you to agree with him? Is this appropriate? Do you already have a strong opinion on the topic? Can you set your opinion aside so that you can read and understand what this writer is saying?

continued on next page

continued from previous page

Clarity: What is clear in this reading? How does the way it's written help make it clear?

Interest: What is interesting in this reading? How does the writing add to the interest?

Purpose: What is the purpose of this reading? How does it relate to the kind of writing you are trying to do?

1. *Where did I find this?*
   Does anyone control in any way what readings are in the location, or can anyone post anything there?

   EXAMPLE

   "Measuring Success" is reprinted in a textbook by a well-known publisher and suggested to you by your instructor. Both of these sources control the material they present to you. This isn't a guarantee of perfect truthfulness in the material, but you do know more about the origins of "Measuring Success" than you do about something you receive in the mail from an unknown address. At least you know that this essay was probably not produced by a hate group, or by someone attempting to sell you something.

   For example, if you search for "Michael Jordan" on the Internet, you may well find a story about him frightening a woman in an elevator. Nothing on that page tells you who wrote or published it. Only if you follow links back to the home page will you discover a statement that the whole story is untrue and that the site is a list of false stories.

2. *Who originally published this?*
   Is the publisher at all well known? What kinds of things does the publisher usually publish?

   EXAMPLE

   "Measuring Success" was originally published in the *Boston Globe Magazine*. Since this is a very well-known newspaper, you know that it would not publish anything that is obviously untrue or libelous. However, since it is a general newspaper, not a special journal, the article might not have the most recent scholarship. That does not matter in this case, because "Measuring Success" is an essay based on the author's personal opinion and experience.

3. *When was this written?*
   Does that matter?

EXAMPLE

"Measuring Success" was originally published in 1997, but the subject matter is not something that would change with time necessarily.

4. *Who wrote this?*
Does this person have enough knowledge to write about this topic? Will this person gain financially or in any other way if readers believe that the writer's view is true?

EXAMPLE

Renee Loth was named Editor of the Editorial Page of the *Boston Globe* in 2001 and has received many awards. She certainly seems qualified to write about success. There's no apparent way that she would gain from persuading readers to agree with her. This would be very different if her essay tried to persuade readers that her newspaper was better than another, for example.

5. *What are the author's sources of information?*
Are those well known? Biased? Recent?

EXAMPLE

Loth's sources are her own experience, so they are appropriate for an essay of opinion. If her essay investigated whether having a college degree made a person more successful or whether most people agree that success leads to happiness, then she would need more general sources based on studies of many people.

6. *Who was the author's target audience (that is, who would be reading this)?*
What did the author expect the audience to know? What did she expect the audience to feel? How are you, the current reader, similar to or different from the target audience?

EXAMPLE

The readers of the *Boston Globe Magazine* are mainly the people who live in the Boston area and have some education. But this essay may be more specifically aimed at two groups: young people who think as she did earlier and older people who are looking back and evaluating their lives. She expects readers to be familiar with office phones and answering machines, with TV interviews and winter vacations, so she assumes a fairly prosperous audience. Her idea of a modest life, in fact, would be very luxurious for many people, so that helps the reader to understand what the vague word *wealth* means to her.

EXERCISE 4.9 | **Evaluate the reading for source, audience, and bias.**

1. Evaluate the publisher(s), author, sources, and target audience of "My Father's Tribal Rule" by Mark Mathabane (pp. 42–46). Decide if you can trust the

information. You should question the article's bias (does the author want you to see only one side of things?), currency of information (have things changed since then?), and intended audience (do you have the background you need to understand this?).

2. Read "Getting Off the Welfare Carousel" by Teresa McCrary (pp. 46–48). What is her background? Does this suggest that she will look at both sides of the welfare question objectively, or will she be likely to favor one side or the other? Why do you think so?

EXERCISE 4.10

Collaboration

As a group, evaluate the publisher, author, and sources of "A Hanging" (pp. 48–51). Decide whether you can trust the information. Question the article's bias (does the author want you to see only one side of things?), currency of information (have things changed since then?), and intended audience (do you have the background you need to understand this?). Assign one part of the evaluation to each group member. Then meet and compile your results. Try to decide on a group opinion about the reading.

Whose Ideas?

Obviously, most ideas in a reading will come from the author, but sometimes the author also uses ideas from other individuals or sources. It is important to not only identify these ideas from other sources but also to understand why the author decides to use them and to recognize the author's opinion of the cited ideas. If you pay close attention to these details as you reread the essay, you will become a more critical reader, better prepared to discuss and write about your response to the reading.

Sometimes a reading, or a part of a reading, will be very much like a conversation that the author is having with other people or sources—the author may report what someone else says in order to agree or disagree with that source. It can be difficult to separate the author's own ideas from ideas of other people or sources, but it is very important to do this or you may get an incorrect idea of the author's meaning. Authors signal that they are reporting the ideas of others in several small ways. In Loth's essay, it's important to distinguish between the ideas she had when she was young and the ones she holds now, so the tense of the verb is important to notice (*I subdivided* compared to ***are** the ones that count*). Be sure not to overlook the use of quotation marks or brief introductory or explanatory remarks, such as *for some people*.

1. What did Loth believe when she was young? How do we know she had those ideas then?

2. In paragraph 3, she refers to some other people's ideas. Who are these people? What did they experience and think? Are their ideas like Loth's, or are they different?

EXERCISE 4.11

Work on determining whose ideas are being expressed.

1. In "Getting Off the Welfare Carousel" by Teresa McCrary (pp. 46–48), look at paragraph 2. What does she mean by "the stereotypical welfare mom"? Who has the stereotype she mentions? Does McCrary agree with this stereotype?

2. In paragraph 4, we see these words: ". . . if we have more than that amount, we should be able to sell some things and live for a year from the proceeds." What words at the beginning of the sentence tell us that these are not Mc-Crary's ideas? In the sentence that follows, what is her response to the idea?

EXERCISE 4.12

Collaboration

Read "A Hanging" (pp. 48–51). Try to locate two places where Orwell gives other people's ideas, and then try to decide whether he agrees or disagrees with the ideas of others. As a group, compare your answers and try to decide as a group what Orwell's ideas are on these points.

Recognizing the Author's Tone

Sometimes authors may say something that is actually the opposite of what they really mean. We call this *irony,* or we say that the author is being *ironic.* You have probably noticed that people do this in conversation, but you may have called it *sarcasm* or being *sarcastic* or *facetious.* Sometimes irony is a way of using another person's ideas. In order to know whether a statement is straightforward or ironic, we need to use all the ways we can to determine what the author's real idea is. We can compare a statement to the rest of the reading, or we can see if the author says anything that seems impossible or greatly exaggerated.

EXAMPLE

In the first paragraph of "Measuring Success" (pp. 41), Loth says, "Back when I was a callow college student . . ." The word callow lets us know that she is going to be a little critical of her earlier ideas, so when we read the rest of the sentence: ". . . I devised a *neat* grid system for what I hoped" would be my life's achievements," we know that she is implying that life might not turn out to be as neat as she thought when she was young. Thus, this part of the sentence is ironic.

EXERCISE 4.13

Look at the last paragraph of "A Hanging." Compare the behavior of the men described here with Orwell's direct statement of his opinion in paragraph 12. What does that suggest about his attitude toward himself and the other men in the last paragraph? How does the final sentence of paragraph 26 remind us of the final sentence of paragraph 12?

EXERCISE 4.14

Collaboration

As a group, compare your answers to Exercise 4.13. Did everyone agree? What other things in the reading support different views of this paragraph?

Recognizing Your Own Biases

Sometimes it's hard to read an article because you have very strong feelings and opinions that make it difficult for you to pay attention to what the author is saying. This can be a problem whether you agree or disagree with the author. To become a really good reader, you need to be aware of your own feelings and opinions and try to separate them from the author's. Pay attention to what the reading actually says.

Paying attention to the reading does not mean accepting everything you read without question, but you won't really be able to ask the specific important questions about a reading—or even disagree with the author's support for the thesis of the reading—unless you first read it carefully and see what the author actually says. Then you will be able to ask about an author's assumptions, evidence, attitude, and everything else that's important.

Recognizing your own biases must begin when you first survey a reading. As soon as you see what the topic is, you should take a moment to think about how you feel and what you think. Then remind yourself to listen, no matter how much you disagree.

Of course, sometimes you might make an exception. You will probably not be able to quietly and objectively read anything that is truly offensive, such as hate literature. You may not want to waste your time with something from a source that you know is unreliable, like the popular tabloid newspapers in the grocery store checkout line. But when you read something that seems to be from a source that has some credibility, try to set your feelings aside the first time you read it so that you can think, rather than simply reacting emotionally.

EXAMPLE

The title "Getting Off the Welfare Carousel" indicates that the reading will be about welfare. At this point you begin to form a reaction, based on your previous ideas about welfare. You go on to read the first sentence: "I am a welfare mom, and I have one thing to say: stop picking on us!" At this point you know that McCrary is arguing in favor of welfare. If you agree that welfare is a good thing, you may not be able to read this article critically and may overlook errors or lack of evidence. If you believe that welfare is harmful to society, you may overlook her arguments in favor of welfare. Whatever your view is, you will not be able to understand and respond well to this article unless you can try to set your own biases aside and pay attention to what McCrary actually says, not to what you think she says or to what others have said before.

| EXERCISE 4.15 | **Do the following to explore your own biases.** |

1. Survey "My Father's Tribal Rule," pp. 42–46. What is the general topic? What are your own feelings when you think about families in conflict and corporal punishment for children? What are your own experiences with children growing up in different cultures from their parents? Will these ideas affect your ability to read this article well?

> 2. Survey "A Hanging," pp. 48–51. How do you feel about the topic being discussed? Can you put those feelings aside and read the essay to discover Orwell's ideas?

EXERCISE 4.16

Collaboration

Look at the following list of titles and guess what the topic of the reading might be. Decide what your own ideas are on those topics. In a group, compare the reactions of different group members. Finally, in your own mind, decide whether you could read each essay in an unbiased way.

a. "Giving Custody to Fathers: Making the Laws Fair to All"
b. "Legalize Marijuana: Time for a Change"
c. "Time to End Summer Vacation: The Case for Year-Round School"
d. "Food for Thought: Antibiotics in Milk Make People Sick"

STEP 6. USE THE READING AS A MODEL

If you're sure you understand what you've read and have begun to give some written responses to a reading, you now may want to look at the reading in a different way—and to decide whether you want to use the reading as a **model** for your own writing. A model is an example that you try to imitate in certain ways. Some of the student essays in Chapter 20 can be used as models, as can the essays written by professional writers in Chapter 21.

ESL

When referring to a model, don't try to imitate everything about it. You should try to write like yourself, not like a copy of another person. Think about the methods you use when learning other skills. If you want to learn to throw a basketball through a hoop, you probably will watch someone else, someone who always makes good shots. You may decide to stand the same way that person stands or hold your hands in the same way. The same is true of singing, driving a car, or even handling a difficult customer at work: you learn how to do things partly by watching or listening to a model. The readings included in this book will thus become your models for how to write. In each one you may find one or two ways of writing that you want to imitate, but you still want to sound like yourself. Here are some points to consider when you evaluate a model.

Clarity   Look back at the reading and decide which parts gave you the most difficulty. Look at this comment on "Measuring Success."

> I found paragraph 9 hard to follow because I didn't expect it and it didn't seem to fit in with her other ideas, also I don't know who Joni Mitchell is and I don't know why she's talking about "always reaching for more."

If you decide that this paragraph is not a good model, you can look at another one.

> Paragraph 2 tells me she found new kinds of success, and then it goes on to tell what those kinds are. This paragraph is clear because it gives examples and states its idea in simple words.

Interest   Look at the parts you enjoyed reading, the parts you remember most clearly after you finish. Try to see what made those parts memorable. Paragraphs 5, 6, and 7 may have been particularly interesting.

> In these paragraphs she gives a lot of weird people who tried to get in touch with her when she was on TV, her boyfriends, agents and people who wrote strange books. I also like the way she talks about things like her answering machine had "maxed out." But I think that's slang—can I really write like that? I could try to use more unusual details.

In these paragraphs it is the details and the language that make everything more interesting.

Purpose   When you begin to think about **purpose**, you may notice details about language and use of slang. For example, some writers may use slang because their main purpose is to entertain. Think about Loth's purpose and whether it's like yours.

> She's trying to get us to understand an idea about how we change. I will write about ideas I want people to understand, too, so her writing is like mine in that way. I don't think she's writing for school, though, so she might be different there.

Loth's purpose is clearly not the same as writing for school, which has a special kind of purpose where using slang may not be appropriate. It is also clear that Loth wants to help her reader understand an idea—a goal that is similar to what you want to do. How does she do this? Should you try to imitate her?

> She gives us some ideas of what she's going to explain and then she gives some examples. I could do that.

EXERCISE 4.17   Evaluate "My Father's Tribal Rule" (pp. 42–46). Decide whether there's anything about the way this essay is written that you'd like to imitate.

1. *Clarity:* Did any parts give you more difficulty than others? How did the writer help you to understand this different culture? How did he help you with language?

2. *Interest:* What do you remember best from the reading? Why is that so easy to remember? Did the details help you really see the people, places, and events he described?

3. *Purpose:* Was Mathabane explaining an idea or telling a story? How does that affect the way that he writes? How is that similar to your own purpose in writing? How is it different?

EXERCISE 4.18

Collaboration

As a group, examine "Getting Off the Welfare Carousel" as a model. Is there anything about this writing that you would like to be able to do in your own writing? Think about language, clarity, and purpose. Is there anything in this writing that you would like to avoid in your own writing?

What You've Done

- ■ *Prepared* to read
- ■ *Surveyed* before reading
- ■ *Read* actively
- ■ *Reviewed* to make sense of what you've read
- ■ *Evaluated* what you've read
- ■ *Modeled* on the writing

For More Reading Strategies

- ■ See Chapter 18 (Research)

The Next Step

- ■ Analyze the assignment (Chapter 5)

5 Analyzing the Assignment for an Essay
Understanding the Question

> ### What You've Done
>
> - Read and analyzed the assigned reading
>
> ### What You Need to Do Next
>
> - Analyze the assignment
>   - Understand the ideas the writing assignment asks you to discuss
>   - Understand the kind of writing the assignment calls for
>   - Understand how to use that kind of writing to focus on the ideas

What a Prompt Does
Identifies your focus
Identifies expected actions
Links focus and actions

Before you begin writing an essay, you must make sure that you understand what you are being asked to do. You can do this by *analyzing the prompt*. A prompt is a statement or a question that directs you to write an essay. When you analyze a prompt, you take the prompt apart and carefully look at its parts. Analyzing the prompt will help you answer the following questions.

WHAT ARE YOU EXPECTED TO FOCUS ON?

To **focus** means to direct your attention to a specific aspect of something. For example, if you are at a football game, you can see many different objects on and off the field: the teams, the band, the cheerleaders, your fellow spectators, and the blimp above the field. Since you can't take in everything at the same time, you direct your attention to—you focus on—one thing at a time. If you were given a writing assignment that asked you to comment on fan behavior, you would spend your time focusing on the spectators. When you write, you also select what you want to pay attention to—where your focus will be.

Study the prompt to see how to focus your essay. Because a reading may contain several different ideas or issues, you will want to see if the prompt points you to a particular idea. To find your focus, look for **key focus words** or **key focus phrases**.

How to Identify Key Focus Words

Key focus words point you to the specific ideas or issues you are to write about. They usually fall into three categories:

People: May include the names of individuals (Katherine, Steve), or categories of people (students, parents, employees).

Things: May be specific (my 1997 Nissan Sentra), general (cars), concrete (bicycle), or abstract (transportation).

Ideas: May be abstractions (love, freedom, happiness, justice, pain, prejudice).

Consider the following prompts.

> *Describe your best friend.*
>
> *Write a letter to the phone company about a mistake that appeared on your bill.*
>
> *Is love at first sight possible?*

The first example is a statement that contains one **key focus** phrase: *your best friend*. To respond to this statement, you would naturally eliminate the other people in your life who are not your best friend—your overbearing boss, your nosy neighbor, your whiny sister. You know that the reader expects you to limit your comments to (that is, to focus on) your best friend.

The second example contains four key focus words: *letter, phone company, mistake, bill*. To respond to this prompt, you would need to limit your discussion to mistakes in your phone bill (not mistakes in your electric bill or the fact that your phone makes a buzzing noise when you hang up the receiver). While you may want both problems fixed, they are not relevant to your immediate task.

The third example is a question that names an idea: *love at first sight*. To answer this question, you must first talk about love (what it is and how it is different from friendship, lust, affection, and so on), and you must further talk about whether it can happen when two people meet for the first time.

WHAT ACTIONS ARE YOU EXPECTED TO TAKE?

Once you have found the focus of your essay, you will need to look at action words to determine what you are expected to do with that focus. For example, when you take your car to the shop, you tell the mechanic to focus on the car's problem, such as faulty brakes, and to take action—to diagnose, estimate the cost for, repair, replace, or adjust the brakes.

Just as the mechanic needs to know what action to take to fix your car, you also need to know what action to take by looking at **key action words**.

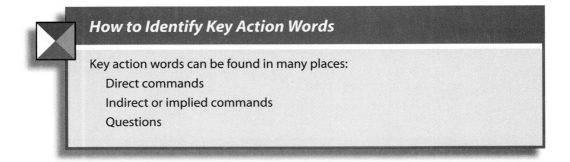

How to Identify Key Action Words

Key action words can be found in many places:

Direct commands

Indirect or implied commands

Questions

Key action words point you to the specific actions you must do to answer the prompt. Let's look again at the following prompts.

Describe your best friend.

Write a letter to the phone company about a mistake that appeared on your bill.

Is love at first sight possible?

The first example contains one key action word—*describe*—which is a direct command. To respond to this statement, you would be expected to describe in detail the key focus word—your best friend.

The second example seems to contain a key action word: *write*. However, this word does not specifically direct you to do anything with the focus—a mistake on your phone bill. To respond to this prompt, you would be expected to *identify* and *describe* the mistake and *argue* for a refund.

The third example is a question that contains no direct or implied command. Instead, the prompt asks a question, and you need to find an action that will allow you to answer it. First, you need to determine what the question is asking you to do—in this case, to prove or disprove that love at first sight occurs. To prove or disprove something, you must *argue* a position.

You need to practice identifying key action words in prompts that are given as direct commands, indirect commands, or questions.

If the Prompt Contains Direct Commands

Some instructors use key action words when creating assignments—a process that is like giving a command. The following list contains the general definitions for commonly used key action words. Since some instructors may use these words with slightly different meanings, you may want to ask your instructor what these words mean. As in all writing tasks, it is always a good idea to keep in mind what your audience expects of you.

Key Action Words That Are Direct Commands

Agree or disagree	To explain why you hold or do not hold an opinion expressed by someone else. During a trial, the prosecution presents a case against the person being tried. Then the jury gives a verdict which shows whether they agree or disagree with the prosecution. When asked, they should be able to explain their position.
Analyze	To examine all aspects of a subject and their relationship to each other. If you are a detective trying to understand what happened at the scene of a crime, you look at the parts of the scene (the bloodstain on the wall, the body on the floor, the knife in the kitchen sink, and the broken window) and make connections between the parts to show how together they present a picture of how the crime was committed.
Argue	To present supporting evidence and reasoning either for or against a view or position. If you are an attorney, you present evidence and reasoning to convince the court of the innocence or guilt of the accused.
Classify	To place various elements of a subject into different categories to reveal their distinctions; for example, criminals can be classified as violent or nonviolent.
Compare	To examine two or more items for their similarities and differences. Compare always means both *compare* and contrast. For example, if you are an investigator, you might look for similarities and differences between two crime scenes to determine whether the crimes were committed by the same person.
Consider	To include in your thinking process. If you must decide whether to walk home by yourself at night, you might think about (or consider) how late it is, how well lit the streets are, what kind of neighborhood you will have to walk through, and whether other people will also be walking.
Define	To clarify the elements that make up the subject. If you are asked to define a word, you give its meaning. If you were to prosecute a defendant for first-degree murder, you would need to present and explain the specific points that make an action murder and not something else.
Describe	To give a visual picture or, if the subject is an idea or argument, to reveal the major characteristics. If you have been mugged, you will want to describe your assailant to the police, giving as many visual details as possible (height; weight; skin, hair, and eye color; identifying marks; dress; etc.). Sensory details are most important here.

continued on next page

continued from previous page

Determine	To weigh evidence and come to a conclusion or make a final decision. If you are asked to determine which of two arguments is the strongest, you will need to decide which is best and why you believe this. If you are serving on a jury, you must decide whether the accused is guilty based on the evidence presented in court.
Discuss	To explore the various aspects of an issue. If you are asked to discuss an author's idea, you must give an in-depth answer rather than a quick summary. Before a jury determines guilt or innocence, members discuss the issues by explaining the evidence that has been presented.
Explain	To give more information about an idea or a situation. If your lawyer advises you to plead guilty, you would want him or her to explain why this would be to your advantage and what your punishment might be.
Identify	To point out specific distinguishing characteristics. If you are asked to identify an author's thesis, you must point it out and separate it from other aspects of the text. Think of it as identifying a person in a police lineup. You're pointing him or her out, differentiating between the person you saw and the other people in the lineup.
Trace	To follow the path or progression of an idea. If you are asked to trace the development of an argument or of a process, you must identify a series of steps. Think of reconstructing a crime. You must pinpoint what a suspect did at different points in time, thus tracing his or her actions.

If the Prompt Contains Indirect Commands

Sometimes a prompt will ask you to perform an action without using any direct action words. In these situations, you must interpret what is being asked for from certain phrases that appear in the prompt. For example, if you take your car to a mechanic and ask her to *look at* the brakes, you will be disappointed if all she does is remove the tires and look at the brakes. You expect her to diagnose the problem, recommend a repair, estimate the cost, and perhaps repair or replace the brakes. When you have a writing prompt that contains an indirect command, you must also identify more specific actions that will address the prompt.

Let's look at an example of a prompt that does not include any of the direct key action words discussed previously.

Write a letter to the governor to ask for more funding for schools in your community.

The key action words in this prompt are *write* and *ask*. But you know that simply writing to the governor and asking for the money will not be very effective, so the instructor must be asking you to do more than that. Your job is to select a direct action word that will allow you to complete the assignment. Your instructor has intentionally not given you a direct action so you can choose the action you think will lead to the best essay. There are many actions that you could use—none are right or wrong. You need to pick the best action or combination of actions to fulfill the assignment.

To write to the governor, you could choose any of the following.

- *Analyze* the schools' budget to show why the money is needed.
- *Argue* your position by presenting evidence showing why the money is needed.
- *Compare* the budgets of school districts to show why more money is needed in your community.
- *Define* quality education and show that more money is needed to provide for it.
- *Describe* the conditions of the schools in your community to show where funding is needed.
- *Determine* the impact of lack of money on students.
- *Discuss* why increasing funding to schools is better than supporting other projects.
- *Explain* what will happen if more money is not given to your community.
- *Identify* sources for increasing money for your community.

Often you will need to use more than one key action word to write an effective essay. Be sure to consider combinations of key action words and to look at the prompt to determine if you are required to complete more than one task.

If the Prompt Contains Questions

Questions always provide a focus, just as indirect or implied commands do. Although questions do not contain direct action words, they do imply more specific actions than sentences with indirect or implied commands. Questions usually require a combination of actions. Your task is again to select the best combination that will allow you to write a thoughtful answer.

✓ Words That Signal Questions

What	How	Which
Who	Why	Whether / If

Many beginning writers skip the implied actions required to answer questions. For example, when asked "What is the purpose of taxes?" beginning writers tend to argue whether taxes should exist. The question, however, implies that taxes do exist and does not ask you to deal with that issue. Instead, the task is to first describe the kinds of taxes (car, sales, property, income) and their purposes. These are the issues your instructor expects you to handle. Once you've done this, you can go beyond the question and argue whether the taxes are fair or whether the revenue is used appropriately, but you cannot substitute these arguments for the implied actions.

Here are sample questions and how to go about answering them.

Who is the best leader?	Define good leadership
	Identify someone who fits this definition
	Describe how this person fits this definition
How can schools be improved?	Identify a problem in schools
	Explain how to solve the problem
Why does racism exist?	Define racism
	Describe it to show it exists
	Determine why it exists
Which candidate should win?	Define the type of person needed for the job
	Identify which person has the qualities needed
	Describe how this person shows these qualities
If we eliminate welfare, what will happen?	Identify the impact of welfare
	Describe what would happen if welfare is stopped
	Compare the results to the present situation

Yes/No Questions   Some prompts involve questions that lead to an answer of yes or no. All of the questions below can be answered with a yes or a no, or even a maybe, but you know that you are expected to write an essay, not a sentence. This kind of prompt asks you to take a position, and, therefore, the key action you are expected to complete is to *argue*. To make your argument convincing, you may also choose other key actions such as *analyze, consider, define, determine,* or *explain*. Consider these questions.

Do you think the welfare system should be eliminated?

Should young adults under 16 be allowed to drive?

Would it be unethical to keep a large sum of money you found on the street?

Is education important?

HOW WILL YOU BRING THE FOCUS AND ACTIONS TOGETHER?

One of the basic requirements of an essay is that you focus clearly on a main idea. Although a prompt may ask you to do several things, you have to find a way to bring the focus and actions together into one essay.

For example, when you are having trouble stopping your car, you may have to take the brakes apart and test each part to find out what you need to do to make everything work properly. Once you have done so, you still have to put the brakes back together before your car will stop safely. In the same way, once you have identified the focus and the actions needed to respond to a prompt, you need to put all your ideas together into one effective essay.

Let's analyze two sample prompts (given here and on page 87). These prompts refer to Mark Mathabane's "My Father's Tribal Rule" (pp. 42–46). In analyzing these prompts, use the questions we discussed.

1. What are you expected to focus on?
2. What actions are you expected to take?
3. How will you bring the focus and actions together?

Sample Prompt 1

Mathabane writes less about his mother than his father or himself. What is her role in the family? Do you think other women play similar roles in their families?

Identifying the Focus

Notice that the first part of the prompt makes a statement about the reading. This statement is an interpretation by your instructor, and it gives you an idea of the direction you are expected to take. You should accept this interpretation as valid for the assignment and write your essay based on it. (The latter part of this chapter will show you how to challenge an interpretation stated in a prompt.) Because this statement contains no direct, indirect, or implied commands and it is not a question, you know that the purpose of this statement is to introduce the assignment, not to give you key action or focus words. To find your action and focus, you must continue reading the prompt.

When you read further, you will see two questions. You should look here for key focus words. They are:

her role   the family   other women   similar roles   their families

These words tell you to focus on the mother rather than on Mathabane or his father, who are mentioned only in the interpretive statement. You know what part of the reading you are expected to focus on—those parts that deal with Mathabane's mother and her role in the family.

Notice also that the key words require you to consider related material beyond the reading. This means that you will have to add material of your own since Mathabane does not discuss women in other families. These key words limit what you will discuss about these other women. You are expected to discuss only women's activities within the family (not at work, church, school, or in the community, unless these activities are clearly related to the family). You now know the focus of your essay will be Mathabane's mother as well as other women and their roles in their families.

Identifying the Actions

Now that you have the focus, you have to determine what you are being asked to do with that focus. Let's look again at the prompt to determine the actions you are expected to take.

> *Mathabane writes less about his mother than his father or himself. What is her role in the family? Do you think other women play similar roles in their families?*

The first sentence contains no key words or phrases describing actions that involve you. The two questions that follow do. (Remember: Questions always require an action on your part.)

The key action words in the first question are *what is*. As described in the example on page 84, *what* indicates that you need to identify the role Mathabane's mother plays and describe what she does to fill that role. Remember that she could play more than one role, and you will want to identify and describe each of them.

The second question in this prompt uses the key action phrase *do you think*. This phrase tells you to consider the roles other women play. When you consider these roles, you will identify and describe them just as you did for the roles played by Mathabane's mother.

To summarize, you need to do the following.

- ▪ *Identify* and *describe* the role of Mathabane's mother.
- ▪ *Identify* and *describe* the role other women play in their families.

Bringing the Focus and the Actions Together

The prompt appears to ask you two different questions, and you have identified two actions that you need to complete. But you are writing one essay, so you must find a way to combine your answers into a single idea. Let's look at the prompt again.

> *Mathabane writes less about his mother than his father or himself. What is her role in the family? Do you think other women play similar roles in their families?*

You have identified all the key focus words (people, things, or ideas) and the key actions (*what is*, or *identify* and *describe*). Many beginning writers stop once they know to identify and describe because they do not notice that the second question requires an additional action. Notice the word *similar* in the prompt. When you are asked whether two things are similar, you are being asked to *compare* (or *contrast*) them. This prompt asks you to compare (or contrast) the roles Mathabane's mother plays and the roles other women play.

You now have three actions to complete.

1. *Identify* and *describe* the role of Mathabane's mother.
2. *Identify* and *describe* the role other women play in their families.
3. *Compare* (or *contrast*) the roles Mathabane's mother plays and the roles other women play.

It is this third action that ties your ideas together to form a complete response to the prompt.

Is All This Really Necessary?   Yes. At first, you will have to consciously and thoroughly analyze the prompt before you begin to write your essay. As you become a more experienced writer, the task of analyzing the prompt will become more automatic, and you will be able to recognize the focus and actions in each prompt quickly and bring them together in your head. Until that time, it is better to address each step individually so that any essay you write will be an effective and complete answer to a prompt. Of course, this process will never become automatic if you don't practice it.

Computer Tip

Use the word processor to help you analyze a prompt. Type the prompt. Then move the key focus words into one list and the key action words into another. You can also separate the prompt into individual sentences to help you be sure that you are addressing each part of the prompt.

To help you move in this direction, let's practice with another prompt.

Sample Prompt 2

Mathabane has a conflict with his father. Do parents and children always have conflicts? Why or why not? Using Mathabane's essay as well as your own observations and experiences, write an essay in which you answer this question.

Here is a much shorter analysis of what the prompt asks you to do.

Identifying the Focus   This prompt directs your attention to the following.

Mathabane	conflict	his father	parents	children	conflicts
Mathabane's essay		your own observations and experiences			

Identifying the Actions   The first part of the prompt is a statement that tells you that Mathabane and his father have conflicts. Your first action is to *identify* these conflicts discussed in the reading and to *describe* them.

The next part of the prompt asks a question. To answer it you first have to determine whether parents and children always have conflicts. There are two answers to this question: *yes* and *no*.

■ If you answer *yes,* you must discuss why this is true, using examples from Mathabane's situation and other families you know of. You will need to *identify* and *describe* the conflicts you know about between parents and their children and *compare* these families and Mathabane's.

■ If you answer *no,* you must show that some parents and children do not have conflicts. Since Mathabane's family did have conflicts, you must *describe* examples of parents and children who do not have conflicts and *compare* these families and Mathabane's.

The third part of the prompt asks you *to explain* why conflicts between parents and children do or do not happen. The last part of the prompt instructs you to use Mathabane's essay as well as your own observations and experiences.

Tying the Focus and Actions Together   As you may notice, we have already brought the focus and actions together by recognizing that we have to compare Mathabane's family and other families. As you get more skilled at analyzing prompts, this third step will often require you to just be sure that you have already responded to all parts of the prompt and that you have tied the focus and the actions together.

| EXERCISE 5.1 | We will be using the following prompt in later chapters to illustrate the entire process of writing an essay in response to a reading. To help you get ready, work with several other students to analyze it. |

Collaboration

Mathabane says he despises rules and rituals. Is he correct in thinking that rules and rituals have no purpose or value?

1. Identify the focus.
2. Identify the actions.
3. Bring the focus and actions together.

| EXERCISE 5.2 | Here are additional prompts for analysis. |

1. The title of Mathabane's essay is "My Father's Tribal Rule." Is it necessary for a family to be descended from a tribe in order for a parent to exercise "tribal rule"? Why or why not?

2. What does Mathabane's mother mean when she says, "Everybody does rituals, Mr. Mathabane. . . . You just don't notice because they do theirs differently" (paragraph 28)?

3. What activities does your family do that could be classified as rituals as Mathabane defines them (in question 2)?

4. Some readers might classify the way Mathabane's father brought up his children as strict. Would he be considered too strict in your community?

5. In "My Father's Tribal Rule," Mathabane says that he hated the rituals that his father made him perform. As an adult, he may have changed his opinion. What makes family relationships change as children get older?

6. Mathabane's family lived in a multiethnic neighborhood in a South African township. His friends spoke different languages from the language of his father's tribe. When Mathabane spoke the languages of his friends, his father threatened and punished him. Does a multicultural situation increase the possibility for conflict between parents and children?

7. Mathabane's family lived in a shantytown in a South African township. Does poverty increase the possibility for conflict between parents and children? How? Why?

8. Mathabane says, "My father belonged to a loosely knit group of black families in the neighborhood to whom tribal traditions were a way of life" (paragraph 3). He also says that he was "learning other ways of life, modern ways, from mingling with children whose parents had shed their tribal cloth and embraced Western culture" (paragraph 5). Mathabane wishes his father did not insist on a traditional way of life. Would you prefer to follow a more traditional or a more modern way of life?

9. Mathabane's mother says, "It's hard to stop doing things when you're old" (paragraph 32). Do people really get too old to change?

ANALYZING MORE DIFFICULT PROMPTS

Responding to what you've read is a common academic assignment, but it is not the only one you will be required to do. You may also be asked to summarize an author's ideas, analyze how the author uses language or strategies, or evaluate how well the author accomplishes what he or she set out to do. These tasks are known as analysis, rhetorical analysis, and critique.

Analysis

To analyze, you must break a text into its parts and explain how the parts relate to each other to create a whole essay. Consider the following prompt.

How does Orwell use the description of the prisoner to attempt to move his reader to a stance against capital punishment?

This prompt directs you to *identify* parts of the text—those parts that describe the prisoner—and to *explain* how they work together to accomplish an effect on the reader.

Rhetorical Analysis

To write a **rhetorical analysis**, you must *identify* and *explain* the strategies or techniques the writer uses to get a point across or to create an effect in the reader. Consider the following prompt.

How does McCrary gain sympathy for herself and other women on welfare?

This prompt directs you to *identify* strategies McCrary uses to gain sympathy and *explain* how those strategies make readers sympathetic.

Critique

To **critique** an essay, you must discuss what the writer is trying to do and how well he or she does it. That is, you must *identify* the writer's strategies, *state* whether they are effective or ineffective, and *explain* why.

This is one of the most difficult assignments for many students, and they often fall back on responding or summarizing, tasks they are more comfortable with. Analyzing the prompts and sticking to the focus and action are critical in writing successful critiques. Consider the following prompt.

How successful is McCrary in presenting her argument that women on welfare need government programs to help them provide for their families until they can gain the education to get good jobs?

To answer this question, you would need to *identify* the strategies that McCrary uses, *describe* each strategy, and *discuss* how effectively she uses each strategy.

Literary Prompts

Literary prompts are a special kind of assignment that requires a response to a reading. They are different for a variety of reasons. First, these prompts ask you to respond to the rhetorical aspects of the reading: how the author presents the ideas and what effect the author expects from the reader. Your role, then, is to serve as an interpreter for your reader who has read the author's work but needs assistance in understanding it. Second, as an interpreter, you are using your own ideas to explain how you understood the author's ideas. But you are also limited to interpretation. You should be sure that you discuss only the author's ideas and not give your own opinions or ideas about the subject matter or evaluate the ideas or the work, unless required by the prompt. Let's consider the following prompt.

Discuss Orwell's ideas toward capital punishment as revealed in "A Hanging."

Key focus words Orwell's ideas (notice that yours are not included)

         Capital punishment (not other topics he discusses)

Key action words Discuss

The **key action word** *discuss,* as you know (see p. 82), gives you a lot of choice as to how to focus what you do in your essay. With a literary prompt, you are not being asked to give Orwell's ideas, but, as the prompt says, to discuss the ideas as they are *revealed.* The use of the word *revealed* is a hint that Orwell may not state his ideas about capital punishment in an argument. Instead, the prompt suggests that he somehow "reveals" them. Your task then is to explain to your reader how Orwell gets his ideas across without stating them as an argument.

It is important for you to recognize the different types of tasks that may be stated or simply implied by a prompt. The following box matches key action words, types of questions, and types of tasks to help you analyze prompts more fully.

✔ Key Action Words

Key Action Word	Question	Task
Agree/disagree React Discuss Explore	What do you think about what the writer has said or done?	Respond
Summarize Trace Restate Discuss Outline Explore	What does the writer say?	Summarize

continued on next page

continued from previous page

Key Action Word	Question	Task
Analyze Examine Consider	What does the writer do?	Analyze Discuss Rhetorical or Literary Aspects
Analyze Examine Consider	How does the writer do it?	Discuss Rhetorical or Literary Aspects
Evaluate Critique Assess Consider	How well does the writer do it?	Criticize

Notice that many of the key action words indicate more than one task. You will need to consider the rest of the prompt to determine which task (or how many of them) you are being asked to do.

If your prompt is in the form of a question, you can determine which action to perform by matching the question to the key action words listed on page 91–92. For example, what would you need to address to be sure you were responding to the following prompt?

Trace Etzioni's argument that it is important and appropriate for communities to agree on and enforce a shared set of values. How does Etzioni counter arguments that the community's moral voice impinges on the individual's right to follow his or her own conscience?

Key focus words	Etzioni's argument
	Important and appropriate
	Communities
	Shared set of values
	Individual's right
	Conscience
Key action word	Trace
Key question	How does

The key action word refers to **summary**. To trace Etzioni's argument, you would have to *restate* how a shared set of values affects a community. "Trace" implies a process of **development**, so it's not enough just to *summarize* each point. You must *explain* how Etzioni moves from point to point (that is, how he describes the relationship between community standards and individual actions).

The key question *how does* refers to analysis. It asks you to *explain* the techniques Etzioni uses during his argument to prove that the community voice and the individual conscience aren't necessary in conflict.

To complete these two actions (*trace* and *explain*), you would need to identify the reasons a shared set of values is important and appropriate, and explain how he shows that the individual voice isn't necessarily drowned out by the community voice. You would also need to look at how he states his audience's objections (the words he chooses, the tone of his language, the types of explanations he offers).

What would you need to address to be sure you were responding to the following prompt?

Etzioni uses a variety of support for his ideas. Analyze his support. What types of support does he use? What is the effect of each type of support? Is his support convincing? Are there other types of support that you would find more effective in this essay?

Key focus words	Variety of support
	His ideas
	Effect of each type of support
	Other types of support
Key action words	Analyze

Analyze is the only specific key action word in the prompt; you could address many topics while performing this task. However, the instructor has given you four questions. You can assume that this additional information is intended to help you focus your answer. If you had no additional questions, you would be asked to shape your own answer. These questions indicate that you should shape your answer to address these issues in your analysis. You must decide what type of information you need to provide to give a full in-depth answer for each question.

What types of support does he use?	*Identify* his support. *Classify* the support by placing it in categories. *Describe* each category.
What is the effect of each type of support?	*Identify* an effect for each type of support. *Describe* each effect. *Explain* how he achieves this effect.
Is the support convincing?	Since there is no standard meaning of "convincing" you will need to *provide your own definition*. (Ask your instructor how he or she is using this term. Also look over your notes from class discussion to see if this has been used before.) *Evaluate* each type *term* of support against your definition of "convincing."

Are there other types of support that you would find more effective?

Suggest other types of support that might prove his points. You might also offer some explanation about why he ignores or neglects these types of support. If this question had been worded "What other types of support does he neglect to use?" the question would then assume that there are other types of support and you are supposed to find them. However, since this question is worded "Are there," you can skip the question if you have tried to find the other types of support and haven't been able to identify any. (Does it make sense to you to write a section of your paper on how Etzioni has used every possible type of support?)

NARROWING THE PROMPT

In the previous prompt, you received a great deal of direction from the instructor as to how to frame your answer. Sometimes, however, you may get a prompt that is so broad that you have no clear indication of what you should be discussing. Your first job is to decide what focus you will choose for your paper rather than attempting to give every possible answer. Look at this example.

Discuss the impact of welfare on your community.

The key focus words and phrases are *impact*, *welfare*, and *community*. *Community* can refer to your neighborhood, or it can refer to a group of people that you identify with. You may need to let your reader know which definition you are planning to use. Giving this definition is one way to narrow the prompt. *Impact* is also a broad term. The impact of welfare might be financial, social, political, psychological, or ethical. You won't be able to discuss every type of effect, so you need to decide which effects are most important or which ones you have the most to say about.

For example, perhaps you consider your community to be young, single, working adults without children, who do not receive welfare. The impact on this community might include financial concerns about tax money spent on welfare and the availability of welfare for single adults without children.

Deciding on this focus would mean that you do not have to talk about mothers with children, married couples, the elderly, or people who are disabled. You could also omit discussions of political, ethical, psychological, and social concerns.

REFOCUSING THE PROMPT

Sometimes you may get an assignment that does not address a topic or issue that you can do your best writing about. Other times, you may have an idea that you know you could write a better paper on, but the prompt doesn't ask you for it. Rather than abandon your idea (and your chance to do your best writing), you need to find a way to refocus the prompt so you can connect your idea to the instructor's assignment. Here is an example.

> *Etzioni says that the moral voice is "unable to force us" because "the ultimate judgment call is up to the individual" (par. 10). To what extent are individuals able to follow their own consciences instead of the will of the community?*

It may occur to you that you could write a better paper if you talked about why it is important for the individual to act on his or her own conscience and not on the extent to which this is possible. You can write this paper: you must acknowledge the original prompt to let the instructor know you understand the assignment but provide a different answer by showing how you will refocus the question. You can do this refocusing either in the introduction or by devoting your first body paragraph to the original question and addressing your own focus in subsequent paragraphs.

Let's look at an example of an introduction in which the writer has decided to refocus the prompt.

> Communities have always tried to control the actions of their members. It is important if people are going to live together to agree on standards of behavior, values, priorities, and rules. People who act inappropriately may be jailed, shunned (as in Amish communities), teased, reprimanded, attacked, or even gossiped about by other members of the community, and this social control is necessary in many circumstances. Sometimes, however, the community standards force individuals to treat others unfairly, and individuals feel justified in breaking those standards. In Harper Lee's novel *To Kill a Mockingbird*, the white lawyer Atticus Finch risks his business, his children, and his life to defend a black man wrongly accused of raping a white woman. Martin Luther King risked jail and lost his life because he insisted on breaking laws he thought unjustly oppressed people. If individuals can live with the consequences applied by their neighbors, they can follow their own consciences, and it is sometimes essential to both the individuals and the health of the community for them to do so.

ARGUING AGAINST THE ASSUMPTION OF THE PROMPT

Some prompts ask you to accept an assumption and then to write your essay based on that assumption. If you feel that you cannot agree with the assumption, you can answer the prompt by pointing out why you think the assumption is not valid. This strategy allows you some leeway to rewrite the question. Consider the following.

Etzioni states that it is always more appropriate to act on judgment: Why is it better for a person to act on judgment than on impulse?

This prompt starts with the assumption that it is always better to act on judgment. One way to respond to this prompt is to challenge this assumption by arguing that acting on impulse is sometimes better than acting on judgment.

To successfully argue against the prompt, you have to explicitly tell your readers that this is what you plan to do. You must tell them in your introduction what the author's (or prompt's) assumption is and that you think it is invalid. In the body of your paper, you would need to explain why you think the assumption is invalid and then show how challenging this assumption reinterprets the reading and sets up the thesis that you will prove in your essay.

To argue against the assumption of this prompt, you would have to argue that acting on impulse is sometimes preferable to acting on judgment. You could challenge this prompt by doing the following.

■ Arguing that some impulses are good
■ Arguing that impulse allows us to act quickly in an emergency

Let's look at an example of an introduction in which the writer challenges the assumption of the prompt and argues against this assumption.

> When I was growing up, my father expected me to be able to explain my actions, particularly if I did something wrong. The only excuse for my actions that I could not get away with in my father's house was "I didn't think." I could tell my father that I did something wrong just because I wanted to or just for spite or to hurt someone, and those excuses did not get nearly the explosive response that followed a claim that I didn't use my judgment. Amitai Etzioni, in his essay "On Restoring the Moral Voice: Virtue and Community Pressure," writes that it is more appropriate to act on judgment than on impulse: "If the judgments always took precedence, we would be saintly; if the impulses always won, we would be psychopaths or animals." Etzioni, like my father, assumes that all impulses are bad and that judgment will always prevent us from doing wrong if only we will take the time to think and then act on our judgments. It's true that people can avoid much trouble by thinking before they act—they can censor what they say before they provoke an argument, they can refrain from striking someone when they are angry, they can choose not to have an affair when they are tempted by lust and desire. I have found, however, that some impulses are good and should be acted on. There are times when our consciences tell us the right thing to do and allow us to act quickly, bravely, and compassionately.

This introduction clearly challenges the assumption that acting on judgment is always better than acting on impulse by stating that it is not always the best way to react. This writer has altered the assignment from "Why is it better to act on judgment than on impulse?" to "Are there times when acting on impulse is appropriate?"

To complete the essay, the writer would need to identify impulses that should be acted on and explain the benefits of acting on these impulses.

EXERCISE 5.3

Analyze the following writing prompts. Try using the techniques in this chapter as they seem helpful.

Teresa McCrary, "Getting Off the Welfare Carousel" (pp. 46–48)

1. How does McCrary use her opposition's arguments to make her own points?

2. Analyze McCrary's use of first-, second-, and third-person pronouns—*I, you, they*. What relationship does she set up with people who aren't on welfare? How does she acknowledge their concerns?

3. McCrary asks if she is the exception to the rule of welfare mothers. Is she typical or is she indeed an exception?

4. McCrary represents herself as being like all welfare moms. Does this undercut her argument or make it stronger?

5. McCrary uses few details about herself and talks about welfare moms in general. Is this more effective than writing a personal narrative? Why or why not? What does this allow her to do that she couldn't do in a personal narrative?

6. McCrary assumes all women on welfare are like herself and the women she knows. Does she have just as stereotypical a view as those who think all mothers on welfare have 10 children?

7. McCrary identifies two outcomes—keep welfare or have all these women and children on the streets. Evaluate the effectiveness of her conclusion.

8. Summarize the alternatives women on welfare have, according to McCrary. Are there other options she's neglected? Explain.

EXERCISE 5.4

Collaboration

Working as a group, analyze the following writing prompts using the techniques in this chapter.

George Orwell, "A Hanging" (pp. 48–51)

1. How does Orwell use the description of the prisoner to attempt to move his reader to a stance against capital punishment?

2. How does Orwell use the superintendent's feelings about the execution to make a statement about capital punishment?

3. What statement is Orwell making about British colonialism in India?

4. What is the effect of the two threads of Orwell's story: capital punishment and British colonialism? Does he seem more concerned with one than the other? Does one issue detract from the other?

5. The superintendent is a doctor. By carrying out this execution, is he going against his beliefs? How do people reconcile following orders and doing what they believe is right?

What You've Done

■ Analyzed the prompt by
   Identifying key focus words
   Identifying key action words
   Bringing focus and action together

The Next Step

■ Understand and practice prewriting (Chapter 6)

6 Prewriting
Freewriting, Listing, Mapping, Questioning

> ### What You've Done
>
> - Analyzed the assignment
>
> ### What You Need to Do Next
>
> - Write to explore your ideas about the reading you will be writing about
> - Write to explore your own ideas and experiences related to the topic of the assignment

In Chapter 5, we discussed how to analyze the prompt to focus your writing. After analyzing an assignment and its **prompt** in depth, you probably think that you are now ready to begin the first draft of your essay. However, if you begin writing your essay at this point, you may discover that you don't have as much information as you thought you had or that your essay is not that interesting. To explore all of your options, you need to begin *prewriting*—a process in which you think about the required tasks and record some of your ideas before you begin to write your first draft.

In this chapter, we focus on prewriting based on a reading as well as on your own material. We also show you how to use the writing prompt to focus your reading and generate information.

WHAT IS PREWRITING?

Types of Prewriting
Focused freewriting
Listing
Mapping, clustering
Questioning

Prewriting is private, not public, writing. It is writing that others will not read, writing in which you generate ideas for yourself, not to produce an essay for your readers. There's more to prewriting than just putting words on paper. Reading, talking to other people, and thinking while you do other things are also ways to explore ideas. While you do some of these things, you may jot down some ideas. These notes may be helpful, but there are also more systematic ways to generate ideas that will help you complete the assignment.

To get the most out of your prewriting, you need to follow certain steps.

■ Write as much as you can. The more you write, the more choices you have.

■ Write down whatever comes to your mind. Don't worry if it seems silly or unrelated.

■ Write without worrying about correctness. Do not correct grammar or mechanics. Do not open a dictionary or thesaurus.

This stage of informal prewriting is often called **freewriting**.

How Much Prewriting Is Required?

The amount of prewriting needed depends on a number of factors.

■ *Time:* The deadline for the assignment will affect how much prewriting you can do. If you must write a timed, in-class essay or essay exam, you will want to prepare at home, reading and thinking. When you begin your in-class assignment, you will need to limit your prewriting to five to ten minutes. If you are writing an essay out of class and you have two or three days to produce a **draft**, you will want to spend one or two days prewriting. It is better to do one prewriting activity at a time and then leave the assignment alone for a period of time. Even if you are not actively writing ideas down, your brain continues to work on the tasks subconsciously. When you return to the assignment and attempt another prewriting activity, you should find that you have lots of new ideas or that you have discovered the connections between your ideas.

■ *Preference:* Another factor determining how you begin to prewrite is the way you prefer to work. Some writers spend lots of time thinking and jot down a quick list of the ideas they want to include in the draft. Other people think on paper and may produce pages of ideas even though they may use only a few of those ideas in their essay. You will need to find the prewriting activities that help you get your ideas on paper most effectively and efficiently.

■ *Assignment:* The nature of the assignment may suggest a particular prewriting activity. For example, if you are writing an essay exam, you may want to list the points that must be included to answer the instructor's question. Some assignments may require you to look carefully at the reading. Other assignments may ask you to think about personal experience or do research in the library or on the Internet. The more difficult assignments may take more time and more attempts at prewriting to find the ideas you want to include in your paper.

While all writers have a favorite method of prewriting, they need to understand how to use several prewriting activities. In this chapter, we introduce four methods of prewriting you can use to generate material from a reading and from your own thoughts. These methods are categorized as focused freewriting, listing, mapping or clustering, and questioning.

PREWRITING ABOUT A READING

Although some college writing assignments will ask you to write only about your own experiences and ideas, other assignments (which we will refer to as prompts), will direct you to respond to ideas in a reading.

When the prompt requires you to respond to a reading, you will probably want to prewrite about the reading before you prewrite to add any of your own material. If you start with your own material, you may generate a lot of information that is not related to the issues in the reading. (See Chapter 5 for more information on analyzing prompts.)

Consider the following prompt related to Mark Mathabane's "My Father's Tribal Rule" (pp. 42–46).

> *Mathabane says he despises rules and rituals. Is he correct in thinking that rules and rituals have no purpose or value?*

Notice that the prompt is specifically concerned about rules and rituals. To prewrite efficiently, you will want to focus your prewriting on those parts of the reading that deal with rules and rituals.

Focused Freewriting

One method of prewriting is to record your first reactions to the general idea about the reading identified in the prompt. The prompt tells you that *Mathabane says he despises rules and rituals.* You might want to write what you think about this idea without looking back at the reading.

Focused freewriting is a prewriting technique that will help you record your first reactions to an idea from a reading. This technique allows you to focus on one idea but gives you the freedom to write anything that comes to your mind while you are thinking about the idea.

You should write in sessions of 15 to 30 minutes. You should try to stay focused on the selected idea. However, if your mind wanders, don't stop writing and don't read what you've already written; just guide your thinking back to the topic.

Let's look at a sample of focused freewriting.

> Tribal rule is wrong. Mathabane wants to be like his friends but his father won't let him. He wants him to speak Venda because his tribe speaks Venda. Mathabane want to speak what his friends speak. The father won't let anyone talk at dinner. This is a dumb rule. Why does his father care? Why can't people talk? Does he talk during dinner? Is this rule only for the children? His mother doesn't speak. Can woman speak at the table? Maybe the rules are for the

father? He wears the tribal clothing. But Mathabane goes to school and needs to fit in. If his father made him wear the tribal clothing he will be laughed at. The rules and ritual may be ok for old people but not for kids who are our future.

If there are mistakes in freewriting, that is all right, since the object is to write down basic ideas in response to the prompt without worrying about being correct.

While focused freewriting is good for recording your first reactions, you will need to examine the reading carefully to make sure you have identified all the rules and rituals discussed in the reading. One good way to identify the places in the reading is to list them.

Listing

This prewriting method allows you to jot down phrases and important words quickly, and it works well for identifying places in the reading that relate to your writing prompt. **Listing** works best when you generate more ideas than you may need in your essay. You want to list everything you might use, knowing that you may choose to eliminate ideas later. Extensive listing gives lots of options and allows you to make the best choices for your essay.

In Chapter 5, we asked you to analyze the prompt to identify the key focus words: *rituals, rules, purpose,* and *value.* To begin dealing with the reading, you first need to identify areas of the reading that relate to these key focus words.

These paragraphs are related to rituals, rules, purpose, and value.

when George is weaned (paragraph 2)

"George's passage from infancy to childhood" (paragraph 2)

return to old traditions when whites leave (paragraph 5)

Mathabane is more interested in modern ways ("we're not living in the tribes"), but father sticks to tradition (paragraphs 5, 24)

daily rituals for protection, good luck, earning money (paragraph 6)

when Mathabane speaks at the table (paragraph 7)

father says he needs to be "taught how to eat properly" (paragraph 11)

when the father wears tribal clothing (paragraph 34)

when Mathabane speaks languages other than Venda (paragraph 34)

You now have a list of areas of the text that relate to the prompt, but it's not clearly organized into specific topics. You can take this first list and break it into separate lists according to the **key focus words**. Your new list might look like this.

Rituals	Rules	Purpose	Value
George's weaning	Not speaking at table	To be prepared	
		To return to tribes	
Daily rituals	Only speaking Venda	To get protection, good luck, money	Safety, prosperity
Tribal clothing		To move to new stage of life	
		To teach manners	

Notice that there is only one item under the heading *value*. When looking at the reading, there are few direct references to what Mathabane and his family get out of these rituals. You may have to decide what value you think the family gets from these rituals rather than finding it clearly in the reading.

As you do other prewriting methods, you may find the ideas you need to fill in the rest of this list.

You will also need to know how these four topics relate to each other. A good way to see the relationship between the parts of your prompt is to draw yourself a picture or a map that shows the connections.

Mapping and Clustering

Mapping and **clustering** allow you to create a visual picture of your ideas and the relationships among them. This method is good if you have found lots of material and ideas but are not sure how all of them fit together. To create a map, you should start by writing one of the central ideas of the topic in the center of the page and then add ideas that you think are associated with this topic. As you generate ideas, you may want to draw lines and circles to show how these ideas are connected.

Mapping is a way to organize and show the relationships that exist between the items in your lists. Since you already have a list organized by topics, you can start your mapping from your list. According to the prompt, you would expect rules and rituals to each have a purpose and a value. You can begin your mapping by showing the connections between the rules and rituals and purpose and value.

Figure 6.1 on page 104 shows a map of the relationships you might find between rituals, rules, purposes, and values. Although some parts of the map

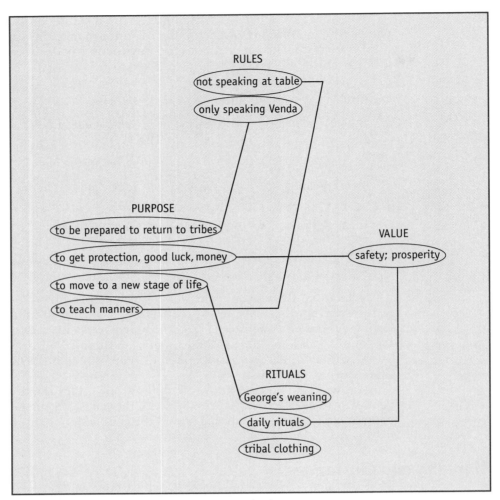

Figure 6.1. Map of Rituals, Rules, Purpose, and Value

still aren't connected to anything else, you may find the connections later or you may find out that they aren't really related and can be eliminated.

At this point, you may want to look back at the prompt to see what else it asks you to consider. The prompt states that "Mathabane says he despises rituals." One of the ideas you'll want to explore is why he despises them. Figure 6.2 illustrates how Mathabane's reasons can be added to the map to give you a better picture of his attitudes toward his father's rules and rituals.

In looking at the reasons Mathabane detests rituals that have been identified, notice that there is one ritual—George's weaning—that he doesn't really despise. Since it doesn't relate to the prompt, you probably won't have to talk about it, and you can cross it off your map.

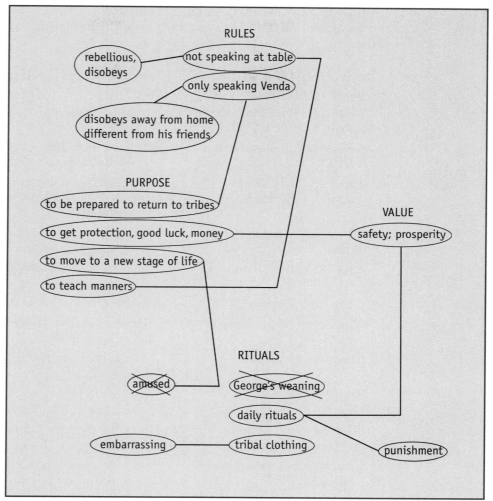

Figure 6.2. Map Including Mathabane's Responses

Questioning

Questioning is a prewriting technique that requires you to ask questions about your topic. The most common question words are the same questions reporters are expected to cover in news stories.

what   who   when   where   why   how

To make questioning an effective prewriting tool, you need to keep asking questions. When you answer one question, ask another question about the answer. The goal is to uncover as much information as you can by asking the difficult and obscure questions as well as the simple, obvious ones. When you continue to ask and answer more specific questions, you get to the core of the issue and reveal the most about the reading.

What rituals does Mathabane and his family participate in?	Weaning George, wearing tribal clothing, daily rituals
What rules does Mathabane have to follow?	Speaking Venda, not speaking at table
Why do they follow these rituals?	Father believes they will return to tribal life, wants them to be ready
Why does Mathabane despise the rules and rituals?	Sometimes used as punishment, his father is unreasonable, he's embarrassed
How does his father punish him?	Beats him, makes him do more rituals
What does Mathabane do?	Sometimes obeys, sometimes disobeys
When does he obey?	Usually when father is there
When does he disobey?	When he's with his friends, when he's mad at his father
How does he disobey?	He talks at the table, he speaks other languages
Why does he disobey?	He wants to be like his friends, he likes modern ways, he's rebellious
What happens when he disobeys?	His father punishes him, his mother talks to him
What does his mother say?	Father is too old to change, all people do rituals, father wants son to be like him
Why does she say this?	Wants him to understand his father

This is not a complete list of the questions you could ask; it is merely a sample to show how to create and answer questions as a prewriting technique. You need to continue asking questions about the reading and about your answers to those questions until you have identified all aspects of the reading that relate to the prompt and understand how that material will help you respond to the prompt.

After using these four prewriting techniques—focused freewriting, listing, mapping and clustering, questioning—you will have identified which parts of the reading deal with rules and rituals. You will also have discovered what Mathabane's attitude is toward rules and rituals and why he feels that way.

PREWRITING ABOUT YOUR OWN IDEAS AND EXPERIENCES

The four prewriting techniques we have just discussed can also be used to help you generate your own ideas and identify experiences that you can use to support your **argument**.

When you prewrite about a reading, you have a ready source of examples—the reading itself. Many beginning writers believe that when an assignment requires their own ideas and experiences, they are allowed to discuss only what they have personally done. In fact, these writers often say things like, "I can't write about capital punishment because I've never committed a serious crime." This view of ideas and experiences is much too narrow. While firsthand experience can be very useful, you can also use the experiences of family and friends, what you've heard in the media, or what you've seen happen in the world around you. These experiences—although secondhand—do influence your thoughts and feelings. Even in extreme situations where you've truly had no experience (firsthand or secondhand), you are expected to show your understanding of the issues by creating hypothetical experiences you can use to place yourself in a relevant situation and complete the assignment.

Therefore, when an assignment requires your own ideas and experiences, you need to consider each of these possible areas of experience.

PERSONAL EXPERIENCE

Have I had any experience with this topic?

EXPERIENCES OF FAMILY MEMBERS OR FRIENDS

Have I heard of anyone else who has experience with this topic?

CURRENT EVENTS, HISTORICAL EVENTS, OR MEDIA (NEWSPAPERS, MAGAZINES, TELEVISION, MOVIES, RADIO)

Have I seen this topic discussed on TV, in a movie, or in a book?

HYPOTHETICAL SITUATIONS

Can I make up a scenario in which the topic would be relevant?

To show you how to use these four sources of examples, let us look again at the prompt we are focusing on in this chapter.

Mathabane says he despises rules and rituals. Is he correct in thinking that rules and rituals have no purpose or value?

The second part of the prompt asks if you think (like Mathabane) that rules and rituals have no purpose or value. To complete this part of the prompt, you will have to present your own experiences with rules and rituals so that you can provide clear examples for your reader.

You may have already decided whether or not rules and rituals have purpose and value. If so, you should prewrite to come up with specifics to support your position. If you are undecided, you will probably want to prewrite to find specifics that support both positions and use this prewriting to help you determine which position you want to take in your essay. You can use prewriting to support your point of view or to find your position on a topic.

Let's examine the four prewriting techniques to show how they can help you produce information and discover your own opinions. Using each of these techniques will help you develop an abundance of material that can be used to strengthen your essay.

Focused Freewriting

A writer did the following focused freewriting on his experiences with the topic of rules and rituals.

> In my family, we have a dinnertime ritual. Before dinner, my brothers and my sister and I are supposed to clean the house and get everything ready for dinner. One day I didn't feel like doing it, because I have to do everything. My brothers and my sister hardly do anything. So, I just sat on the couch and watched TV. My father came in and saw me and started to yell at me. He said he worked hard every day to put food on the table and that I was showing disrespect to him, my mother, my brothers and my sister. He sent me to bed without supper.

> At first I was really mad. I thought my father was being unfair to me. I'm the oldest, so I wind up doing most of the work. Why should I have to clean the house every day and get the table ready? The more I thought about it, the more I felt bad. He did do a lot for us. Besides providing us with a house and food, he paid for my music lessons, he takes us to the beach in the summer, he drops us off at the movies. He really does do a lot for us and sometimes I think we forget to say thank you. I felt bad for not respecting my father.

This writer has focused on one specific ritual performed in his family. At the end of his entry, he seems to feel regret that he didn't participate in the ritual. His feelings of regret suggest that he does see the value in performing rituals.

He will have to generate other examples to see if he feels the same way about other rules and rituals. If most of his experiences are positive, then he will probably write an essay disagreeing with Mathabane's attitude toward rituals.

Here is another example of focused freewriting.

The instructor in my history class had a ridiculous rule: no gum chewing. One day I forgot that I was chewing gum and went into his class. As he was walking between the rows of desks he saw my jaw moving and then seemed to go nuts. "I warned the class about gum chewing," he shouted at me. "Spit it out and go to the principal's office." This outburst completely disrupted the class and ruined my day. What did I do? I quietly chewed gum with my mouth closed. He couldn't have heard me. I got punished for breaking a stupid rule that authority figures like force on us. These rules make no sense and should be abolished.

This writer has focused on one specific rule. At the end of the paragraph we see this student taking a strong stance against it. If this writer can provide more strong examples showing his disgust with rules and rituals, he will be able to write an essay supporting Mathabane's attitude.

Both of these writers clearly included their attitudes toward rules and rituals as they described their experiences. They now need to come up with additional strong examples to support their positions.

Sometimes you may freewrite about an experience but not clearly understand what it reveals about your opinion. Look back at the prompt and identify the key focus words and **key action words**. Use them to create questions that you can ask about your freewriting. The following questions are based on the prompt for this chapter.

- Is this focused freewriting about a *rule* or *ritual*?
- Is there a *purpose* or *value* to this rule or ritual?
- What is the *purpose* or *value*?

If you ask these questions about all the experiences you write down, you'll be doing a focused freewriting on each of them.

While focused freewriting is good for recording the specifics related to the experience you're discussing, the prompt may require you to come up with several different kinds of experiences. If you are having difficulty remembering other experiences, you will want to try another prewriting technique: listing.

As explained on page 102, listing is a prewriting technique that allows you to jot down words and phrases that come to you as you think about the assignment. The benefits of listing are that you don't have to write in complete sentences or in a logical order. Listing is particularly useful when you have so many ideas that you can't take the time to write in complete sentences without losing some of them.

Listing

The following lists focus on a writer's own experiences related to the two terms *rituals* and *rules*.

Rituals	**Rules**
Helping with dinner	No TV until homework is done
Cleanup before bedtime	Can't stay out past 10:00
Sunday—church	Chores before play on Saturday
Sunday cookouts	No allowance until chores done

Rituals	**Rules**
Christmas—Thanksgiving	Only one hour TV per night
Birthdays	No phone calls after 8:00
Saturday morning yard work	Can't stay over at friends' houses
Halloween costume party	

This type of list helps you to identify those areas you need to explore in more depth, and it can become the source for more detailed lists. In the following list, this writer has taken one item from the list on rules—only one hour of TV per night—and expanded it, providing more details.

One hour of TV

Each person has their night to choose shows

Parents think one hour of TV is enough

Parents think TV shows "rot your brain"

I miss shows all my friends watch because my brothers choose on those nights

Forced to watch my brothers' stupid action shows

Forced to watch my parents' news shows

Dad can override anybody if there is something he really wants to see—we can't

Mom says it teaches "time management" and "cooperation"

On weekends we vote for shows, but I always lose

This more detailed list begins to reveal attitudes about this rule. Words like *forced*, *stupid*, and *lose* suggest that the rules are unreasonable. This information could be used to support Mathabane's dislike of rules.

Mapping and Clustering

The lists on rituals and rules presented in the previous section give the writer basic ideas or experiences he can examine. However, lists don't necessarily help the writer see how he feels or thinks about the items in the lists.

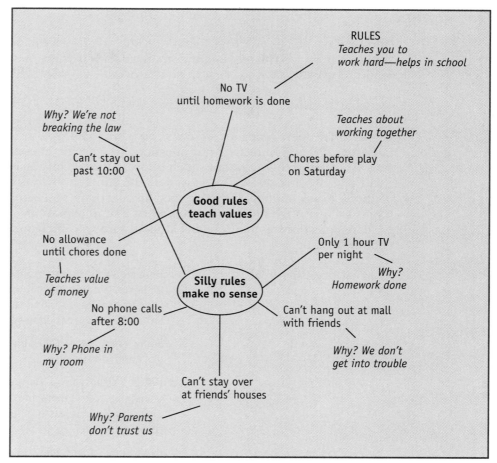

Figure 6.3. Map of Writer's Own Experiences

Figure 6.3 illustrates how the writer has taken his general list on rules and mapped it.

The diagram identifies which rules are good—and thus have value—and which ones are without value. It identifies the basic reason why each rule is or is not valuable.

Three of the rules have value, but in five of the rules, no value is noted. Since this mapping has identified more rules without value, it could become the basis for an essay agreeing with Mathabane's dislike of rules. Consider the rules with value that are identified. Which are the best examples? Which are most closely related to the prompt and the reading? Examples are provided in the mapping that could be used to agree or disagree with Mathabane's attitude about rules. If this were your mapping, you would now need to decide which position you wish to defend.

Questioning

Questioning is a prewriting technique that requires you to ask questions about your topic. The most common question words are the same questions reporters are expected to cover in news stories.

what   who   when   where   why   how

To make questioning an effective prewriting tool, you need to keep asking questions. When you answer one question, ask another question about the answer. The goal is to uncover as much information as you can by asking the difficult and obscure questions as well as the simple, obvious ones. When you continue to ask and answer more specific questions, you get to the core of the issue and reveal the most interesting ideas and information.

This questioning focuses on a student's prewriting from his own experiences with *rituals*.

What rituals do I do?	Helping with dinner, clean-up before bedtime, church, Sunday get-togethers, Christmas, Thanksgiving, Birthdays, Saturday yard work, Halloween party.
When do we do them?	Some every day. Others on special occasions, holidays.
Why do I do rituals?	Holiday rituals fun—Halloween costumes, Christmas tree decorating. Dinner ritual and clean-up rituals not fun but have to be done.
Who has to do them?	Everybody except Dad.
Why doesn't he do them?	He works all day and gets to relax while we work.
Is that fair?	Not sure. He's at work all day but we're at school working all day.
What happens if we don't do them?	Dad gets angry at us. May punish us.
Why does he get angry?	Feels like we're not helping. Shows disrespect to him and Mom.
How does he punish?	Extra chores, go to room, yells and makes you feel bad.

One question has led to another, and the process has helped this writer expand his knowledge of this subject. Notice that there is a question that doesn't contain one of the words *what, who, when, where, why, how*. That's fine. As long as you're asking questions about your subject, you're doing the right thing.

> ### Summary of Prewriting Techniques
>
> Remember that you have many options when prewriting. You can choose the most useful method by thinking about what you need to accomplish in your prewriting.
>
> | When you want to | Use |
> | --- | --- |
> | Record your own reactions and explore your ideas | Focused freewriting |
> | Come up with as many ideas as possible | Listing |
> | Explore relationships between ideas | Mapping and clustering |
> | Generate details and pinpoint meaning | Questioning |

PREWRITING THROUGH COLLABORATION

Collaboration

Other people—classmates, friends, family members, acquaintances—can be a valuable resource for you when you are generating ideas for an essay. Your instructor may assign you to a small group of students and ask that you complete prewriting exercises together. This type of activity allows you to hear several viewpoints and sets of experiences connected to your writing prompt. Not only will you come away from this exercise with other people's perspectives, but you will probably think more deeply about your own. If your instructor does not assign small group work, you can form your own group outside of class and share ideas and examples.

This is the process for brainstorming or listing collaboratively.

1. Review the prompt together and agree on what ideas you will prewrite about.
2. Accept all responses just as you would when you are prewriting for yourself. Remember that you can choose the ideas that will work the best for your paper, so you don't have to argue about them now.
3. Discuss examples from current events, history, or other areas that might help illustrate the topic. Be specific. For example, instead of saying that movies are often violent, name movie titles and, if possible, describe a particularly violent scene.

EXERCISE 6.1

Analyze the following sample prompt.

Mathabane writes less about his mother than his father or himself. What is the significance of her role in the family? Do you think other women play similar roles in their families?

Prewriting About the Reading

Identify places where Mathabane's mother figures in the reading.

Prewriting About Your Own Experiences

1. Select a prewriting activity to help you add your own examples. Remember to consider the following sources of examples.
   - ■ Personal experience
   - ■ Experiences of family members or friends
   - ■ Current events, historical events, or media (newspapers, magazines, television, movies, radio)
   - ■ Hypothetical situations
2. Prewrite about women you know.
3. Choose one of these women and use a prewriting activity to identify the roles she plays or the kinds of things that women are expected to do.

EXERCISE 6.2

Collaboration

In a group, analyze the following sample prompt.

Mathabane has a conflict with his father. Do parents and children always have conflicts? Why or why not?

Prewriting About the Reading

1. Identify places where Mathabane mentions conflicts in his family.
2. Use a prewriting technique to determine how each of these places in the reading relate to the prompt.

Prewriting About Your Own Experiences

Select a prewriting activity to help you add your own examples to answer the prompt. Remember you need to complete the following tasks to answer the prompt.

- ■ Identify and describe the conflicts you know about between parents and children.
- ■ Identify the similarities between these families and Mathabane's family.
- ■ Identify parents and children who do not have conflicts.
- ■ Describe how these families are different from Mathabane's family.
- ■ Explain why conflicts between parents and children happen (or don't happen).

What You've Done

■ Explored four basic types of prewriting.
    Focused freewriting
    Listing
    Mapping or clustering
    Questioning
■ Applied these methods to the following.
    Writing in response to reading
    Writing from your own experience and ideas

The Next Step

■ Organize your material (Chapter 7)

Organizing the Material
Planning, Outlining, and Thinking About Audience

What You've Done

- Completed prewriting activities, applying one or more methods to writing either from reading or research, or from your own experience

What You Need to Do Next

- Review reading and writing assignment and make sure you understand it
- Decide what you can use from the writing you've already done
- Use that writing to determine the main idea of your own essay
- Draft a thesis

After you have completed **prewriting** activities, it's time to evaluate what you have written and decide what material you can use to write your essay, as well as how you can use it.

You probably won't be able to use everything you wrote during prewriting. Don't be surprised or discouraged if you have to cross off some of your ideas because they aren't relevant to the question you are answering. It is much easier to eliminate what you don't need than to make up new ideas or to try to make irrelevant ideas fit into an **essay**. However, do not throw anything away until you have finished **drafting** your paper.

REVIEWING THE PROMPT AND EVALUATING YOUR PREWRITING

Organizing Steps
Review prompt
Review prewriting to
eliminate
combine
link ideas to details
identify key ideas
Draft a thesis

The first step in organizing your material is to review the **prompt**. Your goal here is to identify material in the prewriting that you can use in the essay and to eliminate any material not related to the prompt.

Let's look again at the prompt related to Mark Mathabane's "My Father's Tribal Rule" (pp. 42–46).

Mathabane says he despises rules and rituals. Is he correct in thinking that rules and rituals have no purpose or value?

Once again, the **key focus words** are *rules, rituals, purpose,* and *value.*

The second step is to examine the prewriting you have done. When evaluating prewriting, ask yourself the following three questions.

- What is unrelated to the topic? (Eliminate it.)
- What is repeated? (Choose the best way of saying it, or combine statements that repeat the same ideas.)
- What is a main idea and what may be support for that idea? (Match general ideas to related specific details and examples.)

You can start by evaluating either the prewriting on the reading or on your own experiences. There is no right way or order, although many writers start by evaluating the prewriting that contains the most information or that is most familiar.

EVALUATING PREWRITING ABOUT A READING

Here is an example of a writer's prewriting.

Tribal rule is wrong. The father won't let anyone talk at dinner. When Mathabane talks anyway, his father beats him. This is a dumb rule. Mathabane doesn't deserve to be beaten for breaking it. Mathabane also gets punished when he doesn't do the daily rituals. His father must be superstitious. No ritual can possibly bring good luck or keep people from getting sick. It doesn't make sense to waste time doing these things every day like Mathabane's father made him. His father also wears the tribal clothing and Mathabane's friends laugh at his father, calling his clothes Tarzan clothes. Mathabane cries when his friends tease him. He shouldn't have been made to feel bad because of his father's rituals.

Eliminating Unrelated Material or Ideas

In many cases, you will easily recognize ideas and examples in your prewriting that are unrelated to your topic, but sometimes you may not be sure. To decide whether material is related to your topic, write one sentence explaining how the idea in your prewriting is related to key focus words. If you cannot explain this relationship, your idea may be unrelated and you may choose not to use it. Let's now look at the prewriting from the preceding excerpt, one sentence at a time.

Tribal rule is wrong.	The word *rule* is one of the key focus words. The word *wrong* implies a judgment, which also implies *value,* another key focus word. The use of these words makes this sentence related.

The father won't let anyone talk at dinner.	This sentence refers to one of the rules discussed in the reading, so it is clearly related.
When Mathabane talks anyway, his father beats him.	This sentence also refers to one of the rules discussed in the reading, so it is clearly related.
This is a dumb rule.	Like the first sentence of the prewriting, this sentence is clearly related. The word *dumb* implies a purpose or value, both key focus words.
Mathabane doesn't deserve to be beaten for breaking it.	This sentence refers to what happens when Mathabane breaks the rule; it is related.
Mathabane also gets punished when he doesn't do the daily rituals	This sentence also refers to a set of rituals mentioned in the reading, so it is related.
His father must be superstitious.	No key focus words are used in this sentence. Unless you can write a sentence connecting it to the prompt, it is unrelated.
No ritual can possibly bring good luck or keep people from getting sick.	This sentence includes the key word *ritual;* it is also related.
It doesn't make sense to waste time doing these things every day like Mathabane's father made him.	*These things* refer to rituals, and the words *make sense* and *waste time* relate to the value of the rituals; this sentence is related.
His father also wears the tribal clothing and Mathabane's friends laugh at his father, calling his clothes Tarzan clothes.	Wearing tribal clothing is another ritual.
Mathabane cries when his friends tease him.	This sentence contains no key words and is not clearly related to the prompt.
He shouldn't have been made to feel bad because of his father's rituals.	This sentence also contains the key word *ritual.*

Most of these sentences clearly relate to rules, rituals, purpose, or value. But there are two sentences that may not be related.

> Mathabane cries when his friends tease him.

> His father must be superstitious.

It is not clear how these ideas relate to the key focus words. Eliminate the ideas if they don't relate. However, before eliminating the sentences, the writer can try to write another sentence or two that shows how the ideas relate to the prompt.

The first sentence refers to Mathabane's reaction when his friends laugh at his father's ritual of wearing tribal clothes. The writer should try to write a sentence that relates Mathabane's reaction to the purpose and value of his father's rules and rituals.

> Mathabane is upset because his friends tease him about his father's ritual of wearing tribal clothes. Therefore, this ritual does not have a positive value for him.

The second sentence is an assessment of the father by the writer. Once again, the writer should try to write a sentence that relates this assessment of the father to the purpose or value of his rules and rituals.

> I think that the father must be superstitious to think that his rituals will actually bring good luck and protection. Since that is the purpose of his father doing the rituals, I don't think the rituals really have a good purpose.

How to Check for Unrelated Material or Ideas

Find the key focus words from the prompt.

State the relationship between the key focus words and the sentence in the prewriting to determine if the material is unrelated.

Finding Repeated Material

Now that you have determined that all the material is related to the prompt or eliminated what is not related, you need to look for repeated information—that is, where you have said the same thing in two different ways. You want to look for two types of repetition of ideas.

- Sentences that mean the same thing.
- Sentences that are close but may contain slightly different or new information.

Sometimes it will be obvious that two sentences are saying the same thing. Other times, you will have to look more carefully at what you have written to discover the repetition because it is easy to confuse repetition with similarity. When you state similar or related ideas, you use many of the same words. Using the same words does not mean that you are repeating yourself. In fact, when you explain ideas fully, you have to repeat key words and phrases so that your reader can understand your ideas and see how they are related. Because you are repeating words, you need to make sure that you are not also repeating ideas.

While there are many ways to check for repetition, one way is to group the sentences you have identified as being related to the same focus words and compare them to each other.

- If you are not sure whether two of the writer's ideas are the same, state the difference between the two ideas.
- If you cannot explain the difference between the two ideas, they are probably so close to being the same that you should treat them as one idea.

Let's look at the grouping of the prewriting sentences to see if there are any repeated ideas.

Tribal rule is wrong.
This is a dumb rule.

These sentences both make a judgment about rules and rituals. The first two sentences may seem the same at first glance, but *dumb* and *wrong* mean different things. When people refer to rules as dumb, they generally mean that the rule has no reason or purpose; when people refer to rules as wrong, they usually mean that the rule has a negative effect. These two sentences discuss the same topic, but they give different information about the topic.

The father won't let anyone talk at dinner.
His father also wears the tribal clothing.

These sentences are both related to rules. Each one lists a rule or ritual that Mathabane's father follows.

Mathabane doesn't deserve to be beaten for breaking it.
Mathabane also gets punished when he doesn't do the daily rituals.

These sentences are related because they discuss the consequences of the rules rituals on Mathabane. The first and two sentences state that he is punished when he doesn't follow one of his father's rules and his daily rituals. In addition, the first sentence states the student's opinion about the punishment (Mathabane doesn't deserve it). These two sentences discuss the same topic, but each adds a different piece of information.

Mathabane's friends laugh at his father, calling his clothes Tarzan clothes.

The remaining sentences in this group deal with Mathabane's experience of his father wearing tribal clothes. The first sentence states the consequence: his friends laugh and call his father's clothes Tarzan clothes.

Mathabane cries when his friends tease him.

Mathabane is upset because his friends tease him about his father's ritual of wearing tribal clothes.

He shouldn't have been made to feel bad because of his father's rituals.

Therefore, this ritual does not have a positive value for him.

His father must be superstitious.

I think that the father must be superstitious to think that his rituals will actually bring good luck and protection. Since that is the purpose of his father doing the rituals, I don't think the rituals really have a good purpose.

No ritual can possibly bring good luck or keep people from getting sick.

It doesn't make sense to waste time doing these things every day like Mathabane's father made him.

The next two sentences describe Mathabane's reaction. The first describes his action (he cries), and the second adds his emotional state (he's upset). These sentences sound very similar, but they do give slightly different information.

The next sentence states the writer's opinion toward the results of the tribal clothing ritual.

This last sentence states the writer's conclusion about the value of this ritual.

These three sentences are related since the middle sentence was the one the writer used to show the connection between the other two sentences and the assigned prompt. She can now keep the middle sentence and put the other two aside since the middle sentence incorporates the ideas of both of the other sentences as well as explaining the connection between them and their relationship to the prompt.

This states the writer's opinion of the value of the daily rituals.

How to Check for Repeated Ideas

State the difference between the two ideas.

Matching Main Ideas to Examples and Details

Once you have eliminated unrelated material and chosen the best way to say repeated material, you will now want to match main ideas to examples and specific details. Main ideas are general, and they apply to various people at different times and places. Examples and details (or **supporting** information) apply to specific people at particular times and places. For example, the statement "Dogs make good pets" is a main idea, since lots of people throughout the world and throughout history have said this. An example or specific detail focuses on one particular event or instance: "Spot loves to play with the children, and no matter what they do, he never bites them or growls at them."

Let's look again at some prewriting to identify sentences that do not refer to specific people, places, or events, but to general groups.

Tribal rule is wrong.	General idea. It does not identify which tribal rules but makes a statement about all rules of this type.
The father won't let anyone talk at dinner.	Specific.
This is a dumb rule.	Refers to a specific rule but is a general statement about that rule.
Mathabane doesn't deserve to be beaten for breaking it.	Specific.
Mathabane also gets punished when he doesn't do the daily rituals.	Specific.
I think that the father must be superstitious to think that his rituals will actually bring good luck and protection. Since that is the purpose of his father doing the rituals, I don't think the rituals really have a good purpose.	Refers to a specific ritual but makes a general statement about that ritual.
It doesn't make sense to waste time doing these things every day like Mathabane's father made him.	Refers to a specific ritual but makes a general statement about that ritual.
His father also wears the tribal clothing, and Mathabane's friends laugh at his father, calling his clothes Tarzan clothes.	Specific.
Mathabane cries when his friends tease him.	Specific.
He shouldn't have been made to feel bad because of his father's rituals.	Refers to a specific ritual but makes a general statement about that ritual.

Determining Which Sentences Are Ideas and Which Are Supporting Examples

Some of these sentences composed during the prewriting stage are clearly general or clearly specific. However, some could be both. General ideas are supported by specific examples or by other ideas that further explain them; general ideas also explain the meaning or significance of specific examples. Some sentences serve as support (that is, they support an idea) while also serving as an idea (that is, they explain the significance of an example).

For example, consider the following statements.

It's good to own an animal.

Animals make good companions.

My cat Sherman greets me at the door after a long day and seems happy to see me.

The second sentence, "Animals make good companions," supports the first sentence, "It's good to own an animal." You can test this by asking the following question: Why is it good to own an animal? It is good because "animals make good companions." But it also serves as a general idea to the third sentence. What are you proving by using the example of "my cat Sherman greets me at the door . . ."? My cat greets me at the door; therefore "animals make good companions." Or you can ask, "How do I know that animals make good companions?" You could then answer, "Because my cat Sherman greets me at the door. . . ."

For each sentence in your prewriting, you need to ask two questions.

1. How do I know that this sentence of prewriting is true?
2. What am I proving with this sentence of prewriting?

Any answer to the first question will provide the related supporting example and specifics for this sentence. Any answer to the second question provides the related general idea.

You'll notice that each sentence of the prewriting has corresponding general and specific material. This is because every idea is both general and specific. When you add or include other ideas, you then create a relationship in which one of these sentences is going to be more general or more specific than the other. This relationship creates what instructors sometimes call the "**ladder of abstraction**." Each idea represents a rung on the ladder, and you can move up or down the ladder, from general to specific or specific to general, depending on where you start and the direction in which you move.

Now you need to identify the examples and specific details that match each main idea, asking why each idea is true and looking for the answers (examples) in the prewriting. For the main idea "Tribal rule is wrong," let's look at each sentence of the focused **freewriting** that would demonstrate why it is true. The writer needs to write additional information to show the connection between the main idea and the example or specific detail.

The father won't let anyone talk at dinner.	This sentence brings in an example of a rule. The father requires that everyone eat in silence. How does this show that tribal rule is wrong? Perhaps this rule is unfair or doesn't make sense.
This is a dumb rule.	This sentence reveals an attitude about the rule, but doesn't reveal why it is wrong. The writer needs to ask, "Why are dumb rules wrong?" The answer might be "Rules should have a reason or purpose."
Mathabane doesn't deserve to be beaten for breaking it.	The words "doesn't deserve" are a judgment on the part of the writer. The writer needs to state the link between "Tribal rule is wrong" and this sentence. Perhaps the writer should state, "Tribal

Mathabane also gets punished when he doesn't do the daily rituals.

rule is wrong because it leads to people being treated unfairly."

This sentence brings in an example of a ritual.

I think that the father must be superstitious to think that his rituals will actually bring good luck and protection. Since that is the purpose of his father doing the rituals, I don't think the rituals really have a good purpose.

This example seems to support the same general idea as the writer stated previously: Rituals should have a reason or purpose or they should benefit somebody.

It doesn't make sense to waste time doing these things every day like Mathabane's father made him.

The writer can restate this sentence in more general terms: Rituals ought to make sense and they have no positive value when they don't. Then the writer can use the daily rituals as examples of rituals that don't make sense.

His father also wears the tribal clothing and Mathabane's friends laugh at his father, calling his clothes Tarzan clothes.

Here is a second example of a ritual— wearing the tribal clothing—as well as an example of the results of the ritual.

Mathabane cries when his friends tease him.

This sentence is a specific example of why rituals have no positive value. It is closely related to the next sentence, which is more general.

He shouldn't have been made to feel bad because of his father's rituals.

Rituals have no positive meaning when they cause embarrassment.

How to Match Ideas and Examples

Label general and specific points.

Match specific ideas and examples to general ideas.

"How do I know this is true?"

"What am I trying to prove with this sentence?"

Write a sentence explaining the connection between ideas and support if the connection isn't clear.

Listing Your Main Ideas

What you have just done is to fill in the connections that were in your head but you did not write down. Many inexperienced writers miss this step, and the reasons for their answers remain unclear to their readers. Let's look at a list of just those connections made from the focused freewriting.

1. Rituals should have a reason or purpose.
2. It leads to people being treated unfairly.
3. Rituals should have a reason or purpose or they should benefit somebody.
4. Rituals ought to make sense and they have no positive value when they don't.
5. Rituals have no positive meaning when they cause embarrassment.

Notice that sentence 1 is actually the first half of sentence 3; you can eliminate sentence 1 from your list.

Writing a Tentative Thesis

After listing the ideas that respond to a prompt, you will be ready to write a tentative **thesis**, which will state in a sentence or two a clear "answer" to the question asked by the prompt. In this case your list should state your opinion on tribal rule and provide reasons that support that position. Let's look at one writer's tentative thesis and list of main ideas. Note that it is presented in an outline form.

Tribal rule is wrong because:

It leads to people being treated unfairly.

Mathabane gets punished and doesn't deserve it.

Rituals should have a reason or purpose or they should benefit somebody.

The daily rituals won't actually bring good luck and protection, so they don't really have a purpose.

There doesn't seem to be a purpose for not talking at the table.

Rituals ought to make sense and they have no positive value when they don't.

Mathabane has to waste time performing daily rituals.

Rituals have no positive meaning when they cause embarrassment.

Mathabane is embarrassed when his friends laugh at his father's clothes and call them Tarzan clothes.

This writer may have more than can be used in one paper, so she must now decide which ideas would be best to keep. One way to do this is to turn to the prewriting from personal ideas and experience.

EVALUATING PREWRITING ABOUT YOUR OWN REACTIONS AND EXPERIENCE

Since the prompt asks you to use the reading and your own ideas and experiences, you must also evaluate the prewriting you did about these areas.

Let's review the prompt. You can use the same steps you used when prewriting about the reading.

Mathabane says he despises rules and rituals. Is he correct in thinking that rules and rituals have no purpose or value?

■ What is unrelated to the topic? (Eliminate it.)

■ What is repeated? (Pick the best way of saying it, or combine statements that repeat the same ideas.)

■ What is a main idea and what may be support for that idea? (Match general ideas to related specific details and examples.)

Eliminating Unrelated Material or Ideas

Eliminate material that is not related to the prompt. Follow the steps shown in the box.

How to Check for Unrelated Material or Ideas

Find the key focus words from the prompt.

State the relationship between the key focus words and the sentence in the prewriting to determine if the material is unrelated.

Below are two lists of a student's own ideas and examples pertaining to this topic that she generated during her prewriting. Let's look at an example of how she evaluates this material.

Work Rituals	Work Rules
Draw names to give gifts (Christmas)	Can't take more than 5 sick days
Showers for newlyweds and parents	Must take lunch hour noon to 1:00
Mandatory Christmas parties	Fill out travel form to leave office on company business

Weekly staff meetings

Cakes on birthdays

Monthly "pep" talks from manager

July 4th picnic

Thanksgiving ham or turkey

Fill out inventory form to move piece of equipment or furniture

The material all seems related to the key focus words, the words in the writing prompt that point you to specific topics or issues (see Chapter 5). Because this writer has made a list focused on the key words, she can expect to have little unrelated material. Her results may have been very different had she chosen to freewrite instead since her thoughts would have been less focused on the key words.

Finding Repeated Material

As you did with the prewriting about the reading, check for places where you have repeated the same ideas. If you are not sure whether the ideas are the same, state the differences between your ideas. If you cannot state the difference, the ideas are probably too similar to use for different paragraphs. Eliminate one of the ideas.

Because this writer has chosen to list material, there is probably not much repetition (just as you would not repeat items on a grocery list). If you did, you would probably just ignore the item the second time (you wouldn't buy pickles twice if you listed them twice).

How to Check for Repeated Ideas

State the difference between the two ideas.

Matching Main Ideas to Examples and Details

Finally, as you did with the prewriting about the reading, match ideas with the specific details and examples that support them.

The lists on page 126–127 give specific examples and details but no ideas. We know this because the writer has listed only rules and rituals that she has experienced; in other words, they apply only to her, not necessarily to everyone. To match ideas to these examples and details, she must do the following.

- Put the examples and details into categories of rules or rituals to help make sense of them.
- Write a statement about the purpose or value of each category of rules or rituals.

We can see that the list of rituals refers to several holidays: Christmas, Thanksgiving, birthdays, 4th of July. Inexperienced writers sometimes think because these are separate days that this material is not repeated. They would try to write a paragraph on each of these days and focus their papers on the purpose and value of rituals and rules that apply to holidays. This paper could be written, but it would be a challenging one to write. To write it well, a writer would have to go back to the list and place any material about holidays into categories. The first might be holidays or special days, the second might have to do with specific events at work (showers, parties, staff meetings, pep talks, picnics), and the third with specific activities that take place at work. A new list of rituals would look like this.

Special Occasions	Events	Activities
Christmas	Showers	Drawing names
Weddings	Parties	
Births	Picnics	
Birthdays	Staff meetings	
4th of July	Pep talks	
Thanksgiving		

The same process can be followed with the rules list. There may be more than one way to group the parts of this list. One way would be to divide the list into rules that apply to how employees spend time and those that apply to paperwork that must be completed. A grouping might look like this.

Time	Paperwork
Can't take more than 5 sick days	Travel forms to leave office on company business
Must take lunch hour from noon to 1:00	Inventory forms to move piece of equipment or furniture

Now the writer can take each category and try to figure out the purpose or value of the entire category, but this can be complicated. Another approach is to choose one rule or ritual from the category and to examine its purpose and value. After the writer has done this, he or she can check the purpose and value against those of the entire category. Regardless of which option is chosen, the writer should come up with very similar ideas.

Let's look at the "paperwork" category. What is the purpose or value of rules governing paperwork that must be completed? The writer might answer that these rules ensure that records are kept accurately. Does this purpose apply to each of these items? Yes. Does the writer have any specific examples? No. While the two items in this list are examples of rules that apply to filling out paperwork, they do not provide specific examples of documenting activities or actions, the purposes of these rules.

You can also start by listing all the purposes or values for one item on the list and applying it to the entire category. This method will lead you to more specific examples of purpose and value. For example, let's take the ritual of drawing names to give gifts at work.

Drawing Names to Give Gifts at Work

$20 limit

Everyone gets a gift

All gifts are of similar value

Gifts are opened at Christmas party

Gives us something to do as a group at the party

We learn names of people we didn't know

I always spend more; I don't want to be thought of as cheap

I never know the person I've drawn

Have to guess at a gift

Everyone pretends to like the gift

Gifts are usually inappropriate or stupid

I gave a basket of meat and wine to a vegetarian who didn't drink

As we did when evaluating pieces of prewriting before, we need to follow the steps of eliminating what isn't related to the prompt, looking for what is repeated, and matching ideas with specific examples and details. Because this list is focused on a single rule, we can assume that everything is related to that rule.

How to Match Ideas and Examples

Label general and specific points.

Match specific ideas and examples to general ideas.

   "How do I know this is true?"

   "What am I trying to prove with this sentence?"

Write a sentence explaining the connection between ideas and support if the connection isn't clear.

Grouping Related Items

We can start by grouping related items.

$20 limit Gifts are opened at Christmas party	Each of these statements explains how the ritual is done.
Everyone gets a gift All gifts are of similar value Gives us something to do as a group at the party We learn names of people we didn't know	These statements may indicate the benefits of the ritual or the reasons for following the ritual.
I always spend more; I don't want to be thought of as cheap I never know the person I've drawn Have to guess at a gift Everyone pretends to like the gift Gifts are usually inappropriate or stupid I gave a basket of meat and wine to a vegetarian who didn't drink	These statements all concern what can go wrong with the ritual or complaints that the writer has about the ritual.

Do the Groups Complete the Actions Required by the Prompt?

At this point the writer has to take each group of items and determine if these groups allow a response to the actions required by the prompt. After grouping these ideas, the writer has generated material that clearly provides examples of rituals and rules. But the prompt also asks the writer to determine what each group reveals about purpose or value.

$20 limit Gifts are opened at Christmas party	These statements just explain the rules of the ritual—that is, how it is performed. If there is a value here, perhaps it is the following: The ritual does limit how much individuals have to spend on gifts.
Everyone gets a gift All gifts are of similar value	These statements seem to explain a common purpose: The ritual ensures that people are treated equally.
Gives us something to do as a group at the party We learn names of people we didn't know	These two statements also seem to explain a purpose or value: This ritual serves a social purpose by providing something for people to do together and a way get to know each other.
I always spend more; I don't want to be thought of as cheap	This statement shows how the ritual some times doesn't fulfill its purpose: Instead of limiting the amount people spend to a reasonable sum, people end up spending more.
I never know the person I've drawn Have to guess at a gift Everyone pretends to like the gift Gifts are usually inappropriate or stupid I gave a basket of meat and wine to a vegetarian who didn't drink	These statements show that people don't feel good about the gifts they've given or received. Instead of bringing people together, this ritual makes people feel even more uncomfortable because they have to lie about liking the gift and because they know their gifts aren't appropriate.

Listing Your Main Ideas

Let's now look at a list of the writer's main ideas.

The ritual does limit how much individuals have to spend on gifts.

The ritual ensures that people are treated equally.

This ritual serves a social purpose by providing something for people to do together and a way to get to know each other.

The ritual sometimes doesn't fulfill its purposes—instead of limiting the amount people spend to a reasonable sum, people end up spending more.

Instead of bringing people together, rituals may make people feel even more uncomfortable.

The writer now has a number of lists and should not throw any of them away. She can refer to these specific examples and ideas as she is drafting her essay.

IS ALL THIS REALLY NECESSARY?

Yes. Good writers go through all of these steps. As you gain more experience and skill, you may find that you can complete these steps faster, perform multiple steps at a time, or think through some of them in your head. Until that time, you should continue to go through these steps on paper.

COMBINING THE PARTS OF YOUR PREWRITING

The prompt we have been working with instructs you to use both the reading and your own ideas and observations. Now that you have generated ideas and examples from each of these sources, you need to combine them so it makes sense to use both in the same paper.

Let's compare this writer's tentative thesis and list of ideas from the reading (first given on page 125) to her list of her own ideas and experiences.

This is the thesis.

> Tribal rule is wrong.

This is the list from the reading.

> It leads to people being treated unfairly.
>
> > Mathabane gets punished and doesn't deserve it.
>
> Rituals should have a reason or purpose or they should benefit somebody.
>
> > The daily rituals won't actually bring good luck and protection, so they don't really have a purpose.
> >
> > There doesn't seem to be a purpose for not talking at the table.
>
> Rituals ought to make sense and they have no positive value when they don't.
>
> > Mathabane has to waste time performing daily rituals.
>
> Rituals have no positive meaning when they cause embarrassment.
>
> > Mathabane is embarrassed when his friends laugh at his father's clothes and call them Tarzan clothes.

List of the writer's own ideas and experiences.

> The ritual does limit how much individuals have to spend on gifts.
>
> > No more than $20
>
> The ritual ensures that people are treated equally.
>
> > Everyone gets a gift of similar value.

This ritual serves a social purpose by providing something for people to do together and a way get to know each other.

We exchange the gifts at the party.

The ritual sometimes doesn't fulfill its purposes.

Instead of limiting the amount people spend to a reasonable sum, people end up spending more.

Instead of bringing people together, rituals may make people feel even more uncomfortable.

Gifts may be inappropriate.

The tentative answer to the prompt is that tribal rule is wrong. Now the writer should read each idea and decide if it supports that answer. If any ideas seem to say that tribal rule is right or good, they need to be eliminated. For example, "The ritual does limit how much people spend," "The ritual ensures that people are treated equally," and "This ritual serves a social purpose by providing something for people to do together and a way get to know each other" sound more like reasons why rules might be good than why they might be wrong, so they will not help this writer's essay.

Since the prompt specifies using both the reading and personal experience, the next step is to match the ideas from each source. By omitting the three ideas that contradict the thesis and by combining the two lists, the writer has ended up with the following list.

Tribal rule is wrong because:

It leads to people being treated unfairly.

Mathabane gets punished and doesn't deserve it.

Rituals should have a reason or purpose or they should benefit somebody.

The daily rituals won't actually bring good luck and protection, so they don't really have a purpose.

There doesn't seem to be a purpose for not talking at the table.

Rituals ought to make sense and they have no positive value when they don't.

Mathabane has to waste time performing daily rituals.

Rituals have no positive meaning when they cause embarrassment.

Mathabane is embarrassed when his friends laugh at his father's clothes and call them Tarzan clothes.

The ritual sometimes doesn't fulfill its purposes.

Instead of limiting the amount people spend to a reasonable sum, people end up spending more.

Instead of bringing people together, rituals may make people feel even more uncomfortable.

Gifts may be inappropriate.

This writer has generated a number of ideas and has a lot of material from prewriting. If all of this material were to be incorporated in a paper, it would be very long. The writer should now choose the best ideas, the ones he or she has the most to say about and the most support for. The writer should also return to his or her other prewriting to find additional examples that fit those ideas. Perhaps the writer might choose the following four ideas.

1. Tribal rule is wrong because it can lead to people being treated unfairly.

   From the reading: Mathabane gets punishment he doesn't deserve.

   From the writer's experience: My pay is docked when I have to take a sick day to care for my children.

2. Rules should have a reason or purpose or they should benefit somebody.

   From the reading:
   The daily rituals won't actually bring good luck and protection, so they don't really have a purpose.
   There doesn't seem to be a purpose for not talking at the table.

   From the writer's experience:
   The ritual sometimes doesn't fulfill its purposes—instead of limiting the amount people spend to a reasonable sum, people end up spending more.

   Instead of bringing people together, rituals may make people feel even more uncomfortable. Gifts are sometimes inappropriate.

3. Rituals ought to make sense and they have no positive value when they don't.

   From the reading: Mathabane has to waste time performing daily rituals.

4. Rituals have no positive meaning when they cause embarrassment.

   From the reading: Mathabane is embarrassed when his friends laugh at his father's clothes and call them Tarzan clothes.

   From the writer's experience: I'm embarrassed when I give inappropriate gifts.

These four ideas with examples from the reading and from prewriting form the plan for an essay. The next step is to **draft** your essay.

| EXERCISE 7.1 | Use the following steps to organize and evaluate the prewriting you produced in the exercises from Chapter 6 (pp. 113–114). |

1. Check for unrelated material or ideas.
   A. In your prewriting on Mathabane's essay
   B. In your prewriting about your own ideas and experiences
2. Check for repeated material.
   A. In your prewriting on Mathabane's essay
   B. In your prewriting about your own ideas and experiences
3. Match main ideas to examples and details.
   A. In your prewriting on Mathabane's essay
   B. In your prewriting about your own ideas and experiences
4. List your main ideas.
   A. Check to see that each idea in your list responds to the prompt.
   B. Check to see if your list provides ideas for all of the actions required to complete the assignment.
5. Write a tentative thesis.

AUDIENCE AWARENESS

Unless you are writing for your eyes only (like a journal or a grocery list), you have an audience. If your audience was in the room with you, you could tell somewhat from their actions whether they were listening to you, understanding you, or offended by you. When you write, you don't get to see your audience's faces or body language, so you have to make decisions about how to get and keep their attention and how to explain your ideas clearly to them. Thinking about who your audience is and how they will respond to you is called audience awareness. One characteristic that distinguishes good writing from mediocre is the attention the writer pays to audience and purpose.

Formulating Your Thesis

Organizing Steps

Formulate your thesis

Think about your purpose

Think about your audience

Order ideas

Review the assignment

Usually, by the time you have completed your prewriting, you have identified your thesis (or answer to the writing **prompt**). When you know your thesis, you should write it down as clearly as possible. You then want to decide how you can best support your thesis, given your purpose and your audience, as described in the following section. Thinking about your purpose and audience is the next step in planning your paper.

In some situations, you may complete your prewriting and still not have a clear answer or thesis. In this case, you will need to consider your purpose, audience, and grouping of ideas to help you formulate your thesis.

Thinking About Your Purpose

One essential part of planning an essay is deciding what you are trying to accomplish. You need to think beyond simply "My instructor assigned it and I want to pass the course." Much of the writing you will do outside of college will not be assigned to you by an instructor. You will have to identify your own purpose for writing to do it effectively. Typically, writers have three purposes.

- ▪ *To explain or inform:* Textbooks and encyclopedias are examples of writing that is intended to inform an audience. Writers of these books provide definitions, facts, and statistics.

- ▪ *To persuade or convince:* Advertisements are examples of writing that is intended to persuade an audience. Writers of ads try to convince readers to buy a product. They typically provide reasons why the reader would benefit by choosing that particular product.

- ▪ *To entertain:* Stories are examples of writing that is intended to entertain an audience. Writers of stories are often trying to cause an emotional response—horror, pity, compassion, fear, enjoyment.

Often you may have to combine purposes to achieve the goal of your paper. For example, advertisers often use entertainment (in the form of a catchy jingle or humor) to capture the audience's attention long enough to persuade them. Other times, advertisers inform the audience about the product as one way of persuading; they talk about the product to show why the reader should buy it. Consider the following prompt on Amitai Etzioni's "On Restoring the Moral Voice: Virtue and Community Pressure."

> *Etzioni says we have reached consensus "about the environment, civil rights, and excessive general regulations and are now beginning to have [one] about gay rights" (para. 17). Do you agree that we have reached consensus on these issues? Choose one of the issues listed by Etzioni and assess whether we have reached consensus.*

This question asks you to *choose* and *assess*. The word *assess* asks you to draw a conclusion and convey that conclusion to your audience. In other words, it asks you to *persuade*. Before you can persuade your audience of anything about consensus on this issue, you will need to ensure that your audience knows what the issue is. So you may need to *inform* your audience by giving a definition or explanation of the issue before you can convince them of your assessment. That suggests that your essay should contain a definition or explanation of the issue followed by your assessment of whether or not people generally agree on it. In this case, thinking about your purpose has also helped you think about the order of ideas in your essay. Consider another prompt.

> *Discuss the impact of welfare on your community.*

As covered in Chapter 5, *discuss* is a **key action word** that can direct you to other actions as well. When your key words do not give you a clear direction, determine the purpose you want to achieve. Deciding what to include in your answer will depend on what you want to accomplish in your answer.

■ If your purpose is to *inform* your reader about the impact of welfare in your community, select facts and statistics from your prewriting.

■ If your purpose is to *persuade* your audience that welfare policies should be changed, you would have to *teach* your audience what the impact was before you could convince them to make changes that would affect this impact.

■ You might decide to *entertain* your audience as a step in *persuading* them by telling compelling stories of families on welfare that would get them interested enough to read the facts also and to be moved to act.

| EXERCISE 7.2 | Identify possible purposes in the following prompts. List how you would go about fulfilling these purposes. |

A. Etzioni argues that the only way the moral voice of the community can be effective in a pluralistic society "lies in seeking and developing an evolving framework of shared values—one which all subcultures will be expected to endorse and support without losing their distinct identities" (par. 11). Would it be possible for all Americans to agree on a "framework of shared values"? Why or why not? If so, what might this framework consist of? If not, what would we disagree about?

B. Etzioni concludes that "it is not enough individually to be able to tell right from wrong, as crucial as that is. We must also be willing to encourage others to attend to values we as a community share" (540). What can individuals do to "encourage others to attend to values"?

C. Under what situations would you speak up if you saw someone doing something wrong?

Thinking About Your Audience

Another way to help you decide what to include in your paper is to think about your audience. It is tempting to assume that the instructor is the audience. This is not necessarily true; the assignment itself may direct you to another audience, or the instructor may specify a different audience (such as your classmates, the governor of your state, or the president of your college).

To address an audience successfully, you need to know who your audience is. For example, if your instructor has assigned an essay in the form of a letter supporting the death penalty, you would want to know whom you are addressing.

■ If you are writing to the readers of the local newspaper, you may need to provide some historical or factual material about the death penalty. If you are writing to lawyers, you might be able to assume they would have this information.

■ If your audience is the members of the local victims' rights group, you would choose a different set of points than if you are addressing a group who wants to abolish the death penalty, since the groups are likely to have different attitudes toward this subject.

In considering your audience, you would need to consider the following.

■ What does your audience already know about the topic?
■ What additional information (or background material) does your audience need to know to understand your ideas?
■ Where might your audience disagree with you?

You may need to do research about your topic so that you are able to write knowledgeably and so that you are able to provide information or background material that your audience might need. You can find a discussion of research in Chapter 18.

What Does Your Audience Know?   You need a sense of what your audience knows and what you might need to tell them. This will guide how much detail or what explanations to provide. For example, if you want to discuss the energy crisis in the early 1970s, you would consider the age of your audience as well as their education.

■ For audiences born during or before the 1960s, you might assume that they are aware of efforts at that time to conserve fossil fuels by decreasing speed limits and monitoring thermostats in public buildings, the high price of gas, and the long lines of people waiting to buy gas.

■ For audiences born during or after the 1970s, you may need to provide an explanation of what was going on at the time and what the public impact was.

Of course, it's not as simple as age. Perhaps your audience consists of younger people who are interested in ecological and environmental issues; they may already be well informed on this issue.

Knowing who your audience is and what they are likely to already know can help you decide how much background material you need to supply in your paper.

What Else Does Your Audience Need to Know?   Perhaps your audience remembers the energy crisis and knows that it led to increased gasoline prices and longer waits at gas stations because they experienced it. However, they might not know what impact this crisis had on public policy, on our current attitude toward speed limits and the size of cars, or on the rates of injuries and deaths as a result of car accidents.

If you want to argue that reducing the speed limit increased the fuel efficiency of cars or decreased the number of deaths and injuries as a result of car accidents, you would include any information that supports your claims and not just assume that your audience knows this.

Where Might Your Audience Disagree with You?   To convince an audience, you must deal with their objections to your argument. For example, your audience might say, "Yes, injuries and deaths did decrease as a result of lowering the speed limit, but that's not really necessary anymore because the safety of cars has improved and our road system is much safer. Both the cars and the roads are more capable of handling high speeds than they were in 1974."

To convince your audience that your argument is sound, you would have to acknowledge their disagreement with you and deal with that. Being able to spot how someone else might disagree with you gives you more information on what you need to include as well as where you might need to include it in your paper. The following box lists ways to anticipate your audience's objections to your ideas.

Anticipating Your Audience's Objections

- Based on your analysis of the audience, where do your audience's views and values conflict with yours?
- What is the weakest part of your argument? Where are you the least sure about yourself?
- Look at each of your statements of opinion. Which ones will your audience easily accept? Of the rest, have you provided support so that your audience will accept your opinion?
- Write the opposite side of your argument. What would people who disagree with you say? Writing the other side of the argument will help you determine the points you need to convince your audience about.

Let's look at an example from a student paper in response to this argument.

> In the past few years, the government has passed several laws meant to control the risks an individual takes. These laws—seat belt, car seat, helmet, and anti-smoking laws—are wrong because they impinge on an person's right to make decisions about his or her own life. These laws are different from laws about driving under the influence, because an impaired driver puts others at risk, but a rider who does not wear a seatbelt or a helmet risks only himself or herself; the parent who does not put his or her child in a car seat risks the life

of only his or her child. *People have the right to make decisions about their own lives and the lives of their children, even if these decisions turn out to be unwise.*

Even readers who may agree that adults have the right to make decisions for themselves may believe that government has an obligation to protect children. They would not readily accept that parents have a right to put their children in risky situations. You would need to prove this statement and not just assume the audience will agree.

Assessing Your Audience

Environment of the Audience

■ What is his or her physical, social, and economic status? (Consider age, environment, health, ethnic ties, class, and income.)

■ What is his or her educational and cultural experience?

■ What are his or her ethical concerns and hierarchy of values? (Consider home, family, job, success, religion, money, car, social acceptance.)

The Subject Interpreted by the Audience

■ How much does the reader know about the subject?

■ What is the opinion of the reader about the subject?

■ How strong is that opinion?

■ How willing is he or she to act on that opinion?

■ Why does he or she react the way he or she does?

The Relationship of the Audience and the Writer

■ What is the reader's knowledge and attitude toward me?

■ What are our shared experiences, attitudes, values, myths, prejudices? In other words, what kinds of experiences have I had that my readers might have had, too?

■ What is my purpose or aim in addressing this audience?

■ Is this an appropriate audience for my subject?

■ What is the role I wish to assign to the audience?

■ What role do I want to assume for the audience?

EXERCISE 7.3 Assume you are writing to the following audiences on the following topics. Analyze the needs of each audience.

A. To sixth graders, explaining why the sky is blue.

B. To your supervisor, asking for an expensive piece of equipment that will help you do your job more efficiently.

C. To your classmates, explaining to them a point you tried to make in a class discussion but don't think you did successfully.

D. To 18-year-olds, trying to get them to vote in the next local election.

E. To Teresa McCrary, explaining that welfare is not the only option for young, untrained single mothers like herself.

F. To a pro-choice group, explaining to them why abortion should be illegal.

Ordering Ideas and Information

To decide the order of your ideas, you again must consider your audience. Think about two helpful questions.

■ What does the reader need to know first to understand your ideas?

■ What order will best convince your reader to accept your ideas?

These questions guide you to think about two issues: What order will make the most sense (be logical and understandable) to your reader? What sequence will be most convincing to your reader?

Common Organizational Patterns

The following are common ways to organize ideas.

■ *Problem/solution:* Describe a problem and then explain what your solution is and how your solution would resolve the problem. For example, you might describe the problems of single mothers on welfare and then recommend a solution that would help.

■ *Overview/parts:* Provide an overview of the topic or issue, and then explain each of the parts in detail. For example, you might explain that everyone takes a variety of risks to his or her life, health, jobs, and relationships and then discuss each type of risk in detail.

■ *Definition/analysis or application:* Define a term and then apply that term to a situation. For example, to argue whether a risk is "acceptable," you might define "acceptable" and then discuss whether a particular risk fits the definition.

■ *Most readily accepted to least likely to be accepted:* Begin with a point that your audience is likely to agree with, and progress to more controversial points. For example, you might argue that adults are responsible for protecting children before you argue that children need to be taught about AIDS in elementary school.

continued on next page

continued from previous page

■ *Reasons/conclusion:* State your reasons for believing as you do and then give your belief. This strategy is most effective when your belief (or solution) would be rejected by your audience if you stated it at the first. For example, you might have to tell your supervisor why you need a new computer before you ask him or her to approve a purchase order for several thousand dollars. If your supervisor sees convincing reasons before he or she knows what you are asking for, he or she is more likely to agree.

EXERCISE 7.4

Collaboration

Working in groups, use the following thesis statement to make a list of at least two possible audiences. What method of organization would your group suggest for each audience? Why?

A. All couples should be required to live together for three years before they are married. This would cut down on the number of divorces.

B. I disagree with Teresa McCrary that welfare is the only option for single mothers who do not have job skills because there are other opportunities for training and job placement.

C. The United States government should require every citizen to carry an ID that could be checked at any time. This measure would enable police to catch terrorists before they can strike.

D. We can help get single mothers off welfare by providing child care and medical insurance.

Rogerian Argument

Psychologist Carl Rogers came up with a way to help people resolve arguments and reach mutual understandings. His technique has been adapted by writers as a **Rogerian argument**.

The organization pattern for a Rogerian argument is based on the theory that an effective way to communicate ideas to an audience is to begin with ideas and values that they accept and believe, and ease them over to a new position or idea one step at a time. Many people write **arguments** as if their audience already agrees with them. Because they make this assumption, they insult people who don't agree with them, mock their beliefs, and do nothing to engage them. There are two problems with this: First, it is a waste of time to write an argumentative essay to an audience who already holds the same views. Second, these essays tend to lack evidence that would convince someone who doesn't agree to ever consider the writer's argument, much less change his or her opinion. Talk shows on television and radio provide many examples of people attacking their opponents without listening to them, trying to understand their point of view, or appealing to them. As a result, we see little resolution of the conflicts presented. Such attacks put the audience on the defensive, and they become unwilling to listen. The relationship falls into argument instead of leading to more understanding because the parties have not listened to each other or responded to each other's concerns.

An effective argument must be addressed to those who don't agree or who have not yet made up their minds. Once you've recognized that this is your audience, what you say and how you say it must be altered, and you must organize and develop your essay in a way that shows your audience that you are someone worth taking seriously because you have considered the issue—including their side of it—thoughtfully and politely.

Rogerian argument allows you to get the other person's attention by showing that you understand their position. It also requires that you take out insulting or mocking language that might make people defensive. By the conclusion of this type of argument, you've established that you are willing to continue the discussion, to compromise, and to maintain a civil relationship with your audience even though you don't agree with them on this particular issue.

An organization in this pattern would contain the parts shown in the following box.

Rogerian Argument

- *Introduction:* State the subject as a problem rather than as an issue, to interest your audience in reading something they may disagree with.

- *Fair statement of the audience's position:* State the reader's position in a way that seems fair and accurate to the reader.

- *Statement of contexts in which that position may be valid:* Show the reader that you can see that his or her opinion is valid in certain circumstances.

- *Fair statement of writer's position:* State your own position as thoroughly and honestly as you have stated your reader's.

- *Statement of contexts in which the writer's position is valid:* Show how your position is valid in other circumstances or is superior or more effective than the reader's.

- *Statement of how the audience would benefit by adopting at least some elements of the writer's position:* Show how the reader would benefit from changing his or her opinion to be more in line with yours.

| EXERCISE 7.5 | **Practice argument.** |

1. In pairs or in small groups, agree on a controversial topic to discuss. After the first person states his or her opinion, the second person must summarize that opinion to the satisfaction of the first person before stating his or her own. Continue with the discussion, with each speaker summarizing the points or opinions of the previous speaker before stating his or her own.

2. Try this technique as a problem-solving method with someone with whom you are having a disagreement.

Combining Organization Strategies

You may need to use more than one organizational strategy in the same paper. For example, suppose you want to persuade your audience that the key to getting single mothers off welfare is providing child care and medical insurance. You know that your audience accepts the current method of providing welfare benefits for a limit of two years. You could use the Rogerian argument style to organize your paper, stating your audience's opinion first, showing how it works in some ways, and then showing how your alternative solves the problem better. But you might also use the problem/solution organization by describing the problem of single mothers on welfare, describing how your audience's solution does (and does not) solve the problem, and then describing how your solution solves the problem more fully or more beneficially.

Finding an Order

When all else fails, or when you have massive quantities of material, you may need to physically move your ideas around to find an order. Moving the ideas around can help you see what ideas you have and how they relate to each other.

✔ Ways of Finding an Organization

The following are alternatives for trying your ideas in different orders.

■ *Notecards:* Write each of your main ideas on a different 3 × 5 card. Then arrange the cards in different orders to see which one would be most effective.

■ *Cut and paste:* Cut apart the ideas and examples in your prewriting that you are planning to use in your paper. Then place the slips of paper into piles according to similar topics. Arrange the piles in an order; then work on ordering the slips within each pile. You will probably have to explain how the

continued on next page

continued from previous page

pieces of paper within a single pile relate to each other; this explanation will be part of your body paragraphs.

■ *Cut and paste on a computer:* Cutting and pasting and the card technique can be very easily accomplished on a computer by using the cut and paste options. By putting each sentence in its own paragraph, you can see each idea individually and move it around easily.

■ *Models of professional writers:* Look for interesting and effective organizations as you read essays by professional writers. Try imitating the organization of one of these essays that seems to apply to your topic. (The essay you are using as a model need not be on the same topic as your essay; it does need to show an organization that will work with your topic and purposes.)

EXERCISE 7.6

Make a photocopy of the following paragraphs and then cut them apart and arrange them into piles to try to find an organization. Remember that the connections between the parts of the prewriting will probably not be here; you haven't discovered them yet. Arranging the parts of your prewriting helps you discover these connections. Remember also that you may not be able to use all of your prewriting in every essay. Try to identify the type of organizations you have found.

Mathabane's father wore the same clothing that his ancestors wore. Even though they no longer lived in tribal lands. The other children who dressed in modern clothes thought his father "was the most hilarious thing they had ever seen since natives in Tarzan movies."

Mathabane wanted to speak the other languages that his friends did, but his father wanted him to speak Venda. Mathabane spoke these other languages when he was around his friends, but when his father found out, he was very angry. Mathabane's father had a rule that they couldn't speak at the table. He tells us that "One day I intentionally broke one of these laws." His father got really mad, he said, "You don't have two mouths to afford you such a luxury." Then he threatened to beat Mathabane.

Mathabane had to do "rituals spanning the range of day-to-day living." These rituals were designed to "Protect the house from evildoers" and "to safeguard his job." Mathabane says that these rituals "awed, confused, and embarrassed me."

My friends always made fun of my father playing his bagpipes. They would laugh and pretend they were marching and playing bagpipes. I couldn't understand why my father would embarrass me so much. My mother told me that my father's parents had moved to America before he was born. He had never been to Scotland and this was one way he kept in touch with his roots. She showed me pictures of my great grandparents and other relatives from Scotland. I had never known this about my family's past.

Before dinner, my brothers and my sister and I are supposed to clean the house and get everything ready for dinner. One day I didn't feel like doing it, because I have to do everything. My brothers and my sister hardly do anything. So, I just sat on the couch and watched TV. My father came in and saw me and started to yell at me. He said he worked hard every day to put food on the table and that I was showing disrespect to him, my mother, my brothers and my sister.

My parents always had a rule that my brothers, sister, and I had to wake them up when we came in from a date. It's not that we stayed out that late; another rule was that we had to be home by midnight. My parents would go on to bed but expected us to knock on the door, tell them we were home, and then they would ask how the date went. A lot of times I felt they were treating me like a baby, but sometimes it was nice to talk about my evening.

Everyone in my family has their own assigned ritual. Every night, it's my job to make sure all the doors are locked and the windows shut and latched. My sister irons my father's shirts for the next day. My father gets lunch ready for everybody. My mother supervises and helps whoever needs help.

REVIEWING THE ASSIGNMENT

Now that you have chosen your material and have an idea of how to order it, you need to be sure that your thesis matches the material you have produced. If you have not written a thesis yet, you should now be ready to.

As always, you will need to review the assignment to be sure that you are still addressing it and fulfilling its terms.

Reviewing the Assignment

- Does your thesis address the prompt you were assigned?
- What are your purposes in this essay? Do these purposes allow you to address the prompt?
- Does your organization lend itself to addressing this thesis? (Does it allow you to tell your readers what they need to know to understand your point? Does it present your points in an order that readers will accept them? Does it allow you to achieve your purposes?)
- Who is your audience? Has your instructor specified an audience, or have you had to identify one on your own?
- Is everything in your paper related to the prompt? To your purposes?
- If research is required, are you incorporating appropriate kinds and amounts?

What You Have Done

- Reviewed the prompt
- Evaluated prewriting
- Drafted a thesis
- Considered purpose and audience to find a possible organization

The Next Step

- Draft the introduction

8 Writing Introductions

Since most college-level writing responds to the ideas of others, the model essay presented in Chapters 8, 9, and 10 will stress a structure in which the writer is responding to a reading. Additional essay structures will also be presented.

Getting started may be one of the most difficult things to do in writing an essay. At first, the assignment might seem to be an overwhelming task. However, if you break down the writing process into steps, as shown in the last few chapters, you will find it easier to decide what you need to do. If you have difficulty starting, don't give up. There are several strategies you can use to get started.

- *Go back to the **prompt** or assignment:* What are you specifically being asked to do? Going back to the prompt may help focus your thinking and get you started writing (see Chapter 5).
- *Go back to the reading:* What topics are being discussed? How do you feel about those topics? Do you agree or disagree with what is said? What related personal experiences have you had? (See Chapter 4.)
- *Go back to your **prewriting:*** Prewriting activities help you generate information and give you more material to work with (see Chapter 6).

CREATING DRAFTS

At the end of Chapter 7, the information generated by the writer's prewriting was organized into a basic outline. The plan developed from your prewriting will serve as a framework for your essay. Chapters 8, 9, and 10 will show you how to expand and strengthen the framework you've created.

After examining the prompt, the reading, and your prewriting, you should be ready to begin creating a **draft**—a preliminary version of a final paper. It's important to realize that well-written essays require several drafts and that your first draft will probably be revised many times. You will find that as you write your ideas will change, and you will have to reconsider your original ideas. As you discover new ideas, you may also need to return to the reading to find quotes for support. Here are some points to keep in mind when you begin your first drafts.

- For all your early drafts, choose whatever method—pen, pencil, typewriter, word processor—is most comfortable to you. Be sure to leave enough room on your paper to be able to make additions and changes. Leave wide margins, and double-space or even triple-space the lines if you are writing on lined paper.

- Don't let fine details of **editing** distract you while you create your first drafts. If you stop to look up words in the dictionary as you write, you will lose your train of thought. But do jot down notes about punctuation, grammar, and spelling so that you won't forget to fix them later on.

- Write the paragraphs in early drafts in any order. If you're having trouble with your introduction, you can leave it and work on body paragraphs. Later you can come back to your introduction. See what works best for you.

Completing the exercises in Chapters 8, 9, and 10 will help you create your own essay.

AN INTRODUCTION THAT RESPONDS TO A READING

An **introduction** is an essential part of an essay. It provides readers with the background information they will need to understand the details presented in the **body** paragraphs. It also determines the scope and thesis of the essay by defining and limiting what you will discuss.

What the Introduction Does

- Provides background information
- Familiarizes your reader with the topic
- Defines and limits your discussion
- Clarifies the thesis or main idea of your essay

The following elements usually appear in the introduction to an essay responding to a reading.

An Introduction Provides
A lead-in
Source of a reading
Overview of a reading
Author's thesis
Your thesis
A plan of development

■ *A general **lead-in** to the topic:* Lets your readers know the basic topic you will be discussing.

■ *Author and title of the reading:* Describes who the author is and which particular work you will discuss.

■ *An **overview** of the reading:* Provides a synopsis of what the reading discusses.

■ *The **author's thesis or point:*** Defines the purpose or main idea of the reading.

■ *Your **thesis** statement:* Clarifies what you will discuss and defines the main idea or purpose of your essay.

■ *A **plan of development:*** Tells your reader how you will approach your subject and/or what specific issues you will discuss.

When responding to a reading, your introduction should look like the following model.

✓ **Components of Introductions That Respond to a Reading**

■ Lead-in

■ Identification of author and title of the work

■ An overview of the author's essay

■ The author's thesis or main point

■ Your thesis

■ Your plan of development

The following paragraph responds to a reading by Teresa McCrary (pages 46–48) and uses the general to specific structure shown in the box.

America is considered the land of opportunity, where anyone who is willing to work hard can support both family and self. As a society, we believe that hard work pays off. It is not surprising that many people see welfare recipients as people who are too lazy to work. — lead-in

Teresa McCrary is a woman who was forced to go on welfare. In her article "Getting Off the Welfare Carousel," she tells of her daily struggles and the obstacles that — author and title

single welfare moms face. She points out that in many cases, ⎤
these women have few real options. McCrary sees herself as a   ⎟— overview
true representative of welfare moms. She is someone working   ⎟
hard to get off welfare and become a productive member of so-   ⎦
ciety. McCrary argues that most people's perceptions of welfare ⎤— author's
recipients are wrong. The image we have of most welfare recipi- ⎦   thesis
ents is false. Most recipients are people who only use the bene- ⎤— writer's
fits for a short time between jobs. Other people are unable to   ⎦   thesis
work due to being left a single parent by an uncaring spouse.   ⎤— plan of
                                                                 ⎦ development

This introduction begins with a **lead-in** that discusses Americans' general attitude toward work. Following the lead-in, the writer identifies the *author and the title* of the essay to which she is responding. An **overview** or brief summary of McCrary's essay is provided for the reader. The **author's thesis**—the point of McCrary's essay—is then presented ("most people's perceptions of welfare recipients are wrong"). McCrary's thesis is followed by the *writer's* **thesis** ("The image we have of most welfare recipients is false"). The last two sentences provide a **plan of development**. This writer's essay will focus on recipients who only stay on welfare for a short time and recipients who have been abandoned by their spouses.

PROVIDING LEAD-INS

Lead-ins introduce your reader to the general topic you are discussing. If you are responding to a writer who favors gun control, then your lead-in would discuss the topic of gun control, but it would not discuss the writer's specific argument on gun control. Providing a lead-in identifies the issue your essay will explore, and it prepares the reader for the more detailed information that you will present.

A lead-in performs these functions.

- Makes your introduction unique.
- Helps you to avoid making a generic introduction (the type everyone uses).
- Clarifies the topic or issue.
- Helps readers understand the specific information that will follow.

Purpose of a Lead-in
Distinguishes your introduction
Clarifies the topic
Provides background

How do you create a lead-in? You begin by asking what is the first and most basic thing the reader needs to know—the general topic under discussion. Are you discussing the auto industry, extraterrestrial life, education, or politics? If you are discussing an essay or story you have read, what is the general topic: war, love, technology? What issue or theme in the reading are you responding to?

To guide your reader into the specific topic of your essay, provide a lead-in that begins with the general topic under discussion in the reading. Rather than starting with a sentence that identifies author and title—"In Mark Mathabane's 'My Father's Tribal Rule' . . ."—focus on the general topic you will discuss. Will you discuss rituals? Will you discuss parent-child conflicts? Will you discuss traditional versus modern ways? ("My Father's Tribal Rule" appears on pages 42–46.)

If you begin your essay with your own discussion of a general topic, your essay will be clearly distinguished from the other essays written in the class, even if everyone is writing in response to Mathabane. Since Mathabane detests rituals, you might begin your lead-in with a discussion of the negative aspects of rituals.

When you're responding to a reading, the lead-in should guide the reader into that reading without discussing the specific ideas that an author is putting forth. A lead-in should not directly discuss what an author says in an essay. It should simply be used to set up the general topic that the author is discussing.

Let's look at some suggestions for creating lead-ins on the topic of capital punishment.

■ Present an opinion on the topic that many people would agree with.

> Many Americans favor capital punishment because they believe it brings about justice. They see capital punishment as a way to make murderers pay for their crimes. Justice requires punishment.

■ Present a view opposite to the one the author holds. (Assume that the author's essay is in favor of capital punishment.)

> There are several reasons why some people believe that capital punishment is wrong. We have laws against killing, yet we murder someone who breaks the law. Only a hypocrite would say don't kill or I'll kill you.

■ Present the same view as the author but provide different ideas. (Assume that the author is in favor of capital punishment because he believes it protects society.)

> Capital punishment is necessary in our society because it serves to deter others from committing the same crime. When a criminal is executed, it sends the message to other criminals that society will not permit their behavior. If criminals know they will be executed for certain crimes, they will be less likely to commit them.

■ Relate a personal experience.

> I never thought much about capital punishment. If someone had asked me if I was for it or against it, I would probably have said I was for it. However, one day when I was listening to the news, I heard that some TV personality

wanted to show an execution on TV live. The more I thought about it, the more disgusted I was. It was then that I decided I was against capital punishment.

■ Provide background information.

Capital punishment is a state sanctioned execution. In other words, it is a killing authorized by a government, either on the state or federal level. In the United States, the death penalty is only used for the most evil crime: first-degree murder. Although capital punishment is legal in the United States, not every state in the union carries it out.

Note that these lead-ins discuss the topic of capital punishment, but they do not discuss the author's argument.

To show how lead-ins can help the flow of your introduction, let's look at two examples, one without a lead-in and one with a lead-in.

EXAMPLE WITHOUT A LEAD-IN

In Mark Mathabane's "My Father's Tribal Rule," he talks about rituals and how he doesn't like them.

Notice that this example leaps right into the author's name and the title of the essay.

EXAMPLE WITH LEAD-IN

Many people feel that rituals are a thing of the past, practiced only by primitive people. They feel that rituals have little place in a modern society that is driven by technology and science. Rituals, they would say, are just superstitions acted out.

This example discusses the general topic of rituals and the attitude many people have toward them. This prepares the reader for Mathabane's essay and what the reading has to say about rituals.

EXERCISE 8.1

Collaboration

Form groups of three or four. Each group should select one of the following issues/topics: crime, space exploration, stereotyping, gun violence, war, adversity, personal courage, overcoming obstacles, relationships, drugs, family conflicts, loyalty. Have each person in the group select one or more approaches to writing his or her lead-in.

■ Present an opinion many people would agree with.

■ Present a controversial opinion on the issue.

■ Present a personal experience.

■ Present a definition.

■ Present background information such as a brief history of the issue.

> **When each member is finished, compare your lead-ins. Even though everyone in the group is writing on the same topic, you'll find that each lead-in is unique. When everyone in the class is writing on the same topic, each person's lead-in will make his or her introduction distinct.**

When you choose to start your essay with a lead-in, consider the effect it will have on the audience. Are you trying to provide background information? Are you trying to draw your reader in by personalizing the issue with a personal example or a story? Also consider the appropriateness of your lead-in to the issues you will discuss in your essay. If you provide a story as a lead-in, it should directly relate to the issues you discuss in your essay.

EXERCISE 8.2

Read the following lead-in to Mark Mathabane's "My Father's Tribal Rule." See if you can determine what subject the writer is intending to focus on.

> As children we are always told what to do by our parents and teachers. We may resent what adults force us to do and become rebellious. We may even grow to hate the adults that are always trying to make us do something we do not want to do. Adults tell us that they know what is best for us, but we think we know what is really best. As we grow older, however, we sometimes come to realize that our parents and other adults really were looking out for our best interests.

The following example of a lead-in takes another approach to the reading. What topic in Mathabane's essay does this lead-in focus on?

> The role that women play in a family is stereotypically the mother and the housekeeper. However, women may perform several other functions in the family that we often don't think about. Sometimes women are the breadwinners. Sometimes they are teachers who instruct their children on manners and etiquette. Sometimes they are like close friends who listen to your troubles or give you advice. Many mothers are more than just caretakers for their children.

EXERCISE 8.3

Collaboration

Form groups of three or four students. Have each group member write several lead-ins for introductions on one of the following prompts. Use the suggestions for creating lead-ins discussed earlier in this chapter. Remember not to discuss what the reading says on these topics. Discuss the general topic suggested by the prompt.

Mathabane writes less about his mother than his father or himself. What is the significance of her role in the family? Do you think most women play similar roles in their families?

Mathabane has a conflict with his father. Do parents and children always have conflicts? Why or why not? Using your own ideas and observations, write an essay in which you answer this question.

AUTHOR, TITLE, AND OVERVIEW OF THE READING

After completing your lead-in, you need to do the following.

- ■ Identify the author and title of the reading you're discussing. These elements do not have to directly follow the lead-in, but they do need to appear early in your introduction.

- ■ Provide an overview or summary of the piece to provide background and context for your reader. Your reader may have never read the story or essay you are responding to. If you are responding to a story or a narrative, the reader needs to know the general **story line**, setting, and cast of important characters. If you are discussing an essay, your reader needs a brief summary of the writer's ideas.

> **Providing Information on a Reading**
>
> Identifies the author discussed
>
> Identifies the reading discussed
>
> Provides an overview of the reading

Let's continue the development of the two lead-ins just discussed by adding the author's name, the title of the reading, and an overview of the reading. If you had never read Mathabane's essay, which introduction would give you a better understanding of the text?

In Mark Mathabane's "My Father's Tribal Rule," he talks about rituals and how he doesn't like them. He talks about his brother, his mother, and his sister. His family had to move to a shack. Mathabane really dislikes his father because his father beats him. The father doesn't beat the other children like he beats his son Mark. Mark Mathabane wants to be like the other boys he plays with. He wants to speak other languages.

Many people feel that rituals are a thing of the past, practiced only by primitive people. They feel that rituals have little place in a modern society that is driven by technology and science. Rituals, they would say, are just superstitions acted out. Mark Mathabane is one of those people who detests rituals. In "My Father's Tribal Rule," he tells us about his experiences growing up in South Africa in a shantytown of rundown huts for people who had been forced off their ancestral, tribal lands. Even though Mathabane and the children in the area were interested in modern ways, Mathabane's father insisted that their family stick to the tribal traditions. If Mathabane failed to follow the tribal rules and rituals, his father would severely punish him. Mathabane eventually came to hate his father for making him follow the tribal rituals.

In the first example, there is no lead-in and very little overview of the text. Someone who had not read Mathabane's essay would not have a clear picture of the particular situation or the setting. The second example gives a good overview of the story that provides more information for the reader (but it doesn't go into specific details—they belong in body paragraphs). Someone who had never read the essay would get a much better understanding of what "My Father's Tribal Rule" is about from the second example.

EXERCISE 8.4

Write overviews for the following two prompts. Provide your reader with a summary of the reading, but focus that summary on the issue raised in the prompt.

Mathabane writes less about his mother than his father or himself. What is the significance of her role in the family? Do you think other women play similar roles in their families?

Mathabane has a conflict with his father. Do parents and children always have conflicts? Why or why not? Using your own ideas and observations, write an essay in which you answer this question.

THE AUTHOR'S THESIS OR MAIN POINT

After you have provided an overview, you need to clarify the author's thesis. A thesis statement is the main point of an author's essay. For instance, in an essay presenting several arguments against capital punishment, the author's thesis would be that capital punishment is wrong. To define the author's thesis, ask the following questions:

Purpose of an Author's Thesis
Defines the writer's argument
Clarifies the writer's message

■ What is the point of the reading?
■ What is the author arguing?

If you are reading an **argumentative** essay—an essay where the writer is arguing for or against something—the writer will generally have a thesis statement that tells the reader what he or she will argue (for example, money should be spent on drug rehabilitation programs rather than new jails). However, a narrative like "My Father's Tribal Rule" or a short story like Flannery O'Connor's "Revelation" may not have a thesis statement that defines the writer's point. Instead the writer may use images, situations, or dialogue to get his or her message across.

If you look back at Mathabane's essay (pp. 42–46), you will see that the point of his **narrative** is never clearly stated. Is his point about rules and rituals, his mother, his father, their life in South Africa? What is Mathabane trying to get across to his readers? You must provide this information to your readers, so they can understand Mathabane's point. In some essays, the author may make several points, and it is up to the writer to decide which one to focus the reader on. Looking again at the topics of rules and rituals in Mathabane's article, we can say that each of the following conveys the general point of the essay.

To Mathabane, rules and rituals make no sense.

Mathabane hated rules and rituals and felt he should rebel against them.

Because he was forced to follow the rules and rituals, Mathabane came to hate his father.

When it comes to the topic of rules and rituals, all of these statements convey the general point of Mathabane's essay. Notice, however, that certain words in each example suggest a different focus on the essay. The first example focuses on Mathabane's lack of understanding, the second stresses Mathabane's rebellion, and the third directs our attention to his relationship with his father.

When providing the author's thesis or point, be sure to word it carefully so that it stresses the idea or topic you will discuss.

Let's attach the author's point to our lead-in and overview. We will use the first example on page 156 but reword it to better flow with the overview.

> Many people feel that rituals are a thing of the past, practiced only by primitive people. They feel that rituals have little place in a modern society that is driven by technology and science. Rituals, they would say, are just superstitions acted out. Mark Mathabane is one of those people who detests rituals. In "My Father's Tribal Rule," he tells us about his experiences growing up in South Africa in a shantytown of rundown huts for people who had been forced off their ancestral, tribal lands. Even though Mathabane and the children in the area were interested in modern ways, Mathabane's father insisted that their family stick to the tribal traditions. Mathabane eventually came to hate his father for making him follow the tribal rituals. *Despite his father's insistence that he follow the rules and practice the rituals, Mathabane thought they made no sense.*

At this point, we have provided a lead-in to introduce the general topic being discussed, the author and the title of the reading, an overview for someone who has never read the essay, and—in the last sentence—the author's thesis, a statement that defines how Mathabane felt about rules and rituals.

EXERCISE 8.5 | **Look for the general topics in the following prompts and then write one or more sentences that clarify what you see as the reading's point or thesis. Is there a specific point that Mathabane is trying to make about these issues? If Mathabane isn't trying to make a point about these issues, what point does the reading convey to you?**

Mathabane writes less about his mother than his father or himself. What is the significance of her role in the family? Do you think other women play similar roles in their families?

Mathabane has a conflict with his father. Do parents and children always have conflicts? Why or why not?

YOUR THESIS STATEMENT

While the author's thesis statement defines the main idea of his or her essay, your thesis statement defines the main idea of your essay. Your thesis statement clarifies where you stand in response to what the author has said.

Purpose of a Thesis
Clarifies the main idea of an essay

After you have explained what the reading says, you need to present a thesis statement—a sentence (or more) that tells your reader what you intend to argue or reveal. It defines the main idea of your essay. Will you argue that the author is right or wrong on an issue? Will you reveal that Mathabane's mother serves more roles in the family than just that of mother? Another way to think about a thesis statement is that it is a sentence that tells the reader what you believe and why you believe it. A thesis statement defines the main idea of your paper and thus must be more than an obvious comment about what you're planning to do.

> In this paper, I will discuss Mathabane's essay.

This statement doesn't clarify your reason for writing. It just leaves your reader wondering: Is your purpose to agree with Mathabane's ideas about rituals? Will you examine the relationship between Mathabane's father and mother? You thus need to provide your reader with more than just a general statement. A good thesis statement clearly defines what you will argue in your essay.

Creating a thesis statement may seem difficult, but a strong one can be developed by doing two basic things. If your instructor's assignment is presented as a question, respond to that prompt. Since this assignment is phrased as a question, your answer is your thesis statement. If your instructor has not given you a specific question and expects you to develop your own thesis, then you should use your prewriting to determine your thesis. The following discussions will explain how to use your instructor's assignment or your own prewriting to develop a strong thesis statement.

Using the Prompt to Determine Your Thesis

Keep in mind that an easy way to create a thesis statement is to respond to the **prompt** directly. Another way is to turn the prompt (a question) into a statement. Let's look again at the prompt we have been using.

> *Mathabane says he despises rules and rituals. Is he correct in thinking that rules and rituals have no purpose or value?*

If you haven't analyzed this prompt, do so by going back to Chapter 5, where you can review the process of analyzing the assignment. Use the exercises there to determine what this prompt asks you to do.

Let's look at the prompt again and the thesis statement from Chapter 7 to see if it fully responds to the prompt.

Prompt/Question

> *Mathabane says he despises rules and rituals. Is he correct in thinking that rules and rituals have no purpose or value?*

Response/Answer

Tribal rule is wrong.

Does this tentative thesis statement fully respond to the prompt? The prompt asks about rules and rituals in general, not about tribal rules. The preceding thesis statement mentions rules but not rituals (although it may be possible to write an essay on one or the other). The second part of the prompt asks if you think Mathabane is correct that rules and rituals have no value. This thesis statement doesn't directly respond to the question contained in the prompt. To complete the thesis, some additions need to be made. The question in the prompt requires a yes or no answer. Is Mathabane right or is he wrong? (If you're not sure, then you need to analyze your prewriting to see what your examples suggest. We'll discuss that later.)

Here is the same thesis statement reworded.

Mathabane is right to think that many rules and rituals serve no purpose.

This thesis statement responds to the question in the prompt (*Is he correct in thinking that rules and rituals have no value?*). This thesis also refers to rules and rituals. (Your prewriting might lead you to focus on one or the other rather than both.) The phrase *serve no purpose* in the thesis lets the reader know what the writer thinks about rules and rituals. Remember, when your instructor gives you a prompt in the form of a question, your *direct response* to that question is your thesis statement.

Using Your Prewriting to Determine Your Thesis

After analyzing a prompt to help you determine your thesis, you should then examine your prewriting. Chapter 6 presented several examples on prewriting. One way to determine what your thesis should be is to reexamine the examples you produced while prewriting about your own experiences. The examples you develop can help you determine what your attitude is about a topic. Let's look again at the prompt that asks if you agree with Mathabane's negative attitude toward rules and rituals. Examine the following examples to see if they suggest whether these experiences confirm or contradict Mathabane's attitude toward rules and rituals.

| EXERCISE 8.6 | Examine the following examples to see if they suggest agreement or disagreement with Mathabane's belief that rules and rituals have no purpose or value. |

EXAMPLE 1

In my family, we have a dinnertime ritual. Before dinner, my brothers and my sister and I are supposed to clean the house and get everything ready for dinner. One day I didn't feel like doing it, because I have to do everything. My brothers and my sister hardly do anything. So, I just sat on the couch and watched TV. My father came in and saw me and started to yell at me. He said he worked hard every day to put food on the table and that I was showing disrespect to him, my mother, my brothers and my sister. He sent me to bed without supper. At first I was really mad. I thought my father was being un-fair to me. I'm the oldest, so I wind up doing most of the work. Why should I have to clean the house every day and get the table ready? The more I thought about it, the more I felt bad. He did do a lot for us. Besides provid-ing us with a house and food, he paid for my music lessons, he takes us to the beach in the summer, he drops us off at the movies. He really does do a lot for us and sometimes I think we forget to say thank you. I felt bad for not re-specting my father.

Does this example suggest rules and rituals do or do not have value?

EXAMPLE 2

Where I work, we are given five sick days a year. After that, your pay is docked for each day you're out. I'm never out sick more than two or three days a year. I don't abuse the policy by taking "mental health" days. However, each of the last two years, I've had my pay docked because I used more than my al-lotted sick days. I wasn't abusing this rule. I was simply taking care of my child as any mother would. I can't help it if my daughter is too sick to go to school or needs to go to the doctor. Women with children should have additional sick leave for these emergencies. When I have to call in with a sick child, my super-visor always makes me feel like I'm avoiding doing my work, like I'm not a good employee. Five days of sick leave is not enough for a mother, because she has to have sick days for herself and her child. Although I don't intentionally break this rule like Mathabane did, I still pay for breaking it. Some rules are good, but this one needs to be rethought.

Does this example suggest rules and rituals do or do not have value?

EXAMPLE 3

I personally have experienced firsthand the negative effects of rituals. There is a ritual we perform every year at work. We select names out of a hat, so we can be someone's Santa for that Christmas. Every year I go through the same thing. I don't know what to buy the person. Although there is a twenty dollar limit on the gift, I always spend more, because I don't want this person I hardly know to think I'm cheap. I'm sure everyone else is going through the same thing. Then on the last day of work before Christmas, we open our gifts and pretend to be overjoyed at a present we don't even want. Last year was the worst. I bought a basket of cheeses, smoked meats, and wine for a coworker who turned out to be an herb tea sipping vegetarian. It wasn't my fault because I didn't really know him, but I was humiliated when I found out.

Does this example suggest rules and rituals do or do not have value?

EXAMPLE 4

My parents believe in doing little rituals, thinking that they will protect them. Recently my dad was helping set the table. He knocked over the salt shaker. He picked up a pinch of salt to throw it over his shoulder. He always said that throwing salt over your shoulder would ward off bad luck. He happened to throw the salt over his shoulder right as my mother was walking in carrying a bowl of mashed potatoes. She ducked to avoid the salt and dropped the bowl. The bowl broke and threw mashed potatoes all over the floor and the wall. Obviously the salt over the shoulder didn't ward off bad luck.

Does this example suggest rules and rituals do or do not have value?

What attitude was expressed in each example? Do your answers match the ones below?

Example 1 suggests that rituals do have a value: they teach respect.

Example 2 suggests that rules don't have value because mothers deserve extra consideration.

Example 3 suggests that rituals don't have value: they lead to humiliation.

Example 4 suggests that rituals don't have value: they are just superstitions.

Since there are more examples saying that rules and rituals don't have value, it is best to create a thesis statement that supports examples 2, 3, and 4.

Earlier in this chapter, we used the prompt to help determine a thesis. Does the following thesis statement point ahead to the ideas in prewriting examples 2, 3, and 4?

Mathabane is right to think that many rules and rituals serve no purpose.

This thesis statement will work for the three topics we've chosen. However, the specific focus that the writer will take is still unclear. A reader might ask why rules and rituals serve no purpose. A thesis can be focused by adding a plan of development.

EXERCISE 8.7

Write your own thesis statement in response to one of the following two prompts.

Mathabane writes less about his mother than his father or himself. What is the significance of her role in the family? Do you think other women play similar roles in their families?

Mathabane has a conflict with his father. Do parents and children always have conflicts? Why or why not? Using your own ideas and observations, write an essay in which you answer this question.

PLAN OF DEVELOPMENT

A **plan of development** tells your reader either which parts of the reading you will focus on or what the focus of your arguments will be. In other words, a plan of development tells your reader what you will and will not be examining. A plan of development is generally one or more sentences after your thesis statement; but it can also be in the same sentence(s) as your thesis. You can determine your plan of development by examining your prewriting. What points did your prewriting lead to? Chapters 6 and 7 explain how your prewriting leads to several points, or supporting ideas, used to plan your essay.

Providing a Plan of Development

Defines what areas of the reading you will discuss

Defines the general points you will bring out

Here are two plans of development that have been attached to our thesis statement. Which one points to the reading and which one focuses the reader on the general points the writer will make?

Mathabane is right to think that rules and rituals serve no purpose. This is especially clear in the scenes where Mathabane speaks at the table, when he decides not to speak Venda, and when his father embarrasses him by wearing tribal clothing.

Mathabane is right to think that many rules and rituals serve no purpose. Rules are supposed to be applied equally; however, they often unfairly punish certain people. Although some rituals have a value, there are many pointless rituals which people blindly follow. Certain rituals force people to do things they don't want to do and can lead to embarrassing situations.

The first example of a plan of development tells the reader which areas of the reading the writer will discuss: when Mathabane speaks at the table, when he refuses to speak Venda, and when he is embarrassed by his father. The second plan of development lets us know what the writer will argue: rules can be unfair, many rituals are pointless, and rituals create embarrassing situations. Either one of these plans of development will give the reader an idea of what will come in the essay.

EXERCISE 8.8

Write two plans of development for each of the following prompts. Write one plan of development that tells the reader what areas of the reading you will discuss. Write the other to suggest the points you will make in your body paragraphs.

Mathabane writes less about his mother than his father or himself. What is the significance of her role in the family? Do you think other women play similar roles in their families?

Mathabane has a conflict with his father. Do parents and children always have conflicts? Why or why not? Using your own ideas and observations, write an essay in which you answer this question.

PUTTING THE INTRODUCTION TOGETHER

At this point you should be ready to put together the various parts of your introduction. Let's first compare two possible introductory paragraphs.

> In Mark Mathabane's "My Father's Tribal Rule," he talks about rituals and rules. He talks about his brother, his mother, and his sister. His family had to moved to a shack. Mathabane really dislikes his father because his father beats him. The father doesn't beat the other children like he beats his son Mark. Mark Mathabane wants to be like the other boys he plays with. He wants to speak other languages. In this paper I will discuss Mathabane's essay.

This example lacks a lead-in to the general topic under discussion. The overview of the reading is too brief to convey an understanding of the essay as a whole. Someone who has not read "My Father's Tribal Rule" would have little understanding of what the reading is about. This example doesn't clarify what the point of Mathabane's writing is. There is no thesis statement, and there is no plan of development. A reader would be confused by this introduction because it lacks the essential information the reader needs to understand what will follow in the rest of the essay. Now compare the previous example with this one.

> Many people feel that rituals are a thing of the past, practiced only by primitive people. They feel that rituals have little place in a modern society that is driven by technology and science. Rituals, they would say, are just superstitions acted out. [*lead-in*] Mark Mathabane is one of those people who detests rituals. In "My Father's Tribal Rule," he tells us about his experiences [*author and title of reading*] growing up in South Africa in a shantytown of rundown huts for people who had been forced off their ancestral, tribal lands. Even though Mathabane and the children in the area were interested in modern ways, Mathabane's father insisted that their family stick to the tribal traditions. Mathabane eventually came to hate his father for making him follow the tribal rituals. [*overview of reading*] Despite his father's insistence that he follow the rules and practice the rituals, Mathabane thought they made [*author's thesis*] no sense. Mathabane is right to think that many rules and rituals [*writer's thesis*] serve no purpose. Rules are supposed to be applied equally; however, they often unfairly punish certain people. Although some rituals have value, there are many pointless rituals that [*plan of development*] people blindly follow. Certain rituals force people to do things they don't want to do and can lead to embarrassing situations.

In the second example, we are given a lead-in that discusses the general topic of rituals and focuses on the commonly held view. The overview of the reading provides more information for the reader who has never read it. The point of Mathabane's essay—his thesis statement—is provided for the reader. The writer's thesis statement clarifies what the writer believes and responds directly to the prompt. It is followed by a plan of development, which lets the reader know that the writer will discuss such topics as the unfairness of some rules. The writer will also discuss how rituals are sometimes pointless and can lead to embarrassing situations. There is a clear response to the prompt; we know that this writer will agree with Mathabane's attitude about rules and rituals.

An Alternative Structure

Remember that the model on the previous pages only shows one possible way to construct an introduction. Other assignments may require a different structure. The structure of the introduction on page 163 is designed to move the reader from the most general information to the most specific.

When writing about a reading, you can also use structures other than the general-to-specific model described at the beginning of this chapter. The elements that make up an introduction can be reorganized, or at times some elements can be eliminated. Examine the following paragraph (on the topic of welfare) and note how its structure is different from the general-to-specific model.

> The image that most people have of welfare recipients is false. Many people look at those on welfare as people who are too lazy to work hard. They believe that welfare recipients are just people who want a free ride. This image is often promoted on television news magazines, which do stories on welfare recipients who abuse the system. We see stories about people illegally trading food stamps or making false claims to bilk the system out of money. We also hear about people who make welfare a lifestyle. However, most recipients are people who want to get off welfare and make a decent living for themselves. Teresa McCrary is one such person. She has worked hard to get herself the education required to get a job that will pay her enough money to support her family. The picture that Teresa McCrary presents of welfare mothers in her essay "Getting Off the Welfare Carousel" is an accurate one. She discusses the problems that welfare mothers face and argues against the image that most people have of welfare recipients. The experiences of two friends of mine, Tanya S. and Cindy R., fully support

writer's thesis

overview of issue

author's name

title and overview of essay

author's thesis

what McCrary is saying about most welfare moms. They repre- ⎤— writer's thesis
sent the real image of welfare mothers, women who are dedi-⎤   restated
cated to their children and women who are working hard to ⎬— plan of
better themselves.   ⎦ development

In this example, a lead-in has been eliminated, and the writer has begun with a thesis statement. The writer has then discussed her concerns about welfare before discussing McCrary's essay. At the end of the introduction this writer has chosen to restate her thesis, in case the reader had forgotten it. The introduction concludes with a plan of development. This structure contains most of the elements of the general-to-specific model, but some of the elements have been rearranged.

EXERCISE 8.9

Examine the prompts below and write an introductory paragraph with the six elements we've just discussed. (Go back to Chapter 5 if you need help understanding what the prompt is asking. Go back to Chapter 4 if you need to analyze the reading or Chapter 6 if you need to develop samples of prewriting.) If you have been following the exercises in this chapter, you will have the elements that make up an introduction. Try to put them all together. You'll need to check your wording to make sure the different parts flow together into a whole.

Mathabane writes less about his mother than his father or himself. What is the significance of her role in the family? Do you think other women play similar roles in their families?

Mathabane has a conflict with his father. Do parents and children always have conflicts? Why or why not? Using your own ideas and observations, write an essay in which you answer this question.

INTRODUCTIONS THAT RESPOND TO ISSUES

The beginning of this chapter points out that when you are writing about a reading, it is generally a good idea to create an introduction that moves your reader from general information to more specific information. A reader unfamiliar with your topic will thus be led step by step from your **lead-in**, through your **overview** and identification of the **author and title of the reading**, to your **thesis** and **plan of development**.

However, for some writing purposes, changing, eliminating, or removing some of these elements will strengthen your introduction. If you choose an alternative structure in your introduction, always be sure to consider how the changes will affect the reader's ability to understand. For example, the model introduction just described begins with a **lead-in**, which is helpful to readers unfamiliar with your topic, but if you know who your **audience** is and know that they are familiar with your topic, a lead-in can be removed. In another situation, you can eliminate all references to a specific author and reading if you are responding to an issue rather than a reading. Even if you are going to supply quotes from one or more authors to support your **argument**, you need not mention the name(s) of the authors or title(s) of the articles you use. Your introduction would contain the elements shown in the box.

✓ **An Introduction to an Essay on an Issue**

■ General lead-in
■ Discussion of the issue
■ Your thesis
■ Plan of develoment

This structure is reflected in the following example.

America is considered the land of opportunity, where anyone who is willing to work hard can support both family and self. As a society, we believe that hard work pays off. We also believe the opposite. If you don't work hard, you deserve what you get—or don't get.   *lead-in*

Many people look at those on welfare as people who are too lazy to work hard. They believe that welfare recipients are just people who want a free ride. This image is often promoted on television news magazines, which do stories on welfare recipients who abuse the system. We see stories about people illegally trading food stamps or making false claims to bilk the system out of money. We also hear about people who make welfare a life style.   *discussion of issue*

Fraud does occur, but the image we have of most welfare recipients is false.   *writer's thesis*

Most recipients are people who only use the benefits for a short time between jobs. Other people are unable to work due to disabilities or due to being left a single parent by an uncaring spouse.   *plan of development*

This paragraph begins with a **lead-in** discussing the values Americans hold regarding work. It is followed by a **discussion of the issue** that the writer is concerned with: the negative image of welfare recipients. The **writer's thesis** is that our image of welfare recipients is wrong. The writer presents a **plan of development**, noting that he or she will focus on the short time period most people use welfare and on the problems that some people have that won't allow them to work.

Do the elements of the introduction have to come in this order? No, they don't. The previous example uses the general-to-specific arrangement of information. A writer could choose to skip the lead-in and begin with a discussion of the issue.

- Discussion of issue
- Your thesis
- Plan of development

Since the issue of welfare is one known to most everyone in the United States, a writer could begin with a thesis statement. When a topic is well known, a writer can start with his or her thesis, using the following organizational pattern.

- Thesis
- Discussion of issue
- Plan of development

Since this structure begins with a thesis, the lead-in is removed. Here is the same paragraph we just examined with this new structure.

> The image that most people have of welfare recipients is false. Many people look at those on welfare as people who are ⟶ *writer's thesis*
>
> too lazy to work hard. They believe that welfare recipients are just people who want a free ride. This image is often promoted on television news magazines, which do stories on welfare recipients who abuse the system. We see stories about people illegally trading food stamps or making false claims to bilk the system out of money. We also hear about people who make ⟶ *discussion of issue*
>
> welfare a life style. However, most recipients are people who only use the benefits for a short time between jobs. Other people are unable to work due to disabilities or due to being left a single parent by an uncaring spouse. ⟶ *plan of development*

Eliminating the lead-in and placing the thesis at the beginning of the introduction required some minor changes in wording, but essentially the paragraph is the same as the previous example. Which one works better? That's a matter of opinion. The first example guides the reader from the general topic of American ideas about the value of hard work to the specific topic of the false image of welfare recipients. The second example begins by seizing the reader's attention with a controversial statement. Both structures will work, but, depending on who the writer's audience is, one might work better than the other.

A plan of development is usually placed last in an introductory paragraph because it tells your reader what specific topics you will address. The issue of capital punishment, for instance, has many subtopics: justice, cruel punishment, protection of society, flaws in the justice system. A plan of development would tell a reader which of those topics you will discuss. However, a plan of development can be incorporated into your discussion of the issue. If your discussion of the issue focuses solely on the topic(s) you will examine, a plan of development is not needed at the end of the introduction. Consider the following.

- Lead-in
- Discussion of issue with plan of development
- Your thesis

Use these alternate strategies if you are not responding to one author's ideas but rather presenting your *own ideas* on an issue. In some essays, you might use quotes from other writers to support your ideas. In that case, you would be examining an issue and not responding to one reading—not to one writer's ideas. Thus, you could create introductions modeled after the examples at the end of this chapter.

Keep in mind that the purpose of an introduction is to set up a context for readers—a framework to help them understand what follows in the essay. In addition, introductions should point ahead to what is to come so readers won't be baffled by a topic that suddenly appears. The elements of the introduction that we've discussed will help you to provide the information your reader needs. How you present it and in what order you present it is determined by you, your topic, and your audience. In the next chapter, we will begin by discussing body paragraphs, structured to respond to Mathabane's "My Father's Tribal Rule."

What You've Done

- Familiarized your reader with the topic and your focus
- Presented your plan of development

The Next Step

- Write body paragraphs (Chapter 9)

9 Writing Body Paragraphs

What You've Done

- Created an introduction

What You Need to Do Next

- Write paragraphs that develop the main idea of the essay
    - Write sentences to state the main idea of each paragraph
    - Make the ideas from the reading clear
    - Use your own ideas and examples to respond to the reading
    - End each paragraph with a point supporting your thesis

In contrast to **introductions**, which supply general information, **body paragraphs** present specific information and details for your reader. The most commonly asked question about body paragraphs is "How many do I need?" Although some writing textbooks suggest that an essay include at least three body paragraphs, we recommend that the number of body paragraphs be determined by the reading or the material you're discussing. For instance, when we discussed Mathabane's essay "My Father's Tribal Rule" in Chapter 3, we saw that this reading discusses two rules: not speaking at the table and speaking only Venda. We also saw that there were three rituals: weaning George, wearing tribal clothing, and doing daily rituals. If your assignment was to write about the rules in Mathabane's narrative, you would most likely have only two body paragraphs because rules are only discussed in two places in the reading. Similarly, if your assignment was to write about rituals, you would have three body paragraphs, one for each ritual in the reading. If you were asked to write about both the rules and the rituals, you could have five body paragraphs.

Even though there are five areas of the reading that discuss rules and rituals, you need to focus on two questions: Which areas can you respond to with the best examples or strongest arguments? Which areas are directly related to your **thesis** or the **prompt**? For instance, there are three rituals discussed in the reading. If the prompt asks you to discuss Mathabane's dislike of rituals, you could eliminate one of the three. Mathabane says nothing negative about the ritual surrounding George's weaning. You could then focus on the two he does dislike.

Remember: Use the reading, your **prewriting**, and the assignment to help you determine how many body paragraphs you need.

BODY PARAGRAPHS THAT RESPOND TO A READING

Body Paragraphs
Topic sentence
Transitions
Discussing author's ideas
Your argument
Conclusion

Because many of the assignments you are given in college will require you to respond to the ideas of others, we will focus on a model of a paragraph that creates a balance between the author's ideas and your own. This is only one way to construct body paragraphs. As your assignments change, other structures might be recommended. Later in this chapter, we will discuss alternative structures for body paragraphs. Although there is more than one way to construct your body paragraphs, they usually contain the general elements that an entire essay does: an introduction (**topic sentence**), a body (discussion of reading and your response), and a conclusion (the point you are trying to make).

The box shows an example of a balanced body paragraph structure.

Components of Body Paragraphs That Respond to a Reading

■ A topic sentence

■ A discussion of one of the author's ideas

(Four or five sentences or more with a quote from the author, clarifying the author's point on this specific issue.)

■ Your example and/or argument

(Four or five sentences or more, worded to respond to the author's idea)

■ A point supportive of your thesis

This structure creates a balance between the author's ideas and your response to those ideas. The author's ideas are usually presented first because you are responding to what the author has said. Since many of your assignments will require you to respond to an author's ideas, you must first clarify what those ideas are. Once you have explained the author's position on one issue, you can then directly respond to what he or she has said.

A body paragraph should contain only *one topic*, and any example or discussion of the reading must relate to that topic. This will help you keep a clear focus in each body paragraph, and it will allow you to better select the examples that relate most effectively to the specific point the author is making. If you have more than one topic in a body paragraph, you may confuse the reader, lose your focus, and never clarify your point.

Throughout the rest of this chapter, we will discuss each element of the body paragraph and provide examples.

TOPIC SENTENCES

Topic Sentences
Introduce the topic
Provide transitions

A *topic sentence* announces the specific subject that will be discussed in the paragraph. Topic sentences let the reader know what you will discuss, and they also help you to keep a sharp focus on one topic. They have two functions.

- They set up the *topic*—the main idea of the paragraph.
- They act as a *transition*—linking the information that will come in the new paragraph to information that has been presented in previous paragraphs.

Topic sentences are important because your reader needs to know what you will discuss. It is important that you present your topic sentence immediately—in your introductory sentence. The topic you set up should be the *only* topic discussed in the paragraph. Look at the following example.

Some rituals are practiced in such a way that they become meaningless.

This introductory sentence to the paragraph sets up the topic of rituals and how they can lose their meaning.

When setting up topic sentences, remember not to start with quotes or examples. Quotes show the reader exactly what the author said, but they do not constitute a topic. Examples illustrate a point the author is trying to make, but they cannot be considered a topic. In other words, a writer may give an example of an incident in a football game to make a point about teamwork. If you begin your paragraph by discussing the author's example, your reader will think the topic of the paragraph is football. Teamwork would be the topic you would set up for your reader. Then you would discuss the author's example to reveal his point about teamwork.

When it's time for you to write your body paragraphs, don't jump right into them. Think about your reader. Provide a topic sentence that clearly reveals whatever single topic you will discuss in your paragraph.

TRANSITIONS

Your first body paragraph doesn't need a transition, because it is not following another body paragraph. However, as you move from one body paragraph to another, it helps if you can link together your discussions for your reader. **Transitions** help the readers to see how the new information is related to the information in the last paragraph they read. To make an opening sentence work as a transition, add a reference to the topic or point of the previous paragraph. If the first body paragraph focuses on meaningless rituals, the following sentence would serve as a transition into the next topic.

> Some rituals seem senseless, but some rituals can make us act in ways we don't want to and can lead to embarrassing situations.

This sentence serves as a transition because it points back to a previous discussion about senseless rituals, and it points ahead to the new topic that will be discussed: rituals force us to do things we don't want to do and can be embarrassing.

Topic sentences that serve as transitions do the following.

■ Refer to the topic and/or point of the previous paragraph.

■ Set up the new topic the writer will discuss.

| EXERCISE 9.1 | **Pretend that you are writing an essay in which these are the main ideas presented in your body paragraphs.** |

Mathabane's relationship with his father

The relationship between Mathabane's father and mother

The relationship between Mathabane and his mother

1. Write topic sentences for each of these ideas.
2. Determine which order these ideas should be presented in an essay. In other words, what order would work for the body paragraphs based on these ideas.
3. Once you have determined the order, add transitional words or phrases to the second and third topic sentences.

Repeat all three steps in the preceding exercise for these main ideas.

Mathabane's feelings about only speaking Venda

Mathabane's feelings about not speaking at the table

Mathabane's feelings about his father wearing tribal clothing

CLARIFYING THE AUTHOR'S IDEAS

If you are responding to a reading, your reader needs to know exactly what the author says on a specific point. After you have set up your topic sentence, you need to do the following.

Body Development
Present author's ideas
Provide evidence
Explain ideas
Respond to author's ideas

- Paraphrase or summarize the author's ideas.
- Quote passages that demonstrate these ideas clearly.
- Explain the author's idea or point in your own words.

Even if you are going to disagree with the author, you need to present his or her ideas clearly and fairly. In the next example, the introductory sentence we discussed earlier will be followed by an explanation of what is said in the reading.

Rituals can make us act in ways we don't want to and can lead to embarrassing situations. Mathabane tells about his father wearing the traditional tribal clothing while he wanted to wear modern clothing. He says that when his father wore his tribal clothes, the other children would laugh at both of them. Mathabane says he became "the laughingstock of [his] friends." He goes on to say, "Whenever they laughed at me I would feel embarrassed and would cry." I'm sure Mathabane wanted to be proud of his father, but this ritual just embarrassed him and made him cry.

Someone who had never read the essay would understand the situation being described here. This example has given enough detail for readers to have an understanding of how Mathabane feels about this ritual. The last sentence uses the phrase "embarrassed him and made him cry," which echoes the subject set up in the topic sentence: rituals can lead to embarrassing situations.

RESPONDING TO THE AUTHOR

After you have presented the author's position, you need to respond with your own ideas and examples to reveal how you feel about the topic you're discussing. To explain whether you agree or disagree with the ideas contained in the reading, you must present arguments and/or examples that provide specific details for your reader. Consider the following example.

We have a lot of rituals around our house. There are rituals from dad's side of the family and some from my mother's side. There's a ritual for every holiday. Sometimes I wish we could just ignore them. I don't see why we need to do the same thing every year in the same way.

This example lacks development and specifics. What are the rituals? Which rituals are from the father's side of the family? Which ones are from the mother's side? Is there any difference between them? Why doesn't the writer want to perform the same rituals every year? There are many things that the reader would be uncertain about. A reader would never remember this example because there is nothing concrete that the reader can hold on to.

Let's look at another sample of prewriting from Chapter 8.

> I personally have experienced firsthand the negative effects of rituals. There is a ritual we perform every year at work. We select names out of a hat, so we can be someone's Santa for that Christmas. Every year I go through the same thing. I don't know what to buy the person. Although there is a twenty dollar limit on the gift, I always spend more, because I don't want this person I hardly know to think I'm cheap. I'm sure everyone else goes through the same thing. Then on the last day of work before Christmas, we open our gifts and pretend to be overjoyed at a present we don't even want. Last year was the worst. I bought a basket of cheeses, smoked meats, and wine for a coworker who turned out to be an herb tea sipping vegetarian. It wasn't my fault. I didn't really know him, but I was humiliated when I found out.

This example provides much more detail for the reader. A specific ritual is discussed. There are details given about a specific incident. The way the writer feels about this ritual is spelled out for the reader. This is an example the reader will remember because it has specific details.

You will notice that this example is different from Mathabane's example about his father's tribal clothes, but the situation is very similar. The reader should be able to see the parallel between the two situations: both Mathabane and the writer have to follow a ritual, and Mathabane is embarrassed by his ritual, just as this writer is humiliated by the ritual in which she must participate.

Your examples don't have to be exactly the same as the author's, but they do need to focus on the same issue. For instance, if you were responding to an article describing how important determination and hard work are in learning to play a musical instrument, you could provide an example discussing how important determination and hard work are in learning math. Math and music are different topics, but the issue of determination and hard work in learning these skills is the same.

CONCLUDING YOUR BODY PARAGRAPH

Examples cannot stand on their own, and they cannot serve as an ending to a body paragraph. An example will illustrate your point, but it isn't *your* point. Body paragraphs need to end with a statement that sums up your point for the reader.

Let's look at the prompt again and see if the last sentence from the preceding writer's example is directly responding to the prompt.

Prompt/Question

Mathabane says he despises rules and rituals. Is he correct in thinking that rules and rituals have no value?

Response/Answer

It wasn't my fault. I didn't really know him, but I was humiliated when I found out.

Do these last sentences from the previous example respond to the prompt and support the writer's thesis? The prompt asks if you agree or disagree with Mathabane's attitude toward rules and rituals. You can see that the last sentence in the example doesn't respond to the prompt or support the writer's thesis, which agrees with Mathabane's attitude.

You must explain how your example is related to the issue in the reading. Since the purpose of your paragraph is to support or clarify your thesis, you need to explain to your reader how the example illustrates your point and supports your thesis. Here is the same example of the writer's personal experience with a concluding point.

I personally have experienced firsthand the negative effects of rituals. There is a ritual we perform every year at work. We select names out of a hat, so we can be someone's Santa for that Christmas. Every year I go through the same thing. I don't know what to buy the person. Although there is a twenty dollar limit on the gift, I always spend more because I don't want this person I hardly know to think I'm cheap. I'm sure everyone else goes through the same thing. Then on the last day of work before Christmas, we open our gifts and pretend to be overjoyed at a present we don't even want. Last year was the worst. I bought a basket of cheeses, smoked meats, and wine for a coworker who turned out to be an herb tea sipping vegetarian. It wasn't my fault. I didn't really know him, but I was humiliated when I found out. *Mathabane's father's rituals brought shame on him, just as this office ritual humiliated me. Some rituals should be abolished because they embarrass people.*

This conclusion to the paragraph explains the point of the example: *Some rituals should be abolished because they embarrass people.* It is worded to relate the writer's example to Mathabane's experience. Furthermore, it is supportive of the thesis that is set up in the introductory paragraph: *Mathabane is right to think that rules and rituals serve no purpose.* Essentially, it summarizes what has been discussed in the paragraph and is worded to support the writer's thesis.

PUTTING THE BODY PARAGRAPH TOGETHER

Here is the whole paragraph with all the components put together.

Rituals can make us act in ways we don't want to and can lead to embarrassing situations. Mathabane tells about his father wearing the traditional tribal clothing while he wanted to wear modern clothing. He says that when his father wore his tribal clothes, the other children would laugh at both of them.

— topic sentence

— discussion of the reading

Mathabane says he became "the laughingstock of [his] friends." He goes on to say, "Whenever they laughed at me I would feel embarrassed and would cry." I'm sure Mathabane wanted to be proud of his father, but this ritual just embarrassed him and made him cry. I personally have experienced firsthand the negative effects of rituals. There is a ritual we perform every year at work. We select names out of a hat, so we can be someone's Santa for that Christmas. Every year I go through the same thing. I don't know what to buy the person. Although there is a twenty dollar limit on the gift, I always spend more, because I don't want this person I hardly know to think I'm cheap. I'm sure everyone else goes through the same thing. Then on the last day of work before Christmas, we open our gifts and pretend to be overjoyed at a present we don't even want. Last year was the worst. I bought a basket of cheeses, smoked meats, and wine for a coworker who turned out to be an herb tea sipping vegetarian. It wasn't my fault. I didn't really know him, but I was humiliated when I found out. Mathabane's father's rituals brought shame on him, just as this office ritual humiliated me. Some rituals should be abolished because they embarrass people.

discussion of the reading

writer's example

concluding point supporting writer's thesis

ADDITIONAL BODY PARAGRAPHS

As we discussed at the beginning of this chapter, an essay needs more than one paragraph to provide support for a thesis. Additional body paragraphs should examine either new issues (related to the focus of your thesis) or different areas of the reading. The body paragraph we have just looked at discusses the section of the reading where Mathabane is embarrassed by his father's tribal clothes. Additional body paragraphs should focus on other sections of the reading where rules and rituals are discussed.

| EXERCISE 9.2 | Examine the body paragraphs that follow. Do they contain the four basic elements of the model paragraph we have been discussing? Answer these five questions for each paragraph. |

1. What is the topic sentence?
2. Is there a discussion of one area of the reading? What is it?
3. Does the writer provide a specific example? What is it?
4. Does the paragraph end with a concluding point?
5. Does the concluding point support a thesis? What would the thesis be?

EXAMPLE 1

Like Mathabane, I find that some rituals don't make sense. There's one specific ritual that makes little sense to me. The fourth Thursday of November, my husband, my daughter, and I go to my parents' house for Thanksgiving. It is always held at my parents' house, even though they live the farthest out of town. My mother won't let anyone else host the gathering. Each member of the family is assigned a specific dish to bring. We arrive along with cousins, aunts, and uncles, many of whom we have little in common with. Then we all try to be pleasant, make small talk, and smile. Dinner is always a disaster. When the potatoes are done, the turkey isn't. When the turkey is done, the potatoes are dry and cold. The women, of course, do all the work. For the most part, we just get in each other's way as we try to prepare the meal. Even before we sit down to eat, I'm battling a severe case of stress. Thanksgiving is the day when you're supposed to give thanks, but the only thing I'm thankful for is when it's over. The Pilgrims celebrated the first Thanksgiving for a reason—they had survived in a new and bountiful land. We never share what we are thankful for. Because our family has lost sight of the purpose of this ritual, it makes no sense to celebrate it.

EXAMPLE 2

Mathabane said he had to do daily rituals. Some of the rituals were to "protect the house from evil doers." The family also did rituals to keep them from being sick or hungry. There were other rituals to keep the police away, but I don't know why you would want to do that. The police are there to protect and serve. I would think that you would want a ritual to keep criminals away. They also had rituals to help them get more money. Mathabane says that these rituals "did not make sense." He had to do a lot of rituals, and if he didn't, his father would threaten to beat him. That's not fair and would be considered child abuse.

EXAMPLE 3

Rules can often lead to certain people being treated unfairly. Mathabane's father didn't allow talking at the dinner table. When Mathabane did talk, he was unfairly punished. Where I work, we are given five sick days a year. After that, your pay is docked for each day you're out. I'm never out sick more than two or three days a year. I don't abuse the policy by taking "mental health" days. However, each of the last two years, I've had my pay docked because I used more than my allotted sick days. I wasn't abusing this rule, I was simply taking care of my child as any mother would. I can't help it if my daughter is too sick to go to school or needs to go to the doctor. Women with children should have additional sick leave for these emergencies. When I have to call in with a sick child, my supervisor always makes me feel like I'm avoiding doing my work, like I'm not a good employee. Five days of sick leave is not enough for a mother, because she has to have sick days for herself and her child.

Example 4

We have a big ritual on the 4th of July. All the families on our street know each other. Most of the families have children. We put on a block party fireworks show. The object is to put on the best display, or my strategy, which is to save the best for last. Some of the neighbors set out picnic tables and we all contribute some food. Someone always has a barbecue going. These are rituals because we do them the same way every year. It's always the same.

Example 5

Another problem with rituals is that they are just based on superstitions. Rituals can't protect you. Although he doesn't explain what he had to do, Mathabane tells us that he had to perform "rituals spanning the range of day-to-day living." He had to do rituals "to prevent us from becoming sick, to safeguard his [father's] job, to keep the police away, to bring [the family] good luck" and more. Mathabane said that these rituals didn't make any sense to him. How can performing rituals bring luck or prevent you from becoming sick? When I was younger, I was like Mathabane's father. I had a ritual for almost everything. I had a ritual for going to sleep: 20 deep breaths and count backward from 100. I had rituals for getting high scores on my tests in school: using a new pen or pencil or repeating the word <u>luck</u> over and over before the test. But as I got older, my views changed and are now like Mathabane's. Luck doesn't have anything to do with knowing the answers on a quiz. I know how well I'll do on a test, because I know how much I've studied. Luck isn't going to make information pop into my head. When I stopped relying on rituals and started to rely on studying, my grades went up. Rituals are just baseless superstitions. Following rituals is senseless and Mathabane is right to think they are useless.

EXERCISE 9.3

Collaboration

Which of the preceding paragraphs lack one or more of the four elements? Working in small groups, see if you can rewrite these paragraphs to better match the structure of the example body paragraph we discussed on page 170.

BODY PARAGRAPHS THAT RESPOND TO ISSUES

At times, your instructor may give you a writing assignment that does not require you to respond to a specific reading. Your instructor may ask you to express your own opinion on a given topic or ask you to present your own opinion and support it with quotes from several authors. In these types of assignments, the structure of your body paragraphs will be different from the balanced structure (half focused on the author's ideas and half focused on your ideas) previously discussed in this chapter: **topic sentence, discussion of the author's idea, your example/argument, concluding point.** When you are responding to an issue, the following structure may be preferable.

- ■ Topic sentence
- ■ Discussion of issue
- ■ Concluding point

This structure begins and ends just as the balanced structure we have examined. What is different is that this structure allows you to approach the discussion of the issue in several different ways. In the section of the paragraph where you discuss the issue, you may use one of the following approaches.

- ■ Provide your own, well-reasoned argument.
- ■ Provide a discussion using one or more of the modes (Chapters 15 and 16).
- ■ Provide your own argument, supported with quotes from professional writers.

Providing Your Own Argument

If you are responding to an issue rather than a reading, your body paragraphs do not necessarily have to contain quotes from professional writers. You may be able to make your point by providing a strong, logical argument of your own. Consider the following paragraph on the topic of marriage.

Marriage is a tradition that has lost its meaning because it is no longer seen as a religiously sanctioned joining of two people. `— topic sentence`

In the past, marriage was considered sacred, a union of man and wife overseen by the church. The ceremony was carried out by a priest or a pastor, someone who represented the church's power and authority. Today, however, a justice of the peace can perform a wedding ceremony. A justice of the peace is a low-ranking officer of the court system with little authority— not a representative of a church. Delegating marriages to a justice of the peace shows how unimportant society thinks `— writer's own arguments/ examples`

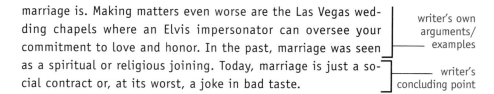

marriage is. Making matters even worse are the Las Vegas wedding chapels where an Elvis impersonator can oversee your commitment to love and honor. In the past, marriage was seen as a spiritual or religious joining. Today, marriage is just a social contract or, at its worst, a joke in bad taste.

writer's own arguments/ examples

writer's concluding point

This body paragraph begins by setting up a topic, which is that marriage is less significant now than in the past, since it is no longer seen in a religious context. The writer then provides her own **argument**, stressing the difference between the religious ceremonies of the past and the civil ceremonies of present day. Her paragraph ends with a concluding **point** about marriages today. This paragraph does not contain any quotes. The writer has put forward her personal beliefs on the topic of marriage.

One can also use the modes when writing body paragraphs responding to or not responding to a specific reading (see Chapters 15 and 16 for a more detailed discussion on the modes). The **modes** are different means to present information to your reader. When you provide a personal experience, you are using the mode of **narration**. Other modes are description, process, definition, **comparison/contrast, classification, cause and effect,** and **illustration**. For instance, if you write in response to the argument that the NASA space program is a waste of taxpayers' money, you might **compare and contrast** the NASA program with other government-supported programs. Through comparing and contrasting, you might be able to show that less money is spent on NASA than on many other programs or that more benefits are derived from the money spent on NASA than on other programs.

The examples that follow in this chapter are paragraphs written in response to an issue rather than a specific reading. The following approaches can be used separately or in combination. In other words, in one body paragraph you might use narration, whereas you might use cause and effect to make a point in another body paragraph.

Narration

Narration is the retelling of an event or experience. In essence, it is relating the story of what occurred. A narration might present the events of a personal experience, like a trouble-filled camping trip or a promising first date. The following example is a narrative about the writer's uncle, but its purpose is to make a point about our perceptions of welfare recipients.

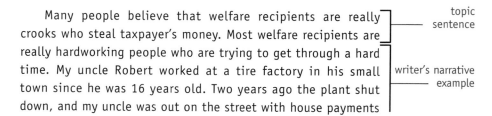

Many people believe that welfare recipients are really crooks who steal taxpayer's money. Most welfare recipients are really hardworking people who are trying to get through a hard time. My uncle Robert worked at a tire factory in his small town since he was 16 years old. Two years ago the plant shut down, and my uncle was out on the street with house payments

topic sentence

writer's narrative example

to make and a family to support. He began looking for work | writer's narrative example
but couldn't find any. Eventually, they were forced to sell the
house. That was humiliating, but what my uncle said was the
worst thing was when he was forced to sign up for welfare benefits. He felt ashamed to ask. He only took it because he had
to feed his family. Although most people on welfare are people
like my uncle, too many of us wrongly think that welfare recipients are lazy bums who steal our tax dollars. He hated being
on welfare so much that he began driving to neighboring
states looking for work. Five months later, he found a job. My
uncle was on welfare, but he was no freeloader. My uncle rep- | writer's concluding point
resents most welfare recipients: hardworking people who work
hard to get off welfare.

This body paragraph's topic is our misperception of those on welfare. The writer then provides a **narration**—a story of his uncle's experiences. Notice, however, that the paragraph doesn't end on the writer's story about his uncle. This narrative example illustrates the writer's point, but it is not the writer's point. The writer ends the paragraph with a **concluding point** about the welfare recipients: most are hardworking people who strive to get off welfare.

Description

Description is a process in which you create a vivid image in the reader's mind, one that will be remembered. The key to description is detail. When describing something for your readers, give them significant details—don't be too vague. Consider the following paragraph.

One of the difficulties for welfare recipients used to be the | topic sentence
welfare office itself. Our local welfare office is designed with
people in mind. As soon as you walk in, you can see that they | writer's descriptive example
want you to feel comfortable. The office is painted in blue and
pink pastel colors, which are very soothing. The welfare workers aren't hidden behind frosted glass panels; instead, they sit
at desks in open areas that give a sense of friendliness. Prints
of impressionist paintings by van Gogh and Cezanne brighten
the walls. Someone expecting a dingy, green government office
will be surprised by the light airy feel of our local office. This
may sound luxurious for a welfare office, but it is actually very
important. Welfare recipients are looked down on by some people. This creates low self-esteem in recipients. Our new office
helps to make recipients feel like they are getting respect. The

look of the new office says to the recipient, we want you to
feel at ease, comfortable—you are important to us. Although
the welfare offices in many cities are dingy, our city's office is
designed to make people seeking welfare more comfortable.
Our new office is large, airy, and bright. The color scheme is
bright and cheery. It's a place where people can feel comfortable. This aids a welfare applicant during this strenuous time
of his or her life. The new office shows respect for applicants
and lets them know they are important.

> writer's
> descriptive
> example

> writer's
> concluding point

Without looking back at the example, name some of the things attributed
to the city's welfare office. The reason you are able to name several things is
because you were provided with detailed descriptions. Notice also that the description is used to get the writer's point across about the office's positive effect on clients.

Description and **narration** are just two modes you can use to create your
own arguments. See Chapters 15 and 16 for more on the modes.

Using Sources to Make Your Point

Research

Another way to present your ideas is to support them with quotes from professional writers. If you can present authoritative statements from published
authors, your argument will be more convincing. What is essential with this
approach is that you must develop your own argument first and then find authors who support your ideas. If you collect your sources first, you may be
overly influenced by what they say and just wind up repeating their ideas
rather than presenting your own ideas with support. The following body paragraph discusses the issue of welfare and incorporates quotes to support the
writer's argument.

One problem with society's ideas about welfare recipients is
our failure to see who the real beneficiaries are—children. Although we think of adults—lazy ones at that—as the ones who
receive the benefits of welfare, it is really the children of welfare parents that our tax dollars support. National studies have
shown, "The majority of those on welfare are women with children under five years of age" (Gregory 31). These are women
who do not choose to be on the welfare roles. One researcher
notes, "Many of the women on welfare rolls are women who are
victims of domestic violence" (Richardson 12). It takes a coura-
geous woman to flee an abusive relationship and try to make a
life for herself and her children. What is most important to these
women is the welfare of their children. These are not women

> topic
> sentence

> writer's
> discussion with
> supportive
> quotes

who have chosen welfare over working. These are women fight-⎤   writer's
ing for their children's safety and security. We forget that chil-⎟ concluding point
dren benefit most from our country's welfare program. ⎦

Research

This paragraph focuses on the topic of children and society's failure to see them as the true beneficiaries of our nation's welfare program. The writer has used quotes from studies on welfare to establish certain facts about welfare recipients. However, the writer is in control of this paragraph and uses the quotes to forward and support her ideas. For more examples on how to use sources, see Chapter 18.

There are many ways to construct body paragraphs. This chapter has shown you just a few. If you are writing an argumentative essay in response to a single reading, the body paragraph structure shown at the beginning of this chapter is recommended. For example, if you are writing in response to the prompt that asks if you agree with Mathabane's attitude toward rules and rituals, the balanced paragraph model presented in the beginning of this chapter is a good one to use. However, for other assignments, some of the structures discussed on the last few pages may be better.

What You've Done

■ Constructed body paragraphs that include the following

    A topic sentence

    A discussion of one of the author's ideas

    Examples and your argument

    A conclusion supporting your thesis

For More Strategies for Body Paragraphs

■ See Chapters 15 and 16 on the modes

The Next Step

■ Write a conclusion (Chapter 10)

10 Writing Conclusions

What You've Done

- Created an introduction
- Created body paragraphs

What You Need to Do Next

- Write a final paragraph to end the essay, in which you will do the following

  Summarize ideas from the reading

  Review the main points you've made responding to the reading

  Review your own main idea
- Put the entire essay together

Many inexperienced writers are so grateful to reach the point of writing a **conclusion** that they are tempted to put almost anything in the last paragraph. Experienced writers remember that the conclusion gives the reader the last impression of their writing and that it's important to end an essay well—with power, with style, with something substantial still to say. The conclusion can make or break the essay.

THE COMPONENTS OF A CONCLUSION

Although a conclusion can function in several different ways, it generally should recap the major ideas presented in your essay. You should quickly remind the reader of the following.

- The author's **thesis** or point of the reading you're discussing
- The main points from the reading you're discussing
- The main points you have made in response to the reading
- Your thesis (reworded so it isn't a repetition of the thesis in your introduction)

The Conclusion
The author's thesis
Main points of the reading
Your main points
Restated thesis

A good conclusion should wrap up an essay and present one final thought. You can discuss how you feel about the issue described in the reading, you can present a solution to a problem described in the essay, you can make a prediction about what will happen in the future, or you can finish something you started in the **introduction**—answer a question, finish a story. What you don't want to do is merely repeat the thesis in your conclusion and do nothing else.

EXAMPLE 1

I think rituals are bad because of the negative effect they have on the family. Mathabane didn't like to participate in them. He was often punished for not following the rules or rituals that his father followed. My experiences have been very similar.

In this conclusion, the writer has only restated the thesis and provided generalizations. Such a conclusion certainly lets the reader know that the writer is at the end, but it doesn't strongly pull together the writer's main ideas and points, indicating to the reader that the writer has nothing more to say. This conclusion makes little reference to the reading. After reading several pages of an essay, a reader needs a good **summary** that reviews the essay's main ideas.

EXAMPLE 2

Rules can help keep things running smoothly, and rituals can help us preserve traditions, but sometimes they can create problems. The rules and rituals Mathabane had to follow ⎤
bewildered and embarrassed him because they were lacking a ⎬ author's thesis and main point
valid purpose. Like Mathabane, I have had to follow senseless ⎦
rules. I have witnessed people engaging in rituals that are ⎤
meaningless, and I have been humiliated by participating in ⎬ writer's main points
rituals. My experiences lead me to agree with Mathabane: ⎦
rules and rituals are often senseless and without purpose or ⎤ writer's thesis
value. ⎦

This conclusion does more than simply restate the thesis. It also refers to the reading as well as the main points the writer has made. These statements sum up the major ideas presented in the essay.

PUTTING IT ALL TOGETHER

Let's now take a look at a whole essay with all the parts put together. We've selected some of the sample **body paragraphs** we examined in Chapter 9. **Transitions** have been added to help unite the body paragraphs. The second body paragraph in the following essay is based on the model paragraph presented in Chapter 9 (p. 170). Because it appears as the second body paragraph, a transition has been added to relate it to the paragraph it follows.

Many people feel that rituals are a thing of the past, practiced only by primitive people. They feel that rituals have little place in a modern society that is driven by technology and science. Rituals, they would say, are just superstitions acted out. Mark Mathabane is one of those people who detests rituals. In "My Father's Tribal Rule," he tells us about his experiences growing up in South Africa in a shantytown of rundown huts for people who had been forced off their ancestral, tribal lands. Even though Mathabane and the children in the area were interested in modern ways, Mathabane's father insisted that their family stick to the tribal traditions. Mathabane eventually came to hate his father for making him follow the tribal rituals. Despite his father's insistence that he follow the rules and practice the rituals, Mathabane thought they made no sense. Mathabane is right to think that many rules and rituals serve no purpose. Rules are supposed to be applied equally; however, they often unfairly punish certain people. Although some rituals have value, there are many pointless rituals that people blindly follow. Certain rituals force people to do things they don't want to do and can lead to embarrassing situations

— lead-in

— author and title of reading

— overview of reading

— author's thesis

— writer's thesis

— plan of development

Even though many rituals are meaningful, some rituals are practiced in such a way that they become meaningless. Although Mathabane doesn't explain what he had to do, he tells us that he had to perform "rituals spanning the range of day-to-day living." He had to do rituals "to prevent [the family] from becoming sick, to safeguard his [father's] job, to keep the police away, to bring [the family] good luck" and more. Mathabane said that these rituals didn't make any sense to him. How can performing rituals bring luck or prevent you from becoming sick? There's one specific ritual that makes little sense to me. The fourth Thursday of November, my husband, my daughter, and I go to my parents' house for Thanksgiving. It is always held at my parents' house. My mother won't let anyone else host the gathering. We arrive along with cousins, aunts, and uncles, many of whom we have little in common with.

— topic sentence

— discussion of reading

— writer's example

Then we all try to be pleasant, make small talk, and smile. Dinner is always a disaster. When the potatoes are done, the turkey isn't. When the turkey is done, the potatoes are dry and cold. The women, of course, do all the work. For the most part, we just get in each other's way as we try to prepare the meal. Even before we sit down to eat, I'm battling a severe case of stress. Thanksgiving is the day when you're supposed to give thanks, but the only thing I'm thankful for is when it's over. The Pilgrims celebrated the first Thanksgiving for a reason— they had survived in a new and bountiful land. We never share what we are thankful for. Because our family has lost sight of the purpose of this ritual, it is as senseless as the confusing rituals Mathabane had to follow.

Some rituals seem senseless, but some rituals can make us act in ways we don't want to and can lead to embarrassing situations. Mathabane tells about his father wearing the traditional tribal clothing while he wanted to wear modern clothing. He says that when his father wore his traditional tribal clothes, the other children would laugh at both of them. Mathabane says he became "the laughingstock of [his] friends." He goes on to say, "Whenever they laughed at me I would feel embarrassed and would cry." I'm sure Mathabane wanted to be proud of his father, but this ritual just embarrassed him and made him cry. I personally have experienced firsthand the negative effects of rituals. There is a ritual we perform every year at work. We select names out of a hat, so we can be someone's Santa for that Christmas. Every year I go through the same thing. I don't know what to buy the person. Although there is a twenty dollar limit on the gift, I always spend more, because I don't want this person I hardly know to think I'm cheap. I'm sure everyone else goes through the same thing. Then on the last day of work before Christmas, we open our gifts and pretend to be overjoyed at a present we don't even want. Last year was the worst. I bought a basket of cheeses, smoked meats, and wine for a coworker who turned out to be an herb tea sipping vegetarian. It wasn't my fault. I didn't really know him, but I was humiliated when I found out. Mathabane's father's rituals brought shame on him, just as this office ritual embarrassed me. Some rituals should be abolished because they embarrass people.

Margin annotations:

writer's example

concluding point supporting the writer's thesis

topic sentence with transition

discussion of the reading

writer's example

concluding point supporting the writer's thesis

Whereas rituals can be embarrassing, rules can often lead to certain people being treated unfairly. Mathabane's father didn't allow talking at the dinner table. Mathabane tells us that "One day I intentionally broke one of these laws: I talked while eating." His father's response was to beat young Mathabane with his belt. Mathabane's father never explains why this rule exists. Like many rules, they exist, but no one questions the fairness of the rule. When Mathabane did, he was unfairly punished. Where I work, we have a rule that causes some people to be unfairly punished. We are given five sick days a year. After that, your pay is docked for each day you're out. I'm never out sick more than two or three days a year. I don't abuse the policy by taking "mental health" days. However, each of the last two years, I've had my pay docked because I used more than my allotted sick days. I wasn't abusing this rule. I was simply taking care of my child as any mother would. I can't help it if my daughter is too sick to go to school or needs to go to the doctor. Women with children should have additional sick leave for these emergencies. When I have to call in with a sick child, my supervisor always makes me feel like I'm avoiding doing my work, like I'm not a good employee. Five days of sick leave is not enough for a mother, because she has to have sick days for herself and her child. Mathabane was unfairly punished for the "crime" he committed, just as I am unfairly punished. Although I don't intentionally break this rule like Mathabane did, I still pay for breaking it. Some rules are good, but some need to be changed or eliminated.

topic sentence with transition

discussion of the reading

writer's example

concluding point supporting the writer's thesis

Rules can help keep things running smoothly, and rituals can help us preserve traditions, but sometimes they can create problems. The rules and rituals Mathabane had to follow confused and embarrassed him because they were lacking a valid purpose. Like Mathabane, I have witnessed people engaging in rituals that are meaningless, and I have been humiliated by participating in rituals. I have also had to follow senseless rules. My experiences lead me to agree with Mathabane: rules and rituals are often senseless and without purpose or value.

author's thesis and main point

writer's main points

writer's thesis

This essay contains all the general elements needed for an essay that responds to a reading.

In Exercise 10.1, we look at another essay written on the same **prompt**. This essay, however, takes the opposite approach to the prompt, arguing that

Mathabane's attitude toward rituals is wrong and that rules and rituals do have value and purpose. In the next chapter, this essay, a first **draft** with many problems, will be revised.

Parts of an Essay

Does the introduction contain the following?

- A lead-in
- An identification of the author and title of the reading
- An overview of the reading
- The author's thesis or point
- A thesis statement (responding to the prompt)
- A plan of development

Do the body paragraphs contain the following?

- A topic sentence (with transitions in paragraphs 3 and 4)
- A focus on a specific area of the reading
- An argument or example from the writer's experiences
- A point to conclude the paragraph supportive of the writer's thesis

Does the conclusion contain the following elements?

- The author's thesis or point of the reading
- The main issues from the reading
- The main points you have made in response to the reading
- A restatement of the thesis (reworded so it isn't a repetition of the thesis in the introduction)

EXERCISE 10.1

Read the following essay to see if it contains the elements discussed in Chapters 8 through 10. What problems do you see? What changes need to be made? Examine this essay and try to identify the problems. Then look at the analysis in the next chapter to see how many of the problems in the essay you identified.

Rules and rituals are things people do. Everyday we follow some kind of rules. We also participate in rituals, although we might not know it. Mark Mathabane knew he participated in rituals. More than he wanted to. He lived with his family in a poor section of South Africa. His father was from the tribes, but they were now living around people who had accepted modern ways. Ways that Mathabane wanted to follow. His father insisted that the whole family follow tribal rules and rituals, he became angry and violent when Mathabane wouldn't obey the rules or follow the traditions. Mathabane writes about his hatred of rules and rituals in "My Father's Tribal Rule" but I think that rules and rituals do have purpose and value.

Mathabane tells about the rule his father had about not speaking at the table. He tells us that "One day I intentionally broke one of these laws." He spoke during dinner and his father got really mad then he threatened to beat Mathabane. What Mathabane didn't understand was that his father got mad because Mathabane wasn't respecting him. In my family, we have a dinnertime ritual too. Before dinner, my brothers and my sister and I are supposed to clean the house and get everything ready for dinner. One day I didn't feel like doing it, because I have to do everything. My brothers and my sister hardly do anything. So, I just sat on the couch and watched TV. My father came in and saw me and started to yell at me. He said he worked hard every day to put food on the table and that I was showing disrespect to him, my mother, my brothers and my sister. He sent me to bed without supper. At first I was really mad. But the more I thought about it, the more I felt bad for not respecting my father. I learned through this rule to respect my father, Mathabane didn't see the valuable things you can learn from rules.

Following rituals can also help us be more mature. Mathabane showed that he was immature because he disobeyed his father simply for the purpose of rebelling. He had no reason to talk at the table except he wanted to make his father angry and see what he would do. When I was younger, I was suppose to clean my room first thing every Saturday morning. Since I would rather play than clean my room, I would put it off as long as possible. If I had been more mature, I would have realized that cleaning my room was my responsibility and I would have done it without trying to get out of it. Also I should have realized that my jobs before dinner were my jobs, whether my brothers and sister did their jobs or not should not have mattered. Being that I was the oldest, I should have had the maturity to set a good example for them by obeying the rules. Mathabane could have shown his maturity by obeying his father's rules rather than disobeying him just because he didn't like it. Doing rituals, particularly if they aren't ones we enjoy, builds maturity because we will have to do things we don't like our whole lives.

Mathabane tells us about his little brother George. It was time for George to be weaned and so "she smeared her breasts with red pepper and then invited my brother to suckle." Of course, George's mouth must of burned like fire so he stopped nursing. Mathabane thought, "It was amusing to witness my mother do it." He just saw this ritual as being funny. He didn't understand that it had a purpose "to mark George's passage from infancy to childhood." My friend Alan went through a passage similar to George's. Alan's family has a lot of money.

His parents had bought cars for his older brother and sister when they turned sixteen. They bought Alan one when he turned sixteen, but they told him that driving a car meant that he had to be very responsible. They told him that driving a car meant that he was no longer a kid, he was now a adult. It's strange, but owning that car really did change him. I guess he realized that you can't act irresponsibly when your driving several tons of steel.

Also, the rituals we do everyday can help the whole family. Mathabane had to do "rituals spanning the range of day-to-day living." Everybody does daily rituals. In our house, these daily rituals are divided up. Every evening before bed, for instance, its my job to make sure all the doors are locked and the windows shut and latched. My sister irons my father's shirts so he'll have a fresh one for work. My father gets lunch ready for everybody. My mother supervises and helps who ever needs help. Although Mathabane may be confused by these rituals, I'm not.

In conclusion, Mathabane just doesn't get it. He thinks rules and rituals are just a waste of time. He doesn't see how they can help us learn to respect others and be more courteous to them. I think that Mathabane was too immature to understand that rituals can help us grow up. They can help develop self-responsibility, which is something most people could use more of. Mathabane only thinks about himself and that's why he doesn't want to do the rituals that help the whole family. Basically he wrong. Rules and rituals are something we should follow and practice.

CONCLUSIONS TO ESSAYS ON ISSUES

There are many ways to conclude your essay. Previously in this chapter, we have discussed the structure of conclusions in essays that respond to a reading. However, your instructor may give an assignment that asks you to respond to an issue rather than a single reading. If you are writing an essay on a controversial issue, you might use your conclusion to do more than just sum up your main points and restate your thesis. Conclusions can also do the following.

- Provide a solution to a problem
- Predict what might happen
- Conclude a story you have begun elsewhere in your essay

The conclusion that follows discusses solutions to some of the problems presented in an essay on welfare.

Many writers point out the problems that people on welfare encounter. One problem discussed by these writers is that welfare benefits are so low, welfare mothers can't afford daycare for their children. As a result, many mothers are forced to stay at home with their children rather than look for work. Welfare mothers are forced into staying at home because they don't have the money they need for childcare. If the government really wants these women off the welfare roles, then the government will have to do more for them. One essential thing the government should do is create daycare centers for those on welfare. These centers should be free to those receiving welfare benefits. This would allow a mother to look for work, knowing that her children are being properly fed and cared for. A mother's first priority is her children. If a mother knows that her children are cared for, she can turn to her second priority, finding a job or receiving the training that will lead to a decent job. Without this assistance, it is unlikely that most mothers will ever get off of welfare. This is probably the most important step the government can take to help welfare moms and, at the same time, reduce welfare roles. Free daycare for welfare recipients should be the next addition to the welfare program.

This paragraph focuses on one of the problems with the welfare system: welfare mothers are forced to stay at home because they can't afford childcare. The writer offers a solution to that problem: free day care for welfare recipients. By providing a solution to the problem raised in the essay, the writer contributes her own original ideas to the issue. Whether or not you are using a reading, offering solutions is often a good way to conclude an essay.

Another strategy is to use your conclusion to make predictions based on the information you have presented in your body paragraphs. Notice how the following conclusion makes some predictions about the future.

Research has revealed several things about the welfare system that need to be changed or our country will continue to suffer the consequences. Since welfare mothers aren't given enough money to pay for day care, they are forced to stay home with their children. Since they must stay home, they can't look for work. Since welfare reform, the amount of time one can stay on welfare is limited. What will happen to these mothers when their time runs out? Five years from now, ten years from now, we will begin to see the results of this policy. Welfare mothers will be expelled from welfare. Where will they go? A likely answer is the streets. Once they are on the streets, who will feed them? These women and their children will probably be fed by relief organizations. And where do these organizations get their money? They get it from the local community. So we will still be paying for these women whether or not they're on welfare. The difference will be that instead of living in the safety of their own homes, they will be living on the streets. If these trends continue, be prepared for the look of your hometown to change. You should be prepared to look the other way when you see a tired mother leading her hungry children down an alleyway searching for food.

This conclusion asked the reader to look five to ten years into the future to see what will happen if welfare mothers are not given the support they need. It paints a grim picture of the streets of America for the reader to consider. One would not have to be responding to a single reading to use this approach.

If you choose the strategy of using a story for your lead-in or a narrative in a body paragraph, you may want to use your conclusion to end the story you've started. In Chapter 9, a writer presented the story of his uncle who was forced out of work and had to rely on welfare. The following conclusion gets back to the story to help the writer make his point.

> Television news shows, even though they purport to be objective, tend to be biased when they do stories on welfare. To boost their ratings, they need a sensational story. They choose to focus on the abuses that take place with welfare. As a result, most people believe that welfare is a lifestyle for people who are conning the system and stealing our tax dollars. However, statistics show that to be untrue. The percentage of people who abuse welfare is very small—smaller than the abuses committed by our elected officials who waste billions of tax dollars. The great majority of welfare recipients are people like my uncle. He was forced to take welfare and he didn't like it. After he got off welfare, he never got back on it again. He has continued to be a hard working taxpayer like everyone else. He, like most welfare recipients, never returned to the welfare rolls. The next time *60 Minutes* or *20/20* does a story on welfare, they should do a piece on my uncle to fairly portray those who have relied on welfare.

Based on this conclusion, we can see that this writer has written an essay attacking the media's biased presentation of welfare recipients. He has brought the story about his uncle back into his conclusion to underscore his point about the false image the public has of welfare recipients.

A conclusion may serve many purposes. It may sum up what has been said in the essay. It may make a recommendation or predict what will happen in the future. These are just a few of the possibilities. As a writer, you must ask yourself what is best for the type of essay you are writing.

Keep in mind that there are a variety of ways to organize the material in your essays. In addition, the content and structure of your introductions, body paragraphs, and conclusions can be changed to meet the needs of the essays you are writing. If you are unsure who your readers are, the general-to-specific structure is advantageous. As a writer, you must consider which structures are best for presenting your subject matter. You must also decide which structures will best convey your ideas to your audience.

The last three chapters have shown you how to develop an introduction, body paragraphs, and a conclusion, and how to put them all together. For good writers, this isn't the end of the process. Revising what you've done may be as important as developing your first draft. The next few chapters will help you polish your essays through revision and editing. In Chapter 11, we will reexamine one of the previous essays on Mark Mathabane's "My Father's Tribal Rule" to determine what needs to be added, deleted, or changed.

What You've Done

- Created a conclusion to summarize the following
    The author's thesis and main points
    Your response and final evaluation
- Put the components of an essay together

The Next Step

- Revise your essay (Chapter 11)

11 Revising
Improving Ideas, Organization, and Style

> ### What You've Done
>
> ■ Drafted your conclusion and seen how it combines with other components of your essay
>
> ### What You Need to Do Next
>
> ■ Prepare to revise the essay
> ■ Make sure the thesis addresses the prompt
> ■ Look again at the organization and structure of the essay
> ■ Look again at the explanations and examples that develop the essay

You have already done more work on this paper than you probably thought possible, and at this point you may be tired of working on it or no longer have the time to work on improving it. However, you should not stop here. Just as the difference between a hacker and a good golfer often involves the follow-through on a shot, the difference between a mediocre essay and a good one is how well the writer follows through in finishing the paper.

To follow through, you need to revise, edit, and proofread. It's important to realize that *each of these is a separate step*. Each step involves making changes to your **draft**, and you may use similar techniques at each of these steps to identify the changes you have to make. Let's look at each step briefly.

1. *Revising:* When you revise your draft, *you are essentially rewriting it*. You will make big changes and may even decide to change your thesis. You may improve your ideas, organization, or development or reconsider the ideas in a reading and how your ideas relate to them. You may also revise at the sentence level, choosing words that are more interesting and creating sentences that express your meaning more clearly.

2. *Editing:* When you edit, *you are making your writing correct* by following the rules of written English. You may edit for clarity, grammar and usage, transitions, punctuation, and spelling.

3. *Formatting and proofreading:* When you proofread, *you are eliminating careless errors.* You are checking to make sure that the words and punctuation on the paper are the ones that you intended to write—not accidents. You will proofread for typographical errors, left-out words, inaccurate quotations, incomplete punctuation, and errors created by revising and editing. You also make sure the format of your essay is correct.

All three of these steps may overlap. You might not realize until you begin editing that you have made a mistake interpreting a quotation, requiring you to revise a whole paragraph. You may edit typographical errors as you are revising for the first time. When you proofread for careless errors, you may find that you need to return to some of the steps of editing to make sure you know correct word forms. That's fine. The point is that you must be sure that you *set aside a separate time for each of the three tasks* because each is essential. This chapter and the next two examine these three steps in detail.

Finishing Your Essay

Revising	Editing	Proofreading
(Chapter 11)	(Chapter 12)	(Chapter 13)
FIRST COMPLETE ROUGH DRAFT	REVISED DRAFT	FIRST GRADABLE DRAFT
Focus on:	Focus on:	Focus on:
Thesis, content, and organization	Language	Corrections and format conventions

THE PROCESS OF REVISION

Steps for Revision

Preparing to revise

Checking the thesis

Checking structure and organization

Checking development

If you think that revision means just recopying everything neatly when your paper is finished, you are mistaken. Revision is a messy process. You are expected to write on your paper, mark out sections, write in the margins or between lines, draw arrows, or even cut your paper into pieces so that you can physically move sections of your essay around. If your draft is neat after you have revised it, you haven't done it right.

It is easier to revise when you have a systematic way of looking for possible improvements. For example, it might be a waste of time to revise your examples if your **thesis** doesn't answer the **prompt**. You would want to be sure that you were fulfilling the assignment before you try to change anything else.

This chapter presents the four main steps that you should follow during revision. It will help you find an organized way to revise all areas of the essay. You may need to repeat some steps, you may need to rethink your thesis, and you may wind up revising your essay several times. Performing these steps carefully will result in a successful final product.

Computer Tips

The revision process is easier if you use a word-processing program such as Word or WordPerfect. These programs allow you to move around parts of your essay and try out different alternatives without recopying or retyping. Here is a list of commands that are useful in revising on a word processor.

- *Cut*—allows you to delete (or erase) text you no longer want
- *Copy*—allows you to make a copy of a section of text so that you can move it somewhere else
- *Paste*—allows you to add text you have copied or cut from another location
- *Save as*—allows you to make a new copy of the file with a new name so you can make changes to it while keeping the old copy intact
- *Insert*—allows you to insert complete files with new material into an existing file

---

STEP 1. PREPARING TO REVISE

Letting the Paper Cool

Once you've finished the first draft of a paper, you may feel you have produced the best paper you can. You may believe you have used all your ideas and have organized them logically. The assignment, any readings you referred to, and your ideas are still fresh in your head, and this can make it hard for you to evaluate your paper objectively. At this point, you should take a break from the paper and let it get "cold," a term writers use to talk about the time they take between the drafting and the revising stages. When you come back to the paper, you are more likely to see ways you can improve on it.

Too often, beginning writers do not allow themselves enough time to adequately complete this step. The amount of time you allow the paper to cool will vary with the amount of time you have. Ideally, wait half a day to a day. If you have less time, at least go do something else so you are not thinking about the paper during this period.

Reading the Paper Again

Pretend that you, like your reader, have not read your essay before. Forget what you meant to say, and try to focus on only what you have said. Read the entire draft all the way through, preferably aloud.

When you read, mark anything that doesn't seem to convey what you meant. Don't worry about **grammar**, **mechanics**, and **usage** at this point. Avoid wasting energy correcting sentence level problems when you may not even keep the sentence. Don't change anything at this point; just mark the places that you have concerns about so you can come back to them in a later step.

Consulting a Reader

Asking someone else to read the paper is another helpful revision technique. This technique is particularly useful if you have problems reading your own words objectively. If you are going to automatically assume that readers will know what you are writing about, it is a good idea to compensate by asking someone to read your paper and then answer questions about it. This way you can find out what parts of your paper other readers might have difficulty understanding.

Involving someone else in your work requires you to think about your attitudes toward constructive criticism. Be aware that it can also be difficult for the reader to feel comfortable offering honest criticism.

Collaboration

Here are some important points to consider when working with another reader in revising.

- Make sure the reader has time to really consider your paper.
- Make sure the reader knows that he or she is helping you improve the paper, not praising or attacking the paper (or you!).
- Tell the reader what your assignment is. Show him or her the written assignment sheet, if possible.
- Tell the reader not to correct grammar or comment on your handwriting or typing skills. Keep the focus on ideas, organization, and development.
- Ask the reader to follow the same steps that you follow in revising. (You can share the lists for evaluating introductions, body paragraphs, and conclusions shown in this chapter.)
- Ask the reader for specific feedback on what works and what doesn't, as well as for suggestions on how to improve your paper.
- Check out possible solutions with your reader. If your reader says that one of your examples is unclear, try out another example before writing it into your paper.

Consider your readers' comments as attempts to be helpful, and don't argue with them. You will decide what to change about your paper, so you don't need to defend your work. You might not agree with all of their suggestions, but you should at least think about them.

Consulting another reader is one way to see if your paper passes the "displacement test." Your paper must communicate effectively—not just to you and not right after you have finished it but to readers who are not familiar with the reading your paper discusses and who do not share your life experiences. If another reader can follow your paper, it is probably clear enough for an instructor to evaluate.

STEP 2: MAKING SURE YOUR THESIS ANSWERS THE QUESTION

Before you begin to revise your essay, make sure your thesis answers the prompt and that the implied connections between it and what will follow in your essay are clear. First, review the prompt. Then look for how the parts of your thesis fit together to provide an answer to the prompt.

Evaluating Your Thesis

 Does Your Thesis Address the Prompt? Remember that your thesis is the answer to a prompt and must clearly respond to it. Let's look again at Mark Mathabane's "My Father's Tribal Rule" (pp. 42–46) and the prompt we have been using.

✔ Checking the Prompt

- ▪ Do the key focus words from the prompt appear in the thesis?
- ▪ Do the actions you are performing in the thesis match the key action specified in the prompt?

Mathabane says he despises rules and rituals. Is he correct in thinking that rules and rituals have no purpose or value?

Before you evaluate how well a thesis provides an answer to a prompt, review the key words and actions you must bring together in the thesis. In the preceding prompt, the key words are "rules," "rituals," "purpose," and "value." The action you have to perform is to agree or disagree with Mathabane's views. Let's now look at some thesis sentences and analyze how well each of them answers the prompt.

- ▪ **Thesis 1: Mathabane talks about rules and rituals. I agree with him.** This thesis does contain the key words "rules" and "rituals," but it does not connect rules and rituals to the remaining key words "purpose" and "value." Also, saying what a writer "talks about" does not explain the writer's idea. Since the idea is not explained or restated, readers will not understand what the writer is agreeing with when the student writes "I agree with him."

- ▪ **Thesis 2: In the essay, Mathabane talks about how he hates the rules and rituals his father made him follow. I have to follow stupid rules, too.** This thesis also contains the key words "rules" and "rituals" and states Mathabane's attitude toward his father's rules and rituals. This statement almost gets to the key words "purpose" and "value" by mentioning hate, which implies that Mathabane does not see any purpose or value in the rules and rituals he discusses. The second sentence of the thesis does contain the writer's response, but it does not fulfill the requirements of the prompt because it does not agree or disagree. It just compares experiences. While the word "stupid" is similar to the word "hate" and implies a judgment of value and purpose, it does not clearly state whether there is purpose and value in the rules and rituals Mathabane and the writer had to follow.

- ■ **Thesis 3: It's wrong for parents to punish their children for not obeying their rules or following their rituals.** This thesis does contain some of the key words, but it does not complete the key action given in the prompt: to agree or disagree with Mathabane's attitude toward the purpose and value of rules and rituals. Whether or not parents should punish their children for not obeying rules or following rituals is not the same issue as whether those rules and rituals have purpose and value. The idea of obedience and punishment is not related to the question posed in the prompt.

- ■ **Thesis 4: Mathabane is wrong because rules and rituals do help young people grow up to be good adults.** This thesis does state the direction of the paper: that rules and rituals help young people grow up to be good adults. However, unless the writer has already explained what Mathabane believes about rules and rituals, this sentence alone does not fully reflect Mathabane's idea, although it is more specific about the writer's idea.

Let's look at the thesis of the paper drafted in Chapter 10 (pp. 189–191) and see if it addresses the prompt.

Mathabane writes about his hatred of rules and rituals in "My Father's Tribal Rule," but I think that rules and rituals do have purpose and value.

This thesis does contain the key words "rules," "rituals," "purpose," and "value." It also implies the key action of disagreeing (as shown in the word "but"). However, it doesn't clearly state Mathabane's ideas.

REVISED THESIS:

Mathabane writes that he hates rules and rituals in "My Father's Tribal Rule." Although Mathabane disliked rules and rituals, he didn't see that they can be valuable and that they do have a purpose.

Using "that" instead of "about" and adding the phrase "although Mathabane disliked rules and rituals" make Mathabane's ideas clearer. The phrase "he didn't see that" shows that the writer sees purpose and value that Mathabane does not, implying disagreement.

Does Everything in Your Thesis Clearly Relate to the Prompt? Once you have determined that you have addressed the prompt by using the key focus words and key action words, you will need to be sure that everything in your thesis is related to the prompt. As you review your thesis, also evaluate how well your plan of development connects to it and the prompt. Many times the parts of your thesis and plan of development will be connected to the prompt, but that connection may not be clear to your reader. In this case, you will need to rephrase the thesis and plan of development to make the connections clear.

Looking for Connections

- State the connection between the parts of your paper.
- Write down that connection.
- Revise the connection to fit in your paper.

For example, consider the following (underlined) thesis and plan of development.

> Mathabane is right to think that rules and rituals are worthless, especially when they have no purpose and they benefit no one. Rules are just something authority figures use to push people around. Furthermore, they can make you feel separated from other people.

The thesis does contain the key words "rules," "rituals," and "purpose," and it refers to "value" by using the word "worthless." It also performs the key action of agreeing (as shown in "Mathabane is right"). The sentence after the thesis, however, is more about why we have rules than whether they have value.

Using the Looking for Connections box, state the relationship between the three ideas in the thesis and the answer that rules and rituals are worthless. The first idea that develops the thesis is already connected.

> *First idea:* Rules and rituals are worthless, especially when they have no purpose and they benefit no one.

What is the connection between the answer the thesis provides and the second idea?

> *Thesis:* Mathabane is right to think that rules and rituals are worthless.

Second idea: Rules are just something authority figures use to push people around.

The second idea defines one function of rules: controlling other people. The second idea does not say directly that this is not valuable. A reader must infer that you believe rules are used only to push people around, have no good purpose, and are worthless. To connect the idea to the thesis, you have to make this clear. Add a phrase that expresses your opinion about the value of rules that have no real function except to let some people control others.

Revised second idea: Rules and rituals are worthless if their only purpose is so authority figures can push other people around.

What is the connection between the thesis and the third idea?

Thesis: Mathabane is right to think that rules and rituals are worthless

Third idea: They [rules] can make you feel separated from other people.

"Making people feel separated" is not really about a purpose; it's more about having a bad effect. Again, explain that "making people feel separated" is not a good purpose for rules. Rules whose only function is to separate others are not valuable.

Revised third idea: Rules and rituals are worthless if they make you feel separated from other people.

Now we can put the parts of the thesis and plan of development back together again, showing the relationship between the answer and each of the main ideas. How? First, you have to express your opinion clearly (it is an "agree or disagree" prompt), using the key words. Then show how undesirable purposes and values of rules have negative consequences.

Rules and rituals are worthless if they have no purpose, and if they benefit no one, if their only purpose is so authority figures can push people around, and if they make you feel separated from other people.

Notice that a clear thesis uses the key words as a starting point and clearly indicates the action needed to answer the question. A thesis can become even more understandable if you show how the rest of the paper will develop its key ideas. This addition is called a plan of development, and it is discussed under Step 4: Checking Development (page 210).

EXERCISE 11.1   Revise thesis sentences 1–4 on pages 199–200.

EXERCISE 11.2   Use the suggestions for revision to evaluate how well the following thesis sentences match the writing prompts. Revise them if necessary.

1. Mathabane writes less about his mother than about his father or himself. What is the significance of her role in the family? Do you think other women play similar roles in their families?

   A. Mathabane's mother plays an important role in his family.

   B. I agree with Mathabane that women play the role of peacemaker in their families.

   C. I think other women play similar roles in their families as Mathabane's mother.

   D. The women I know are caregivers, peacemakers, and housewives, just like Mathabane's mother.

2. Mathabane has a conflict with his father. Do parents and children always have conflicts? Why or why not?

   A. No, they don't have to have conflicts if parents would just consider their children's feelings.

   B. I have conflicts with my parents just like Mathabane.

   C. Yes, because the older generation never understands the younger generation.

   D. Parents and children have to have conflicts in order for the children to grow into independent adults.

3. Mathabane says he despises rules and rituals. Is he correct in thinking that rules and rituals have no purpose or value?

   A. I disagree with Mathabane because rituals do have a purpose even though children are not able to understand.

   B I agree with Mathabane because I had to make similar choices, and I resented them.

   C. Mathabane is correct in saying that rules and rituals have no purpose or value.

   D. Although rituals do have good purposes, parents should allow their children the freedom to choose between the family's rituals and those of their friends.

EXERCISE 11.3   **Evaluate and revise the thesis and plan of development of one of your own papers. Use the Checking the Prompt box (page 199) and Looking for Connections box (page 201).**

EXERCISE 11.4	Work with a classmate to evaluate each other's thesis statements and plans of development. Use the Checking the Prompt and Looking for Connections boxes on pages 199 and 201. Review the suggestions for working with another reader (on page 198) before you begin. Use the suggestions from your partner to revise your work.

Collaboration

STEP 3. CHECKING STRUCTURE AND ORGANIZATION

Are All the Parts of the Essay Present?

Label the parts of your paper (**introduction**, **body** paragraphs, and **conclusion**). If you cannot find one of the parts, chances are your reader won't find it either. You will need to write the missing part.

As we discussed in Chapters 8–10, you would expect to have the following components shown here in any essay responding to a reading.

Parts of an Essay

Introduction
- A lead-in
- An overview of the reading
- A thesis statement (responding to the prompt)
- A plan of development

Body paragraphs
- A topic sentence (with transitions in paragraphs 3 and 4)
- A focus on a specific area of the reading
- An example from the writer's experiences
- A point to conclude the paragraph

Conclusion
- The author's thesis or point of the reading you're discussing
- The main points from the reading you're discussing
- The main points you have made in response to the reading
- A restatement of the thesis (reworded so it isn't a repetition of the thesis in the introduction)

EXERCISE 11.5	Using the box above, label the parts of the following essay.

Rules and rituals are things people do. Every day we follow some kind of rules. We also participate in rituals, although we might not know it. Mark Mathabane knew he participated in rituals. More than he wanted to.

He lived with his family in a poor section of South Africa. His father was from the tribes, but they were now living around people who had accepted modern ways. Ways that Mathabane wanted to follow. His father insisted that the whole family follow tribal rules and rituals, and he became angry and violent when Mathabane wouldn't obey the rules or follow the traditions. Mathabane writes about his hatred of rules and rituals in "My Father's Tribal Rule" but I think that rules and rituals do have purpose and value.

Mathabane tells about the rule his father had about not speaking at the table. He tells us that "One day I intentionally broke one of these laws." He spoke during dinner and his father got really mad then he threatened to beat Mathabane. What Mathabane didn't understand was that his father got mad because Mathabane wasn't respecting him. In my family, we have a dinnertime ritual too. Before dinner, my brothers and my sister and I are supposed to clean the house and get everything ready for dinner. One day I didn't feel like doing it, because I have to do everything. My brothers and my sister hardly do anything and I didn't think it was fair that they played in the yard with their friends while I was working. So, I just sat on the couch and watched TV. My father came in and saw me and started to yell at me. He said he worked hard every day to put food on the table and that I was showing disrespect to him, my mother, my brothers and my sister. He sent me to bed without supper. At first I was really mad. But the more I thought about it, the more I felt bad for not respecting my father. I learned through this rule to respect my father, Mathabane didn't see the valuable things you can learn from rules.

Following rituals can also help us be more mature. Mathabane showed that he was immature because he disobeyed his father simply for the purpose of rebelling. He had no reason to talk at the table except he wanted to make his father angry and see what he would do. When I was younger, I was suppose to clean my room first thing every Saturday morning. Since I would rather play than clean my room, I would put it off as long as possible. If I had been more mature, I would have realized that cleaning my room was my responsibility and I would have done it without trying to get out of it. Also I should have realized that my jobs before dinner were my jobs, whether my brothers and sister did their jobs are not should not have mattered. Being that I was the oldest, I should have had the maturity to set a good example for them by obeying the rules. Mathabane could have shown his maturity by obeying his father's rules rather than disobeying him just because he didn't like it. Doing rituals, particularly if they aren't ones we enjoy, builds maturity because we will have to do things we don't like our whole lives.

Mathabane tells us about his little brother George. It was time for George to be weaned and so "she smeared her breasts with red pepper and then invited my brother to suckle." Of course, George's mouth must have burned like fire so he stopped nursing. Mathabane thought, "It was amusing to witness my mother do it." He just saw this ritual as being funny. He didn't understand that it had a purpose "to mark George's passage from infancy to childhood." Some rituals help us to grow up and realize our new responsibilities. My friend Alan went through a passage similar to George's. Alan's family has a lot of money. His parents had bought cars for his older brother and sister when they turned sixteen. They bought Alan one when he turned sixteen, but they told him that driving a car meant that he had to be very responsible. They told him that driving a car meant that he was no longer a kid, he was now a adult. It's strange, but owning that car really did change him. I guess he realized that you can't act irresponsibly when you're driving several tons of steel.

Also, the rituals we do every day can help the whole family. Mathabane had to do "rituals spanning the range of day-to-day living." Everybody does daily rituals. In our house, these daily rituals are divided up. Every evening before bed, for instance, its my job to make sure all the doors are locked and the windows shut and latched. My sister irons my father's shirts so he'll have a fresh one for work. My father gets lunch ready for everybody. My mother supervises and helps who ever needs help. Although Mathabane may be confused by these rituals, I'm not.

In conclusion, Mathabane just doesn't get it. He thinks rules and rituals are just a waste of time. He doesn't see how they can help us learn to respect others and be more courteous to them. I think that Mathabane was too immature to understand that rituals can help us grow up. They can help develop self-responsibility, which is something most people could use more of. Basically he wrong. Rules and rituals are something you should follow and practice. If everyone followed the rules and rituals they were taught at home, the world would be a better place.

When you read over the essay, did you notice any missing parts to the introduction, the body paragraphs, or the conclusion? If so, make a note of them. They will have to be added.

Before you add a lot to your essay, check once again to see that each body paragraph supports the thesis. The best way to do that is to first find the main idea of each paragraph. The simplest way to check that a body paragraph supports the thesis is to look for one sentence that expresses this idea clearly, a topic sentence. This sentence is often at the very beginning of each body paragraph.

Does the Main Idea of Each Body Paragraph Correspond to Some Part of the Thesis?

Since the main ideas of each body paragraph are ways of supporting the thesis, the main ideas and the thesis should match. If they don't match, you have two options. You can revise the main idea and paragraph that does not match the thesis, or you can revise the thesis so that it includes the main idea. However, if you choose this second option, you must be sure that your thesis still answers the prompt. In other words, after revising your thesis, you might have to revise the entire essay again.

Look at the revised thesis sentence from the essay drafted in Chapter 10 and reprinted on pages 204–206, along with a list of the main ideas from each of the body paragraphs.

> Mathabane writes about his hatred of rules and rituals in "My Father's Tribal Rule," but I think that rules, and rituals do have purpose and value.

■ **Main idea of body paragraph 1:** There is no clear main idea in this paragraph that states a general purpose or value of rules and rituals. The two examples (Mathabane's experience and the writer's experience) are related, but there is not one sentence that clearly ties them together. Using the Looking for Connections checklist on page 201, state the connection between the two examples, and write that connection down.

> Rules and rituals help us learn to show respect for others.

While the main idea of a body paragraph does not have to be the first sentence, it is often helpful to have a clear topic sentence to begin the first body paragraph. Inserting this sentence at the beginning of the paragraph helps your reader connect your thesis and your first body paragraph.

■ **Main idea of body paragraph 2:**

> Following rituals can also help us be more mature.

This main idea is the first sentence of the paragraph and is clearly related to the thesis, since it states another benefit or value of rituals.

■ **Main idea of body paragraph 3:**

> Some rituals help us to grow up and realize our new responsibilities.

In other body paragraphs, it may be helpful to give some introductory information before the main idea. The first six sentences of this paragraph provide that information, which leads into the seventh sentence. It is this sentence that really states the idea that governs the body paragraph.

■ **Main idea of body paragraph 4:**

> Also, the rituals we do every day can help the whole family.

This main idea is the first sentence of the paragraph and is clearly related to the thesis, since it states another benefit or value of rituals.

The main ideas of body paragraphs 1–4 are related to the thesis. We don't have to eliminate any main ideas in the body completely, but we will check how the main ideas are developed in Step 4: Checking Development (page 210). We may still want to revise the body paragraphs to make our ideas clearer and to arrange our ideas in the most effective way.

EXERCISE 11.6

Use the suggestions for revision to evaluate how well the following main ideas match the corresponding thesis sentences.

1. Parents and children have to have conflicts in order for the children to grow into independent adults.
   A. Children have to learn to think for themselves.
   B. It's normal for children to break rules just for fun and to find out what will happen.
   C. Parents are old-fashioned, and children want to keep up with the times by listening to the newest music and wearing the coolest clothes.
   D. Parents do know what's best, but children still have to rebel.

2. If children honor their parents the way they should, then parents and children won't have conflicts.
   A. Honoring parents means obeying them.
   B. Children should obey their parents until they are at least 18 and out on their own.
   C. Conflicts are okay between parents and children as long as children learn that their parents are always right.
   D. When children have kids of their own, then they'll understand that their parents were right.

3. Like Mathabane's mother, the women I know act as peacemakers, caregivers, and teachers in their families.
   A. Many women act as peacemakers, making sure family members talk to each other instead of sulking.
   B. Most women take care of the children and the men in the family.
   C. Many modern men are also taking care of the children.
   D. Whenever I didn't understand why my parents wouldn't let me do something I wanted to do, my aunt would always explain it to me in a way that I could understand their point.

Are the Paragraphs Arranged in the Best Order?

You will want to give your ideas in an order that your reader will understand and that will have the effect on the reader that you want. Since the purpose, audience, and effect for every writing task is different, no one **organization** will fit every time. You will want to choose the organization that is most appropriate for what you are trying to do in your essay.

The order of the paragraphs should reveal a reason—in other words, the reader can see why the paragraphs are ordered as they are. (Review the types of organization presented on drafting in Chapter 7.)

Often when responding to a reading, inexperienced writers organize their paper by discussing the reading in one section and their own ideas and experiences in another. While this can be an acceptable way to organize an essay, it also tends to be simplistic and should be avoided.

EXERCISE 11.7

Turn back to the essay on pages 204–206, and do the following.

1. Write down the thesis of the paper. Then list the main idea of each paragraph below the thesis.

2. Using the suggestions for organization presented in this chapter, determine the organizational pattern the writer has used for ordering the body paragraphs.

3. Suggest a more effective order for the body paragraphs. Be sure that you can explain why you think your order is more effective.

EXERCISE 11.8

For more practice, complete steps 2 and 3 with the following thesis and main ideas.

■ Thesis

Mathabane is right to think that rules and rituals are worthless. Rules and rituals are worthless when they have no purpose and benefit no one, if their only purpose is so authority figures can push people around, and if they make you feel separated from other people.

■ Main idea of body paragraph 1

Rules and rituals are worthless if they make you feel separated from other people.

■ Main idea of body paragraph 2

Parents should always explain why they want their children to follow their rules when they are different from their friends' rules.

■ Main idea of body paragraph 3

The problem is not that parents insist that the children keep the ritual; it's that parents don't explain to the children what the ritual means and why it is important.

■ Main idea of body paragraph 4

In addition to lessons about respecting others, rituals can teach us about traditions.

EXERCISE 11.9

Collaboration

Work with a classmate to evaluate each other's essays for structure and organization. Use the Parts of an Essay checklist on page 204. Review the types of organization presented in Chapter 7 for help in determining if the paragraphs are arranged in the best order (pages 141–142). Keep in mind the suggestions for working with another reader (on page 198) as you work. Use the suggestions from your partner to revise your work.

STEP 4. CHECKING DEVELOPMENT

Evaluating Your Introduction

How many paragraphs make up your introduction? In short papers, usually one paragraph is enough. Often students will write one paragraph for the **lead-in**, one for the summary of the reading, and one for their thesis. However, if these sections are relatively short, they should be combined into one introductory paragraph.

In Chapter 8, we suggested a five-part introduction when responding to a reading. At this point, you should check your introduction to ensure that the essay includes these sections and that what you have written fits together. Beginning writers tend to evaluate the introduction as a whole to see if it all makes sense together. However, good revising requires that you break the introduction into its parts and evaluate each part by itself to ensure that it can stand alone and still make sense to the reader.

Evaluating Your Lead-in   The lead-in includes all material from the very beginning of the essay until the summary of the reading. Now that you have separated it from the rest of the introduction, evaluate your lead-in based on the following checklist.

✓ *Checklist for Lead-ins*

■ Does the introduction include a lead-in?

■ Is the lead-in too long and/or too detailed for the paper?

■ Is the lead-in too short and/or too sparse for the paper?

■ Does the lead-in relate to the summary of the reading and the thesis?

■ Does the lead-in present interesting material that makes the reader want to continue reading?

Let's look at the following lead-in for an essay.

> Rules and rituals are things people do. Every day we follow some kind of rules. We also participate in rituals, although we might not know it. Mark Mathabane knew he participated in rituals. More than he wanted to.

The lead-in introduces the topic of rules and rituals but says nothing about purpose and value. In addition, the information provided is not especially helpful; "things people do" does not distinguish rules and rituals from many other things, nor is this information interesting.

To revise, you might want to go back to Chapter 8 and review the types of lead-ins you can choose from. Here's an example of a more compelling lead-in.

> As a child, I assumed that every family did things exactly like mine did. It wasn't until I spent a summer vacation with my best friend's family that I realized this wasn't true. The members of his family got up and grabbed bagels for breakfast, while my family always sat down to pancakes or scrambled eggs every morning. In my family, we all had assigned chores, but in his family, his mother took care of the house by herself. That summer I learned that I participated in rules and rituals that other families didn't necessarily follow. Mark Mathabane knew he participated in rituals. More than he wanted to.

This new lead-in provides a story, a technique that often can catch a reader's interest. The story also provides an example of a ritual and of a rule so the writer doesn't have to actually define them. In addition, this lead-in provides a direct connection to the summary of the reading, the idea of realizing that the writer participated in rituals.

EXERCISE 11.10 **Using the checklist for lead-ins on page 210, evaluate the effectiveness of the following lead-ins to essays on this topic.**

1. My father had weird rules when I was young.
2. Do you have to follow rules?
3. Rules are good for young people.
4. *Webster's* defines rules as "an authoritative prescribed direction for conduct." *Webster's* defines rituals as "a ceremonial act or series of such acts."
5. Have you ever been to South Africa? Have you ever had to wear tribal clothes?

Evaluating the Summary Based on the model we've discussed in this book, the **summary** of the reading is the material between the lead-in and the thesis. It includes information about the reading and the author's thesis. Once

you have separated your summary of the reading from the rest of the introduction, evaluate it based on the following checklist.

Summary of the Reading

- Does the summary adequately introduce the reading and the author of the reading?
- Does the summary really address the main point of the reading?
- Does the summary provide adequate information for the reader to under-stand how the summary relates to the lead-in?
- Does the summary provide adequate information for the reader to under-stand how the summary relates to the thesis?

Let's look at the summary from the essay.

> He lived with his family in a poor section of South Africa. His father was from the tribes, but they were now living around people who had accepted modern ways. Ways that Mathabane wanted to follow. His father insisted that the whole family follow tribal rules and rituals, and he became angry and violent when Mathabane wouldn't obey the rules or follow the traditions.

This summary does include the author of the reading but not the title.
You may remember that the title is mentioned in the thesis, but it may be
more helpful to your reader to move it to where you first mention the author.

> In Mathabane's essay "My Father's Tribal Rule," he says that he lived with his family in a poor section of South Africa.

The rest of the summary does give background information that helps the
reader understand the context of the main idea, but it does not clearly state
the main idea that relates to the thesis. Remember that the thesis also refers
to Mathabane's attitude toward rules and rituals, so you may be able to state
the main idea there.

> Mathabane writes about his hatred of rules and rituals in "My Father's Tribal Rule," but I think that rules and rituals do have purpose and value.

This sentence doesn't state Mathabane's attitude toward rules and rituals;
it merely mentions his hatred of them. The word "about" identifies a topic,
but it does not state a specific idea, point, or opinion. Try using the word
"that" to clearly introduce Mathabane's opinion instead. You have already
used the title of the reading, so you can omit it here. In addition, you need to

connect Mathabane's hatred of rules and rituals and your view that rules and rituals do have value and purpose. His hatred makes him unable to to see rules and rituals objectively. It is a cause.

> Mathabane writes that he hates his father's rules and rituals. Because he disliked rules and rituals, he didn't see that they can be valuable and that they do have a purpose.

Put back together, the new summary might look like this:

> In Mathabane's essay "My Father's Tribal Rule," he says that he lived with his family in a poor section of South Africa. His father was from the tribes, but they were now living around people who had accepted modern ways. Ways that Mathabane wanted to follow. His father insisted that the whole family follow tribal rules and rituals, and he became angry and violent when Mathabane wouldn't obey the rules or follow the traditions. Mathabane writes that he hates his father's rules and rituals. Because he disliked rules and rituals, he didn't see that they can be valuable and that they do have a purpose.

EXERCISE 11.11   **Using the suggestions for writing summaries, evaluate the effectiveness of the following summaries for essays on this topic.**

Mark Mathabane tells how he grew up in South Africa. His brother was weaned and his father wears tribal clothes. His father beat him for talking at the table. Now Mathabane hates his father and his tribal rules.

In this story Mark Mathabane is embarrassed by his father who wears tribal clothes and follows tribal rules.

Mark Mathabane writes how he hates rules and rituals because his father beat him.

Mark writes about the rules and rituals his father made him follow when he was living in South Africa. He writes about not being able to talk while eating and about how embarrassed he was when his friends teased him about his father's old fashioned clothes.

In this story, Mark Mathabane writes that he disliked following his father's rules and rituals. When his mother weans his brother by smearing hot stuff on her breast, he thinks this is funny. But when his father insists on wearing tribal clothes, he is embarassed. His father won't let him speak any language other than the one his tribe speaks, so Mathabane gets in trouble when he speaks the languages his friends speak because he doesn't want to be different. Mathabane also speaks at the dinner table even though his father tells him not to. As punishment, Mathabane has to perform even more rituals that are supposed to help keep the family safe and bring them more money, and he ends up hating his father even more.

Evaluating the Thesis and Plan of Development   The last part of your introduction should be your thesis and plan of development. Once you have separated these parts from the rest of the introduction, evaluate them based on the following checklist.

Checking the Thesis and Plan of Development

- ▪ Does the thesis clearly relate to the lead-in and the summary of the reading?
- ▪ Does the thesis clearly relate to the plan of development?
- ▪ Is the plan of development necessary for the paper?
- ▪ Is the plan of development clearly stated?

Since we have revised the thesis, we need to check again to see that it addresses the prompt.

Mathabane writes that he hates his father's rules and rituals. Because he disliked rules and rituals, he didn't see that they can be valuable and that they do have a purpose.

The thesis contains the key words "rules," "rituals," "valuable," and "purpose," and it implies the key action "disagree" by the phrase "he didn't see that."

This thesis clearly relates to the summary, since the summary and thesis sentence are combined. However, the thesis has no plan of development. Since the thesis does not indicate how the writer will support his idea that rules and rituals do have value and purpose, it would be helpful to have a plan of development.

To write a plan of development, the writer would need to look back at the main ideas of each paragraph and include an indication of these ideas in the thesis or in another sentence immediately following the thesis.

- ▪ Main idea of body paragraph 1

Rules and rituals help us learn to show respect for others.

▪ Main idea of body paragraph 2

Following rituals can also help us be more mature.

▪ Main idea of body paragraph 3

Some rituals help us to grow up and realize our new responsibilities.

▪ Main idea of body paragraph 4

Also, the rituals we do every day can help the whole family.

These main ideas can be summarized into the following plan of development.

Rules and rituals can teach us many things. They can teach respect, growing up, and helping the whole family.

In summarizing the main ideas, you may notice that the main ideas of paragraphs 2 and 3 are very similar; in fact, we have summarized them into a single idea in our plan of development. We will have to look at these paragraphs when we revise them to be sure that we do indeed have two different ideas and aren't writing two paragraphs on the same idea.

The new introduction would read as follows.

As a child, I assumed that every family did things exactly like mine did. It wasn't until I spent a summer vacation with my best friend's family that I realized this wasn't true. The members of his family got up and grabbed bagels for breakfast whenever they were hungry, while my family always sat down to pancakes or scrambled eggs every morning. In my family, we all had assigned chores, but in his family, his mother took care of the house by herself. That summer I learned that I participated in rules and rituals that other families didn't necessarily follow. Mark Mathabane knew he participated in rituals. More than he wanted too. In Mathabane's essay "My Father's Tribal Rule," he says that he lived with his family in a poor section of South Africa. His father was from the tribes, but they were now living around people who had accepted modern ways. Ways that Mathabane wanted to follow. His father insisted that the whole family follow tribal rules and rituals, and he became angry and violent when Mathabane wouldn't obey the rules or follow the traditions. Mathabane writes that he hates his father's rules and rituals. Because he disliked rules and rituals, he didn't see that they can be valuable and that they do have a purpose. Rules and rituals can teach us many things. They can teach respect, growing up, and helping the whole family.

Evaluating Your Body Paragraphs

What Is Development?   **Development** is the pairing of an idea with an illustration or example and with an explanation. This pairing has to be present; it is not enough to give just the idea or just the example. You must provide both the example and the idea you are trying to prove as well as show the connection between them. As you evaluated your prewriting (see Chapter 7), you paired your ideas with examples that supported them, identifying them as general or specific. You also stated how the example supported the idea or what you were trying to prove with the example. It is this explicit connection that many beginning writers omit. When you revise, you should look for places where you need to add these explanations.

Is Each Idea Adequately Supported?   Beginning writers tend to write too little when explaining their ideas. They assume that their readers know more than they do and that the readers can understand the whole idea from being told just a little of it. Experienced writers have a different attitude. They assume that they know more about their ideas and how they connect to the reading than readers do. They are skilled at explaining ideas as fully as possible. These explanations are the supporting information that you promised your readers in the plan of development that you wrote in your introduction.

Let's look at an example that shows the impact of adding adequate development. Suppose you are writing an essay in which you are arguing that some families are abusing the welfare system. You may use a neighbor as an example.

> Some families abuse the welfare system. For example, my neighbors Lou and Ellen receive food stamps to help feed their five kids. Ellen is also pregnant with her sixth, so she'll be getting even more of my tax money. Her husband drives a very nice truck, while my husband drives an old truck that his father gave him. It's not fair that they get help and have a better truck than we do.

The writer has a main idea (some families abuse the welfare system) and a specific example but has not connected the example to the main idea. Adding an explanation of how this example shows families abusing the welfare system will provide adequate development. The writer might add the following sentences to her paragraph.

> Families like my neighbors, who accept welfare money to pay for essentials such as food and diapers so they can afford big, fancy cars, are abusing the welfare system. They could be more like my family and drive a less expensive truck so they could buy their own food and clothing without help from the government.

"Adequate" development is defined as development that is explained in enough detail that the reader understands why it is in the paper, how it connects to the main idea, and how it proves or supports that idea. One way to check for the adequacy of your development is to ask yourself if you would accept the development as a convincing and understandable explanation of the main idea.

Development Using the Reading   Beginning writers tend to use ideas and specifics from the reading without showing the connection between the idea from the reading and the ideas in their essay. Revision is the time to add these connections so that readers will know why the material from the reading is being used and how it relates to the writer's ideas. To evaluate your use of the reading, use the following checklist.

Checking the Use of the Reading

- Does the material from the reading clearly relate to your idea?
- Have you used the reading accurately?
- Have you acknowledged the author when using his or her ideas or words?
- Have you used the reading appropriately and adequately?

We have spent much time on connecting ideas, so you should be well prepared to attempt the first question. Now we will help you address the other questions in the checklist.

Beginning writers tend to use ideas, examples, and thoughts from the reading but without letting the reader know that these ideas and examples *came* from the reading. Beginning writers also tend to use parts of an essay out of **context**—that is, they select words or details to fit into their essay but misrepresent what the original author intended or change the meaning or purpose of the original author's words. You may be more familiar with how some politicians use the same tactic. They may intentionally take a phrase from an opponent's speech and use it to mean something entirely different from what the opponent originally said.

During revision, you need to find each place in your essay where you have used words, ideas, or examples from the reading. Then use the following steps to help you identify ways to improve your use of the reading.

1. Underline each place in the essay where you have used the reading.
2. Find the specific part of the reading that you have used.
3. Reread the section from the reading and the place in your essay. If your essay does not accurately and fairly reflect that section of the reading, revise that part of your essay.

4. Ask yourself, "What would the author say about how I've used this part of the reading?" If you can imagine the author protesting that you are being unfair, you need to revise.

Remember that you can show that you agree or disagree with an author without misrepresenting that person's words or ideas by writing careful connections between the material from the reading and your own ideas.

For the third question in the reading checklist, you will need to look at two parts of your essay.

- Look at the parts of your essay you've underlined to indicate that they refer to the reading. Be sure that your readers will be able to tell which part of your essay came from the reading and which part is your own. If the difference is not clear, revise to give credit to the author for his or her words, ideas, or examples.
- Look at the rest of your essay (that is, the parts of your essay that you haven't underlined). Have any of the author's words or examples slipped into these parts as well? If so, acknowledge that they belong to the author.

Finally, you will want to look at the amount of your essay that you've underlined to judge whether you have used enough development from the reading. You don't want to use so much of the reading that your ideas are getting lost or that the reading takes up more of the essay than your own ideas. On the other hand, you don't want to use so little of the reading that you aren't fulfilling the assignment.

TIPS   **Development Using Your Own Ideas and Experiences** In Chapter 7 we looked at establishing the relationship between examples and ideas. At the beginning of this section, we reviewed this crucial part of development. Just as you checked the parts of your essay where you've used the reading to be sure that you have explained how the reading is connected to your ideas, you must use the same process when you are working with examples from your own ideas and experiences.

In addition, you will want to make sure that your examples truly **support** your ideas and don't contradict them. Finally, you will want to be sure that your examples are different from those used in the reading and not just a rewriting of the author's examples. For example, if the author uses his cousin who dropped out of school as an example and you use your aunt who dropped out of school as an example to prove the same point, your readers will think that you are imitating the author, not adding your own example.

Use the following checklist as a reminder of these steps as you evaluate your development using your own ideas and experiences.

Using Your Own Ideas and Experiences

- Do your own examples clearly relate to your idea?
- Do your own examples truly support your idea?
- Are your examples different enough from the author's that it's clear you aren't just repeating the same example?

Revising a Body Paragraph   Let's look at the first body paragraph from the essay on pages 204–206 including the changes made so far in the revision process.

> Rules and rituals help us learn to show respect for others. Mathabane tells about the rule his father had about not speaking at the table. He tells us that "One day I intentionally broke one of these laws." He spoke during dinner and his father got really mad then he threatened to beat Mathabane. What Mathabane didn't understand was that his father got mad because Mathabane wasn't respecting him. In my family, we have a dinnertime ritual too. Before dinner, my brothers and my sister and I are supposed to clean the house and get everything ready for dinner. One day I didn't feel like doing it, because I have to do everything. My brothers and my sister hardly do anything and I didn't think it was fair that they played in the yard with their friends while I was working. So, I just sat on the couch and watched TV. My father came in and saw me and started to yell at me. He said he worked hard every day to put food on the table and that I was showing disrespect to him, my mother, my brothers and my sister. He sent me to bed without supper. At first I was really mad. But the more I thought about it, the more I felt bad for not respecting my father. I learned through this rule to respect my father, Mathabane didnt see the valuable things you can learn from rules.

This paragraph has the necessary parts: a main idea, an example and explanation from the reading, an example and explanation from the writer, and a concluding point that ties the two examples back to the main idea.

The example from the reading accurately describes Mathabane's experience and clearly relates it to the main idea of the paragraph. The writer has included enough information from the reading so that readers understand what happened and that Mathabane misunderstood the purpose of the ritual, showing respect for his father.

The example from the writer's own experience also gives enough information—it describes the rule and it shows how the writer learned to show respect for his father. However, the paragraph also loses its focus and talks about the rule being unfair. One sentence is off track.

My brothers and my sister hardly do anything, and I didn't think it was fair that they played in the yard with their friends while I was working.

Because body paragraphs should be clearly focused on the main idea, this sentence should be omitted.

Body Paragraphs 2 and 3   When we looked at the main ideas of these two paragraphs to ensure that they matched the thesis, we noted that they seemed very similar. To revise these paragraphs, we need to look at both of them together and decide if we have two different ideas or if we are writing two different paragraphs about the same idea.

Following rituals can also help us be more mature. Mathabane showed that he was immature because he disobeyed his father simply for the purpose of rebelling. He had no reason to talk at the table except he wanted to make his father angry and see what he would do. When I was younger, I was suppose to clean my room first thing every Saturday morning. Since I would rather play than clean my room, I would put it off as long as possible. If I had been more mature, I would have realized that cleaning my room was my responsibility and I would have done it without trying to get out of it. Also I should have realized that my jobs before dinner were my jobs, whether my brothers and sister did their jobs are not should not have mattered. Being that I was the oldest, I should have had the maturity to set a good example for them by obeying the rules. Mathabane could have shown his maturity by obeying his father's rules rather than disobeying him just because he didn't like it. Doing rituals, particularly if they aren't ones we enjoy, builds maturity because we will have to do things we don't like our whole lives.

Some rituals help us to grow up and realize our new responsibilities. Mathabane tells us about his little brother George. It was time for George to be weaned and so "she smeared her breasts with red pepper and then invited my brother to suckle." Of course, George's mouth must have burned like fire so he stopped nursing. Mathabane thought, "It was amusing to witness my mother do it." He just saw this ritual as being funny. He didn't understand that it had a purpose "to mark George's passage from infancy to childhood." Some rituals help us to grow up and realize our new responsibilities. My friend Alan went through a passage similar to George's. Alan's family has a lot of money. His parents had bought cars for his older brother and sister when they turned sixteen. They bought Alan one when he turned sixteen, but they told him that driving a car meant that he had to be very responsible. They told him that driving a car meant that he was no longer a kid he was now a adult. It's strange, but owning that car really did change him. I guess he realized that you can't act irresponsibly when you're driving several tons of steel.

Checking for Repeated Ideas

■ Can you state the difference between the two ideas? If you can, the ideas are different.

■ Can you switch the examples supporting one idea with the examples supporting the other idea and still have valid support? If you can, your ideas are probably the same.

In the preceding body paragraphs, let's focus on the difference between the following two ideas.

Following rituals can also help us be more mature.

Some rituals help us to grow up and realize our new responsibilities.

Most people would define "mature" as meaning "growing up" and "becoming more responsible"; thus, these two ideas are very similar.

Is it possible to switch the examples in each paragraph? While we couldn't just pick up the support from one paragraph and use it as support for the other with no changes, we could very easily reword the examples to fit the idea in the other paragraph.

All of this shows us that we do not need both paragraphs. We now have two choices.

1. Combine the paragraphs in some way

    or

2. Eliminate one paragraph

Although either choice may work, we need to make the choice that strengthens this particular paper. We are going to eliminate the second paragraph and keep the third because it allows us to bring in two entirely new but relevant examples instead of reusing the same ones we discussed in the first body paragraph.

Notice that there is some good writing in the discarded paragraph. However, leaving it there would have made the paper less effective because it simply repeats what is better said somewhere else. As painful as this process may be, we often have to throw out perfectly good examples, ideas, or even whole paragraphs for the sake of an entire paper. As you eliminate ideas and even whole paragraphs from your paper, it is a good idea to save them in a "discard file." You may be able to use them later in the conclusion or perhaps in another revision in which you try out different ways of developing your body.

Now we need to evaluate how well we have used the reading and our own examples in the third body paragraph.

> Mathabane tells us about his little brother, George. It was time for George to be weaned and so his mother "smeared her breasts with red pepper and then invited my brother to suckle." Of course, George's mouth must have burned like fire, so he stopped nursing. Mathabane thought, "It was amusing to witness my mother do it." He just saw this ritual as being funny. He didn't understand that it had a purpose "to mark George's passage from infancy to childhood." Some rituals help us to grow up and realize our new responsibilities.

The reading is used accurately, and the writer has quoted the words taken from Mathabane's essay. But is it clear how George's weaning is related to helping George to "grow up and realize new responsibilities"? Perhaps adding another sentence or two would help explain what has changed for George:

> . . . He didn't understand that it had a purpose "to mark George's passage from infancy to childhood." <u>George would no longer be nursed like a baby. He would now have to eat and act like a child. Like the ritual to wean George,</u> some rituals help us to grow up and realize our new responsibilities.

The underlined sentences help explain how the weaning ritual fits the category of rituals that "help us to grow up and realize our new responsibilities." Now let's look at an example from the writer's own experience.

> My friend Alan went through a passage similar to George's. Alan's family has a lot of money. His parents had bought cars for his older brother and sister when they turned sixteen. They bought Alan one when he turned sixteen, but they told him that driving a car meant that he had to be very responsible. They told him that driving a car meant that he was no longer a kid; he was now an adult. It's strange, but owning that car really did change him. I guess he realized that you can't act irresponsibly when you're driving several tons of steel.

This example is clearly connected to the rest of the paragraph by the first sentence. While the story itself is a good example, we have no sense of what changed for Alan, so adding a couple of details to show the difference would help.

> . . . It's strange, but owning that car really did change him. <u>Instead of urging his friends to drive faster, Alan was very careful to drive the speed limit. Instead</u>

<u>of blowing his money on the latest CD or a few slices of pizza, Alan saved his money to pay for gas and insurance.</u> I guess he realized that you can't act irresponsibly when you're driving several tons of steel.

These underlined sentences, like the ones added to the example of George's weaning, help to show the growth that results from the ritual.

Body Paragraph 4   This paragraph does contain a main idea, an example from the reading, and an example from the writer.

> Also, the rituals we do every day can help the whole family. Mathabane had to do "rituals spanning the range of day-to-day living." Everybody does daily rituals. In our house, these daily rituals are divided up. Every evening before bed, for instance, it's my job to make sure all the doors are locked and the windows shut and latched. My sister irons my father's shirts so he'll have a fresh one for work. My father gets lunch ready for everybody. My mother supervises and helps whoever needs help. Although Mathabane may be confused by these rituals, I'm not.

However, it does seem to be lacking. The example of the reading is only one sentence; this alone may be a clue that more information about these daily rituals could be added.

The transition between the two examples focuses on the fact that everyone does daily rituals. However, the focus of the paragraph is that daily rituals benefit everyone in the family. This is another area that can be revised.

Finally, the writer's example does list each person's rituals but does not relate each ritual to how it benefits the entire family.

The revised paragraph might look like this.

> Also, the rituals we do every day can help the whole family. Mathabane had to do "rituals spanning the range of day-to-day living." <u>These rituals are intended to bring good luck to the entire family, to protect the household, to keep family members healthy, and to ensure that the father keeps his job. All of these rituals benefit Mathabane, George, their mother, and their father. Each member of my family also does daily rituals that help the rest of the family out.</u> Every evening before bed, for instance, it's my job to make sure all the doors are locked and the windows shut and latched, <u>my ritual keeps us safe from intruders.</u> My sister irons my father's shirts so he'll have a fresh one for work, <u>which helps him make a good impression on his job.</u> My father gets lunch ready for everybody <u>so we don't go hungry the next day</u>. My mother supervises and helps whoever needs help. <u>Our rituals help us work together to everyone's benefit.</u> Although Mathabane may be confused by these rituals, I'm not.

Evaluate the development in each of these paragraphs from different papers. The main idea is underlined for you.

Another purpose of rituals is to teach family members to work together. For example, Mark says that his father made him and his brother wear the ritual garb of the Venda tribe even though Mark's friends had shed their tribal cloth and embraced Western culture. The reason his father did this was so that the family would fit in with others in their tribe when the whites left South Africa and they revert to their old ways of living. Teaching children to work with other members of the family is good. The family needs to fit in with the rest of the tribe, too. In my family, my brothers and sisters and I had to clean up the house before dinner. As we got older, we got better and faster at having the house straight for my parents before dinner, this made supper time much calmer and meant that we sometimes had free time after dinner.

Within families, parents make their children do things that they think are valuable. Sometimes these things are different from what the children's friends do. Parents should always explain why they want their children to follow their rules when they are different from their friends. Of course, children still won't always agree with their parents reasons, and then their parents should allow them to choose which rituals to obey unless their is a very good reason. Mark's father should have let him wear Western clothes and speak Zulu with his friends instead of insisting that he stick to the tribal way of living. He certainly should not have beaten Mark for disobeying these rules. He also should have explained why he thought Mark should follow these rituals instead of just telling him he had to. My parents never let me go out on Halloween night with my friends. They never explained why I couldn't go and I thought it was a really stupid rule. All of my friends would come back to school talking about how much fun they had and asking me why I hadn't gone. I would always make up something like I was sick so I wouldn't have to tell them my parents wouldn't let me. If my parents had explained, I might have not have lied.

Most women take care of the children and the men in the family. Although this is changing as more women go back to work, in most families it's the woman who stays home with the children, feeds them, changes diapers, takes care of them when they are sick, makes sure they have clean clothes and cleans the house. Even though my father knew how to do all of these things, he sat and watched television while my mother rushed around taking care of everything after she had worked as a waitress all day. On weekends when they were both off work, the children stayed with my mother. Even if she needed to go shopping and he was staying home, we all piled into the car with her so she could look out for us. Usually when we got back with the groceries, my dad had cut the grass and was asleep on the couch with the television on. When my mother had put up all the groceries, she would cook dinner for my father.

Evaluating Your Conclusion

The conclusion of a paper, like the last song in a concert, is the part of the performance that the audience or reader is most likely to remember. If you want a standing ovation, you need to conclude your paper with skill.

Use the following checklist to help you write a strong conclusion.

✔ Checklist for Conclusions

- Does the conclusion wrap up all the ideas in the essay without restating them exactly?
- Does the conclusion avoid contradicting your paper or apologizing for your ideas and opinions?
- Does the conclusion provide one more thing without bringing in new information or making wild claims?

Here is the conclusion from the essay on pages 204–206:

> In conclusion, Mathabane just doesn't get it. He thinks rules and rituals are just a waste of time. He doesn't see how they can help us learn to respect others and be more courteous to them. I think that Mathabane was too immature to understand that rituals can help us grow up. They can help develop self-responsibility, which is something most people could use more of. Basically he is wrong. Rules and rituals are something you should follow and practice. If everyone followed the rules and rituals they were taught at home, the world would be a better place.

This conclusion begins with a cliché opener (see Chapter 10 on drafting conclusions). You should not have to tell your readers you are presenting your conclusion. Your ideas, not this cliché, will make it clear that you are finishing your paper.

This conclusion also restates only two of the main ideas: learning respect and growing up. To conclude the entire essay, the conclusion should also refer to the other main ideas.

In addition, it is jarring that the end of the conclusion switches to the second person (you).

Rules and rituals are something you should follow and practice.

This switch sounds strange coming at the end of this paper, since the writer changes the tone and tells the reader how to behave. Changing "you" to "people" will help.

The end of this conclusion also makes a claim.

If everyone followed the rules and rituals he or she was taught at home, the world would be a better place.

This is a rather large claim that readers may find unbelievable. The revised version of this conclusion might look like this.

Mathabane just doesn't get it. He thinks rules and rituals are just a waste of time. He doesn't see how they can help us learn to respect others and be more courteous to them. I think that Mathabane was too immature to understand that rituals can help us grow up. They can help develop self-responsibility, which is something most people could use more of. In addition, if Mathabane had been less selfish, he'd know that rituals benefit everyone in the family. Basically he is wrong. Rules and rituals are something people should follow and practice. If everyone followed the rules and rituals they were taught at home, they could learn respect, responsibility, and how to help others.

EXERCISE 11.13   **Evaluate the following conclusions.**

In conclusion, Mathabane is right to think that rules and rituals are worthless. Rules and rituals are worthless when they have no purpose and benefit no one, if their only purpose is so authority figures can push people around, and if they make you feel separated from other people.

Rules and rituals are worthless when they have bad effects on people. Some rules are good because they teach us about tradition.

I agree with Mathabane that rules and rituals are worthless. For example, my high school wouldn't let us wear baseball caps in class. There was no purpose for this rule. Wearing caps didn't hurt anyone. The teachers just wanted to prove to us that they were in charge. Rules that have no purpose, that are used to push people around, and that separate people are worthless.

Mathabane is right that rules and rituals have no purpose or value. All children should refuse to follow their parents stupid rules. Then the world would be a much better place for us all.

The following box lists the steps we have taken to revise this essay.

The Steps for Revision

Step 1: Preparing to Revise
- Let the paper cool.
- Read the paper.

Step 2: Making Sure You Answer the Question
- Check to see that the thesis matches the prompt.
- Revise your thesis so that it matches the parts of your paper.

Step 3: Checking Structure and Organization
- Ensure that all parts of the essay are present.
- Ensure that all main ideas relate to the thesis.
- Ensure that your paragraphs are in the best order.

Step 4: Checking Development
- Evaluate your introduction.
- Ensure that each main idea is adequately supported.
- Evaluate your conclusion.

THE REVISED ESSAY

The entire revised essay now reads as follows (however, according to the chart on page 196, we still have to edit and proofread this essay before the paper is finished).

As a child, I assumed that every family did things exactly like mine did. It wasn't until I spent a summer vacation with my best friend's family that I realized this wasn't true. The members of his family got up and grabbed bagels for breakfast whenever they were hungry, while my family always sat down to pancakes or scrambled eggs every morning. In my family, we all had assigned chores, but in his family, his mother took care of the house by herself. That summer I learned that I participated in rules and rituals that other families didn't necessarily follow. Mark Mathabane knew he participated in rituals more than he wanted too. In Mathabane's essay "My Father's Tribal Rule," he says that he lived with his family in a poor section of South Africa. His father was from the tribes, but they were now living around people who had accepted modern ways. Ways that Mathabane wanted to follow. His father insisted that the whole family follow tribal rules and rituals, he became angry and violent when Mathabane wouldn't obey the rules or follow the traditions. Mathabane writes that he hates his father's rules and rituals. Because he disliked rules and rituals, he didn't see that they can be valuable and that they do have a purpose. Rules and rituals can teach us many things. They can teach respect, growing up, and helping the whole family.

Rules and rituals help us learn to show respect for others. Mathabane tells about the rule his father had about not speaking at the table. He tells us that "One day I intentionally broke one of these laws." He spoke during dinner and his father got really mad then he threatened to beat Mathabane. What Mathabane didn't understand was that his father got mad because Mathabane wasn't respecting him. In my family, we have a dinnertime ritual too. Before dinner, my brothers and my sister and I are supposed to clean the house and get everything ready for dinner. One day I didn't feel like doing it, because I have to do everything. So, I just sat on the couch and watched TV. My father came in and saw me and started to yell at me. He said he worked hard every day to put food on the table and that I was showing disrespect to him, my mother, my brothers and my sister. He sent me to bed without supper. At first I was really mad. But the more I thought about it, the more I felt bad for not respecting my father. I learned through this rule to respect my father, Mathabane didn't see the valuable things you can learn from rules.

Mathabane tells us about his little brother George. It was time for George to be weaned and so "she smeared her breasts with red pepper and then invited my brother to suckle." Of course, George's mouth must have burned like fire so he stopped nursing. Mathabane thought, "It was amusing to witness my mother do it." He just saw this ritual as being funny. He didn't understand that it had a purpose "to mark George's passage from infancy to childhood." George would no longer be nursed like a baby. He would now have to eat and act like a child. Like the ritual to wean George, some rituals help us to grow up and realize our new responsibilities. My friend Alan went through a passage similar to George's. Alan's family has a lot of money. His parents had bought cars for his older brother and sister when they turned sixteen. They bought Alan one when he turned sixteen, but they told him that driving a car meant that he had to be very responsible. They told him that driving a car meant that he was no longer a kid he was now an adult. It's strange, but owning that car really did change him. Instead of urging his friends to drive faster, Alan was very careful to drive the speed limit. Instead of blowing his money on the latest CD or a few slices of pizza, Alan saved his money to pay for gas and insurance. I guess he realized that you can't act irresponsibly when you're driving several tons of steel.

Also, the rituals we do everyday can help the whole family. Mathabane had to do "rituals spanning the range of day-to-day living." These rituals are intended to bring good luck to the entire family, to protect the household, to keep family members healthy, and to ensure that the father keeps his job. All of these rituals benefit Mathabane, George, their mother, and their father. Each member of my family also does daily rituals that help the rest of the family out. Every evening before bed, for instance, it's my job to make sure all the doors are locked and the windows shut and latched, my ritual keeps us safe from intruders. My sister irons my father's shirts so he'll have a fresh one for work, which helps him make a good impression on his job. My father gets lunch ready for everybody so we don't go hungry the next day. My mother supervises and helps whoever needs help. Our rituals help us work together to everyone's benefit. Although Mathabane may be confused by these rituals, I'm not.

Mathabane just doesn't get it. He thinks rules and rituals are just a waste of time. He doesn't see how they can help us learn to respect others and be more courteous to them. I think that Mathabane was too immature to understand that rituals can help us grow up. They can help develop self-responsibility, which is something most people could use more of. In addition, if Mathabane had been less selfish, he'd know that rituals benefit everyone in the family. Basically he wrong. Rules and rituals are something people should follow and practice. If everyone followed the rules and rituals they were taught at home, they could learn respect, responsibility, and how to help others.

EXERCISE 11.14	Work with a classmate to evaluate each other's essays for development. Keep in mind the suggestions for working with another reader (on page 198) as you work.
Collaboration	Use the checklists for the parts of an Introduction: Lead-in (page 210), Summary, (page 212), and Thesis and Plan of Development (page 214).
	Check the development of each body paragraph. Use the checklists for Use of the Reading (page 217), Using Your Own Ideas and Experiences (page 219), and Repeated Ideas (page 221).
	Finally, evaluate the conclusion, using the Checklist for Conclusions (page 225). Use the suggestions from your partner to revise your work.

USING CHECKLISTS

To revise effectively, you should have a systematic way to identify the parts of the essay that you can improve. Using a checklist is a good strategy for being sure that you are looking at many ways to improve your essay.

Sometimes, an instructor will provide a checklist for a specific assignment, especially if the assignment is not a general persuasive or expository essay. For example, you might be writing a critique of an assigned reading. Another type of paper that is evaluated according to very different criteria is a research paper.

If your instructor does not give you a checklist, how can you create your own checklist for an assignment? First, review your syllabus and course description to discover the emphasis of the course. Then read the assignment carefully to determine what is important about that particular paper. For a

persuasive essay, clear organization with particular emphasis on **thesis**, **topic sentences**, and **support** are important. For a paper using more than source, such as a research paper, attention to the source of ideas and accurate citation of sources and documentation are important.

A revision checklist is intended to help you determine if your essay has the content and organization of a good essay and meets the requirements of particular assignment. To be useful, a checklist needs to help you evaluate not only basic essay structure and development but the effectiveness of your essay in response to a particular assignment.

To use a checklist, you need to answer the questions honestly and thoroughly. The purpose of a checklist is not to say you've completed it but to actually use your answers to improve your paper. The questions will help you identify weaknesses in your paper or essential steps that you have not completed. When you find an omission or a weakness, address it before moving on to the next set of questions.

A suggested detailed checklist based on the revision guidelines is given here. It can be adapted to specific assignments. Simply modify, add, or delete points to the list before you begin to revise a specific paper.

Be prepared to revise   Beginning writers usually complete the **draft** of a paper by making a clean copy of it, and then they do not complete the necessary revisions because they don't want to mark up the clean and neat draft. However, effective revising requires that you be willing to destroy that clean copy by making marks and notes that help you improve the paper. The following checklist has check mark icons (✓) that signal when you should be writing on your draft.

Revision Checklist

- **Does your essay address the assignment effectively?**
  - **What is your thesis?**
    - ☑ Put an * before and after the sentence(s) that express your thesis.
  - **Does the thesis provide an appropriate response to the assignment?**
    - ☑ Underline the **key focus words** from the **prompt** in your thesis. Have you used all key focus words from the prompt? If not, should you revise your thesis to include them? Does your thesis match the **key action** in the prompt?
  - **Where is your thesis stated? Is this an appropriate place for your thesis?**
  - **Have you used the reading accurately? Have you documented your use of it appropriately?** The following suggestions are based on a response to a single reading. For some types of papers, such as a research paper or a paper comparing one reading to another, you will need to adapt how you evaluate your use of ideas from another writer.

continued on next page

continued from previous page

☑ Write **RID** (Reading Identification) in the margin where you introduce the reading. Have you included the author's name, the title, and a statement of the main idea?

☑ Write **R** (Reading) in the margin beside all of the other places use the reading.

  ☑ Write a question mark (**?**) beside where it is not clear that you are using the author's material rather than your own.

  ☑ Write an equal sign (=) beside ideas from the reading that support your ideas and show that you agree with the author.

  ☑ Write a does-not-equal sign(≠) beside ideas from the reading that you use to show where you disagree with the author.

■ **Check for an appropriate balance of ideas from the reading and your own ideas.**

  If you have more material from the reading than from your own ideas and experiences, then you have probably used the reading too much.

  Have you **summarized** large portions of the reading instead of explaining how points of the reading connect with your own ideas? Cut out unnecessary summaries.

  Do you need to develop your own ideas? You may need to add more of your own ideas, explanations, and examples.

Is Your Essay Organization Effective?

Introduction

■ **Is the introduction a clearly defined section of your essay?**

  ☑ Draw a line between your introduction and first body paragraph.

  ☑ Label the parts of your introduction.

■ **Do you need to add or improve any of the following parts of your introduction?**

  Lead-in: Is the introduction interesting? Is it related to your thesis?

  Background (including the summary from the reading): Does the introduction have the necessary general background information? Does it introduce relevant ideas from an assigned reading?

  Thesis: Is the thesis the main point (or just part) of your whole essay? Your thesis is the key to a good essay. Take time now to ensure that your thesis answers the question and clearly states your response.

  Plan of development: Does the introduction suggest how the thesis will be supported?

continued on next page

continued from previous page

Body

■ **Is the body divided into parts? Is it more than one paragraph?**

☑ *Number the body paragraphs:* Do you have more than one? Do you support your thesis in at least two separate body paragraphs? Does the number of paragraphs seem to match the thesis?

☑ Put an * before and after the sentence that expresses the main idea of each body paragraph (the topic sentence). Ask yourself: Is the point of each body paragraph clear? Is each paragraph clearly on a different point, or do the points overlap too much? Does each paragraph support the thesis? How?

If the main idea of a body paragraph does not support your thesis, you have two choices: change your main idea and body paragraphs to match your thesis, or rewrite the thesis to reflect your main ideas.

If the main ideas of your body paragraphs overlap, decide if you can rewrite them so they develop different points, or think about combining and eliminating ideas. Prewrite and draft a new body paragraph if you have to.

☑ Count the number of sentences in each body paragraph; write this number at the end of the paragraph. Although there is no set number of sentences that you must have in a paragraph, counting the number of sentences may help you identify paragraphs that are undeveloped.

☑ Write **OWN** beside your own ideas, experiences, and observations.

☑ Is each example related to the main idea of the paragraph?

If not, find a different example, one that is related to the main idea of the paragraph, or add enough explanation showing how the example is related to the main idea.

☑ What does each example illustrate? Is each explanation detailed enough to be clear to another reader?

☑ Put **DEV** beside each example and explanation that needs more development to be clear. You will need to come back to the sections marked DEV and add more material. You may even have to do research to find information to develop your ideas more effectively (see the section on revising with research below).

☑ Does any example have *too much* detail? Does your reason for using it get lost?

Developing ideas from the Reading: For each place you wrote **R** earlier.

☑ Write **SUM** beside each summary.

☑ Write **PARA** beside each paraphrase.

continued on next page

continued from previous page

☑ Write **QUO** beside each quotation.

Do you introduce and explain each use of the adding, especially each paraphrase and quotation?

Organizing Ideas within Each Body Paragraph

Beginning writers tend to write paragraphs in the order in which they thought of the ideas. During the revision stage, you need to reconsider how you have organized each paragraph.

☑ Determine how many points you make in the paragraph by numbering each point (1, 2, 3, . . .).

☑ Be sure that all sentences related to a point are grouped together. If they are not grouped together, move them or provide adequate transitions so that your reader will know why you are moving back and forth between points.

☑ Consider the order of these points: Move each grouping around, read the paragraph with this new order, and then determine which order works best.

☑ Once you have chosen the best order for these points, check the transitions between these points to see if they match this new order.

Conclusion

■ **Is the conclusion a separate part (paragraph) of your essay?**

☑ Draw a line between the body of your paper and the conclusion.

■ **Does the conclusion include a summary and a final thought that is related to the whole essay?**

☑ Underline the restatement or summary of your thesis. If this restatement is identical to your thesis, reword it.

☑ Put [ ] around the final thought.

■ **Have you contradicted the rest of your paper?**

■ **Have you introduced new ideas or examples that belong in a body paragraph?**

DEVELOPING YOUR IDEAS WITH RESEARCH

Sometimes you will realize that you need more examples or other information to be able to develop the essay completely, but your personal experiences and observations aren't related. If you have time, you can use research to develop your ideas.

Questions for Revising with Research

Introduction

■ Would more background on the topic help the reader understand my thesis?

■ Would more background on the author make the essay more interesting?

Body

■ Where would more examples be helpful?

■ Where would specific facts or figures support my ideas?

Conclusion

■ Would a final example make my conclusion more convincing?

When you find answers to any of the questions listed in the preceding box, the next step is to locate the material in outside sources. See pages 330–333 and 335–337 for details on how to locate and use material and pages 335–344 on how to document sources.

EXERCISE 11.15   **Use the checklists in this chapter to revise your own essay.**

After you have worked through the revision checklist and have added, changed, moved, or eliminated ideas to improve your essay, you need to be sure that each paragraph and sentence is clear. The next chapter provides a short style checklist and a grammar and mechanics checklist to help you check this area of your writing.

What You've Done

■ Drafted your complete essay

■ Revised it in terms of thesis, organization, and development

■ Learned to use checklists to evaluate your own writing for checking a thesis, organization, and development

The Next Step

■ Editing your essay (Chapter 12)

12 Editing
Improving Grammar, Usage, and Punctuation Skills

> ### *What You've Done*
>
> - Drafted and revised your essay
>
> ### *What You Need to Do Next*
>
> - Notice any errors in grammar, spelling, usage, or punctuation
> - Learn to use tools to correct the errors you've found
> - Keep an editing log to avoid future errors
> - Use suggestions from instructors and other students
> - Edit for style

When you've carefully constructed an essay, you've worked hard to create something to be proud of. But if you don't take the final steps of making sure that the details are correct, you may leave your readers with a bad impression of your work. **Editing** is the step that finishes your essay. It's very much like brushing your teeth or washing your car—the final touch that makes everything presentable. In an essay, you want the words, grammar, punctuation, spelling, and appearance to be as neat and clear as possible.

WRITING AND SPEAKING STANDARD ENGLISH

The language you use when you speak and the language you use when you write are very similar but not exactly the same. Sometimes your spoken language is similar to your written language; other times the two are very different from each other.

All of us—from different parts of the country, of different ages and social groups, with different abilities—have special kinds of English that we use with friends and families, a language that makes us feel comfortable and with which we can communicate easily. But sometimes we encounter problems when we try to communicate with groups who might not understand or feel comfortable with our own style of English. So all of us need to be able to use a common or general kind of English when we're communicating with people we don't know well in the academic, professional, and business worlds.

The accepted practice in these situations is to use **standard written English**. This means that when you write essays for a class, you need to use this general kind of English unless there's a special reason not to. In fact, for most school and business writing, standard written English is best.

Some aspects of language—such as punctuation and spelling—are the same, no matter what kind of English you write. They follow definite rules that, fortunately, most of us have learned by now. And if we haven't, there are two tools that help us with the rules we don't remember: handbooks (such as Chapter 19 of this book) and dictionaries. These tools will provide crucial help in those cases where standard English is different from spoken English.

Taking Time to Edit

Sometimes using standard English may be difficult. It's hard to think about grammar rules when you're concentrating on understanding a reading and communicating your ideas about it. If you stop in the middle of drafting or revising to look up words in a dictionary or punctuation rules in a handbook, you will probably lose your train of thought. This is why it is best to plan a separate period of time for editing. You will quickly learn how long that time needs to be for your own style of editing and the type of assignment. There are two important steps in editing: locating errors and correcting errors.

Computer Tip

Most people aren't able to pay attention to details on a computer screen. So it's a good idea to print out a draft to use just for editing. Be sure that it's double-spaced. Some people like to use a larger font so they can see individual letters more clearly.

LOCATING ERRORS

Editing Steps
Locating Errors
Correcting Errors

ESL

The first step in editing should be locating the problems you'll need to repair. This is a little trickier than it may seem. Because you're the author of your paper and already familiar with its ideas and organization, *you will tend to see what you meant to write, rather than what you actually wrote. Note:* You may have already used some of these techniques when you were revising (Chapter 11), but this time you are not looking for ways to make your meaning clear. You are looking for ways to make sure you have followed the rules of standard written English. You'll need some tools and tricks to help you see what is actually on the page.

■ *Edit pen:* Always use a pen or pencil that is a bright, strong color to edit your **draft**. An edit pen should catch your attention and be easy to read. Any pen will do, but you may find it helpful to use several colors: one color for corrections and another for points you need to look up. A pencil or erasable pen is helpful if there's a chance you'll change your mind. Experiment to find what works best for you. Marking words or punctuation and also writing notes in the margin will help you keep track of where you are.

▪ *Pointer:* Use something physical like your finger or your edit pen to actually touch each word. This action will help you see what's really there. Using your edit pen will mean that it's handy when you see something you need to mark or correct.

▪ *Read backward:* Read the last sentence of your essay. See any problems? If so, correct them. Then read the next-to-last sentence and make any needed corrections. Then move on to the sentence before that, and continue to read backward, correcting errors until you've completed the essay. This technique works because good readers automatically predict what will appear in a sentence or what should come next. When good readers read forward, moving from one sentence to the next, they often subconsciously fill in blanks or skip over repeated words. Good readers may "read" words, spellings, and punctuation that aren't actually written. Reading backward will help you think about the way you've written each sentence. It will help you see each sentence individually and make mistakes easier to see.

▪ *Read aloud:* Reading aloud will help you in two ways. First, because reading aloud slows down your processing of each sentence, it will help you see the actual words on the page. Second, because punctuation signals how parts of sentences relate to each other, reading aloud will help you decide if the pauses and breaks in sentences—the commas and periods—are correct (see fragments pp. 365–368 and run-ons pp. 368–372).

▪ *Peer editing:* Another way to locate errors in papers is through **peer editing**, a technique that is explained and illustrated on pages 247–248. Because peer editing involves working with someone else, it is necessary to consider the roles and responsibilities of both the writer and the reader. Instructors also often assign peer editing as a class activity, so it will be necessary to learn how to follow your own instructor's specific directions.

Combining Tools to Locate Your Own Errors

Using several or all of these techniques to locate your own errors will help you focus even more on the language and individual style of your paper instead of on the general ideas.

Look for the most typical types of errors when editing a draft of your paper, including the following.

▪ Careless mistakes in typing
▪ Misquoting a reading or other source

- Omitting or repeating a word
- Spelling errors
- Punctuation errors

Some of these trouble spots are considered in Chapter 11 (revision), in this chapter (proofreading), and in Chapter 19 (the Handbook).

EXERCISE 12.1

Collaboration

Look at this **introductory paragraph** from an essay. Read it aloud and mark the errors you find with a colorful edit pen. Try reading from the end of the paragraph sentence-by-sentence to find more errors. One error has been underlined. Compare your ability to locate errors with someone else. Divide a piece of paper into two columns labeled "errors" and "corrections." List the errors you find on the left and write the correction for each error on the right. (See the example following the paragraph.) Compare the number and kinds of errors you find with someone else. Compare your suggestions for correcting these errors.

Rules and Rituals (Introduction)

Rules and rituals are <u>thing</u> people do, every day we follow some kind of rules. We also paticipate in rituals, although we might not no it. Mark Mathaban knew he participated in rituals. More than he wanted too. He lived with his family in a poor section of South Africa. His father was from the tribes, but they were now living around people who excepted modern ways. Ways that Mataban wanted to follow. His father insist that the whole family follow tribal rules and rituals, he became angry and violent when Mathabane wouldnt obey the rules or follow the traditions. Mathabane writes about his hatred of rules and rituals in My fathers tribal rule. Although Mathabane dislike rules and rituals he didn't see that they can be valuable and that they do have a pupose. Rules and rituals can teach us many things. They can teach respect, growing up, and helping the whole family.

EXERCISE 12.2

Locate errors with each of the following methods on the first **body paragraph** (paragraph 2) of this essay (1) using an edit pen, (2) using a pointer, (3) reading backward, and (4) reading aloud.

After you have finished editing the page, think about what you have done.

- What types of errors did you find in the sample paragraph?
- How many mistakes did you find?
- Which techniques did you find most helpful? (These are the ones you might find most helpful in locating errors in your own essays.)
- Could you correct some of these errors?
- Compare the edited paragraph to the original paragraph with mistakes. You should be able to see how your corrections help improve the paragraph.

> **Rules and Rituals (Body Paragraph 1)**
>
> First, rules teach respect. Mathabane tells about the rule his father had about not speaking at the table. He tells us that "One day I intentionally broke one of these laws. He spoke during dinner and his father got really mad, he said, "You don't have two mouths to afford you such a luxury." Then he threatened to beat Mathabane. By Mathabane not respecting him made his father get mad, but Mathabane did'nt understand it. One time my father got at me to. In my family, we have a dinnertime ritual. Before dinner, my brothers and my sister and I are suppose to clean the house and get everything ready for dinner. One day I didn't feel like doing it, because I have to do everything. My brothers and my sister don't do hardly anything. So, I just sat on the couch and watch TV. My father come in and saw me and started to yell at me. He said he worked hard every day to put food on the table and you are showing disrespect to me, your mother, your brothers and your sister. He sent me to bed without supper. At first I was really mad. Being that my father was unfair to me. I'm the oldest, so I wind up doing most of the work. I don't see why should I have to clean the house every day and get the table ready? The more I thought about it, the more I felt bad. He did do a lot for us. Besides providing us with a house and food, he paid for my music lessons, he takes us to the beach in the summer, he drops us off at the movies. He really does do a lot for us and sometimes I think we forget to say thank you. I felt bad for not respecting my father. I learn through this rule to respect my father, Mathabane didnt see the valuable things you can learn from rules.

EXERCISE 12.3 **With some or all of the following methods, locate errors in an essay you have written. Do this (1) using an edit pen, (2) using a pointer, (3) reading backward, and (4) reading aloud.**

CORRECTING ERRORS

For many people, locating errors is the most difficult part of editing. You will probably know how to correct most of the errors you find. It's important to mark everything that you recognize as an error and everything you suspect may be an error. You can then correct what you have marked in two stages.

1. Correct the errors you know.
2. Find help in correcting the ones you don't know or the ones you think might be wrong, even though you're not sure.

Correcting Errors You Understand

Make the correction on the draft as soon as you locate it. Don't expect to recognize the error again later and remember how you planned to correct it if you will be recopying your essay. Write clearly so that you can read what you've written. When you located the errors in the paragraph on page 238 (in Exercise 12.1), you knew how to correct many of these errors.

Computer Tip
Handwrite the correction on your draft if it is short. If it is more complicated, requiring many changes, write a note on the draft to remind yourself. When you return to the computer, mark off each correction as you find it so you won't skip over it.

1. *Rules and rituals are <u>thing</u> people do.* [You know the phrase *rules and rituals* is plural, so *things* must be plural, too.]
2. *. . . although we might not <u>no</u> it.* [You know *no* is the opposite of *yes*, but the word makes no sense in this context. What you want is the word that means *be aware of*. You change the spelling of *no* to *know*.]
3. *Ways that <u>Mathaban</u> wanted to follow.* [You check the spelling of the author's name and correct *Mathaban* to *Mathabane*.]
4. *His father <u>insist</u> that the whole family follow tribal rules and rituals.* [You've been writing about this story in the past tense (*wanted, was, were now living*), so you change *insist* to *insisted*.]
5. *Mathabane <u>wouldnt</u> obey the rules.* [You know *wouldnt* is a contraction of *would* + *not* and needs an apostrophe between *n* and *t*. You correct this word to be *wouldn't*.]

Finding Help for Errors You Don't Understand

ESL

There are several steps you can follow in finding help. The first is deciding what kind of help you need.

Spell Checkers   The **spell checker** is a computer device that checks each word that is typed in your essay against a list in the computer's memory. Spell checkers are helpful, but they don't fix everything. The computer can't understand the meaning of words or sentences in a word-processing program, so it can't decide which correctly spelled word is correct for your sentence. You must make the decision as to whether to change the word and how to change it, if you do. Sometimes the spell checker will tell you that a word is wrong even when it's right, because not every word can be on the computer's list. Most proper names are left off those lists, as are specialized words such as technical words from many fields and words from other languages used in English sentences.

Computer Tip
Spell checkers don't know which words are the best corrections for misspelled words. Don't simply accept the first suggestion the spell checker offers. You will have to think about the meaning of each word to see which fits best in your sentence, and you may need to use a dictionary to help you. Turn off the "Autocorrect" feature so that you will be able to make your own decisions about correcting words. Also, many proper names will be marked as misspelled even if they aren't.

The following list shows that some errors can be corrected using a spell checker and others cannot. Be careful. You, not the spell checker, must correct your errors.

1. Your spell checker highlights *Mathabane.* You don't need to change this word because it is the correct spelling of the author's name.

2. Your spell checker highlights *paticipated* and suggests *participated.* This seems correct to you, and, in fact, it is. If you aren't sure that it is correct, look up *participate(d)* in the dictionary.

3. Your spell checker highlights *pupose* and suggests *puppies.* You read the sentence with *pupose* and determine that *puppies* makes no sense in that sentence. Another choice the spell checker offers is *purpose,* which you recognize as the word you meant to write.

4. Your spell checker doesn't highlight *no* in *we might not no it,* because *no* is a word that would be correct in some sentences. It's not the correct word in this sentence, but the computer doesn't understand the meaning of the sentence.

Grammar Checkers and Style Checkers   Grammar checkers and style checkers are often included as part of the software of a word-processing program. Again, these mechanical aids simply compare your phrases and sentences against a list in the computer. But the computer does not understand the meaning of the sentence—it just looks for patterns of words on a list. Unfortunately, sentences and phrases are much more complicated than words, so the checker's suggestions are wrong more often than they are right. Most students find them very confusing. It is probably better to learn how to recognize and correct your own errors.

Dictionaries   Dictionaries are helpful for correct spellings and definitions of words. Don't give up immediately if you can't find the words you're looking for, since not all words are spelled the way they sound. Try to think of other letters that might make the same sound (for example, *chaos* is spelled with *ch*, not *k*).

Also, the word you're looking up may have prefixes like *re-* or suffixes (endings added to make a word a different part of speech) like *-ance* or *-ence.* If you have trouble finding the whole word, try to figure out the root and look that up. See page 66 in Chapter 4 for help in finding roots.

1. You try to look up the word *participate*, but you have spelled it *paticpate.* You won't find the word listed under *pat-*, but if you continue to look under *pa-*, you eventually find *participate.*

2. You aren't sure you've spelled *disrespect* correctly, but you don't find it under *dis-*. You know that *dis-* is a prefix meaning *not*, so you look for the word *respect*. You find that *disrespect* is the correct spelling of the word.

Use a college dictionary to edit your work. Other dictionaries have far fewer words and fewer and less complete definitions of words.

Handbooks   Handbooks can be very helpful for punctuation, grammar, and usage questions. In some courses you will need to learn to use a complete handbook for many different questions, but in this course you can use the shorter handbook that begins on page 358. *The key to using a handbook is being able to name the error you are trying to correct.* You may already know the names of some problems, but you may need to learn the names of others.

Common Problems Covered in the Handbook

Period or comma
- Fragments (sentence basics, pp. 359–364; fragments, pp. 365–368)
- Run-ons (run-ons and comma splices, pp. 368–372)
- Other commas (commas, pp. 393–396)

Other punctuation
- Question marks (question marks, p. 396–397; question word, p. 367)
- Quotation marks, pp. 399–400)
- Titles (pp. 397–398)
- Capitals (pp. 398–399)

Word endings (pp. 372–383)
- *-s* on words
    - Plural nouns (p. 373–374)
    - Verbs (recognizing verbs, p. 360; final *-s* verbs, pp. 376–377; subject-verb agreement, pp. 383–385)
    - Apostrophes (pp. 374–375)
- *-ed, -ing* on words (recognizing verbs, p. 360; past tense verb endings, pp. 380–383)
- More on verbs (irregular verbs, pp. 381; helping verbs, pp. 378; modals, pp. 378)
- Verb tense overview (pp. 382)

Using other writers' work
- Quotation marks and italics (pp. 397–398)
- Documentation
    - Parenthetical citations (p. 400)
- Paraphrase (pp. 391–392)

continued on next page

continued from previous page

Unclear sentences (p. 388–393)

- Prepositional subjects (pp. 388); recognizing prepositional phrases (pp. 364); subject-verb agreement (pp. 383–385); prepositions (pp. 405–410)
- Articles (pp. 404–405)
- Indirect questions (pp. 391)
- Verb tenses (pp. 410–418)

Parallelism (clarity, p. 393)

Pronouns

- Pronoun agreement (pp. 385–386)
- Pronouns and point of view (pp. 386)

Word choice

- Similar words and spelling (pp. 386–388)

Problems You Can Name   Many times you will know the name of the problem you are trying to correct. To find the section of the handbook that describes that problem, you can do either of two things.

1. Look at the list of items that begins on page 242 (also printed on the back inside cover).
2. Look in the index at the back of the book under the name of the problem.

When you edit, you should check every period and comma. Let's say you are not sure the period is correct in this group of words.

Mathabane knew he participated in rituals. More than he wanted to.

You know that using a period sometimes creates a **fragment**. You can now look for the section of the handbook that describes fragments to help you decide whether a period should be used. You find that "more than" is a kind of connecting phrase, so "More than he wanted to" will be a fragment if you put a period before it and after it. You correct the fragment by connecting it to the preceding sentence, since it goes with it.

Mathabane knew he participated in rituals more than he wanted to.

Problems You Can't Name   If you don't know the name of a problem, it will be hard to use a handbook. You will need to ask an instructor, tutor, or classmate for help.

They can teach respect, growing up, and helping the whole family.

You know that this last sentence in Body Paragraph 1 sounds a little strange. You ask your instructor about the sentence, and she tells you that the list at the end of the sentence involves a problem in parallel structure. She explains that the grammatical forms of all items in a list should match—that is, they should all be *-ing* words, or *to* words, or parts of sentences that are alike. You have several options.

■ Use simple verbs after *to.*

They can teach us to have respect, to grow up, and to help the whole family.

■ Use *-ing* words.

They can teach us about having respect, growing up, and helping the whole family.

■ Use separate sentences.

They can teach us to have respect, they can aid us in growing up, and they can help the whole family.

You might decide that the last sentence is the closest to expressing the meaning you want because each sentence adds emphasis to the three separate points your paper will make.

Handbook Tip

When you find the section of the handbook that describes the problem you are trying to correct, or when someone has suggested that you look at a particular section of the handbook, read over the explanations and examples carefully. Then practice correcting the problem by doing the exercises in the handbook. Write down your answers and check them in the back of the book. (Answers for exercises in Chapters 19 are found on pp. 545.) If you have successfully completed the exercise, return to your paper and make the correction. You can then look at the rest of your paper for similar problems.

EXERCISE 12.4   Use a spell checker, dictionary, and handbook to correct the errors you located in Exercise 12.2.

EXERCISE 12.5   Use a spell checker, dictionary, and handbook to correct the errors you located in your own essay.

ESL

Editing Log   To be able to write independently and avoid repeating the same mistakes, you need to learn the names of the problems you commonly have. One good way to do this is with an **editing log**—a written record that is kept in a notebook. Each time your instructor returns a paper or you edit a paper, write down the names of the errors in your log. Also, copy the part of the sentence with the error and mark the correction in a different color. This will help you to learn to recognize and name your own particular errors.

Editing Logs

Part 1. Creating an Editing Log

1. Make an entry for the paper you are editing—for example, *English 101, Essay 1, 1/21/03: Just Following Orders.*

2. Read your paper carefully, sentence-by-sentence, looking for errors.

3. Copy any sentence with an error. Mark the error so you can easily see what part of the sentence is the problem.

4. If others have read your paper and marked a sentence, include any comments they have made beside the error.

5. Identify the error type by name; use the Handbook if necessary.

6. Using suggestions in the Handbook or your instructor's comments, decide how to correct the error.

7. Write the correction next to the error in your editing log.

Part 2. Making a Summary of Error Types

1. List each error type by name.

2. Count how many times each mistake was made.

3. Identify any problems you should spend extra time working on.

An editing log is often most useful if it is divided into two parts:

Part 1—the log itself. Record the name of the mistake you made and how to correct it. Some mistakes can be easily corrected by adding verb endings or punctuation. If you decide to just correct the mistake in the log entry, use a different color pen or circle it, so you can identify it. Include any notes to yourself about checking your corrections with your instructor or in a handbook if you are unsure about them. See the following sample entries in the editing log.

Part 2—a short summary of the errors you made for a particular assignment. Make a list of each error type and the number of times you made this error. This summary will help you see if a particular problem is typical of your writing or perhaps just a careless mistake. The summary will help you see if your errors fall into a particular pattern. It can help you identify problems you need to spend more time on or ask for help in learning how to correct. If your instructor has not assigned a format for an editing log, follow the steps in the box on page 245.

Sample Entries in an Editing Log

This example illustrates an editing log entry for a daily reading response assignment to George Orwell's essay "A Hanging."

Lena Martin
Reading Response, 1/20/03
George Orwell,"A Hanging"

Errors	**Corrections**
1. Error/Context: . . . in George Orwell's "A Hanging.	Correction: Close quotation.
Type of error: Closing quotation marks around title	Note: Look up the order of quotation mark and period.
2. Error/Context: After the hanging is over, a Eurasian boy referred to the dead prisoner as . . .	Correction: Change referred to present; maybe change is to was.
Type of error: Tense shift	Note: Ask instructor about which tense would be best to use.
3. Error/Context: Shortly before, the superintendent pokes the dead body and replies . . .	Correction: Change pokes to poked. and replies to replied
Type of error: Wrong tense	Note: This is pretty clearly past, because this is at least before the Eurasian boy talks.

When to Use Your Editing Log

It is often easiest to learn to use an editing log after you have had help from someone else in recognizing what—or at least where—your errors are on a rough draft. After you have practiced identifying and correcting many of the common problems in your writing, you will be able to use an editing log more independently. You'll also determine the best times to use your editing log.

■ Your instructor reads over and comments on a complete rough draft of your paper before you submit it for a final grade. Use your editing log to respond to these comments. Instructors often include the names of an error along with an indication of where the problem is, so identifying the type of error and deciding how to correct it may be easier.

■ You have gotten some feedback from peer review. Remember, many times a fresh reader—even a fellow student—can detect problems more easily than the writer. If your peer editor has marked any particular sentences or phrases as being unclear, awkward, confusing, or wrong, then look at them to see if the problems could be caused by one or more of the common errors you make.

■ As you edit, read your paper twice. The first time, look specifically for common errors you noted from your editing log; the second time, look for anything else that seems less than satisfactory: organization, ideas, use of the reading, grammar, mechanics, and format.

EXERCISE 12.6 Make mock entries in an editing log for the errors in Exercises 12.1 and 12.2 on pp. 238–239.

EXERCISE 12.7 Make real entries for the errors you find in an essay you have written.

Collaboration **Peer Editing** Even the best writers will not be able to locate and correct every error in their writing. A new reader will see your essay with different eyes and will find errors that you understand but overlooked as well as others that you didn't understand. For this reason, many instructors will offer time in class for peer editing—an exercise in which peers look at each other's papers to find errors and make corrections.

Sometimes students feel that other students can't really help them learn to write or that they have nothing to offer other students. If you feel that way, you should think about a parallel situation: how you learned to use a computer. You may have learned many things about word processing from an instructor, but you probably also learned from other students. Even beginning students can help each other learn about word processing or using the Internet. Many times, students can help each other more easily than an instructor in a formal lesson can. Learning to write is a similar situation. You will be able to read a classmate's paper and recognize some errors, and that same classmate will recognize different errors in your paper. You can become each other's teachers. During this process, everyone—even good students—can learn from helping students with problems. Looking at other people's errors sharpens your own eyes, and explaining problems to others helps you understand and remember them yourself.

If your instructor doesn't give you time to peer edit, you might want to form a group outside of class with other students because this is one of the best ways to work on your editing. You can also e-mail drafts to other students for peer editing.

Editing Tip

Peer editing is a cooperative exercise that requires you to correct problems in your own paper. It is very different from handing your paper to a friend and asking him or her to make corrections for you. You won't learn from your friend's corrections, and your instructor might think that you are plagiarizing or cheating by turning in someone else's work as your own. If peer editing has not been assigned by your instructor, make sure that she knows that you are working on papers together and approves of your methods.

Here are some peer editing pointers.

Attitudes

- Give your partner a legible draft for peer editing so that reading each word is not a struggle.
- Accept the idea that the papers you write will be read by another person besides your teacher. Be prepared to read your paper aloud to another student.
- Don't be hurt by helpful, constructive criticism. Use your partner's suggestions as ways to learn and improve your paper.
- Don't belittle your partner, laugh at mistakes, or insult another's writing.
- Don't be afraid to offer constructive criticism. You won't be helpful to your partner if you say that a paper is correct when it is actually full of errors.

Actions

- Exchange papers with a partner, and use a pen or pencil that's a different color from that used in the paper.
- Read the paper aloud to the writer, if possible. If not, read it twice. Skim the paper once to see the overall meaning. Then read slowly and carefully.
- Do not write corrections on your partner's paper. Instead, mark a small X or dot in the margin. Make one mark for each error you think you see in the line.
- When the paper has been checked, return it to the writer. When you receive your checked paper from your partner, look at each mark in the margin, and try to locate and correct one error for each mark.
- If you can't find an error your partner marked or don't understand how to correct it, ask your partner to explain.
- If you are not sure that your partner's idea is correct, look in the handbook or ask a tutor or your instructor to verify the corrections.

EXERCISE 12.8

Pretend that the following body paragraph was written by one of your class-mates. Follow the preceding "actions" for peer editing to help your classmate improve the essay. Use the techniques discussed earlier under "Locating Errors" to find mistakes that you think your classmate should correct. Be prepared to explain everything you have marked.

Rules and Rituals (Body Paragraph 2)

Second, although rules can teach us things, rituals can help you grow. Mathabane tell us about his little brother George. It was time for George to be weaned and so "she smeared her breasts with red pepper and then invited my brother to suckle.. Of course, Georges mouth must of burned like fire soon he stopped nursing. Mathabane thought, it was amusing to witness my mother do it. He just saw this ritual as funny. He didn't understand that it had a purpose it was to mark George's passage from infancy to childhood. My friend Alan went though a passage similar to Georges. Alans family has a lot of money. Since they were rich, he did what ever he wanted cause he could afford too. He was really irresponsible and wasted money on stupid stuff that he would get tired of in two days. When they were sixteen, his parents bought cars for his older brother and sister. They bought Alan one when he turned sixteen, but they told him that driving a car ment that he had to be very responsable. They told him that driving a car meant that he was no longer a kid he was now a adult. It's strange, but owning that car really did change him. I guess he realized that you can't act irresponsably when your driving several tons of steel. This ritual of getting a car was good for Alan. Georges ritual was good for him because it meant he was no longer a baby. Mathabane was just amused by the weaning rit-ual, not realizing how rituals help you grow and become more mature.

EXERCISE 12.9

Exchange essays with another student and follow the previous suggested activ-ities. Keep your partner's feelings in mind.

Collaboration

Responding to Instructor Comments

Understand the comments

Correct the errors

Enter errors in your editing log

ESL

Instructor Comments If your instructor has looked at an earlier draft of a paper, she may have made comments on the editing. These will be use-ful suggestions for improving your writing. So be sure to think about and act on these comments. Here are some guidelines:

■ *Understand the comments:* When your instructor comments on your drafts, she may use symbols or abbreviations. Look at the back inside cover for some common symbols and abbreviations. If your instructor has her own system, be sure to ask her to explain anything you don't recognize.

■ *Correct the errors:* It's extremely important to correct errors as soon as the paper is returned to you. If you don't, you may not have the opportunity to ask the instructor for assistance later, and you may forget to make the corrections, causing problems in subsequent drafts.

■ ***Enter the errors in your editing log:*** Remember that the goal of correcting your editing is not just to make this one paper correct but to learn to correct your own errors when a teacher is no longer available. Otherwise you may continue to make the same mistakes over and over again. You will need to enter the errors in your editing log (see pp. 245–247) each time you receive a draft from your instructor.

An Instructor's Comments on a Paper

annotations
(teacher's comments)

annotations
(teacher's comments)

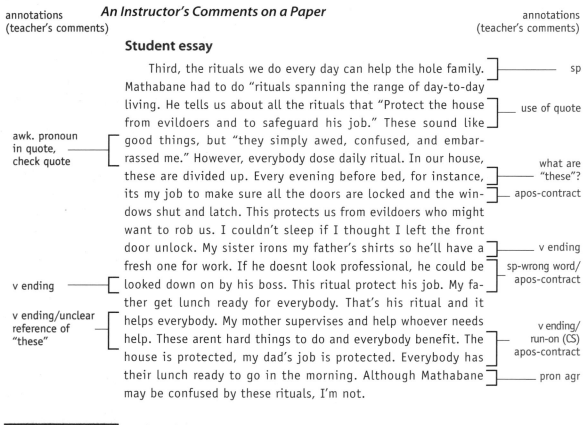

Student essay

Third, the rituals we do every day can help the hole family. — sp
Mathabane had to do "rituals spanning the range of day-to-day living. He tells us about all the rituals that "Protect the house — use of quote
from evildoers and to safeguard his job." These sound like
good things, but "they simply awed, confused, and embarrassed me." However, everybody dose daily ritual. In our house,
these are divided up. Every evening before bed, for instance, — what are "these"?
its my job to make sure all the doors are locked and the win- — apos-contract
dows shut and latch. This protects us from evildoers who might
want to rob us. I couldn't sleep if I thought I left the front
door unlock. My sister irons my father's shirts so he'll have a — v ending
fresh one for work. If he doesnt look professional, he could be — sp-wrong word/ apos-contract
looked down on by his boss. This ritual protect his job. My father get lunch ready for everybody. That's his ritual and it
helps everybody. My mother supervises and help whoever needs — v ending/ run-on (CS) apos-contract
help. These arent hard things to do and everybody benefit. The
house is protected, my dad's job is protected. Everybody has
their lunch ready to go in the morning. Although Mathabane — pron agr
may be confused by these rituals, I'm not.

awk. pronoun in quote, check quote

v ending

v ending/unclear reference of "these"

EXERCISE 12.10   **Look at the instructor's comments above.**

1. Think about the differences between revising (Chapter 11) and editing (this chapter). Which comments refer to editing and which to revising?
2. What does each comment mean?
3. Make a correction for each editing comment.
4. Enter the errors in your mock editing log.

| EXERCISE 12.11 | **Work with your instructor's comments on one of your own papers.** |

1. Think about the differences between revising (Chapter 11) and editing (this chapter). Which comments refer to editing, and which refer to revising?
2. What does each comment mean?
3. Make a correction for each editing comment.
4. Enter the errors in your own editing log.

EDITING FOR STYLE

After you have revised and edited your paper, you also need to be sure that each paragraph and sentence is clear. A short style check can do this.

A Simple Style Checklist

Pronouns

- Is it clear what each pronoun refers to?
- Does each pronoun agree with what it refers to (its antecedent)?
- Avoid *it, there, this,* and *that.*
- Use *you, I,* and *we* only when you mean it.

Verbs

- Shift tenses only with a reason.
- Avoid passive: *be + ed* verbs.

Word choice

- Say what you mean.
- Vary your word choice: Avoid repetition.

Sentence variety

- Use a mix of long and short sentences.
- Avoid very long sentences.
- Start sentences in a variety of ways.

Sentences that are unclear, confusing, or simply awkward will distract a reader from your ideas. You can find these weak sentences by looking for the parts of sentences that typically cause the problem. Follow the style checklist in the box to identify the parts of a sentence that are unclear, confusing, or awkward. There is further discussion of each part following the checklist. After you identify each part, you must decide if it is clear or if you can improve the sentence.

If you still have trouble, ask your instructor or lab tutor for help, or go to the relevant section of the Handbook (Chapter 19). You may need to review the meanings of some of the grammar terms or look up correct forms of words. *Note:* You will also find that some of the points in this style checklist are the same or similar to certain points in the **grammar** and **mechanics** checklist on page 242–243.

Pronouns

Clear and correct pronoun use requires you to constantly put yourself in the place of your audience. Check for pronouns separately.

Pronouns That Identify Which One   Put every use of *it, this, that,* and *there* in square brackets. Use these words only when they seem to be the only way to express something. Can you rewrite any sentence to eliminate these words? Can you add something after *this* or *that* to make them clear?

> **EXAMPLE:** Mathabane addresses <u>this</u> to the general public in America as his audience.
> [What is <u>this</u>? What does Mathabane address to the general public—the entire essay "My Father's Tribal Rule" or only one part of the essay?]

For additional help, see Handbook section 4.2 (p. 385–386).

Pronouns That Identify the Reader and the Writer   Put every *you, I,* and *we* in square brackets. Ask yourself: Does *you* really mean all of your readers? If not, rephrase the sentence to eliminate this word. Don't say *if <u>you</u> are a troubled parent, . . .* unless you are sure all of your readers are troubled parents. Say *if <u>someone</u> is a troubled parent,* or *if a <u>parent</u> is <u>troubled</u>.*

Often *I* is unnecessary and just weakens academic writing. Not only will sentences seem wordy, but the main idea will be buried in the middle of a longer sentence. If you really need to use *I* to explain an experience, using *I* is all right, but don't explain the obvious.

> **EXAMPLE:** <u>I personally think that</u> no-fault divorce weakens the institution of marriage because immature partners can marry without a strong sense of commitment and they can avoid taking responsibility for their selfish actions.
> [It is clear to a reader that you are the writer and that you are making a point. Ask yourself: What is the main point of my sentence—that "I personally think" something or *what* I am thinking? If you eliminate *I* (and more), you will have a more forceful and convincing sentence.]

CORRECTION: No-fault divorce weakens the institution of marriage because immature partners can marry without a strong sense of commitment and they can avoid taking responsibility for their selfish actions.

Verbs

Verb Tenses   Underline each verb. Write SHIFT beside each change in verb tense. Are these shifts necessary and appropriate, or are they lapses to spoken style or a misunderstanding about the time frame of examples?

> **EXAMPLE:** Mark Mathabane <u>was</u> a young boy who <u>was</u> growing up in South Africa. He <u>had</u> many conflicts with his father. Mathabane <u>blames</u> his father for treating him harshly. [Notice that all of the verbs are past tense except the last one. Is it appropriate to use present tense for an action done in the past? No. Change *blames* to *blamed.*]

For additional help, see Handbook sections 3.2 (pp. 376–383) and 7.3 (ESL; pp. 410–418).

Passive Verbs   Underline all forms of the verb *be*—which would include *is, are, was, were, am, been,* and *being.*
  Do some *be* forms occur with *-ed* verb forms? These are probably passive sentences. Can you rephrase them?

> **EXAMPLE:** Mathabane's mother is viewed as a mediator between him and his father. [This idea can be more directly expressed as *Mathabane views his mother as a mediator between him and his father.*]

Word Choice (Diction)

See Handbook section 5.1 (pp. 386–388).

Correct Word Choice   Put an X over any word that you are unhappy with. Then think about why the word isn't right, why it does not express exactly what you want to say. You'll probably find it most helpful to use a dictionary or a thesaurus to find the word that best suits your ideas.

> **EXAMPLE:** His mother's explanations have an <u>impounding</u> effect on Mathabane. [A quick check in a thesaurus will show that *impounding* means "confining" or "caging." What the writer probably means is simply *great* or *convincing.* The thesaurus gives *important* and *compelling* as synonyms for these words. *Compelling* is probably

the best choice because the mother's words are persuasive: She wants to *compel* Mathabane to agree with her.]

Variety and Word Choice   Within each paragraph, put XX over every word or word combination that you repeat. Do you use the same word many times? If the repeated word is a key word, repetition is fine. Repeating a key word can hold an essay together and keep it focused on the main point. But if a frequently repeated word is not a key word, use a synonym. Use a thesaurus if you need help.

Look at the preceding example again.

McCrary defends welfare supplements to mothers **because they** contribute to children's welfare.
[This sentence uses *welfare* twice. The first use could be replaced by *financial* or *governmental* and/or the second by *health*.]

Sentence Variety

Sentence Length   Count the number of words in each sentence. Put that number in parentheses at the end of each sentence. If many sentences are about the same length, rewrite some to vary sentence length.

Here are some ways to add variety.

▪ Combine shorter sentences by using words to show how they are related to each other.

▪ Break up very long sentences by using sentence adverbs to show how the shorter parts are related. Which is better—more long sentences or more short sentences?

▪ Learn when to use a few short sentences to get across your important ideas directly.

  EXAMPLE: Mathabane learns more than his father intends. He learns to hate his father.
  [While it would be possible to combine the two sentences above using *because,* using two sentences gives emphasis to the second idea (*learns to hate his father*) as well as the first (*learns more than his father intends*).]

▪ Avoid a succession of many long sentences. Watch out for sentences that are more than three typed lines. (They make your ideas hard to follow.) Try to break long sentences up or eliminate unnecessary or repeated ideas.

  EXAMPLE: <u>In reading the essay</u> "My Father's Tribal Rule" written by <u>Mark Mathabane, Mathabane</u> attempts to illustrate the ways in which his father attempts to change him by forcing him to conform to the vanishing customs of his father's people <u>in spite of the fact that</u> they now live in a world that is changing.

This sentence could be improved in several ways.

■ Eliminate some repeated phrases: *written by Mathabane* and *Mathabane*.
■ Delete unnecessary words: *In reading the essay*.
■ Break up the sentence to focus on the two main ideas: (1) Mathabane's purpose in writing and (2) his father's erroneous ideas.
■ Use one word instead of several to express one idea: *although* instead of *in spite of the fact that*, and *how* instead of *the ways in which*.

Here's an edited version.

> In "My Father's Tribal Rule," Mathabane attempts to illustrate how his father attempts to change him. His father wants him to conform to the vanishing customs of his father's people although they now live in a changing world that is changing.

These two sentences can be further improved by making them more active and eliminating words that do not contribute to the main idea of the sentences.

> In "My Father's Tribal Rule," Mathabane illustrates how his father attempts to change him. His father wants him to conform to the vanishing customs of the Venda.

See Sentence Basics, Handbook section 1 (pp. 359) and Sentence Boundaries, Handbook section 2 (pp. 364) for help in understanding sentence structure. See Handbook section 5 (pp. 386) for help in clarity.

Phrasing   Circle the first five words of each sentence. Read through the essay, reading only these circled words. If many sentences start with the same pattern, rewrite some to have more variety. For example, in one paragraph, a writer has used these first five words to begin sentences.

According to the author, his father . . .

According to Mathabane, his father was . . .

According to Mathabane's portrayal . . .

According to "My Father's Tribal Rule" . . .

Some of these can be started in different ways.

Mathabane states that his father . . .

Mathabane portrayed his father as . . .

"My Father's Tribal Rule" implied/suggested that . . .

Before continuing, review the box on page 251, which summarizes points that can be style problem areas.

Before continuing, review the box on page 251, which summarizes points that can be style problem areas.

| EXERCISE 12.12 | **Using all the methods suggested in this chapter, edit the following conclusion. Compare your results with those of your classmates.** |

Collaboration

Rules and Rituals (Conclusion)

In conclusion. Mathabane just doesn't get it. He thinks rules and rituals are just a waste of time. He doesn't see how they can help us learn to respect others and be more courtous to them. I think that Mathabane was to immature to understand that rituals can help us grow up. They can help develop self-responsibility and to become more mature, which is something most people could use more of. Mathabane only thinks about himself and thats why he doesn't want to do the rituals that help the whole family. Basically he wrong. Rules and rituals are something you should follow and practice.

What You've Done

■ Learned techniques to locate errors in your revised essay
■ Learned to use tools to correct errors
    Checkers for spelling
    Dictionaries and handbooks
■ Learned the usefulness of editing logs and peer editing
■ Learned to edit to improve style

The Next Step

■ Format and proofread your essay (Chapter 13)

13 Finishing the Essay
Formatting and Proofreading

What You've Done

- Checked and edited the essay

What You Need to Do Next

- Prepare the final copy of the essay in the correct format
- Check the final copy for careless errors

FORMATTING YOUR ESSAY

Now that you have **edited** your essay, you're ready to put it into the final **format**. You want to use a format that is clear and easy to read, so that your instructor will be able to concentrate on your writing.

Your instructor may require that papers be written on a computer, but some instructors will accept handwritten **drafts** for evaluation. As far as possible, try to follow the same rules for formatting, whether you're writing on a computer or by hand.

Formatting on a Computer

Writing on a computer is covered in Chapter 2 (pp. 33–37).

Computer Tip

Most word-processing programs have preset margins and fonts called the *default settings.* Use them. If you must set them yourself, set them as follows.

Use 1-inch margins on top, sides, and bottom.

Use a clear, simple font: 12 pt Times New Roman is most common.

Do not use italics or bold unless you need them for titles or subheads. Use black ink, not colors.

Use left justification only; do not use full justification. Left **justification** means that the left margin is a straight line. Full justification means that the right margin is a straight line, too. (In the production of this book, full justification is generally used, although in lists such as this you will see left justification.)

Double-space your essay (set line spacing to 2) and write on one side of the paper only.

If you have problems with your printer, bring the disk to class, along with the last draft you were able to print out.

Handwritten Papers

Handwritten papers are not as easy to read as word-processed papers. But you can make a handwritten paper easier to read if you follow these formatting suggestions. Most instructors will accept printing as well as cursive writing, but check with your instructor to be sure.

- Write in black ink, one side of the paper only.
- Leave 1-inch margins on all sides, including the bottom.
- Double-space. On lined notebook paper, skip lines and write on alternate lines.
- You may use white-out for some errors, but if you make many corrections, begin the page again.

Headings and Page Numbers

Whether you use a computer or write by hand, you should do the following (or follow the equivalent directions from your instructor).

1. Put your name, instructor's name, course and section, and the date in the upper left corner of page 1.
2. Center the title two spaces below the date or on the first line of lined paper. Do NOT use bold, italics, all capitals, underlining, or quotation marks, but DO capitalize the first letter of all important words.
3. Indent each paragraph, usually one TAB on most computers. If you are writing by hand, indent the beginning of each paragraph the equivalent of five spaces.
4. Put your last name and the page number in the upper right corner of every page.

Cover Page and Works Cited List

Most instructors do not require a separate cover page for short papers because they waste paper. Also, most instructors let you put a Works Cited list on the last page of your paper if you have enough space. But some instructors require a separate Works Cited page, which follows the style guidelines of the Modern Language Association (see pp. 337–339).

- ▪ A cover page has the title of your paper (without any special font and without quotation marks), plus all of the information needed to identify you, the course, the instructor, and the specific assignment. This may include the due date of the paper and the name of the paper, such as Paper 3 or Mathabane Response Paper. All of the information on the cover page should be centered. Lower the title of your paper until it is about one-third of the way down the page.

- ▪ Center the heading for a separate Works Cited page at the top of the paper. Follow the documentation format your instructor requires. For more information on how to write a Works Cited list, see pages 337–339.

Here is part of the essay "Rules and Rituals" that has been edited (in Chapter 12, pp. 235–256) and formatted. But the essay has not yet been **proofread**, so there are still errors. The complete, finished essay is at the end of this chapter (pp. 266–268).

Sanchez 1

Maria Sanchez
Dr. Simpson
ENG 100G10
December 12, 2003

Rules and Rituals

Rules and rituals are things people do. Everyday we follow some kind of rules. We also participate in rituals, although we might not know it. Mark Mathabane knew he participated in rituals, more than he wanted too. He lived with his family in a poor section of South Africa. His father was from the tribes, but they were now living around people who excepted modern ways, ways that Mathabane wanted to follow. His father insisted that the whole family follow tribal rules and rituals. He became angry and violent when Mathabane wouldnt obey the rules or follow the traditions. Mathabane writes about his hatred of rules and rituals in <u>My Father's Tribal Rule</u>. Although Mathabane disliked rules and rituals, he didn't see that they can be valuable and that they do have a purpose. Rules and rituals can teach us many things. They can teach respect, growing up, and helping the whole family.

First, rules teach respect. Mathabane tells about the rule his father had about not speaking at the table. He tells us that "One day I intentionally broke one of these laws" (42). He spoke during dinner and his father got really mad, he said, "You don't have two mouths to afford you such a luxury" (42). Then he threatened to cut out Mathabane's tongue. What Mathabane didn't understand was that his father got mad because Mathabane wasn't respecting him. One time my father got at me to. In my family, we have a dinnertime ritual. Before dinner, my brothers and my sister and I are supposed to clean the house and get everything ready for dinner. One day I didn't feel like doing it, because I have to do everything. My brothers and my sister don't do hardly anything. So I just sat on the couch and watched T.V. My father come in and saw me and started to yell at me. He said he worked hard every day to put food on the table and that I was showing disrespect to him, my mother, my brothers and my sister. He sent me to bed without supper. At first I was really mad because I thought that my father was unfair to me. I'm the oldest, so I wind up doing most of the work. Why should I have to clean the house every day and get the table ready? The more I thought about it, the more I felt bad. He did do a lot for us. Besides providing us with a house and food, he paid for the movies. He really does do a lot for us and sometimes I think we forget to say thank you. I felt bad for not respecting my father. I learn through this rule to respect my father, Mathabane didn't see the valuable things you can learn from rules.

[the essay continues below]

In conclusion, Mathabane just doesn't get it. He thinks rules and rituals are just a waste of time. He doesn't see how they can help us learn to respect others and be more courtous to them. I think that Mathabane was too immature to understand that rituals can help us grow up. They can help develop self-responsibility and to become more mature. These are two things most people could use more of. Mathabane seems only to thinks about himself and that's why he doesn't want to do the rituals that help the whole family. Basically he wrong. Rules and rituals are something you should follow and practice

[the following starts a new page]

Sanchez 9

Works Cited

Mathabane, Mark. "My Father's Tribal Rule." *The User's Guide to College Writing*. Ed. N. Kreml et al. New York: Longman, 2004. 42–46.

PROOFREADING YOUR ESSAY

As you look at the edited draft of your paper in its final format, you're probably assuming it's ready to be turned in.

However, if you look closely, you'll see that there are still some other errors to deal with. As the last step, the edited and formatted paper must be proofread. And proofreading must be a separate, careful step, not just a quick glance.

Proofreading as a Reading Process

When you proofread a paper, you are not trying to improve or change what you have written. You are trying to look at the words you have actually written on the page. Is this what you intended to write? When you were **drafting**, **revising**, and **editing**, you were paying attention to one problem at a time, and you may have missed some small errors. Also, if you have written your paper by hand or if you have waited to enter it on the word processor as a final step, there's a very good chance that you may have made some errors when you copied it.

Computer Tip

If you write your first draft on a word processor, you'll find it much easier to create a final draft with fewer errors. You won't need to do any recopying, which means you won't make any new errors.

Looking for Typical Trouble Spots in the Final Draft

As you proofread, you may discover that revising and editing has caused your earlier draft to lose some coherence. That is, changes in word choice or carelessly added examples may make your paper jumpy and hard to follow. If you discover that this has happened, you will need to go back to the earlier steps of revising (Chapter 11) or editing (Chapter 12) to make whatever larger changes are necessary. A change in one place in a sentence in your paper may lead to a complication later. If you revise and edit, you will have to proofread the new draft. Don't be afraid to return to an earlier step if you must.

After you have corrected all of your careless mistakes, you need to read your paper again to be sure what you have written is what you meant to write. Even if you are an excellent speller and know all your punctuation rules, you've probably made some mistakes even on the final draft. You may have relaxed your attention to details like spelling or punctuation, or you may have just become too tired or distracted to notice certain mistakes.

AN OVERVIEW OF PROOFREADING TECHNIQUES

Proofreading, like any step in writing, takes time. Expect that you'll need to read the essay at least two more times—once to be sure that it all fits together and at least once to look for specific errors. In fact, most writers find that they proofread more than twice. To be sure that you do see exactly what you've written, you'll need to use some of the same tools and techniques you used in locating your errors for editing (see pp. 236–238 for more details).

Proofreading for Coherence: Does It All Fit Together?

Read each sentence and paragraph to see if they still say what you want them to. Focus on each sentence or paragraph as a meaningful unit. This is an essential step for locating problems in coherence: missing words, wrong words, sentences copied twice, and so forth. After you are satisfied that your essay expresses your ideas clearly, you are ready to proofread for specific errors.

Tools and Techniques for Locating Specific Errors

The tools and techniques for proofreading are the same as those for revising and editing (see Chapters 11 and 12). But you are not reading to rephrase or reorganize your ideas. You are checking to make sure that all of the choices you have made in phrasing, sentence structure, and formatting are accurate and that changes made in revising and editing have not caused other mistakes. As explained in Chapter 12 (see pp. 236–238), you need a variety of tools.

- ■ *Edit pen*
- ■ *Pointer*
- ■ *Reading aloud*
- ■ *Reading backward*
- ■ *Your editing log:* Your **editing log** will help you proofread because it will remind you about the errors you usually make. Use the list in your log and check through the paper for each of your typical errors. For example, you might want to check each place you know the reading is used separately for accuracy and proper documentation, or you might know that you often confuse *to* and *too*. Remember that checking your editing log for the mistakes you commonly make is one of the most important steps in proofreading.

Combining Proofreading Tools to Locate Your Own Errors

Using several or all of these methods together will help make your proofreading more effective. Remember that proofreading for coherence, specific errors, and your own typical errors is important and none of these steps should be skipped.

When finishing all your final drafts, remember to be patient and to take a few moments to look over everything one more time. Although someone might be able to understand your paper without one more proofreading, your essay will present your ideas more clearly if there are no little mistakes to confuse or distract the reader. As you proofread, remember to check for all potential trouble spots.

Typical Trouble Spots
Coherence
Typos and carelessness
Misquoting of reading or other sources
Small words
Spelling
Punctuation
Spacing between words
Entries in your editing log

Examples of Errors Corrected in Proofreading

When you proofread, you are checking that earlier revisions and editing are accurate and that they have not caused a new problem. Sometimes one correction may introduce a new problem. Also, some types of errors are simply hard to catch, even at the editing stage. Mistakes involving small words, repeated words, word endings, spelling, and punctuation can be hard to notice. The following examples illustrate the types of errors that can still occur in an edited draft.

Overall Coherence   Check once again to make sure that everything fits together smoothly and makes sense. Were any problems introduced in revising and editing?

Computer Tip

Did you move, add, or delete any words or phrases or sentences? Be sure you didn't create any strange problems by leaving out a word or adding an extra one.

Verb Endings   If you change sentence structure or a verb tense, the ending may change and this will affect the spelling of the word. For example, if you combined the following two sentences into one using *besides* or *in addition to* to emphasize the contrast between the ordinary and the extra, *provide* now has the suffix *-ing* and this changes the spelling. This means that adding or deleting endings always requires checking the spelling of a word.

ORIGINAL

He <u>provides</u> us with a house and food.

He pays for my music lessons, he takes us to the beach in the summer, and he drops us off at the movies.

CHANGED IN EDITING

Besides <u>provideing</u> us with a house and food, he pays for my music lessons, he takes us to the beach in the summer, and he drops us off at the movies.

CORRECTED IN PROOFREADING

Besides <u>providing</u> us with a house and food, he pays for my music lessons, he takes us to the beach in the summer, and he drops us off at the movies.

Rephrasing   Rephrasing can also change forms and spellings of words. For example, if you decide to change the phrase *by intention* to the single word *intentionally,* you will need to be sure that you have spelled it correctly. You can't always just add *-ly* as you do in some words—for example, *slow+ly* Look up any of these changes you are unsure of.

ORIGINAL PHRASING

I also broke one of my father's rules <u>by intention</u>.

CHANGED IN EDITING

I also broke one of my father's rules <u>intentionly</u>.

CORRECTED IN PROOFREADING

I also broke one of my father's rules <u>intentionally</u>.

Typographical Errors and Carelessness   Some spelling mistakes are the result of typing errors or carelessness. Letters can be easily switched, left out, or repeated when typing or writing quickly. In the example below, the spell checker will not identify the misspelling *eve*, but it will probably identify the author's name as a misspelling.

Mathabane <u>eve</u> describes his father as ugly.

Since *eve* is a word, the **spell checker** won't underline it. Both the correct *Mathabane* and the incorrect *Mathaban* will be treated as equally incorrect by most spell checkers. It is up to you to check all names for correct spelling.

Misquoting a Reading or Other Sources   If you've quoted from a reading, you must use exactly the words and punctuation that the author used. Double-check the accuracy of your quote by looking back at the reading. Sometimes paraphrasing the author's ideas is better than quoting the original. However, even a paraphrase must accurately represent the content of the original.

The Little Words

Misspelling or Misusing Little Words   Little words can be easily overlooked by spell checkers since the program will not understand which meaning you intend.

Did you mean *of* or *off*?

Do you mean *he* or *she*?

Did you intend to write *doe snot* or *does not*? Your spell checker probably will not recognize the difference.

Leaving Out Little Words   Little words, like *to* and *be*, often do not contribute much to the meaning of a sentence and are often left out in hurried writing. Reading the final draft aloud slowly can catch small words omitted in the editing and proofreading process. For example, what word has been left out of the sentence below?

They can teach respect, growing up, and helping whole family.

Spacing Between Words   Proofread for spacing between words and sentences. Changes in editing a paper may affect spaces between words, sentences, and punctuation. For example, words can run together.

It was time for George tobe weaned.

Unnecessary spaces can appear before commas.

First , rules teach respect.

Parts of sentences can become fused together. In the following example, correcting a fragment by adding it to the previous sentence has resulted in a spacing problem.

His father was from the tribes, but they were now living around people who accepted modern ways, <u>ways that Mathabane wanted to follow</u>.

Spelling, Punctuation, and Accuracy   Here are some points to focus on.

- *Spelling and capitalization:* Don't forget to check names and titles.
- *Mistaken identities:* Check words like *except* and *accept,* or *it's* and *its* (more apostrophes to check).
- *Periods and commas:* Are you sure that each of these is at the proper place?
- *Question marks:* You may notice these more easily if you read your essay aloud. Does each question end with a question mark?
- *Accuracy:* Check what you quoted and what you paraphrased or summarized. Are the quotes accurate? Do you use quotation marks only where needed? Do you include quotation marks at the beginning *and* the end of each quote? Check the rest of the punctuation in the quote and the punctuation of any sentence you are combining with the quote.
- *Format:* Do you have appropriate headings, titles, indentations, and page numbers?

Proofreading: Checking and Rechecking

- ☑ Revision and editing often create new mistakes.
- ☑ Read every sentence and paragraph at least one more time.
- ☑ Read your paper aloud.
- ☑ Read backward from the end of the paper.
- ☑ Check the format one more time.

It's not realistic to expect every final draft you turn in to be absolutely perfect, but the more you check, the sharper your eye for details will become. This is the point at which your paper will be ready to turn in. The results of your paper should be evident on every page.

EXERCISE 13.1   **Proofread the final paragraph of the paper.**

In conclusion, Mathabane just doesn't get it. He thinks rules and rituals are just a waste of time. He doesn't see how they can help us learn to respect others and be more courtous to them. I think that Mathabane was to immature to understand that rituals can help us grow up. They can help develop self-responsibility and to become more mature, which is something most people could use more of. Mathabane only thinks about himself and thats why he doesn't want to do the rituals that help the whole family. Basically he wrong. Rules and rituals are something you should follow and practice

EXERCISE 13.2 **Proofread an essay that you have written.**

THE FINAL PRODUCT

Let's now look at the final version of "Rules and Rituals," a finished essay that has been proofread carefully and is ready to turn in.

Sanchez 1

Maria Sanchez
Dr. Simpson
ENG 100G10
December 12, 2003

Rules and Rituals

Rules and rituals are things people do. Every day we follow some kind of rules. We also participate in rituals, although we might not know it. Mark Mathabane knew he participated in rituals, more than he wanted to. He lived with his family in a poor section of South Africa. His father was from the tribes, but his family was now living around people who accepted modern ways, ways that Mathabane wanted to follow. His father insisted that the whole family follow tribal rules and rituals. He became angry and violent when Mathabane wouldn't obey the rules or follow the traditions. Mathabane writes about his hatred of rules and rituals in "My Father's Tribal Rule." Maybe because Mathabane disliked rules and rituals, he couldn't see that they can be valuable and that they do have a purpose. Rules and rituals can teach us many things. They can teach us to have respect, they can aid us in growing up, and they can help the whole family.

First, rules teach respect. Mathabane tells about the rule his father had about not speaking at the table. He tells us that "one day [he] intentionally broke one of these laws" (42). He spoke during dinner, and his father got really mad and said, "You don't have two mouths to afford you such a luxury" (42). Then he threatened to cut out Mathabane's tongue. What Mathabane didn't understand was that his father got mad because Mathabane wasn't respecting him. One time my father got mad at me, too. In my family, we have a dinnertime ritual. Before dinner, my brothers, my sister, and I are supposed to clean the house and get everything ready for dinner. One day I didn't feel like doing it because I usually end up doing most of the work. My brothers and my sister do hardly anything. This one time I just sat on the couch and watched TV. My father came in and saw me, and then he started to yell at me. He said he worked hard every day to put food on the table and that I was showing disrespect to him, my mother, my brothers, and my sister. He sent me to bed without supper. At first I was really mad because I thought that my father was unfair to me. I'm the oldest, so I wind up doing most of the work. Why should I have to clean the house every day and get the table ready? But the more I thought about it, the worse I felt. My father does a lot for us. Besides providing us with a house and food, he pays for us to go to the movies. He really does do a lot for us and sometimes I think we forget to say "thank you." I felt bad for not respecting my father. I learned through this rule to respect my father. Unlike me, Mathabane didn't see the valuable things you can learn from rules.

Second, while rules can teach us things, rituals can help us grow. Mathabane tells us about his little brother George. It was time for his mother to wean George and so his mother "smeared her breasts with red pepper and then invited my brother to suckle" (41). Of course, George's mouth must have burned like fire. Soon he stopped nursing. Mathabane thought, "It was amusing to witness my mother do it" (41). He just saw this ritual as funny. He didn't understand that its purpose was "to mark George's passage from infancy to childhood" (41). My friend Alan went through a passage similar to George's. Alan's family has a lot of money. Since they are rich, he used to do whatever he wanted because he could afford to. He was really irresponsible and wasted money on stupid stuff that he would get tired of in two days. When his older brother and sister were sixteen, his parents bought cars for them. They bought Alan one when he turned sixteen, too, but they told him that driving a car meant that he had to be very responsible. They told him that driving a car meant that he was no longer a kid. He was now an adult. It's strange, but owning that car really did change him. I guess he realized that you can't act irresponsibly when you're driving several tons of steel. This ritual of getting a car was good for Alan. George's ritual was good for him because it meant he was no longer a baby. Mathabane was just amused by the weaning ritual, because he did not realize how rituals help you grow and become more mature.

Third, the rituals we do every day can help the whole family. Mathabane had to do "rituals spanning the range of day-to-day living" (42). He tells us about all the rituals that his father made the family do. He mentions rituals to "protect the house from evildoers and to safeguard his job" (42). These sound like good things, but "they simply awed, confused, and embarrassed" Mathabane (42). However, as Mathabane's mother observed, "everybody does rituals" (43). In our house, the daily rituals are divided up. Every evening before bed, for instance, it's my job to make sure all the doors are locked and the windows shut and latched. This protects us from evildoers who might want to rob us. I couldn't sleep if I thought I had left the front door unlocked. My sister irons my father's shirts so he'll have a fresh one for work. If he doesn't look professional, he could be looked down on by his boss. This ritual protects his job. In the morning, my father gets lunch ready for everybody. That's his ritual and it helps everybody. My mother supervises and helps whoever needs help. These aren't hard things to do and everybody benefits. The house and my dad's job are protected. Everybody has their lunch ready to go in the morning. Although Mathabane may be confused by the purpose of rituals in his family, I'm not confused about their purpose in my family.

In conclusion, Mathabane just doesn't get it. He thinks rules and rituals are just a waste of time. He doesn't see how they can help us learn to respect others and be more courteous to them. I think that Mathabane was too immature to understand that rituals can help us grow up. They can help us to learn responsibility and to become more mature. These are two things most people could use more of. Mathabane seems to think only about himself and that's why he doesn't want to do the rituals that help the whole family. Basically he is wrong. Rules and rituals are something you should follow and practice.

[the following starts a new page]

Sanchez 5

Works Cited

Mathabane, Mark. "My Father's Tribal Rule." *The User's Guide to College Writing.* Ed. N. Kreml et al. New York: Longman, 2004. 42–46.

What You've Done

- ■ Read thoughtfully
- ■ Analyzed the assignment
- ■ Done prewriting and organized your ideas
- ■ Drafted introductory, body, and concluding paragraphs
- ■ Revised
- ■ Formatted and proofread

PART THREE

Essay Options

14 Writing for Evaluation

As you have seen, the writing process has many steps. However, not every writing task will require—or even allow—you to spend a lot of time on each step. You will also find that different tasks call for different strategies. It is important for you to modify the process to match your own strengths and weaknesses, as well as to match your specific task. This chapter explains how to adapt the process to timed writing, since essay exams are one way instructors use to evaluate your writing. Another way instructors evaluate writing is through **portfolio** assessment. This chapter also provides some specific tips on preparing an assessment portfolio.

MODIFYING THE PROCESS TO MEET YOUR NEEDS

Writing for Evaluation: Learning to Adapt the Process

Modifying the process to meet your needs

Modifying the process for the writing task

Adapting the process to timed writing.

Preparing a portfolio of your work: Self-evaluation

All parts of the writing process are necessary if you are going to produce good writing. However, some of the tasks will come more naturally and more easily to you than others. You must be mindful of the way you write so you can recognize those parts of the process you can complete quickly and naturally as well as those you really need to concentrate on.

For example, some writers have a great deal of life experience and can come up with their own ideas and topics quickly. Their **prewriting** tasks are usually brief and easily completed. However, these same writers often have difficulty using material from other sources. They may have to devote more time to studying an author's ideas, summarizing them, and prewriting about them.

To be a successful writer, you will need to identify the steps that are difficult for you and to decide how much time you need to spend on these steps to complete them successfully. Think about where you have spent the most time when writing your essays. Here are some common problem areas for writers that can cause difficulties in timed essays.

1. **Getting started on the topic.** Ask yourself why it was so difficult to get started. Was it because you discovered you were not really familiar enough with the reading assignment to begin prewriting and planning your essay? If so, that tells you that you must read more actively and do the focused prewriting activities that will help you become familiar with the reading and use it more quickly in writing. Look over the suggestions for active reading in Chapter 4. Practice writing sum-

maries and outlines of the assigned reading. Practice focused prewriting about a reading (Chapter 6).

2. **Answering the question exactly.** Although you may be able to write an essay, you might stray from the assigned topic. Writers whose essays stray might need to practice the step of analyzing the prompt (Chapter 5), or they might need to practice organizing their prewriting and planning an essay (Chapter 7).

3. **Getting ideas into a clear, organized essay structure.** If you have found that your ideas do not fit into an easily recognizable structure but tend to wander around the topic, you should also practice organizing your prewriting and planning your essay before you write (Chapter 7). Your prewriting should suggest not only an answer (a thesis) but also a plan of development.

   Have you overlooked a step in analyzing the prompt? Does the prompt suggest an organizational structure that you did not use to plan your essay? Questions such as "Are there other ways a lack of money causes disruption in the family?" suggest an organization with one problem caused by lack of money in each body paragraph. Look at the section in Chapter 5, "Analyzing the Prompt," which discusses how analyzing the prompt can lead you to a thesis and a plan of development.

   A third way you can easily improve your organization is to think about paragraph structure, especially for the body of your paper. Do you use topic sentences effectively? If not, practice stating the main idea or generalization that each example illustrates. Practice explaining how the example relates to the thesis. As you write, be conscious of the beginning and ending of each body paragraph. Review the structure of body paragraphs in Chapter 9.

4. **Editing and Proofreading.** You will become a more efficient editor of your own writing if you know your weaknesses in grammar and mechanics. Review your previous rough drafts and make a list of the commonly recurring errors. Do you have a lot of added-on detail fragments? Do you have a tendency to create run-ons in your drafts? Do you frequently leave off word endings, especially verb endings, when drafting? Do you always confuse "their" and "there"? Do you forget to close your quotation marks and include page numbers of quotations?

   Do you know how to correct the errors you found when looking over your drafts? If not, review the sections in the Handbook that explain and show how to correct these errors (see Chapter 19). Practice correcting these errors by completing some exercises in the Handbook. The answers are in the back.

   If you have kept an editing log, look over your most recent entries (see Chapter 12, pp. 245–247). This will help you recognize them in your own writing. Be sure to practice how to correct these errors in your own writing, too.

> ### Modify the Process for Your Own Writing
>
> Before you are evaluated, modify the writing process to your own writing.
>
> Review the entire writing process.
>
> > See Part Two (Chapters 4–13).
>
> Know your strengths and weaknesses.
>
> > Focus on revising (Ch. 11) and editing (Ch. 12).
>
> Review and practice the skills that will improve your own writing.
>
> > See the exercises in Part Two and the Handbook (Ch. 19).

MODIFYING THE PROCESS TO MATCH YOUR TASK

Even after you have experimented with the process enough to know which parts come naturally and which parts you have to wrestle with, you will still have to adapt your process for each task. Different tasks place different demands on writers. Constraints of time, formality and correctness, subject matter, complexity—any of these may require you to modify the process you are most comfortable with.

Subject Matter Constraints   Many beginning writers are very articulate when it comes to topics they have an opinion about. These writers do not need a great deal of time because ideas and examples come easily to them. But when they come across a topic they know little about or that they find less appealing, it is harder for them to think of anything to say. The temptation is often to just say, "This topic is boring, so I can't write about it." Instructors (or employers) are not likely to let these writers switch their topics simply for this reason.

If you feel you have little to say about a topic, you need to fall back on prewriting techniques or research to find a way to have more to say and to make the topic more appealing The good news is that writing depends on techniques that can be learned, not just inspiration that either hits you or doesn't. When you are feeling uninspired or lost, you can follow the techniques to get restarted.

Time Constraints   Often, time limits will require you to alter your process. If you have about an hour to write an in-class essay, you have a limited amount of time to **prewrite**, **organize**, **draft**, **revise**, and **edit**. If you are accustomed to taking a few hours or days to prewrite before you begin to organize and draft, you obviously must try a different strategy. We will discuss writing in timed situations in the next section.

Task-Based Constraints You will also want to modify steps for the unique challenges presented by different assignments. For example, some writers find that organizing their ideas for shorter papers is easily done by writing a list of their ideas in the order they plan to include them. However, for longer papers, these same writers have difficulty seeing how to fit more ideas and examples into their writing. For these tasks, they might write sections of their prewriting on index cards so that they can physically move the pieces around and try out different organizations.

If a significant portion of your evaluation is based on creating a folder or **portfolio** of your work for the semester, you will need to create and organize your writing in a way that's easy for your reader. Grouping together similar assignments and making an outline or table of contents to introduce this portfolio is helpful. See the suggestions for creating and organizing a portfolio below.

The important thing is to experiment. Try new things, and try old things in new ways. The more you experiment, the more tools you can develop and the more flexible you can be in approaching each new writing situation.

Modify the Process for the Writing Task

Identify the Constraints Imposed by the Task

Prepare for constraints imposed by the subject matter.

Read, annotate, and analyze the assignments.

    See Chapter 4.

Research topics you are unfamiliar with.

    See Chapter 18.

Think About the Time Constraints

Identify what can be done ahead of time.

    See Chapters 4, 5, 6, and 7.

Think about possible questions and practice writing

    See Chapters 5, 6, and 7.

Think About Task-Based Constraints

Practice listing to organize and plan timed writing.

    See Chapters 6 and 7.

Use index cards to organize research papers.

    See Chapters 18 (Research) and 19 (Documentation section of Handbook).

MODIFYING THE PROCESS FOR ESSAY EXAMS

Writing essay exams is perhaps the most difficult writing task for many students. The idea of writing an essay with limited time and limited sources (such as notes, textbooks, or outlines) leaves students feeling powerless. Don't be intimidated—there are many ways to alter your writing process that will help you to be successful.

Prewriting for Essay Exams

To prepare to write in a timed situation, you should complete your prewriting activities in two steps. First, complete the reading and writing activities that will help you study and organize the information you will need for the exam ahead of time. Second, prewrite briefly during the exam period. You may want to merge the analysis of the **prompt**, prewriting, and planning into one brief session at the beginning of the exam. Here are some tips for prewriting in a short period of time.

Preparing for Timed Writing Before Class

- Review the materials—textbook chapters, handouts, essays, articles, literary works—that you are required to use for the exam, and complete the activities discussed in Chapter 4. Allow adequate time for reading and for completing the necessary prewriting and studying activities.

- Think of possible exam questions and essay topics. Now practice with these topics! Prewriting will also help you learn the material.

- As you prewrite, determine which writing modes could help you answer your practice questions: Is comparison and contrast or cause and effect more appropriate? If you need to explain and illustrate ideas, is description or chronological narration more effective?

- Review other essay exams and papers you have completed for this instructor. This will help you to identify weaknesses in your writing that your instructor has previously noted so that you can work to improve in these areas.

- Prepare for the exam conditions. If your instructor gives open-book exams or allows you to use notes, review these materials and mark them so you can find information quickly.

- Gather the materials you will need early. Bring plenty of paper or pens and correcting liquid or erasers. If you can use a dictionary, the textbook or other readings, a page of notes, or study guides, gather these and bring them to class as well.

Some of the pressures of timed writing can be eliminated if you are prepared. Following the preceding list will help you to prepare. It is also important to adapt the writing process to timed writing. This often means shortening the time you spend prewriting. Here are some suggestions for previewing the exam, analyzing the prompt, and prewriting in timed writing.

Prewriting in Class: Previewing, Analyzing the Prompt, and Prewriting

- *Preview the exam.* Look over the entire exam so you will know how much you need to write. How many questions? What type of answers? Are there choices? If you have to write more than one essay, decide how to divide your time.

- *Analyze the prompt.* Read the assigned topic carefully, and be sure you understand exactly what you are asked to do. If you have a choice of topics, choose the topic you plan to answer carefully. Underline the **key focus words** and **key action words**. If key action words are not provided, determine what writing **mode** will help you focus, develop, and organize your essay in a way that addresses the prompt.

- *Prewrite.* Do not prewrite topics that you do not intend to answer. Allow 5 to 10 minutes to prewrite a full-length essay. Allow about 2 to 3 minutes for short-answer questions.

- *Create lists to plan your answer.* First, list the two or three main ideas that you will need to develop your essay. For each main idea, make a list of one or two examples and details from your own ideas and experiences, the assigned readings, and your notes.

After you have made notes on the main ideas and the supporting examples and details, you are ready to plan and organize your essay. This step should only take a minute or two.

Planning and Organizing Your Essay in Class

- Write a **thesis**. Be sure that the thesis clearly responds to the topic or exam question. Use the language of the prompt in your thesis.

- Decide the order of the discussion of the main ideas. Look at your prewriting list. It can help you to decide on an organizational pattern. Any of the following common patterns (see Chapters 15 and 16) will work.

  Chronological

  Least important to most important

  Cause and effect

  Problem and solution

  Side by side or point by point for compare/contrast

- Write **topic sentences** for each main idea. Look at your thesis as you start each body paragraph. Connect each main idea in the topic sentence to the thesis and prompt by using the same language.

Once you have a clear thesis and have planned how to organize your main ideas, you are ready to complete drafting your paper. You may decide to use the thesis and topic sentences you have just developed as an outline for your paper and rework them as you complete the draft.

Drafting the In-Class Essay

Since you will have time to write only one draft, skip lines to leave room for revision. Don't write on the back of the paper—especially if you are writing in ink. (The ink may bleed through, making the back side of the page difficult for you to revise and for your instructor to grade.)

Budget your time. If you have 30 minutes, don't spend more than 6 or 7 minutes on each paragraph.

Don't stop to do complicated editing as you go. Underline words you'll need to look up in a dictionary, but wait until after completing the draft to actually look them up. (That's why you're skipping lines.)

Revising, Editing, and Proofreading: Readability vs. Neatness

Once you have drafted your essay, allow yourself 10 to 15 minutes to revise, edit, and proofread it. At this point, it is important to focus on correctness and clarity rather than on neatness. Don't spend time recopying your response. Neatness rarely counts in an in-class essay, but readability always does, so spend your time making your essay easier to understand and follow.

While making changes that strengthen your content, you will want to be sure that your reader can tell where you are inserting material and which material you are deleting. Unless you are given an additional class period to complete a major revision for the exam, you will not have time to do more than this. However, as you edit and proofread your writing, you should check the following basic aspects of the essay.

Revising an In-Class Essay

- Are your paragraph breaks logical? You can always change the beginnings and endings of paragraphs by drawing lines and paragraph symbols (¶).
- Do the thesis and main ideas match? Check for key focus words in both. If you changed your mind about which main ideas to use in developing your paper or if you changed your **plan of development** while drafting, check to see if your thesis still fits the body of your paper.
- Eliminate paragraphs that do not fit your thesis or that repeat the same ideas. Cross out the paragraph with an X over the deleted material. If you have time at the end of class, you can write another paragraph to insert in the essay to replace the deleted material.

▪ Run each paragraph through a mental checklist. Add a topic sentence to each paragraph that lacks a clear controlling idea. Use the key focus words from the prompt that will tie the paragraph back into the thesis. Add a summary statement at the end of each paragraph to make the the point of the paragraph clear. Use the key focus words from the prompt that will tie the paragraph back into the thesis here, too.

Once you are sure that the content of your paper clearly develops a thesis that answers the question, you can spend a few minutes on editing and proof-reading. You should combine these two steps in in-class writing because of time constraints.

Editing and Proofreading

▪ Recopy only what is absolutely necessary. If you have made so many changes in one paragraph that it is not legible, recopy only that paragraph. Write a note in the margin indicating where your reader can find the new paragraph.

▪ Edit for word choices and correctness. Ask yourself these four questions.

  1. Do you need to change some words to clarify your point?

  2. Do you need to add words to clarify how your ideas and sentences relate to each other?

  3. Have you omitted words when writing or changing sentences? Add missing words and endings.

  4. Have you checked quotations for accuracy, punctuation, and documentation (by page, paragraph, or line, as needed)?

▪ Check for potentially confused words that would alter the meaning of your essay. For example, you don't want to confuse words such as *accept* and *except.*

▪ Check for these major grammar and usage issues (see Chapter 19 for details).

  Sentence boundaries—**fragments** and **run-ons**

  Verb endings and verb forms

  Punctuation

  Spelling

Although you may prefer to edit and proofread using liquid paper to make essays look neater, draw a line through the words you want to change and neatly write the new words above them. This will save you valuable time.

As in all skills, the more you write timed essays, the better you will become at producing them. Until writing in-class essays becomes natural for you, focus on each of the steps discussed in this chapter. Practice at home. A few hours spent preparing and practicing essay writing under testing conditions may make a big difference.

Timed Writing: Writing Essay Exams

Modifying Prewriting: Before and During the Exam

Preparing for timed writing: Prewriting before the exam

    See Chapters 4, 5, 6, and 7.

Prewriting during the exam: Combining steps

    See Chapters 5, 6, and 7.

Planning and Organizing Your Essay

    See Chapters 6 and 7.

Drafting a Complete First Draft

    See Chapters 7 and 8–10.

Revising Within the First Draft

    See Chapter 11.

Editing and Proofreading: Correctness and Clarity Counts

Don't recopy unless absolutely necessary.

    See Chapters 12 and 19.

CREATING A PORTFOLIO

The development of a portfolio allows writers to demonstrate the breadth and depth of their writing and to show an understanding of writing as a process. There are many ways to organize a portfolio: It can be a tool for organizing all of your writing in a course, or it may be a folder of what you consider your best writing.

What Do All Portfolios Have in Common?

Portfolios show an overview of the writer's skills, and they represent the best efforts of a writer. They include a number of assignments, sometimes all major course assignments and sometimes only a selection of assignments.

Portfolios are usually evaluated for product and process. As a product, a portfolio represents the accomplishments of a writer in a course. As a process, a portfolio shows how the writer developed each assignment through steps. Writers who try to skip steps and cut corners may develop sloppy habits, so ensuring that the writing process is well represented is the key for any portfolio.

Portfolios and the Writing Process   Your portfolio should show that you understand the writing process and that you have followed all of the steps necessary to develop good writing. Your portfolio should reflect these aspects of your writing.

Drafting. Are early drafts available for comparison with final drafts? Instructors usually want to be able to evaluate the progress you have made in a course. Are these drafts thoughtful and on target (related to the writing prompt or question)? Do they show a plan for organizing ideas? Do they show connections between ideas that may have been given as part of the assignment and the writer's own ideas?

Revising. Is there evidence of revision for content, development or ideas, and structure and organization? Is the purpose of each paper clear? Are the connections between the parts of your essays clear? If there are comments from the instructor, did you respond to the suggestions for improving your writing?

Editing. Is there evidence of editing? Has each sentence been evaluated for clarity, effectiveness, structure, grammar, and correct word forms?

Proofreading and Formatting. Did you really proofread your work, especially your final drafts? Are the final drafts largely free of punctuation, spelling, and word-processing errors?

Portfolio Evaluation

Portfolio evaluation is very common in composition courses. Portfolios can be evaluated in different ways. Ask your instructor how your portfolio will be evaluated at the beginning of the course. A few weeks before the portfolio is due, look over your work and ask for clarification of any points you do not understand fully. Many instructors will want you to continue improving your essays throughout the course. Look over comments and suggestions for improving each paper and continue to revise and edit your papers. After you have mastered more skills toward the end of the course, revisit the papers you wrote early in the course to see how they can be further improved.

Self-evaluation: Checklists and Cover Letters   Often an instructor will require self-evaluation and reflection by the writer on individual essays or on the entire portfolio. Most portfolios include a cover letter or a checklist to establish that the portfolio is complete and organized according to requirements. Be sure that any required self-evaluation is in the correct format.

If you are not formally required to evaluate your portfolio, it is still a good idea to save time to do this. You may discover some weaknesses in the final draft of some papers or some areas that need to be clearer.

Checklists. Use the checklist provided by your instructor to judge whether your papers meet the course standards. You can also use the checklists for essay organization and development in Chapters 8, 9, and 10, and the checklists for revising, editing, formatting, and proofreading in Chapters 11, 12, and 13.

Cover letter or memo. Another form of self-evaluation is to write a reflective letter or memo that assesses the strengths and weaknesses of the essays in the portfolio. The letter usually identifies problems encountered in developing each assignment and how these problems were addressed. The letter should also include a discussion of how the writer's writing has changed over the course of the semester. It should identify aspects of writing and the writing process that the writer now feels more comfortable with and aspects that the writer feels may still need improvement.

Writing a Cover Letter

- Introduce all of the work in the portfolio in the first paragraph of your cover letter. Identify the essays and other assignments in your portfolio.

- Discuss each major assignment in the body of your cover letter. Write a separate paragraph for each major assignment in your portfolio. Identify the problems you encountered as you developed the paper. Consider all of the steps involved: reading an assignment, analyzing the prompt, prewriting, organizing and planning, drafting, revising, editing, formatting, and proofreading. Which of these skills required the most work? Why?

- If your portfolio includes other daily assignments such as summaries, reading responses, or other short assignments, develop another paragraph to comment on them. What skills do you think you developed as you did each task? How did these other daily writing assignments affect your writing in the course?

- Conclude the cover letter by writing a paragraph explaining how your writing has changed as a result of taking the course. Comment on the challenges you faced during the term and how your portfolio reflects your writing skills.

Instructors will evaluate your writing for how well you meet the requirements of your assignments. In most courses, these assignments vary and may include timed writing. The writing process can be successfully adapted to timed writing with adequate preparation, analysis of your own strengths and weaknesses, and practice. The key is to realistically prepare for the task.

Creating a Portfolio

Portfolio as Product and Process

Portfolio as product

Review checklists in Chapters 11, 12, and 13 (revising, editing, formatting, and proofreading).

Portfolio as process

Review Part Two (Chapters 4–13).

Portfolio self-evaluation: checklists and cover letters

Review Part Two: all of the steps.

Review checklists in Chapters 11, 12, and 13 (revising, editing, formatting, and proofreading).

Instructors will also evaluate your writing by reviewing a portfolio of your writing that represents both product and process. Before submitting your portfolio, you should evaluate your work according to the standards set for the course. Use any checklists provided by your instructor. Organize your portfolio according to the specific instructions given by your instructor. Save adequate time to write a cover letter to introduce your portfolio.

15 Writing in the Expository Modes

Expository Modes of Writing
Narration
Description
Definition
Classification
Comparison and contrast
Illustration
Process
Cause and effect

In many college writing tasks, you will be asked to respond to an assignment with a specific **critical thinking**, **developing**, and **organizing** strategy—what composition instructors often call call modes of writing. For example, a history instructor may ask you to compare America's attitudes toward World Wars I and II; a computer instructor may ask you to explain the process of segmenting a hard drive; or an English instructor may ask you to write a character analysis. These tasks may require a few paragraphs or a full-length essay. No matter what the length requirements are, you can use the same steps for generating and organizing material. The only difference will be the amount of material you need.

Exposition is basically explaining a subject to an audience and making that subject clear. While exposition is not an argument in itself, you can use exposition to make your argument or persuade your audience. In this chapter, we provide tips for the common expository modes, including narration, description, definition, classification, compare/contrast, illustration, process, and cause/effect.

NARRATION

Narrative writing is used to describe a sequence of events or actions, and it is very similar to fiction writing found in short stories, novels, plays, and movies.

Purpose

When writing a narrative, you need to reveal a **purpose** that allows the reader to determine the meaning of events and why they matter. For example, are you trying to convey conflict or tension and how this was resolved? Are you trying to demonstrate how you or a place has changed—or stayed the same—over time?

Development

Good narrative writing includes many of the same features as **descriptive writing** a combination of general and specific information and the use of concrete nouns with descriptive adjectives and adverbs. Vivid descriptions of the places, people, and events involved in a narrative add life and meaning to all writing.

Many inexperienced writers tend to give too many or too few details. They don't always understand that readers do not need a description of everything that happened or was said. For example, if you were describing a car accident, you would not discuss every detail: the man grabbed the door handle, pulled the handle, pushed the door open, put one leg on the ground, then the second leg, then stood up, then prepared to walk, and he stopped and said, "Are you okay?" Such minute detail would distract and bore a reader. Although you may want to write down everything that happened and was said during the **prewriting** and planning steps, you need to select the relevant details that convey your purpose and meaning.

Organization

When organizing a narrative, you may choose to tell the events in the order or sequence in which they occurred. To do this, you can make a list of events that happened and then rearrange them in the order they happened. To signal the order of events, writers use words like *first, next, then, after that, while, when,* and *before.*

Sometimes it is more effective to rearrange the order of events, especially if you are trying to create suspense. Flashbacks and flash-forwards are two techniques for altering the sequence of events. In a flashback, the narrator goes back to a time before the present sequence of events being described; in a flash-forward the narrator describes a sequence of events in the future. Both techniques allow a writer to show relationships among events that may be separated by a long period of time or that may be connected in the narrator's mind even though others may not see the connection.

The following box highlights some techniques useful in writing narration.

Tips for the Narrative Mode

Point of view is the position from which the narrative is told. One way to understand point of view is to consider who is telling the story (or narrating it). Think about those involved in and those who witnessed a car accident. Everyone at the scene of the accident would have a different story. The different ways of telling the story of this wreck represent different points of view.

Verb tenses show the passage of time and indicate clearly the order of events. For example, "We walked to the store" indicates an event that has already happened. If your next sentence is "We watched the movie," your reader needs to know the order in which these events occurred as well as their relationship.

The time and relationship of the two events mentioned in the box can be conveyed in many ways.

We walked to the store before we watched the movie.

We watched the movie, and then we walked to the store.

We were expected to walk to the store before we watched the movie.

We walked to the video store so we could rent a movie to watch that night.

The list of possibilities is endless, but the point is simple. To demonstrate time and relationship, we varied the verb tenses and the way words were used in the sentence. This same level of attention to verbs is required throughout a narrative so that your readers will not get confused about the sequence of events and how they fit together to create meaning.

EXERCISE 15.1

Here are some prompts to help you practice using the narrative mode.

1. Recall an event in your life during which you learned an important lesson. Write an essay in which you tell the story of the lesson you learned.

2. Conduct an interview of someone in your family, and relate an important experience in his or her life.

Collaboration

3. Working as a group, identify an event that all of you have witnessed or experienced, either as individuals or as a group. Brainstorm the events that occurred, and then organize the details into a narrative paper.

Collaboration

4. Working as a group, identify a historical event, and conduct research on the details of this event. Then, as a group, write a narrative of this event as if you were there to witness it.

Examples of Essays Written in the Narrative Mode

Malcolm X, "A Prison Education," pp. 461–464

Maya Angelou, "Champion of the World," pp. 504–508

DESCRIPTION

Description involves putting into words how something looks or appears or the way something acts. Description focuses on details, especially details that reveal the essence of what is being described.

Often you will be asked to describe something that you are very familiar with (your house, a person close to you, your favorite place) or something very new to you (a painting for an art class, a character in a work of literature, a piece of new machinery used in your field of study). For familiar objects, you need to find a new way to see them. For new objects, you have to study them closely to understand them. In either case, you will be asked to examine an object in depth, to give all relevant details, and to make the subject come alive.

Purpose

When you begin writing a description, consider your purpose for writing and what the reader is going to do with this knowledge. If you are writing an ad to sell your car, your readers will want to know what the car looks like and its condition. They will not be interested in details about personal items in the car or how you feel about it. However, if you are writing an essay on car ownership, you may want to show how cars reflect personality or values, and you may want to include personal information.

There are two types of descriptive writing: technical and evocative. In **technical description**, the writer provides pictorial data in an orderly manner that reveals the purpose, function, or appearance of a subject. This kind of description is most often found in instructional materials, such as user manuals and technical manuals. The order of the details provided should focus on how the object is constructed and how all the parts relate to each other. Since the writer is not trying to convey any emotional connection to the subject, the tone needs to remain objective and the language will need to be precise and technical. For example, to describe the CPU of your computer you would need to mention the visible parts, such as the power button, the reset button, the 3½-inch disk drive, the CD-ROM drive, and the zip drive. You would also need to describe clearly where these parts are in relation to each other—above, below, 3 inches to the left, and so on. Many technical descriptions include a drawing of the subject with the important components labeled.

In **evocative description**, the writer emphasizes the emotional aspects of the subject to create a vivid impression. In this type of writing your goal is to reveal the personal aspects of the subject, to move your readers from being detached to being emotionally involved. While you may be tempted to include a painting, drawing, or photograph of the subject being described, this will not make your task any easier.

Let's say you have been asked to describe a favorite place, and you have chosen to write about your bedroom. In an evocative description, you would want to emphasize some aspects of the subject more than others to encourage an emotional response. You would focus more on **connotation** (the emotional aspect) than **denotation** (the objective meaning). For example, instead of using the word "closet" you might use the phrase "overflowing river" to create an image of a closet so crammed full that stuff spills out when you open the door.

Development

When prewriting and planning a descriptive paper, you need to answer these questions.

- ▪ What is the subject?
- ▪ What are its dimensions (size and shape)?
- ▪ What materials is it made of?
- ▪ What is its purpose or use?
- ▪ Where is it made or manufactured?
- ▪ Where is it most commonly found?

- ▪ When does it appear?
- ▪ When does one need it?
- ▪ Why is it of value?
- ▪ Why is it important for the reader to understand it?
- ▪ Who needs or uses it?
- ▪ Who made it?
- ▪ How does it work?

Organization

When organizing a piece of descriptive writing, it is important to choose a consistent angle or **point of view** that establishes how each new detail is related to the previous ones. One method is to describe every detail from a single reference point or viewpoint. This works best if you are describing a stationary object or if you want to capture everything that the reader would see from one particular place. For example, you may be describing something you see when you look out your bedroom window: a new car parked in the driveway. Or you may choose to describe *everything* you see when you look out the window. Once the reader has an angle or point of view, you can then use words and phrases like *to my left* or *in front of the car*.

Another method for organizing descriptions is *spatial*, which means to move around the object or through the place or scene being described. Instead of describing how the car looks in the driveway, you may choose to walk around the car to describe how it looks up close. Instead of looking out the window to describe your neighborhood, you may choose to walk down the street. If you are moving, your reader will need words such as *down, along,* and *next* to understand the relationship of details.

Regardless of the organizational pattern you select, you need to connect the details with transitions and ideas so that the reader can understand the details and how they relate to each other. These connections help you establish your purpose for writing. The box below highlights some techniques useful in writing description.

Tips for the Descriptive Mode

Use concrete nouns to refer to specific places and physical objects. These nouns help your readers visualize the place or thing you are describing. For example, *transportation* is an abstract noun that refers to an idea, not to a specific object; *bicycle, subway, train, airplane, car,* and *bus* are concrete nouns that name a specific vehicle.

continued on next page

> *continued from previous page*
>
> *Sensory words* are related to our senses of sight, touch, taste, smell, and sound, and they create a picture for readers. An effective descriptive paper will focus on all five senses.

EXERCISE 15.2

Here are some prompts to help you practice the descriptive mode.

1. Describe a place that reveals or reflects your personality.
2. Find a work of art that you enjoy and describe it.

Collaboration

3. Working as a group, select an item with which you are all familiar. List all the details about that item and then organize these details into a descriptive paper.

Collaboration

4. Working as a group, choose a historical or famous person, and conduct research about this person, identifying both biographical and physical information. Then, organize the information you find into a descriptive paper.

Examples of Essays Written in the Descriptive Mode

Randall Williams, "Daddy Tucked the Blanket," pp. 436–440

Mark Mathabane, "My Father's Tribal Rule," pp. 42–46

George Orwell, "A Hanging," pp. 48–51

DEFINITION

Definition essays help readers understand the meaning of words or concepts, particularly those that are abstract or complex. Let's say you are writing about welfare. You might begin by defining this term as government assistance to individuals. But then you'll need to explain that there are several kinds of government programs for assisting both individuals and businesses. One person's use of the word *welfare* may be in reference to one particular type of assistance for unwed mothers, whereas another person may be referring to medical assistance for the elderly, and yet a third person may mean tax breaks given to individuals and businesses.

Purpose

There are three common purposes of definition papers.

- To explain how a word or phrase should be used (*technical definition*)
- To explain the writer's attitude toward a word or phrase (*personal definition*)
- To show how the meaning of a word has changed or is changing (*historical definition*)

Development

In a definition essay, your role will be to provide more than just a repetition of the meaning listed in a dictionary entry, but the dictionary is a good place to start when prewriting for this kind of essay. You will probably have to read through the several definitions given, each providing a slightly different meaning. Locate one or two words that fit your purpose and use them as the basis of your essay.

For example, here are some definitions you might find if you look up the word *love.*

Strong affection for another arising out of kinship or personal ties, such as maternal love for a child

Attraction based on sexual desire, or the affection and tenderness felt by lovers

Attraction based on admiration, benevolence, or common interests, such as love for a friend

Warm attachment, enthusiasm, or devotion to something, such as the love of a sport or place

A person's adoration of a god or religious figure

Obviously, when you use the word *love* in a particular situation, you would not expect the reader or listener to think of all these meanings, but your reader or listener may be thinking of a definition of the word that you did not intend. Therefore, it is important when writing or giving a presentation that you establish the meaning of a word for your audience.

You must also consider whether to discuss the *denotations* of a word—the direct, specific meaning—as well as the *connotations*—the meanings or emotions triggered by the use of the word. For example, the denotations of the word *welfare* are (1) the state of doing well, especially in respect to good fortune, happiness, well-being, or prosperity, and (2) relating to the improvement of disadvantaged social groups. However, each reader of those meanings will also have certain emotional reactions—connotations—to the word *welfare,* depending on their personal experiences and beliefs. A person who has family members receiving welfare benefits may have a different reaction than a person who has never known anyone who received this assistance.

There are several ways to write a definition. During the prewriting stage of your paper, you may want to try all the methods listed below to determine which works best for you or whether you want to include more than one of these methods of development.

You can define a word by using the following methods.

■ Provide other words that mean the same thing; these are known as *synonyms.*

■ Compare two or more meanings to distinguish among the meanings.

■ Explain the function of the word.

■ Provide examples to demonstrate how the word is used.

■ Explain what the word does *not* mean.

For technical definitions, you need to analyze the object by naming it and all of its parts.

■ What is the object and its history?

■ What is object made of, or what does it look like?

■ What does it do?

■ How does it work?

■ Who uses it?

■ How is the object similar to other words like it?

■ How is it different than these objects?

Organization

The organization of a definition paper should suit the purpose and the methods of development used. For historical definitions, you would probably begin with the original use of the word and trace the changes in meaning through the present. In some situations, it might be better to start with the present meaning and trace it back in time to its roots. Either method requires that you organize your material in chronological order.

For technical definitions, you may want to organize the paper by focusing first on the object being defined as a whole: what does it mean in general and what are its *major* features? Then, you would discuss the individual features of the object—the details of how it is made and used.

For personal definitions, you have more flexibility in organizing the paper, but you do need to be careful to remain focused on your readers' needs and expectations. Remember that your readers may not share your personal definition and will respond emotionally to your words.

Let's look again at how we organized the two denotations of the word *welfare.* We began with the least-used denotation, or definition—the state of doing well, especially in respect to good fortune, happiness, well-being, or prosperity. This placement was intentional, and we suspected that very few readers would think of this meaning of the word. We knew that they would have stronger feelings about the second denotation, or definition—relating to the improvement of disadvantaged social groups. Since we expected strong personal reactions to the second, we thought they would not really pay serious attention to the other denotation. We also wanted to remind them of the original meaning of the word *welfare*—how someone is doing— a meaning having a positive connotation. We realized that the negative connotations most often associated with the second definition may have prevented readers from acknowledging this positive connotation of the original definition.

The following box highlights an important technique useful in definition.

Tip for the Definitive Mode

Focus on *word choice* and *phrasing*. These are particularly important when writing definitions because you are expected to be as precise as possible in relating the meaning of the term you are defining.

EXERCISE 15.3

Here are some prompts to help you practice the definition mode.

1. Define a word that is important to you or reflects who you are.

2. Define a term that is relevant to your major or career.

Collaboration

3. Working as a group, define a slang term that is currently in use to label a group of people. Explain the term to someone who has never heard the word. You may want to explore whether the word is appropriate to use.

Collaboration

4. Working as a group, select an abstract term and brainstorm possible meanings of this word. Then as a group, write a definition paper that reflects the group's consensus of what the word means.

Examples of Essays Written in the Definitive Mode

Dorsett Bennett, "I, Too, Am a Good Parent," pp. 443–445

Amatai Etzioni, "On Restoring the Moral Voice," pp. 535–541

Ian Frazier, "Pride," pp. 482–484

CLASSIFICATION

In a **classification** essay, you will be analyzing a group of things that have similarities and perhaps breaking certain elements into smaller groups. For example, you might classify types of music—classical, pop, big band, jazz, hip-hop, rap, R&B, and so on.

In another type of classification, you might be separating one object into parts, pieces, sections, or categories for a close examination of the object. For example, an automobile can be analyzed in terms of thousands of parts or it can be more generally categorized into major parts—its engine, drive or transmission, exterior or body, interior.

Purpose

The purpose of classification essays is to analyze similar things and to show the relationships, differences, connections, and associations among them.

Development

Part of the prewriting process for classification is to find or create clear categories. These categories need to meet the following guidelines.

■ The categories need to be the *major* categories of the whole or the general classification. For example, if we are discussing a classification system for transportation, we might use the following major categories, each of which has its own subcategories.

Airplanes

Trains

Ships

Automobiles

We would not expect to see a category called *ski lift* because it is not a major mode of transportation.

■ The level of categories discussed should be *consistent*. We would not expect to use any of the following words to classify modes of transportation because they are categories of automobiles and, therefore, subcategories and not major modes of transportation.

Sports utility vehicles (SUVs)

Subcompact cars

Indy cars

■ A *component* of the whole should not fit into two categories. If this occurs, it probably means that the two categories are really two subcategories of a larger group and should be combined into the major category. For example, if we had used the category *subcompact cars* in our list of types of transportation, we would be able to fit a Nissan Sentra in two categories, *automobiles* and *subcompact cars*.

■ The list of categories needs to be *complete*. When we look back at our list of the major modes of transportation, we should have a list that is complete so that we could find a category for any vehicle that transports people or goods.

■ The categories should be *significant* and useful to your readers, who should be convinced that you have conducted an in-depth analysis of the topic. For example, a reader would not find the following classification of modes of transportation very useful.

Air transportation

Land transportation

Sea transportation

However, if you did choose to use these categories, you would still need to create subcategories for each group so that the number of vehicles in each category would not be overwhelming to the reader.

Organization

One way to organize a classification paper is to discuss each of the major categories in an order determined by their relationships. For example, if you are tracing the history of the modes of transportation, you would use a chronological order. If you were conducting an analysis of the best mode of transportation, you might organize your information by moving from worst to best records. The following box highlights some techniques useful in writing classification.

Tips for the Classification Mode

Don't oversimplify. Beginning writers tend to create categories that are too broad. A paper classifying movies should do more than provide a discussion of good movies and bad movies.

Don't stereotype. Too often categories of groups of people tend to be stereotypes, lacking any fair and clear distinctions. Let's say you have been asked to create categories of TV shows. If you decide to create categories based on what shows certain ethnic groups watch, it would be stereotyping to distinguish them by stating that a group watches shows that include only people in that ethnic group or that are about a topic associated with that group. For example, you wouldn't categorize TV shows with Jewish actors (such *Seinfeld*) as those watched by Jewish viewers or shows about the mob (*Wiseguy, The Sopranos*) as those watched by people of Italian descent.

EXERCISE 15.4

Collaboration

Collaboration

Here are some prompts to help you practice the classification mode.

1. Working as a group, write a paper in which you discuss the different kinds of parenting styles. You may substitute the styles of supervisors, workers, teachers, or students.

2. Select a subject in your field of study or career, and write an essay in which you classify the types of jobs available.

3. Working as a group, write a paper in which you identify a general group of people (students, bosses, shoppers), and classify them into more specific groups.

4. Write an essay in which you select a general category (music, sports, hobbies, movies, television programs), and classify the category into more specific groups.

Example of Essays Written in the Classification Mode
Meg Greenfield, "Why Nothing Is 'Wrong' Anymore," pp. 542–544
Vincent Ryan Ruggiero, "How Good Are Your Opinions?" pp. 476–481

COMPARISON AND CONTRAST

Comparison and contrast papers provide an analysis of the similarities and differences among related items. For example, if you were preparing to buy a car, you would compare the different makes and models of cars to decide which one would best suit your needs.

Purpose

The purpose of comparison and contrast papers is to organize information on related items so that readers can make the best decision about them. Comparison papers can be objective or **persuasive**. If the paper is objective, the reader expects a comparison and contrast of the topic without a recommendation, which means the reader expects to make the decision based on the information provided. If the paper is persuasive, the reader expects to be given a recommendation based on the comparison and contrast of the subject. Whether the purpose is objective or persuasive, the reader expects a fair and complete comparison.

Development

In a comparison paper, you provide the criteria for comparison and then apply all of the criteria to each item being discussed. The first step in prewriting to develop your paper is determining the criteria. For example, when comparing cars, you might select any of these criteria: size, price, reliability, gas mileage, style, optional features, cost of maintenance and repair, resale value, expected life of the car, performance of the engine, or safety features. Once you have selected the criteria, you then need to prewrite to find the supporting evidence and the criteria for each item. For example, if you chose resale value as a means of comparison and you were comparing six cars, you would need to find the resale value for all six cars.

After you have gathered your information, you will need to analyze it. If you are writing an objective paper, you may choose to simply list the details. But you can also provide some interpretation or scale for your reader. You might rank the items based on the criteria. For example, if you are comparing the resale values of six cars, you might give a rank from 1 to 6 for the highest to lowest resale value, an analysis that will help readers interpret the information. However, such rankings do not imply a recommendation of which car to buy because there are other criteria to consider.

If you are writing a persuasive comparison paper, you will need to determine the recommendation by weighing all the criteria. Since one product or item is usually best for one criterion and not as good for another, you will need to discuss fully how you determined which item or product to recommend.

Organization

Comparison papers can be organized in two ways: side-by-side and point-by-point.

Side-by-side organization is arranged according to the items being compared. You would first discuss each item individually and then, in a separate section, discuss the similarities and differences among the items. For example, if you were comparing three political candidates, you might begin by discussing each one of them individually (in three separate paragraphs). You would then write several more paragraphs in which you compared candidates based on selected criteria. This organizing method works best if you are comparing two or three items; if there are more, the reader is likely to get lost. Beginning writers tend to discuss each of the items well, but they are less likely to provide an adequate and fully developed comparison of items. Without this comparison, the paper is a description, not a comparison, and does not fulfill the readers' expectations.

Here is an example of side-by-side organization for an assignment comparing the types of daytime TV shows.

1. Talk shows
2. Soap operas
3. Game shows
4. Comparison of all three based on the selected criteria
5. Contrast of all three based on the selected criteria

Point-by-point organization is arranged according to the criteria selected for comparison. Let's look again at three criteria you might use to compare the three political candidates. If you decide to discuss all three candidates as you discuss each criterion, you will need to choose the order in which to discuss the criteria; usually from least to most important or from most to least important will work. You can probably choose any order for the items being compared under each criterion, but the order of these items should be the same in each paragraph of criteria.

Here is an example of how point-by-point organization might be used in the assignment comparing daytime TV shows.

1. Educational value
   a. Talk shows
   b. Soap operas
   c. Game shows
2. Entertainment value
   a. Talk shows
   b. Soap operas
   c. Game shows

3. Appropriateness for children
   a. Talk shows
   b. Soap operas
   c. Game shows

The following box highlights some techniques useful in writing comparisons and contrasts.

Tips for the Compare/Contrast Mode

Pay close attention to *transitions* in all comparison and contrast essays. Since you will be discussing at least two items, your reader may get confused if you are not clear about which item you are discussing. For that reason, you must clearly indicate when you switch from one item to the next. Also, you need transitions to indicate if you are comparing or contrasting, since most comparison papers include discussions of both similarities and differences. Transitional words and phrases such as *on the other hand, similarly,* and *in contrast* will help readers follow your ideas.

Another way to help readers understand all the information provided in a comparison essay is to use *graphics* such as charts and graphs. These visual aids both help organize the ideas and provide a quick reference to the information at a later time.

EXERCISE 15.5

Here are some prompts to help you practice the comparison and contrast mode.

Collaboration

1. Working as a group, watch two movies or television shows. Then select an organization pattern, and write a paper in which you contrast the shows.
2. Write an essay in which you compare two relationships with friends or with romantic partners.
3. Choose an experience you had, and write about what you expected to happen and what really happened.

Collaboration

4. Working as a group, compare the roles of men and women or of mothers and fathers.

Example of Essays Written in the Compare/Contrast Mode

Judith Ortiz Cofer, "The Myth of the Latin Woman: I Just Met a Girl Named Maria," pp. 525–531

Margaret Visser, "Fingers," pp. 446–451

ILLUSTRATION

Illustration, sometimes called **exemplification**, is a mode that uses examples to **support** an idea. In previous chapters, we have demonstrated how to use examples to support ideas for all assignments. However, in an illustration essay, the examples are much more fully developed, and the writer may include several examples. Since the focus of the paper is the illustrations, the writer does not provide much discussion of the relationships between the thesis and the illustrations or examples.

Purpose

Illustration papers provide the audience with extensive examples that are designed to draw a picture of a situation, place, or event in much the same way description papers do. The difference is that illustration papers usually combine the elements of narration (what happened) with description (what something looks like) so that the reader will have a more in-depth example or several different examples. It is this accumulation of examples and illustrations that allows the reader to find the patterns and relationships among the examples and, therefore, understand the author's point.

Development

When prewriting an illustration paper, you will want to create a list of all possible examples and illustrations that will help make your point or prove your thesis. In fact, sometimes this kind of list is used as a list in the essay to demonstrate the amount of evidence. A list works well if your readers are familiar with the topic and will quickly understand how most of the list proves your point. However, if your list includes only what they previously knew, this method of development will not work. You need to either add more items to the list that provide new information or make an unusual or surprising point by using a list of items.

If a list of the examples will not work for your assignment, you need to choose a number of examples from the list and prewrite to develop fully the ones you plan to include in your paper. You can use the same techniques for developing narration and description to provide the necessary details and specifics needed for extended illustrations.

When choosing which details and specifics to include in the essay, you want to focus on those that not only establish the story and describe the situation but also show (or imply) the connections between the illustration and your thesis. This is important because in illustration papers the bulk of the focus is on the example itself rather than on the writer's explanation of it. Another common feature of illustration papers is the use of several extended examples that at first glance appear to be random choices. But the writer ties together these examples to support his point and fulfill his purpose.

Organization

To organize an illustration paper effectively, you must find the order of examples that will best build your case or support your thesis. One way to organize the material is to move from shorter to longer examples. Another way is to move from least important to most important, and yet another is to move from most familiar to least familiar.

The following box highlights some techniques useful in writing illustrations.

Tips for the Illustrative Mode

Carefully determine the types and number of *examples* you need to include in your essay. If you use too many, you might bore your readers. If the examples are too obvious, your readers may be insulted. For example, if you are writing an essay on welfare and include every example you can think of related to unwed mothers on welfare, you need to make sure that these examples are not repetitions. Each example should add a new idea or a greater level of understanding for the reader. Also, if you can't think of other examples of people receiving welfare benefits, you may be stereotyping and your illustrations will not lead to new information or understanding for the reader.

Review all *transitions*, an important aspect of an illustration paper. Beginning writers tend to use transitions such as *first, second, third,* and so on, while others use *also, and, another example,* and so on. Neither of these patterns for transitions will work well in an illustration paper. Examples should be organized so that their relationships create the necessary transition. For example, two examples may include similar language or use a word in two distinct ways; putting these examples close together can help establish the pattern you want your readers to find. If there are no obvious connections between examples, you will need to provide informative transitions that let the reader know that you have changed from one example to another.

EXERCISE 15.6

Collaboration

Collaboration

Here are some prompts to help you practice the mode of illustration.

1. Working as a group, write an essay in which you discuss current fads in television shows, giving examples to illustrate each of these fads.
2. Working as a group, write a paper, using illustrations, discussing if your group thinks song lyrics are too violent.
3. Illustrate how your life is different from your grandparents' lives.
4. Illustrate a major concept in your field of study or career.

Examples of Essays Written in the Illustrative Mode
Jack G. Shaheen, "The Media's Image of Arabs," pp. 516–519
Renee Loth, "Measuring Success," pp. 41–42
Mary Arguelles, "Money for Morality," pp. 532–535

PROCESS

Process papers explain how to do something or how something works. Some are instructions that show readers how to perform a process—for example, how to configure the hard drive on a computer. Others are descriptions that help readers understand what is being done, has been done, or will be done. An example of this would be a description of how to reform the welfare system.

Purpose

The purpose of process papers is to provide readers with the sequence of actions involved in a process or procedure. Process descriptions are intended for those who need to understand the process so that they can make a decision; these readers do not need to perform the process, just to understand it. Process instructions should be written so that readers can successfully perform the sequence of actions that lead to, or should lead to, a predictable result.

Development

Process papers, whether descriptions or instructions, must be accurate and specific. Imagine that you are trying to explain why you need more staff working in your department. To demonstrate that more help is needed, you would have to provide detailed and specific evidence of what you do, how you do it, and how long it takes. Without adequate details, a supervisor may argue that you don't do enough and that you don't perform your job efficiently.

When you prewrite, you want to create a list, or **flowchart,** of steps involved in the process. If you are writing instructions, you need to include each step in detail. In fact, you need enough detail that the reader will be able to complete the process without having to discuss it with anyone else (including you, the writer). If you have ever purchased an item that required assembly, you probably know how poorly some instructions are written. Your goal is to provide enough detail for your reader to be successful on the first attempt at completing the process.

If you are writing a process description, you need to determine what details and specifics to include in the overview of the process or procedure. You also need to determine what the reader already knows about the process. For example, your approach for a paper on reforming the welfare system would be very different if your audience were taxpayers rather than politicians.

You also need to consider adding graphics, such as drawings and flowcharts, so that your reader can visualize the process. Flowcharts are useful if the process is one of sequential steps, while charts and drawings are useful when there are steps that occur at the same time or when the order of steps is not important.

Organization

To organize a process paper, you must follow the logical order of actions required to perform or understand the process or procedure. In most situations, you will introduce the process by identifying its purpose and major steps. If you are writing instructions, you need to include a list of equipment and materials in this introduction.

When organizing the body of the paper, you should group the steps into manageable chunks. For example, if the process requires 50 pieces of equipment that are used to manufacture five large sections of something, you can divide your process description into five sections as well. The order of these five sections would be determined by their relationships. If one part must be completed before moving to the next, you would organize according to that order. If the five sections can be completed in any order and then merged into one unit, then you would have six sections in your paper: one for each of the five parts and a sixth to show how to combine the five parts.

If you are writing instructions, you will want to include a troubleshooting section at the end of the paper. For process descriptions, you need to conclude the paper by providing readers with information on the next step or what to do with their knowledge of the process.

The following box highlights some techniques useful in writing processes.

Tips for the Process Mode

Start your sentences with verbs that direct readers to the *action to be performed.* An instruction that says, "First, you should insert the disk in your computer at home" would be better if written as follows: "Insert disk into the 3$\frac{1}{2}$-inch disk drive." Your readers should obviously know where their computer is, and they probably know that the disk is to be inserted somewhere in the computer.

Don't assume that your reader knows any of the steps in a process or that a particular step is obvious. Most likely it won't be. For example, purchasers of new computer software will probably know that the disk containing the new program must be inserted into the floppy drive, but they may not know how to create or change the path the computer looks for when the program is installed.

Remember to *list* which actions readers should avoid when you are giving instructions. If you are providing instructions on how to load a computer program onto the hard drive of a computer, you should include a warning that all virus scanning programs must be disabled before installing the new program. It's best to include such warnings early in the instructions, not at the end.

EXERCISE 15.7	**Here are some prompts to help you practice the mode of process.**

1. How have you changed? You may discuss physical, emotional, intellectual, or occupational changes.
2. Select an important process in your field of study or career, and explain the process in detail.

Collaboration

3. Working as a group, select one aspect of society that your group thinks has changed, and explain how this change has occurred. Your group may choose to conduct research to find details for supporting evidence.

Collaboration

4. Working as a group, explain how people go about finding someone they want to spend their lives with.

Examples of Essays Written in the Process Mode
Guanlong Cao, "Chopsticks," pp. 500–504
Barbara Dafoe Whitehead, "Where Have All the Parents Gone?" pp. 451–457

CAUSE AND EFFECT

Purpose

Cause-and-effect essays provide readers with an analysis of the reasons for and the results of an event and an examination of the relevant causal relationship. Cause-and-effect assignments might include the following.

Discuss the causes of the Revolutionary War.

Analyze the effects of the Revolutionary War.

What are the causes and effects of the Revolutionary War?

Do we need welfare programs such as Medicare and food stamps? Why or why not?

What effect does being on welfare have on children?

Whether you include cause and effect in the same essay depends on the wording of the assignment. If both words are not used, then you need to ask your instructor if you can make any changes to the assignment.

Development

You must use your critical thinking skills to prewrite a cause-and-effect paper, where you will be asked to describe and make clear connections between events or situations and their consequences. Specific prewriting steps can help you do the thinking necessary to make these connections.

1. Make a list of possible causes and effects. Be sure to make the distinction between causes and effects.

2. Group or map major and minor causes and effects. Note that this technique is similar to that of classification; you may want to refer to this mode (pp. 290–292) for more ideas on categorizing.

After you have completed the lists of the causes and effects, you need to prewrite to find the connections between the event and each cause and effect listed. If you cannot discuss this connection clearly so that your reader can also understand this connection, you need to reconsider whether it is related, whether it is a cause or an effect, or if further research is needed to find this connection. When you provide the evidence or the logical connections, you have analyzed the causes and effects.

The connection between an event and its causes and effects does not require that you judge or evaluate the situation. For example, current welfare policies have, according to McCrary, a negative impact on single mothers, but she does not fully develop the causes and effects for each idea used in her essay. An adequately developed essay would include extensive discussion of the causes and effects but not necessarily your attitude toward them. You need to check with your instructor to determine if it is appropriate to include a discussion of personal attitudes.

Organization

Once you have determined the major causes and effects, you then need to decide the order in which you will discuss them in your essay. Many writers choose to move from least to most important. If you are required or choose to include a discussion of your attitudes toward the topics identified in your paper, this discussion would probably work best if placed after an analysis of the causes and effects. This placement ensures that your readers will know that you have fully discussed the causes and effects and that you have the necessary background to make sound judgments. This placement also ensures that readers will not confuse the causes and effects with your attitudes.

The following box highlights some techniques useful in writing cause and effect.

Tips for the Cause/Effect Mode

Separate causes clearly and consistently from effects. One way to think about this separation is to place your ideas into two lists or categories: *before* and *after*. For example, to find the causes of poverty, list things that you think happen before a person is impoverished. To find the effects of poverty, make a list of things that happen after a person becomes impoverished. It is obviously not possible to list everything, but you might try to make a list of related concepts and then make your choices based on logic and supporting evidence.

continued on next page

continued from previous page

Discuss clearly the *connection* between an event and its causes and effects—a process similar to drawing a road map that enables you to make logical connections between points. For example, suppose that you have a framed picture on the wall and that a train passes by your house every day at 4 P.M. One day as the train is passing, a family member runs into the room, trips, and hits the wall. The picture then falls to the floor. What would you say caused the picture to fall? Who is responsible—the train or the family member? What is your evidence? If you try to blame either the railroad company or your family member, you need to sound rational and to provide convincing evidence.

| EXERCISE 15.8 | **Here are some prompts to help you practice the cause-and-effect mode.** |

1. Have you ever done something you did not think you ought to do? Why did you do it? What were the effects of this action?

2. Choose a relationship you presently have or have had. Write an essay in which you discuss why this relationship is/was positive or negative.

Collaboration

3. Working as a group, choose a habit, and discuss what makes people develop this habit and what happens because of the habit.

Collaboration

4. Working as a group, select a social problem and conduct research on this problem. Then, in the group's paper, discuss either the causes or effects of this problem.

Examples of Essays Written in the Cause/Effect Mode

John Leo, "Punished for the Sins of the Children," pp. 440–442

Cindi Ross Scoppe, "Every Choice Has Its Consequences—Or At Least It Should," pp. 484–487

For more help using any of these modes, see Chapter 9, which provides paragraph-length examples of these modes.

16 Writing in the Argument and Persuasive Modes

You use the modes of persuasion and argumentation when you want to (1) help others to better understand a controversial subject or (2) convince readers to change their minds or behavior as the result of your writing. You will be writing in these modes to a varied audience who are indifferent to the topic, who disagree with your position, or who need to understand better the complexities of the topic to make their own decisions.

The expository modes discussed in Chapter 15 can be used effectively in persuasion and argumentation papers. Each of these modes can be used to develop your ideas as supporting evidence in a paper.

PERSUASIVE MODE

Persuasion is a powerful type of writing because it seeks to move the reader either emotionally or intellectually. When you are asked to write a persuasive paper, you will be expected to convince your readers to reconsider their views and opinions about a particular subject and as a result act in a different way. For example, you may be writing to a government official asking for a specific action to be taken. You may be asked to write a paper to convince someone in your family to change his or her behavior or attitude toward a family problem. In other words, persuasive papers are not written for you or for those who already agree with you and act as you do, but are meant to cause change in those around you.

Purpose

Because the purpose of persuasion papers is to change the way readers think or act, understanding your audience is essential. Remember, your audience does not share your beliefs, and you want them to act in a particular way as a result of reading your paper. For example, if you are writing to voters about a particular bill or candidate, you are asking the reader to vote in a specific way. If you are writing to resolve a problem within your family or at work, you are asking for a change in action as well as attitude.

To help you understand your audience and meet the demands of the assignment, consider what you know about your audience as well as what they know about the subject. Here are some questions that you need to answer to help you write a successful persuasive paper.

- ▪ Who is my audience? Consider demographics and personal experiences.
- ▪ What does my audience already know or believe about this subject? What are the possible reasons why my audience holds these beliefs about the subject?
- ▪ Based on what I know about my audience, what kinds of information or evidence will convince them? How would I respond to my paper if I were part of the audience?
- ▪ How will my audience respond to my ideas? If the audience will be hostile, what can I write to make the readers more willing to consider my position? What concessions about their stance can I make to help my audience realize that I understand their current position?
- ▪ What do I want my reader to do after reading my paper?

Tone is extremely important when addressing your audience. Your tone, or attitude, reveals what you think of them. If you are insulting or make fun of their beliefs, your audience will not take you or your writing seriously. Select words that are appropriate for your audience. If you are writing to a lay audience, your word selection would be very different from that used to address decision makers or experts in the field. When writing to a general audience, you must define technical terms or words that have more than one meaning.

Development

Even though persuasive papers often appeal to a reader's emotions as well as intellect, you will want to include logical reasons for your position and convincing evidence to support it. Make a list of all the reasons why you hold a certain position, and select the ones that are most logical and convincing. You should ask yourself three questions when choosing the reasons to include in your paper.

1. How does this reason support my position?
2. Why is this reason important?
3. Will the reader be convinced by this reason? Why or why not?

While the reasons for your position are important, the bulk of the paper will be the evidence you use to support your position. As you prewrite, you want to select the most convincing evidence—examples, personal anecdotes, statistics, and testimony. You should also include **quotations**, **paraphrases**, and **summaries** and be able to document all such evidence thoroughly.

After you have listed your reasons and provided supporting evidence, you need to answer questions that will show the logic of your thinking and anticipate your readers' reactions to your paper.

- ▪ Are the reasons logical and convincing rather than based solely on personal taste (likes or dislikes) or unimportant criteria (since person X has this position, I have to take the same position)?

- Can you provide logical explanations to connect the reasons and evidence?
- What are the weaknesses in the reasons and evidence?
- What counterarguments will readers think of while reading the paper?

For persuasive papers, include a discussion of what you want readers to think or do—ideally a specific action as well as something that will impact the situation.

Organization

The first section of a persuasion paper should include background information on the issue or an explanation of why the issue is an important one. This is typically followed by a **thesis,** or position, on the issue.

The body of the paper includes reasons that support your thesis and the details and evidence for the thesis and topic sentences. The order of ideas and evidence in a persuasion paper should be logical and convincing, usually arranged with the most important reason placed either first or last. If the most important or convincing reasons take up the most space in your paper, it's best to place them at the beginning or end of your essay. If your paper is long, place the strongest point at the beginning so that your readers will be compelled to read on; if they don't finish reading the paper, at least they have read the most convincing evidence. If your paper is short, you probably want the strongest point to end the essay, since this is the idea that readers will most likely remember about your position.

The conclusion of a persuasive paper clearly establishes your purpose, or what you want your reader to do based on your paper. Often conclusions for persuasive papers point to the future, particularly if you have clearly established what action you expect them to take. Refer to Chapter 10 on writing conclusions for other types of information you can add to the conclusion.

The following box highlights some techniques useful in writing persuasion.

Tips for the Persuasive Mode

Understand your audience. Too often beginning writers forget that they are writing to those who don't agree with them or who don't care about the topic.

Never attack the reader for his or her beliefs and opinions.

Establish your purpose in writing, or what you want your reader to do after reading your paper. Persuasive writing calls for change.

EXERCISE 16.1   **Here are some prompts to help you practice the persuasive mode.**

1. Write a letter to a school or government official to persuade this person to change a policy or reconsider the way she plans to vote on an important issue.

Collaboration

Collaboration

2. Write a persuasive paper in which you try to solve a problem at home or work.

3. Working as a group, write a paper to your instructor to convince him or her to change something about the course or to select the readings from the textbook that should be assigned for the course.

4. Working as a group, select a social problem or a problem on your campus and conduct research on this problem. Then, write the appropriate audience to change a policy related to the problem or to intervene in the problem.

Examples of Essays Written in the Persuasive Mode
Lynda Barry, "The Sanctuary of School," pp. 464–468
Sally Thane Christensen, "Is a Tree Worth a Life?" pp. 487–490

ARGUMENTATIVE MODE

Argumentation papers present reasons and evidence to support a position without necessarily intending a change in action. A persuasion paper would include an argument with reasons and evidence, but it would also include a call for action by the readers. An argument paper would focus on analyzing a topic or explaining a position to simply convey information to the reader and then let the reader decide what, if any, action is called for.

Purpose

The purpose of argument papers is to inform or educate readers by explaining a position on an issue. To do this, you will need to show that you have considered your position thoroughly and that you understand thoroughly the positions of others.

As with persuasive writing, argumentation requires an understanding of your audience. Before beginning your paper, you need to refer to the questions about audience discussed earlier in this chapter (page 304).

Development

The discussion of development of persuasive papers can be applied to argumentative papers as well. However, argumentative papers avoid emotional appeals and rely heavily on logic and reasoning.

You need to make your points reasonably and give relevant evidence. You can rely on many types of evidence: personal experience and observations, research, or testimonies from others. The topic will partly guide you in determining what kinds of evidence you need. For example, a paper on a public policy may be effective if it relies on facts and statistics about the impact of the policy on a large group of people, not just you personally. However, if you are writing to someone close to you to resolve a problem, personal experience is the most effective kind of evidence, since it helps the reader understand the situation better. You can use research to help you make your points, but you do not want to lose sight of your audience and purpose.

Your argument is based on assumptions, which you may or may not be aware of. You need to determine what assumptions underlie your beliefs as well as the beliefs of your reader. Also, your argument reveals your values, just as the audience's position and beliefs reveal their values. As you develop your paper, you will want to show the reader how your assumptions, values, and evidence are connected.

Recognize the complexity of the issue. This often involves explaining what others believe and showing either the faults in their reasoning or how to reach another conclusion. You do not want to attack a person's reasoning by simply writing, "Anyone who believes this is wrong." Instead, you need to show alternative ways of thinking about the subject. You may show that the readers' assumptions might lead them to one conclusion, but if they accepted your assumptions, they may reach another conclusion.

Often instructors will ask you to include the claims you are making and then connect your assumptions and claims with supporting evidence. Some instructors will use the term "warrant" to describe the connection between your claim and the evidence you provide. Including all these aspects of an argument—assumptions, claims, evidence, and warrants—will show that you have purposefully thought through your argument and presented that argument in a logical and reasoned manner.

In addition to following these guidelines for writing an argumentative paper, you should review the discussion of development of a persuasive paper.

Organization

When organizing an argumentative paper, you want to present your position or argument by moving from point to point or from reason to reason. The same methods of organization suggested for persuasive papers can help guide you.

One way to organize an argumentative paper is to structure paragraphs based on your claims, evidence, and warrants. If you establish your claim as a topic sentence for your paragraph, you can then include a piece of evidence. After each piece of evidence, you would then establish the warrant, which simply means explaining how the evidence you have given supports your claim.

The following box highlights some techniques useful in writing argumentation.

Tips for the Argumentative Mode

Avoid logical fallacies. Do not rely on emotional appeals. Be logical and show your reasoning.

continued on next page

continued from previous page

Demonstrate that you *recognize the weaknesses* in your own argument or position. This acknowledgment shows your reader that you have fully considered the argument and have identified the weaknesses but are still convinced that your position is valid and worth sharing.

Anticipate and *refute* any counterarguments that readers may think of when considering your position. Including differing viewpoints shows that you understand the counterarguments and can use them to make your case even stronger.

BEING LOGICAL

Since argument papers are based on logic and reasoning, you should understand the common problems or errors in logic that writers (and speakers) often make. Here is a list of what are often called "logical fallacies." You need to read your argumentative paper closely to make sure you have not made these mistakes in logic.

Hasty Generalization. Relying on inadequate evidence to reach a conclusion. Avoid jumping to conclusions by adding evidence or alternative types of evidence.

Sweeping Generalizations. Using words such as *always, never, everybody,* and *none*. These words indicate that there can be no exceptions, and your reader can find exceptions to every claim you make.

Either-Or Thinking. Presenting only two solutions to a problem. This type of argument does not allow for other possibilities.

Character Attack (Argumentation ad hominem). Faulting a person instead of focusing on the actual beliefs of the person and how they relate to your argument.

Begging the Question (Argumentation ad ignorantiam). Asserting that a proposition is true (because it has not been proved false) or false (because it has not been proved true), instead of providing evidence for your argument.

Jumping on the Bandwagon (Argumentation ad populum). Appealing to popular opinion and bias by stating that since everyone is doing it, it must be right.

Appealing to an Inappropriate Authority (Argumentation ad verecundian). Using testimony from someone who has no qualifications in the field or who has no expert knowledge of the topic being discussed.

Non sequitur. Making a conclusion that does not follow logically from the claim or premise of the argument.

Straying from the Point (Ignorantia elenchi). Trying to prove one point but accidentally proving something else.

Illogical Causality (Post hoc, ergo propter hoc). Asserting that because A came before B, A caused B. For example, a person my say, "I washed my car. Therefore, it rained." These events may have occurred sequentially, but there is no evidence of a cause/effect relationship.

Promise of Doom (Argumentation ad baculum). Threatening that something will happen if your argument or point is not accepted by the reader.

Stereotyping. Making assumptions about your audience, events, places, and so on, without sufficient evidence.

Circular Reasoning. Stating the same idea in different words but not providing evidence or reasons that support your idea.

Red Herring. Introducing an argument that sidetracks the reader with a discussion of ideas that are irrelevant to your argument.

False Analogy. Comparing two situations that are more unlike than alike.

You need to be aware that these fallacies weaken your argument. However, many writers and speakers rely on them and use them successfully if the reader does not demand logical proof. They tend to be successful in persuasive writing, although many readers may see through the use of these fallacies and choose not to be persuaded. They need to be avoided in argumentative papers.

| EXERCISE 16.2 | **Here are some prompts to help you practice the argumentative mode.** |

Collaboration

Collaboration

1. Working as a group, select an issue that is important to your community and explain the group's position on the issue. You may want to conduct research on the issue to help your group support its position.

2. Working as a group, choose a controversial topic. Divide your group into two sides, and have each side brainstorm support for two positions on the topic. Then, work as a group to write a paper that presents both sides of the issue and, as a group, develop the position that you think is most logical. You may want to conduct research on the topic.

3. Write a letter to a family member, a coworker, or a supervisor and make a recommendation to resolve a problem. Your goal is to demonstrate that you have thought carefully about all sides of the problem and your recommendation is the most logical conclusion.

4. Select a social problem that you care about deeply. Analyze the problem, present a solution, and show how your solution will be effective.

Examples of Essays Written in the Argumentative Mode
Amatai Etzioni, "On Restoring the Moral Voice," pp. 535–541
Barbara Dafoe Whitehead, "Where Have All the Parents Gone?" pp. 451–457

17 Writing About Literature

ANALYZING LITERATURE

We may understand why we need to read and write about factual, real-world ideas, but we may wonder why so many English classes require us to read and write about characters in stories, novels, and plays, and about feelings and ideas expressed in poetry. Literature helps to connect us to other people, especially to other people whose lives are very different from our own. Literature also helps us to understand ourselves more thoroughly.

Nevertheless, practical reasons for reading and writing about literature do exist. Literary analysis requires us to use all the skills we use in other reading and writing tasks but to do so more intensely, in greater depth, and with more care for detail. Exercising our skills on very difficult texts, like Japanese poetry and Shakespearean plays, makes it easier for us to analyze the texts we encounter in our lives and careers.

Analyzing literature uses all the skills we have discussed in this book, but it also involves a few new skills. For this reason, you'll often be asked to review other chapters and then go on to practice more detailed versions of the same skills. Also, since some terms, like **irony**, have a different meaning, or additional meanings, when applied to literature, we may return to the definition of those terms.

READING LITERATURE

Most of us have read literature since we were very young. We may read mystery or romance novels, or we may read children's books to our families. We even encounter literature without reading when we watch dramas or comedies on television, see action movies, or listen to the lyrics of songs. In college, we read literature to write about what we have read. We can write about other topics without reading anything, but in literary analysis, reading and writing go hand in hand.

Because some aspects of reading—like previewing, reading actively, and evaluating—are the same for all kinds of readings, review Chapter 4 before you read this chapter. You'll use the same tools for reading literature that you used for other kinds of reading: prepare to read, survey before reading, read actively, review, and evaluate. However, you may add some parts to these tasks.

Prepare to Read and Survey

First, you need to recognize the genre that you are reading. Genres are different types of literature, and each genre will call on certain types of reading skills.

- *Fiction:* Novels and stories; imagined narratives written in prose
- *Poetry:* Feelings and ideas expressed in various forms
- *Drama:* Plays written to be performed

We will focus on fiction because it is a good starting place, but your teacher may add or substitute another genre. Some of the reading techniques and many of the writing techniques will be similar for all types of literature. Your survey will let you know immediately what genre you are reading, because the genres have different appearances on the page. Poetry will be in verse form, with lines of different lengths, and drama will be in dialogue form. Only fiction will be in paragraph form.

Once you know that you are reading fiction, you need some knowledge about the background of the reading. The time and location of a story or the life of the author are often parts of this preparation. For example, if you are assigned to read "The Story of an Hour" on pp. 52–53, your teacher might want you to have the following information.

- *Social customs of the time and place:* In the last part of the nineteenth century and the early twentieth century, women frequently had little control over their own lives. A woman's parents told her whom she should marry, and her husband made the decisions about where and how to live, spend money, and so on. Women usually could not get jobs, and divorce was very difficult to obtain.
- *Author's life:* Kate Chopin, an American, wrote around the beginning of the twentieth century. She was educated in the Midwest and wrote books about the problems of women of her time.

If your teacher does not give you background for the reading, you can consult books and Internet sources to learn about the social customs during that time period. To survey a work of literature, you may follow the suggestions from pages 58–60 in Chapter 4, looking at the title, the beginning, and the end of the work. In works like "The Story of an Hour" (pp. 52–53), for example, the story might be more interesting if you don't know the ending when you read the story for the first time. For this reason, looking at the title and the beginning of the story might be enough to help you develop a framework for understanding what you read. Thus, you might come to the following conclusions from an early survey of "The Story of an Hour."

Date and author: This was written over a century ago. Will it still be interesting or make sense?

Title: Sounds like an event that's over quickly. What could happen in an hour that would be worth a whole story?

First paragraph: This story may be about the death of this woman's husband or about how someone is taking care of her. This is written in a slightly formal style or maybe the way that people spoke at that time.

EXERCISE 17.1	**As a group, discuss the following, or on your own, think about the questions or write a brief response.**

Collaboration

1. What do you already know about the background of the story? What do you know about the lives of women in the United States 100 years ago? Have you learned anything from history or sociology classes or from talking to family members about how women lived differently at that time?

2. What can you find online about Kate Chopin? Was her life different from the lives of most women of her time?

3. What do you expect the story to be about?

Read Actively and Form Interpretations

When you read a story, you must read it actively. You won't have much choice, since the author won't be able to give you every piece of information you need and can only suggest or imply some facts, details, and ideas. (Follow the techniques suggested on pp. 61–68 to help you find this information.) You'll need to look for *implied* ideas, especially when you try to determine the main idea or **theme** of a work of literature. The author frequently tells you about people and events but leaves it up to you to decide what they mean. You may remember hearing the story of "The Three Little Pigs." Parents and teachers often tell this story and assume that children will learn an idea from it: that careful preparation can prevent many difficulties. Although the pig who took time to build a solid brick house was safe from the wolf, the pigs who quickly built shoddy houses of sticks and hay were eaten. However, the story itself doesn't state the idea; it tells you what each pig did and what happened, and you must decide for yourself how the third pig is different from the first two. Another child might find a very different idea in the story: the idea that crime is eventually punished or even that revenge is enjoyable. Teachers and parents can't control how the children decide to read the story, since each reader can have his or her own **interpretation.** Many children may not even think much about the story but may just enjoy the idea of pigs singing and dancing and the wolf's destruction.

However, some interpretations clearly don't make much sense. If a child decided that the idea of the story was that wolves should not be mistreated, we'd want to read the story to the child again and discuss the wolf's behavior. The events in the story don't fit with that interpretation. When we write about literature, our goal is to show that our interpretation does make sense. For that reason, we must include evidence that shows our interpretation is reasonable or plausible—not that it is the only possible correct interpretation. Thus, reading actively means you are doing two things: developing an interpretation (deciding what the story means) and finding evidence to show that your interpretation makes sense.

Develop an Interpretation

An interpretation of a story is developed as you read and then expressed when you write, so this process is at the heart of writing about literature. To come to a conclusion about what the story means, you may need to look at it in many different ways. You may use some tools that make the story easier to analyze, often called the **elements of fiction**, which are useful because they help you to break the story into different parts. Looking at the parts, or analyzing, can help you reach a more meaningful interpretation. The elements of fiction include the following.

- *Plot:* What happens in a story
- *Character:* A person in a story
- *Setting:* When and where the story happens
- *Point of view:* Who tells the story
- *Style:* The way the story is written
- *Symbol:* Something physical, possibly an object or place, that stands for an idea or feeling

In the story, these elements blend together and overlap—the plot develops from the action of the characters, the setting may turn out to symbolize some of the ideas. However, analyzing a story means looking at each part separately to be sure you have not missed anything and have made all the necessary connections.

For each of these elements, it's important to do these steps in order to develop your interpretation.

- Attempt to identify and summarize each element of fiction.
- Highlight words, sentences, and paragraphs in the story that show each element.
- Decide which elements are most important in the story.

Use these steps as you look at each of the elements in a story, but don't expect that all stories will use the elements in the same way.

Plot: In most stories, the **plot** is not just a series of events but a narrative that fits together through cause and effect. It begins and ends at a definite point. For example, a list of your activities this morning would just be a list, not a plot: *Got up, took a shower, ate breakfast, got dressed, drove to school, took test, met friends, went to computer lab, ate lunch.* However, in the story of "The Three Little Pigs," the plot begins when the pigs leave home and are warned by their mother to be careful. It continues when the first two pigs build their houses carelessly and are eaten by the wolf and when the third pig is careful and builds a sturdy house. The story ends when the wolf is killed by the third pig. One aspect of the plot that can be very important is **irony**. A plot is ironic if the events turn out the opposite of the way we might expect or the opposite of the way the characters expect. In "The Three Little Pigs," the ending is ironic because the wolf expects to eat the third pig but is instead killed by that pig.

| EXERCISE 17.2 | Discuss the following in groups, or on your own, think about the answers to the questions or write brief responses. |

Collaboration

1. In "Story of an Hour," the plot begins with the news of the death of Mrs. Mallard's husband in a train wreck. It continues as she grieves as a result of the news and then goes upstairs because she is grieving. What are the other steps in the plot? What happens when she goes upstairs, and what happens at the end of the story? Highlight any words or sentences that show important steps in the plot.

2. What causes Mrs. Mallard's death? Draw a flowchart showing the steps of cause and effect in the plot.

3. What in this plot shows irony? Does anything happen that is the opposite of what any characters expect or the opposite of what the reader expects?

Character   **Character** is not just the external identification of the people in the story but also their personalities, pasts, motivations, expectations, mannerisms, and relationships to others. Often we speak of **round characters** (usually these are the important characters), about whom we know much information, such as their earlier lives, their opinions and reactions, and more than one aspect of their personalities. Often we are given more details about their appearance and personality, and, most important, we often see them change in the course of the story or we learn about a new aspect of them. Like people in photographs, they seem to have several dimensions. If you have ever watched a long-running TV series and felt as though you knew some of the characters, those were probably round characters. Other characters are sometimes called **flat characters**. Like cartoon characters, they seem to have only one dimension to their personalities. We know them only in one way and do not see them change. We don't learn much about their opinions or how they developed into the people they are now. The people in jokes and fairy tales are usually flat.

| EXERCISE 17.3 | Discuss the following in groups, or on your own, think about the answers to the questions or write brief responses. |

Collaboration

1. How can you classify the characters in "The Story of an Hour"? Which are round and which are flat?

2. In what ways is Mrs. Mallard a round character? What are some of the different things we know about her? Does she change in the course of the story?

We also have to consider how we know the characters. Sometimes the author will give us a straightforward description, as Chopin does when she discusses Mrs. Mallard's feelings for her husband: "And yet she had loved him—sometimes. Often she had not" (p. 53). But there are many other ways that a character's thoughts, feelings, plans, reactions, and essential nature can be revealed to the reader.

- The author's direct description
- The character's thoughts, words, and actions
- Other characters' thoughts, words, and reactions to the character

EXERCISE 17.4

Collaboration

Discuss the following in groups, or on your own, think about the answers to the questions or write brief responses.

1. Find an example of how Chopin uses each of the preceding techniques to reveal the character of Mrs. Mallard, and highlight the words that show this.

2. Based on this evidence, write three sentences that describe Mrs. Mallard, her feelings about her husband, and reasons why she reacts as she does to the news that he is dead and to the news that he is alive.

Setting The setting is literally the time and place of the story. Sometimes these details are stated directly, but often they are implied or suggested. Authors may not offer many clues to the time, so it is helpful to know when a story was written. Also, time and place can be important in many different ways. The physical location might be very important for an adventure story where the hero struggles against a storm *or* for a ghost story set in an old mansion. The social and political setting might be important for a story set during a war or in a time and place very different from our own, such as a historical story about ancient China or science fiction set on another planet in the distant future.

EXERCISE 17.5

Collaboration

Discuss the following in groups, or on your own, think about the answers to the questions or write brief responses.

1. When did Chopin write "The Story of an Hour"? Are there any clues to suggest that the story took place during that time? Highlight any words that give us a clue about the time or place of the story.

2. Where does the story take place? Why is that important? Highlight any descriptions of the place. Do different parts of the story happen in different parts of the place? Why is that important?

3. What do we know about the time and place of the story? What kind of social class did characters like Mrs. Mallard belong to? What were women's lives like at that time? Were there rules she had to follow?

Point of View   The **point of view** is the way the reader sees the story. Whose eyes are we looking through? Who tells the story? In a story such as "The Three Little Pigs," we hear from a **narrator**, who sees the events of the story but not what any of the characters are thinking. In other stories, the narrator might actually be one of the characters, in which case the narrator would let us know what that character thinks but not the others. Sometimes a narrator who is not a character can still know what one of the characters thinks, almost as if that character were telling the story, and occasionally the narrator will let us know what many characters think. Also, remember that the point of view can change as the story proceeds.

We distinguish these different points of view according to the pronouns the narrator uses.

- *First person point of view:* Used by a narrator who refers to himself or herself or is a character in the story
- *Third person limited:* Used by a narrator who is not in the story, and does not know what all the characters are thinking
- *Third person omniscient:* Used by a narrator who knows what all the characters are thinking

EXERCISE 17.6	**Discuss the following in groups, or on your own, think about the answers to the questions or write brief responses.**

Collaboration

1. Who tells the story? Can we know what any of the characters are thinking, or can we only see what they say or do? Highlight any passages that show the character's thoughts and internal feelings.
2. How would the story be different if it were written from a different point of view? How is the point of view important at the end of the story?

Symbol   A **symbol** is an object, place, or person that represents more than itself. A dollar bill, for example, is not worth anything in itself; it is only valuable because it symbolizes the ability to buy things. A flag is just a piece of cloth; it is important because it stands for a country and the people, history, and values of that country. Often in literature, a symbol is a simple, physical object that stands for ideas and feelings that are very complicated. In the story of the pigs and the wolf, the house built of sticks is a symbol of carelessness, whereas the house made of brick is a symbol of planning ahead and working hard to provide for the future. However, not every object in a story is symbolic, and symbols are not always simple codes for other simple ideas. Symbols aren't always immediately evident, and a reader may have to think about the ideas in a story for a while before he or she can recognize symbols and their meanings. However, writers don't use symbols to play a guessing game with readers or hide the real truth in a story. Instead, they use symbols to make us see and feel things more clearly.

EXERCISE 17.7

Collaboration

Discuss the following in groups, or on your own, think about the answers to the questions or write brief responses.

1. In "The Story of an Hour," physical objects are not mentioned very often. Therefore, we can guess that the ones that are mentioned might be symbolic in some way. Find and highlight any mention of a physical object.

2. When physical objects are mentioned, what feelings are described or mentioned at the same point in the story? Are there any similarities between the feelings and the objects?

Review and Evaluate

When you have read a story actively, you have used the elements of fiction to help you analyze it. Now you are ready to try to state the theme of the story for yourself, just as you did with nonfiction readings on pp. 67–68. Do not assume that every story has a clear thesis sentence like an essay or that all stories teach lessons, as the story of "The Three Little Pigs" does. Sometimes the theme may seem very obvious when you state it. For example, a very good and complicated story might have a theme that is very simple, such as "Life is short" or "People don't always receive what they earn." Literature is not just about ideas but also about emotions and values, so stating the theme as an idea may not completely capture the essence of the story. Nevertheless, seeing the story as a whole is helpful if you are trying to state the theme.

Evaluating literature is a little different from evaluating nonfiction, which you learned to do in Part Two of this book. You probably are not trying to write stories yourself right now, so you are not looking at the story as a model. However, you will still evaluate literature. You will have an opinion about whether a story is interesting or boring, and you might want to think about whether the author has tried to write about real life or a fantasy, whether the writer achieves his or her goal in writing, or whether you as a reader have a bias that affects how you will read it. One important step in the evaluation process of reading literature is to become aware of your own responses to what you have read. As you analyze the story your responses may change from your first reading (sometimes your first response may be that you don't understand the story or that it's meaningless). Sometimes your teacher may ask you to respond only at one point in the process of reading, but it's very important to recognize your response after active reading, analysis, and class discussion.

EXERCISE 17.8

Collaboration

In a group of five members, each member should be responsible for one of the elements of fiction (plot, character, setting, point of view, symbol, style) in "The Story of an Hour."

1. Highlight each phrase or sentence or more that gives evidence for your element.

2. Summarize what you have learned about the story from an examination of your element.

3. In a group, share the summaries of each member.

4. Individual or group: Based on these summaries, try to write a statement of the theme of the story. What is your interpretation of the story—that is, what feelings or ideas can you find in it?

5. Individual: How do you feel about this story now that you have analyzed it? Is it similar to or different from anything you have experienced or that someone you know has experienced?

DEVELOPING A WRITING TOPIC

Once you have developed an interpretation of a story, your next task is determining the topic you'll write about. Many instructors will assign a topic; in that case, you should follow the guidelines in Chapter 5, pp. 90–94 for analyzing the assignment. If you are expected to develop your own topic, you should be sure you understand the type of topic your instructor expects. Here are some common types of topics, but your instructor may combine topics, add to this list, or use different names for the types of topics.

■ *Summary:* Retell the story briefly, using your own words.

■ *Response:* Discuss your reaction to the story.

■ *Analysis:* Break the story down into parts, and discuss one, showing how that helps you understand the story.

■ *Explication:* Take one passage in the story, and look at the figures of speech, the word choices, and other details to reveal the ideas in the story.

For this example, we'll focus on **literary analysis**, since that's a common assignment. To develop a topic for literary analysis, you may use the interpretation you developed using the elements of fiction on pp. 313–316.

Note: Unless your teacher clearly assigns a *summary* or *response,* you should avoid simply retelling the story or only writing about your initial feelings about the story.

Analysis in writing is not difficult if you have already done analytical reading to develop and interpret. Begin to develop your **literary analysis** topic by looking back at the parts of the story you noticed as you read for plot, character, setting, point of view, and symbol. For example, while reading "The Story of an Hour," you may have noticed that the plot was very intriguing, and you learned a lot about the characters, but you were given very little information about the setting, except for the open window in Mrs. Mallard's room. Then you see that Mrs. Mallard's room is also described, and you think about the contrast between the closed door of her room and the open window. You see how this is connected with plot and character, but you decide that you can focus on the setting. So your rough version of your topic becomes something like this.

The setting of "The Story of an Hour" is related to the changes in the character and plot.

Now you have a first attempt at a **thesis** for your essay. A good thesis will help you write a good essay, so be sure your thesis will not lead only to a summary. Remember, too, that your thesis is an idea, not just a feeling about the story.

> ## Checklist for Literary Analysis
>
> A thesis should have the following elements.
> - It should be clear.
> - It should be related to the story.
> - It should *not* be just a summary of the plot.
> - It should *not* be just feelings about the story.
> - It must be supported by evidence in the story.

EXERCISE 17.9

Use the tools in Chapter 5 to analyze this assignment: Explain how the point of view changes in "The Story of an Hour."

1. Look back at the plot of the story. How could you develop a topic related to the plot? Does everything happen as characters expect it to happen?
2. Use one of these ideas to write a first-try thesis for a literary analysis paper on "The Story of an Hour."
3. As a group, look at the thesis written by each member of the group. Use the preceding checklist to determine if each thesis could lead to a good literary analysis essay.

Collaboration

PREWRITING AND PLANNING

Sometimes it's helpful to prewrite to develop ideas. You might review the techniques in Chapter 6 and experiment with them, or you may find that moving directly to planning may work well. As you read analytically to develop your interpretation, you did a good bit of the work of prewriting. Your instructor might ask you to write a reading response, journal entry, or discovery draft, which may or may not be a graded assignment. These activities can help you find your topic and additional ideas that will form the basis of your essay. You might want to use brainstorming, listing, or mapping to help you prepare to plan (see pp. 101–106). Sometimes analysis can begin with very simple steps in prewriting, like making simple lists of things you notice. For example, suppose you developed this list for your topic on the setting (Exercise 17.5).

Room	Trees	Sky
Chair	Sounds	Closed door
Open window	Wind	Stairs

Now you have something you can work with as you move through the other steps of analysis.

EXERCISE 17.10

Collaboration

Discuss the following in groups, or on your own, think about the answers to the questions or write brief responses.

1. Map what you noticed about the point of view in the story. Whose eyes are we looking through at the beginning of the story? The middle? The end?

2. Brainstorm a list of points where the plot is ironic, where events occur differently from the way the reader expects, or where the characters misunderstand what is really happening.

When you are ready to plan your essay, you should first think of your intended audience. Writing to your reading group may help you remember that your essay will be read by people who have already read the story. You are not trying to tell them the story; instead, your goal is to convince your audience that your interpretation is the best, or at least that it is reasonable. Since you have already developed a topic and found some specifics as you read, you have an idea to prove, and you have some evidence. Now your job is to make clear the connections between idea and evidence.

Start by planning: Use the ideas about grouping from Chapter 7. For example, you may look at your brainstormed list on p. 320 and see that you really have two kinds of items: the objects found in the house and the objects seen through the window. Now you have the basics of a plan.

House	**Open window**
Room	Trees
Chair	Sounds
Closed door	Wind
Stairs	Sky

This is the point at which you will make an important step in writing your paper. You need to plan to show the connections between the idea and the evidence. In your first try at a thesis, you wrote the following.

The setting of "The Story of an Hour" is related to the changes in the character and plot.

So now you will add to your plan some ways that the objects in your list of items in the setting relate to the way Louise Mallard changes during the story. You see that the room and the house are in some ways like her life with her husband: She is comfortable; she may have some privacy, but she is shut in, away from the rest of the world. Also, what she sees outside the window is similar to the feelings she has about the kind of life she can lead now that her husband is gone: It is open, new, fresh, unknown, and free. You can revise your thesis to be more specific.

> The setting of "The Story of an Hour" is related to the changes in the character and plot. The house resembles her marriage, and the open window is like the life she could have without her husband.

Now your plan is expanded

> <u>Thesis:</u> The setting of "The Story of an Hour" is related to the changes in the character and plot. The house resembles her marriage, and the open window is like the life she could have without her husband.

<u>House:</u> Like her life with her husband	<u>Open window:</u> Like her life without her husband
Room—her own	Trees—outside
Chair—she's comfortable	Sounds—seem happy
Closed door—shut away	Wind—free
Stairs—removed	Sky—fresh, free

EXERCISE 17.11

Discuss the following in groups, or on your own, think about the answers to the questions or write brief responses. Use the list you brainstormed in the last exercise.

1. Group the items in the list.
2. Make sure the connection is clear. How are the items in the list related to the theme you stated?

DRAFTING

Actually writing the literary analysis essay, or **drafting**, is very much like writing other essays. You can use the guidelines in Chapters 8–10 to help you with this. However, writing about literature is different in a few ways.

> ### Drafting Literary Analysis Essays
>
> ■ Avoid summarizing the entire story in analysis papers.
> ■ Provide evidence for your statements using quotations, paraphrases, or summaries.
> ■ Explain how the evidence is connected to the ideas.

Remember that your readers have already read the story, so you do not need to tell them everything that happens, but you may retell part of the story if you need it as evidence. For example, if you are making the point that Louise Mallard's room is a place where she is shut away from other people, you might prove it by summarizing it like this.

Her sister has to beg her to open the door and come out.

There is no need to go on to tell every step of the story—only the events that prove your point. Because summarizing is very easy to do, it's important to check your plan as you write, making sure that you are not getting away from the point of your paragraph. Remember that you are trying to convince your readers to accept your point.

When you make a statement about the story, you need to prove it by giving evidence. The evidence comes from the actual words of the story, but you don't always have to supply direct quotations. Sometimes paraphrasing or summarizing will fit more smoothly into your paragraph. Even if you plan to use your own words, look carefully at the words of the story, because sometimes you'll find words that state your ideas more clearly than you can.

As you draft, be sure that you are not just listing the evidence. Your paragraph should not contain a string of quotations from the story. Connect your evidence to your ideas by explaining what the quotations or paraphrases show or mean, or why they are important.

At the same time, remember that you will be revising and writing more drafts, so don't expect to write a perfect paper with your first draft. It's important to go ahead and get your ideas down, and then you can return and improve the essay in later drafts. Here is a possible first draft of an essay based on the plan on p. 321.

Jeanine Wu
ENG 102
June 9, 2004

Setting in "The Story of an Hour"
Where does Louise Mallard live? We know very little of the answer to that question. Kate Chopin does not tell us very much about the setting of "The

Story of an Hour." We don't know whether it takes place in a city or a small town, in the West or in the East. However, we do know a good bit about some parts of the setting. We know that most of the story takes place inside the house, and we know what Louise Mallard can see from her open window. Since we do hear about this small area so much, we can see that it must be a clue to the events of the story.

The first thing we know about the setting is that it takes place in the house where Louise Mallard lives. "She went away to her room alone" (52). While she is there, she looks out the window and begins to have different feelings. Because of the things she sees outside the window, she knows she can be free and happy without her husband. Her sister has to beg her to open the door and come out. She and her sister "descended the stairs" (53). When she comes out, she feels much better. Obviously she has undergone a great change while alone in her room. However, when she finds that her husband is still alive, she realizes that she can't have her freedom, and she dies, but other people don't understand why. The doctors think she dies of "joy" (53), but they were wrong.

Looking out the window changes her feelings about her husband's death. Through the window, she can see the open square. She can also see the sky and hear the sound of birds, of peddlers calling out, and of someone singing. "She felt it, creeping out of the sky, reaching toward her *through* the sounds, the smells, the colors in the air" (52). Eventually she can understand that the feeling is her awareness that she is now able to live her own life the way she wants to live: "Free, free, free!" she says to herself (Chopin 53). She realizes that her husband has controlled her and that she will be free now that he is dead. But then he turns out to be alive, and so she dies of grief, although the doctors don't understand this.

The setting of the story is similar to the feelings that go on inside her. Therefore the setting of "The Story of an Hour" is much more important than it might have seemed at first reading.

Work Cited

Kreml, Carr, Capps, Jake, and May. <u>The Story of an Hour</u> by Kate Chopin. 2003.

EXERCISE 17.12   **Write a draft of an essay based on one of the plans you developed in Exercise 17.11 (p. 321).**

REVISING

Revising is an essential step, so don't try to jump immediately to editing. However, you may certainly make editing corrections if you see them as you revise. Most of the problems in writing about literature are similar to those found in other kinds of writing, so first be sure to check the revising and editing suggestions in Chapters 11 and 12. Here are some additional points to add to the checklist if you are revising a literary analysis essay.

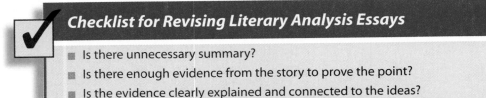

Checklist for Revising Literary Analysis Essays

■ Is there unnecessary summary?

■ Is there enough evidence from the story to prove the point?

■ Is the evidence clearly explained and connected to the ideas?

Summary can be useful as evidence, but it's not useful if it's not related to the point you are making. In the draft paper on pp. 322–323, look at the first body paragraph. The writer is making the point that the room resembles Louise Mallard's marriage, and the first part of the paragraph focuses on this. However, in the middle, the paragraph turns toward summary. The last part of the paragraph is a summary of the story.

> When she comes out, she feels much better. Obviously she has undergone a great change while alone in her room. However, when she finds that her husband is still alive, she realizes that she can't have her freedom, and she dies, but other people don't understand why. The doctors think she dies of "joy" (53), but they were wrong.

These sentences are not related to the idea that the room is like her marriage. The end of the paragraph should be revised to stay focused on the point.

The details, including the exact words, can often be essential in proving a point, so summary can also be overused when important details are omitted. You should be careful not to be too vague and general when explaining your own ideas as well as the events of the story. Look at the first paragraph.

> While she is there, she looks out the window and begins to have different feelings. Because of the things she sees outside the window, she knows she can be free and happy without her husband.

What are the "different feelings" she has? This is one of the most important ideas in the essay, but it is not clearly explained with details. Also, the related evidence from the story is treated the same way: "Because of the things she sees outside the window. . . ." This gives us no idea of what she sees. Thus, the paragraph really doesn't convince us of the idea the writer wants to prove.

In both body paragraphs, quotations and other evidence are given with no connection to the ideas. Look at the beginning of the first paragraph.

The first thing we know about the setting is that it takes place in the house where Louise Mallard lives. "She went away to her room alone" (52). While she is there . . .

The first quotation is not introduced or explained, so we don't understand why the quotation is there or why it is important.

EXERCISE 17.13

In the following exercises, practice the revision techniques discussed in this section.

1. Examine the rest of this draft, using the revising checklists on pp. 230–233 as well as the one on p. 324. What other changes should be made?
2. Examine the draft you wrote for Exercise 17.11, using the revising checklists on pp. 230–233 as well as the one on p. 324. What changes should be made?

Collaboration

3. Using photocopies of one group member's essay, check for revisions, using the revising checklists on pp. 230–233 as well as the one on p. 324. What changes should be made?

EDITING AND PROOFREADING

Remember that editing and proofreading are separate steps! Read Chapters 12 and 13 to review how to do these important tasks. Use the checklists on pp. 242–243 and 251 to help you focus on the details. Also remember that you will need to be especially careful when handling quotations and following the details of MLA style. Here are a few areas you might want to emphasize when editing and proofreading literary papers of all kinds.

■ Are the author's exact words used in direct quotations?
■ Are quotation marks used correctly, especially for quotes within quotes?
■ Are titles punctuated correctly?
■ Is correct MLA style used?

EXERCISE 17.14

In the following exercises, use the editing and proofreading techniques discussed in this section.

1. Review the draft on pp. 322–323 for editing and proofreading problems. Use the checklists on pp. 242–243 and 251 as guides.
2. Review the draft you revised in Exercise 17.12 for editing and proofreading problems. Use the checklists on pp. 242–243 and 251 as guides.

Collaboration

3. Exchange essays with other group members, or use photocopies. Look for problems in editing and proofreading. Use the checklists on pp. 242–243 and 251 as guides.

Here is an example of a final draft of a literary analysis essay that has been revised and edited.

Jeanine Wu
ENG 102
June 9, 2004

The Room and the Open Window:

Setting in "The Story of an Hour"

Where does Louise Mallard live? We know very little of the answer to that question. Kate Chopin does not tell us very much about the setting of "The Story of an Hour." We don't know whether it takes place in a city or a small town, in the West or in the East. However, we do know a good bit about one part of the setting. We know that most of the story takes place inside the house, and we know what Louise Mallard can see from her open window. Since we do hear about this small area so much, we can see that it must be a clue to the events of the story.

The first thing we know about the setting is that it takes place in the house where Louise Mallard lives. We know this because "she went away to her room alone" (52) after expressing her grief at hearing of her husband's death, and later, when she returns, she and her sister "descended the stairs" (53). Thus, we know she lives in a house where she has a room of her own, which includes a comfortable armchair. This shows us that she is fairly well-to-do and also that she has a certain amount of independence and privacy. Her sister has to beg her to open the door, showing that Louise cuts off the rest of the world when she goes into her room. When she is alone in the room, she can face her real feelings, because we see her very differently when she goes in and when she goes out. When she goes upstairs, she is "pressed down by a physical exhaustion that haunted her body and seemed to reach into her soul" (52), which shows that grief has overwhelmed her. When she comes out, "she carrie[s] herself unwittingly like a goddess of Victory" (53). Obviously she has undergone a great change while alone in her room.

Because we can see what happens inside the room and inside Louise Mallard's mind, we can understand what happens to her there. But we can also see that it is not the room that causes the change. Instead, it is the open window and the world outside that is described at the same time that the changes in her feelings are described. Through the window, she can see the open square, filled with trees "all aquiver with the new spring life" (52). She can also see the sky and hear the sound of birds, of peddlers calling out, and of someone singing. As she sits there, she no longer cries or even thinks, but gradually she begins to have a feeling very different from grief, and this new feeling is connected with the open window and the world outside the house: "She felt it, creeping out of the sky, reaching toward her *through* the sounds, the scents, the color that filled the air" (52). Eventually she can understand that the feeling is her awareness that she is now able to live her own life the way she wants to live: "Free, free, free!" she says to herself (53). She realizes that her husband has controlled her and that she will be free now that he is dead. In a way, his death has opened a window in her life. As Chopin says, "She was drinking in a very elixir of life through that open window" (53). Thus, the open window, the square with trees, the blue sky, and all the other things outside the window help her to see all the new things that can be in her life now that she is no longer controlled by her husband.

The setting of the story—the room and the open window—helps Mrs. Mallard to reach a new understanding of her life, but they are also similar to the feelings that go on inside her. In her room, she is safe and comfortable but controlled and shut away from the rest of life, but through her window she can learn about the possibilities of the future. Thus, the room and the window are similar to the life she leads and the life she hopes for.

Work Cited

Chopin, Kate. "The Story of an Hour." <u>The User's Guide to College Writing: Reading, Analyzing, Writing.</u> Ed. Nancy Kreml et al. 2nd ed. New York: Longman, 2003. 52–53.

18 Conducting Research

Imagine that you are having a conversation with a group of friends. If you express an opinion without first listening to the others and shaping your words to acknowledge what has already been said, you may appear rude or foolish. To join the conversation, you need to listen to your friends and then explain how your opinion fits into what other members of the group are saying. **Academic writing** is like a conversation among scholars. To join the conversation, you will need to conduct research to find out what has already been said by other scholars.

By using research material in your paper, you are showing that you have something useful to add to the conversation. Even if you don't think you have something to add, you still want to show that you have been listening and that you understand the conversation.

There are two types of research.

1. **Primary** (or field) **research**—collecting data and interpreting it
2. **Secondary research**—using someone else's report on *his or her* primary research

Throughout your academic career, you will be expected to conduct both types of research; occasionally you will have an assignment that requires you to include both kinds in your paper.

In this chapter, we discuss how to use research as a prewriting strategy. We first examine how to conduct secondary research (since it is the most common in academic settings) and then how to conduct primary research. Finally, we discuss how to select material from your research to use in your writing.

CONDUCTING SECONDARY RESEARCH

Secondary research is useful when you want to use information gathered by authorities on a topic. The authorities have conducted primary research and have written books or articles on their findings. Secondary research provides you with some authority without having to conduct the primary research yourself, and it enables you to find out what other people have already done to investigate a topic.

Types of Sources

There are two types of sources for secondary research: print and electronic. Print sources are those you find on library shelves: books, magazines, newspapers, journals, encyclopedias, dictionaries. Electronic sources are materials published in cyberspace or for use on a computer: Internet, CD-ROM, intranet, discussion groups, listservs, or chat rooms.

Evaluating Your Sources

Any time you are using research, you should evaluate the accuracy of your sources. Many print sources have already been evaluated through the publication process. To be printed, the author has had to prove his or her credentials and the validity of his or her ideas. Articles found in journals have been juried, which means that a board of professionals has agreed that the article is worth publishing.

Some print sources may not be valid for use in academic writing. Some books and magazines are published by the author, using what is known as a "vanity press," which allows an author to pay a company to print the materials. You will need to evaluate printed materials to determine if they are reliable and accurate sources.

On the Internet, anyone can publish materials. This means that electronic sources are not consistently reliable. Some electronic sources have printed equivalents, which means that they were juried in the same manner as reliable print sources. Those that do not have printed equivalents may or may not be reliable.

Electronic sources found on Websites that are maintained by universities and colleges, professional groups, publishing companies, government agencies, and research companies have been juried. Sites maintained by individuals are self-published and therefore not juried; such electronic sources need to be evaluated to determine if they are appropriate for the assignment.

Most instructors want you to avoid using sources that contain only general information (information that can be found in three or more sources), such as material contained in encyclopedias and textbooks. Although these sources are good for giving you background information, college instructors usually do not consider these valid research sources and do not want you to cite them as sources.

The Internet has many sites that are for student use in conjunction with classes. These sites may post papers written by students. However, most instructors consider student papers to be invalid sources for research.

Evaluating Websites You may want to use Websites that have already been evaluated, or you may want to evaluate a site yourself. Some Websites offer a service of filtering and evaluating research on the Internet. If you do not feel comfortable evaluating a site yourself, you may want to use one of these screening services, since someone has already checked the sites, at least to some extent, for accuracy and usefulness.

Evaluated Websites

AltaVista	http://www.altavista.com
Argus Clearinghouse	http://www.clearinghouse.net
AskJeeves	http://www.askjeeves.com
Best of the Web	http://www.botw.org
Excite	http://www.excite.com (Choose one of the categories, such as "education.")
Google	http://www.google.com
HotBot	http://www.hotbot.com
Lycos	http://point.lycos.com (Choose from the Topic Directory.)
Magellan	http://www.mckinley.com (Choose "Green Lite Sites Only.")
Webcrawler	http://www.webcrawler.com (Choose one of the "Channels.")
Yahoo	http://www.yahoo.com (Yahoo does not guarantee the quality of all sites.)

Conducting Searches

Even though you need to be open to what you find during a research project, you must have a starting point. The first step is to conduct a search for material related to your topic. Obviously you don't have time to wander through the library and look at every book and magazine to find information. Fortunately, others have created devices called **search engines**—research tools that might include a computerized listing of the library's holdings, an index on a CD-ROM, or an Internet browser. Whether you are in the library or on the Internet, you need to understand how to search for the topic and how the search engine provides the information related to your topic.

Computer Tip

Here are some options for reading the information provided by the search engine.

■ Read the material on the screen; this will require lots of time in the library or on the computer, and you can't take the information with you unless you make notes, but it is cost effective if you aren't paying for the Internet access or if you pay a flat fee for it.

■ Print the information and take it with you; this saves time but is not cost effective because many libraries charge for excess printing. You will want to be selective about what you print.

■ Download this information; this requires that you provide your own disk and that you have access to a computer so you can read the information later, but it does save time in the library, it is cost effective, and it allows you to take all the information you want with you.

Identifying Keywords for Searches   The most common way to search for a topic is to provide the search engine with a **keyword**, an identifying word or phrase usually taken from the writing **prompt**. However, you don't want to stop there. An author of an article or book may have used a different term, and you need to search with similar keywords in order to find as much information as you can. For example, if you are searching for information on the death penalty, you would obviously use the words *death penalty* in your search and then search with other closely related terms such as *execution* and *capital punishment*. If you can't think of related keywords on your own, a good strategy is to look at a few articles or books and make a list of terms that the authors use when discussing the death penalty.

| EXERCISE 18.1 | **Brainstorm keywords that might help you locate information on the following topics.** |

   A. Terrorism
   B. Health insurance
   C. Domestic violence
   D. Homelessness
   E. Cancer
   F. World Series champions

Narrowing the Subject with Keywords   Sometimes keywords provide you with so much information that you can't possibly look at everything, and you will likely miss the best information because you are overwhelmed. A search on *welfare* will provide you with a list of thousands of books and articles published on the topic. You will want to narrow your search by combining keywords to make your topic more specific. For example, to search for information on welfare in your home state of California, you would conduct a search combining both keywords *California* and *Welfare*.

Some search engines provide you with a list of categories for broad topics, such as *welfare*. Instead of getting a list of articles on welfare, the computer may give you a list that looks something like this.

Welfare—federal
Welfare—reform
Welfare—state
Welfare—women

You need to select the category you are interested in, and then the computer will show you a list of articles related to that category and ignore other categories related to welfare.

| EXERCISE 18.2 | **Brainstorm a list of terms that would help you narrow the focus of the following broad topics.** |

A. Terrorism

B. Health insurance

C. Domestic violence

D. Homelessness

E. Cancer

F. World Series champions

Using the Results of a Search   The kind of information provided by search engines varies, so you need to understand what they will and will not do. For example, a search engine may provide you with the following.

- A list of articles and books
- A list with short summaries of the article, or annotations
- A list and the full text of the article

What you do next will depend on the kind of list provided by the search engine. Here are some suggestions.

If You Get a List of Books and Articles . . .

- Determine whether you want to read the article by looking at the title of the article, the author, or the title of the publication.
- Determine if you want to find an annotation or summary of the article before you try to find the article.
- Find the articles and skim them to ensure their relevancy to your assignment.
- Print or photocopy the article, download it to a computer disk, or make notes.
- Document all information about the article, including where and how you found the article.

If You Get a List with Annotations . . .

- Skim the annotation to determine if you want to find the article.
- Find the articles and skim them to see if they are relevant to your assignment.
- Photocopy the article or make notes.
- Record all the information for documentation of where and how you found the article.

If You Get a List with Full-Text Articles . . .

- Skim the articles to see if they are relevant to your assignment.
- Print or download the article or make notes.
- Record all the information for documentation of where and how you found the article.

Making Notes

When you are making notes from research materials, you want to follow these steps.

- Skim the article or book to discover the focus of the article and to determine if you need to do a close reading.
- Look for the author's use of keywords in your topic and for interesting or useful ideas, facts, or quotes.
- When you find something that you might want to use in your own paper, read the section closely to make sense of the author's ideas or data.
- Copy the information carefully, making sure you record it accurately.
- If the material is a direct quote, be sure to use quotation marks or some other notation so you will remember that these are the exact words used by the author and that they require proper documentation.
- Be sure to copy the page number, the name of the article and/or book, the author's name, and all publication information related to the idea. This will keep you from having to repeat this step when you get ready to draft your paper and your bibliography or **Works Cited page**.

After you have gathered all notes from the research information, you will want to identify the connections among the ideas as well as identify how they relate to your own ideas and opinions.

COLLECTING INFORMATION DURING RESEARCH

Too often students find appropriate materials while conducting secondary research but forget one of the most important steps: recording the information required to create a paper that follows the research style guidelines required in academic writing. Two types of information must be recorded correctly. First, you must take notes on relevant information you find, including the numbers of the page or pages on which you found the information. Second, you must take notes on how to find the material in case your instructor or reader would like to read the article, book, or Website that you referred to or used in your paper.

Research Tip
As you do your research, be sure that you have all the information about the book or other source that you will need for your works cited list. See pages 337–339 for a list of details needed for different kinds of sources. If you have the information, you won't have to go back to the library to try to locate a lost Website when you're trying to finish your paper.

Before you begin this task, you will need to find out from your instructor which style guidelines you are expected to follow. The following are the two most common types in academic writing.

- Modern Language Association (MLA)
- American Psychological Association (APA)

In the sections that follow, you will be given examples on how to use direct quotes, how to paraphrase and summarize, and how to create a bibliography or works cited page for both MLA and APA. Before you begin your research, read this material closely. You will also find it helpful to use your textbook during your research to remind you of which details you need to record about the documents you find. Completing this step carefully will prevent extra work later when you need this information to complete your research paper.

For more information on MLA style, consult Joseph Gibaldi's *MLA Handbook for Writers of Research Papers*, 6th ed. New York: MLA, 2003. For more information on APA style, consult *The Publication Manual of the American Psychological Association*, 5th ed. Washington, DC: APA, 2001.

Computer Tip
Listings from databases usually give information that will allow you to complete a Works Cited or References list. However, this information is not placed in any order that follows either MLA or APA guidelines; putting the information in the correct format is your job. Also, verify that the information given in these listings is correct, and get the appropriate page numbers for internal documentation.

MLA STYLE GUIDELINES

Spacing   In MLA format, *everything is double-spaced.*

Citations   Citations are a reference to the sources you are using in your essay. To avoid plagiarism, you must cite your sources within the body of your essay. Some beginning writers think that they can avoid internal documentation, or citing their sources, by changing one or two words in the source. You must cite, or document, all ideas, whether they are quoted, paraphrased, or summarized in your paper.

Quoting Sources

Attaching Quotes to Your Writing   Avoid floating quotes. Quotes cannot stand alone.

> The author makes some good points. "Concern for student learning should come before all other concerns" (Jones 5).

This is a floating quote because the introduction of the quote is not connected to the quotation used. You must attach quotes to your sentences and supply whatever punctuation is required by the structure of your sentences.

COMMA REQUIRED

Newman states, "The process for elections will have to be changed" (43).

NO COMMA REQUIRED

Newman states that "the process for elections will have to be changed" (43).

OR

Newman believes the system has failed, and the current "process for elections will have to be changed" (43).

COLON REQUIRED (WRITER'S SENTENCE IS A COMPLETE SENTENCE)

Newman believes the old system has failed: "The process for elections will have to be changed" (43).

Quoting a Single Source   If you are only quoting one author in your essay, identify the author and the title of his or her work in your introduction. Thereafter, only place page numbers in the citation.

> Mary Jones states, "Many new students are overwhelmed by the demands of college work" (67). They have not been "sufficiently prepared by their high school experience" (68), she tells us.

Quoting More Than One Source   If you are quoting from more than one work, you must identify the author and page number in your citation each time you quote. If you give the author's name in your sentence, use only the page number in the citation.

> Stewart suggests, "Colleges need to do more to recruit students" (87).

If you do not use the author's name in your sentence, then the author's name must appear in the citation.

> He goes on to say, "Enrollments will fall if colleges don't do more" (Stewart 89).

Quoting Sources Without an Author Given   At times, you may come across articles that do not give the author's name. In this case, provide the title of the article (or an abbreviation) in quotation marks (to indicate it is an article) and provide the page number.

> One study shows college enrollment "has risen sharply in the last few years" ("College Update" 12).

> OR

> The article "College Update" notes that college enrollment "has risen sharply in the last few years" (12).

Quoting Articles from the Internet   Articles on the Internet often do not provide authors' names. If no name is given, use the title of the article. The Internet has no page numbers. If you identify the author (or title of the article if no author is given) in your sentence, you will have no citation following the quote.

However, if an article is clearly divided with page numbers, use them. If an article has numbered paragraphs, place them in your citation using the abbreviation *par.* (for one paragraph) or *pars.* (for multiple paragraphs). Place a comma after the author's name as shown in this example.

> (Williams, par. 3).

Sometimes Internet articles do not provide numbered pages or numbered paragraphs. In these cases, you will need to provide the author's name. The examples below show two acceptable methods for documenting this type of article.

> Russell believes the current trends in technology "will lead America to a new economic dominance."

OR

One writer believes the current trends in technology "will lead America to a new economic dominance" (Russell).

Works Cited Page

At the end of your essay, you must provide a Works Cited page for your reader. This page provides all the information a reader would need if he or she wanted to examine the works you quoted from. The words *Works Cited* appear centered at the top of the page. Remember that MLA requires that your paper be double-spaced. Do not use bold, italics, or a different font for the words *Works Cited*. (See example page 352.)

The entries in your Works Cited page should be listed in alphabetical order. Only list works in your Works Cited that you have quoted or made direct reference to in your essay. If you looked at a book or essay but did not quote it or directly refer to it, *do not* put it in your Works Cited. Only list works that you have directly cited in the body of your essay.

If no author is given for a work you cite, use the first major word of the title ("The College Crisis"—alphabetize using the word *College*). The entry should begin flush with the left-hand margin. If the entry runs more than one line, indent subsequent lines one tab (five spaces).

A Book with One Author

Last, First. Title of Book. City of Publication: Publisher, Year of

publication.

Smith, Thomas L. Academic Futures. New York: Haven Press, 2001.

A Book with More Than One Author

Last, First, First Last, and First Last. Title of Book. City of Publication:

Publisher, Year of Publication.

Brooks, Heyward A., Bridget R. Young, and Brian Held. Reassessing

Assessment. Chicago: Davis, 1999.

Anthology—One Work

Last, First. "Title of Essay/Poem/Short Story." Title of Anthology.

Editor(s). Edition (if applicable). City of Publication: Publisher, Year
of Publication. Page Spread.

Morris, Gina. "Blue Café." <u>Modern Women Writers</u>. Ed. Sherry Rich, Barbara Sutton, and Joan Nance. 2nd ed. Chicago: Worton, 2000. 191–99.

Anthology—Two or More Works from the Same Anthology

When quoting from two or more works from the same anthology, you must provide an entry for each author as well as an entry for the editors. The entries should be in alphabetical order, even if they are separated by other entries. The following entries are for Gina Morris, "Blue Café" and Linda Wesley, "Open Road." The editors are Rich, Sutton, and Nance (editors' names should be presented in the order given in the book—in this case they aren't presented alphabetically).

Works Cited

Albert, Thomas. "Modern Influences." <u>New Fiction</u>. 2nd ed. Ed. Mary Tinsley. New York: Hudson, 1998.

Morris, Gina. "Blue Café." Rich, Sutton, and Nance 191–99.

Nathan, Mary A. <u>Women Writers: 1990 to 2000</u>. London: Boxford House, 2001.

Rich, Sherry, Barbara Sutton, and Joan Nance, eds. <u>Modern Women Writers</u>. 2nd ed. Chicago: Worton 2000.

Wesley, Linda. "Open Road." Rich, Sutton, and Nance 99–105.

Magazine Article

Last, First. "Title of Article." <u>Title of Magazine</u> Date: Page Spread.

Long, Rita J. "Information Theory." <u>News Front</u> 12 Apr. 2001: 7–9.

Journal Article

Last, First. "Title of Article." <u>Title of Journal</u> Volume Number (Year): Page Spread.

Weatherby, Thomas A. "Illusory Patterns: Chaos Theory." <u>Science and Theory</u> 22 (1997): 77–81.

Newspaper Article

Last, First. "Title of Article." <u>Title of Newspaper</u> Date: Section and Page Number (plus symbol (+) to indicate additional pages).

Cappela, Marcus. "City Lights Affect Palomar Observatory." <u>San Diego Post</u> 12 Oct. 1992: B2+.

Internet Articles posted on the Internet may not list an author's name. If no author is given, use the title of the article (if given) or the title of the home page. Use an abbreviation for long titles. Be sure to look for all information (author, title of article, and the home page); you may need to look at more than one "page" of the Website to determine this information.

URLs should not be printed as hyperlinks. If after typing the URL, your computer changes it to a hyperlink (it turns blue and the font changes), use the following procedure for Microsoft Word. Highlight the URL. On the toolbar select "Insert." At the bottom of the dropdown menu, select "Hyperlink." In the bottom corner of the dialogue box that appears, select "Remove Hyperlink." You may still have to manually edit the URL after the hyperlink is removed.

When providing entries in your Works Cited page, you should always type to the far right margin. If your entry has a long URL, it may be dropped down to the next line if there isn't enough room for the entire URL. As a result, your entry may have a large gap. If the URL will not fit on one line, divide the URL; the place for this break is following a backslash (/) or a double backslash (//).

INTERNET—PERSONAL SITE

Last, First. <u>Title of Site</u> (if given; otherwise the term "Home page" can be used without quotation marks, no underline). Posting Date. Access Date URL.

Keesley, Roberta. *Dangerous Writers*. 3 May 2002. 20 Jan. 2003 <http://www.writershome.com/20thcentury/women/ shortstories>.

INTERNET—PROFESSIONAL SITE

<u>Title of Professional Site</u>. Name of Site Editor (if given). Date of Last Update (if given). Name of Organization Associated with the Website (if given). Access Date. URL.

<u>Language Assessment Program Dept. Homepage</u>. 12 May 2002. Northwest University. 6 Nov. 2002 <http://www.nwuniv.edu/academics/ assessment>.

INTERNET—ARTICLE FROM A MAGAZINE

Last, First. "Title of Article." <u>Title of Magazine</u> Date of Publication. Access Date URL.

Kays, Richard. "Educational Reform." <u>Modern Teaching</u> 5 May 2002. 14 Dec. 2002 <http://www.academicpages.com/mathematics/review>.

APA STYLE GUIDELINES

Spacing In APA format, *everything is double-spaced.*

Citations Citations are reference to the sources you are using in your essay. To avoid plagiarism, you must cite your sources within the body of your essay. Some beginning writers think that they can avoid internal documentation, or citing their sources, by changing one or two words in the source. You must cite, or document, *all* ideas, whether they are quoted, paraphrased, or summarized in your paper.

Quoting Sources

Attaching Quotes to Your Writing Avoid floating quotes. Quotes cannot stand alone.

> The author makes some good points. "Concern for student learning should come before all other concerns" (Jones, 1998, p. 5).

This is a floating quote because it is not connected to the writer's sentence. You must attach quotes to your sentences and supply whatever punctuation is required by the structure of your sentences.

COMMA REQUIRED

Newman (1999) states, "The process for elections will have to be changed" (p. 43).

NO COMMA REQUIRED

Newman (1999) states that "the process for elections will have to be changed" (p. 43).

OR

Newman (1999) believes the system has failed, and the current "process for elections will have to be changed" (p. 43).

COLON REQUIRED (WRITER'S SENTENCE IS A COMPLETE SENTENCE)

Newman (1999) believes the old system has failed: "The process for elections will have to be changed" (p. 43).

Quoting a Single Source   In subsequent references to the same source within the same paragraph, the date is left out.

> Mary Jones (1993) states, "Many new students are overwhelmed by the demands of college work" (p. 67). They have not been "sufficiently prepared by their high school experience" (p. 68), she tells us.

If you do not use the author's name in your sentence, then the author's name must appear in the citation.

> He goes on to say, "Enrollments will fall if colleges don't do more" (Stewart, 1992, p. 89).

Quoting Sources Without an Author Given   At times, you may come across articles that do not give the author's name. In this case, provide the title of the article (or an abbreviation). Do not place quotation marks around the title of articles

> One study shows college enrollment "has risen sharply in the last few years" (College Update, 1996, p. 12).

> **OR**

> The article "College Update" (1996) notes that college enrollment "has risen sharply in the last few years" (p. 12).

Quoting Articles from the Internet   Articles on the Internet often do not provide authors' names. If no name is given, use the title of the article and posting date. The Internet has no page numbers. If you identify the author (or title of the article if no author is given) in your sentence, you will have no citation following the quote.

However, if an article is clearly divided with page numbers, use them. If an article has numbered paragraphs, place them in your citation, using the symbol for paragraph, ¶, or the abbreviation *para*. Place a comma after the author's name and date of posting as shown in this example.

> (Williams, 2000, ¶ 3).

Often the pages and paragraphs on a Website are not numbered. To cite these types of articles, use one of the formats below.

> Russell (2002) believes the current trends in technology "will lead America to a new economic dominance."

Another example follows here.

One writer believes the current trends in technology "will lead America to a new economic dominance" (Russell, 2002).

References Page

At the end of your essay, you must provide a References page for your reader. This page provides all the information a reader would need if he or she wanted to consult the works from which you took your quotes. The word *References* should be centered at the top of a new page. Be sure to double space. Do not use bold, italics, or a different font for the word *References*. (See the example on page 353.)

The entries in your References page should be listed in alphabetical order. List only works that you have quoted or made direct reference to in your essay. If you looked at a book or essay but did not quote it or directly refer to it, do not include it in your References. Only list works that you have directly cited in the body of your essay.

If no author is given for a work you cite, use the first major word of the title (The College Crisis—alphabetize, using the word *College*). The citations within the body of your text would use the title of the article or an abbreviation for a long title.

The entry should begin flush with the left-hand margin. If the entry runs more than one line, indent subsequent lines five spaces.

Titles of articles are not placed in quotation marks. Titles of books or major works are italicized.

A Book with One Author

Last, Initial. (Year of Publication). *Title of book*. City of Publication: Publisher.

Smith, T. L. (1998). *Academic futures*. New York: Haven Press.

A Book with More Than One Author   Use an ampersand (&) rather than the word *and* before the last author's name

Last, Initial., Last, Initial., & Last, Initial. (Year). *Title*. City of Publication: Publisher.

Brooks, H., Bridget, R. Y., & Held, R. B. (2002). *Reassessing assessment*. Chicago: Davis Inc.

Anthology—One Work

Last, Initial. (Year). Title of essay. In Editor(s)' Name(s) (Eds.), *Title of anthology* (Edition [if applicable]. Page Spread). City of Publication: Publisher.

Morris, G. (2000). Blue café. In S. Rich, B. Sutton, & J. Nance (Eds.), *Modern women writers* (2nd ed. pp. 191–199). Chicago: Worton.

Periodicals   Do not place titles of articles in quotation marks. Only capitalize the first word of the article's title.

MAGAZINE ARTICLE

Last, Initial. (Year, Month Day). Title of article. *Title of Magazine, Magazine Number* (if given), Page Spread.

Long, J. (2000, April 3). Information theory. *News Front, 135,* 7–9.

JOURNAL ARTICLE

Last, Initial. (Year). Title of article. *Title of Journal, Volume Number,* Page Spread.

Weatherby, T. R. (1994). Illusory patterns: Chaos theory. *Science and Theory, 22,* 77–81.

NEWSPAPER ARTICLE

Last, Initial. (Year, Month Day). Title of article. *Title of Newspaper,* Section and Page Numbers.

Cappela, M. (2002, June 5). City lights affect Palomar Observatory. *San Diego Post,* pp. B2, B4.

Internet   Articles posted on the Internet may not list an author's name. If no author is given, use the title of the article (if given) or the title of the home page. Use an abbreviation for long titles.

URLs should not be printed as hyperlinks. If after typing the URL, your computer changes it to a hyperlink (it turns blue and the font changes), use the following procedure for Microsoft Word. Highlight the URL. On the toolbar select "Insert." At the bottom of the dropdown menu, select "Hyperlink." In the bottom corner of the dialogue box that appears, select "Remove Hyperlink." You may still have to manually edit the URL after the hyperlink is removed.

When providing entries in your References page, you should always type to the far right margin. If your entry has a long URL, it may be dropped down to the next line if there isn't enough room for the entire URL. As a result, your entry may have a large gap. If the URL will not fit on one line, divide the URL after a slash (/) or before a period (.).

INTERNET—PERSONAL SITE

Last, Initial. (Date). *Title of article*. Retrieval Date from URL.

Keesley, R. (2002). *Dangerous writers*. Retrieved January 12, 2003, from
   http://www.writershome.com/20thcentury/women/shortstories

INTERNET—PROFESSIONAL SITE

Provider. (Posting Date). Title of Home Page. Retrieval Date from URL.

Northwest University. (2002, May 12). Language assessment program.
   Retrieved November 6, 2002, from http://www.nwuniv.edu/
   academics/assessment

INTERNET—ARTICLE FROM A MAGAZINE

Last, Initial. Date of Publication. Title of article. *Title of Magazine, Volume
   number* (if given), Page Spread. Retrival Date from URL.

Kays, R. (2002, May 29). Educational reform. *Modern Teaching,
   5,* 15–18. Retrieved December 10, 2002, from http://www.
   academicpages.com/mathematics/review

CONDUCTING PRIMARY RESEARCH

Advantages to Primary Research

Primary research is a useful procedure because it provides you with new information and gives you some authority to write about a subject and to find
out firsthand what people think or feel about a subject. For example, if you
are writing a paper on welfare, you may want to interview someone who is (or
was) on welfare. You can also use the Internet to access newsgroups, online
discussion groups, and listservs related to the subject. These are all electronic
means for people who are interested in a topic to exchange ideas and information through the computer.

   In addition, primary research may allow you to challenge or verify
another writer's claims. For example, some media critics claim that prime-
time television is full of sex, violence, and other negative influences that have
no positive value for viewers, particularly young ones. To test this hypothesis, you might list the programs shown during prime-time, watch some of
them, and then use your observations to agree or disagree with the media
critics.

Disadvantages to Primary Research

Primary research is very time consuming. You have to design your own research plan, complete the plan yourself, and finally, make sense of the information you've gathered before you report your findings in your paper. Another disadvantage can be the personal aspect of some types of primary research, such as interviews and surveys. While your grandmother may have experienced the Great Depression, others may not consider her an authority on the subject, even though she has firsthand knowledge of the event. Therefore, when using primary research, you need to decide if you need an expert witness. If you are trying to add details and emotions about a topic, you may interview and/or survey anyone—friend, relative, classmate. If you are more interested in interpretations of the event, you will want to rely on expert witnesses, professionals who are qualified to help others understand the topic.

While there are many ways to conduct primary research, we discuss only the following two types.

1. Interviews and surveys
2. Observations

Interviews and Surveys

In-depth Interviewing   Some of the best resources for information may be people who live in your own community. Before conducting any interview, take some time to learn as much about the topic as you can. You want to convince the person you are interviewing that you are serious and well prepared. If you do not have a good background understanding of the topic, you will not understand enough of what you have been told to ask follow-up questions or to know if you are getting information that you can use.

You should also be professional when conducting an interview. Any subject who is worth interviewing deserves your professional courtesy. Here are some guidelines for good conduct during an interview.

1. Call for an appointment. Although you need to find a time that is convenient for both of you, you should expect to have to adjust *your* schedule. Be sure to write down the time and date, as well as the directions to the location of the interview.

2. Do your homework. Complete any background reading and prepare a list of questions. (See the "Designing Opinion Questions" section on p. 347.)

3. Gather the necessary equipment: paper, writing instruments, a tape recorder (be sure it works), and tapes. Be sure to take extras of everything.

4. Dress appropriately for the environment in which the interview will be conducted.

5. Arrive early for the appointment.

6. Ask permission to record the interview. If you can record it, you should write down only follow-up questions that you think of, not everything

the person says. If you cannot record anything, you will need to write everything that is said; you may read your notes to the person to verify your understanding.

7. Record the full name of the person you are interviewing and the date of the interview. You can add this later to your Works Cited or References list.

8. Write a thank you letter to the person you interviewed.

Designing Primary Research Questions Before you interview or survey others, you want to carefully plan your questions. This type of prewriting allows you to be prepared so you don't forget important questions. More importantly, this **prewriting** activity helps you focus on the material that you have decided is important.

Two kinds of information are gathered during an interview or survey:

1. Demographic
2. Opinion

Designing Demographic Questions Demographic information about your subjects is an important but often overlooked aspect of research. For example, you may find that five out of six people support welfare reform. To understand your data, the reader will want to know who these six people are, and you should be prepared to include relevant details about the people you interviewed or surveyed.

You will need to add other demographic questions based on the writing prompt or on the group of people you are interviewing or surveying. For example, if you are conducting research on people's perception of those who have cancer, you may want to include age.

What Do Demographic Questions Usually Include?

Age	Race	Educational level
Gender	Geographic location	Religion
Marital status	Income level	

Demographic questions reveal a great deal about a person's personal life, and many people don't want you to reveal their income level or sexual orientation. For this reason, you need to be clear with the people you survey or interview about how you plan to use the information. If you plan to quote an individual by name, you will need to have permission to use any demographic information. If you plan to report trends, you are then promising to leave out any information that would identify individual participants.

Designing Opinion Questions   Opinion questions get to the heart of primary research. This is the information that, when linked to demographics, can provide insight into the situation. If you are writing a paper on the Great Depression, someone who experienced the event could offer his or her opinion about the facts we all know.

When writing opinion questions, you need to consider two types of questions: *Limited questions* direct the answer in some way and are useful if you want to gather the same information from all people interviewed or surveyed. Such information usually leads to a yes/no answer or to an answer placed on a scale (strongly agree, agree, neither agree nor disagree, disagree, strongly disagree). Here are some examples of limited questions.

Do you know anyone on welfare?

Have you ever received welfare benefits?

Do you think the mentally or physically disabled should receive financial support from the government?

Open-ended questions allow the person being interviewed or surveyed to provide any kind of response or information he or she wants. If you want to know the reasons or emotions behind an answer, you will want to include such questions. Here are some examples of open-ended questions.

What do you think about welfare?

Who do you believe should receive welfare benefits?

How did you feel when you applied for welfare benefits?

To help you write questions, refer to the section on questioning in Chapter 6 on page 112.

EXERCISE 18.3

Collaboration

Working as a group, write five limited questions and five open-ended questions that you might ask on a survey or in an interview on the following topics.

A. Terrorism   C. Health insurance   E. Homelessness

B. Cancer   D. Domestic violence   F. Cloning

Observations

Observing may include watching a scene or an event, but it is not limited to that. You can test a hypothesis by checking out someone's claims.

Designing Observational Research   The key is to identify a question you want to answer or a theory you want to prove or disprove and then design a way of gathering the information that will allow you to find an answer to the question or to prove (or disprove) the theory. Your research design will vary based on the information you want to find, the resources you have available to you, and the time you have to complete your project. There are basically two phases of setting up observational research.

1. **Forming a question, answer, or hypothesis**

   Suppose you have read an article in which the author claims that prime-time television is filled with sex and violence, and you want to test this claim. You might come up with a question or a statement you want to test.

   ■ Does prime-time television present a lot of sex and violence?

   OR

   ■ Prime-time television does (or does not) present a great deal of sex and violence.

2. **Designing research to answer a question or test a hypothesis**

   Once you have pinpointed your question or hypothesis, you must design a plan to find an answer. For the preceding question or hypothesis, you might decide to do one or more of the following.

   ■ Watch television shows that you feel are representative of those shown on prime-time. As you watch, keep track of features you think are presentations of sex and violence. For example, you might count the number of times that characters refer to sex or are shown (or indicated) having sex and the number of times a character physically attacks or threatens another character.

   ■ Enlist several people to watch shows with you; then interview them about the amount and appropriateness of sex and violence they found in the shows.

Completing the Research

The process of primary research involves three steps.

1. **Conducting the research**

   Be sure to allow yourself enough time to complete your research. If you are conducting interviews or surveys, you are partially dependent on other people's schedules and cooperation, so allow more time.

   Take notes at the time you are conducting your interviews or observing events. You will find it difficult to remember exactly what you heard and saw if you wait to do so after the fact.

   Jot down any ideas or trends you notice while conducting the research. Be sure to keep it separate from the information you are gathering, but you will need to note your ideas and trends for use later.

2. **Compiling the findings**

Once you have completed your surveys, interviews, or observations, you need to compile your findings. That is, you need to place the answers you received or the insights you gained next to each other to look for patterns. Where are you finding the same type of information? Where are you getting different answers?

If you are conducting surveys or interviews in which you have asked limited-answer questions, count the number of persons who gave the same answer to the same question.

3. **Drawing conclusions**

Once you have placed the answers or insights next to each other and looked for patterns, you need to draw some conclusions: What does the information you gathered mean? How do you make sense of it? What does this information tell you?

If you have conducted interviews or surveys, you might compare the demographic information about your subjects with their answers. Do younger participants tend to answer differently from those who are older? Do female participants tend to answer differently from those who are male? Can you offer an explanation of why answers differ among groups?

Evaluating Your Research

What did you believe or think about the topic prior to starting the research?

Have you changed your mind about the topic as a result of what you discovered during your research?

Why did you choose the topic?

Why is the topic an important one?

What did you learn during your research that surprised you?

List one to five interesting statistics or facts that you discovered.

List one to five interesting quotes that you discovered.

What did you learn about the topic as a result of your research?

What data did you find hard to believe?

What categories or parts of the topic did you find?

What contradictions about the topic did you find?

What errors in fact or perception did you find?

What recurring ideas did you find?

Working in a group, brainstorm ways to investigate the following statements.

1. All rap music contains negative influences, such as profanity, sex, and violence.

2. Children who listen to rap music may repeat the words, but they don't understand the meaning of the songs.

3. Talk shows encourage guests and viewers to consider personal experience (or testimony) but not to think about the larger issues. Guests, studio audiences, and hosts alike concentrate on individuals' personal experience instead of looking objectively at causes, effects, and solutions on a larger scale.

4. *Sports Illustrated* magazine is unfair to female athletes, showing more women in the swimsuit issue than in all other issues during the rest of the year.

5. Parents who want to limit the sex and violence their children are exposed to in music, television, and movies can do so without the help of ratings systems or parental warnings that may entice children.

6. Even though experts says that Americans spend too much time watching TV, in truth most people are doing other things while the TV is on.

7. Adults as well as teenagers are affected by suspenseful and violent movies.

SELECTING MATERIAL TO USE IN YOUR WRITING

Once you have gathered your research material, whether primary or secondary, you must decide how you will use the material in your writing. Consider your research prewriting, and use the same strategies we discussed in Chapter 7 to evaluate your research as prewriting.

One particularly useful strategy to use with research is to start with the conclusions drawn as you've conducted the research, taken notes, compiled your findings, and evaluated them. These conclusions represent your ideas and could become your **thesis** or **supporting** ideas for your writing. The information that led you to your conclusions then becomes your supporting evidence. Reorganizing your prewriting (by clustering, **listing**, charting) into this format may help clarify your ideas and evidence about the topic.

SAMPLE MLA STYLE PAPER

Basically, there are two parts to any citation: (1) a parenthetical citation in the body of an essay that tells your reader exactly which words or ideas are yours and which are someone else's and (2) a Works Cited list that gives all the information about the sources used in the essay.

The two parts of a citation work together. You must first make the end list, which we call the **Works Cited** list. The first word or words in each entry in the list will be used as a shorthand in your paper each time you use material from that source. Here's an example of two paragraphs and part of the Works Cited list from a paper using outside sources. This example follows MLA style. Notice that every quotation or paraphrase is clearly linked to the first words of one of the entries in the list that follows.

The image that most people have of welfare recipients is false. Many people look at those on welfare as people who are too lazy to work hard. They believe that welfare recipients are just people who want a free ride. According to Chou, "Newt Gingrich [said that they] posed a threat to American civilization" (B15). This image is often promoted on television news magazines which do stories on welfare recipients who abuse the system. We see stories about people illegally trading food stamps or making false claims to bilk the system out of money. We also hear about people who make welfare a lifestyle. However, most recipients are people who want to get off welfare and make a decent living for themselves (McLeod and Donalds 12–27). Teresa McCrary is one such person. She has worked hard to obtain the education required to get a job that will pay her enough money to support her family. The picture that Teresa McCrary presents of welfare mothers in her essay "Getting Off the Welfare Carousel" is an accurate one. The fact is that life is very difficult for women like her, who usually have poorer working conditions than other people (Clemons). She discusses the problems that welfare mothers face and argues against the image that most people have of welfare recipients. The experiences of two friends of mine show this daily, as they struggle to take care of children by volunteering at the elementary school and going to school themselves at night. They represent the real image of welfare mothers, women who are dedicated to their children and women who are working hard to better themselves, yet I've heard neighbors call them "bums," just because they get a few dollars to help feed their children.

The welfare system seems to be designed to work against those who receive benefits. McCrary explains to us how the system really works. When a woman with children finds herself divorced, she has to clothe and feed her offspring even though she may have no job skills (Myron 107). Of course, her first step is to apply for welfare to protect her children. However, welfare is barely enough to survive on. The woman's next step is to get a job, but because she has no work experience or job skills, "The only jobs open [to her] are maid work, fast-food service and other low-paying drudgery with no benefits," McCrary tells us (11). According to the Clearinghouse for Welfare Information, women are "steer[ed] . . . into working for minimum wage rather than training for better jobs." This situation leads women on welfare to "take money under the table for odd jobs" (McCrary 11) so they can make a little more money but not lose their benefits. The system forces women to stay on welfare and take money under the table—for which the government receives no taxes. This system does not benefit the women on it or the government who wants them off it.

[Start New Page]

Works Cited

Chou, Linda. "Off the Welfare Rolls, On the Payrolls." New York Times 2 July 2000: B15.

Clearinghouse for Welfare Information. "You Never Get Free: Transition from Welfare to Work." Social Work Site. 15 Jan. 1998. Online. 18 March 2000 <http://www.clearinghouse.org/socialworksite/welfare/transition.htm>.

Clemons, Laurie G. "Welfare Reform and Working Women." Review of Welfare May 1999: 79–109. Online. Stanton, MT: LEXIS-NEXIS Academic Universe, 7 April 1998. 21 May 2000 <http://web.lexis-nexis.com/cis>.

McCrary, Teresa. "Getting Off the Welfare Carousel." Newsweek 6 December 1993: 11.

McLeod, Peggy, and Samuel Donalds. The Stories of Women at Work and on Welfare. New York: Ramparts, 1998.

Myron, Wessinger. "Making It Alone: The Single Parent." Welfare Reform. Ed. Sandra Mayson. New York: Clarks, 1999. 98-119.

SAMPLE APA STYLE PAPER

Basically, there are two parts to any citation: (1) a parenthetical citation in the body of an essay that tells your reader exactly which words or ideas are yours and which are someone else's and (2) a References list that gives all the information about the sources used in the essay.

The two parts of a citation work together. You must first make the end list, which we call the **References page**. The first word or words in each entry in the list will be used as a shorthand in your paper each time you use material from that source. Here's an example of two paragraphs and part of the References page from a paper using outside sources. This example follows APA style. Notice that every quotation or paraphrase is clearly linked to the first words of one of the entries in the list that follows.

The image that most people have of welfare recipients is false. Many people look at those on welfare as people who are too lazy to work hard. They believe that welfare recipients are just people who want a free ride. According to Chou, "Newt Gingrich [said that they] posed a threat to American civilization" (2000). This image is often promoted on television news magazines which do stories on welfare recipients who abuse the system. We see stories about people illegally trading food stamps or making false claims to bilk the system out of money. We also hear about people who make welfare a lifestyle. However, most recipients are people who want to get off welfare and make a decent living for themselves (McLeod and Donalds, 1998). Teresa McCrary is one such person. She has worked hard to obtain the education required to get a job that will pay her enough money to support her family. The picture that Teresa McCrary presents of welfare mothers in her essay "Getting Off the Welfare Carousel" is an accurate one. The fact is that life is very difficult for women like her, who usually have poorer working conditions than other people (Clemons, 1999). She discusses the problems that welfare mothers face and argues against the image that most people have of welfare recipients. The experiences of two friends of mine show this daily, as they struggle to take care of children by volunteering at the elementary school and going to school themselves at night. They represent the real image of welfare mothers, women who are dedicated to their children and women who are working hard to better themselves, yet I've heard neighbors call them "bums," just because they get a few dollars to help feed their children.

The welfare system seems to be designed to work against those who receive benefits. McCrary explains to us how the system really works. When a woman with children finds herself divorced, she has to clothe and feed her offspring even though she may have no job skills (Myron, 1999). Of course, her first step is to apply for welfare to protect her children. However, welfare is barely enough to survive on. The woman's next step is to get a job, but because she has no work experience or job skills, "The only jobs open [to her] are maid work, fast-food service and other low-paying drudgery with no benefits," McCrary (1993) tells us. According to the Clearinghouse for Welfare Information, women are "steer[ed] . . . into working for minimum wage rather than training for better jobs." This situation leads women on welfare to "take money under the table for odd jobs" (McCrary, 1993) so they can make a little more money but not lose their benefits. The system forces women to stay on welfare and take money under the table—for which the government receives no taxes. This system does not benefit the women on it or the government who wants them off it.

[Start New Page]

References

Chou, L. (2000, July 2). Off the welfare rolls, on the payrolls. *New York Times*, B15.

Clearinghouse for Welfare Information. (1998, January 15). You never get free: transition from welfare to work. *Social Work Site*. Retrieved March 18, 2000, from http://www.clearinghouse.org/socialworksite/welfare/transition.htm

Clemons, L. G. (1999, May 5). Welfare reform and working women. *Review of Welfare*, 79–109. Retrieved April 7, 1998, from http://web.lexis-nexis.com/cis

McCrary, T. (1993, December 6). Getting off the welfare carousel. *Newsweek, 11*, 25–27.

McLeod, P. & Donalds, S. (1998). *The stories of women at work and on welfare.* New York: Ramparts.

Myron, W. (1999). Making it alone: The single parent. In S. Mayson (Ed.) *Welfare reform* (pp. 98–119). New York: Clarks.

DOCUMENTATION PUNCTUATION EXERCISES

EXERCISE 18.5

Assume that the following passage was found on page 156 of the book *Guide to China* by J. L. Sims. Use this paragraph for the exercises that follow.

The city of Beijing is the capital of China and is located in the northeast section of the country. Although Beijing was not the first capital of this ancient country, it has held that position since the fourteenth century. When China's rulers were emperors, they lived in the center of Beijing in a great palace called the Forbidden City. This palace is now a cultural and art museum, open to all of China's people. Also in Beijing are many temples and other museums, but Beijing is not a city of the past. Most visitors delight in the many restaurants serving different kinds of food from every part of China and the world. On one street the restaurants have blazing fires and whole sheep hanging outside; on another street are elegant Sichuanese restaurants where twenty-course meals are served on rare porcelain dishes, and on yet another street Pizza Hut competes with McDonald's.

Correct the use of quotation marks in the following student paragraph. Be sure to check with the preceding original to see where the student is quoting and where she is paraphrasing.

The capital of the United States is Washington, D.C., and the capital of China is Beijing (Sims 156). Beijing is like Washington is in some ways and different in others. Beijing once had emperors who lived in the center of Beijing in a great palace called the Forbidden City. Washington has the White House and our president lives there now, but the leader of China does not live in the Forbidden City "which is now open to all of the people of China" (Sims 156). Washington and Beijing both have many museums and restaurants, and in both you might find exotic ethnic foods, elegant cuisine, and streets where Pizza Hut competes with McDonald's (Sims 157).

Note: When using **parenthetical citations,** the parentheses come after any quotation marks but before the period. (See pp. xxx on documentation for more information on citing sources.) Here's an example.

In *An Anthropologist on Mars,* Robert Kellogg says that we are all "wishing for the past" (185).

EXERCISE 18.6	Write a paragraph comparing your city to Beijing, using quotations from the selection on page xx. Be sure to introduce and explain your quotes.

EXERCISE 18.7	Here is a paragraph from a book. It will be the original text to use in the exercise that follows.

Volcano eruptions are not as common as earthquakes, hurricanes, and tornadoes. Volcanoes look very much like big mountains—they sit there quietly, wearing their snow and glaciers like kindly white-haired grandparents. This is deceptive. Under the cold ice lies a raging furnace that may spew tons of suffocating ashes, torrents of hot mud, or fiery rivers of lava. Any of these eruptions will destroy all life in the path of the outpouring. Mt. St. Helens erupted with ashes and caused destruction in the United States; Mt. Pinatubo in the Philippines and Mt. Fako in Cameroon have also erupted in the last ten years.

Improve the sentences in the student paragraph below by selecting better material from the preceding original or by rewording the sentence.

Among the natural disasters in the United States recently was "Mt. St. Helens erupted with ashes." We don't expect volcanoes. The source says "like kindly white-haired grandparents." We should be afraid of volcanoes "spew tons of suffocating ashes."

EXERCISE 18.8	Improve the use of quotation by using ellipses in the following sentences (the original text is on p. 355).

1. Some results of volcano eruptions include: "Under the cold ice lies a raging furnace that may spew tons of suffocating ashes, torrents of hot mud, or fiery rivers of lava."

2. Three volcanoes that have erupted recently are "Mt. St. Helens erupted with ashes and caused destruction in the United States; Mt. Pinatubo in the Philippines and Mt. Fako in Cameroon have also erupted in the last ten years."

Adding Words   If you want to add your own explanatory words or comments to a direct quote, place them in square brackets, *not* parentheses. Make sure the meaning is not changed.

SAME MEANING   Beber says that it was difficult to be a complete feminist in law school because "wanting to be a lawyer
means identifying with the people [men] you are trying to defeat" (207).

MEANING CHANGED (AVOID)   Beber says that it was difficult to be a complete feminist in law school because "wanting
to be a lawyer means [not] identifying with
the people you are trying to defeat" (207).

Changing Words   If you want to substitute a word or phrase for something
in a direct quote, use square brackets. (Do not use ellipses.) Make sure the
meaning is not changed.

SAME MEANING   When they met Irina, the reporters knew that she
"[had become] a legend" (87).

MEANING CHANGED (AVOID)   When they met, the reporters knew that "Irina
[was going to be] a legend" (87).

EXERCISE 18.9   Use brackets to add or change the wording to make the sentences fit smoothly.
Be careful not to distort the meaning.

1. People who live near a volcano should be concerned about the eruptions
   because "these eruptions will destroy all life in the path of the outpouring."
2. Anyone who was climbing a volcano and thought that it was peaceful
   should have realized that "this is deceptive."

EXERCISE 18.10   Use the following sources to create a Works Cited list using MLA style guidelines or a References list using APA style guidelines.

1. title of article: electronic café author: margaret wertheim month: january
   year: 1993 magazine: omni pages: 66–68, 70
2. year: 1994 date: 16 month: may magazine: newsweek article: gender gap
   in cyberspace page numbers: 82–83
3. author: gerard van der leun magazine: wired year: 1993 pages: 74, 109
   access: online Website: hotwired date accessed on the Internet: august 22
   1995 URL: http://vip.hotwired.com/wired/1.1/features/cybersex.html
4. book: island in the net. author: bruce sterling publisher: morrow year: 1998
   published in New York, NY
5. book main title: silicon snake oil book subtitle: second thoughts on the information highway year: 1995 published in New York, NY published by
   Doubleday Publishers Author: Ralph Smith
6. Journal: humanist pages: 5–14 year: 1991 published in September/October
   volume number 51 author: gregory ulmer article title: trouble in cyberspace

PART FOUR

Working on Sentences

19 A Handbook for Writing Correct Sentences

19 A Handbook for Writing Correct Sentences

HOW TO USE THE HANDBOOK

This handbook explains the most common problems you are likely to find when **editing**. If you discover that you make the same errors frequently in your writing, or if a teacher, tutor, or writing partner suggests that you need to review a certain kind of problem, then you should follow the steps listed here.

How to Use This Handbook

1. Read the explanation of the problem in the handbook.
2. Try the exercise.
3. Check the answers on pages 545–558.
4. Ask your instructor for help with any problems you don't understand.
5. Check your writing for the problem and make corrections.

After reading the explanation of each problem area, you should try the corresponding exercise and check the answers in the back of the book. If you didn't miss any, go on to check your paper for the same problem. If you did miss something in the exercise, reread the explanation. If you continue to have difficulty understanding the problem, talk with your teacher or tutor.

Here is an overview of this handbook. Note the abbreviations in the parentheses; they are found on tabs in this chapter to help you locate the specific explanation you need at any given time.

Problems Discussed in the Handbook

1. Sentence basics (BAS)
   1.1 Recognizing verbs (p. 360)
   1.2 Recognizing subjects (p. 361)
   1.3 More complicated subjects and verbs (p. 361)
   1.4 Recognizing prepositional phrases (p. 364)

continued on next page

1. SENTENCE BASICS

Before you can understand how to deal with the problems in your writing, you will need to know how the basic building blocks of sentences—verbs, subjects, and prepositional phrases—are used in sentences.

1.1 RECOGNIZING VERBS

<table>
<tr><td>

**The Building
Blocks of a
Sentence**

Verbs

Subjects

Prepositional phrases

</td></tr>
</table>

You must first learn to recognize a **verb**—a word that shows action or state of being.

ACTION The firefighter **will extinguish** the fire.

ACTION We **considered** our choices.

STATE OF BEING Sri Lanka **is** the name of the island country just south of India.

If this definition seems confusing, you might find it helpful to use an additional definition: *A verb is a word in a sentence that changes when the time of the sentence is changed.*

PRESENT The firefighter **will extinguish** the fire tomorrow.

PAST The firefighter **extinguished** the fire yesterday.

PAST We **considered** our choices last week.

PRESENT We **are considering** our choices today.

PRESENT Sri Lanka **is** now the name of the island country just south of India.

PAST Ceylon **was** once the name of the island country just south of India.

As you can see in these examples, sometimes a verb is just one word, and sometimes it is several words, called a **verb phrase.** The word that carries the meaning of the verb is called the **main verb,** and the other parts of the verb are known as the **auxiliary** or **helping verbs** or helpers.

Auxiliary	**Main**
will	*extinguish*
are	*considering*

BAS EXERCISE 1   Underline each verb twice. Be sure to underline all the parts of the verbs, including main verbs and all auxiliaries (or helping verbs).

The story of the Heike is a very sad story from Japanese history. The emperor (whose family was called the Heike) was fighting his enemies, who chased him until finally he boarded a ship with his family and followers. A nurse carried the baby, the son of the emperor. When the enemies captured the ship, she took the baby emperor to the prow of the ship and jumped into the water where she and the baby drowned, but escaped their enemy in death. All the family and soldiers of the Heike were killed and their bodies were lost at sea. Now the crabs who are caught in that part of the ocean have strange markings on their shells. Local people call them the faces of the Heike.

1.2 RECOGNIZING SUBJECTS

After locating the verb in a sentence, you must now find the **subject**—the word that tells you who or what performed the action of the verb. Just read the sentence again and find the verb.

> The firefighter **will extinguish** the fire.

Now put a mental blank before the verb, and fill it in:

> _____ will extinguish
>
> **firefighter** will extinguish

Now you know that *firefighter* is the subject.

> We **considered** our choices.
>
> _____ considered
>
> **We** considered

This process works the same way with verbs that don't name an action:

> Sri Lanka **is** the name of the island country just south of India.
>
> _____ is
>
> **Sri Lanka** is

BAS EXERCISE 2

In the following paragraph, underline the verb in each sentence twice. Underline the subject once.

A very old story from the Middle East is called *Gilgamesh*. Gilgamesh was the ruler of his country, and he was very strong and handsome. Another man in that country was called Enkidu. Enkidu lived in the forest and had only animals for friends. Gilgamesh sent a woman to Enkidu, and when the animals saw him with another human, they became afraid of him. Enkidu left the forest. He and Gilgamesh fought each other, but finally became good friends. The importance of friendship is a theme of the story.

1.3 MORE COMPLICATED VERBS AND SUBJECTS

Not every sentence you write will be as simple as the preceeding ones. Here are some hints about how to deal with the more complex sentences you will be writing. If you remember the basic rules, you'll see that problems can be easily avoided.

> ### *What Do We Know About Verbs and Subjects?*
>
> Verbs are words that must be changed when the time of the sentence changes.
>
> Subjects are words that tell who or what performed the action of the verb.

Now let's look at some ways the words in your sentences may change.

1.3.1 Infinitives

A *to* + word (infinitive) or an *-ing* word with no helper (gerund or participle) cannot be the verb of the sentence. An infinitive (*to* + **word**) is a phrase such as the following.

> to sing   to explain   to capture   to inspect

A gerund or participle **(*-ing*, no helper verb)** is a word ending in *-ing* that does not have auxiliaries or helping verbs such as *is, were, will be, have been*.

> peeling the potatoes taking the test remembering the past a flying bird

You might see sentences like these.

> I wanted **to paint** the room yellow last week.
>
> Right now, the supervisor calls Gina **to repair** the gears.
>
> **Waiting** makes me nervous these days.
>
> **Speeding** down the street last night, the truck passed every car.

What is the verb in each sentence? To determine that, you can always apply the first verb rule: **Verbs are words that change form when the time of the sentence changes.** If you change the time of each sentence, you can see which words change form—those are verbs. The words that do not change are not being used as verbs.

> I **want** <u>to paint</u> the room yellow this week.
>
> Tomorrow, the supervisor **will call** Gina <u>to repair</u> the gears.
>
> <u>Waiting</u> **made** me nervous when I was younger.
>
> <u>Speeding</u> down the street, the truck **passes** every car right now.

The boldfaced words in the preceding sentences are verbs because they required different forms when the time of the sentence changed. The underlined words may seem like verbs, but they did not change in form when the time of the sentence changed. To save time, you can remember that a word with *to* before it is not the verb in the sentence and that a word that ends in *-ing* cannot be the verb *unless* it has auxiliaries or helping verbs.

BAS EXERCISE 3   In the following paragraph underline the verb twice (be sure to include all helping verbs). Draw a circle around the infinitives (*to* + word) and the gerunds or participles (*-ing*, no helper verbs).

> From an ancient African county in Mali comes the story of Son-Jara, who was born a prince. His mother was one of the king's wives, but another of the king's wives hated her. Being jealous was a common problem among the king's wives in those days. This woman cursed Son-Jara so that he was unable to walk when he was a child. To be a king's mother was his mother's ambition, so she wanted him to be stronger than other men, but instead he was weaker. His mother's hopes for her son seemed impossible, but she went to ask help from a Djinn, a supernatural creature. Following the Djinn's instructions was difficult, but she obeyed. She sent her son on a Haj, which is a pilgrimage to Mecca. Finally the curse was destroyed, and Son-Jara became a great king.

1.3.2 Parts of Verbs

The parts of a verb phrase can be separated, and some parts can come before the subject. Don't expect that the auxiliaries or helping verbs will always come right before the verb. Other words can be placed between the helper and the main verb, and some helpers may even come before the subject.

> Nathaniel **was** already **going** on to the last part of the test.
>
> After Saturday, Marta **will** not **live** with her sister.
>
> **Are** we really **expecting** to find a good car here?
>
> **Don't** you **want** to enroll in the payroll deduction plan?

BAS EXERCISE 4   In the following paragraph, underline the verb in each sentence twice. Underline the subject once.

> Do all people have the same idea about how the world was created? People in different parts of the world can sometimes have very different ideas. Many cultures have asked these questions: Where do we come from? How were we made? The question is often answered by a story. The Mayan people of ancient Guatemala long ago told the story of creation, which, according to the stories they told, had been accomplished by a group of gods. These gods were called Bearer, Begetter, Maker, and Modeler (also called Plumed Serpent). They used many grains, fruits, and vegetables to create the first people.

1.4   RECOGNIZING PREPOSITIONAL PHRASES

A **prepositional phrase** is a **noun** (or **pronoun**) and the preposition that connects it to the sentence. It is a part of a sentence but can never be the subject or the verb. If you're not sure whether a word is a preposition, try inserting it in the blank in the following sentence.

> The airplane flew _____ the cloud.

Most prepositions will make sense in that blank: *by, beside, under, through, around, with, beneath, after, before.* *Note:* One very common preposition that does **not** fit in that sentence is the preposition *of.*

Prepositional phrases can occur in many places in a sentence.

> Elevated trains and subways both provide transportation **in Chicago.**

> Mathematics is an easier subject **for me** than history.

> **In summer,** days are long and nights are short.

In a prepositional phrase, the preposition does not always come right before the noun. Words can be added to describe the noun, and sometimes they can be combined with a gerund or participle (-ing, no helper verb) to describe the noun or even to become the noun itself.

> **Beside the beautiful princess** sat a frog.

> We waited **for the slowly passing cars.**

> One **of the most wonderful sights on earth** is Mt. Fuji **in Japan.**

BAS EXERCISE 5   **In the following paragraph, put parentheses around each prepositional phrase.**

> Many of the stories we find in one country are also found in the tales from other countries. For example, the story of a great flood that destroys the earth is found in many stories from all over the world. In ancient China, in Babylon, in Israel, in South America, and probably in many other lands as well, we can read or hear of one man who survives the flood with his family and starts the world again. The story of the flood appears in the Bible and in the Koran. One man suggested a theory about these universal stories. In his book *Man and His Symbols,* Carl Jung called these stories *archetypes* and reminded us that people in all parts of the world tell similar stories, and also dream similar dreams.

2. SENTENCE BOUNDARIES

Do you have problems choosing between commas and periods? Do your papers often have notes about fragments, run-ons, and comma splices? If so, you need to work on understanding **sentence boundaries**—that is, on knowing what makes a complete sentence and how sentences can be combined.

2.1 FRAGMENTS

A **sentence fragment** is a group of words that does not form a sentence. To avoid writing fragments, you will need to recognize sentences.

What Is a Sentence?

A sentence always has a subject and a verb.

A sentence never has a subordinating word, unless the sentence is joined to another sentence.

2.1.1 Check for Subject and Verb

Review the explanations for locating subjects and verbs in Section 1 (pp. 360–363) if you don't remember them clearly.

- ■ Verbs are words that must be changed when the time of the sentence changes.
- ■ Subjects are words that tell who or what did the action of the verb.

Any group of words that does not have a subject and a verb is a fragment. Here are examples of fragments caused by the lack of verb and subject.

<u>NO VERB</u> I was really tired. **Studying all day and working all night.**

Studying all day and working all night has no verb. Try changing the time, and you will see that no words must be changed.

<u>NO SUBJECT</u> **Studying** all day today and **working** all night tonight.
Studying all day yesterday and **working** all night last night.

Note: A verb that ends in *-ing* must have a helping verb. The helper shows the time change.

When we ask "Who?" before the *studying* or *working,* we cannot find the answer in that sentence. We can thus conclude that *Studying all day and working all night* has no subject.

To revise this fragment, add it to the sentence before it.

<u>REVISION</u> I was really tired, studying all day and working all night.

It can also be revised by adding a subject and verb.

REVISION I was really tired. **I was** studying all day and working all night.

BND EXERCISE 1 Underline each fragment. On a separate sheet of paper, make whatever revisions are needed to create complete sentences. You may either add a fragment to another sentence or add subjects and verbs to create new sentences.

> A writer of many plays and poems. William Shakespeare is considered to be the greatest writer in the English language. We usually think of Shakespeare as the writer of tragic plays. Plays about murder and unfortunate deaths. However, Shakespeare also wrote plays referred to as the histories and the romances. Also, twelve plays called the comedies. His plays were very popular in his own time. Performed at the Old Globe theater. Today, his plays are perhaps most often seen in movie theaters. Some film directors will update the play and set it in modern times. Rewriting the play's original language so it is more accessible for today's audiences. These directors may also film the play outdoors. Instead of indoors on the stage.

2.1.2 Check for Subordinating (Fragment) Words

Words that are used to connect two sentences are sometimes called **subordinating words** or **fragment words**. (You also might have learned to call these subordinating conjunctions and relative pronouns.) Here are some examples of subordinating words.

although	since	when
after	that	who
because	through	which
if	so that	while
before	how	what
as	until	unless

Because subordinating words connect two sentences, **a group of words that has a subject and verb** *and also* **has a subordinating word is often a fragment.**

> **Although I had followed the directions.** My hair turned a horrible shade of orange.

Although is a fragment word. It shows the relationship between the two groups of words. Revise this fragment by removing the period and adding a comma between the two parts of the new sentence.

REVISION Although I had followed the directions, my hair turned a horrible shade of orange.

Note: When revising, use a comma if the fragment word is at the beginning of the sentence. Do not use a comma if the fragment word is inside the sentence.

> My hair turned a horrible shade of orange <u>although</u> I had followed the directions.

BND EXERCISE 2	**Underline each fragment. Then on a separate sheet of paper, if needed, revise to create complete sentences. You may add the fragment to another sentence, or you may delete the fragment word.**

> William Shakespeare, who wrote the play *Hamlet*. Was born in England in 1564. The town of his birth was Stratford-on-Avon, and after his death, he was buried there. Little is known about his father, who some biographers say was a merchant. However, Shakespeare's father may also have been a mayor. Although it is not known for certain. It is believed that Shakespeare attended grammar school. Where he learned to read and write. At the age of eighteen he became a husband. When he married Anne Hathaway. We think of Shakespeare as a playwright, but he was also known for his acting. While most people have heard of *Hamlet* and *Romeo and Juliet*. Many of us don't realize that he wrote more than thirty other plays. In addition, he was an accomplished poet. Who wrote some of the greatest sonnets in the English language. Because he wrote plays that are still popular today and wrote poems that are still models for aspiring poets. He is considered one of the greatest writers who ever lived.

2.1.3 Check for Fragment Words or Question Words

If sentences that begin with *who, which,* or *that* do not ask a question, they are probably fragments.

> SENTENCE **Who** was the woman in the red Miata?

> FRAGMENT She was the one. **Who** was in the club.

Sentences that begin with expressions like "The one *who . . .*" or "The car *that . . .*" may also be fragments. Check to be sure that the fragment word joins the sentence parts.

> FRAGMENT The cat **who wore the hat.** [*The cat* is not a sentence.]

> SENTENCE The woman **who called the police** was furious.
> [*The woman was furious* is a sentence.]

Delete the fragment word.

> REVISION The cat ~~who~~ wore the hat.

Or add the fragment to another sentence.

> He wanted to read about the cat **who wore the hat.**

> She was the one **who was in the club.**

BND

BND EXERCISE 3   Underline each fragment. Revise as needed, on a separate sheet of paper, to make complete sentences. You may either delete the fragment word or add the fragment to another sentence.

One of Shakespeare's outstanding works is *Hamlet*. Which is about a young prince trying to avenge his father's death. The play begins with the ghost of Hamlet's father appearing to Horatio and the sentries on duty. They tell Hamlet about their experience. That night, Hamlet also sees the ghost of his father. Who was the former king of Denmark. The experience that young Hamlet has. Deeply disturbs him. Hamlet discovers that his father was murdered by Hamlet's uncle, Claudius. Who is now the king of Denmark and who has married Hamlet's widowed mother. Hamlet is commanded by his father's ghost to kill Claudius. Although Hamlet seems to know that he must take revenge, he delays. Which leads to the deaths of other characters in the play. It can even be argued that Hamlet's inability to carry out the act of revenge leads to the death of Ophelia. Who was Hamlet's true love. That the play ends on a tragic note. Is a vast understatement. In the final scene there are four dead bodies sprawled across the stage.

BND EXERCISE 4   Underline each fragment. Be sure that you have underlined fragments, not questions. Revise as needed, on a separate sheet of paper, to make complete sentences. You may either delete the fragment word or add the fragment to another sentence.

Because this play has so many problems. Readers have always argued about Hamlet's character. They can't decide whether he is a brave and cautious man. Or just can't make up his mind. A really indecisive character! Why should we care about a fictional character? Some readers see themselves reflected in characters like Hamlet. Who may seem to have unusual problems, but are very human all the same.

2.2 RUN-ON SENTENCES, COMMA SPLICES, AND FUSED SENTENCES

2.2.1 Recognizing Run-on Sentences

A **run-on sentence** is just the opposite of a fragment: It is two or more complete sentences joined together without the correct punctuation. You may hear different terms used for this kind of error. If a comma is used instead of a period, some teachers call it a **comma splice**; if no punctuation is found between the two sentences, it may be called a **fused sentence**. Because the grammatical error is so similar in all three cases, many teachers call all three errors run-ons.

To understand run-ons, you must remember the following:

■ Verbs are words that must be changed when the time of the sentence changes.

■ Subjects are words that tell who or what did the action of the verb.

One kind of run-on is very easy to understand, because it simply consists of two sentences that are not separated by a period.

RUN-ON Ryan stepped on the accelerator the car sped away.

In the first group of words, *stepped* is the verb and *Ryan* is the subject. In the second part of the sentence, *sped* is the verb and *car* is the subject. These are two separate sentences and cannot be written as one.

A comma is not the correct punctuation between two sentences.

RUN-ON Ryan stepped on the accelerator, the car sped away.

This is still a run-on because commas are used within sentences, not between them.

BND EXERCISE 5 | **Locate each run-on. Draw a vertical line between the two sentences.**

One of the most interesting characters in the play *Hamlet* is Ophelia, who is Hamlet's love interest. She is often portrayed as a weak-willed person she is dominated by her father Polonius. In the beginning of the play, Ophelia tells her father that Prince Hamlet has been expressing his love to her. Polonius tells her that she should ignore Hamlet's vows of love, Ophelia obeys him she doesn't even protest. Even though she loves Hamlet and wants to see him, she follows her father's orders. Later in the play when Polonius and the king want to spy on Hamlet, she allows herself to be used she talks to Hamlet while Polonius and the king hide behind the curtains and listen. After this scene, Hamlet never sees her alive again, she is later found dead in a stream. It is said that Hamlet couldn't decide what to do Ophelia couldn't stand up for what she wanted.

2.2.2 Revising Run-ons

Period   The simplest way to correct a run-on is to use a period between two sentences.

SENTENCES Ryan stepped on the accelerator. The car sped away.

Joining Word   There is a small group of joining words that can be used between two sentences.

and	so	or	for
but	yet	nor	

Always put a comma *before* these joining words when you use them between sentences.

SENTENCE Ryan stepped on the accelerator, **so** the car sped away.

SENTENCE Ryan stepped on the accelerator, **and** the car sped away.

Subordinating Word   Subordinating words or fragment words can be used to make one sentence a part of another. (See the list of fragment words in Section 2.1.2 p. 366.) If the subordinating word is at the beginning of a sentence, use a comma between the two parts of the new sentence. If the subordinating word is in the middle of the sentence, do not use a comma.

SENTENCE **When** Ryan stepped on the accelerator, the car sped away.

SENTENCE Ryan stepped on the accelerator **before** the car sped away.

Semicolon   A semicolon (;) can be used instead of a period between two sentences.

SENTENCE Ryan stepped on the accelerator; the car sped away.

Transitional Words with Periods or Semicolons   A word that is often found between sentences (but can also be found within sentences) is called a transitional word.

however	thus	for example
then	therefore	moreover
next		

These words do *not* join sentences; they simply give us some information. When transitional words come between sentences, a semicolon or a period must also be used before the transitional word and a comma must follow the transitional word.

SENTENCE Ryan stepped on the accelerator; **therefore,** the car sped away.

SENTENCE Ryan stepped on the accelerator; **then,** the car sped away.

BND EXERCISE 6   **Locate the run-on sentences. Use one of the preceding five types of revision to make them complete sentences.**

An often overlooked character in the play *Hamlet* is Fortinbras, however, he is very important. Hamlet and Fortinbras are in the same situation, they have both lost their fathers. At the beginning of the play, we learn that Fortinbras has raised an army and is demanding that Denmark return the lands his father lost. This is Fortinbras' way of avenging his father's death Fortinbras is a man of action. Hamlet, like Fortinbras, formulates plans to take revenge for his father's murder he delays he doesn't act. In the middle of the play, Fortinbras' army is allowed to cross Denmark on its way to do battle with the Poles. Again we see that Fortinbras craves action Hamlet, at this point in the play, is being shipped off to England he still hasn't taken action against Claudius, his father's murderer. Fortinbras only appears in the play once. In the very last scene, Fortinbras arrives at the castle he finds Hamlet dead. The man of action has survived, the man of thought has perished.

2.3 DISTINGUISHING FRAGMENTS AND RUN-ONS

As you learn to correct fragments, you may find that at first you create run-ons. And as you learn to correct run-ons, the opposite may happen—you find more fragments in your writing. Don't be discouraged by this. It's normal because you're trying to establish a clear model of a sentence in your mind. You'll also find that the sentences you write yourself are sometimes more complicated than the examples in books and exercises and that the errors are more difficult to find in your own writing. For more practice, work on the exercises in this section, which contain both run-ons and fragments.

The Difference Between a Fragment and a Run-on

A fragment

■ lacks a subject and/or verb.

OR

■ has a subordinating word that does not join it to another sentence.

A run-on is two or more complete sentences

■ joined only by a comma.

OR

■ without any punctuation.

BND EXERCISE 7

In the following paragraph, locate all fragments and run-ons. Revise so that all sentences are complete.

Hamlet believes that his mother, Gertrude, has betrayed his father's memory. After the death of King Hamlet, Gertrude marries Claudius. Who is King Hamlet's brother this infuriates Hamlet. Hamlet sees his father as a god, he sees Claudius as a satyr, a creature half goat. Hamlet cannot understand how his mother could so quickly forget his godlike father, therefore he concludes that women are faithless. In addition to feeling betrayed by his mother, Hamlet also feels that Ophelia has betrayed him. At her father's command, Ophelia rejects Hamlet and she returns the letters and gifts he has given her. This sends Hamlet into a rage, it confirms his belief that women are weak and unfaithful.

END

BND EXERCISE 8   In the following paragraph, locate all fragments and run-ons. Revise so that all sentences are complete.

Although *Hamlet* is one of Shakespeare's tragedies, it has moments of humor. One of the most humorous scenes takes place in a graveyard, Hamlet has a dialogue with a gravedigger who won't give Hamlet a straight answer. When Hamlet and his friend Horatio enter, they find the gravedigger in the act of digging a grave. Hamlet asks to whom the grave belongs, the gravedigger responds that it is his own grave. Hamlet wants to know who will be buried in the grave, however, the gravedigger's logic is that the one who makes the grave owns the grave. This gravedigger is fond of wordplay he is also fond of riddles. Prior to the arrival of Hamlet and Horatio, the gravedigger has asked his fellow worker who builds stronger than a mason, a shipwright, or a carpenter. His co-worker's answer is good he says a gallows-maker. After all, the man who makes the gallows lives longer than those who find themselves on the gallows. The gravedigger, however, has a better answer. Which he gives to his co-worker. The gravedigger says that a grave maker builds stronger than a mason, a shipwright, or a carpenter, his logic is twisted but sound. The grave you are buried in lasts longer than the house a mason might build, therefore, the grave maker builds the strongest.

BND EXERCISE 9   In the paragraph below, locate all fragments and run-ons. Revise so that all sentences are complete.

Hamlet's negative view of life is in part the result of the betrayals he has experienced. Which leave him with few people to trust. His mother betrayed both King Hamlet and Hamlet by quickly marrying Claudius Ophelia betrayed Hamlet by rejecting his affections. In addition to these betrayals, Hamlet is also betrayed by Rosencrantz and Guildenstern. Who are friends of Hamlet's. Although Hamlet doesn't know it, his two friends are really spying on him for Claudius. Hamlet finds out they are spying on him, therefore, he decides to toy with them. He asks Guildenstern to play a recorder. Which is a wooden flute. Guildenstern says that he doesn't know how to play the instrument, then Hamlet tells his two friends what he thinks of them. Hamlet says that they think they can play him more easily than one can play a flute. This is not however the end of their betrayal. The King has Hamlet sent to England so he can have Hamlet executed. Rosencrantz and Guildenstern accompany Hamlet they are carrying a letter which requests that Hamlet be killed immediately upon his arrival in England. Hamlet changes the letter now it says that Rosencrantz and Guildenstern should be killed immediately. Rosencrantz and Guildenstern pay dearly for the betrayal of their friend.

3. WORD ENDINGS

ESL   Many English words change their meanings slightly when the endings of the words are changed. You know that a person is referring to more than one bird if an *s* is added to make the word *bird* into the word *birds*. You know that the action happened in the past if the verb ends in *-ed*. When you are writing, you may concentrate on the ideas you are expressing and forget to add these important endings, or you may accidentally use the wrong one. If this is a problem in your writing, you must learn to form the habit of checking carefully for all word endings as a part of your editing. If you find that you don't understand which endings you need to use, study some of the explanations in this section.

3.1 NOUN ENDINGS: PLURALS AND APOSTROPHES

You must often make decisions about the letter *s* at the end of a noun. There are two key rules that tell you how to use the letter *s*.

Choosing Noun Endings

■ To show that a noun is plural, add the letter *s*.

■ To show that a word is possessive, add an apostrophe and the letter *s* (usually).

3.1.1 Forming Plurals

If you want to show that you are talking about more than one of a thing, you usually add an *s* to the word.

    three boy**s**   some automobile**s**

    those idea**s**   many national**s**

The plurals of some words are formed differently. Here are two other ways words might become plural.

■ Form the plural of words that end in *y* or *s* or *sh* or *ch* by changing the spelling.

    abili**ties**   los**ses**   ra**shes**   chur**ches**

■ Form the plural of some words by changing the spelling **inside** the word, not at the end.

    wom**en**   m**ice**   g**ee**se

END EXERCISE 1   Underline each noun that should be plural. Add an *s* to each of those words, or change the spelling if necessary.

    Many single mother who work have too many responsibility—they can't find enough hour in one day to do all the job that must be done. Their children need lunch for school, the dish need washing, the car needs

END

gas—all at the same time. No magic will give those mother the five extra minute in each hour, but some trick will help them. Mother with too many chore can try this: set a timer for fifteen minute after each meal, and each member of the family must spend those minute putting away object that are out of place. Keep a table or a shelf by the door, and put on it all the book, coat, lunch, key, and other thing that need to be taken when the family leaves.

3.1.2 Forming Possessives

When Should *-'s* **Be Used?**   Generally, use an apostrophe (') and an *s* with a noun or a proper name (even if it ends in *-s*) to show possession (ownership).

That is Charlie**'s** house.

The dog**'s** bowl is empty.

END EXERCISE 2   **Circle each word that shows possession. Draw an arrow to the word it possesses. Add an apostrophe (') or 's to the possessive words.**

Another problem for single mothers families is keeping the children rooms neat. When a childs toys are scattered everywhere, children fight about them more often. Is the truck in the living room Renita or Roberts truck? Is that Lara paintbrush or her brothers? If the children know each toy place, they will be more likely to put their toys away.

Where Should the Apostrophe Be Placed?   With plurals, the final letter is the key. *Note:* A plural noun ending in *-s* requires only an apostrophe.

the shoes that belong to the boy**s** = the boy**s'** shoes

the choice made by the ladie**s** = the ladie**s'** choice

If a word does not end in *-s,* add an apostrophe and an *-s.* It does not matter whether the word is singular or plural.

the pen that belongs to a studen**t** = the student**'s** pen

the skates of the childre**n** = the children**'s** skates

END EXERCISE 3   **Underline the possessive words. If the possessive word already has an *-s,* add an apostrophe after the *-s.* If the possessive word does not already have an *-s,* add an apostrophe and then an *-s.***

Keeping children clothes clean is yet another problem for single mother families. If the laundry is just the mother job, then she will be washing her family clothes all day. Each child must learn to be responsible for clothes.

> If Tara shirt is dirty, or if her brothers sheets need washing, the children themselves must be sure to put them in the hamper. Each child room should have a hamper, and it should also be the children job to put towels in the bathroom hamper.

There are certain times when an apostrophe should **not** be used.

- **Do not** use an apostrophe with a plural noun that is *not* possessive.

  <u>PLURAL</u> The **roses** are beautiful.

  <u>PLURAL</u> The **shirts** were at the laundry.

- **Do not** use an apostrophe with a *pronoun* to show possession.

  The book lost **its** cover.

  That house is **theirs.**

Here are some pronouns that end in -*s* and show possession; you should **not** use an apostrophe with them.

yours   ours   hers   his   theirs   its

END

END EXERCISE 4

Underline all the words that show possession, and draw a circle around the pronouns. Cross out any unneeded apostrophes. Add apostrophes where needed.

What are the most important foods to eat? Whether it's dieters waistline's or athletes muscles, many people are trying to change their bodies', but they need to know their bodies needs. Everybody should eat some foods with protein, some with carbohydrate's, some with fats. Your muscles strength comes from protein—it's found in meats, soybeans, and dairy products. Carbohydrate's give us quick energy for the days work. Carbohydrates are found in bread, candy, alcohol, potatoes, rice, and cereal. Fats store energy to meet your bodys needs at any time. Be sure to give your body enough to meet it's needs. Without any fats, we'd be like bunnies' without batteries, but we only need a few batteries at a time.

END EXERCISE 5

Add apostrophes where needed, and cross out any that are not needed.

A students future may not totally depend on her grade's, but grades will help when she looks for job's, so a course in study skills might make a difference in a student's life. Student's sometimes don't want to take these course's, because the credits aren't required for degree's, but they don't realize that what's most important is having a good GPA. When credit's are analyzed at graduation time, a course's grade might be just as important as its credit's.

END

3.2 VERB ENDINGS

3.2.1 Final -s verb endings

Before you read this section, consider these two questions.

- ■ Can you always pick out the complete verb in a sentence? If not, see Section 1.1 (p. 360) before you continue.
- ■ Can you always recognize the subject of a verb? If not, see Section 1.2 (p. 361) before you continue.

The verbs in a sentence provide all kinds of information, as do the endings on every verb. Besides telling us the meaning of the word itself, the ending tells us when the sentence takes place, and it may indicate whether the subject is singular or plural. Because many people do not pronounce these verb endings when they speak, they also forget to add the endings when they write. When you write, be sure that all verbs have the necessary endings.

Note: Adding an ending may change the spelling of the word. For example, *carry* becomes *carries.*

Simple (One-Word) Verbs   A **simple (one-word) verb** in a sentence that describes the present *may* end in -*s.* To determine whether a simple verb should have an -*s,* we must find the subject. If the subject is *I, you, we,* or *they,* a present tense verb does not need an -*s.* Also, if the subject is a word that could be replaced by *they,* the verb does not need an -*s.*

I walk	you cook	they sing
we settle	dogs bark	airplanes fly

A simple verb needs an -*s* only if it happens in the present and the subject is singular.

Now he *plays* guard.

Today the house *looks* clean.

Every day she *waits* for the bus.

END EXERCISE 6   Underline the verbs in the following sentences. Write P above the ones that happen in the present and add an -*s* to those verbs.

When Lisa plant a garden, she always use lots of fertilizer, just as her mother did when she was a little girl. Her mother told her how to plant, and now Lisa follow that advice. Lisa sometimes buy fertilizer at a discount store but she also get compost from the city. Last fall the city took all the leaves people had raked, and ground them up. Now the compost is ready to use. Each weekend, Lisa spread the compost on her garden and dig it in. Then she rake it smooth.

A simple verb needs an *-s* if the subject is third person *singular.* The third person singular subjects are *he, she,* or *it* **or** a word that can be replaced by one of these words.

(HE)	(SHE)	(IT)
he *walks*	She *cooks*	it *flies*
Alvin *seeks*	Suzette *laughs*	the computer *works*

Do not add an *-s* if the subject is *they* or a word that could be replaced by *they.*

(THEY)	(THEY)
They *walk*	We *cook*
Raymond and John *seek*	Those women *laugh*

END

END EXERCISE 7   **Underline the verbs in the following sentences. Draw an arrow to the subject. Then add an *-s* to the verb if the subject is *he, she, it,* or a word that could be replaced by one of those words.**

Sean always take care of his car. He clean it every weekend, he change the oil every three thousand miles, and he take it for a tune-up every thirty thousand miles. The tires take some of his attention, too, because they need to be rotated often so that they wear evenly. Sean's brother Charles take care of the tires for him, but he charge Sean a small amount. Rotating the tires take time and tools, Charles say. Time and tools cost him money, so he want Sean to pay.

Verbs Ending in *-s*

Remember: Add *-s* to a verb only if the tense is present and the subject is third person singular.

Check:

1. When is the verb happening?
    - ■ now (use *-s*)
    - ■ in the past (no *-s*)
2. What word would replace the subject?
    - ■ he, she, it (use *-s*)
    - ■ they, you, we (no *-s*)

END *(vertical tab in left margin)*

| END EXERCISE 8 | Underline each verb in the following sentences. Add an *-s* if the verb is in the present tense and the subject is singular. |

> Computers do exactly what we tell them to do. If we tell a computer to type a letter, the computer type a letter. If we tell a computer to sing a song, it will sing a song. Sometimes when I write, I look back and see that what I have written look really strange. It look strange because I told the computer to write in capital letters or italics. Of course the computer did exactly what I told it to do. Sometimes my hands write words that my brain know, and other times my hands seem to write on their own. It take time to go back and correct these mistakes, but it save more time, since I just type the corrections, not the whole paper.

Helping Verbs   Often a verb is actually several words—the main verb and its helpers. **Helping verbs** (also called **auxiliary verbs**) are short, common verbs that give more information about the main verb but do not change its meaning. Here are some examples of helping verbs.

are	does	is
can	have	will

In *most* cases, use the rules above to decide if a verb needs an *-s*. Then find the *first* helping verb and use the *-s* form (most helping verbs have many forms).

she *was* skipping	we *were* finished
Marcia and Tom *are* driving	the cat *is* mewing

| END EXERCISE 9 | Underline each verb phrase once, and then underline twice any helping verbs that are part of the verb phrase. Draw a line to the subject. Use the checklist from p. 377 to decide if the helping verb should be put in the present tense. |

> Trying to lose weight have been really confusing. (It also take a lot of willpower, of course.) Some experts were saying that bread make you fat and others have said that butter and cheese make you fat. My friend were reading a book that say exercise work best. My friends Marla and Rene were trying to run a mile every day, and Mike went with them. Mike have been losing weight by not eating any dessert, because he had heard that sugar make you fat.

Modal Verbs   A modal verb is a special kind of helping verb that *slightly* changes the meaning of the main verb. Modal verbs tell more than just the time when a verb happens. They suggest ideas like possibility and necessity. Future verbs, especially, use modals.

may	might	can
would	could	will
must	ought (to)	should

Even when these verbs seem to have a present meaning and a third person singular subject, they do not end in -s.

he **can** stay   Lorraine **must** sell

END EXERCISE 10   **Correct the use of -s in the following paragraph. Use the checks in the box on Verbs Ending in -s (p. 377) as well as the information in this section on helping verbs, p. 378. Add -s when it is needed and cross it out when it is not.**

We sometimes wonder what would have happened if things in history had been different. For example, things might have been safer for everyone if the nuclear bomb had never been invented. Maybe scientists should think more carefully about what will happen to their inventions. An inventor who make a new way to run cars may think she will help the world but she may really finds that the new invention can kill many people.

Infinitives (to + verbs)   Most of the verbs we encounter are real verbs, which means that they show time. The **infinitive** is a special kind of verb that does not show time. (You might find the word *infinitive* hard to remember. If so, call it a **to + verb**.) It is written with a *to* before the verb and never has an -s added to it.

I want *to eat* now   they have *to leave* now

END EXERCISE 11   **Correct the use of -s in the following sentences.**

We'd like to think that the invention of medicine was one way to improves the world. It is certainly better that no child has to catch polio and that no one even has to get a smallpox vaccination anymore. But now that fewer people die from infectious diseases, there is not enough room for all of us to lives well. We are going to become even more crowded every year. So even the miraculous inventions of a vaccine to cure a terrible disease can turn out to be a problem no one knows how to solves.

Sometimes the *to* in an infinitive is understood (like the subject *you* in a command), but the rules are still the same.

I heard you **sing.** She lets the dog **eat.**

The infinitive can never be the only verb in a sentence.

END EXERCISE 12   **Underline the verbs twice and the subjects once. Circle the infinitives. Add -s where needed and correct the helping verbs as necessary.**

Sometimes a person want to go on a trip but don't know how to get to her destination. Now there is a site on the Internet that tell you how to get from one place to another. The traveler have to type in the city she is leaving from and the place where she want to go. Then the computer tell her what route to take and also warn her to avoid any delays.

3.2.2 Past Tense Verbs

Regular Verbs   The following discussion covers simple verbs and verbs without helpers. (Can you always recognize the complete verb phrase? If not, review Section 1.1 on p. 360 before working on this section.)

When a sentence describes the past, the verb should reflect that time. Most simple verbs show past time by ending in *-ed* although the ending may change the spelling.

The men gossip**ed**	Maynard exercis**ed**	she suggest**ed**
A train pass**ed**	the babies cri**ed**	MacIntosh produc**ed**

END EXERCISE 13   Underline the verbs that happen in the past. Add *-ed* to those verbs.

> Yesterday Alicia want some ice cream, so she borrow her sister's car. Then she remember that she also need some money, so she ask her sister for money. Her sister laugh. She want some ice cream, too, so she call to Alicia: "When you get to the store, please buy two cones! I want chocolate!" Alicia use the money for the cones of ice cream. She and her sister lick the cones while they watch TV yesterday evening.

In some past tense forms, both the helping verb and the main verb will change. The helping verb usually changes form (see pp. 378–379), but a regular main verb may need an *-ed* ending. Here's a checklist to help you determine when to use *-ed*.

When to Use *-ed* on a Past Tense Verb

- If the tense is past (which means that the verb happened in the past)
- If the helper is *is, are, was, were, has,* or *had* and the verb is past tense

macaroni **was** serv**ed**	a form **had been** fil**ed**
they **were** tir**ed**	those horses **have** jump**ed**

- If the verb is passive, even if it is present tense

Note: Even present tense verbs with the helpers *is* or *are* need *-ed* endings if the verb is passive (if the action happens *to* the subject).

the toast is burned	the houses are painted
the tires are mended	the hose is filled

| END EXERCISE 14 | Underline helping verbs once and main verbs twice. Add an *-ed* if needed (use the checklist above), and remember that *to* + verbs don't show change in time. |

> If you have ever use a car with a manual shift, you must have notice the clutch. In most cars, clutches are locate on the floor to the left of the brake pedal. When the clutch is push in, the driver is able to change gears with the right hand, using a gearshift on the floor. Drivers who are use to this arrangement are sometimes confuse when they change to an automatic transmission. In these cars, there is no clutch, and the gears are changed by a gearshift that is locate on the steering column.

Do not use *-ed* with the helping verbs *do, does, did, don't, doesn't, didn't.*

I do believe

the car didn't stall

| END EXERCISE 15 | Underline the helping verbs once and the main verbs twice. Circle the helping verbs *do, does, did, don't, doesn't, didn't.* Add *-ed* to main verbs that have helping verbs that are not circled. Change the spelling of main verbs if necessary. *Note:* Remember that helping verbs are often found in questions or in contractions. Look carefully at the entire verb. |

> Did the weather seem warmer this year? Has it rain as much as it usually does? If you aren't worry about the icebergs melting, maybe you don't worry about the ocean rising near the beach, either. When the temperature of the water has been raise only a few degrees, the level of the water will have been raise by a few feet. That's not much, but it doesn't take much to make a difference if you live in Miami or Charleston or Boston.

Do not use *-ed* with modal helpers such as *can, could, may, must, should, would, will, might.* Modal helpers change the meaning of the verb slightly, not the time.

| END EXERCISE 16 | Underline the main verbs twice. Underline the *-ed* helpers once and draw a circle around the modals. Add an *-ed* where needed. *Note:* Remember that one helping verb might fit with two main verbs joined by *and* or *or.* |

> Have you ever been charge a lot for medicine? People who would pay $50 to see a basketball game will not pay $50 for medicine, will they? Most people say they would think about whether they could find cheaper medicine, and then they might try to wait a few days. If they had learn about another medicine that they could buy, they would buy it. If they hadn't ask their doctor for cheaper medicine, they might call the office and ask the nurse.

| ESL | **Irregular Verbs** Some verbs show past time by changes in the spelling of the entire word: |

the quartet **sang**   the boat **sank**

he was **caught**   it has been **said**

END

Here is a list of some common irregular verbs and the changes in their endings. Three different forms are given for each irregular verb. Here are the ways that each form is used.

1. *Present form:* Use for present tense, or use with *do, does, did,* and so on, and with modals (*can, may,* etc.).
2. *Past form:* Use for simple past tense.
3. *Past participle:* Use with *-ed* helping verbs (*had, has, have, is, are, was, were*).

Present	Past	Past Participle
beat	beat	beaten
break	broke	broken
bring	brought	brought
buy	bought	bought
catch	caught	caught
come	came	come
drink	drank	drunk
eat	ate	eaten
fight	fought	fought
find	found	found
get	got	gotten
go	went	gone
hold	held	held
know	knew	known
lose	lost	lost
make	made	made
put	put	put
say	said	said
see	saw	seen
seek	sought	sought
send	sent	sent
sing	sang	sung
sink	sank	sunk
spend	spent	spent
teach	taught	taught
wind	wound	wound

Computer Tip

Be sure to proofread all verb endings carefully.

END EXERCISE 17 Underline the verb phrase once and the irregular verbs twice. If the irregular verb is not in the correct form, cross it out and write in the correct form.

Why do athletes receive so much money? When a major league pitcher has brung in as much money as Greg Maddux, the fans have gave him their respect. But other athletes haven't came as far as he has, and they don't deserve the salary he makes.

4. AGREEMENT

In order to make writing clear, certain words must *agree* with certain other words. Specifically, pronouns and verbs must match the nouns they're related to in certain ways.

4.1 SUBJECT-VERB AGREEMENT

> ### To Solve Problems in Subject-Verb Agreement
>
> Be sure you understand the following material:
> Recognizing subjects and verbs (pp. 360–363)
> Recognizing prepositional phrases (p. 364)
> Verb endings: present tense (*-s*) (pp. 376–379)

Subject-verb agreement means that a verb must match its subject in several ways, the most important being number (whether a word is singular or plural). As we saw in Section 3.2.1, present tense verbs with singular subjects must end in *-s*, so you must be able to recognize the correct subject for the verb. There are many rules for special situations, but those presented in the sections that follow are the ones that most writers use. You can find additional rules in complete handbooks.

To be sure that verbs agree with their subjects, keep the following points in mind.

> ### Checking for Singular or Plural Subjects
>
> ■ Subjects are never in prepositional phrases.
> ■ Two or more singular subjects joined by *and* form a plural subject.
> ■ Usually there is an *-s* on either the subject or the verb, but not both.

AGR

4.1.1 Subjects and Prepositional Phrases

There are two ways to be sure that you have located the correct subject of a verb, which can never be in a prepositional phrase.

- ■ Locate the verb. Then ask *Who?* or *What?* before the verb.

  The man in the jacket with the red initials has turned the corner.

  If you locate the verb, *has turned*, and asked **who** or **what** *has turned*, you will see that the subject must be *man*. Therefore, you will use the verb *has*.

- ■ Cross out any prepositional phrases (either on the paper or in your mind). The subject will then become clear.

  The painters in the truck with the loud radio have turned the corner.

  If you cross out the prepositional phrases *in the truck* and *with the loud radio*, you will find that the subject must be *painters*. Therefore, you will use the verb *have*.

AGR EXERCISE 1   **Draw a line through all prepositional phrases. Underline the verb twice and the subject once. Correct any problems in subject-verb agreement.**

> One of the biggest problems for students are finding time to keep in shape. In the morning, a student could get up early to run if it is the time of year when mornings are lighted, but in the winter the light of the sun don't appear until almost seven. A woman by herself in the darkness have to be a little more careful than usual. After school, a student could go to the gym, but a student with expenses must work. At night, a student with a family make dinner for them, and a student without a family try to have a little time to be with her friends. Nevertheless, most of the students I know have found some time to get the exercise they needs.

4.1.2 Subjects Joined by And

Remember that one way to recognize a plural subject is to think of the pronoun you would use instead of the nouns. If you choose *they*, the subject will be plural.

> Tamara and Ben have bought a new car.

When you find the verb *have bought* and ask *Who?* or *What?* before it, you will find that two people *have bought* the car: *Tamara and Ben*. The pronoun *they* would be used for these two people, so the subject is plural. Therefore, you would use *have bought* as the verb.

AGR EXERCISE 2   **Underline the verb twice and the complete subject once. Correct any errors in subject-verb agreement.**

> If you want to be healthy, eating and exercising is very important subjects to understand. Being a healthy vegetarian requires a little knowledge

about the foods your body and your health needs. Protein and iron is nutrients you must be sure to have. A milk product and a bean dish usually
provides enough protein, but iron is more difficult. A vegetarian often
must take an iron supplement.

4.1.3 Only One -s

Language is not always logical. When you think of verbs matching subjects,
you may begin to think that a subject that ends in -s should go with a verb
that ends in -s, but the opposite is true. You might want to think that you
have only one -s to use and that you can't use it on both the subject and the
verb—only one -s to a pair. Review pages 376–379, which discuss the simple
present.

AGR EXERCISE 3   Underline the verb twice and the complete subject once. Correct any errors in
subject-verb agreement.

My friends thinks that getting in shape mean getting smaller, period. They
don't realize that muscles is healthy and also attractive, even on a woman.
Diets and pills is a bad way to lose weight, but eating well and exercising
are good ways. Even weightlifting can be healthy for a woman. If she don't
want big muscles, small weights helps you to be strong. Muscles and
bones benefits from weightlifting, because the pressure of the weights
makes bones tougher.

4.2   PRONOUN AGREEMENT

ESL

A pronoun is a word that stands for a noun (remember that -*ing* words and *to*
+ words can be nouns). This means that the pronoun should match the noun
it stands for. Usually this means that you must use a plural pronoun to stand
for a plural noun.

The crops were withering in the heat. **They** would soon be dead.

The corn was withering in the heat. **It** would soon be dead.

Watering the crops will be expensive. **It** can cost many dollars a day.

The noun that the pronoun stands for should be clear. Avoid using pronouns
that could possibly refer to more than one noun in a sentence.

UNCLEAR   **Tomas** drove **Luke** to **his** house.

CLEAR   **Luke** went home in **Tomas's** car.

Avoid using *you* to mean *people in general.* You may use *you* to speak directly
to the reader.

INCORRECT   When **you** get drunk, **you** do not use good judgment.

CORRECT   When **people** get drunk, **they** do not use good judgment.

AGR

You should also be careful to stay with the same person, especially when you are using pronouns to stand for your reader or for people in general.

INCORRECT   **You** must follow these directions whenever **you** attempt to start this machine. Otherwise, **operators** might damage the machine or hurt **themselves.**

CORRECT   **Operators** must follow these directions whenever **they** attempt to start this machine. Otherwise, **they** might damage the machine or hurt **themselves.**

CORRECT   **You** must follow these directions whenever **you** attempt to start this machine. Otherwise, **you** might damage the machine or hurt **yourself.**

Always try to use the most accurate pronoun for a noun. Avoid using *he* to stand for a noun like *student* that could refer to either a male or female student. One simple way to achieve this is by using plural nouns and pronouns.

INCORRECT   **A student** must be careful to put **his** name on all **his** books.

CORRECT   **Students** must be careful to put **their** names on all **their** books.

AGR EXERCISE 4   **Underline the pronouns in this paragraph. Draw an arrow to the noun each pronoun stands for. If the pronoun does not agree with the noun, change the pronoun, using a separate sheet of paper if necessary.**

Traveling in the summer can be very unpleasant. It can make you want to stay at home forever. Travelers sometimes forget their manners. You have to expect the worst from an airline trip. They can sometimes take twice as long as scheduled. When the traveler comes home, he calls the airline to complain, but they don't offer him a refund.

5. CLARITY

5.1   CHOOSING THE RIGHT WORD

ESL

Because many words look or sound very much alike, you must be extremely careful to choose the one you really want. Here are some commonly confused words that you'll probably be seeing often. There are many others to watch for in grammar reference books and dictionaries.

Word	Meaning
already	earlier, before
all ready	completely ready
course	subject of study, path
coarse	rough, not fine
cloths	more than one cloth
clothes	attire: shirts, pants, shoes, etc.

hear	perceive with ears, listen to
here	in this place, not there
hole	empty space
whole	complete, all
know	be aware of, understand
no	opposite of yes, negative
knew	past tense of *know*, understood
new	not old
lose	misplace
loose	not tight
lost	(verb) past tense of *lose*, misplaced
loss	(noun) something that is gone
passed	past tense of *pass*, went by or succeeded in a course
past	time before now
peace	quiet, harmony, no conflict
piece	section, segment, part
sense	feeling or understanding
since	after
their	belongs to them
there	not here
they're	they are
to	into, in the direction of, toward (used with verb in infinitive)
too	also, very
two	one plus one
want	desire
won't	will not
would of	(no meaning; not standard English)
would have	wanted to
where	in what place
were	past tense of *are*
your	belonging to you
you're	you are

CLR

CLR EXERCISE 1   **Cross out any incorrectly used words and substitute appropriate ones.**

Mathabane was embarrassed because his father insisted on wearing tribal cloths and his friends referred to him as Tarzan. He wanted to live a modern life like his friends did instead of the traditional weigh of life his father wonted him too. My parents always wonted me to dress like nice young man but the cloths that were in style when I was a teenager were those jeans with wholes in the knees. Even though I new that my parents thought that I looked like a hood in those pants, I would change into my favorite jeans the minute I left the house so I would be dressed the way my friends where when I got to school.

| CLR EXERCISE 2 | **Cross out any incorrectly used words and substitute appropriate ones.** |

When my brother and I would play basketball, I would always loose because I was shorter than him and he used to block every shot I tried to make. In fact, he would tease me sense he could just stand their and still reach higher than me even when I jumped as high as I could. But now that I'm taller than he is, I'm the one who's winning every game. Its nice to get him back for all those games I loss.

5.2   WRITING CLEAR SENTENCES

Some sentences may sound correct when you are speaking but are confusing when written down. In this section we'll show you several kinds of sentences that have this problem. First, we'll explain why these sentences don't work. If you find the grammar in that part confusing, you can skip to the next part: how to repair these sentences.

5.2.1 Prepositional Phrases as Subjects

Note: Before you begin this section, you may want to review Section 1, Sentence Basics (pp. 360–364).

Here are some examples of sentences that have prepositional phrases as subjects.

INCORRECT **A.** In the article by Samuel Watson says that computers are essential in business.

INCORRECT **B.** By her taking so long to get dressed made us both late to school.

Following are some rules that will help you to understand the errors in these sentences.

A Word Can Do Only One Job in a Sentence   Words can do many different jobs in sentences. They can be verbs, subjects, objects of prepositions, and so on. Words can do different jobs in different sentences, but in any one sentence, a word *cannot* do two jobs. If a word is a subject, it cannot also be a verb or an object of a preposition.

The problem in sentence A is that the word *article* is being forced to do two jobs, which it can't do. Here are the two ways *article* is used in sentence A.

■ *In the article:* Here *article* is the object of the preposition *In.*

■ *The article . . . says:* here *article* is the subject of the verb *says.*

To repair this kind of error, you must choose which job you want the word to do and then either add or drop a word to take care of the other job. If you choose to make *article* the subject of the verb *says*, you can choose to drop the preposition *In*.

> CORRECT   The article by Samuel Watson says that computers are essential in business.

Another way to correct the sentence is by making another word act as the subject of the verb *says*.

> CORRECT   In the article by Samuel Watson, **he** says that computers are essential in business.

This sentence is grammatically correct but wordy and possibly confusing. You could also drop a different preposition to make a slightly different correction that's not so wordy. *Samuel Watson* is the object of the preposition *by*. You can drop this preposition and make *Samuel Watson* the subject.

> CORRECT   In the article, Samuel Watson says that computers are essential in business.

A Prepositional Phrase Can't Do the Job of a Subject of a Sentence   In sentence B, the prepositional phase is used as the subject.

> INCORRECT   By her taking so long to get dressed made us both late to school.

The verb in this sentence is *made*. If we try to find the subject asking <u>*who*</u> or <u>*what*</u> *made us late to school*, the answer we will get is the prepositional phrase *by her taking so long to get dressed*. This phrase can't also be a subject.
   To repair a sentence with this problem, you'll often need two steps.

1. Make the prepositional phrase into a *because* clause.
2. Add a word that can be the subject of the sentence.

> CORRECT   Because she took so long to get dressed, we were both late to school.

Sometimes you'll see sentences that have only done the second part of the repair, adding only a new subject. This makes a sentence that's incorrect because it breaks another rule.

> INCORRECT   By her taking so long to get dressed, it made us both late to school.

A Pronoun Cannot Stand for a Prepositional Phrase   In the preceding sample sentence, the pronoun *it* stands for the prepositional phrase *By her taking so long to get dressed*. A pronoun cannot stand for a prepositional phrase, so this sentence is still incorrect.

CLR

Revisions   If you see sentences that start with prepositional phrases in your writing, check to make sure that you are not using the phrase or part of the phrase as the subject of the verb. To repair these sentences, you may do the following.

■ Drop words

INCORRECT In the article by Samuel Watson says that computers are essential in business.

CORRECT The article by Samuel Watson says that computers are essential in business.

CORRECT In the article, Samuel Watson says that computers are essential in business.

■ Add words

CORRECT In the article by Samuel Watson, he says that computers are essential in business.

■ Change words

CORRECT Samuel Watson's article says that computers are essential in business.

■ Drop, add, and change words

INCORRECT By her taking so long to get dressed made us both late to school.

CORRECT Because she took so long to get dressed, we were both late to school.

CLR EXERCISE 3   Mark the verb with a **V** and the subject with an **S** in the following five sentences. Put prepositional phrases in parentheses. If the subject is a prepositional phrase, rewrite the sentence so that the subject is not a prepositional phrase. You may use any method to rewrite: drop, add, and/or change words.

EXAMPLE:

S   V

(With me being an only child) meant that I was sometimes lonely.

Because I was an only child, I was sometimes lonely.

OR

As an only child, I was sometimes lonely.

1. By me working very hard pulled up my grade in math.
2. With them taking care of my children helped me to have time to study.
3. In the textbook for my math class says that calculators are sometimes necessary.
4. With two children at home, I can't always have time for myself.
5. By knowing about my problems helped my teacher understand how to help me.

5.3 INDIRECT QUESTIONS

5.3.1 Sentences and Questions

Word Order In English, we don't use the same words in the same order to ask a question and to make a statement. One difference between questions and statements is the order of the subject and the verb.

> STATEMENT You can leave.

> QUESTION When can you leave?

In the statement, the subject *you* comes **before** the verb *can*. In the question, the subject *you* comes **after** the verb *can*.

Question Words Another difference between statements and questions is the use of question words. The word *when* can be used as a **question word** in a question or as a **connecting word** in a statement.

> QUESTION **When** did you leave? [*When* is a **question word** here]

> STATEMENT I told you **when** I left. [*When* is a **connecting word** here]

You can make a statement about asking a question. The following sentence does not ask what you are going to do but states what I did—I asked you a question.

> STATEMENT I asked you **when** you left. [*When* is a connecting word here]

In this statement, the word *when* is used as a **connecting word**, not a question word. Also, the subject *you* comes before the verb *left*. Because it's a statement and not a question, it follows the rule for a statement.

5.4 DIRECT AND INDIRECT QUOTES AND PARAPHRASING

Research

ESL

Students often have problems fitting the material from a reading into their own sentences. The first step in learning to do this is to recognize the difference between a direct quote, an indirect quote, and a paraphrase. Let's start with an example of a conversation between Gus and his friend Lara.

CLR

<u>ORIGINAL MATERIAL</u>

Gus says: *I've been working too hard. I need to get away.*

Lara says: *I have some free time this weekend. Maybe we could go some-where together.*

Gus says: *Sounds great. Let's go to the mountains.*

Lara says: *When can you leave?*

<u>QUOTE</u>   Gus's friend Lara said, "I have some free time this weekend. Maybe we could go somewhere together."

The words inside the quotation marks, *"I have some free time this weekend. Maybe we could go somewhere together,"* are a **direct quote**—the exact words spoken by Lara. Whatever appears inside the quotation marks is like a photocopy of her words—which have not been changed in any way.

<u>PARAPHRASE</u>   Gus told Lara that he had to have a change of scenery because he was tired.

A **paraphrase** expresses an idea from the original in different words. Gus said, *"I've been working too hard. I need to get away."* If you repeat those words, you are quoting, but if you change the words but keep the same idea, you are paraphrasing. Notice how the ideas stay the same although the words change.

<u>ORIGINAL</u>   I've been working too hard.

<u>PARAPHRASE</u>   He was tired.

<u>ORIGINAL</u>   I need to get away.

<u>PARAPHRASE</u>   He had to have a change of scenery.

CLR EXERCISE 4   Paraphrase Gus's answer to Lara.

Sometimes you can make your writing clearer and easier to follow by combining quotes and paraphrases. This is sometimes called an **indirect quote** because it uses some original words and some that are changed.

<u>INDIRECT QUOTE</u>   Gus said that he wanted "to get away."

The words in quotation marks, *"to get away,"* are like a photocopy of the actual words that Gus used. The words not in quotation marks—*that he wanted*—are not his exact words but express his ideas in the writer's words. The rest of Gus's words (*"I want"*) are not quoted but paraphrased as *he wanted*. This allows the quote to fit smoothly into a paragraph.

Gus was talking to Lara yesterday and said that he wanted "to get away." She suggested that they could go somewhere that weekend.

Notice that the pronoun *I* is changed to *he* in the paraphrase, and the verb tense is changed to past to fit with the rest of the paragraph.

CLR EXERCISE 5   Restate the rest of the conversation, using indirect quotes.

5.5 PARALLELISM

When words in a sentence express similar ideas, they should be stated in a similar form. That means that items in a list or joined by the conjunctions *and, but, not, for, or* should all be words, or phrases, or even complete sentences.

<u>INCORRECT</u> For breakfast, we ate **fish, tomatoes,** and **were toasting some good bread.**

<u>CORRECT</u> For breakfast, we ate **fish, tomatoes,** and **bread.**

<u>CORRECT</u> For breakfast, we **were broiling fish, slicing tomatoes,** and **toasting some good bread.**

<u>INCORRECT</u> I wanted to learn **to make** multimedia presentations and **using** a spreadsheet.

<u>CORRECT</u> I wanted to learn **to make** multimedia presentations and **to use** a spreadsheet.

CLR EXERCISE 6 Underline the items that are in lists or joined by conjunctions such as *and*. If the items are not in similar form, rewrite them, using a separate sheet of paper if necessary.

Pollution is everywhere: out in the country, in the city, and also found in our homes. Pollution is caused by manufacturing processes and we drive cars, as well as to waste many products. For example, when consumers buy broccoli at the store, the vegetable has a wire around it and in a plastic bag, then puts it in a bigger bag with other vegetables. This makes three different wrappings for the broccoli, when one would be enough.

6. FREQUENTLY USED PUNCTUATION AND STYLING MARKS

Frequently Used Punctuation
Commas
Question marks
Titles
Capitals
Quotation marks

This section focuses on some basic rules of punctuation that may seem very small but are in fact an important part of good writing. Again, you will need to consult a complete handbook for many details in unusual sentences. Here we give you the simplest rules for the most common problems.

6.1 COMMAS

Commas are not decorations that you can just sprinkle randomly through your sentences. Every comma added to a sentence has a clear job that is determined by the rules of punctuation. Think about the two general concepts below, and the rules that go with them.

PUNC

Using Commas

Comma Guide 1: Use a comma only within a sentence or between the parts of one sentence. A comma can do many things in a sentence:

■ Separate introductory material before the subject.

■ Set off words or phrases that could be removed or moved to other places in the sentence.

■ Separate items in a series.

■ Separate two complete sentences if they are joined by conjunctions (and, but, or, nor, for). See Section 2.2.

Comma Guide 2: Use a comma only when you have a reason. If in doubt, leave it out.

6.1.1. Using a Comma to Separate Introductory Material Before the Subject

When you have any introductory words at the beginning of a sentence, the sentence may be hard to follow. Use a comma right *before* the subject to make the main part of the sentence clear.

> <u>CONFUSING</u> When students are painting their hands may feel cramped.
> <u>CLEAR</u> When students are painting, their hands may feel cramped.

PUNC EXERCISE 1   **Correct the comma usage in this paragraph.**

> On my way home I passed a group of older women. Since I could see that they were walking slowly I felt that I should ask, if they needed any assistance. One of them thanked me and said she was able to walk but just not very quickly. Although I worried about them I felt that I needed to get to my destination. When I came back, I saw the same ladies. They had walked just one more block while I had walked five.

6.1.2 Using a Comma to Set Off Words or Phrases That Could Be Removed or Moved to Other Places in the Sentence

Commas can be used almost like parentheses to show words and groups of words that are not needed to make a complete sentence. Use commas around material that can be omitted from the sentence.

<u>COMPLETE SENTENCE</u> My sister, the woman in the green boots, has enrolled in computer classes this fall.

Use commas before and after the phrase *the woman in the green boots*. It could be removed from the sentence without creating a fragment:

<u>COMPLETE SENTENCE</u> My sister has enrolled in computer classes this fall.

Use commas around material that can be moved to another place in the sentence without changing the meaning:

<u>SENTENCE</u> I told him, however, that we would also require a written request.

<u>SENTENCE WITH UNCHANGED MEANING</u> I told him that we would also require a written request, however.

<u>SENTENCE WITH UNCHANGED MEANING</u> However, I told him that we would also require a written request.

Note: Be sure to use commas both *before* and *after* this kind of material, unless it comes at the beginning or end of a sentence; see rules for using commas on p. 394.

PUNC EXERCISE 2   **Correct the comma usage in this paragraph.**

When a single parent is a man he may have more problems however than a woman. My brother the parent of a three-year-old has to work and arrange for child care. With these problems he's just a like a single mother. In the evening though it's hard for him to find another single father to share child care or to trade babysitting jobs. Surprisingly he doesn't know any other single fathers. He knows single women who have children but they live far away from him.

6.1.3 Using Commas to Separate Items in a Series

When you have a list of words, phrases, or clauses, you should put a comma after each item except the very last one.

<u>LIST OF WORDS</u> Jogging, rowing, and skating are all good aerobic exercise.

<u>LIST OF PHRASES</u> We put notices on the bulletin boards, on the windows, and on the doors to advertise the sale.

<u>LIST OF SENTENCES JOINED WITH CONJUNCTIONS</u> In this computer lab students are typing papers, lab assistants are sending e-mail, and people are learning to use software.

PUNC EXERCISE 3   **Correct the comma usage in this paragraph.**

The best rituals in my family were those around holidays birthdays and vacations. Those were the times when we cooked special food visited family, and went on trips. We might visit our cousins they might visit us or we might all go to the beach together. When we went to the beach with my older cousin her favorite rituals were singing silly songs in the car telling ghost stories and playing card games in the middle of the night.

6.1.4 Using a Comma to Separate Two Complete Sentences Joined by Conjunctions

Review the rules on fragments (pp. 365–368) and run-on sentences (pp. 368–372), and make sure you know that you may join two complete sentences with a conjunction (*and, but, or, nor, for, so*). When you do this, you should use a comma *before* the conjunction, not after.

<u>CORRECT</u> Alicia wanted to improve her children's musical ability, so she enrolled them in guitar lessons.

<u>CORRECT</u> The transmission of the car was working well, but the fuel pump needed to be replaced.

Note: Do *not* use a comma before conjunctions that join only two words or two phrases. Be sure the conjunction joins two *complete* sentences.

<u>CORRECT</u> I wanted to visit Africa, so I signed up for the tour.

<u>INCORRECT</u> I wanted to visit Africa, and Korea.

<u>INCORRECT</u> I wanted to visit Africa, and stop in Europe on the way.

PUNC EXERCISE 4   Correct the comma usage in this paragraph.

We all react differently to feelings of guilt. Orwell and the prison officials may have felt guilty about hanging the man but they denied their feelings and hid from them by drinking and joking. Other people may use these same ways to hide from guilt or they may get angry at the person they have hurt. Admitting that you feel guilty is a difficult thing to do and many people never can take that step. Thinking about your feelings and your reactions is difficult but necessary.

PUNC

6.2   QUESTION MARKS

Questions can be direct or indirect (see Section 5.3). **Always use a question mark at the end of a direct question.**

What would be the point of writing all the papers and taking all the exams if you withdrew from the course at the very end?

Why did you come?

Never use a question mark after an indirect question.

She asked me why I came.

| PUNC EXERCISE 5 | **Correct the use of question marks in this paragraph.** |

The interview with the new governor was really boring, wasn't it. First a reporter asked him if he planned any changes in the next year? He said that he would wait and see what happened. Then another reporter asked, "Will you approve a bill to raise taxes?" The governor replied, "Didn't I just answer that." Would you listen to an interview as boring as that. Why do the sponsors want to pay for boring news. I just don't get it?

6.3 TITLES

| Research |

6.3.1 Capitals in Titles

There are two basic rules that tell you which words to capitalize in a title.

■ Capitalize the first word and the last word in a title.

In his essay "A Hanging," George Orwell describes his own experience.

To Have and Have Not is the movie assigned for this discussion.

"On His Blindness" is the poem Milton wrote.

■ Capitalize all other words *except* articles, conjunctions, and prepositions.

The Old Man and the Sea is my favorite book.

In "Getting Off the Welfare Carousel," McCrary says that welfare recipients are stereotyped.

Note: Do *not* copy the capitalization as you find it on the title page or in a library or electronic listing. Many times you will see that book covers and title pages do not follow the rules of capitalization. The title may appear in all capital letters or with no capitals at all. When you find a reference to a book in a database or on the Internet, only the first word may be capitalized.

6.3.2 Underlining, Italics, and Quotation Marks

When you want to indicate that a group of words is a title, you must follow certain rules.

■ Underline (or italicize) long, complete works such as books, plays, and movies.

Gone With the Wind is my favorite movie.

<u>In Our Time</u> is the book assigned for this discussion.

PUNC

■ Use quotation marks for short works or parts of longer works.

In "Getting Off the Welfare Carousel," McCrary says that welfare recipients are stereotyped.

"On His Blindness" is the poem Milton wrote.

■ Choose the correct format and use only that; do *not* use both underlining and quotation marks for the same title.

INCORRECT In his essay "<u>A Hanging</u>," George Orwell describes his own experience.

CORRECT In his essay "A Hanging," George Orwell describes his own experience.

■ Be consistent throughout your essay in the use of either italics or underlining for titles of long and complete works. Do *not* use both.

INCONSISTENT *Gone With the Wind* is my favorite movie now, not <u>The Wizard of Oz</u>.

CONSISTENT *Gone With the Wind* is my favorite movie now, not *The Wizard of Oz*.

CONSISTENT <u>Gone With the Wind</u> is my favorite movie now, not <u>The Wizard of Oz</u>.

PUNC EXERCISE 6   **Correct the punctuation and capitalization of titles in this paragraph.**

I found a number of good sources for my paper. I'm going to use a novel called The scarlet Letter, a story entitled "<u>Where I'm calling from,</u>" and a poem called MY PAPA'S WALTZ. The best book I read was **the Firm,** but I don't think I'll use that. I might also discuss the movie <u>How Green Was My Valley</u>, or another movie, *American Beauty*. My little sister used the movie "Beauty And The Beast" for her project.

6.4   CAPITALIZATION

Using a capital letter for the first letter of a word has a specific meaning for most readers. Capitalization can be confusing unless it is done correctly, so use capital letters only when you know why you are doing so. Here are some simple rules for capitalization.

■ Capitalize proper names of people (including titles and honorifics), ethnic groups, places, countries and states, holidays, institutions, and religions.

the Armenian people	Sri Lanka	Juneteenth
Easter	South Dakota	Ms. Chung
Victory Savings Bank	Buddhism	Pope John Paul II
the Inuit	Nelson Mandela	Prime Minister Blair

■ Capitalize the first word in a sentence or a quoted word, phrase, or sentence of dialogue. Do not capitalize the first word of an indirect quote in paraphrase (see pp. 391–392).

> The most important thing is her answer. If she says, "The men weren't here," then we will know that they were not the criminals.

■ Do *not* capitalize words to emphasize them in academic writing.

> INCORRECT That was MY First Real Job.

> CORRECT That was my first real job.

PUNC EXERCISE 7 **Correct the capitalization in this paragraph.**

> Marla went to visit her Aunt in Buffalo, New york. Aunt Mary told her, "don't expect it to be as warm here as it is in California," but marla thought it would be warm anywhere by easter. She took her Tee shirts and plenty of Levis. Her Cousins laughed at her idea of warm clothes, and told her, "you need to go to the Mall to get some REALLY Warm Clothes."

6.5 QUOTATION MARKS

Research

6.5.1 When to Use Quotation Marks

Use quotation marks whenever you use the *exact words* of a speaker or a book, even if it is only a few words or something that someone *might* have said.

> The essay describes "the poets in the kitchen."

> Formal writers should avoid slang, meaning terms like "cool" and "laid back."

Note: If a speaker's or writer's words are introduced by words like "said" or "replied," use a comma to set off the quotation. Don't use a comma after "that."

> Robert said, "I'll do it!"

> Jefferson says that "life, liberty, and the pursuit of happiness" are every human being's "inalienable rights."

Do not use quotation marks for paraphrases or summaries. Also, single, *very common* words that might be found often in many works do not require quotation marks.

> PARAPHRASE Robert thinks he can take care of the problem.

> SUMMARY Jefferson described universal entitlements.

> COMMON WORD Jefferson lists our **rights.**

PUNC

Note: Don't mix the speaker's (or writer's) words with yours. Anything in quotation marks should be exactly what was said by someone else; anything *not* in quotation marks should be entirely your own words.

<u>INCORRECT</u> Jefferson described universal entitlements, such as life, liberty, and the pursuit of happiness.

<u>CORRECT</u> Jefferson described universal entitlements, such as "life, liberty, and the pursuit of happiness."

PUNC EXERCISE 8

Assume that this paragraph is found on page 156 of the book *Guide to China* by J. L. Sims. Use this paragraph for the exercises that follow.

The city of Beijing is the capital of China and is located in the northeast section of the country. Although Beijing was not the first capital of this ancient country, it has held that position since the fourteenth century. When China's rulers were emperors, they lived in the center of Beijing in a great palace called the Forbidden City. This palace is now a cultural and art museum, open to all of China's people. Also in Beijing are many temples and other museums, but Beijing is not a city of the past. Most visitors delight in the many restaurants serving different kinds of food from every part of China and the world. On one street the restaurants have blazing fires and whole sheep hanging outside; on another street are elegant Sichuan restaurants where twenty course meals are served on rare porcelain dishes, and on yet another street Pizza Hut competes with McDonald's.

Correct the use of quotation marks in the following student paragraph. Be sure to check with the original paragraph to see where the student is quoting and where she is paraphrasing.

The capital of the United States is Washington, D.C., and the capital of China is Beijing (Sims 156). Beijing is like Washington is in some ways and different in others. Beijing once had emperors who lived in the center of Beijing in a great palace called the Forbidden City. Washington has the White House and our president lives there now, but the leader of China does not live in the Forbidden City "which is now open to all of the people of China" (Sims 156). Washington and Beijing both have many museums and restaurants, and in both you might find exotic ethnic foods, elegant cuisine, and streets where Pizza Hut competes with McDonald's (Sims 157).

Note: When using parenthetical citations, the parentheses come after any quotation marks but before the period. (See pp. 335–337 on documentation for more information on citing sources.) Here's an example.

In *An Anthropologist on Mars,* Robert Kellogg says that we are all "wishing for the past" (185).

6.5.2 Quoting Too Much

Is it possible to quote too much? In most cases, you should try to avoid quoting so much material that your own ideas are overshadowed. Quoting too much can confuse your readers because the quotations may not fit together well with each other or with your ideas. Quote only as much as you need to give evidence for your opinions, and quote only the phrases or sentences that are directly related to what you are saying.

GOOD George Orwell knows that the people of Burma do not like the Europeans. The young priests "stand on street corners and jeer" (175).

AVOID (TOO MUCH QUOTATION)

At that college, you may take courses to improve your basic skills. "Business Math I stresses the basic operations of addition, subtraction, multiplication, and division as applied to whole numbers, decimals, fractions, and percentages. Speed and accuracy are emphasized along with some application to consumer and business problems. The course is not open to students who have completed BUS 109 or its equivalency" (Catalogue 143). You may also take courses to improve reading speed and comprehension, spelling, and study skills that will prepare you for many career majors.

6.5.3 Fitting Quotations Smoothly into a Paragraph

Quotations as long as a complete sentence or more need an introduction and explanation to fit them smoothly into the paragraph. Here are some techniques for doing this.

■ Introduce a quotation with a sentence or phrase.

Ellis explains what khakis mean to Americans. She says, "The pants have become a tradition" (31).

According to Leibowitz, "Irina was already a legend" (87).

■ After giving a quotation, explain what it means or why it is important.

Ellis explains what khakis mean to Americans. She says, "The pants have become a tradition" (31). **We like them because of their history as well as their usefulness.**

According to Leibowitz, "Irina was already a legend" (87). **They thought she was beautiful partly because of her reputation for courage.**

PUNC EXERCISE 9 Write a paragraph comparing your city to Beijing, using quotations from the selection on p. 400. Be sure to introduce and explain your quotes.

PUNC

6.5.4 Fitting Quotations Smoothly into a Sentence

Shorter quotations—words, phrases, parts of sentences—can fit into sentences without a separate introduction and explanation, but they must fit in smoothly with the grammar of your sentence, and they must make sense. You can do this in several ways.

■ Begin and end quotations at points that fit well with your sentence.

INCORRECT Beber says that being a law school feminist is hard because of "a lawyer means identifying with the people you are trying to defeat" (207).

CORRECT Beber says that it was difficult to be a complete feminist in law school because wanting to be "a lawyer means identifying with the people you are trying to defeat" (207).

■ Reword your sentence to help it fit with the quotation.

INCORRECT Xanadu is a house that "Hearst appeared to have furnished Xanadu largely from estate sales" (112).

CORRECT A visitor might think that "Hearst appeared to have furnished Xanadu largely from estate sales" (112).

PUNC EXERCISE 10 **Here is a paragraph from a book. It will be the original text to use in the exercise that follows.**

Volcano eruptions are not as common as earthquakes, hurricanes, and tornadoes. Volcanoes look very much like big mountains—they sit there quietly, wearing their snow and glaciers like kindly white-haired grandparents. This is deceptive. Under the cold ice lies a raging furnace that may spew tons of suffocating ashes, torrents of hot mud, or fiery rivers of lava. Any of these eruptions will destroy all life in the path of the outpouring. Mt. St. Helens erupted with ashes and caused destruction in the United States; Mt. Pinatubo in the Philippines and Mt. Fako in Cameroon have also erupted in the last ten years.

Improve the sentences in the following student paragraph by selecting better material from the preceding original or by rewording the sentence.

Among the natural disasters in the United States recently was "Mt. St. Helens erupted with ashes." We don't expect volcanoes. The source says "like kindly white-haired grandparents." We should be afraid of volcanoes "spew tons of suffocating ashes."

6.5.5 Changing Quotations

If necessary, you can make *very small* changes that do not affect the meaning of the original sentence. You may add, delete, or change words. For example, you may need to change the person or number of pronouns or verbs, or substitute a noun for a pronoun.

Leaving Out Words　If you want to leave out some words within quoted material, you must indicate that you have done this with ellipses—three spaced dots that take the place of the words you have left out. Be sure that the meaning is not changed.

> <u>SAME MEANING</u>　Xanadu is a house that "Hearst appeared to have furnished . . . largely from estate sales" (112).

> <u>MEANING CHANGED (AVOID)</u>　Not many people know that "Hearst . . . furnished Xanadu largely from estate sales" (112).

PUNC EXERCISE 11　Improve the use of quotation by using ellipses in the following sentences (the original text is on p. 402).

1. Some results of volcano eruptions include: "Under the cold ice lies a raging furnace that may spew tons of suffocating ashes, torrents of hot mud, or fiery rivers of lava."
2. Three volcanoes that have erupted recently are "Mt. St. Helens erupted with ashes and caused destruction in the United States; Mt. Pinatubo in the Philippines and Mt. Fako in Cameroon have also erupted in the last ten years."

Adding Words　If you want to add your own explanatory words or comments to a direct quote, place them in square brackets, *not* parentheses. Be sure that the meaning is not changed.

> <u>SAME MEANING</u>　Beber says that it was difficult to be a complete feminist in law school because "wanting to be a lawyer means identifying with the people [men] you are trying to defeat" (207).

> <u>MEANING CHANGED (AVOID)</u>　Beber says that it was difficult to be a complete feminist in law school because "wanting to be a lawyer means [not] identifying with the people you are trying to defeat" (207).

Changing Words　If you want to substitute a word or phrase for something in a direct quote, use square brackets. (Do not use ellipses.) Be sure that the meaning is not changed.

> <u>SAME MEANING</u>　When they met Irina, the reporters knew that she "[had become] a legend" (87).

> <u>MEANING CHANGED (AVOID)</u>　When they met, the reporters knew that "Irina [was going to be] a legend" (87).

PUNC

| PUNC EXERCISE 12 | Use brackets to add or change the wording to make the sentences fit smoothly. Be careful not to distort the meaning. |

1. People who live near a volcano should be concerned about the eruptions because "These eruptions will destroy all life in the path of the outpouring."

2. Anyone who was climbing a volcano and thought that it was peaceful should have realized that "This is deceptive."

7. ENGLISH AS A SECOND LANGUAGE (ESL)

7.1 ARTICLES

ESL

Articles, also called *determiners,* are words that precede many nouns (and any adjectives that go with the nouns). The greatest problems in using determiners arise when you must choose whether to use *a/an* or *the.* Some general rules will guide you correctly for many sentences, but there are many exceptions to these rules. As you read and hear American English, you will gradually develop an intuition for using articles and determiners. Your instructors, tutors, and fellow students who are native speakers will be able to tell you which determiner "sounds right," so use peer editing and teacher comments as much as possible. This is a special use of **collocation**, so you might want to add sentences that are new examples of article use to your vocabulary/collocation log. Nevertheless, the following rules will give you some basic guidance. There are two important things to know about a noun when you choose an article or determiner.

1. **Is the noun definite or indefinite?**

   The article *a/an* is **indefinite**: it is used to refer to an item that is not specific, but can be any one of a group. The article *the* is **definite**: it is used for specific or unique items.

   An airplane flew overhead. It was not **the** plane I was meeting.

   A manager gave me **the** application for **the** job.

   The teachers met to grade **the** papers.

   Exception: Many proper names take no article.

   The programmer worked for **Microsoft.**

   Sevena worked for **the software company.**

2. **Can the noun be counted?**

   Use articles to refer to items that can be counted. Use *a/an* if singular, and *some* if plural. If the item cannot be counted, use no article.

   Education is important for a student.

One of **the** ways to lose **weigh**t is to exercise.

To cook **rice,** use water and salt; make sure a lid is on the pot.

Exception: If a number or quantity comes before a count noun, no article is needed.

Three children sat waiting in **the chairs.**

The children sat waiting in **three chairs.**

ESL EXERCISE 1 In the following paragraph, add the correct article. If no article is needed, do not add anything.

Even though United States is one country with official language which is called English, many people speak dialect which means that they use language differently from people in other parts of country. Person who lives in North Carolina mountains might not understand person who lives in northern city like New York. Sometimes misunderstanding is funny, but sometimes big problem can result.

7.2 PREPOSITIONS

Prepositions are very common in English, but there are few rules to tell which preposition is best for a particular sentence. Choosing the right preposition for a particular phrase can be very difficult. To become more fluent in choosing and using prepositions, make a special place in your log of English phrases, idioms, and collocations. Sometimes a preposition adds real meaning to a sentence, and then the choice of preposition is not difficult. For example, *before* allows us to relate ideas about time and space.

Leslie left **before** lunch.

Alex stood in line **before** Sam.

Note on dialect variation: The use of prepositions can vary from dialect to dialect. For example, in many parts of the United States, people stand *in line*, but in parts of the Northeast (New York or New Jersey, for example), people stand *on line.* But they are doing the same thing; they are waiting for their turn to do something (maybe to see a bank teller).

7.2.1 Prepositions with Verbs (Phrasal or Prep + Verbs)

Many times the choice of a preposition depends on the other words around it. This means that the preposition is in an **idiom** or a more general collocation—that is, words that are often used in combination with each other. For example, *run into* can mean meet by chance as well as physically run into. These two sentences mean very different things.

ESL

Alex **ran into** Leslie at the store. (met by chance)

The truck **ran into** Mary's car at the corner of Main Street and Rosewood Avenue. (had a wreck)

As you add prepositions to your vocabulary log, notice the differences in meaning in different phrases. *Run into* is an example of a verb + preposition combination called "phrasal verbs" or "prep + verbs." These types of verbs should be learned as a unit, not as separate words. For example, there are different types of phrasal verbs. Some are called *separable*, which means that the preposition can come after the noun it goes with, too. For example, you can say both <u>throw away</u> *the garbage* and <u>throw *the garbage* away</u>. A list of common phrasal verbs in English is found on pages 407–409. The list shows which prepositions can be separated from their verbs and which cannot.

Verb-Preposition-Verb   When a phrasal verb is followed by another verb, the second verb is usually a gerund or *-ing* verb. It's different when a verb is followed by another verb; in that case, usually the second verb is an infinitive or *to* + verb. Often the preposition is dropped before the infintive.

PHRASAL VERB FOLLOWED BY *-ING* VERB: We **planned on going** to the store.

PHRASAL VERB FOLLOWED BY *-ING* VERB: We **thought about going** to the store.

VERB FOLLOWED BY *TO* + VERB: We **planned to go** to the store.

VERB FOLLOWED BY *TO* + VERB: We **wanted to go** to the store.

INCORRECT: We planned on to go to the store.

Differences Across Languages   One way languages differ that does not seem to follow a pattern is the use of prepositions to add another element to a sentence. For example, English allows some verbs, such as *tell* or *give*, to have two objects without requiring a preposition for the second object: *Tony told Alex a story*. However, not all verbs that express similar ideas have similar patterns. For example, you can *explain the answer to him*, but you cannot *explain him the answer*. Verbs that can have two objects without the use of a preposition are called *double object verbs*. But even these double object verbs occur with prepositions (usually *to* or *for*): *Tony told a story to Alex*. There are only a few double object verbs in English, and most verbs with two objects will need a preposition to express the second object, but verbs like *tell* and *give* are very common.

7.2.2 Prepositions with Other Kinds of Words

Adjectives   Many adjectives occur with prepositions when the situation that the adjective is describing is being explained in more detail. For example, a sentence like *Marie is angry* gives less information than a sentence like *Marie is angry **at Tony*** or *Marie is angry **about the meeting.*** It is best to learn the whole adjective + preposition phrase as a unit. You can enter common uses of

Prepositions with Verbs: Phrasal or Prep + Verbs

In the following list, verbs are listed with the prepositions that often follow them to make up Prep + Verbs. The verbs are in alphabetical order, and the prepositions are in bold. Words in parentheses are optional (they can be left off without changing the meaning of the verb). Separable prep + verbs are marked with an asterisk (*). The meanings of phrases that might not be clear if you have only a dictionary definition are given in italics.

account **for** one's actions, an idea, or a situation
*add something **to** something else
agree **on** something
agree **with** someone
apologize (**to** someone) (**for** something)
apply (**to** a place) **for** something
*apply oneself **to** something
approve **of** something or someone
argue **with** someone **about** something
arrive **at** a specific place (*airport, stadium, building, room, meeting*)
arrive **in** a larger open place (*a city, country*)
*ask (someone) (**about** something or someone)
ask (someone) (**for** something)
*ask someone **out** (**on** a date or **to** an event)

believe **in** something or someone
belong **to** someone or something
*blame someone **for** something
*blame something **on** someone
*borrow something (**from** someone or a source)

*call someone **back**
*call something **off**
call **on/upon** someone (to do something)
*call someone **up** (*on the telephone*)
care **for** someone or something
come **from** somewhere (**to** another place)
*compare something or someone **with/to** someone or something

complain **to** someone **about** something
*compliment someone **on** something
concentrate **on** something (or someone)
consent **to** something or a verb
consist **of** something
*convince someone **of** something (or **to** verb)
*cross something **out**

decide **about** something
depend **on** someone or something (**for** something or **to** verb)
disagree **with** someone (**over** or **about** something)
*discuss something **with** someone
*divide something **up** (or **into** parts)
* divide something **by** something
*do something **over** (redo)
dream **about** something or someone or verb + ing
drop **in** (**on** someone) (*visit informally*)
drop **out** (**of** something) (*quit school*)

escape (**from** something)
*excuse someone (**from** a duty)
*excuse someone (**for** a mistake)

*figure **out** something or figure something **out**
*fill **in** something
*fill **out** something
*fill **up** something or fill something **up**
*find **out** something
fool **around** (**with** something/

someone, *sometimes with a sexual meaning*)
*forgive someone (**for** something)

get **along** (**with** someone)
get **back** (**from** a place)
get **in/into** (a car)
get **off** (*a means of transportation*)
get **on** (*a means of transportation*)
get **out of** (*a means of transportation or avoiding something*)
get **over** something (*such as an illness or problem*)
get rid **of**
get **through** (*with a task*)
*give something **back** (**to** someone)
give **up** (verb + ing/a goal or project)
graduate (**from** an educational institution)
grow **up**

*hand **in** something (**to** someone) or hand something **in**
*hand **out** something (**to** someone)
*hang **up** something (**on** a hanger or hook) or hang something **up**
*hang **up** the phone
happen **to** someone (involve someone)
*have respect **for** someone or something
hear **about/of** someone or something
hear **from** someone or something
*help someone (**with** something)
*hide something (**from** someone)
hope **for** something (to happen)
*hunt **down** something/someone (*find*)

insist **on**
*introduce someone **to** someone else or something new
*invite someone **to** (an event/a place /verb)

keep **on** (verb + ing) (*continue*)
know **about** something or someone

laugh **at** something/someone
*leave **out** something or leave something **out**
listen **for** (*something/someone*)
listen **to** (*something/someone*)
look **after** someone (*watch, care for*)
look **at** (*something/someone*)
look **down on** someone (*disregard*)
look **for** (*something/someone*)
look **forward to** (something/an event/verb + ing)
*look something/someone **over** (*inspect*)
*look **up** some information

*make **up** something (*invent, create*) or make something **up**
make **up** (**with** someone) (*settle disagreements or differences*)
make **up** one's face (*use cosmetics*)
matter **to** someone
(what is the) matter **with** someone or something (*what is the problem*)

object **to** something/an idea/verb + ing

*pay **back** money (**to** someone) (**for** something)
pay **for** something
*pick **up** something (**from** a place or **for** someone)
plan **on** something/an event
point **at/to** something or someone
protect something or someone (**from** something or someone)
provide **for** something/someone
*provide someone **with** something
*put **away** something or put something **away**
*put **back** something (*in the original place*) or put something **back**
*put **down** something (in a place) or put something **down**
*put **down** someone or an idea (*criticize*) or put someone or something **down**

*put **off** something (*postpone*) or put something off

*put **off** someone (*avoid giving a direct answer to someone or discourage someone*)

recover **from** (an illness/an error)

rely **on** someone or something (*for something*)

remind someone **of/about** something

result **from** something

run **into** something or someone (*meet by chance*)

run **into** something or someone (*crash or wreck*)

*run **off** someone (*make someone leave*) or run someone **off**

run **out** (**of** something)

run **over** something or someone

run **over** (**to** a place) (*visit*)

search **for** something/someone

see **about** something/someone

*separate something or someone **from** someone or something else

*shut **off** something or shut something **off**

speak **to** someone (**about** something)

stare **at** something or someone

*start (something) **over**

substitute (something) **for** something/someone

*subtract something **from** (something else)

take care **of** something

*take something **off** (**of** something)

talk (**to/with** someone) (**about** something/someone/verb + ing)

talk **of/about** something or someone or verb + ing

*tear **down** something (*destroy*) or tear something **down**

*tear **off** something (*of something else, like a credit card receipt*) or

tear something **off**

*tear **out** something (*of something, like paper out of a notebook*) or tear something **out**

*tear **up** something (*into pieces*) or tear something **up**

*tell (someone) (**about** something)

*thank someone (**for** something)

think **about/of** something/ someone/an idea

*throw **away** or **out** something or throw something **away** or **out**

*tie **up** something/someone or tie something **up**

travel **to** a place

*try something **on** (*clothing*)

*try something **out** (*an idea*)

*turn something **down** (*decrease volume or speed*)

*turn someone or something **down** (*refuse*)

*turn something **off** (*a machine, light, noise*)

*turn someone **off** (*offend or repel someone*)

*turn something **on** (*a machine, light, noise*)

*turn someone **on** (*arouse, usually with a sexual meaning*)

*turn someone **on to** something (*make aware of*)

*turn something **up** (*increase volume or speed*)

wait **for** something/someone

wait **on** someone (serve; same as *wait for* in some dialects)

*wake (someone) **up**

watch **out** (*be careful*)

watch **out** (**for** something or someone)

worry **about** someone or something

write (**to** someone) (**about** something)

*write something **down**

ESL

adjectives + preposition phrases in your English log to help you remember these phrases.

Nouns (Possessive *of*)   English has two ways to express possession and other related meanings: the apostrophe + *s* (*Tony's friend*) and the preposition *of* (*a friend of Tony*). Possessive *'s* is discussed on pp. 374–375.

ESL EXERCISE 2   **In the following paragraph, correct the use of prepositions and prep + verbs.**

When Adam first arrived to this college, he insisted to buy new books. He worried for having the books because he hoped on a good grade in his classes. When he went at the bookstore, he looked to many books. He didn't want to leave out any of his courses. He listened at the salesman explain around new books and used books, and finally Adam decided for the ones he needed to buy. While he stood in line, he met a friend who introduced him with another student who wanted to sell his used books.

ESL EXERCISE 3   **In the following paragraph, correct the use of prepositions.**

Many people have difficulty by living in a climate that is different from their home. They may complain for the cold or the heat. If they become ill, they blame on their illnesses to the climate. They fool over the thermostat in their homes. After living in a new climate for several years, they may get used of the new climate, and may no longer ask of changes in the office's temperature.

7.3   VERB TENSE

Verbs in English can be simple (or one word), but they can also be longer (combining helping verbs and verb endings). Sections 1.1, 1.3, 3.2, and 4.1 give some basic information about verbs, but additionally you will need to understand some other qualities of English verbs.

- **tense** (the time when a verb happens)
- **aspect** (how the verb happens)
- **modals** (the possibility of something happening)
- **voice** (whether the subject does the action or receives the action of the verb)

First, be sure that you understand each of these qualities separately, and then see how they are combined.

7.3.1 Tense

Tense in English identifies when an event happens or describes a state. It can be in the **past**, the **present**, or the **future**. One form of the future is a modal: *will*. There is another way to express future that is very common in American English: *be going to* + verb. The form of *be* agrees with the subject. In the last example here, *are* agrees with students.

<u>PRESENT</u> The students **write** in their journals twice a week.

<u>PAST</u> The students **wrote** in their journals twice a week.

<u>FUTURE (MODAL)</u> The students **will write** in their journals twice a week.

<u>FUTURE (*BE GOING TO*)</u> The students **are going to write** in their journals twice a week.

If a verb is present tense and the subject is, or can be replaced by, *he, she,* or *it,* the verb must agree with the subject and have an *-s* ending (see Section 4.1). In the following example, *the student* can be replaced by *she.* This form of the verb is called third person singular (present tense).

<u>THIRD PERSON SINGULAR PRESENT</u> The student **writes** in her journal every evening.

Writers use past tense to describe and narrate an event or situation that occurred in the past and is over. Notice how the specific age of *twelve* sets the scene for this narrative.

When I **was** twelve, I **broke** my leg. I **slipped** on the playground on a cold winter morning and **fell.** The bone near my ankle **snapped** with a loud "pop!" Even my friends **heard** it. The teachers **called** my parents, who **came** quickly. . . .

Writers use present tense to describe an event or situation that is typical and that can be predicted to occur in the same way again. Notice the phrase *every spring* in the first sentence.

The alligators **come** back to the nesting grounds **every spring.** The grass **grows** thick again and the egrets **build** nests in the trees over the water. If a chick **falls** out of the nest, an alligator **is** there. When the chicks **are** mature and **fly** well, the alligators **move** back to the black water swamp.

7.3.2 Aspect

Aspect locates an event in relation to another time, often the present. *Progressive* or *continuous* aspects show that events or states are happening at a particular time. *Perfect* aspect shows that events are completed by a certain time. Progressive and perfect are illustrated here, along with combinations of tense and aspect.

Progressive **Progressive** verbs contain a form of *be* and add *-ing* to the main verb.

Li **is** work**ing.**   Thomas **will be** earn**ing** more next year.

Gloria **was** listen**ing** to the radio.   I **am** try**ing** to help.

Progressive aspect focuses on the action of an event. *Note:* When people write quickly, they sometimes leave out the *be* verb. Be careful in your writing to

ESL

include both parts of the progressive. Remember that aspect is an additional quality of verbs, so they may also have tense and modals.

In this example, the action of writing is occurring now (today or this semester).

PRESENT PROGRESSIVE   **Today** some of the students **are writing** in their journals and others **are starting** to prewrite the next essay.

This semester we **are studying** *Don Quixote*.

In this example, the action of writing was an activity in the past (the class period, the course, or the semester).

PAST PROGRESSIVE   The teacher **was conferencing** with some students, while other students **were revising** their rough drafts.

In this example, future progressive represents a prediction or guess.

FUTURE PROGRESSIVE   Lena **will be sleeping** if you arrive after ten o'clock.

What is the difference between progressive and habitual? Progressive aspect is most commonly used for events in the present—events that are going on as we speak but may end at some definite time. On the other hand, the simple present tense (one word) often suggests that an event happens regularly or that it is habitual. In the following pair, the first sentence suggests that this is a goal of the course, not a specific activity.

The students **learn** about documenting quotes (every semester when this course is taught).

The students **are learning** about documenting quotes (during this class period).

Simple present is most commonly used for verbs that describe a state, not an activity—verbs such as *is, are, seem, taste, feel*, and others. Using present progressive for this kind of verb suggests that something is not typical about the situation.

Miles **lives** in Charleston.

Miles **is living** in Charleston. [but he hasn't always lived there]

Sally **is** a cooperative child.

Sally **is being** a cooperative child. [but she isn't usually or might not be expected to be cooperative in all situations]

Perfect   **Perfect aspect** has two parts: *have* and a past participle ending of the verb (an *-en* or an *-ed* ending or an irregular form such as *bought* (see Section 3.2.2 for more about past participles of irregular verbs). Perfect means that an activity or situation has been completed by a certain time or began to happen at a certain time. Many verbs must be stated in the present perfect because we often discuss one event as happening before some other event.

                   present perfect   *began in past*

<u>PRESENT PERFECT</u> Maureen **has lived** in Charleston since last summer.
[The situation was true in the past (last summer) and is also still true now.]

    If the past event was an activity (rather than a state), the verb may also be progressive. In this example, notice that college graduation is a one-time event, but working is an activity that can start in the past and be continuing in the present.

                          present perfect

<u>PRESENT PREFECT PROGRESSIVE</u> Maureen **has been working** with that

          simple past

company since she **graduated** from college.

    Past perfect is often used to relate two events in the past, especially if one is a specific event and the other is ongoing. In this example, an ongoing past activity (*had been working*) is related to an activity that happened at one specific time in the past (*decided*).

                   past perfect progressive

<u>PAST PERFECT</u> Maureen **had been working** in Washington, but she

simple past
decided it was too expensive.

    The future tense can also occur with the perfect aspect. Future perfect makes a prediction that an action will be completed by a certain time in the future. Future perfect can also be progressive.

                   future perfect

<u>FUTURE PERFECT</u> Caroline **will have finished** her driver's education class
definite time in the future
by December.

       future perfect progressive
She **will have been practicing** for four months by December.

ESL EXERCISE 4 | **In the following paragraph, correct the use of verb tense and aspect.**

> Tomorrow we will going to our new apartment. We are owning too much furniture, so we will hiring a van to help us move. We will had worked all day packing things when the van arrives. Last time we were moving, we had tried to do all the work ourselves. We are having better judgment this time, even though it will be costing us more money. However, we will saved money if the dishes are not breaked and the chairs is not lose.

7.3.3 Modals

    Modals express possibility, obligation, or inferences about what the speaker believes to be true.

ESL

> ### The Use of Modals
>
> ■ Modals are often used in polite forms (instead of simple commands).
>
> ■ Modals can mean different things in different sentences. The context makes clear which meaning is intended.
>
> ■ When modals are combined with other verb forms, the meaning usually changes.

Modals do not combine with tense, although some modals (such as *could* or *would*) look as if they could be a past tense form. Also, using modals with the perfect aspect can express a past meaning (for more on modals, see page xxx). One modal, *can,* does not occur with perfect aspect. The following list gives the meanings of modals with other aspects.

Modal	*They **could go.***	(ability, possibility, permission; a polite form)
Modal + progressive	*They **could be going.***	(a prediction or guess)
Modal + perfect	*They **could have gone.***	(a guess or a past possibility or a missed possibility)
Modal + perfect progressive	*They **could have been going.***	(a missed or past possibility or a guess)

There are two types of modals: true modals that are simple (one word + verb) and phrasal modals (several words + verb or infinitive).

SIMPLE **might** read

PHRASAL **might be able** to read

Only one modal can be used with each verb, but a simple modal can occur with a phrasal modal.

Lena **might be able** to read that story by tomorrow.

Note: Using two modals, such as *might could,* is a regional spoken dialect and never written unless you are quoting someone who speaks this local variety of English.

The following modals occur with bare verb forms (bare verbs do not have tense; they are usually the same as the simple present):

can

could

had better

may

might

must

shall

should

will (future)

would

The following phrasal verbs are like modals, but they occur with an infinitive (*to* + verb). (The forms preceded by an asterisk can be stated in different tenses.) They usually have the same meaning as a simple modal.

*be able to (can)

*be going to (will)

*be supposed to (should)

*have to (must)

*have got to (must)

ought to (should)

supposed to (should)

used to (would)

In speaking, modals are often used to express polite requests for oneself.

May I go? **Could** I go? **Can** I go?

I **would** like some coffee.

Some modals are used to ask someone to do something.

Could you do this? [the speaker is not sure you can]

Would you do this? [the speaker assumes you can]

Can you do this? [a little more informal than **could**]

Some modals express obligation, advice, or necessity.

All students **should** keep their journals up to date. [advice, an obligation]

All students **must** take the placement exam. [a necessity]

All students **have to** take the final exam. [a necessity]

All students **had to** take the final exam. [a past necessity]

All students **have got to** turn in their final essays on Monday. [a necessity]

Some modals express degrees of certainty.

■ With verbs that show a state rather than an activity, *must, may, might,* and *could* represent a belief or a guess.

Maureen **must be** tired; she usually goes to bed later. [sure]

Maureen **could be** sick. [less sure]

ESL

■ With actions, the perfect is used to express certainty or guesses.

Maureen **must have done** her assignment. [sure]

Maureen **could have done** well on the test. [less sure]

Maureen **might not have gone** to the library. [less sure]

Some modals show predictions can be made about the future.

Maureen **will do well** on the test. [sure future]

Maureen **should do well** on the test. [sure future]

Obligation plus perfect implies expectations may not be met.

Maureen **should have done well** on the test, but maybe she didn't. [unsure future]

Some modals change their meaning when they are negative, and others do not.

NEED We **have to tell** the rest of the class about the project before the end of the semester.

NO NEED We **do not (don't) have to tell** the rest of the class about the project before the end of the semester.

NEED We **must tell** the rest of the class about the project before the end of the semester.

PROHIBITED We **must not (mustn't) tell** the rest of the class about the project before the end of the semester.

Some other modals with special meanings are often used.

■ *Used to* expresses a typical past state or activity that is no longer true.

They **used to** live in Illinois.

Before Jim got ill, he and Marie **used to** travel more.

■ *Supposed to* expresses an obligation, like *should,* but also suggests that the obligation may not be met.

They were **supposed to** arrive at noon, but they didn't.

■ *Had better* is usually stronger than other modals of obligation or advice.

Students **had better** get their papers in on time, or their grades will be lowered.

ESL EXERCISE 5   **In the following paragraph, correct the use of modals.**

Lee must hopes to make a high salary, because he will majoring in computer science. He thinks he ought start at a salary as high as many people make with several years' experience because he goes to study many new aspects of computers. He can be very unhappy if he received a lower salary. He can would make more than his friends who study art, but they might enjoys their work, even if their salaries may be low.

7.3.4 Voice

Verbs in English also have the quality of "voice," which tells whether the subject does the action of the verb (**active voice**) or receives the action of the verb (**passive voice**).

> <u>ACTIVE</u> The dinosaur ate the tree. [*dinosaur*, the subject, performs the action]
> <u>PASSIVE</u> The tree was eaten by the dinosaur. [*tree*, the subject, receives the action]

Passive sentences use the helping verb *be,* and the past participle form of the verb occurs (usually the *-ed* or *-en* form, or an irregular form like *bought* from *buy*—see Section 3.2.2 for more on verb parts and endings). The agent (the doer of the action) occurs at the end of the sentence after the preposition *by,* but it can be left out. Many times people use the passive voice because only the thing affected by the verb is important and they want to leave out the agent or they don't know the agent.

> The accident occurred around midnight. The windshield of the minivan **was broken** and the fender of the hatchback **was smashed.** A guardrail **was bent** and **may have to be replaced.** Fortunately, the teenaged drivers of the two cars **were not** seriously **injured,** although they **were taken** to the hospital for observation. The parents of the drivers **have been notified.**

The form of *be* depends on the modal, tense, and aspect of the verb in the active form.

Tense, Aspect (Modal)	Active	Passive
Past, simple	The lawyer **wrote** the letter.	The letter **was written** [by the lawyer].
Past, simple	Someone **knocked** over my bicycle.	My bicycle **was knocked** over [by someone].
Past, perfect	The company **has bought** the building.	The building **has been bought** [by the company].
Past, progressive	Someone **was telling** the rumors at work.	Rumors **were being told** at work [by someone].
Past, simple, possibility	The class **might finish** the project soon.	The project **might be finished** [by the class] soon.

ESL

If a verb has more than one object, only the first object can become the passive subject.

<u>ACTIVE</u>	<u>PASSIVE</u>
The family sent a **nice birthday present** to Caroline.	**A nice birthday present** was sent to Caroline [by the family].
The family gave **Caroline** a nice birthday present.	**Caroline** was given a nice birthday present [by the family].

Sometimes *get* occurs with past participles with a passive-like meaning.

> The couple **got married** last week [by someone].
>
> The children **are getting excited** about the state fair [by someone/something].
>
> The squirrel almost **got run over** in the street [by a car].

7.3.5 Verb Form Combinations

Helping verbs are often combined, as some examples have shown. The different forms must be placed in a certain order: tense or modal, perfect, progressive. Passive can follow either tense or a modal. The endings that express the concepts of tense, perfect, progressive, and passive are added to the verb after the helper or modal.

Past	+	**Progressive**	+	**Passive**	+	**Verb**
Past form		***be*** + *ing*		***be*** + *-en/-ed*		*eat*
was		***be****ing*				*eat**en***

The corn **was being eaten** by wild animals all summer, so none is left now.

For more details about verb endings, see these sections of the handbook: past forms (pp. 380–383), irregular verbs (pp. 381–383), present third person singular -*s* (Section 3.2.1). Also, you should check every sentence with a helping verb for endings on the verb, since any verb using the helpers *be* or *have* also needs an ending (see p. 378). Look as well at subject-verb agreement (pp. 383–385). You should keep a record of mistakes you make using verb forms in your editing log to help you discover any pattern of error in verb forms.

ESL EXERCISE 6   **In the following paragraph, correct the verb usage.**

I am owning a car now, and it can being a big responsibility. I must to worry about gasoline, repairs, and insurance. Because my car is paint white, it is getting dirty very easily. My brother teaches me how to take care of the car. He is driving to work every day, and he must parks in a garage, which is also costing him more money. One day I was driving my car and I can hear a terrible sound. I was very worried, but then I saw that the door was open and the seat belt dragged on the road.

PART FIVE

Essays and Readings

Essays by Student Writers

Rituals . . . for the Love of a Parent

by Keenan Johnson

In this essay, Keenan Johnson uses vivid details to demonstrate that the apparently unreasonable rules and rituals of a parent may in fact have a serious purpose in the future lives of the children, which the children do not understand. He first gives the example of a friend whose father hoped to instill a respect for culture in children by punishment and then goes on to show how he himself has adopted his own rituals of luck as a result of his family's practices. Most complete of all is his explanation for the rational basis of the prohibition against talking while eating.

1   In the essay, "My Father's Tribal Rule," Mark Mathabane portrays his hatred toward his father's tribal rituals. All through the story Mathabane tells of his father making him practice tribal rituals and his rebellion toward these rituals. Although his father is doing all of this for his own reasons, he is also doing it for love. Mathabane has a hatred for all the rituals that his father forces him to participate in, as do most children who are unwillingly forced to do certain rituals, although all parents who make their children perform such rituals have some purpose for doing this.

2   One purpose for forcing rituals upon young children is the parent's desire for the preservation of culture. In Mathabane's essay, Mathabane is forced to speak his father's native language of Venda. When he is caught speaking another language, his father gets angry and punishes him by lashing him and making him participate in more daily rituals. Mathabane's father just wants his son to grow up knowing the culture and language that the father grew up with. I agree that Mathabane's father went about making his son learn about his culture the wrong way, but he is raising his children the way he was raised.

3   Many people today have the same type of problem Mathabane faced as a child. My best friend's father is from a small island named Guam. The island is a very different place than the States. My friend's father was raised in a harsh way. When he disobeyed his father he was hit, not just spanked with a belt, but hit with a fist. When my friend was growing up, his father tried to force the native language on him. He refused to learn the language, saying, "We aren't on the islands and I probably will never go there." My friend's father was furious at this and hit him, just like the father had been hit when he

was a child. Now that my friend is older, he understands that his father was just trying to keep the island culture alive through him.

4   Some of the rituals described were supposed to bring good luck, money, and safety. Mathabane as a child hated doing these rituals because in his youth he did not understand the necessity of them. As a young kid I did not understand some of the rituals my parents made me do. Some include eating collard greens on New Year's Day. This was said to bring money. Also, I didn't understand why my grandfather kept a horseshoe hung over the barn door. This was to ensure luck. Now that I am older, I have some rituals that I participate in that I believe help me. Before every football game I wore the same shirt and boots. Now every time I need luck I wear them. Also, when I need luck I carry around a green Monopoly hotel. I think it is lucky because all hotels in that game are red, and I got a green one the only time I have ever won that game. Every culture and every person has different ways of trying to make luck and has different superstitions about things. Just as my parents did for me, Mathabane's father was just passing down the ways to get these things.

5   In one part of the essay, Mathabane is punished for talking at the dinner table. His father gets very angry about this and tells him, "You don't have two mouths to afford such luxury!" (44). I believe that Mathabane's father is just looking out for the well-being of his children. By that I mean if a family is poor and doesn't have much to eat, they need to spend all their meal time eating and not talking. One of my good friends just moved to Greenville, South Carolina, where she teaches the second grade. During lunch time she has to punish her children when they talk, so that they will get finished eating in time to get back to work. I think it is necessary to keep the talking down during a meal because it is a time of nourishment and not a social time.

6   Although as a child I hated the rituals my parents forced upon me as much as Mathabane hated the rituals forced upon him, they all had a purpose. In every instance Mathabane was forced to do rituals, his father had a clear purpose for enforcing them. Mathabane's father might have had a harsh way in teaching the rituals to his children, but he did it for the love he had for his children. He loved his children enough to take the time to teach his kids these rituals and punish them for not doing them. When a parent punishes children for not doing something, it is done in love. All these rituals did have a pupose in one way or another to his father and his father just wanted Mathabane to learn them as the father did.

Rituals: A Way of Life

by J. P. Myers

The following essay by Mr. Myers argues that children resent being forced to follow rules and customs that they do not understand. He uses a brief description of his bitterness toward his father after being forced to do his sister's chores, and follows with a concrete and memorable description of the clothes he was re-quired to wear, showing how similar his problems were to those experienced by Mathabane. An obvious conclusion would be the restatement of the thesis that parents cannot accomplish their goals by intimidation, since that only creates more resistance.

1 Growing up through life, my father had rules and values to which I never grew accustomed. Their purpose was to mold me into the best person my father could imagine. In the essay "My Father's Tribal Rule," Mark Mathabane reflects on his life growing up with his father's tribal rules and rituals. He discusses the differences between the way everyone else around him lives, and the strict rules and rituals his father instills in the household. Mathabane despises his father's rules so much that he develops animosity toward his father and the beliefs. I agree with Mathabane on his belief that rules and rituals have no purpose or value because my father's rules and rituals served only to intimidate, embarrass, and develop resentfulness in me because he felt I should be like him.

2 My father, whom I feared, stood six feet tall and weighed three hundred pounds and intimidated me something fierce. Although rebellious against certain rules, I had no alternative but to follow them or get switched. Mathabane says, "Somehow they did not make sense to me; they simply awed, confused, and embarrassed me, and the only reason I participated in them night after night was because my father made certain that I did by using, among other things, the whip, and the threat of the retributive powers of my ancestral sprits, whose favor the rituals were designed to curry" (44). For example, one afternoon I was asked by my father to do one of my sister's chores. Although I disagreed, my father stood up with the belt and that intimidation alone frightened me into doing his wishes. I will never forget the control my father had over me when it came to obedience.

3 As a child and a teenager, my father set strict rules pertaining to the type of clothes I was allowed to wear. His philosophy was that I should wear plaid shirts with pockets and a collar, corduroy pants, and loafers. He felt that this type of attire would help me to look presentable and gain respect from others, at least in his eyes. Mathabane says "Participation in my father's rituals sometimes led to the most appalling scenes, which invariably made me the laughingstock of my friends, who thought that my father, in his ritual garb, was the most hilarious thing they had ever seen since natives in Tarzan movies" (45). For example, one day I had to wear brown corduroy pants, a plaid shirt, and cowboy boots to school. At this time kids normally wore blue jeans, cool T-shirts, and Nikes. Every kid in class made fun of me all the time because I looked ridiculous, like a geek. However, for this embarrassment my father never seemed to care and never respected my wishes to wear what I felt was normal clothes.

4 When it came time for dinner, my father's rules seemed to aggravate me most. He believed you should eat poultry, beef, and lots of green vegetables. Every meal my mother cooked consisted of these items. Mathabane says, "This diet he administered religiously, seemingly bent on moulding George

and me in his image. At first I had tried to resist the diet, but my father's severe looks frightened me" (43). For example, my mother always seemed to prepare liver and broccoli a numerous amount of times in my life. This particular meal was my father's favorite. I remember having to eat this horrid meal, and having really no chance to be excused from the table. All I ever wanted was a peanut butter sandwich or even a cheeseburger and french fries every now and again.

5   In conclusion, my father's rules and values were supposed to serve a purpose. In fact the only purposes they served were intimidation, fear, embarrassing clothes, and resentfulness for eating horrible foods. Consequently, it was my belief and aggravation that my father imagined me as if he was growing up himself all over again. I can't say that I hated him for his values, but I believe it would have been very close. Mathabane says, "As further punishment, he increased the number of rituals I had to participate in. I hated him more for it" (44). I believe my father enjoyed having control and developing rules and values that he knew must be obeyed growing up. My hatred is not so much at him but for his lack of understanding that times do and always will change.

WORKS CITED

Mathabane, Mark. "My Father's Tribal Rule." *The User's Guide to College Writing: Reading, Analyzing, and Writing.* Nancy Kreml et al. New York: Longman, 2004. 42–46.

The Woman Chain: A Reflection of Women's Roles

by Meg Christmas

In this essay, the strong introduction and conclusion help focus on the thesis that the roles of women are roles of strength rather than weakness. In the body paragraphs, the deft paraphrases and quotes chosen by Meg Christmas show the details of the roles of women in Mathabane's writing, and parallel examples from her own experience show how much information can be inferred from small details, such as the fact that the mother was busy while the rest of the family ate. Ms. Christmas also explains how the role of peacemaker played by Mathabane's mother does not really undercut her support of her husband, showing how the mother cooperates with the father in maintaining a united front. The wealth of detail and thoroughness of examples make the argument convincing.

1   We come from our mothers. They have been with us over the course of our entire lives. Whether we were brought up by our natural mothers, grandmothers, adopted mothers, aunts, or a father that played the role of an absent mother, these people were the ones that cared for us when we were ill. They fought with us when we were at battle, and provided for us a sense of love and

belonging that only a mother can provide for her child. Women have played an integral part in most people's lives, whether directly or indirectly, throughout history. In Mathabane's essay, "My Father's Tribal Rule," he shows us how his mother and his experiences with her parallel other experiences we might have had in our own families. Mothers and women throughout time have proclaimed love and family above all else, not only in our era, but in any time, any place, and in any country in the world. A mother's love shines as the brightest beacon in the night, provides a safe harbor in any storm, and comforts in any tragedy.

2   Mathabane first introduces us to his mother in a positive light. He says, "It was amusing to witness my mother do it [wean George]." This shows us that he likes her, which reflects that she is, in turn, a good mother. It shows us her human side, not just a mother-like characteristic; it makes her a person. It brings us to a place in our hearts that is instinctively sensitive and warm when we think about our mothers. He shows her as a friend, someone he can take delight in and feel comfortable around. Women throughout time have played a similar role in the family, whether it be Elizabethan-Age to Turn-of-the-Century mothers or mothers of the 1960s or mothers of the 1990s. I believe we all strive to maintain good rapport with our children. Providing love and affection, helping our children grow up healthy and happy in their lives, is the role of most mothers.

3   Mathabane also shows his mother as a nurturer. The woman is usually in charge of preparing meals, feeding children, washing clothes and washing dishes. He illustrates this point when he was talking about mealtime. He says, "We were sitting on the floor, about the brazier, and my mother was in the bedroom doing something" (44). This might have been part of a tribal rule, one that states that women must wait to eat after everyone else has had their fill. I know that to be true because in my family, the men and children are always seated at the table and served before the women even think about sitting down themselves. If in a large family group and eating, the women are busy serving and making sure everything has been taken care of. One might be tending to children and the other in the kitchen washing dishes. But when it is just my mother and no other woman around, she still waits for every one to get a plate and then eats afterwards. Some might call it being polite, but I think it's much deeper than that. She is putting the family before herself. And I see that as what Mathabane is saying about his mother when she is found in the other room while all the others are eating. Women sacrifice. I also see Mathabane placing his mother in the role of protector. He says in his essay, "My mother led me into the kitchen and pleaded for me" (44). He also states, "She tried to intervene" (44). This evokes scenes of mother bears and their cubs, the natural feeling a female gets in protection of her offspring. No mother wishes harm to befall her child. In my experiences, I have seen mothers fight tooth and nail for the well-being of their children from bodily harm and from emotional distress. Women are inbred with this natural protection device, some say to ensure the progression of the species, and I am sure that it is so in some cases. But to protect what is hers, what a mother or woman loves, especially a child, is a far greater inbred desire than any survival of the species theory I have ever heard.

4   Women are also disciplinarians. Mathabane uses his mother as an example of this when he begins to tell her he hates his father. Her reaction is one of a loyal wife. She begins by saying, "Don't say that!" followed by Mathabane's interpretation "My mother reprimanded me . . . 'He's your father, you know . . . Shut that bad mouth of yours!'" and he says she threatened to smack him (45). In saying these things to her son, she is ingraining the values and rituals her husband has taught in the home. This enlightens us in that we see her as a loyal wife and a believer in the customs that her husband dictates. In a wife-husband relationship, it is customary that the wife is submissive to the husband. What the husband enforces, the wife follows and teaches to her children. I say this because it is usually the mother that can better relate to her children than the father, simply because she is usually the one to take more time with them. This enables her to communicate better than the father. In threatening to hit her son, she is also being a loyal wife by using the same method of hand-to-rod discipline that the father doles out. This leaves no room for the children to be confused by a different method of treatment. Instead of her just talking to the children and offering some lesser punishment such as not being able to have dinner, she is right on the heels of her husband in promising the same punishment for her children as the father would give if he were there himself. This shows unity in the couple—a trait that all women hope to find in a good marriage.

5   Mathabane also shows us a softer side of his mother. After disciplining her son, she begins to teach him by example why things are the way they are. She defends her husband and says, "He's trying to discipline you. He wants you to grow up to be like him" (45). She then goes on to explain calmly and rationally the reasons why. "Well, in the tribes sons grow up to be like their fathers" (43), and goes further by saying, "But we're still of the tribes" (45) at Mathabane's "indignation." She includes not only her husband and her son when she says "we" but also herself, now showing a family unity, not just a wife-husband unity. She then is seen in the role of philosopher. "Everybody does rituals, Mr. Mathabane" (45). She elaborates so that the child can understand her. She is not forceful in tone or in body, but simply states to him the reasoning behind her statement. Women generally take up a steady vigil of maintaining peace in their homes. They play the part of peacemaker and justifier, teacher and judge of what is said and how it means to be interpreted. In this case, the son is having problems with what his father is enforcing, and the mother has stepped in to aid in the communication process. Just as in any modern day home, the woman plays the same role. We might call it refereeing in this day, but the task remains the same: keeping peace in the home and explaining why certain rules are in place.

6   "My mother laughed" (45). Mathabane brings us to his mother again in a personal way. At the end of his essay, he brings us to her as a solitary person, not in conjunction with his father, showing us that he still likes her, that his mother is a person of positive reflection and that she can laugh in the midst of things when they seem heavy. But at the very closing of Mathabane's essay, he last mentions his mother with his father. His father asks, "Whose son are you? . . . Yours and Mama's . . . Whose? . . . Yours" (45). I hear Mathabane saying

that no matter what he might think of his mother, once the father steps in she is no longer an issue in what he deems as right and necessary. Again I see this submissive female role in society even today in a world where we all try to see everyone as a person, not as male or female. It wasn't until recently that women were actually credited with equal stature as men as far as their capability is concerned. Women were thought to be inferior to men and not deemed worthy of equal work for equal pay.

7   Women have always been in the forefront of their family's lives. They have played the same roles, taught the same lessons, and eaten of the same philosophies that their societies have given them. In valuing family above all, women have nurtured the well-being of their loved ones in a way that only a woman can. Throughout history, women have been the backbone of their families. They administer the same strength and knowledge that was taught to them by their mothers. Women are ensuring the role of the woman by handing down the teachings of our mothers to our children, and by our children to our children's children, generation after generation, until the end of time.

Single Parents' Adversities

by Larry Evans

In a brief response to Teresa McCrary's "Getting Off the Welfare Carousel," Larry Evans asks if welfare assistance is warranted for single parents experiencing financial difficulties and concludes that some assistance is better than the alternative. His reflections focus on two benefits of welfare assistance—health care and housing. His observations regarding the complex issue of health care are more complete, although the reader is left to make the connection between his points and the argument he cites from McCrary. Regarding housing, Mr. Evans suggests that poverty creates living arrangements that are especially stressful for the children involved. Finally, in a very brief conclusion, Mr. Evans hints that political energy would be better spent on trying to find solutions to poverty rather than trying to avoid a situation because we do not feel responsible for it.

1 Single parents with children experience hardship in raising their children. It is almost impossible for single parents to raise children without an adequate job or any type of assistance. In a recent article, Teresa McCrary, a single parent on welfare, wrote that "single mothers were told to get off of welfare and get a job." I agree that single parents can not raise their children without any type of assistance from welfare or another government source.

2   Health care is probably the most important concern for single parents because parents want to know that their children have secure health coverage. Welfare provides health care for parents and their children. If single parents with children did not have any type of health coverage, they would be putting

their children in a state of health poverty. Health care for one child alone can cost thousands of dollars a year. A recent article in *USA Today* tells how some health providers have organized a low income plan for single parents with children to provide adequate health coverage for them. McCrary said, "When the only jobs open to us are maid work, fast-food service and other low-paying drudgery with no benefits, how are we expected to support our children? Minimum wage will not pay for housing cost, health care, transportation and work clothes that an untrained, uneducated woman needs to support even one child. Although welfare pays very little, it provides adequate health coverage for single parents with children."

3   Single parents without any assistance can not afford adequate housing for their children. A house on the market today is very expensive for a person who has a secure job and can afford it. An apartment can cost hundreds of dollars a month. Many single parents and their children stay with other family members or friends because they can not afford adequate housing of their own. This may create a situation where too many are in the home and cause hardship on the children. The Department of Housing and Urban League has a program set up for families. Without this type of government assistance, many single parents could not afford housing for their children.

4   Parents and their children are in such a position that no matter what they do, the solution is that they will suffer. No, we did not put them in the position they are in, but we can help them find a solution to their problem, by voicing our opinion to Congress or our state Representative.

Give the Needy a Break

by Rodell S. Johnson

Rodell S. Johnson's discussion of issues raised in Teresa McCrary's essay "Getting Off the Welfare Carousel" suggests that the failures of the welfare system are a consequence of the system itself. His topic sentences in paragraphs 2 and 3 clearly present his two main ideas: Minimum wage is not enough to support a family, and the system penalizes those who try to get ahead. Building on McCrary's comments, Mr. Johnson shows some of the absurd and unreasonable consequences of a system that seems designed to punish the poor. Overall, Mr. Johnson's paper reflects an appreciation of McCrary's position and argues that we should "Give the Needy a Break."

1   We Americans dramatize ourselves as being a kind, friendly, and caring nation which reaches out to help other countries in their time of need. Yet, why does the United States of America, a country that represents a great pillar for humanity, find it so difficult to lend a giving hand to single parents with children? In the article "Getting Off the Welfare Carousel," by Teresa McCrary, she

describes how single mothers who are supported by the welfare system find it difficult to raise their families because of the inadequate support in today's society. I agree with the author that single parents find it difficult to raise their families because of inadequate support.

2   It is very difficult for a single woman with kids to support her family financially while earning minimum wages. McCrary cites how single parents who undertake the impossible task of managing, with minimum wage support, a family with one child. McCrary explains in paragraph 3 how single mothers take money from other sources, such as "odd jobs, and cash from generous friends, and relatives" to make ends meet without reporting it to the Aid To Families With Dependent Children. They are allowed to have up to three thousand dollars in total assets, and possessing anything more would reduce their benefits. I understand that the government wants to prevent people from taking unfair advantage of the system. For example, a welfare recipient could be receiving aid while owning an expensive automobile valued at thirty-five thousand dollars. I am sure if such recipients can afford to own an expensive vehicle and make the monthly payments, they should not be supported by financial aid at the taxpayers' expense. However, it doesn't take a degree in accounting to figure out a recipient's problem. Earning the minimum wage of five dollars and seventy-five cents an hour and at forty hours a week, totaling fifty-two weeks a year, minus twenty-five percent in taxes, she will earn an average salary of eight thousand and nine hundred dollars a year to support her family. Out of her net income she must make allowances for rent, daycare, clothes, insurance, utilities, school supplies, and a used car that isn't valued over her allowed assets. As a result of her net worth totaling three thousand dollars, she cannot afford a good car or the repairs. A single parent must balance her limited income and overcome the financial strains that choke her family out of their independence and deprive her children of social normalcy.

3   Welfare recipients shouldn't be penalized for people wanting to help them. The author goes on to explain that unless child support from fathers is paid to the state and is greater than AFDC benefits, the mother is given only fifty dollars more, while at the same time reducing her allowances in food stamps. She also mentions that the state keeps collected back child support that is paid by fathers and none of the money is given back to the children. I ask you, is this concept conducive to improving their economics? Instead, our government has developed a system to keep families who are dependent on welfare wondering about their next meal. They live from paycheck to paycheck, because they have no contingency plan to obtain financial freedom from poverty. The system amputates any means of families having a better life. Let's consider that the deadbeat dad finally comes out of his comatose state of mind, and he decides to do the morally right thing. That is, he starts being responsible and supports his children in the principal state of fatherhood. Maybe their dad is earning minimum wages too, and he can only afford to give a small amount of what he earns. Should we deduct the amount from the family's total assets worth three thousand dollars? In addition, a neighbor who is a good samaritan has purchased a new living room set, and he wants to donate to the welfare recipient his used set that's valued at fifteen hundred

dollars. Now the AFDC penalizes her, and literally reduces her support, because her total net worth is more than three thousand. It is appalling to think how the United States has supported other countries with billions of dollars, such as Bosnia, to improve their economic situation, which I have seen with my own eyes, while at the same time, the government puts a choke chain on welfare recipients and deprives their families of the right to a better life.

4   Our government should not penalize the needy for their economic situation and social status. Just because they are poor, society should not have a prejudiced heart. I have seen pets receive better treatment. For example, a pet obeys a command, or does a trick; we reward them with a bone. A welfare recipient does more to improve on their economics and what is expected of them, and the government penalizes them by cutting back on their benefits, as if they were being punished by taking their bone back, and treating them like pets.

The Single Female Families
by Benjamin W. Munden, Sr.

Benjamin W. Munden, Sr., explores his own response to times when his wife was essentially a single parent while he was posted overseas with the military. The strengths of this essay lie in Munden's ability to connect the details of his own family's limited single-parent experience with the larger picture of hardships Teresa McCrary discusses in "Getting Off the Welfare Carousel." Mr. Munden points out there was an emotional toll to his long military-related absences, even though his family was not poor. In addition to the emotional toll the "second shift at home" took on his wife, Mr. Munden also offers his children's reactions to their mother's stress, and he also recognizes that in some single-parent situations, physical hardship and stress may lead to abuse. In his conclusion, Mr. Munden returns to McCrary's position that public assistance should provide opportunities for education and training, including life skills that encourage single parents to learn to better balance education and child care.

1   A single-parent family is likely to be headed by a woman. Most women who live in a single-parent family do not choose to do so. The single mother has the enormous responsibility of taking care of a child's emotional and physical well-being. The biggest problem of being a single mother is financial. I agree with Teresa McCrary's idea that it is almost impossible for a single parent to rear children with no assistance.

2   As Teresa McCrary says, "We may not have paying jobs, but any mother, married or single, working or retired, will tell you that motherhood is a career in itself" (46). I empathize with any mother who works and has the responsibility of caring for her children. For example, during my military career, my

wife and children remained in the States several times when the military transferred me to a foreign country. We thought at the time that it would enable the children to remain in the same school system. As we discussed it, I thought that remaining in the States was more beneficial for the children's education. My wife and I felt that it would also be wise for economical reasons. Meanwhile, my wife was employed full time on a job and pulled second shift at home with housework, children, and checking homework. I felt guilty about the situation for leaving her behind with the children and I couldn't help her as I wanted. In fact, I felt I was not doing my part as a spouse. Nevertheless, my guilty feeling was replaced by the justification that I was supporting my family. At times, I wondered whether it would be more beneficial if she did not work. Her salary was spent on babysitters and transportation. Adding more to the downside, she didn't spend enough quality time with the children.

3   My wife stated that the children asked her not to check their homework, because she used their papers as pillows when she fell asleep from fatigue. Her make-up was a telltale sign on their papers. She said, "The only consolation I had was the knowledge that you'd come eventually, to help with the children." She stated, "During those times, I often thought about the single mothers' plight with no help in sight." I questioned myself about the pressure and stress that single mothers undergo when the threat of utilities being disconnected presents itself. It's difficult enough caring for children alone. Add the fear of no shelter, food, or clothing, and get total disaster. Many times abuse comes into play. Teresa McCrary says, "These fears cause stress that may result in child abuse" (47). When some single mothers worry about how they are going to help their children without assistance from welfare, family, or friends, they hurt the children. They seem to use this as an outlet. Most often, help from family, friends, or welfare assistance can alleviate this. However, single mothers should not turn welfare assistance into careers. They should use these measures as a measure to get off that role into a more independent role of self-sustaining.

4   Teresa McCrary says, "I believe that we single mothers must become self-sufficient through education and training" (47). Education and training are vital elements in moving to the right direction. Through self-motivation a single mother can devise a plan or schedule to accommodate time for studying and caring for her children.

Capital Punishment

by Lois Johnson

Lois Johnson has clearly presented her analysis of Orwell's essay. She uses detailed evidence to demonstrate how Orwell "manipulates" rather than makes an argument. She presents this analysis by writing a clear thesis that indicates the areas she will discuss, providing transitions between body paragraphs, and including specific details and quotes from Orwell. The strength of her essay lies mainly in her explanations of the details and quotes she uses as support for each of her main ideas and in her concluding sentences that remind readers how her examples are related to her main ideas.

1   What does one have to do to be put on death row? Is capital punishment right or wrong? In George Orwell's narration of "A Hanging," he tells us of a prisoner being put to death in the early 1900s, in Burma. Orwell manipulates the reader against capital punishment by not telling the reader what the prisoner did to be put to death. Although Orwell doesn't present an argument, he uses the prisoner's religion, size, personality and physiological description to persuade us that capital punishment is wrong.

2   One of the things Orwell wants us to see is that the prisoner is a religious man. Orwell tells us he is "a Hindu," (48) who worships all life. The prisoner is described as having "a shaved head" with "a lock of hair" (48). He was demonstrating his religion. Even when the prisoner was about to be hanged, he cried "RAM! RAM! RAM!" (50) All he was thinking about was his god and he was calling out to him. When we think of a religious man, we have the impression that he is a good, nice man and one who tries not to do anything wrong. This is what Orwell wants us to see, that the prisoner is a religious man who is nice and friendly.

3   Another thing Orwell wants us to see about the prisoner is his personality. Orwell tells us that, when the warders were taking the prisoner to the gallows, he "stood quite unresisting, yielding his arms limply to the ropes" (48). Even though they had his arms bound to his sides, he was calm. This tells us that the prisoner is not violent, that he is peaceful and calm. When the dog came out of nowhere and was excited to see many people, he picked the prisoner out of every person there to jump on him and lick his face. That tells us the prisoner is a friendly man, because dogs are known to have a sixth sense. When we think of someone who is peaceful and calm, we think of them as nice and easygoing, even when mad. The calmness suggests that he's an OK guy. Orwell wants us to see that the prisoner was calm even when he knew he was going to die. Orwell wants us to see that the prisoner is a calm, easygoing and friendly man.

4   Orwell also wants us to take into consideration the prisoner's size. Orwell tells us that the prisoner was a "puny wisp of a man" with a "thick, sprouting mustache, absurdly too big for his body" (48). We picture somebody who's small and skinny. Orwell tells us there were "six tall Indian warders" (48) guarding the prisoner. Orwell describes the warders as being tall standing beside the prisoner, so the prisoner must also be short. Orwell wants us to see that the prisoner is short and skinny, which means that he is a small man.

5   The last thing Orwell wants us to see about the prisoner is that he is a living human being just like everybody else. Orwell says that "all the organs of his body were working—bowels digesting food, skin renewing itself, nails growing, tissues forming—all toiling away in solemn foolery" (49–50). Orwell is trying to tell us that the prisoner is alive, that all his body parts are working,

even though he is being put to death. When we think of someone whose organs are working in his body and their tissues forming, we picture someone who is alive just as we are. That is what Orwell wants us to see about the prisoner: he is alive and breathing, just like all us other humans.

6   Orwell manipulates the reader into thinking that capital punishment is wrong by using the description of the prisoner. He tells us that the prisoner is a religious man, he has a good personality, and he is short and skinny and that he is just like all other human beings. From the descriptions, we picture this man as nice and friendly. If the prisoner is all these nice things, then what could he have possibly done to be put to death? Orwell wants us to see that the prisoner was just like us and since he's just like us he shouldn't be put to death. Therefore, capital punishment is wrong.

Exposure of Public Executions

by Jane Smith

This essay discusses whether executions should be televised—a topic that has been debated in recent years. In her introduction, Jane Smith uses quotes from George Orwell's "A Hanging" to show the reader where she stands on this issue. She returns to Orwell in her last body paragraph, quoting a passage that condemns the death penalty. In the rest of her essay, Ms. Smith presents her own ideas as to why executions shouldn't be televised and strengthens them with passages from Orwell's description of an execution.

1   If public executions were televised or made admissable to the public by any means, I believe society would become so accustomed to the exposure of people murdered legally as an everyday occurrence that executions may become common enough not to affect the general public in a conscious fashion. In George Orwell's essay "A Hanging," he says, "but till that moment I had never realized what it means to destroy a healthy, conscious man" (49). Life is very precious to me, no matter what form it may be in, and to purposely take a life has to be wrong, unless in self-defense. Publicizing executions is wrong. It could give people that are watching them the idea that somehow killing someone is O.K. as long as you have a good reason. In Orwell's essay he says, "an enormous relief had come upon us now that the job was done. One felt an impulse to sing, to break into a run, to snigger. All at once everyone began chattering gayly" (51). Viewing an execution could become such a common occurrence that we might just find it easier not to feel anything as long as it doesn't take longer than our lunch hour.

2   A lot of people in the past have murdered in cold blood and felt no remorse. Soldiers have to be trained to kill the enemy soldiers. With every body count, killing becomes maybe not easier, but perhaps automatic. Television

sometimes puts crazy ideas into people. There is enough violence on television today even though most of it may be fiction. We don't need to give people in our society, especially those people that are already unstable, any reasons to think that killing is fine as long as you have a good reason. Look what Hitler did to the Jews. Who knows where he got his ideas for his executions of Jews? There are just too many unstable people in the world today. There seem to be no good reasons why we should add more exposure to killing than society is already exposed to by television, or in our homes, or streets.

3   What effect would it have on young minds to see someone being killed? Children are so vulnerable at young ages. What they see and hear sometimes may have everlasting effects on children. This public display of executions would be wrong because the very young mind might not be able to grasp the legal ethics of killing someone, whatever the reason. There are enough statistics involving children, children that are committing crimes and crimes that are committed on them, without exposing our young ones to this kind of killing, even though it is supposed to be legal.

4   The public should also take into consideration, especially if people have never witnessed someone dying, that it's not a pretty sight to see. Taking someone's life away may affect the human side of people more than we would expect. I don't believe God created people so that they could kill one another for any reason other than self-defense. There is a lot of humanity left in our society, even though people might have to remind themselves of this at times. For some people it just comes naturally to let the "human" side of them show. Orwell says, "When I saw the prisoner step aside to avoid the puddle I saw the mystery, the unspeakable wrongness, of cutting a life short when it is in full tide" (49).

5   It is not in our human nature to take a life for any other reason than survival unless there is an unbalanced side to us. Having to carry out the task of escorting someone to their death could not be a very pleasant job. Public executions should not be completely open to the public, unless you have a good reason to witness such displays.

A Cry of Grief, or a Cry of Relief?

by Marilyn Mallory

Marilyn Mallory analyzes the way that setting can reveal character and affect plot in "The Story of an Hour" in this essay. The aspect of setting she addresses is time—she shows how the time of year (spring) is related to Louise Mallard's hopes for a new life. The essay also shows how this setting becomes ironic when those hopes are not fulfilled. Note Mallory's use of detail and quotations as evidence for her points and the clear connection she makes between this material and the ideas that are supported.

1   We aren't always happy with the way we live our lives. We tend to give up our own thoughts and ideas to follow those of our families. We forget our own needs in order to do as they would want because we love them. We begin to feel a sense of imprisonment within our lives. "The Story of an Hour," by Kate Chopin, depicts a character who realizes that she does feel imprisoned by her marriage. However, her family and friends do not know of these feelings and take great care in telling Mrs. Mallard the news of her husband's death. In response to her husband's death, she retreats to her room. In the solitude of her room, Mrs. Mallard begins to feel a shocking revelation within herself. Like a new spring, Mrs. Mallard realizes her chance for the start of a new life, where she can live her own life, not for someone else.

2   In the spring, we find new formations of life: leaves budding on trees, the birds singing, and in the air the fresh smell of rain. I see spring as a new beginning, a fresh start, while others may see it as a sense or freedom or an open door. Either way, it is a time to start over. Mrs. Mallard's old life had been very protected. Chopin tells us that, due to Mrs. Mallard's heart trouble, her sister and a family friend gently break the news of her husband's death to her. Chopin explains, "It was her sister Josephine who told her, in broken sentences, veiled hints that revealed in half-concealing" (52). Josephine found it hard to tell Louise Mallard about the tragedy. She knew that her sister's heart was not strong, and that there was a high risk of heart attack from shock. After hearing the news, Mrs. Mallard begins to cry uncontrollably and withdraws alone to her room. There she sits in front of an open window, staring out at the blue sky. "She could see in the open square before her house the tops of the trees that were all aquiver with the new spring life," Chopin states (52). It's the start of spring, and with that, a feeling begins to overcome Mrs. Mallard. She tries to fight the feeling, but the signs of spring seem to make the feeling stronger: "She felt it, creeping out of the sky, reaching toward her through the sounds, the scents, the color that filled the air" (52). As I see the new spring, she saw her life, a new and fresh beginning.

3   Mrs. Mallard begins to realize that her freedom in this new life would mean that there would be no one to live for, that she would now live for herself. We all feel imprisoned sometimes in our lives, whether by our spouse or even our children. We tend to get so caught up in their lives that we can forget to live our own. Even though we may be doing it out of love, the end result is still that we feel a lack of fulfillment within ourselves. And it's that feeling of loss that can make us bitter and sometimes grudging toward the ones we love. Mrs. Mallard would grieve her husband's death. Chopin tells us, "She knew that she would weep again when she saw the kind, tender hands folded in death; the face that had never looked save with love upon her" (53). Chopin goes on to say, "And yet she had loved him—sometimes. Often she did not" (53). So Mrs. Mallard admits to herself that her husband could be kind and tender and that she has had no doubt that he loved her. At the same time, she is saying that though his intentions could be good, they were cruel nonetheless. She sometimes felt as if he were a powerful will in her life, binding her. And now . . . she can whisper to herself that she is "Free, free, free!" (53). She

will live by her own will. Although Mrs. Mallard loves her husband and will grieve his death, she now no longer feels imprisoned in that life.

4   Mrs. Mallard finally comes to grasp with her new feelings and embraces them in the new spring. Soaking in the thought of many days that would be her own, she leaves the solitude of her room and joins her sister. As they descend the stairs, her husband enters through the front door. Chopin tells us, "He had been far from the scene of the accident, and did not even know that there had been one" (53). It has all been a huge mistake; her husband is not dead—he is very much alive. At the sight of seeing her husband standing there, Mrs. Mallard's weak heart gives out. "When the doctors came they said she had died of heart disease—of joy that kills" (53), Chopin concludes. The doctors think she has died due to the fact that her heart could not take the joy of seeing her husband alive. However, in truth she dies because she has lost her new spring in a moment's time and become like the winter—dead.

5   Freedom comes in many forms, whether it is the start of something new or the end of something old. Though Mrs. Mallard loves her husband, she finds his death to be the sign of her new freedom. Mrs. Mallard dies in the end from the shock of seeing her husband alive. The true irony of it all is that only now is she truly "free, body and soul, free!" She finds her new freedom only in death.

21 Readings by Professional Writers

Family

Exploring the Theme

- What helps a family stay united? Do difficult times bring family members together, or do they tear them apart?
- How should parents shape and guide their children's behavior? What works best to help children grow into responsible adults—punishment or reward?
- How do our cultural, ethnic, or religious backgrounds support our families?
- How do institutions and bureaucracies help families? How do they cause harm to families?
- What should our society do to protect families? Should there be limits on government interference with family problems?
- What is a good parent? Who should decide?

Daddy Tucked the Blanket*

by Randall Williams

Randall Williams describes his own experiences in this essay. He later went to college on a scholarship and became a writer, but vividly recalls the problems of his earlier life. This article was first published in 1975 in The New York Times.

PREREADING QUESTIONS

1. Can you recall a house or an apartment that you lived in when you were a child? Write a brief passage describing that place and your feelings about it.

2. What to you would be the most damaging part of being poor?

1   About the time I turned 16, my folks began to wonder why I didn't stay home any more. I always had an excuse for them, but what I didn't say was that I had found my freedom and I was getting out.

2   I went through four years of high school in semirural Alabama and became active in clubs and sports; I made a lot of friends and became a regular guy, if you know what I mean. But one thing was irregular about me: I managed those four years without ever having a friend visit at my house.

3   I was ashamed of where I lived. I had been ashamed for as long as I had been conscious of class.

4   We had a big family. There were several of us sleeping in one room, but that's not so bad if you get along, and we always did. As you get older, though, it gets worse.

5   Being poor is a humiliating experience for a young person trying hard to be accepted. Even now—several years removed—it is hard to talk about. And I resent the weakness of these words to make you feel what it was really like.

6   We lived in a lot of old houses. We moved a lot because we were always looking for something just a little bit better than what we had. You have to understand that my folks worked harder than most people. My mother was always at home, but for her that was a full-time job—and no fun, either. But my father worked his head off from the time I can remember in construction and shops. It was hard, physical work.

7   I tell you this to show that we weren't shiftless. No matter how much money Daddy made, we never made much progress up the social ladder. I got out thanks to a college scholarship and because I was a little more articulate than the average.

8   I have seen my Daddy wrap copper wire through the soles of his boots to keep them together in the wintertime. He couldn't buy new boots because he had used the money for food and shoes for us. We lived like hell, but we went to school well-clothed and with a full stomach.

9   It really is hell to live in a house that was in bad shape 10 years before you moved in. And a big family puts a lot of wear and tear on a new house, too, so you can imagine how one goes downhill if it is teetering when you move in. But we lived in houses that were sweltering in summer and freezing in winter. I woke up every morning for a year and a half with plaster on my face where it had fallen out of the ceiling during the night.

10   This wasn't during the Depression; this was the late 60's and early 70's.

11   When we boys got old enough to learn trades in school, we would try to fix up the old houses we lived in. But have you ever tried to paint a wall that crumbled when the roller went across it? And bright paint emphasized the holes in the wall. You end up more frustrated than when you began, especially when you know that at best you might come up with only enough money to improve one of the six rooms in the house. And we might move out soon after, anyway.

12   The same goes for keeping a house like that clean. If you have a house full of kids and the house is deteriorating, you'll never keep it clean. Daddy used to yell at Mama about that, but she couldn't do anything. I think Daddy knew it inside, but he had to have an outlet for his rage somewhere, and at least yelling isn't as bad as hitting, which they never did to each other.

13   But you have a kitchen which has no counter space and no hot water, and you will have dirty dishes stacked up. That sounds like an excuse, but try it. You'll go mad from the sheer sense of futility. It's the same thing in a house with no closets. You can't keep clothes clean and rooms in order if they have to be stacked up with things.

14   Living in a bad house is generally worse on girls. For one thing, they traditionally help their mother with the housework. We boys could get outside and work in the field or cut wood or even play ball and forget about living conditions. The sky was still pretty.

15   But the girls got the pressure, and as they got older it became worse. Would they accept dates knowing they had to "receive" the young man in a dirty hallway with broken windows, peeling wallpaper and a cracked ceiling? You have to live it to understand it, but it creates a shame which drives the soul of a young person inward.

16   I'm thankful none of us ever blamed our parents for this, because it would have crippled our relationships. As it worked out, only the relationship between our parents was damaged. And I think the harshness which they expressed to each other was just an outlet to get rid of their anger at the trap their lives were in. It ruined their marriage because they had no one to yell at but each other. I knew other families where the kids got the abuse, but we were too much loved for that.

17   Once I was about 16 and Mama and Daddy had had a particularly violent argument about the washing machine, which had broken down. Daddy was on the back porch—that's where the only water faucet was—trying to fix it and Mama had a washtub out there washing school clothes for the next day and they were screaming at each other.

18   Later that night everyone was in bed and I heard Daddy get up from the couch where he was reading. I looked out from my bed across the hall into their room. He was standing right over Mama and she was already asleep. He pulled the blanket up and tucked it around her shoulders and just stood there and tears were dropping off his cheeks and I thought I could faintly hear them splashing against the linoleum rug.

19   Now they're divorced.

20   I had courses in college where housing was discussed, but the sociologists never put enough emphasis on the impact living in substandard housing has on a person's psyche. Especially children's.

21   Small children have a hard time understanding poverty. They want the same things children from more affluent families have. They want the same things they see advertised on television, and they don't understand why they can't have them.

22   Other children can be incredibly cruel. I was in elementary school in Georgia—and this is interesting because it is the only thing I remember about that particular school—when I was about eight or nine.

23   After Christmas vacation had ended, my teacher made each student describe all his or her Christmas presents. I became more and more uncomfortable as the privilege passed around the room toward me. Other children were reciting the names of the dolls they had been given, the kinds of bicycles and the grandeur of their games and toys. Some had lists which seemed to go on and on for hours.

24   It took me only a few seconds to tell the class that I had gotten for Christmas a belt and a pair of gloves. And then I was laughed at—because I cried—by a roomful of children and a teacher. I never forgave them, and that night I made my mother cry when I told her about it.

25   In retrospect, I am grateful for that moment, but I remember wanting to die at the time.

READING QUESTIONS

1. Why was the author ashamed of his home? What were some of the physical problems in the house he lived in? Why does the author think that the house was a bigger problem for the girls in the family than for the boys?

2. Why did his parents argue about the washing machine? When the author's father watches the mother sleeping, why does he cry? Why do you think they divorced?

3. How do the children expect other people to react to their poverty? Do other people react as the children expect them to? Why does the author say he's "grateful" for the laughter of the children in his class?

4. What is the effect of poverty on children, according to this writer? How does he suggest poverty affects family relationships?

5. Poverty can affect many parts of life: medical care, education, food, clothing, and so forth. What aspect of poverty does this essay emphasize? Why is that aspect so important?

WRITING TOPICS

1. Williams suggests that the house we live in can affect our lives in many ways. Write an essay showing how a house can cause problems or benefits for the people who live in it.

2. Williams shows how children and adolescents often judge other people by their money and possessions. Is this still true in our society? Write an essay explaining your views.

3. Williams's parents divorced, and he suggests that the problems of their housing could have been one of the causes. Can money problems cause disruption in a family? Write an essay arguing your point.

GROUP ACTIVITIES

1. This essay shows how lack of money affects people psychologically and socially. List and discuss other ways that poverty can affect people.

2. Find specific details describing the problems of the house that the Williams family lived in. Why are the details important?

RESEARCH TOPICS

1. Find information to support or refute Williams's ideas. Do poor families have more divorces?

2. Find information on problems of poverty in another part of the world. How do those problems compare with those Williams describes?

Punished for the Sins of the Children

by John Leo

John Leo has written for well-known magazines and newspapers for many years, including The New York Times *and* Time. *He was also a commissioner for the New York Environmental Protection Agency. This article was first published in 1995 in* U.S. News & World Report.

PREREADING QUESTIONS

1. Recall a time when your parents or guardians tried to control your behavior. What was the result?
2. Briefly describe a recent crime committed by teenagers or children.

1   In a burst of mostly patronizing publicity from the national media, the small town of Silverton, Oregon, and the Oregon state legislature have moved to hold parents responsible for offenses committed by their children.

2   "Both stigmatize parents with their assumption that a child's misbehavior results from a failure of parental supervision," clucked a Page 1 *New York Times* report. And the reporter for public TV's "MacNeil/Lehrer Newshour" explained that Silverton's belief that parents are responsible for children up to age 18 is "a homespun philosophy from a homespun town." (Translation: We are dealing here with a town full of rubes.)

3   What the reporter seemed to think was some sort of rural aberration is actually part of a fast-growing national trend. Hundreds of exasperated communities, large and small, are holding parents responsible for curfew violations, graffiti damage and crimes by their children. Often they impose fines or community service and sometimes require attendance at basic classes on how to parent.

4   Many changes in welfare plans also make parents responsible for their children's attendance at school, and in some public housing, a parent can be evicted if a child is found to be dealing drugs out of the family apartment.

5   In some cases, these laws are popping up in basically stable, but apprehensive, communities. By big-city standards, the level of vandalism and youth crime in Silverton seems quite low. And in the dozens of Chicago-area communities that now have parental responsibility laws, the targets seem to be illegal teen drinking parties and drunken driving. In these cases, the tactic is chiefly to embarrass well-off parents into taking charge.

6   In devastated urban areas, however, the practical and ethical problems are very different. It can look as though poor mothers are being punished for the

sins of children they can't control. Patricia Holdaway, the first parent charged under the curfew law of Roanoke, Virginia, said: "I went through so much with these kids. I'm just ready to just call it quits." Her 16-year-old son, arrested at 5 a.m. for his fifth curfew violation and for driving without a license, said, "I just left. It's not her fault. She shouldn't be held responsible. I know right from wrong."

7   Roanoke's policy is a reasonable one—it wants to work with at-risk youngsters and keep things out of court, if possible. It wants to establish the principle that parents should supervise a youngster in trouble. But in this case, the policy led to a $100 fine and a 10-day jail sentence for a woman who already agreed with the principle of parental responsibility but couldn't enforce it. She is appealing the conviction.

8   Very few parental responsibility laws allow jail terms. But given the stresses on the poor, many of them single mothers, even mandatory community service or $100 fines can be very punitive. That's why parental responsibility laws catch so many of us leaning both ways, pro and con. Are these laws attempts to reassert reasonable civic expectations about parenting, or are they desperate attempts to use the coercive force of the state to solve a cultural problem?

9   "When a culture is in free fall, as ours is, and our nonlegal institutions are falling apart, there's a temptation to move in with laws and government," said David Blankenhorn, president of the Institute for American Values. And the laws work best with parents who are already in control and merely need a wake-up call; they work poorly, or not at all, when the no-parenting ethic is ingrained or passed on from one generation to the next.

10   Still many communities are so besieged that something must be tried. It's hard to keep kids off the streets during early morning hours when gangs are roaming if parents don't cooperate. And the detachment of many parents from the fate of their young is a crucial problem—many don't even bother to go down to a police station to collect an arrested son or daughter.

11   "These laws are signs that the antibodies are starting to kick in," said Roger Conner, head of the American Alliance for Rights and Responsibilities. "But they have to be regarded as experiments. We have to find out what works, what encourages responsibility without resorting to draconian penalties." Conner thinks the Silverton ordinance is too strong—it allows a fine for a first offense, requires parental responsibility to age 18, and has been applied to cover teens caught smoking.

12   The statewide Oregon measure, which has passed the legislature and has to be signed into law by the governor, is more carefully constructed. The law covers responsibility for children up to age 15—a way of recognizing that older teens are much harder to deal with and sometimes beyond parental control. The first offense draws only a warning. The second time a parent faces mandatory attendance at a parenting class. Only after a third offense is a fine likely, and even then not if a parent can show reasonable efforts to control the child. The offense is civil, not criminal, and parents cannot be jailed.

13   With feedback from the community, these laws can be adjusted depending on results and a changing social consensus. Let the experiments continue.

READING QUESTIONS

1. What new laws does this article describe in the first paragraphs? What does the *New York Times* reporter say about those laws? Paraphrase his statement.

2. Does Leo agree with the reporters? How can you tell?

3. What similar laws does he describe next? How do these laws affect poor parents more than wealthy ones?

4. Why are such laws needed, according to Leo?

5. What are some more reasonable penalties in other communities? Why are these penalties better?

6. What is Leo's position? Does he favor or oppose laws that hold parents responsible for their children's behavior?

WRITING TOPICS

1. Is it necessary to have laws that make parents responsible for their children's behavior? Why or why not?

2. Do you believe that it is possible for a single mother to control the behavior of an older teenager? Write an essay explaining why it would or would not be possible.

3. Do you agree or disagree that some punishments are less fair to poor parents than to rich ones? Write an essay supporting your views.

GROUP ACTIVITIES

1. Leo suggests that laws are used because cultural controls, like families, neighborhoods, or communities no longer work. Is there any other way, besides laws, to help families and neighborhoods restore control over children? Brainstorm ideas.

2. Leo uses a very difficult vocabulary. Pick three difficult sentences and paraphrase them in language a young teenager could understand. Then compare your paraphrases. Which is closest to the original in meaning?

RESEARCH TOPICS

1. Conduct your own research to find ways that children and teenagers were controlled in the past.
   a. Interview members of your family or community.
   b. Look for material in the library and on the Internet comparing parental control over teenagers in the past and in the present.

2. What are the laws in your state concerning parents' responsibility for teenagers' actions?

I, Too, Am a Good Parent

by Dorsett Bennett

This essay was originally published in the "My Turn" column in Newsweek *magazine. Dorsett Bennett lives in Roswell, New Mexico, where he is an attorney. This article was first published in 1994.*

PREREADING QUESTIONS

1. Do you know families in which the father is the parent who contributes most to the children's care? Write a brief description of their abilities.
2. Why is it sometimes difficult for a father to be a good parent?

1 Divorce is a fact of modern life. A great number of people simply decide that they do not wish to stay married to their spouse. A divorce is not a tremendously difficult situation unless there are minor children born to a couple. If there are no minor children you simply divided the assets and debts. But you cannot divide a child. The child needs to be placed with the appropriate parent.

2 In my own case, my former wife chose not to remain married to me. That is her right and I do not fault her decision. My problem is that I do not believe it is her right to deny me the privilege of raising our children. Some fathers want to go to the parent/teacher conferences, school plays, carnivals, and to help their kids with homework. I have always looked forward to participating on a daily basis in my children's lives. I can no longer enjoy that privilege—the children live with their mother, who has moved to a northern Midwest state.

3 I tried so hard to gain custody of my children. I believe the evidence is uncontradicted as to what an excellent father (and more important, parent) I am. My ex-wife is a fairly good mother, but unbiased opinions unanimously agreed I was the better parent. Testimonials were videotaped from witnesses who could not attend the out-of-state custody hearing. I choose to be a father. When I was three years old, my own father left my family. While I've loved my father for many years, I did and still do reject his parental pattern.

4 A couple of centuries ago, a father and mother might have shared equally in the care and raising of children above the age of infancy. But with the coming of the Industrial Revolution the father went to work during the day, leaving the full-time care of the young to the mother, who stayed at home. It was easier to decide who should get child custody under those circumstances. That would be true today even if the mother were put into the position of working outside the home after the divorce.

5 Now, a majority of married mothers are in the workplace—often because the family needs the second income to survive. With the advent of the working mother, we have also seen a change in child care. Not only have we seen an increase in third-party caregivers, there is a decided difference in how fathers

interact with their children. Fathers are even starting to help raise their children. I admit that in a great many families there is an uneven distribution of child-care responsibilities. But there are fathers who do as much to raise the children as the mother, and there are many examples where men are full-time parents.

6   But, because we have this past history of the mother being the principal child caregiver, the mother has almost always been favored in any contested child-custody case. The law of every state is replete with decisions showing that the mother is the favored custodial parent. The changes in our lifestyles are now being reflected in our laws. In most, if not all, states, the legislature has recognized the change in child-care responsibilities and enacted legislation that is gender blind. The statutes that deal with child custody now say that the children should be placed with the parent whose care and control of the child will be in the child's best interest.

7   This legislation is enlightened and correct. Society has changed. We no longer bring up our children as we did years ago. But it is still necessary to have someone make the choice in the child's best interest if the parents are divorcing and cannot agree on who takes care of the kids. So we have judges to make that enormous decision.

8   The state legislature can pass laws that say neither parent is favored because of their gender. But it is judges who make the ultimate choice. And those judges are usually *older males* who practiced law during the time when mothers were the favored guardians under the law. These same judges mostly come from a background where mothers stayed home and were the primary caregivers. By training and by personal experience they have a strong natural bias in favor of the mother in a child-custody case. That belief is regressive and fails to acknowledge the changed realities of our present way of life. Someone must be appointed to render a decision when parents cannot agree. I would ask that those judges who make these critical decisions reexamine their attitudes and prejudices against placing children with fathers.

9   After the videotaped testimony was completed, one of my lawyers said he had "never seen a father put together a better custody case." "But," he asked me, "can you prove that she is unfit?" A father should not be placed in the position of having to prove the mother is unfit in order to gain custody. He should not have to prove that she has two heads, participates in child sacrifice or eats live snakes. The father should only have to prove that he is the more suitable parent.

10   Fathers should not be discriminated against as I was. It took me three years to get a trial on the merits in the Minnesota court. And Minnesota has a law directing its courts to give a high priority to child-custody cases. What was even worse was that the judge seemed to ignore the overwhelming weight of the evidence and granted custody to my ex-wife. At the trial, her argument was, "I am their mother." Other than that statement she hardly put on a case. Being the mother of the children was apparently deemed enough to outweigh evidence that all the witnesses who knew us both felt I was the better parent; that those witnesses who knew only me said what an excellent parent I was; that our children's behavior always improved dramatically after spending time with me; that my daughter wished to live with me, and that I had a better child-custody evaluation than my wife.

11   So I say to the trial judges who decide these cases: "Become part of the solution to this dilemma of child custody. Don't remain part of the problem." It is too late for me. If this backward way of thinking is changed, then perhaps it won't be too late for other fathers who should have custody of their children.

READING QUESTIONS

1. Why does Bennett want custody of his children?
2. Trace the changes in the history of parenting, according to Bennett. How does he think changes in women's work patterns have affected child care? How does this new legislation in many states reflect these changes?
3. If the new laws are fair to fathers, why are mothers often given custody? Who decides how the laws are applied? Do the people who make the decisions have backgrounds that would cause them to be biased? How?
4. What proof did Bennett feel he needed to produce? What evidence did his wife need to give? Why does he feel that the courts were unfair?

WRITING TOPICS

1. Can fathers ever be better parents than mothers? Write an essay illustrating your answer.
2. What are some standards for being a good parent that courts should use for determining child custody? Write an essay explaining why these are important characteristics of a parent.
3. Bennett says that "the child needs to be placed with the appropriate parent" (paragraph 1). In your opinion, what is more important: the parent's behavior in the marriage or the parent's ability to care for the child? Write an essay arguing your point of view.
4. This essay focuses on a parent's ability to care for children. Why is this so important in the case of divorce? Write an essay explaining some of the ways that divorce can affect children. *Optional:* Do research to learn about some of these effects.
5. Is it possible for divorced parents to share the custody of the children? Write an essay examining the dangers as well as the benefits of sharing custody.

GROUP ACTIVITIES

1. Act as judges in the case of Bennett versus his wife. Find the evidence supporting each one's case for custody of the children.
2. List the qualities of an ideal parent. Give an example of each.

RESEARCH TOPICS

1. Find the laws governing child custody in your state.
2. Find statistics on the percentages of single fathers in your state or in the country.

Fingers

by Margaret Visser

Margaret Visser has written extensively on the relation of culture and rituals to life. Her research into the sometimes forgotten significance of the ordinary includes The Geometry of Love: Space, Time, Mystery, and Meaning in an Ordinary Church *(2001) and* Much Depends on Dinner *(1990). She is perhaps best known for her research into eating habits across cultures. "Fingers," from* The Rituals of Dinner *(1991), offers a survey of eating habits across time and cultures and explores what it means to have good table manners.*

PREREADING QUESTIONS

1. What rules of good table manners were dominant in your home as you grew up? What was the purpose of these manners? Did the rules vary according to occasion or according to the guests present?

2. Have you ever been a dinner guest at someone else's home and felt unsure of yourself? What do you think caused this uncomfortable feeling?

1   One of the more spectacular triumphs of human "culture" over "nature" is our own determination when eating to avoid touching food with anything but metal implements. Our self-satisfaction with this marvellous instance of artificiality, however, should not lead us to assume that people who habitually eat with their hands are any less determined than we are to behave "properly"; for they too overlay "animal" instincts with manners, and indulge in both the constraints and the ornamentations which characterize polite behaviour. Forks, like handkerchiefs, look dangerously grubby objects to many people encountering them for the first time. To people who eat with their fingers, hands seem cleaner, warmer, more agile than cutlery. Hands are silent, sensitive to texture and temperature, and graceful—provided, of course, that they have been properly trained

2   Washing, as we have already remarked, tends to be ostentatious and frequent among polite eaters with their hands. Ancient Romans, like the modern Japanese, preferred to bathe all over before dinner. The etiquette of hand-washing in the Middle Ages was very strict. During the washing ritual, precedence was observed as it was in the seating of diners at the table; the bows, genuflections, and ceremonial flourishes of the ewerers or hand-washers were carefully prescribed. It was often thought disgusting, as it is in India today, to dip one's hands into the basin of water: a servant had to pour scented water *over* the hands so that it was used only once. (The modern North American preference for showers over baths is similar.) In modern Egypt, the basin is sometimes provided with a perforated cover so that the dirty water disappears at once from view. Hand-washing rules always insist that one must not splash or swish the water; be careful to leave some dry towel for a person washing next; and above all touch as little as possible between washing and beginning

to eat. If an Abbasid (ninth-century Arab) guest scratched his head or stroked his beard after washing, everyone present would wait before beginning to eat, so that he could wash again. An Abbasid, like a modern Egyptian, host would wash first, so that guests need not look as though they were anxious to start the meal; alternatively, washing was done outside, and the meal began directly after the seating, usually when the guest of honour stretched his hand to take the first morsel.

3   Desert Arabs go outside the tent, both before and after the meal, to perform ablutions by rubbing their hands with sand; they often prefer to perform this ritual before washing, even when there is plenty of water available. It is thought very rude to perform one's final washing before everyone else has finished eating; it would be the equivalent of our leaving the table while the meal is in progress. The corollary of this is that people who eat with their hands usually try to finish the meal together, since it is uncomfortable, for one thing, to sit for long when one has finished eating, holding out one greasy hand. Where family eating is done from a shared pot, there are rules about leaving some food over for the children, who eat more slowly than adults do. A great deal of attention, forethought, and control is required in order to finish a meal together, or at a moment agreed on in advance; it is a manoeuvre few of us have been trained to perform.

4   A monstrously greedy Greco-Roman banqueter is said to have accustomed his hands to grasping hot things by plunging them into hot water at the baths; he also habitually gargled with hot water, to accustom his mouth to high temperatures. He would then bribe the cook to serve the meal straight from the stove, so that he could grab as much food as possible and eat it while it was still hot—before anyone else could touch it. The story reminds us that eating food while it is hot is a habit both culture-specific and modern; a taste for it has developed in us, a taste which is dependent both on technology and on the little brothers of technology, the knife, fork, and spoon. People who eat their food with their hands usually eat it warm rather than steaming, and they grow up preferring it that way. (It is often said that one of the cultural barriers that divide "developed" from "developing" peoples is this matter of preference in the temperature at which food is eaten.) Where hot drinks are served, on the other hand (an example is the Arab coffee-drinking habit at mealtimes), people tend to like them very hot, as a contrast, and because the cups or glasses, together with the saucers under them, protect their hands.

5   Delicacy and adroitness of gesture are drummed into people who eat with their hands, from childhood. It might be considered polite, for example, to scoop food up, or it could be imperative to grasp each morsel from above. Politeness works by abjuring whole ranges of behaviour which the body could easily encompass—indeed , very often the easier movement is precisely what is out of bounds. It was once the mark of the utmost refinement in our own culture to deny oneself the use of the fourth and fifth fingers when eating: the thumb and first two fingers alone were allowed. Bones—provided they were small ones— could be taken up, but held between thumb and forefinger only. We hear of especially sophisticated people who used certain fingers only for one dish, so that they had other fingers, still unsticky and ungreasy, held in reserve for taking

food or sauce from a different platter. This form of constraint was possible only if the food was carefully prepared so that no tugging was necessary: the meat must be extremely tender, cut up, or hashed and pressed into small cakes. None but the rich and those with plenty of servants were likely to manage such delicacy; it followed that only they could be truly "refined."

6   Distancing the fourth and fifth fingers from the operation of taking food can be performed by lifting them up, elegantly curled; the constraint has forced them to serve merely as ornament. A hand used in this manner becomes a dramatic expression of the economy of politeness. When a modern tea-drinker is laughed at for holding her cup-handle in three fingers, lifting the two unused digits in the air, we think it is because we find her ridiculously pretentious. What we really mean is that she is conservative to the point that her model of social success is completely out of date, and the constraints and ornaments with which she clothes her behaviour are now inappropriate—which is another way of saying that, although she is trying very hard to be correct, she succeeds merely in being improper. Modern constraints and ornaments are, quite simply, different. We should remember that snobbery has usually delighted in scorning what is passé.

7   Left hands are very commonly disqualified from touching food at dinner. The *Li Chi* tells us that ancient Chinese children were trained from infancy never to use their left hands when eating. Ancient Greeks and Romans leaned on their left elbows when reclining at meals, effectively withdrawing their left hands from use. You *had* to lean on the left elbow even if you were left-handed: if you did not, you ruined the configuration of the party by facing the wrong way. The same problem confronted, even more vitally, an ancient Greek hoplite soldier. He formed part of a phalanx of shields, all of which had to be held on left arms so that they could overlap; fighting was done with swords grasped in the right. A shield on the right arm would have created a gap in the closed phalanx. It must have been very difficult to be left-handed in the ancient world.

8   Abbasid Arabs used to hold bread in their left hands because this was the part of the meal not shared from a common dish, and even strict modern Middle Eastern manners permit the use of the left for operations such as peeling fruits; the main thing is not to take from a communal dish with the left, and to avoid bringing the left hand to the mouth. The left hand is traditionally discouraged at table because it is the non-sacred hand, reserved for profane and polluting actions from which the right hand abstains. One example of these tasks is washing after excretion. Now it is invariably important for human beings both culturally and for health reasons to understand that food is one thing and excrement another: the fact that they are "the same thing," that is, different phases of the same process, merely makes it imperative that we should keep the distinction clear, and continually demonstrate to others that we are mindful of it.

9   Eating together is a potent expression of community. Food is sacred, and must also be pure, clean, and undefiled. It crosses the threshold of the mouth, enters, and either feeds or infects the individual who consumes it: anything presented to us as edible which is perceived as impure in any sense immediately

revolts us. Homage is paid to the purity of what we eat, and precaution taken to preserve it, in many different ways: we have already considered washing, white cloths and napkins, dish covers, poison-tastings, prayers, and paper wrappings, and we shall see many more of these. In our culture, lavatories (literally, "wash places"—only euphemisms are permissible for this particular piece of furniture) are kept discreetly closeted, either alone or in a bathroom; a "wash-room" or a "toilet" (literally, a "place where there is a towel") is nearly unthinkable without a door for shutting other people out. The lavatory bowl is covered (sometimes the cover is covered as well), usually white, wastefully water-flushed (people even like to tint this water an emphatically artificial blue), and hedged about with special paper rolls and hand-washings.

10   Our fascination when we learn that people exist who will not touch food with their left hands is rather interesting. It begins with our conviction that "civilized" people (ourselves, of course) should eat with knives and forks in the first place—that is, try not to handle food at all. We do not like the reason left hands are most often said to be banned among certain "foreigners," fastening as we do upon one reason when it is only one from a whole category of "profane" actions, because our taboo about washrooms is so strong that we cannot bear to be reminded of excretion—which we are, by the prohibition. In other words, our taboo is even stronger than theirs. Moreover, left hands have in fact an "unclean" connotation in our own culture.

11   "Right," after all, means "correct" or "okay" in English. "Sinister" originally meant "left." In French, a just man is *droit*, meaning both "right" and "straight," while *gauche* ("left") describes one who lacks social assurance, as well as dexterity and adroitness (both of which literally mean "right-handedness"). We raise right hands to take oaths and extend them to shake hands: left-handed people just have to fall in with this. In fact, left-handed people, like left-handed ancient Greeks, have always been regarded as an awkward, wayward minority, to the point where left-handed children have been forced, against their best interests, to use their right hands rather than their left. When sets of opposites (curved and straight, down and up, dark and light, cold and hot, and so forth) are set out, our own cultural system invariably makes "left" go with down, dark, round, cold—and female. Males are straight, up, light, hot—and right. Our metal eating implements free us from denying the left hand—but most of us are right-handed anyway, and knives (quintessentially "male" weapons, by the way) are held in right hands. And as we shall see, North Americans still prefer not only to cut with the right, but to bring food to their mouths with the right hand as well.

12   Eating with the help of both hands at once is very often frowned upon. The Bedouin diner is not permitted to gnaw meat from the bone: he must tear it away and into morsels using only the right hand, and not raise the hand from the dish in order to do so. Sometimes right-handed eaters confronted with a large piece of meat, a chicken, for instance, will share the task of pulling it apart, each of two guests using his right hand and exercising deft coordination; no attention should be drawn to this operation by any movement resembling a wrench or a jerk. Even on formal occasions our own manners permit us, occasionally, to use our fingers—when eating asparagus for example (this is an

early twentieth-century dispensation), or radishes, or apricots. But all of these are taken to the mouth with one hand only. We are still advised that corn kernels should be cut off the cobs in the kitchen, or that corn should, better still, be avoided altogether unless the meal is a very intimate affair. One reason why this vegetable has never become quite respectable is that corn cobs demand to be held in two hands. (More important reasons are of course that teeth come too obviously into play when eating them, and cheeks and chins are apt to get greasy.) When we chew, we should also be careful to fill only one cheek—not too full, to be sure. Two hands and two cheeks both signify indecent enthusiasm; cramming either hands or mouth is invariably rude.

13   People whose custom it is to eat with their hands make a further rule: Never take up and prepare a new morsel while you are still chewing. When left hands are allowed as well as right, it is quite dreadful to be feeding one's mouth with one hand while the other is groping in the dish for more. (We are far more lax than they on this point: we are permitted to use the knives and forks in our hands, and chew at the same time.)

READING QUESTIONS

1. Does Visser regard eating with utensils as necessarily more polite than eating with one's fingers?
2. How is cleanliness dealt with by cultures of people who eat with their fingers?
3. How does eating with one's fingers affect how a meal is served and eaten?
4. In what ways can good table manners be shown by people who eat with their fingers?
5. What observations does Visser offer about the differing roles of right and left hands in eating? In life in general?
6. What are different approaches to eating difficult or messy food such as meat on a bone or corn on the cob?

WRITING TOPICS

1. Visser's essay describes how meals can provide social connections and cultural identity. Discuss ways in which your own eating experiences with family and/or friends reflect these notions.
2. Americans eat some types of food with their hands. Identify and describe the different situations in which a meal is primarily eaten with one's hands. Are all of the situations similar to each other, or are there differences?
3. Families often eat special foods on holidays or other important occasions. Select one such occasion and discuss the significance of the preparation, serving, and eating of the meal.

GROUP ACTIVITIES

1. Compare eating habits of your classmates. When do they eat their meals? What do they usually eat? Where do they eat these meals? What

generalizations can you reach about nutrition, social, and cultural values represented by these eating habits?

2. Survey your classmates. What special meals are most important to them? Why? Is there a consensus about which meals are most important?

3. Keep a food diary for about a week. What does this diary reveal about your eating habits, both nutritionally and socially? Compare your results with your classmates. How are your habits similar? How are they different? Can your group make any generalizations about eating habits?

RESEARCH TOPICS

1. For many cultures, not eating with the left hand represents a taboo, or rule that cannot be broken. Research another culture to discover if there are other eating taboos. How strict are these taboos? What seems to be origin of the taboos? Some taboos may relate to eating particular types of food, such as pork, or preparing certain types of food together, such as meat and dairy. Others may relate to who can eat with whom.

2. Food is a part of certain religious ceremonies. Research one you are familiar with. What is the significance of food in the ritual celebration?

Where Have All the Parents Gone?

by Barbara Dafoe Whitehead

Barbara Dafoe Whitehead writes about issues involving families and children. She serves on the Massachusetts Governor's Commission on Responsible Fatherhood and Family Support and the Religion and Public Values Task Force of the National Campaign to Prevent Teen Pregnancy. She has published articles in many magazines and newspapers and is probably best known for her book The Divorce Culture *(Knopf, 1997).*

PREREADING QUESTIONS

1. Freewrite about the word *parent*. What comes to mind when you hear the word?

2. What makes a good parent? A bad parent? Which do you think is more common?

1 "Invest in kids." George Bush mused during his 1988 presidential campaign. "I like it." Apparently so do others. A growing number of corporate CEOs and educators, elected officials and child-welfare advocates have embraced the same language. "Invest in kids" is the bumper-sticker for an important new cause, aptly tagged the *kids as capital* argument. It runs as follows:

2   America's human capital comes in two forms: the active work force and the prospective work force. The bulk of tomorrow's workers are today's children, of course. So children make up much of the stockpile of America's potential human capital.

3   If we look at them as tomorrow's workers, we begin to appreciate our stake in today's children. They will determine when we can retire, how well we can live in retirement, how generous our health insurance will be, how strong our social safety net, how orderly our society. What's more, today's children will determine how successfully we compete in the global economy. They will be going head-to-head against Japanese, Korean, and West German children.

4   Unfortunately, American children aren't prepared to run the race, let alone win it. Many are illiterate, undernourished, impaired, unskilled, poor. Consider the children who started first grade in 1986: 14 percent were illegitimate; 15 percent were physically or emotionally handicapped; 15 percent spoke another language other than English; 28 percent were poor; and fully 40 percent could be expected to live in a single-parent home before they reached eighteen. Given falling birth rates, this future work force is small—all the more reason to worry about its poor quality. So "invest in kids" is not the cry of the soft-hearted altruist but the call of the hardheaded realist.

5   *Kids as capital* has caught on because it responds to a broad set of national concerns. Whether one is worried about the rise of the underclass, the decline of the family, our standing in the global economy, the nation's level of educational performance, or intergenerational conflict, *kids as capital* seems to offer an answer.

6   Further, *kids as capital* offers the rationale for a new coalition for child-welfare programs. The argument reaches beyond the community of traditional children's advocates and draws business into the child-saving fold. American corporations clearly have a stake in tomorrow's work force as they don't have in today's children. *Kids as capital* gives the toughminded, fifty-five year-old CEO a reason to "care" about the eight-year-old, Hispanic school girl.

7   Nevertheless, the argument left unchallenged could easily become yet another "feel-good" formula that doesn't work. Worse, it could end up betraying those it seeks to save—the nation's children.

8   First, *kids as capital* departs from a classic American vision of the future. Most often, our history has been popularly viewed as progressive, with each generation breaking with and improving on the past. As an immigrant nation, we have always measured our progress through the progress of our children; they have been the bearers of the dream.

9   *Kids as capital* turns this optimistic view on its head. It conjures up a picture of a dark and disorderly future. Essentially, kids as capital is dystopic—closer to the spirit of *Blade Runner* and *Black Rain* than *Wizard of Oz* or *It's a Wonderful Life*. Children, in this view, do not bear the dream. They carry the seeds of our destruction. In short, *kids as capital* plays on our fears, rather than our hopes. It holds out the vision of a troubled future in order to secure a safer and more orderly present.

10   There is something troubling, too, in such an instrumental view of children. To define them narrowly as tomorrow's wonders is to strip them of their

full status as humans, as children: Kids can't be kids; they can only be embryonic workers. And treating *kids as capital* makes it easier to measure them
solely through IQ tests, class standing, SAT scores, drop-out ratios, physical
fitness tests. This leaves no place in the society for the slow starter, the handicapped, the quirky, and the nonconforming.

11   Yet kids-as-capital has an even more serious flaw. It evades the central fact
of life for American children: They have parents.

12   As we all know, virtually every child in America grows up in a family with
one or more parents. Parents house children. Parents feed children. Parents
clothe children. Parents nurture and protect children. Parents instruct children in everything from using a fork to driving a car. To be sure, there have
been vast changes in family life, and, increasingly, parents must depend on
teachers, doctors, day-care workers, and technology to help care for and educate their children. Even so, these changes haven't altered one fundamental
fact: In American society, parents still bear the primary responsibility for the
material and spiritual welfare of children. As our teachers and counselors and
politicians keep reminding us, everything begins at home. So, if today's children are in trouble, it's because today's parents are in trouble.

13   As recently as a dozen years ago, it was the central argument of an ambi-
tious report by the Carnegie Council on Children. The Council put it plainly:
"The best way to help children tomorrow is to support parents today." Yet,
that view has been lost. The *kids as capital* argument suppresses the connection between parents and children. It imagines that we can improve the standing of children without improving the standing of the parents. In the new
rhetoric, it is hard even to find the word "parent." Increasingly, kids are portrayed as standing alone out there somewhere, cosmically parent-free.

14   As a result, *kids as capital* ignores rather than addresses one of the most
important changes in American life: the decline in the power and standing of
the nation's parents.

15   Only a generation ago, parents stood at the center of society. First of all,
there were so many of them—fully half the nation's households in 1960 were
parent households with one or more children under eighteen. Moreover, parents looked alike—Dad worked and Mom stayed at home. And parents
marched through the stages of childbearing and child rearing in virtual lock-
step: Most couples who married in the 1940s and 1950s finished having their
3.2 children by the time they were in their late twenties.

16   Their demographic dominance meant two things: First, it made for broad
common ground in child rearing. Parents could do a great deal to support
each other in raising the new generation. They could, and did, create a culture
hospitable to children. Secondly, it made for political clout. When so many
adults were parents and so many parents were part of an expanding consumer
economy, private and public interests converged. The concerns of parents—
housing, health, education—easily found their way into the national agenda.
Locally, too, parents were dominant. In some postwar suburbs like Levittown,
Pennsylvania, three-quarters of all residents were either parents or children
under ten. Not surprisingly, there was little dissent when it came to building a
new junior high or establishing a summer recreation program or installing a

new playground. What's more, parents and kids drove the consumer economy. Every time they bought a pair of sneakers or a new bike, they were acting in the nation's best interest.

17   Behind this, of course, lurked a powerful pronatal ideology. Parenthood was the definitive credential of adulthood. More than being married, more than getting a job, it was having a child that baptized you as an adult in postwar America. In survey after survey, postwar parents rated children above marriage itself as the greatest reward of private life. For a generation forced to make personal sacrifices during the Depression and the war, having children and pursuing a private life represented a new kind of freedom.

18   By the 1970s, parents no longer enjoyed so central a place in the society. To baby boom children, postwar family life seemed suffocating and narrow. Women, in particular, wanted room to breathe. The rights movements of the sixties and seventies overturned the pronatal ideology, replacing it with an ideology of choice. Adults were free to choose among many options: single, married, or divorced; career-primary or career-secondary; parent, stepparent, or child-free.

19   Thus, parenthood lost its singular status. It no longer served as the definitive credential of maturity and adult achievement. In fact, as careers and personal fulfillment beckoned, parenthood seemed just the opposite: a serious limitation on personal growth and success. As Gloria Steinem put it, "I either gave birth to someone else or I gave birth to myself."

20   As the pronatal ideology vanished, so did the close connection between private families and the public interest. Raising children was no longer viewed as a valuable contribution to the society, an activity that boosted the economy, built citizen participation, and increased the nation's confidence in the future. Instead, it became one option among many. No longer a moral imperative, child rearing was just another "lifestyle choice."

21   Viewed this way, raising children looked like an economic disaster. Starting out, parents had to shell out $3,000 for basic prenatal care and maternity costs; $3,000–$5,000 per child for day care; and $2,500 for the basic baby basket of goods and services. Crib-to-college costs for middle-class Americans could run as high as $135,000 per child. And, increasingly, the period of economic dependency for children stretched well beyond age eighteen. College tuitions and start-up subsidies for the new college graduate became part of the economic burden of parenthood. In an ad campaign, Manufacturers Hanover Trust gave prospective parents fair warning: "If you want a bundle of joy, you'll need a bundle of money."

22   Hard-pressed younger Americans responded to these new realities in several ways. Some simply chose not to have children. Others decided to have one or two, but only after they had a good job and solid prospects. Gradually, the number of parent households in the nation declined from one-half to one-third, and America faced a birth dearth.

23   For those who chose the parent option, there was only one way to face up to the new economic pressures of child rearing: work longer and harder outside the home. For all but the extremely well-off, a second income became essential. But in struggling to pay the bills, parents seemed to be short-changing

their children in another way. They weren't taking their moral responsibilities seriously enough. They weren't spending enough time with their kids. They weren't reading to the children or playing with the kids or supervising home-work. And, most important, they weren't teaching good values.

24   This emerging critique marked a dramatic change in the way society viewed parents. In the postwar period, the stereotypical parent was self-sacri-ficing, responsible, caring, attentive—an impossible standard, to be sure, but one that lent enormous popular support and approval to adults engaged in the messy and difficult work of raising children. Cruel, abusive, self-absorbed par-ents might exist, but the popular culture failed to acknowledge them. It was not until parents began to lose their central place in society that this flattering image faded. Then, quite rapidly, the dominant image of The Good Parent gave way to a new and equally powerful image—the image of The Bad Parent.

25   The shift occurred in two stages. The first-stage critique merged in the seventies and focused on an important new figure: the working mother. Work-ing mothers were destroying their children and the family, conservative crit-ics charged. They weren't feeding kids wholesome meals, they weren't taking the kids to church, they weren't serving as moral exemplars. Liberals sided with working mothers, but conceded that they were struggling with some new and difficult issues: Was day care as good as mother care? Was quality time good enough? Were the rewards of twelve-hour workdays great enough to make up for the loss of sleep and leisure-time? Where did the mother of a feverish child belong—at the crib or at her desk?

26   On the whole, the first-stage critique was a sympathetic critique. In its view, parents might be affected by stress and guilt, but they weren't yet af-flicted by serious pathology. After all, in the seventies, the nation's most sus-pect drug was laetrile, not crack or ice. Divorce was still viewed as a health al-ternative to an unhappy family life. But as the eighties began, a darker image of parents appeared. In the second-stage critique, . . . parents became toxic.

27   Day after day, throughout the eighties, Americans confronted an ugly new reality. Parents were hurting and murdering their children. Day after day, the newspapers brought yet another story of a child abandoned or battered. Day after day, the local news told of a child sexually abused by a father or a stepfa-ther or a mother's boyfriend. Week by week, the national media brought us into courtrooms where photographs of battered children were held up to the camera. The sheer volume of stories suggested an epidemic of historic propor-tion. In even the most staid publications, the news was sensational. The *New York Times* carried bizarre stories usually found only in tabloids: a father who tortured his children for years; a mother who left her baby in a suitcase in a building she then set on fire; parents who abandoned babies dead or alive, in toilets, dumpsters, and alleyways.

28   Drug use among parents was one clear cause of abuse. And, increasingly child abuse and drug abuse were linked in the most direct way possible. Pregnant women were battering their children in the womb, delivering drugs through their umbilical cords. Nightly images of crack-addicted babies in neonatal units destroyed any lingering public sympathy for mothers of the underclass. And as the highly publicized Joel Steinberg case made clear,

middle-class parents, too, took drugs and killed babies. Even those parents who occasionally indulged were causing their children harm. The Partnership for Drug-Free America ran ads asking: "With millions of parents doing drugs, is it any wonder their kids are too?"

29　　More than drugs, it was divorce that lay at the heart of middle-class parental failure. It wasn't the crackhouse but the courthouse that was the scene of their collapse. Parents engaged in bitter custody battles. Parents kidnapped their own children. Parents used children as weapons against each other or simply walked away from their responsibilities. In an important new study on the long-term effects of divorce, Judith Wallerstein challenged the earlier notion that divorce is healthy for kids. She studied middle-class families for fifteen years after divorce and came up with some startling findings: Almost half of the children in the study entered adulthood as worried, underachieving, self-deprecating, and sometimes angry young men and women; one in four experienced a severe and enduring drop in their standard of living; three in five felt rejected by at least one parent. Her study concluded: "Divorce is almost always more devastating for children than for their parents. . . . [W]hile divorce can rescue a parent from an intolerable situation, it can fail to rescue the children."

30　　As a group, today's parents have been portrayed as selfish and uncaring: Yuppie parents abandon the children to the *au pair*; working parents turn their kids over to the mall and the video arcade; single parents hang a key around their kids' necks and a list of emergency numbers on the refrigerator. Even in the healthiest families, parents fail to put their children first.

31　　The indictment of parents is pervasive. In a survey by the Carnegie Foundation, 90 percent of a national sample of public school teachers say a lack of parental support is a problem in their classrooms. Librarians gathered at a national convention to draft a new policy to deal with the problem of parents who send unattended children to the library after school. Daycare workers complain to Ann Landers that all too often parents hand over children with empty stomachs and full diapers. Everywhere, parents are flunking the most basic tests.

32　　Declining demographically, hard-pressed economically, and disarrayed politically, parents have become part of the problem. For proponents of the *kids as capital* argument, the logic is clear: Why try to help parents—an increasingly marginal and unsympathetic bunch—when you can rescue their children?

33　　To blame parents for larger social changes is nothing new. In the past, child-saving movements have depended on building a public consensus that certain parents have failed. Child reformers in the Progressive Era, for example, were able to expand the scope of public sector responsibility for the welfare of children by exploiting mainstream fears about immigrant parents and their child-rearing practices. But what is new is the sense that the majority of parents—up and down the social ladder—are failing. Even middle-class parents, once solid, dependable caretakers of the next generation, don't seem to be up to the job.

34   By leaving parents out of the picture, *kids as capital* conjures up the image of our little workers struggling against the little workers of Germany and the little workers of Japan. But this picture is obviously false. For the little workers of Germany and Japan have parents too. The difference is that their parents are strongly valued and supported by the society for their contributions *as parents*. We won't be facing up to reality until we are ready to pit our parents against their parents, and thus our family policy against theirs.

READING QUESTIONS

1. What is the "kids as capital" argument? Why is it so popular?
2. What flaws does Whitehead find in "kids as capital"?
3. What, according to Whitehead, has led to "the decline in the power and standing of the nation's parents"?
4. In what ways have parents come to be viewed as "toxic"?
5. What is Whitehead's argument in this essay? What solution does she offer?

WRITING TOPICS

1. Whitehead argues that current American society does not value or support parents "for their contributions as parents." In your experience, is this true? Why or why not?
2. Whitehead writes that "parents still bear the primary responsibility for the material and spiritual welfare of children." Yet, schools have also begun character education, conflict resolution, and antidrug campaigns. Who is bearing the primary responsibility for children's welfare?

GROUP ACTIVITY

In a small group, do a quick survey of parenting: Who has children? How many? Who has siblings? How many? At what age did the members of your group have children? At what age did the parents of members of your group have children? Do your findings match Whitehead's claims about the changes in the age of parents and the number of children they have? What explanations can you offer for your group's findings?

RESEARCH TOPICS

1. Research some of the programs provided for children through government agencies, schools, and communities. Evaluate the extent to which these programs acknowledge or ignore the role of parents in children's lives.
2. Whitehead says that there were always bad parents, but they didn't receive much attention until the loss of respect for parents in our society. Research the rates of child abuse, drug use, and other signs Whitehead mentions that may mark bad parenting. How do rates today compare to those of 20 years ago? 50 years ago?

The Struggle to Be an All-American Girl

by Elizabeth Wong

Elizabeth Wong grew up in the United States, but her family came here from China. She describes problems caused by her two cultures in this essay. This article was first published in 1980 in the Los Angeles Times.

PREREADING QUESTIONS

1. Have you ever been embarrassed by feeling different from other people?
2. Think of someone you've learned to appreciate better as you grew more mature.

1   It's still there, the Chinese school on Yale Street where my brother and I used to go. Despite the new coat of paint and the high wire fence, the school I knew ten years ago remains remarkably, stoically the same.

2   Every day at 5 P.M., instead of playing with our fourth- and fifth-grade friends or sneaking out to the empty lot to hunt ghosts and animal bones, my brother and I had to go to Chinese school. No amount of kicking, screaming, or pleading could dissuade my mother, who was solidly determined to have us learn the language of our heritage.

3   Forcibly, she walked us the seven long, hilly blocks from our home to school, depositing our defiant tearful faces before the stern principal. My only memory of him is that he swayed on his heels like a palm tree, and he always clasped his impatient twitching hands behind his back. I recognized him as a repressed maniacal child killer, and knew that if we ever saw his hands we'd be in big trouble.

4   We all sat in little chairs in an empty auditorium. The room smelled like Chinese medicine, an imported faraway mustiness. Like ancient mothballs or dirty closets. I hated that smell. I favored crisp new scents. Like the soft French perfume that my American teacher wore in public school.

5   There was a stage far to the right, flanked by an American flag and the flag of the Nationalist Republic of China, which was also red, white and blue but not as pretty.

6   Although the emphasis at the school was mainly language—speaking, reading, writing—the lessons always began with an exercise in politeness. With the entrance of the teacher, the best student would tap a bell and everyone would get up, kowtow, and chant, "Sing san ho," the phonetic for "How are you, teacher?"

7   Being ten years old, I had better things to learn than ideographs copied painstakingly in lines that ran right to left from the tip of a *moc but*, a real ink pen that had to be held in an awkward way if blotches were to be avoided. After all, I could do the multiplication tables, name the satellites of Mars, and write reports on *Little Women* and *Black Beauty*. Nancy Drew, my favorite book heroine, never spoke Chinese.

8   The language was a source of embarrassment. More times than not, I had tried to disassociate myself from the nagging loud voice that followed me wherever I wandered in the nearby American supermarket outside Chinatown. The voice belonged to my grandmother, a fragile women in her seventies who could outshout the best of the street vendors. Her humor was raunchy, her Chinese rhythmless, patternless. It was quick, it was loud, it was unbeautiful. It was not like the quiet, lilting romance of French or the gentle refinement of the American South. Chinese sounded pedestrian in public.

9   In Chinatown, the comings and goings of hundreds of Chinese on their daily tasks sounded chaotic and frenzied. I did not want to be thought of as mad, as talking gibberish. When I spoke English, people nodded at me, smiled sweetly, said encouraging words. Even the people in my culture would cluck and say that I'd do well in life. "My, doesn't she move her lips fast," they would say, meaning that I'd be able to keep up with the world outside Chinatown.

10   My brother was even more fanatical than I about speaking English. He was especially hard on my mother, criticizing her, often cruelly, for her pidgin speech—smatterings of Chinese scattered like chop suey in her conversation. "It's not 'What it is,' Mom," he'd say in exasperation. " It's 'What *is* it, what *is* it, what *is* it'!" Sometimes Mom might leave out an occasional "the" or "a," or perhaps a verb of being. He would stop her in midsentence: "Say it again, Mom. Say it right." When he tripped over his own tongue, he'd blame it on her: "See, Mom, it's all your fault. You set a bad example."

11   What infuriated my mother most was when my brother cornered her on her consonants, especially "r." My father had played a cruel joke on Mom by assigning her an American name that her tongue wouldn't allow her to say. No matter how hard she tried, "Ruth" always ended up "Luth" or "Roof."

12   After two years of writing with a *moc but* and reciting words with multiples of meanings, I finally was granted a cultural divorce. I was permitted to stop Chinese school.

13   I thought of myself as multicultural. I preferred tacos to egg rolls; I enjoyed Cinco de Mayo more than Chinese New Year.

14   At last, I was one of you; I wasn't one of them.

15   Sadly, I still am.

READING QUESTIONS

1. What was "Chinese school"? How did Wong feel about going there?
2. Was the principal really a child killer? Why does she say that she recognized him as one?
3. What was Wong proud of knowing?
4. How did she feel about the Chinese language? How did she and her brother react to their mother's way of speaking?
5. Why does she say she was "granted a cultural divorce" (paragraph 12)? How does she feel about that now?

WRITING TOPICS

1. Has there ever been a time when you wanted to be very different from the rest of your family? Write an essay comparing your experience to Elizabeth Wong's.

2. Should parents force their children to follow the ways of a culture that is different from the ones their friends follow? Write an essay supporting your opinion.

3. Wong did not want to learn about her family's culture when she was young, but now she feels sad that she is not more like her family. How can adults learn more about the cultures of their families? Write an essay explaining how a person could learn about your family's background.

GROUP ACTIVITIES

1. Elizabeth Wong is an adult writing about her feelings and behavior as a child. Find three places where she hints that as a child she misunderstood something.

2. What are the best ways for parents to help children appreciate their own culture when it is different from that of their friends?

RESEARCH TOPICS

1. Research some information on the background of your family and write an essay explaining what is most important to you.

2. Are there any cultural schools in your community? Locate one resource that would help a person learn more about one culture in your area.

Education

Exploring the Theme

▪ Why is education so important? Has the need for education changed in the last fifty years? In what ways?

▪ What motivates people to learn?

▪ Why are some students better than others? How are some teachers and schools better than others?

▪ Does our family or cultural background influence our education? Should it? Does education affect the way we relate to our friends and family?

▪ Who should make decisions about what is taught in our schools? Is going to school the only way to become educated?

A Prison Education

by Malcolm X

Malcolm X was a famous and controversial African-American leader. After his release from prison in 1949, he went on to become a great writer, speaker, and leader, first in the Nation of Islam, then in his own organization. He was assassinated in 1965. This selection is from The Autobiography of Malcolm X *(1965).*

PREREADING QUESTIONS

1. Do you remember when you first learned to read? Write a brief description of how this happened.
2. What are your reasons for needing an education?

1 It was because of my letters that I happened to stumble upon starting to acquire some kind of a homemade education.

2 I became increasingly frustrated at not being able to express what I wanted to convey in letters that I wrote, especially those to Mr. Elijah Muhammad. In the street, I had been the most articulate hustler out there—I had commanded attention when I said something. But now, trying to write simple English, I not only wasn't articulate, I wasn't even functional. How would I sound writing in slang, the way I would *say* it, something such as, "Look, daddy, let me pull your coat about a cat, Elijah Muhammad—"

3 Many who today hear me somewhere in person, or on television, or those who read something I've said, will think I went to school far beyond the eighth grade. This impression is due entirely to my prison studies.

4 It had really begun back in the Charlestown Prison, when Bimbi first made me feel envy of his stock of knowledge. Bimbi had always taken charge of any conversation he was in, and I had tried to emulate him. But every book I picked up had few sentences which didn't contain anywhere from one to nearly all of the words that might as well have been in Chinese. When I just skipped those words, of course, I really ended up with little idea of what the book said. So I had come to the Norfolk Prison Colony still going through only book-reading motions. Pretty soon, I would have quit even these motions, unless I had received the motivation that I did.

5 I saw that the best thing I could do was get hold of a dictionary—to study, to learn some words. I was lucky enough to reason also that I should try to improve my penmanship. It was sad. I couldn't even write in a straight line. It was both ideas together that moved me to request a dictionary along with some tablets and pencils from the Norfolk Prison Colony school.

6 I spent two days just riffling uncertainly through the dictionary's pages. I'd never realized so many words existed! I didn't know *which* words I needed to learn. Finally, just to start some kind of action, I began copying.

7   In my slow, painstaking, ragged handwriting, I copied into my tablet everything printed on that first page, down to the punctuation marks.

8   I believe it took me a day. Then, aloud, I read back, to myself, everything I'd written on the tablet. Over and over, aloud, to myself, I read my own handwriting.

9   I woke up the next morning, thinking about these words—immensely proud to realize that not only had I written so much at one time, but I'd written words that I never knew were in the world. Moreover, with a little effort, I also could remember what many of these words meant. I reviewed the words whose meanings I didn't remember. Funny thing, from the dictionary first page right now, that "aardvark" springs to my mind. The dictionary had a picture of it, a long-tailed, long-eared, burrowing African mammal, which lives off termites caught by sticking out its tongue as an anteater does for ants.

10   I was so fascinated that I went on—I copied the dictionary's next page. And the same experience came when I studied that. With every succeeding page, I also learned of people and places and events from history. Actually the dictionary is like a miniature encyclopedia. Finally the dictionary's A section had filled a whole tablet—and I went on into the B's. That was the way I started copying what eventually became the entire dictionary. It went a lot faster after so much practice helped me to pick up handwriting speed. Between what I wrote in my tablet, and writing letters, during the rest of my time in prison I would guess I wrote a million words.

11   I suppose it was inevitable that as my word-base broadened, I could for the first time pick up a book and read and now begin to understand what the book was saying. Anyone who has read a great deal can imagine the new world that opened. Let me tell you something: from then until I left that prison, in every free moment I had, if I was not reading in the library, I was reading on my bunk. You couldn't have gotten me out of books with a wedge. Between Mr. Muhammad's teachings, my correspondence, my visitors—usually Ella and Reginald—and my reading of books, months passed without my even thinking about being imprisoned. In fact, up to then, I never had been so truly free in my life.

12   The Norfolk Prison Colony's library was in the school building. A variety of classes was taught there by instructors who came from such places as Harvard and Boston universities. The weekly debates between inmate teams were also held in the school building. You would be astonished to know how worked up convict debaters and audiences would get over subjects like "Should Babies Be Fed Milk?"

13   Available on the prison library's shelves were books on just about every general subject. Much of the big private collection that Parkhurst had willed to the prison was still in crates and boxes in the back of the library—thousands of old books. Some of them looked ancient: covers faded, old-time parchment-looking binding. Parkhurst, I've mentioned, seemed to have been principally interested in history and religion. He had the money and the special interest to have a lot of books that you wouldn't have in general circulation. Any college library would have been lucky to get that collection.

14   As you can imagine, especially in a prison where there was heavy emphasis on rehabilitation, an inmate was smiled upon if he demonstrated an unusually intense interest in books. There was a sizable number of well-read inmates, especially the popular debaters. Some were said by many to be practically walking encyclopedias. They were almost celebrities. No university would ask any student to devour literature as I did when this new world opened up to me, of being able to read and *understand.*

15   I read more in my room than in the library itself. An inmate who was known to read a lot could check out more than the permitted maximum number of books. I preferred reading in the total isolation of my own room.

16   When I had progressed to really serious reading, every night at about ten P.M. I would be outraged with the "lights out." It always seemed to catch me right in the middle of something engrossing.

17   Fortunately, right outside my door was a corridor light that cast a glow into my room. The glow was enough to read by, once my eyes adjusted to it. So when "lights out" came, I would sit on the floor where I could continue reading in that glow.

18   At one-hour intervals the night guards paced past every room. Each time I heard the approaching footsteps, I jumped into bed and feigned sleep. And as soon as the guard passed, I got back out of bed onto the floor area of that light-glow, where I would read for another fifty-eight minutes—until the guard approached again. That went on until three or four every morning. Three or four hours of sleep a night was enough for me. Often in the years in the streets I had slept less than that.

19   Every time I catch a plane, I have with me a book that I want to read—and that's a lot of books these days. If I weren't out here every day battling the white man, I could spend the rest of my life reading, just satisfying my curiosity—because you can hardly mention anything I'm not curious about. I don't think anybody ever got more out of going to prison than I did. In fact, prison enabled me to study far more intensively than I would have if my life had gone differently and I had attended some college. I imagine that one of the biggest troubles with colleges is there are too many distractions, too much panty-raiding, fraternities, and boola-boola and all of that. Where else but in a prison could I have attacked my ignorance by being able to study intensely sometimes as much as fifteen hours a day?

READING QUESTIONS

1. How well could Malcolm X read and write when he went to prison? What motivated him to learn to read well?

2. What was the process he used to begin learning to read?

3. What was the next stage in his education? What problems did he have in continuing to educate himself in prison?

4. What does he say about prison as a place to become educated, compared to college?

5. How did his ability to read change his life?

WRITING TOPICS

1. Write an essay comparing Malcolm X's educational experience to your own.

2. Malcolm X was inspired to become educated by two people. What motivates you to become educated? Write a paper explaining your reasons for needing an education.

3. Malcolm X says that prison was probably a better place to become educated than a college. Do you agree or disagree? Write a paper supporting your argument.

4. Prison was a terrible place, but Malcolm X turned that disaster into an opportunity. Write a paper narrating a time when you turned a bad experience into a good one.

GROUP ACTIVITIES

1. In paragraphs 1–5, Malcolm X narrates some events that led to his beginning to educate himself. He tells those events out of order. As a group, make a list of the events in those paragraphs, and rearrange them in chronological order. Why did he write them out of order?

2. Have all group members discuss what motivates them to become educated. Has their motivation changed as they have gotten older?

RESEARCH TOPICS

1. Research more about the life of Malcolm X. In what ways was he a person of great moral courage?

2. Malcolm X became a Muslim. What are some beliefs of Islam?
   a. What are the Five Pillars of Islam?
   b. What was Malcolm X's Muslim name? What does "El Hajj" mean?
   c. What is the Nation of Islam? How many Americans are members of that group?

The Sanctuary of School*

by Lynda Barry

Lynda Barry is a cartoonist and writer. In "The Sanctuary of School," she reflects on her own experience in grade school in Seattle, Washington. This article was first published in the "Educational Life" section of the New York Times *in 1992.*

PREREADING QUESTIONS

1. What does sanctuary mean?
2. When you were seven, where did you feel safest? Why?
3. What is the purpose of school?
4. What role should school play in the life of a child?

1 I was 7 years old the first time I snuck out of the house in the dark. It was winter and my parents had been fighting all night. They were short on money and long on relatives who kept "temporarily" moving into our house because they had nowhere else to go.

2 My brother and I were used to giving up our bedroom. We slept on the couch, something we actually liked because it put us that much closer to the light of our lives, our television.

3 At night when everyone was asleep, we lay on our pillows watching it with the sound off. We watched Steve Allen's mouth moving. We watched Johnny Carson's mouth moving. We watched movies filled with gangsters shooting machine guns into packed rooms, dying soldiers hurling a last grenade and beautiful women crying at windows. Then the sign-off finally came and we tried to sleep.

4 The morning I snuck out, I woke up filled with a panic about needing to get to school. The sun wasn't quite up yet but my anxiety was so fierce that I just got dressed, walked quietly across the kitchen and let myself out the back door.

5 It was quiet outside. Stars were still out. Nothing moved and no one was in the street. It was as if someone had turned the sound off on the world.

6 I walked the alley, breaking thin ice over the puddles with my shoes. I didn't know why I was walking to school in the dark. I didn't think about it. All I knew was a feeling of panic, like the panic that strikes kids when they realize they are lost.

7 That feeling eased the moment I turned the corner and saw the dark outline of my school at the top of the hill. My school was made up of about 15 nondescript portable classrooms set down on a fenced concrete lot in a run-down Seattle neighborhood, but it had the most beautiful view of the Cascade Mountains. You could see them from anywhere on the playfield and you could see them from the windows of my classroom—Room 2.

8 I walked over to the monkey bars and hooked my arms around the cold metal. I stood for a long time just looking across Rainier Valley. The sky was beginning to whiten and I could hear a few birds.

9 In a perfect world my absence at home would not have gone unnoticed. I would have had two parents in a panic to locate me, instead of two parents in a panic to locate an answer to the hard question of survival during a deep financial and emotional crisis.

10 But in an overcrowded and unhappy home, it's incredibly easy for any child to slip away. The high levels of frustration, depression and anger in my house made my brother and me invisible. We were children with the sound turned off. And for us, as for the steadily increasing number of neglected children in this country, the only place where we could count on being noticed was at school.

11   "Hey there, young lady. Did you forget to go home last night?" It was Mr. Gunderson, our janitor, whom we all loved. He was nice and he was funny and he was old with white hair, thick glasses and an unbelievable number of keys. I could hear them jingling as he walked across the playfield. I felt incredibly happy to see him.

12   He let me push his wheeled garbage can between the different portables as he unlocked each room. He let me turn on the lights and raise the window shades and I saw my school slowly come to life. I saw Mrs. Holman, our school secretary, walk into the office without her orange lipstick on yet. She waved.

13   I saw the fifth-grade teacher Mr. Cunningham, walking under the breezeway eating a hard roll. He waved.

14   And I saw my teacher, Mrs. Claire LeSane, walking toward us in a red coat and calling my name in a very happy and surprised way, and suddenly my throat got tight and my eyes stung and I ran toward her crying. It was something that surprised us both.

15   It's only thinking about it now, 28 years later, that I realize I was crying from relief. I was with my teacher, and in a while I was going to sit at my desk, with my crayons and pencils and books and classmates all around me, and for the next six hours I was going to enjoy a thoroughly secure, warm and stable world. It was a world I absolutely relied on. Without it, I don't know where I would have gone that morning.

16   Mrs. LeSane asked me what was wrong and when I said "Nothing," she seemingly left it at that. But she asked me if I would carry her purse for her, an honor above all honors, and she asked if I wanted to come into Room 2 early and paint.

17   She believed in the natural healing power of painting and drawing for troubled children. In the back of her room there was always a drawing table and an easel with plenty of supplies, and sometimes during the day she would come up to you for what seemed like no good reason and quietly ask if you wanted to go to the back table and "make some pictures for Mrs. LeSane." We all had a chance at it—to sit apart from the class for a while to paint, draw and silently work out impossible problems on 11 × 17 sheets of newsprint.

18   Drawing came to mean everything to me. At the back table in Room 2, I learned to build myself a life preserver that I could carry into my home.

19   We all know that a good education system saves lives, but the people of this country are still told that cutting the budget for public schools is necessary, that poor salaries for teachers are all we can manage and that art, music and all creative activities must be the first to go when times are lean.

20   Before- and after-school programs are cut and we are told that public schools are not made for baby-sitting children. If parents are neglectful temporarily or permanently, for whatever reason, it's certainly sad, but their unlucky children must fend for themselves. Or slip through the cracks. Or wander in a dark night alone.

21   We are told in a thousand ways that not only are public schools not important, but that the children who attend them, the children who need them most, are not important either. We leave them to learn from the blind eye of a

television, or to the mercy of "a thousand points of light"* that can be as far away as stars.

22   I was lucky. I had Mrs. LeSane. I had Mr. Gunderson. I had an abundance of art supplies. And I had a particular brand of neglect in my home that allowed me to slip away and get to them. But what about the rest of the kids who weren't as lucky? What happened to them?

23   By the time the bell rang that morning I had finished my drawing and Mrs. LeSane pinned it up on the special bulletin board she reserved for drawings from the back table. It was the same picture I always drew—a sun in the corner of a blue sky over a nice house with flowers all around it.

24   Mrs. LeSane asked us to please stand, face the flag, place our right hands over our hearts and say the Pledge of Allegiance. Children across the country do it faithfully. I wonder now when the country will face its children and say a pledge right back.

READING QUESTIONS

1. Why did Barry sneak out of the house?
2. Why does Barry discuss her and her brother's watching television? What is the relationship between her feelings about television and school?
3. Paraphrase paragraphs 9 and 10.
4. Why does Barry describe all those who spoke to her? What effect does this have on a reader?
5. What discovery does Barry make while writing about the morning at school?
6. What role did art play for Barry when she was a child? What role does art play in her adult life?
7. What does Barry mean when she says "I learned to build myself a life preserver that I could carry into my home" (paragraph 18)?
8. Why is Barry telling the story of her experience at school? What does she want the reader to do or to think after reading her story of her grade school?
9. Why does Barry refer to the Pledge of Allegiance in her concluding paragraph?

WRITING TOPICS

1. Describe a place that you thought of as a sanctuary when you were a child.
2. Barry points out that school is often a substitute home for some and that society should recognize and financially support this role. Do you agree? Why or why not?
3. Do you think art, band, and other creative activities should be part of the school curriculum and supported by public funds? Why or why not?

---

*"A thousand points of light" is a phrase from President George Bush's State of the Union Address.

GROUP ACTIVITIES

1. Identify the places where Barry is narrating the story of her morning at school when she was seven and the places where she is commenting on those events as an adult.

2. Work as a group to conduct research on the school schedule and budget in Research Topic 1.

3. Working as a group, make a list of all the purposes—official and unofficial—of school.

RESEARCH TOPICS

1. Conduct research to determine if the local school provides time and supplies for creative activities, such as music, art, and band. What percent of the time and budget goes to the personnel and supplies for these activities? What academic subjects are taught? How much time is given to each? What other kinds of activities such as PE, sports, clubs, and so on does the school support financially and by allotting students the time to participate? Using your findings, write a letter to the school board asking for more money and support for a particular activity you think is important but not adequately supported. (Or you can write asking for a decrease in funding and support for an activity you think is less important.)

2. Conduct research to determine if public funding for schools has changed in the last five years. How much of this money reaches the classroom? What is the dollar amount spent per student in the state or in the school district? How does this compare to other states or school districts? Write a report in which you provide the results of your research.

Lives on the Boundary*

by Mike Rose

This reading is an excerpt from Rose's Lives on the Boundary: The Struggles and Achievements of America's Underprepared. *In this excerpt, he discusses how his life was different when he was placed in the college prep track and talks about a teacher he met then. Rose went on to become a university teacher and researcher who studies how students learn to write, especially students who, like him, were not originally planning to go to college. His books, including* Possible Lives: The

Reprinted with the permission of The Free Press, an imprint of Simon & Schuster Adult Publishing Group, from Lives on the Boundary: The Struggles and Achievements of America's Underprepared by Mike Rose. Copyright © 1989 by Mike Rose.

Promise of Public Education *(Penguin, 1999), have inspired many writing teachers to find new ways to work with their students.*

PREREADING QUESTIONS

1. When you were in middle school and high school, what did you expect your own future would be like? Did school seem likely to help you reach that future?

2. Recall your high school teachers. Who were the ones who really made a difference in their students' lives? Who were the ones who didn't seem to care much for students? How were their students affected by the teachers' feelings about them?

1 Students will float to the mark you set. I and the others in the vocational classes were bobbing in pretty shallow water. Vocational education has aimed at increasing the economic opportunities of students who do not do well in our schools. Some serious programs succeed in doing that, and through exceptional teachers—like Mr. Gross in *Horace's Compromise*—students learn to develop hypotheses and troubleshoot, reason through a problem, and communicate effectively—the true job skills. The vocational track, however, is most often a place for those who are just not making it, a dumping ground for the disaffected. There were a few teachers who worked hard at education; young Brother Slattery, for example, combined a stern voice with weekly quizzes to try to pass along to us a skeletal outline of world history. But mostly the teachers had no idea of how to engage the imagination of us kids who were scuttling along at the bottom of the pond.

2   And the teachers would have needed some inventiveness, for none of us was groomed for the classroom. It wasn't just that I didn't know things—didn't know how to simplify algebraic fractions, couldn't identify different kinds of clauses, bungled Spanish translations—but that I had developed various faulty and inadequate ways of doing algebra and making sense of Spanish. Worse yet, the years of defensive tuning out in elementary school had given me a way to escape quickly while seeming at least half alert. During my time in Voc. Ed., I developed further into a mediocre student and a somnambulant problem solver, and that affected the subjects I did have the wherewithal to handle; I detested Shakespeare; I got bored with history. My attention flitted here and there. I fooled around in class and read my books indifferently—the intellectual equivalent of playing with your food. I did what I had to do to get by, and I did it with half a mind. . . .

3   My own deliverance from the Voc. Ed. world began with sophomore biology. Every student, college prep to vocational, had to take biology, and unlike the other courses, the same person taught all sections. When teaching the vocational group, Brother Clint probably slowed down a bit or omitted a little of the fundamental biochemistry, but he used the same book and more or less the same syllabus across the board. If one class got tough, he could get tougher. He was young and powerful and very handsome, and looks and physical strength were high currency. No one gave him any trouble.

4 I was pretty bad at the dissecting table but the lectures and the textbook were interesting; plastic overlays, that, with each turned page, peeled away skin, then veins and muscle, then organs down to the very bones that Brother Clint, pointer in hand, would tap out on our hanging skeleton. Dave Snyder was in big trouble for the study of life—versus the living of it—was sticking in his craw. He worked out a code for our multiple-choice exams. He'd poke me in the back, once for the answer under A, twice for B, and so on; and when he'd hit the right one, I'd look up to the ceiling as though I were lost in thought. Poke: cytoplasm. Poke, poke: methane. Poke, poke, poke: William Harvey. Poke, poke, poke, poke: islets of Langerhans. This didn't work out perfectly, but Dave passed the course, and I mastered the dreamy look of a guy on a record jacket. And something else happened. Brother Clint puzzled over this Voc. Ed. kid who was racking up 80s and 90s on his tests. He checked the school's records and discovered the error. He recommended that I begin my junior year in the College Prep program. According to all I've read since, such a shift, as one report put it, is virtually impossible. Kids of that level rarely cross tracks. The telling thing is how chancy both my placement into and exit from Voc. Ed. was; neither I nor my parents had anything to do with it. I lived in one world during spring semester, and when I came back to school in the fall, I was living in another. . . .

5 Switching to College Prep was a mixed blessing. I was an erratic student. I was undisciplined. And I hadn't caught on to the rules of the game: why work hard in a class that didn't grab my fancy? I was also hopelessly behind in math. Chemistry was hard; toying with my chemistry set years before hadn't prepared me for the chemist's equations. Fortunately, the priest who taught both chemistry and second-year algebra was also the school's athletic director. Membership in the track team covered me; I knew I wouldn't get lower than a C. U.S. history was taught pretty well, and I did okay. But civics was taken over by a football coach who had trouble reading the textbook aloud—and reading aloud was certainly an improvement over the vocational program—at least it carried some status—but the social science curriculum was weak, and the mathematics and physical sciences were simply beyond me. I had a miserable quantitative background and ended up copying some assignments and finessing the rest as best I could.

6 Let me try to explain how it feels to see again and again material you should once have learned but didn't.

7 You are given a problem. It requires you to simplify algebraic equations or to multiply expressions containing square roots. You know this is pretty basic material because you've seen it for years. Once a teacher took some time with you, and you learned how to carry out these operations. Simple versions, anyway. But that was a year or two or more in the past; and these are more complex versions, and now you're not sure. And this, you keep telling yourself, is ninth- or even eighth-grade stuff.

8 Next it's a word problem. This is also old hat. The basic elements are as familiar as story characters; trains speeding so many miles per hour or shadows of buildings angling so many degrees. Maybe you know enough, have sat through enough explanations, to be able to begin setting up the problem: "If one train is going this fast . . ." or "This shadow is really one line of a trian-

gle. . . ." Then: "Let's see . . ." "How did Jones do this?" "Hmmmm." "No." "No, that won't work." Your attention wavers. You wonder about other things: a football game, a dance, that cute new checker at the market. You try to focus on the problem again. You scribble on paper for a while, but the tension wins out and your attention flits elsewhere. You crumple the paper and begin daydreaming to ease the frustration.

READING QUESTIONS

1. What does this sentence mean: "Students will float to the mark you set"? How does that happen in Mike Rose's life?

2. What is the "vocational track"? What should it be like? What kind of student was placed in that track in the school Rose describes?

3. What expectations did the school have for the students in the vocational track? How did Rose react to those expectations?

4. What kind of teacher was Brother Clint? How does he treat the students from the vocational classes?

5. How did Rose help Dave Snyder with the questions in the biology class? What did Brother Clint discover about Rose's real abilities?

6. What problems does Rose encounter when he is moved into college prep classes? Why does he have those problems?

7. What does this reading show about the ways that schools can affect the students who attend them? What future does a student like Rose have?

WRITING TOPICS

1. Write an essay explaining what a vocational track is and what it should demand of the students enrolled in it.

2. "Students will float to the mark [teachers] set." Write an essay agreeing or disagreeing with this statement. Use your own observations and experiences as well as Rose's essay to support your points.

GROUP ACTIVITIES

1. Assume that your group is a school board. Based on the information in Rose's essay, decide what should be done to improve high school education for students like Mike Rose.

2. Each member of the group should select one paragraph in Rose's essay. Determine the main idea of the paragraph, and then underline or make note of details used to support this idea. Compare results with the group, and discuss how the essay would be changed if the details had not been included.

RESEARCH TOPICS

1. What is vocational education? Use your library to find out the different ways that high schools teach work skills.

2. Use the Internet, local newspapers, or interviews to find out as much as you can about what vocational subjects are taught in the schools in your community.

Thinking in Pictures
by Temple Grandin

Dr. Temple Grandin holds a Ph.D. in animal science from the University of Illinois. She teaches and does research in livestock behavior at Colorado State University and consults for the livestock industry in facility design, livestock handling, and animal welfare. Dr. Grandin has also written widely about her experiences growing up as an autistic child. This selection from her autobiography Thinking in Pictures: And Other Reports from My Life with Autism *explains how difficult it is for even highly verbal autistic children to learn to read and understand words with abstract concepts such as "peace" and "trespassing." Her essay not only explains part of the isolation faced by autistics but also reminds us that language and literacy are complex systems that many take for granted.*

PREREADING QUESTIONS

1. What is autism?
2. Think about idiomatic expressions such as "a piece of cake" or to be "all tied up." What do the words mean literally? What do the expressions usually mean in ordinary communication? What other figurative expressions can you think of where the meaning of the expression does not add up exactly to the combined meanings of the parts?

Processing Nonvisual Information

1 Autistics have problems learning things that cannot be thought about in pictures. The easiest words for an autistic child to learn are nouns, because they directly relate to pictures. Highly verbal autistic children like I was can sometimes learn how to read with phonics. Written words were too abstract for me to remember, but I could laboriously remember the approximately fifty phonetic sounds and a few rules. Lower-functioning children often learn better by association, with the aid of word labels attached to objects in their environment. Some very impaired autistic children learn more easily if words are spelled out with plastic letters they can feel.

2 Spatial words such as "over" and "under" had no meaning for me until I had a visual image to fix them in my memory. Even now, when I hear the

word "under" by itself, I automatically picture myself getting under the cafeteria tables at school during an air-raid drill, a common occurrence on the East Coast during the early fifties. The first memory that any single word triggers is almost always a childhood memory. I can remember the teacher telling us to be quiet and walking single-file into the cafeteria, where six or eight children huddled under each table. If I continue on the same train of thought, more and more associative memories of elementary school emerge. I can remember the teacher scolding me after I hit Alfred for putting dirt on my shoe. All of these memories play like video-tapes in the VCR in my imagination. If I allow my mind to keep associating, it will wander a million miles away from the word "under," to submarines under the Antarctic and the Beatles song "Yellow Submarine." If I let my mind pause on the picture of the yellow submarine, I then hear the song. As I start humming the song and get to the part about people coming on board, my association switches to the gangway of a ship I saw in Australia.

3   I also visualize verbs. The word "jumping" triggers a memory of jumping hurdles at the mock Olympics held at my elementary school. Adverbs often trigger inappropriate images—"quickly" reminds me of Nestle's Quik—unless they are paired with a verb, which modifies my visual image. For example, "he ran quickly" triggers an animated image of Dick from the first-grade reading book running fast, and "he walked slowly" slows the image down. As a child, I left out words such as "is," "the," and "it," because they had no meaning by themselves. Similarly, words like "of" and "an" made no sense. Eventually I learned how to use them properly, because my parents always spoke correct English and I mimicked their speech patterns. To this day certain verb conjugations, such as "to be," are absolutely meaningless to me.

4   When I read, I translate written words into color movies or I simply store a photo of the written page to be read later. When I retrieve the material, I see a photocopy of the page in my imagination. I can then read it like a TelePrompTer. It is likely that Raymond, the autistic savant depicted in the movie *Rainman*, used a similar strategy to memorize telephone books, maps, and other information. He simply photocopied each page of the phone book into his memory. When he wanted to find a certain number, he just scanned pages of the phone book that were in his mind. To pull information out of my memory, I have to replay the video. Pulling facts up quickly is sometimes difficult, because I have to play bits of different videos until I find the right tape. This takes time.

5   When I am unable to convert text to pictures, it is usually because the text has no concrete meaning. Some philosophy books and articles about the cattle futures market are simply incomprehensible. It is much easier for me to understand written text that describes something that can be easily translated into pictures. The following sentence from a story in the February 21, 1994, issue of *Time* magazine, describing the Winter Olympics figure-skating championships, is a good example: "All the elements are in place—the spotlights, the swelling waltzes and jazz tunes, the sequined sprites taking to the air." In my imagination I see the skating rink and skaters. However, if I ponder too

long on the word "elements," I will make the inappropriate association of a periodic table on the wall of my high school chemistry classroom. Pausing on the word "sprite" triggers an image of a Sprite can in my refrigerator instead of a pretty young skater.

6   Teachers who work with autistic children need to understand associative thought patterns. An autistic child will often use a word in an inappropriate manner. Sometimes these uses have a logical associative meaning and other times they don't. For example, an autistic child might say the word "dog" when he wants to go outside. The word "dog" is associated with going outside. In my own case, I can remember both logical and illogical use of inappropriate words. When I was six, I learned to say "prosecution." I had absolutely no idea what it meant, but it sounded nice when I said it, so I used it as an exclamation every time my kite hit the ground. I must have baffled more than a few people who heard me exclaim "Prosecution!" to my downward-spiraling kit.

7   Discussions with other autistic people reveal similar visual styles of thinking about tasks that most people do sequentially. An autistic man who composes music told me that he makes "sound pictures" using small pieces of other music to create new compositions. A computer programmer with autism told me that he sees the general pattern of the program tree. After he visualizes the skeleton for the program, he simply writes the code for each branch. I use similar methods when I review scientific literature and troubleshoot at meat plants. I take specific findings or observations and combine them to find new basic principles and general concepts.

8   My thinking pattern always starts with specifics and works toward generalization in an associational and nonsequential way. As if I were attempting to figure out what the picture on a jigsaw puzzle is when only one third of the puzzle is completed, I am able to fill in the missing pieces by scanning my video library. Chinese mathematicians who can make large calculations in their heads work the same way. At first they need an abacus, the Chinese calculator, which consists of rows of beads on wires in a frame. They make calculations by moving the rows of beads. When a mathematician becomes really skilled, he simply visualizes the abacus in his imagination and no longer needs a real one. The beads move on a visualized video abacus in his brain.

Abstract Thought

9   Growing up, I learned to convert abstract ideas into pictures as a way to understand them. I visualized concepts such as peace or honesty with symbolic images. I thought of peace as a dove, an Indian peace pipe, or TV or newsreel footage of the signing of a peace agreement. Honesty was represented by an image of placing one's hand on the Bible in court. A news report describing a person returning a wallet with all the money in it provided a picture of honest behavior.

10   The Lord's Prayer was incomprehensible until I broke it down into specific visual images. The power and the glory were represented by a semicircu-

lar rainbow and an electrical tower. These childhood visual images are still triggered every time I hear the Lord's Prayer. The words "thy will be done" had no meaning when I was a child, and today the meaning is still vague. Will is a hard concept to visualize. When I think about it, I imagine God throwing a lightning bolt. Another adult with autism wrote that he visualized "Thou art in heaven" as God with an easel above the clouds. "Trespassing" was pictured as black and orange no trespassing signs. The word "Amen" at the end of the prayer was a mystery: a man at the end made no sense.

11   As a teenager and young adult I had to use concrete symbols to understand abstract concepts such as getting along with people and moving on to the next steps of my life, both of which were always difficult. I knew I did not fit in with my high school peers, and I was unable to figure out what I was doing wrong. No matter how hard I tried, they made fun of me. They called me "workhorse," "tape recorder," and "bones" because I was skinny. At the time I was able to figure out why they called me "workhorse" and "bones," but "tape recorder" puzzled me. Now I realize that I must have sounded like a tape recorder when I repeated things verbatim over and over. But back then I just could not figure out why I was such a social dud. I sought refuge in doing things I was good at, such as working on reroofing the barn or practicing my riding prior to a horse show. Personal relationships made absolutely no sense to me until I developed visual symbols of doors and windows. It was then that I started to understand concepts such as learning the give-and-take of a relationship. I still wonder what would have happened to me if I had not been able to visualize my way in the world.

READING QUESTIONS

1. Why were words like "of," "an," and "be" more difficult for Grandin to learn than "under" and "jumping"?

2. How do associations from memory and pictures of what words refer to help Grandin understand their meanings?

3. Young people change a great deal during their high school years and often find this period of their lives confusing and challenging. Why was high school particularly difficult for Grandin? When did the concept of personal relationships begin to make sense to her?

WRITING TOPICS

1. Grandin's essay discusses some of the obstacles she faced in learning to communicate verbally. In what ways is her essay of interest to teachers and other educators? Try to illustrate your discussion with specific examples, real or hypothetical.

2. Have you ever tried to learn another language? If so, compare your experiences with Grandin's experiences as an autistic learner. Do you find any similarities?

3. Companies often name products because consumers already know one meaning of a word and this first meaning becomes associated

with the product. Look at some of the connections suggested by common products. What is the history of the product name (its etymology)? What types of associations do the companies want consumers to develop?

GROUP ACTIVITIES

1. Find a passage from a work of literature that you like. Analyze it to see how much of its meaning is literal and/or concrete and how much is based on either abstractions or comparisons and associations. Compare your results with classmates.
2. Make a list of words that you found difficult to understand as a child. Can you identify why you found them difficult? Compare your list of words with your classmates' lists.
3. Watch the film *Rainman*. What makes the behavior of Raymond, Dustin Hoffman's character, unusual?

RESEARCH TOPICS

1. Look up autism. Is it a single condition, or is it a more complex condition? Summarize your findings.
2. Find out more about Dr. Grandin's accomplishments. Use an electronic database such as Infotrac or Lexis-Nexis to investigate the connection between autism and her profession. Summarize your findings.
3. Linguists speak of the process of language acquisition. Look up the theories that have been proposed for child language acquisition. How well does Grandin's experience fit these models? What is similar and what is different?

How Good Are Your Opinions?*

by Vincent Ryan Ruggiero

Vincent Ryan Ruggiero is a professor emeritus at State University of New York at Delhi. He has written numerous books on critical thinking, philosophy, and the humanities, including textbooks designed to help students become critical thinkers and learners. The following is an excerpt from his textbook Beyond Feelings: A Guide to Critical Thinking *(McGraw-Hill, 2000).*

PREREADING QUESTIONS

1. Define the word *opinion*.
2. What is critical thinking?
3. Do you base your actions primarily on your opinions or on critical thinking?

1 "Opinion" is a word that is often used carelessly today. It is used to refer to matters of taste, belief, and judgment. This casual use would probably cause little confusion if people didn't attach too much importance to opinion. Unfortunately, most do attach great importance to it. "I have as much right to my opinion as you to yours," and "Everyone's entitled to his or her opinion," are common expressions. In fact, anyone who would challenge another's opinion is likely to be branded intolerant.

2 Is that label accurate? Is it intolerant to challenge another's opinion? It depends on what definition of opinion you have in mind. For example, you may ask a friend "What do you think of the new Buicks?" And he may reply, "In my opinion, they're ugly." In this case, it would not only be intolerant to challenge his statement, but foolish. For it's obvious that by opinion he means his *personal preference*, a matter of taste. And as the old saying goes, "It's pointless to argue about matters of taste."

3 However, consider this very different use of the term. A newspaper reports that the Supreme Court has delivered its opinion in a controversial case. Obviously the justices did not state their personal preferences, their mere likes and dislikes. They stated their *considered judgment*, painstakingly arrived at after thorough inquiry and deliberation.

4 Most of what is referred to as opinion falls somewhere between these two extremes. It is not an expression of taste. Nor is it careful judgment. Yet it may contain elements of both. It is a view or belief more or less casually arrived at, with or without examination of the evidence.

5 Is everyone entitled to his or her opinion? In a free country this is not only permitted, but guaranteed. In Great Britain, for example, there is still a Flat Earth Society. As the name implies, the members of this organization believe that the earth is not spherical, but flat. In this country, too, each of us is free to take as bizarre a position as we please about any matter we choose. When the telephone operator announces "That'll be 95 cents for the first three minutes," you may respond, "No it won't—it'll be 28 cents." When the service station attendant notifies you "Your oil is down a quart," you may reply "Wrong—it's up three."

6 Being free to hold an opinion and express it does not, of course, guarantee favorable consequences. The operator may hang up on you. The service station attendant may threaten you with violence.

7 *Acting* on our opinions carries even less assurance. Consider the case of the California couple who took their eleven-year-old diabetic son to a faith

healer. Secure in their opinion that the man had cured the boy, they threw away his insulin. Three days later the boy died. They remained unshaken in their belief, expressing the opinion that God would raise the boy from the dead. The police arrested them, charging them with manslaughter. The law in such matters is both clear and reasonable. We are free to act on our opinions only so long as, in doing so, we do not harm others.

Opinions Can Be Mistaken

8 It is tempting to conclude that, if we are free to believe something, it must have some validity. That, however, is not the case. Free societies are based on the wise observation that people have an inalienable right to think their own thoughts and make their own choices. But this fact in no way suggests that the thoughts they think and the choices they make will be reasonable.

9   Evidence that opinions can be mistaken is all around us. The weekend drinker often has the opinion that as long as he doesn't drink during the week, he is not an alcoholic. The person who continues driving with the oil light flashing on the dashboard may have the opinion that the problem being signaled can wait until next month's service appointment. The student who quits school at age sixteen may have the opinion that an early entry into the job market ultimately improves job security. Yet however deeply and sincerely such opinions are held, they are wrong.

10   Research shows that people can be mistaken even when they are making a special effort to judge objectively. Sometimes their errors are caused by considerations so subtle they are unaware of them. For example, before Taster's Choice coffee was introduced, it was tested and sampled with three different labels—brown, yellow, and red. People who sampled the coffee in the container with the brown label reported that it was too strong and kept them awake at night. People who sampled the yellow-labeled coffee found it weak and watery. Those who samples the red-labeled coffee judged it just the right strength and delicious. All this even though the coffee in all jars was exactly the same. *The people had been unconsciously influenced by the color of the label!*

Even Experts Can Be Wrong

11 History records numerous occasions when the expert opinion has been the wrong opinion. In ancient times the standard medical opinion was that headaches were caused by demons in the skull. The accepted treatment ranged from opening the skull to let the demons out to giving medicines derived from cow's brain and goat dung. (The American Indians preferred beaver testicles.)

12   When the idea of inoculating people against such diseases as smallpox first arrived in the colonies in the early 1700s, most authorities regarded it as nonsense. Among them were Benjamin Franklin and a number of the men who later founded Harvard Medical School. Against the authorities stood a relatively unknown man who didn't even have a medical degree, Zabdiel Boylston. Whose opinion was proved right? Not the experts' but Zabdiel Boylston's.

13   In 1890 a Nobel prize-winning bacteriologist, Dr. Robert Koch, reported that he had found a substance that would cure tuberculosis. When it was injected into patients, though, it was found to cause further illness and even death.

14   In 1904 psychologist G. Stanley Hall expressed his professional opinion that when women engage in strenuous mental activity, particularly with men, they experience a loss of mammary function and interest in motherhood, as well as decreased fertility. If they subsequently have children, the children will tend to be sickly.

15   Between 1919 and 1922 the Metropolitan Museum of Art in New York City bought seventeen gold vessels that experts determined were authentic treasures from a 3,500-year-old Egyptian tomb. In 1982 they were discovered to be twentieth-century fakes.

16   In 1928 a drug called thorotrost was developed and used to outline certain organs of the body so that clearer X rays could be taken. Nineteen years later, doctors learned that even small doses of the drug caused cancer.

17   In 1959 a sedative called thalidomide was placed on the market. Many physicians prescribed it for pregnant women. Then, when a large number of babies were born deformed, medical authorities realized that thalidomide was to blame. . . .

Kinds of Error

18 There are four general kinds of error that can corrupt anyone's opinions. Francis Bacon classified them as follows: (1) errors or tendencies to error common among all people by virtue of their being human; (2) errors that come from human communication and the limitations of language; (3) errors in the general fashion or attitude of an age; (4) errors posed to an individual by a particular situation.

19   Some people, of course, are more prone to errors than others. John Locke observed that these people fall into three groups. He described them as follows:

> Those who seldom reason at all, but do and think as those around them do—parents, neighbors, the clergy, or anyone else they admire and respect. Such people want to avoid the difficulty that accompanies thinking for themselves.
>
> Those who are determined to let passion rather than reason govern their lives. Those people are influenced only by reasoning that supports their prejudices.
>
> Those who sincerely follow reason, but lack sound, overall good sense, and so do not look at all sides of an issue. They tend to talk with one type of person, read one type of book, and so are exposed to only one viewpoint.

20   To Locke's list we should add one more type—people who never bother to reexamine an opinion once it has been formed. These people are often the most error-prone of all, for they forfeit all opportunity to correct mistaken opinions when new evidence arises.

Informed vs. Uninformed Opinion

21 If experts can, like the rest of us, be wrong, why are their views more highly valued than the views of nonexperts? Many people wonder about this, and conclude that it is a waste of time to consult the experts. Let's look at some situations and see if this conclusion is reasonable.

22   What are the effects of hashish on those who smoke it? We could ask a person who never saw or smelled it, let alone smoked it. It would, of course, make better sense to get the opinion of a smoker or to take a poll of a large number of smokers. Better still would be the opinion of one or more *trained* observers, research scientists who have conducted studies of the effects of hashish smoking. (At least one such group, a team of army doctors, has found that heavy use of hashish leads to severe lung damage. Also, if the smoker is predisposed to schizophrenia, it can cause long-lasting episodes of that disorder.) . . .

23   Can a whale communicate with another whale? If so, how far can he transmit his message? Would our auto mechanic have an opinion on that matter? Perhaps. And so might our grocer, dentist, banker. But no matter how intelligent these people are, chances are their opinions about whales are not very well informed. The people whose opinions would be valuable would be those who have done some research with whales. (They would tell us that the humpback whales can make a variety of sounds. In addition to clicking noises, they make creaking and banging and squeaking noises. They've been found to make these sounds for as long as several minutes at a time, at an intensity of 100 to 110 decibels, and for a distance of 25,000 miles.)

24   Similar examples could be cited from every field of knowledge: from antique collecting to ethics, from art to criminology. All would support the same view: that by examining the opinions of informed people before making up our minds, we broaden our perspective, see details we might not see by ourselves, and consider facts we would otherwise be unaware of. No one can know everything about everything; there is simply not enough time to learn. Consulting those who have given their special attention to the field of knowledge in question is therefore not a mark of dependence or irresponsibility but of efficiency and good sense. . . .

READING QUESTIONS

1. How does Ruggiero distinguish between "opinion" and "personal preference"?

2. What according to Ruggiero is the definition of opinion?

3. What is Ruggiero's thesis? Where is it located in the reading?

4. What is the impact on the reader of the numerous examples Ruggiero uses to support his thesis?

5. What is the difference between "informed" and "uninformed" opinions?

6. According to Ruggiero why should we, as learners, rely on informed opinion?

WRITING TOPICS

1. Write about an experience in which you let your opinion lead you to a bad decision about someone or something.

2. Based on Ruggiero's ideas, write an essay in which you explain how a person should evaluate his or her opinion before acting on it.

3. In paragraph 4, Ruggiero defines opinion. Do you agree with this definition? If so, explain why. If you disagree, explain why, and give your own definition of the word.

GROUP ACTIVITIES

1. Working as a group, make a list of the examples Ruggiero uses to demonstrate potential problems with opinions. Explain how each example is used to support his thesis.

2. Working as a group, brainstorm a list of times when people are most likely to rely on their opinion instead of thinking critically about the situation. Is there a pattern? What advice would you give to people who rely too heavily on personal opinions?

RESEARCH TOPICS

1. Who are Francis Bacon and John Locke? What is the impact of Ruggiero's quoting these two men?

2. Select one of Ruggiero's examples of experts being incorrect. Research the event or practice. Write a paper in which you explain how "experts" developed the practice, what events led to the discovery that the "experts" were wrong, and what was done to correct the mistake.

Choices

Exploring the Theme

■ What types of factors do you consider when making a choice about your own actions? (For example, other people's opinions, the likely consequences, your own beliefs, and so on.) Which of these factors are more important? Less important? Why?

■ What should be the role of society in regulating the individual's actions? What should the individual do if society requires him/her to act against his/her conscience?

Pride

by Ian Frazier

Ian Frazier began writing professionally for The New Yorker. *Many of these essays are collected in his first two books* Dating Your Mom *and* Nobody Better, Nobody Better. *Since leaving* The New Yorker, *Frazier has traveled across the American west, writing about some of his experiences in* Great Plains. On the Rez *offers Frazier's observations about his experiences with Oglala Sioux in South Dakota. His most recent book is* The Fish's Eye: Essays About Angling and the Outdoors. *Frazier's writing shows how an essayist makes connections between different life experiences and in so doing offers us new ways of looking at familiar notions. "Pride" points out connections between acting out of pride and acting out of stupidity.*

PREREADING QUESTIONS

1. Are you familiar with the proverb "pride goeth before a fall"? What does this saying suggest? Have you observed any experiences that validate this expression? Describe one or two in detail and explain the connection between pride and "the fall."

2. Think about groups that frequently use the word *pride*. What do you think it means to the members of these groups? Does it always mean the same thing?

1   One time I stopped on an icy road in Montana in my van and then couldn't get going again. The road was so slippery and my tires so bald that I had no traction either in forward or reverse. All I needed was a push, but unfortunately I was alone. I sat there spinning. Nobody came along. When I got out to take another look, I forgot I had left the car in drive. That made no difference, because the wheels continued spinning as before. Experimentally, I gave the van a shove from the rear. I could see it would be easy to rock it out of the rut. The idle on that van was set so that even with no foot on the gas it went about eight miles an hour. I opened the driver's side door, went back to the rear of the vehicle, checked again for traffic, and pushed. One heave, another, and the van was off and heading down the road. I ran after it, slipped, and fell. When I got up the van had a 50-foot lead. I ran at top speed, caught up, jumped in, and drove away.

2   No one but me saw me do that. The exclusivity of this feat made me think even more highly of myself as I tooled on into town. I was the top celebrity in that van. Of course, I was also an idiot.

3   What I'm trying to describe here is the fine line between pride and stupidity. Actually, there's a fine line between stupidity and lots of things (bravery, love, being funny), so many that the line probably should be redrawn as a circle, with those important accessories of humanity in the middle, and a vast parade ground of stupidity all around. Of those accessories, none will fraternize with stupidity as readily as pride. Pride and stupidity are thick. Except for the

part that keeps you from going on *The Ricki Lake Show*, pride almost is stupidity. This is revealed most comically and horribly in what we do outdoors.

4   Going down a flooded creek in a boat we'd found, me bailing and my friend Kent fending off obstacles with a surveyor's stake, both of us about 13; up ahead, unexpectedly, a large deadfall lying clear across the creek; and Kent said, "Don't worry, I've got everything under control." I used to tell the rest of that story, but now I understand that I don't have to. Certain prideful declarations— "I know this road like the back of my hand"—seem to exist mainly as preludes to the inevitable disaster. We Americans like to think of ourselves as thumbs-up, can-do types. More recently, we have begun to suspect that the cocky, grinning bush pilot who flies twice a week across the Arctic Circle and back carrying no emergency supplies but a Clark Bar may actually be insane. That we took on the alteration of this continent in the first place now looks more and more like hubris on a gigantic scale. "Manifest Destiny" may be a fancy, nineteenth-century way of saying "I know this road like the back of my hand."

5   But what the heck. We're here. For better or worse, our pride/stupidity has a lot to do with bringing us this far. Pride, the deadliest sin, is a crime of attitude—of overweening ambition, of imagining ourselves equal to powers beyond our range. Oddly, though, it's a sin whose punishment equals its failure: We approach too near the sun, the wax melts, the wings fall off, and we plunge into the sea. Yet once in a while we don't fail, miraculously, and instantly the sin is erased, and all is glory. In the town where I live—Missoula, Montana—someone recently climbed the tallest building on the campus of the University of Montana and impaled a pumpkin on the spire atop the uppermost tower. In the night, the perpetrator or perpetrators scaled several steeply pitched tile roofs, ascended the tower, carried or hoisted an extra-large pumpkin, and left it there for the school to see when the sun rose in the morning. The administration grumbled about the irresponsibility of this act, and about how expensive it would be to take the pumpkin down. But they didn't take it down, and it's been there ever since. I've looked at it from many angles, wondering how the feat was managed, admiring the mountaineering skill it took, and in the process noticing the architecture of this estimable old building much more closely than I ever would have otherwise. If the pumpkin-impalers had fallen and hurt or killed themselves, public opinion would rightly have regarded them as worse than stupid. But fate turned out better, and the lofty pumpkin remains, making us proud to live in the same town as the idiot or idiots who put it there.

READING QUESTIONS

1. What is your opinion of Ian Frazier's slick Montana road experience? If you had been in Ian Frazier's situation, would you have done what he did? Why or why not?

2. What is "hubris" (paragraph 4)? What is "Manifest Destiny" (paragraph 4)?

3. Frazier writes, "Certain prideful declarations—'I know this road like the back of my hand'—seem to exist mainly as preludes to the inevitable disaster" (paragraph 4). If we accept this connection, what is Frazier suggesting when he says that the notion of "Manifest Destiny" may have been an example of this statement?

4. Frazier ends his essay with an anecdote about a pumpkin on a tower. What does this story illustrate to you?

WRITING TOPICS

1. Do you agree with Frazier that there is a connection between pride and stupidity? Why or why not?

2. Frazier's essay suggests that the notion of national hero is complex. Do you think he is correct in suggesting that some heroic actions share a connection with stupidity? Why or why not? Illustrate your answer with specific examples.

3. Have you ever done something out of a sense of pride or because you felt challenged to prove yourself? How did the episode go? Were you successful, or embarrassed, or disgraced? How does your experience compare with the experiences and ideas discussed in Frazier's essay?

GROUP ACTIVITY

In a group, make a list of prideful experiences of the group members or experiences that members have observed (experience of relatives or close friends). Try to identify common features of the episodes. Consider age and gender of the participants, location of the action, and activity before, during, and after the episode. Are there any similarities between episodes, or are they all different?

RESEARCH TOPICS

1. Research U.S. history and identify specific acts that were justified under the slogan of "Manifest Destiny." Were there any negative consequences to these acts of national expansion?

2. Do an Internet search using terms like *pride* and *nationalism*. Look at the topics for 20 to 50 sites. (You will get thousands of results.) Classify the results by subject matter. Select one interesting Website and identify specifically the connection you see between these two notions.

3. Make a list of famous historical figures. Look up their personal lives and public activities. Are there both positive and negative aspects to their lives? Summarize your results.

Every Choice Has Its Consequences— Or at Least It Should

by Cindi Ross Scoppe

Cindi Ross Scoppe is an editorial writer for The State *newspaper in Columbia, South Carolina. This article was first published in 1999 in* The State *newspaper.*

PREREADING QUESTIONS

1. Have there been any laws regulating public behavior that you or others you know have not wanted to accept? What are they? Why have you or others rejected these laws?

2. Do you think health insurance rates or car insurance rates are equitable? Or do you think your rates are unfairly high because of the risky behavior of other people?

1 Once again, it seems, highway safety will be done in by the cholesterol police. When his colleagues tried recently to make the state's safety belt law enforceable, Senator Glenn McConnell decried the idea of "government getting involved in micromanaging people's lives." Since fried foods lead to poor health and higher insurance rates, he warned, the state will soon try to ban them.

2 Yes, dictating diets sounds outrageous. And in a world in which we were all responsible for our actions, it would be. But we're not living in that world. Not anymore.

3 Once upon a time, we understood that with rights come responsibilities. When my rights come into conflict with the rights of others, a balance must be struck. Striking that balance is what society—and our mechanism for maintaining society, government—is all about. Before we exercise our rights, our covenant with society requires us to consider the impact our actions will have on others.

4 But little by little, we have put the rights of some individuals above the legitimate interests of society, which just happens to be made up of individuals. We have constructed our laws so that individuals don't have to suffer the consequences of their actions. Society as a whole (in other words, all the other individuals in the community) pays for their irresponsibility, usually through higher insurance rates or taxes or higher prices on goods and services.

5 These protections become so normal that people tend to forget about them. So when society as a whole tries to impose reasonable restrictions on individuals' activities in order to reduce the burden the rest of us must bear, a few people scream bloody murder.

6 So we back down, and we are left with an inherently unfair situation—most of us must subsidize the irresponsibility of a few.

7 Of course, there is an alternative. Instead of imposing reasonable restrictions on your activities, we could tear down those artificial protections that society offers you from yourself. And the rest of us could take back *our* rights.

8 Go ahead, exercise your right to drive without a seat belt. Then when you slam head-on into another car and your body goes flying through the windshield, the insurance company can refuse to pay your hospital bills. After all, the rest of the people who have the same insurance company have the right to refuse payment for higher premiums to cover your irresponsibility.

9 Don't want Image Data to have your picture in its database? Fine. Let's give your bank the right to make you cover the checks that thief wrote on your account—as well as all the five-figure credit card bills he ran up.

10 Smoke all you want. It's your right. But shouldn't it be the right of businesses to refuse to hire you, since your employment will make the company's

insurance rates skyrocket? Or maybe we should just let insurance companies exercise the right to refuse to cover you and other people who make unhealthy lifestyle choices—even through group insurance coverage. And as a society, shouldn't we have the right to refuse to subsidize unhealthy behavior through Medicare and Medicaid? (Economists estimate that within the next decade, a full 17 percent of the nation's gross domestic product will be devoted to treating preventable diseases.)

11   Need to cut a few corners on safety measures in order for your company to save money? OK. Do it. But then when your product inevitably injures your customers, they have the right to sue for damages. (Yes, that right already exists. But the same legislators who want to protect your right to drive without a seat belt also want to take the right to sue away from your customers.)

12   You want your own children so much that you're willing to use fertility treatments that exponentially increase the chance of expensive and dangerous multiple births? Go ahead. But certainly you'll understand when the rest of us exercise our right to refuse to have our insurance rates go up to pay for the treatment.

13   If we carry the idea of removing artificial protections to its logical conclusion, we would also exercise our right to refuse to pay for the extra expense of all those extra births. (Of course, even the most radical libertarians understand that we don't condemn children for the choices of their parents.)

14   My colleague Claudia Brinson tells me that a similar approach is fashionable in parenting. It's called "logical consequences." You teach your children about the consequences of their actions by allowing those consequences to play out naturally. When your child leaves his keys at home for the 10th time, you let him sit on the stoop for an hour before you come to his rescue.

15   I imagine that could be pretty effective. But I would guess that most parents would rather come up with a combination of reasonable limits and protections that would prevent them from having to subject their children to the consequences of bad behavior. Do we, as a society, really want anything different for ourselves?

READING QUESTIONS

1. What does Senator Glenn McConnell's criticism of the "'government getting involved in micromanaging people's lives'" (paragraph 1) mean? Give some examples of this type of legislation.

2. What fault does Scoppe find with putting "the rights of some individuals above the legitimate interests of society" (paragraph 4)?

3. What alternative to subsidizing the irresponsible behavior of theirs does Scoppe give? What is problematic about this solution?

4. What are some examples that Scoppe gives of irresponsible behavior?

5. Scoppe points out that an approach to parenting "called 'logical consequences'" is popular (Brinson, quoted in paragraph 14). Does she suggest that we follow this approach in dealing with the irresponsible behavior in society? Why or why not?

WRITING TOPICS

1. Scoppe says "we are left with an inherently unfair situation—most of us must subsidize the irresponsibility of a few" (paragraph 6). Do you agree that this is unfair? Why or why not?

2. Scoppe provides several examples of behavior that can be classified as irresponsible. There are, of course, other types of risky behavior. Present an analysis of another type of behavior that is in some ways socially irresponsible. How should society respond to individuals who practice this type of behavior? Is there a simple solution to the problems associated with this type of behavior?

3. Is it overly simplistic to suggest that individuals who practice irresponsible or risky behavior must accept all of the consequences of their actions? Why or why not?

4. Do you agree with the title of Scoppe's essay? Why or why not?

GROUP ACTIVITIES

1. Think about your lifestyle. Do you have any habits or activities that someone could label "bad"? What is bad about these habits? Whom do they negatively impact? Compare the results of your self-assessment with the self-assessment of others in your group.

2. List other habits or activities that society pays for. As a group, discuss which ones should be solely the responsibility of the individual and which should be subsidized by others. Then state guidelines that would help another group come up with the same decisions your group made.

RESEARCH TOPICS

1. Explore car/driver insurance rates. What factors affect the cost of insurance? What is your opinion of these relative costs?

2. Explore health insurance rates. What factors affect the cost of health insurance? Can individuals be considered responsible for these factors? Explain.

Is a Tree Worth a Life?

by Sally Thane Christensen

Sally Thane Christensen (1954–1992) was a federal attorney who represented the U.S. Forest Service and whose battle with ovarian cancer caused her to question the choices we make between individuals and the environment. This article, written for Newsweek's *"My Turn," was published the year prior to Christensen's*

death. The University of Montana honors Ms. Christensen with a Single-Parent
Law Student Scholarship in her name.

PREREADING QUESTIONS

1. Do you think the protection of endangered species is more important than the local economy?
2. Do you think the protection of endangered species is more important than an individual's health?

1 For most of the last decade, federal timberlands in the West have been held hostage in a bitter fight between environmental groups and the timber industry. The environmentalists want to save the forests and their wildlife occupants. The timber industry wants to cut trees and provide jobs in a depressed economy. Caught in the middle is the United States Forest Service, which must balance the conflicting concepts of sustained yield and multiple use of national forest land.

2 The latest pawn in this environmental chess match is the Pacific yew tree, a scrubby conifer found from southern Alaska to central California and in Washington, Oregon, Idaho and Montana. Historically the yew has not been harvested for value but often has been treated as logging slash and wasted. Not any longer. An extract of the bark of the Pacific yew known as taxol has been found to have cancer-fighting properties, particularly with ovarian cancer. As many as 30 percent of those treated with taxol have shown significant response. Some researchers call taxol the most significant new cancer drug to emerge in 15 years.

3 For the first time, the environmental debate over the use of a natural resource involves more than a question of the priority of the resource versus economic considerations. At stake is the value of a species of tree and the habitat it provides for wildlife as opposed to the value of the greatest of all natural resources, human life.

4 When I was first diagnosed three years ago, no one had an inkling that I would become caught in the center of what may become the most significant environmental debate of my generation. Although as early as 1979 researchers had discovered that taxol killed cancer in a unique way, imprisoning malignant cells in a cage of scaffoldlike rods called micro-tubules, lab tests on animals were inconclusive. By 1985, however, a woman with terminal ovarian cancer was treated with taxol and had a dramatic response. Six years later, the once lowly yew tree is at the threshold of a controversy that challenges the fundamental precepts of even the most entrenched environmentalist.

5 It takes about three 100-year-old Pacific yew trees, or roughly 60 pounds of bark, to produce enough taxol to treat one patient. When the bark is removed, the tree dies. Environmental groups like the Oregon Natural Resources Council and the Audubon Society are concerned that the Pacific yew as a species may be decimated by the demand for taxol. But this year alone, 12,000 women will die from ovarian cancer. Breast cancer will kill 45,000 women. Is preservation of the Pacific yew worth the price?

6 It is sublimely ironic that my fate hinges so directly on the Pacific yew. As a federal attorney representing the Forest Service, I have witnessed the environmental movement in the West from its embryonic stages. I have seen

such diverse groups as the National Wildlife Federation and the Sierra Club challenge the Forest Service's ability to sell and harvest its trees. Win or lose, the forests are often locked up during the lengthy legal process.

7   The viability of the national forests does not rise or fall with the Pacific yew. But, unfortunately for cancer victims, the tree is most abundant on national-forest lands which are subject to environmental review by the public. Already challenges to the federal harvest of the yew have begun. In Montana, the Save the Yaak Committee has protested the Kootenai National Forest's intention to harvest yew trees and make them available for experimental use. The committee contends that the yew may be endangered by overharvesting.

8   I have news for the Save the Yaak Committee. I am endangered, too. I've had four major abdominal surgeries in two years. I've had the conventional chemotherapy for ovarian cancer, and it didn't work. Though I was in remission for almost a year, last August my cancer returned with a vengeance. Taxol may be my last hope.

9   Because of the scarcity of supply, taxol is not commercially available. It is available only in clinical trials at a number of institutions. Bristol-Myers, working with the National Cancer Institute in Bethesda, Md., is asking the Forest Service to provide 750,000 pounds of bark for clinical studies this year.

10   The ultimate irony of my story is that I am one of the lucky ones. This May I was accepted by the National Cancer Institute for one of its clinical trials. On May 8 I was infused with my first treatment of taxol. Hospitalized in intensive care at NCI, I watched the precious, clear fluid drip into my veins and prayed for it to kill the cancer that has ravaged my body. I thought about the thousands of women who will die of cancer this year, who will not have my opportunity.

11   Every effort should be made to ensure that the yew tree is made available for the continued research and development of taxol. Environmental groups, the timber industry and the Forest Service must recognize that the most important value of the Pacific yew is as a treatment for cancer. At the same time, its harvest can be managed in a way that allows for the production of taxol without endangering the continued survival of the yew tree.

12   The yew may be prime habitat for spotted owls. It may be esthetically appealing. But certainly its most critical property is its ability to treat a fatal disease. Given a choice between trees or people, people must prevail. No resource can be more valuable or more important than a human life. Ask my husband. Ask my two sons. Ask me.

READING QUESTIONS

1. How is Christensen's job important to her argument?
2. What is Christensen's thesis? Where in the article is this most clearly stated?
3. What distinction does Christensen make between the need to protect the national forests and the Pacific yew tree?
4. What evidence does Christensen give to indicate that harvesting the Pacific yew can be done so that its survival can be ensured?
5. What is the impact of the last paragraph on the reader?

WRITING TOPICS

1. Evaluate the logic in Christensen's essay.

2. Which do you think is more important: preservation of the environment or medical assistance to an individual or group? Why?

3. Brainstorm to create a list of issues in which the individual's needs and rights are in conflict with the needs and rights of society. Write an essay in which you explain the two sides of the issue, and provide a resolution to the conflict.

GROUP ACTIVITIES

1. Working as a group, outline Christensen's argument. Be sure to identify all the appeals to logic and to emotion, labeling each one, and explaining how the appeal supports her position.

2. Working as a group, review the section on logic (pages 308–309) and determine how many, if any, fallacies Christensen's essay includes. If your group identifies a fallacy, explain the impact of the fallacy on her reader.

RESEARCH ACTIVITIES

1. Conduct research on the drug Christensen discusses in her essay. Does the drug come only from the trees she mentions? Is there an artificial chemical equivalent of the natural drug from the tree? How many women are afflicted with ovarian cancer every year? Are there other types of treatment than the one she describes? After you have conducted your research, write an essay in which you evaluate Christensen's argument.

2. Conduct research to determine what other kinds of plants or animals are protected by environmental laws. Select one plant, animal, or region that is protected, and discuss how this protection impacts the local economy or people's health.

Beat on the Brat: The Economics of Spanking.*

by Steven E. Landsburg

Steven Landsburg is an adjunct associate professor of economics at the University of Rochester. He has published six books and has been a regular contributor to Forbes Magazine *and an occasional contributor to* The New York Times, The Washington Post, *and* The Wall Street Journal. *His upcoming book,* More

Sex Is Safer Sex, and Other Surprises, *continues to describe how economic theory can be used to understand many other aspects of life.*

PREREADING QUESTIONS

1. What methods of disciplining children do you find most effective? Why?
2. Should parents spank their children as a means of disciplining them?

1 In child discipline, as in pretty much everything else, the rich have more options than the poor. If you're rich (or even modestly middle-class), you can take away the Game Boy, confiscate the car keys, or turn off the Instant Messenger. But for families with no Game Boys, no cars, and no Internet access, that whole range of punishments is unavailable.

2 If you're rich or middle-class, you can cut your kid's allowance; if you're poor, your kid might need the allowance to live on. When a middle-class kid loses his allowance, he makes do with fewer CDs or video games. When a poor kid loses his allowance, he makes do with fewer school lunches. Depriving a kid of luxuries can be an effective punishment; depriving a kid of necessities can be a form of child abuse.

3 Spanking, by contrast, is an equal-opportunity punishment; it works equally well whether you're rich or poor. So simple economics suggests that the very poor, with fewer alternatives available, should spank their kids more—and they do. Professor Bruce Weinberg of Ohio State University has studied this. He found that if you're a kid in a $6,000-a-year household, you probably get spanked every six weeks or so. If your parents' annual income goes up to $17,000, you'll get spanked about once every four months. As income rises above about $17,000, spanking falls off more slowly; $40,000 and $120,000 households are not much different from $17,000 households. That makes sense; in today's America, you don't have to be very wealthy before your kid has a Game Boy, so even a $20,000 household has good non-spanking alternatives.

4 For allowance withdrawal, the numbers go exactly the opposite way, Weinberg found. If you're a kid in a typical $6,000-a-year family, you'll almost never lose your allowance, but in a family that makes $17,000 or more, you'll lose your allowance four or five times a year.

5 It might seem like a stretch to explain spanking with economics, but what else could account for these patterns? Well, there's always culture. The very poor are disproportionately black, and blacks physically discipline their children more than whites do. But according to Weinberg, the effect of income persists even after you've controlled for race and other cultural variables.

6 Anyway, black parents punish their children more than white parents in *all* ways. If you're black and you misbehave, you're both more likely to get spanked *and* more likely to lose your allowance than your white neighbor, who in turn is both more likely to get spanked *and* more likely to lose his allowance than the Hispanic kid down the street. So on average, poor people spank more and withdraw allowances less, whereas black people spank more

and withdraw allowances *more*. The income pattern fails to match the racial pattern, so the income pattern can't be fully explained by race.

7   It is true, though, that racial differences are more pronounced for spanking than for allowance denial: In both cases blacks punish the most, then whites, then Hispanics, but the gaps between racial groups are much bigger for corporal than for financial punishment.

8   There are other cultural factors: Boys are punished more than girls, with substantially more spankings and a bit more in the way of allowance withdrawals. Single mothers spank a little less, and withdraw allowances quite a bit less, than other parents. Older and better-educated parents are a bit less likely to spank and a bit more likely to withdraw allowances. Bigger families spank less and withdraw allowances more. But Weinberg's study finds that the poor spank more even *after* you've accounted for all of these effects. The question is why.

9   Here's one good alternative to the economic explanation: University of New Hampshire sociologist Murray Straus has published multiple studies concluding that children who are spanked are less successful as adults. If the link is causal—that is, if being spanked actually lowers your earnings potential—and if spanking runs in families, then we have an alternative explanation for Weinberg's numbers: Low-income parents are more likely to spank their children because low-income parents are more likely to have been spanked themselves. Or maybe it's as simple as this: Poverty breeds frustration, and frustrated parents lash out at their kids. Does any reader have a better story?

READING QUESTIONS

1. According to Landsburg, why do wealthy parents have more options than poor parents when disciplining their children?

2. Why, according to Landsburg, do poor parents spank their children more often than rich parents? What evidence does he cite to show this is true?

3. To what extent can differences in spanking and withholding allowances be explained by race instead of by income level?

4. What other factors affect whether children are spanked or don't receive an allowance as discipline?

5. What alternative does Landsburg present to his economic explanation of discipline methods?

6. Does Landsburg approve of spanking as a method of discipline? How do you know?

WRITING TOPICS

1. Agree or disagree with Landsburg's idea that wealthier families have more ways to discipline their children than poorer families do.

2. Landsburg implies that poor parents spank their children out of frustration. Do you agree that spanking is an expression of the parents' frustration?

GROUP ACTIVITY

With a small group of students, brainstorm a list of methods parents use to discipline children. Discuss each method, trying to determine whether economics, race, or culture influence the methods parents use.

RESEARCH TOPICS

1. Landsburg cites Murray Straus's studies that conclude "children who are spanked are less successful as adults," and he speculates that the link may be "causal"—"being spanked actually lowers your earnings potential." Is there any evidence that the link is causal? What other factors may be involved to explain this finding rather than a direct causal link?

2. Much has been written on the appropriateness of spanking as a method of disciplining children. What are parenting experts currently saying about this?

Missed Time

by Ha Jin

Ha Jin is the pen name of Xuefei Jin. He was born in northern China and grew up during the Cultural Revolution. After serving in the People's Liberation Army for six years, he taught himself English while working as a telegraph operator for the railroad. When the universities in China reopened, he passed the entrance exam and earned a B.A. and an M.A. in English literature. He came to the United States to work on his doctorate at Brandeis University in 1985. Government repression of students at Tiananmen Square made him decide to remain. Ha Jin has published several collections of poetry and fiction. His novel Waiting *won the National Book Award. Ha Jin is professor of English and creative writing at Emory University in Atlanta.*

PREREADING QUESTIONS

What is more important to you, accomplishing things or feeling happy? What makes you happy?

My notebook has remained blank for months
thanks to the light you shower
around me. I have no use
for my pen, which lies
languorously without grief.

Nothing is better than to live
a storyless life that needs
no writing for meaning—

when I am gone, let others say
they lost a happy man,
though no one can tell how happy I was.

READING QUESTIONS

1. Read the first verse of "Missed Time" aloud. Who do you think is the speaker? What has the speaker not done recently? How does he feel about this lack of productivity?

2. How can a person "shower" light around another person? What feeling does this suggest?

3. What does the word "languorously" mean? Is this a word you could use to describe a pen? What is the pen being compared to? Why doesn't the pen feel sad?

4. In the second verse, the speaker of the poem declares, "Nothing is better than to live / a storyless life that needs / no writing for meaning—." What do think a "storyless life" is? What kind of stories is the speaker talking about? Do you agree that living such a life is best? Why or why not?

5. How does writing give meaning to lives? Why doesn't his life need writing for meaning?

6. Why can't others know about his happiness?

WRITING TOPICS

1. Can one person make another person happy or give meaning to another person's life? Write an essay comparing your ideas about this question to the ideas in Ha Jin's poem.

2. Ha Jin's poem contrasts writing about life with living life. Do you see these as necessarily incompatible?

3. What do you think the title "Missed Time" means? What do you think the poem means?

4. Ha Jin's poem hints that a person who is truly happy does not need to try to convey his or her happiness to others. Do you agree with this suggestion? Why or why not?

GROUP ACTIVITIES

1. Think about the two characters in the poem. What type of person is the "I" of the poem? Who is the "you" of the poem? What is their relationship? Discuss your ideas with your classmates.

2. Look for things in the poem that are compared to other things. Ask each member of the group to find one comparison and explain it.

RESEARCH ACTIVITIES

1. What was China like during the time that Ha Jin lived there? What can you find out about the Cultural Revolution? What happened to writers during that time?

2. What are Ha Jin's books about? Is this poem similar to those books in ideas, or is it different?

Survivor

by James Scott, as told to Paige Williams

Huntington's disease is a degenerative brain disorder that gradually takes away a person's ability to function independently. Because it is hereditary, it can strike several members of the same family.

PREREADING QUESTIONS

1. Have you ever had a serious injury or illness? Have you cared for someone with a serious injury or illness? If so, write about this experience.

2. If you could find out whether you would develop terminal illness for which there is no effective treatment, would you want to know? Why or why not?

1 We lived in Riverdale, Ga., me and my dad and my mother and my two brothers. We didn't know nothing about Huntington's disease back then—even the doctors didn't know much. We didn't know the chances of us getting it till later on. Now it feels like a family curse. My dad's brother had it. He shot and killed himself. My grandmother got put in a sanitarium and died there.

2 We first knew my dad was sick in the 70's. He was coaching my baseball team then. He went from being everywhere outdoors to not doing practically nothing at all. It got to where somebody had to watch him all the time. Huntington's eats part of your brain, the part that controls the nervous system. I took care of him for a couple of years during the day, and my mom took care of him at night after work. He kept walking out the door, going toward the mailbox, probably 20 or 30 times a day, and finally we had to start locking the door to keep him from getting out. He always talked about going to work, needing to go to work, and we would have to tell him he didn't work anymore.

3 Randy came down with it about the time we put my dad in the nursing home. There wasn't any test back in the early 80's; you pretty much just waited for symptoms. Randy started wandering off, too, going to the neighbor's house, thinking one of his friends lived there. He would get upset over the least little thing. We'd go out in public, and one of us would ask, "Where do you want to sit at?" and he would start raising Cain: "That's my seat." If he lost his cigarettes or something, he'd blame it on somebody. Only thing we could do was take him back home, get him away from people and talk to him. I was pretty much the only one who could talk to him. Sometimes that wouldn't work, and we'd wind up fistfighting. I'd try to calm him down before he hurt somebody, but mainly to keep him from hurting Mama.

4   Andy got sick, too. Randy more or less had jerky motions, but Andy shook all the time, worse and worse. Randy never shook the way Andy did. It advanced a lot faster with him for some reason. I tried to hide it for years. I wouldn't tell nobody what was wrong with my dad, tried to keep it from my friends what was wrong with my brothers. It was kind of embarrassing to me.

5   When they told me I had it, it wasn't nothing I wasn't expecting. I started showing symptoms in my late 20's: memory loss, jerking, muscle spasms like in my eyebrows. I'd start shaking, and it would keep going for two or three hours, sometimes longer, sometimes all day. There are certain things you can do to hide it, like if you get your hands in your pockets or you hold on to something, people don't see you shaking. I've been doing that for a long time. I just didn't want to be treated different. Sometimes I stumbled when I walked. I lost my temper a lot; you get aggravated and get ill at somebody.

6   I have to live. I can't just lay down and die. The more I do for myself, the more I keep my balance and memory; that's what the doctors told me. I drive and do my own cooking and cleaning. My daughter is 12. I've got her here every other weekend. I take care of myself. Don't nobody has to do nothing for me. If I quit doing it all, they say I could advance faster. I have nightmares about it a lot, Stephen King nightmares.

7   Really, I went public, let all my friends know, when all this happened with my mother. The night it happened, the sheriffs knocked on the door. They told me to come outside. They opened the back of my truck and told me to sit down on the tailgate. They said something happened down there at the nursing home: my brothers had been shot. At first I didn't know what to think. I didn't know my mom had got arrested until about 2 or 3 in the morning.

8   The last time I saw her was earlier that day. I had went out and bought something from Kentucky Fried Chicken. She said she wasn't hungry. She told me she was going down to see my brothers. I didn't know she was upset. I can't let myself go wondering what I could have done or what I couldn't have done. I can't change things now. My mom is in jail. There's people down here all over the place saying she needs to be freed, that she's already suffered enough. I agree with that. She raised them from babies; when they got old, she had to take care of them again. I know my brothers better than anybody else, and they didn't want to suffer like that. I know they're not suffering anymore.

9   I'm not worried about dying, but I am worried about going into a nursing home. I've grown up going to them, and I know how miserable they can be. At the end, my brothers were technically brain dead. I don't think they died that night my mother went to the nursing home. I think they died a few years ago. Randy was 42, and Andy was 41. I'm 38. The day I can't get around and walk and fish and do other stuff, I think my life is over then. Why drag it on after that? You just hurt the people around you.

READING QUESTIONS

1. How did Huntington's disease affect Scott's family?

2. How does Scott tell us what his mother has done? How would the reader be affected differently if he described her actions more directly? Why do you think he chose to say so little about it?

3. What is Scott's purpose in telling his story? What point is he trying to make? How effectively does he achieve his purpose and make his point? Why?

4. How does Scott feel about his mother's act? How do you know?

5. How does Scott feel about his own future?

6. Williams did not change Scott's grammar or sentence structure. Why not? Was this an effective choice? Why or why not?

WRITING TOPICS

1. Scott says, "There's people down here all over the place saying [my mother] needs to be freed, that she's already suffered enough. I agree with that." Should Scott's mother serve jail time for killing her sons?

2. Although there is a test to determine if someone carries the gene for Huntington's (and other similar degenerative illnesses), many people decide not to be tested because no cure exists. If a genetic illness for which there was no cure ran in your family, would you be tested to find out if you had inherited the gene? Why or why not?

3. Scott responds to his own illness by insisting on doing things for himself and to his mother's actions by telling his friends what had happened. What strategies do you think are helpful for people trying to manage personal and family tragedy?

GROUP ACTIVITIES

As a group, pick one of the following positions to argue: (1) Scott's mother should be imprisoned for murder, (2) Scott's mother should be set free from prison because she has suffered enough. After you have listed the points to support your position, debate the issue with another group that picked the opposite stance.

RESEARCH TOPICS

1. What is Huntington's disease? What are its major symptoms? Who gets it? What is the prognosis for someone with this illness?

2. Scott's mother is not the only person to kill a family member who had an incapacitating or terminal illness. Research another situation in which this happened. Why did the family member kill the person who was ill? What were the legal and personal consequences of this act?

Haves and Have-Nots

Exploring the Theme

■ What is your community doing to address the needs of poor people? What should it be doing?

■ Homelessness and poverty are usually depicted as having a negative impact on people. Can these situations have a positive impact as well? Why or why not?

■ This unit describes how little many people live with. What would you need for you (and your family) to survive? What would you be willing to do to get these needs met?

Experiencing Poverty Might Do Us All Good

by Ernest L. Wiggins

Ernest Wiggins is a journalism professor at the University of South Carolina. He has written editorials for The State *newspaper, often focusing on minority issues. This article was first published in 1998 in* The State *newspaper.*

PREREADING QUESTIONS

Our culture tends to think of poor people in two opposite ways: either as dirty and criminal or as honest and good-hearted. What examples in the media or popular culture can you think of that support each view?

1   A student came to me, concerned that the use of the phrase "poor people" in an exercise was inappropriate. I said I didn't understand her concern. She said she'd been taught the expression is rude.

2   This struck me as odd, odder yet when other students voiced the same opinion. Why would "poor people" be considered rude by some folks? In its context in the exercise it was accurate and meaningful. But then I thought about it.

3   Perhaps it is considered damning by some. There is, after all, the Protestant ethic of hard work and thrift in which poverty is tantamount to godlessness, prosperity to righteousness.

4   Or, perhaps, it is thought ill-mannered to point out the deficiencies in others of God's children. Maybe they believe it is like referring to another's disability.

5   Whatever the reason, I was, and am, intrigued.

6   Millions of us in this country know or have known need. We are the most acquisitive society in the world, and yet 16 percent of us live *below* the poverty

level. For those of us who are black and brown, the figure is 30 percent, though the rate is decreasing for blacks.

7   And yet, I fear, not nearly enough of us have known need.

8   I believe that need—be it hunger or chill—can enliven as well as destroy. Need inspires in many of us the resolve to overcome obstacles and venture forward. In this way we survive.

9   And yet, if the obstacles are tremendous and we are without the resources—spiritual or material—to scale them, we will, most assuredly, perish. In these instances, we need the help of others to pull ourselves up and over. It is because too many of us have not known need that so many others are despairing of life. It is in this way that our lack of need can actually be destructive.

10   For the lack of need skews our values.

11   I was stunned by reports of McDonald's customers throwing away scores of Happy Meals after pulling the prized Beanie Babies out of them. Unless I'm mistaken, much of the public outrage has been over the measures some folks have used to acquire these plush toys. Little was said about the waste of food. Would one who had known hunger be so cavalier?

12   Likewise, the lack of need numbs us to people's suffering. We spend hundreds of dollars for purebred canines to do "potty" at the curb and avert our eyes from the poor living on the streets.

13   How many of us have even faced uncertainty day after day as we tried to ensure the survival of our children, wondering if the day would ever come when we would accept that our children will never thrive as others do? Would we maintain a vise grip on the hope that more and better is in store for our offspring if we press on?

14   And yet we daily hear men and women—associates and leaders—who cannot understand how hope might be crushed under the unyielding pressures of modern living. I'm not talking about the urbane pressure of choosing between investments or refinancing schemes, but the maddening pressure of choosing between keeping a fatiguing, low-paying job and gambling on a "retraining" opportunity that might pay off, and then might not.

15   If more of us had known need, plans to scuttle public assistance would not have overlooked such disheartening dilemmas.

16   Those of us who have not known need cannot fabricate an experience so that we might, if we desired, know better how to assist the poor. But we can listen, without bias and with compassion, maybe even trust, when the poor talk to us.

17   Our public leaders and the media rarely do listen. That lends credence to my belief that the most destructive consequence of our lack of need is our blindness to the poverty of humanity within us.

READING QUESTIONS

1. Who can benefit from experiencing poverty? How can they benefit?
2. What is the Protestant work ethic? How does it affect people's attitude towards poverty?
3. What solutions does Wiggins offer to getting out of poverty?

4. What does Wiggins mean by "the lack of need skews our values" (paragraph 10)?

5. What would happen if more people had experienced need?

6. What alternative does Wiggins offer to direct experience of need?

WRITING TOPICS

1. Wiggins says that poverty "can enliven as well as destroy" (paragraph 8). Using Wiggins's essay and your own ideas and experiences, write an essay in which you discuss whether poverty is more likely to enliven or to destroy.

2. Wiggins says that "our lack of need can actually be destructive" (paragraph 9). Write an essay in which you discuss how lacking bad experiences may be detrimental.

GROUP ACTIVITIES

1. Wiggins says that his student expressed concern over his use of the term "poor people" because she thought it was rude. Make a list of terms your group has heard used to refer to poor people. Are some of these undesirable terms? Why or why not?

2. Pick another group of people (the disabled, mentally ill, etc.) and make a list of terms used to refer to this group. Are some of these undesirable terms? Why or why not?

RESEARCH TOPICS

1. Wiggins says in 1998 that 16 percent of Americans lived below the poverty line. Conduct research to find out the dollar amount of the poverty line and how many Americans live below this line today. Has this number increased or decreased? If there is a difference, what do you think has caused this change?

2. Using the current government definition of the poverty level you researched in question 1, make a budget, using typical prices for your community. What can you afford? What can you not afford? What choices will you have to make to ensure your survival? How would you make those choices?

Chopsticks

by Guanlong Cao

Guanlong Cao grew up in Shanghai, China, during the Chinese Cultural Revolution. During the 1950s to the 1970s, he and his family of five were assigned to live in a tiny attic because his father was deemed a "class enemy." The Attic: Memoirs of a Chinese Landlord's Son *(1996) offers personal observations about these extraordinary and difficult times. Cao writes both fiction and nonfiction. His writing has been recognized in China and the rest of the world. In 1987, Cao came to the United States. He graduated from Middlebury College and holds a Master of Fine Arts degree from Tufts University. His artwork includes sculpture, paintings, prints, and photographs. In "Chopsticks," an excerpt from his memoir, Cao describes the values placed on these ordinary eating tools by students at the automotive school he attended.*

PREREADING QUESTION

Have you ever attached special significance to an ordinary object? Describe the intended use of the object in everyday life. How does the significance you attached to it make it different?

1 I always think chopsticks are an invention unique to Asian culture. Its historical and cognitive significance is no less than that of the Great Wall, the compass, gunpowder, and paper.

2 The greatest wisdom appears to be foolishness. Complexity ultimately ends in simplicity. Maybe it is because chopsticks are so simple that, just as air's weight was long ignored and white light was mislabeled as colorless, in thousands of years no one has ever scientifically or conscientiously researched them. A sensitive probe for examining the characteristics of Asian culture has been ignored. In my four years at the automotive school, I witnessed and experienced a splendid chopsticks civilization. I record it here for the benefit of future researchers.

3 In those days almost every male student carried an elongated pouch hanging from his belt. It was fashioned from canvas, leather, or leatherette. Like a warrior's dagger, it dangled all day from the student's waist.

4 Female students didn't wear belts, so the slim bags usually hung from a cord around their necks. Their materials were more delicate: nylon, silk, or linen. Embroidery was often added as an embellishment.

5 Within these bags were chopsticks.

6 Because the rationed food offered insufficient calories, oxygen-intensive activities were not encouraged. Chess, card games, and calligraphy were the officially recommended pastimes. But the most popular activity was making chopsticks.

7 The number of students at the school increased each year, and new dormitories were constantly being built. Owing to limited funds, the dormitory roofs were constructed out of tar paper, straw, and bamboo. That bamboo became the primary source of chopstick lumber.

8 The selection of material was critical. Segments close to the plant's roots were too short. The meat between the skin and hollow core of the segments close to the top was too thin. A bamboo tree about one inch thick provided only a few middle segments that could be used to make quality chopsticks.

9 The bamboo poles were covered with a tarp and stored on the construction site. In the evenings, taking advantage of the absence of the construction workers, we started looting.

10   If only a few trees were missing, nobody would have noticed. But when an idea becomes a fad, things can easily get out of hand. There were hundreds of students. A newly delivered pile of bamboo would be half gone the morning after an all-out moonlit operation.

11   The superintendent of the construction site was furious and demanded that the student dormitories be searched. We got scared and threw our booty out the windows. The superintendent called a meeting of the school leaders to deal with the problem. He arrived with both arms laden with cut segments of bamboo. With a crash, he slammed the sticks down on the meeting table. The leaders, gathered around the table, looked like diners at an exotic feast.

12   The next day, a large notice was posted listing the price of the transgression: one bamboo tree = one big demerit. But the punishment was never really put into effect. After the immediate storm passed, the bamboo continued to go missing, but not in the same flagrant quantities.

13   After a bamboo segment was split open, it had to be dried in the shade for about a week. Experienced students put their bamboo strips on the mosquito netting over their beds. Their rising body heat helped evaporate the moisture.

14   Although the bamboo's skin is hard, it must be stripped away. If left on, the different densities of the inner and outer materials cause the chopsticks to warp. The best part comes from the quarter inch of meat just inside the skin. There the texture is even and dense, and the split will go precisely where the knife directs it.

15   The student-made chopsticks usually had a round cross-section. Round chopsticks require little skill to make. Wrap sandpaper around the strip of bamboo and sand for an hour or two, and a round cross-section is the result.

16   Only experts dared to make square cross-sectioned chopsticks. To make the four sided straight and symmetrical from tail to tip required real expertise. Sandpaper could not be used, because it would wear away the sharp edges you were trying to create.

17   To begin the procedure, you have to soak a fine-grained brick in water for a couple of days, and then grind it flat on a concrete floor. Laying the roughed-out chopstick on the brick, with one finger applying pressure to the tail and another to the top, you slowly ground the stick on the brick. Water was dripped on the brick to ensure fine grinding. Only by this painstaking process could chopsticks be formed with clear edges and smooth surfaces.

18   A boy student unprecedently produced a pair of five-sided chopsticks, which created a sensation on campus. The boy dedicated his efforts to a girl on whom he had a crush. Unfortunately, his gift was spurned and, desolate, he broke the chopsticks in front of his peers. This became the classic tragedy of the school year.

19   In addition to varying cross-sections, the top two or three inches were another place to show off your skill. The usual decoration was a few carved lines with inlaid color. Some students borrowed techniques from seal carving and sculpted miniature cats, turtles, and dragons out of the upper portions of the sticks. One student, who was good at calligraphy, carved two lines of a Song dynasty poem on his chopsticks:

"Vinegar fish from the West Lake," read one of them.
"Cinnamon meat from East Hill," read the other.

20   He cherished the chopsticks as sacred objects, not intended for daily use. He employed them only on special occasions or festival days when excitement rippled through the student body:

21   "Today we are going to eat meat!"

22   Only then would he take his chopsticks from his trunk. Applying a thin layer of beeswax, he would polish them for at least ten minutes with a piece of suede. Then they were ready to be brought into the dining room.

23   Following the epochal five-sided masterpiece, chopsticks became a popular gift for boys to give to girls. If the girl liked the boy, she would accept his present and later give a gift to her admirer—a sleeve for chopsticks. The painstaking needlework expressed her sentimental attachment. We had never heard about Freud, but with our raw wisdom we subconsciously felt that there was some symbolic meaning, which could hardly be expressed in words, in this exchange, in the coming and going of the chopsticks and the sleeves. But school regulations clearly stated:

NO DATING ON CAMPUS

24   I think the regulation was well supported by science. Dating belonged to the category of oxygen-intensive activities. Before you could open your mouth, your heart started jumping and your cheeks were burning, clearly indicating a rapid consumption of valuable calories.

READING QUESTIONS

1. What other inventions does Cao compare chopsticks to?

2. Describe the bags that students wore to carry chopsticks.

3. How did students get materials for making chopsticks? What does this episode tell the reader about the relationship of the students and the school administration?

4. Cao describes different types of chopsticks the students made. What do these differences tell the reader about the students at the school?

5. At the beginning of the essay, Cao says he is going to describe a "splendid chopsticks civilization" created by the students of his automotive school. Do you agree that what he describes is such a development? Why or why not?

6. Is there a relationship between the shortage of food at the school and making chopsticks? What evidence in the reading supports your answer?

WRITING TOPICS

1. Cao's essay describes how chopsticks came to play a significant role in students' lives. Do you think that ordinary objects become more significant under certain conditions? Why or why not?

2. What aspects of student life were most affected by chopsticks? Why do you think that these were the aspects most affected?

3. Chopsticks were personally significant to students, but they also came to dominate student life. Have you observed a similar situation in which something ordinary (an object or an activity) develops into something significant for a larger group? Analyze the factors that contributed to this added significance. Are they similar to or different from the factors playing a role in the rise of the "chopstick civilization" in Cao's automotive school?

GROUP ACTIVITIES

1. In a group, make a list of different eating utensils and dishes. Compare experiences you have had in using these items. Do certain utensils or dishes affect your attitude toward the meal you are eating or the people you are eating with? How?

2. In Cao's school, chopsticks became a symbol of attraction between students. What objects have you observed used similarly? Compare your observations with your classmates' observations.

RESEARCH TOPICS

1. Research the social, political, and economic conditions in China before communism. Concentrate on the conditions in the second half of the nineteenth century and the early 1900s.

2. Look up Mao Tse-tung and the Chinese Cultural Revolution. How does this information help you understand the larger context of Cao's essay?

3. Research authentic Chinese food. How is it different from Western food? How is its preparation different? Analyze and discuss factors you think account for some of these differences. (You may want to limit your research to food from a specific part of China, such as Shanghai or Beijing.)

Champion of the World

by Maya Angelou

Maya Angelou, born in 1928, is a poet, author, and director. She has won numerous awards and honors, including a Grammy award for her poetry readings. She read her poem "On the Pulse of Morning" at the inauguration of Bill Clinton in January 1993. She holds a lifetime appointment as a Reynolds Professor of American Studies at Wake Forest in Winston-Salem, North Carolina. The following work is taken from her autobiography I Know Why the Caged Bird Sings *(1969).*

PREREADING QUESTIONS

1. Who was Joe Louis? If you are not sure, use the Internet to determine his importance.

2. Do you remember an event from your childhood that seemed especially significant to the adults around you? What was that experience? What impact did it have on you?

1 The last inch of space was filled, yet people continued to wedge themselves along the walls of the Store. Uncle Willie had turned the radio up to its last notch so that youngsters on the porch wouldn't miss a word. Women sat on kitchen chairs, dining-room chairs, stools, and upturned wooden boxes. Small children and babies perched on every lap available and men leaned on the shelves or on each other.

2 The apprehensive mood was shot through with shafts of gaiety, as a black sky is streaked with lightning.

3 "I ain't worried 'bout this fight. Joe's gonna whip that cracker like it's open season."

4 "He gone whip him till that white boy call him Momma."

5 At last the talking finished and the string-along songs about razor blades were over and the fight began.

6 "A quick jab to the head." In the Store the crowd grunted. "A left to the head and a right and another left." One of the listeners cackled like a hen and was quieted.

7 "They're in a clinch, Louis is trying to fight his way out."

8 Some bitter comedian on the porch said, "That white man don't mind hugging that niggah now, I betcha."

9 "The referee is moving in to break them up, but Louis finally pushed the contender away and it's an uppercut to the chin. The contender is hanging on, now he's backing away. Louis catches him with a short left to the jaw."

10 A tide of murmuring assent poured out the door and into the yard.

11 "Another left and another left. Louis is saving that mighty right . . ." The mutter in the Store had grown into a baby roar and it was pierced by the clang of a bell and the announcer's "That's the bell for round three, ladies and gentlemen."

12 As I pushed my way into the Store I wondered if the announcer gave any thought to the fact that he was addressing as "ladies and gentlemen" all the Negroes around the world who sat sweating and praying, glued to their "Master's voice."

13 There were only a few calls for RC Colas, Dr. Peppers, and Hires root beer. The real festivities would begin after the fight. Then even the old Christian ladies who taught their children and tried themselves to practice turning the other cheek would buy soft drinks, and if the Brown Bomber's victory was a particularly bloody one they would order peanut patties and Baby Ruths, also.

14 Bailey and I laid coins on top of the cash register. Uncle Willie didn't allow us to ring up sales during a fight. It was too noisy and might shake up the atmosphere. When the gong rang for the next round we pushed through the near-sacred quiet to the herd of children outside.

15   "He's got Louis against the ropes and now it's a left to the body and a right to the ribs. Another right to the body, it looks like it was low . . . Yes, ladies and gentlemen, the referee is signaling but the contender keeps raining the blows on Louis. It's another to the body, and it looks like Louis is going down."

16   My race groaned. It was our people falling. It was another lynching, yet another Black man hanging on a tree. One more woman ambushed and raped. A Black boy whipped and maimed. It was hounds on the trail of a man running through slimy swamps. It was a white woman slapping her maid for being forgetful.

17   The men in the Store stood away from the walls and at attention. Women greedily clutched the babes on their laps while on the porch the shufflings and smiles, flirtings and pinching of a few minutes before were gone. This might be the end of the world. If Joe lost we were back in slavery and beyond help. It would all be true, the accusations that we were lower types of human beings. Only a little higher than apes. True that we were stupid and ugly and lazy and dirty and, unlucky and worst of all, that God Himself hated us and ordained us to be hewers of wood and drawers of water, forever, and ever, world without end.

18   We didn't breathe. We didn't hope. We waited.

19   "He's off the ropes, ladies and gentlemen. He's moving towards the center of the ring." There was no time to be relieved. The worst might still happen.

20   "And now it looks like Joe is mad. He's caught Carnera with a left hook to the head and a right to the head. It's a left jab to the body and another left to the head. There's a left cross and a right to the head. The contender's right eye is bleeding and he can't seem to keep his block up. Louis is penetrating every block. The referee is moving in, but Louis sends a left to the body and it's an uppercut to the chin and the contender is dropping. He's on the canvas, ladies and gentlemen."

21   Babies slid to the floor as women stood up and men leaned toward the radio.

22   "Here's the referee. He's counting. One, two, three, four, five, six, seven . . . Is the contender trying to get up again?"

23   All the men in the store shouted, "NO."

24   "—eight, nine, ten." There were a few sounds from the audience, but they seemed to be holding themselves in against tremendous pressure.

25   "The fight is all over, ladies and gentlemen. Let's get the microphone over to the referee . . . Here he is. He's got the Brown Bomber's hand, he's holding it up . . . Here he is . . ."

26   Then the voice, husky and familiar, came to wash over us—"The winnah, and still heavyweight champeen of the world . . . Joe Louis."

27   Champion of the world. A Black boy. Some Black mother's son.

28   He was the strongest man in the world. People drank Coca-Colas like ambrosia and ate candy bars like Christmas. Some of the men went behind the Store and poured white lightning in their soft-drink bottles, and a few of the bigger boys followed them. Those who were not chased away came back blowing their breath in front of themselves like proud smokers.

29   It would take an hour or more before people would leave the Store and head home. Those who lived too far had made arrangements to stay in town. It wouldn't do for a Black man and his family to be caught on a lonely country road on a night when Joe Louis had proved that we were the strongest people in the world.

READING QUESTIONS

1. According to Angelou, what is the relevance of the fight in the segregated South of the 1930s?

2. Approximately how old is Angelou when the fight occurs? What is her role at the store?

3. How does the adult Angelou view the fight? What points in the narrative reveal that it is the adult Angelou telling the story?

4. What is the significance of paragraphs 16 and 17?

5. What does the final paragraph of the reading reveal about the impact of Joe Louis's victory?

WRITING TOPICS

1. Write an essay in which you describe a historical event and its impact on you, your family, and/or your community.

2. Write an essay about an individual of your choice who you think stands for more than just his or her job. Be sure to explain how this individual reflects the values you are attributing to him or her.

3. Angelou describes how a race placed all of their hopes and dreams upon one sporting event. Do you think it is fair to athletes to be expected to behave as symbols and role models for a particular political or social cause?

GROUP PROJECT

1. Working in groups, identify other sports figures whose actions impact more than just the sports world. Select one of these athletes, and write a paper, as a group, explaining what our attitudes toward this athlete reveal about our society.

2. Working in groups, brainstorm to identify other athletic events that have had political or social significance. Select one of these events, and write a paper in which you explain the relationship between the athletic event and what it stood for.

RESEARCH TOPICS

1. Research Joe Louis's career and the significance of the particular fight discussed in Angelou's work. Based on your research do you think both whites and blacks responded to the fight in the ways that Angelou describes?

2. Research Maya Angelou, and select another of her works. Compare and contrast how Angelou uses her own experience to express the social and political issues facing America.

The Prisoner Who Wore Glasses

by Bessie Head

Bessie Head (1937–1986) had the unusual distinction of being born in a mental hospital in Pietermaritzburg, South Africa. Her mother had been forcibly admitted to the mental hospital because she was white and the father of her child was black. A mixed-race family adopted Bessie, and she was able to get an education and become a teacher. Eventually, she left teaching and began writing both novels and short stories. She is considered to be one of Africa's most outstanding writers.

PREREADING QUESTIONS

1. For what beliefs would you be willing to go to prison?
2. Can enemies ever learn to work together? If your answer is yes, what must happen for them to come together?

1 Scarcely a breath of wind disturbed the stillness of the day and the long rows of cabbages were bright green in the sunlight. Large white clouds drifted slowly across the deep blue sky. Now and then they obscured the sun and caused a chill on the backs of the prisoners who had to work all day long in the cabbage field. This trick the clouds were playing with the sun eventually caused one of the prisoners who wore glasses to stop work, straighten up, and peer shortsightedly at them. He was a thin little fellow with a hollowed-out chest and comic knobbly knees. He also had a lot of fanciful ideas because he smiled at the clouds.

2   "Perhaps they want me to send a message to the children," he thought tenderly, noting that the clouds were drifting in the direction of his home some hundred miles away. But before he could frame the message, the warder in charge of his work detail shouted: "Hey, what you tink you're doing, Brille?"

3   The prisoner swung round, blinking rapidly, yet at the same time sizing up the enemy. He was a new warder, named Jacobus Stephanus Hannetjie. His eyes were the color of the sky but they were frightening. A simple, primitive, brutal soul gazed out of them.

4   The prisoner bent down quickly and a message was quietly passed down the line: "We're in for trouble this time, comrades."

5   "Why?" rippled back up the line.

6   "Because he's not human," the reply rippled down and yet only the crunching of the spades as they turned over the earth disturbed the stillness.

7   This particular work detail was known as Span One. It was composed of ten men and they were all political prisoners. They were grouped together for convenience, as it was one of the prison regulations that no black warder should be in charge of a political prisoner lest this prisoner convert him to his views. It never seemed to occur to the authorities that this very reasoning was the strength of Span One and a clue to the strange terror they aroused in the warders. As political prisoners they were unlike the other prisoners in the sense that they felt no guilt nor were they outcasts of society. All guilty men instinctively cower, which was why it was the kind of prison where men got knocked out cold with a blow at the back of the head from an iron bar. Up until the arrival of Warder Hannetjie, no warder had dared beat any member of Span One and no warder had lasted more than a week with them. The battle was entirely psychological. Span One was assertive and it was beyond the scope of white warders to handle assertive black men. Thus, Span One had got out of control. They were the best thieves and liars in the camp. They lived all day on raw cabbages. They chatted and smoked tobacco. And since they moved, thought, and acted as one, they had perfected every technique of group concealment.

8   Trouble began that very day between Span One and Warder Hannetjie. It was because of the shortsightedness of Brille. That was the nickname he was given in prison and is the Afrikaans word for someone who wears glasses. Brille could never judge the approach of the prison gates and on several previous occasions he had munched on cabbages and dropped them almost at the feet of the warder, and all previous warders had overlooked this. Not so Warder Hannetjie.

9   "Who dropped that cabbage?" he thundered.

10   Brille stepped out of line. "I did," he said meekly.

11   "All right," said Hannetjie. "The whole Span goes three meals off."

12   "But I told you I did it," Brille protested.

13   The blood rushed to Warder Hannetjie's face. "Look 'ere," he said. "I don't take orders from a kaffir. I don't know what kind of kaffir you tink you are. Why don't you say Baas? I'm your Baas. Why don't you say Baas, hey?"

14   Brille blinked his eyes rapidly but by contrast his voice was strangely calm. "I'm twenty years older than you," he said.

15   It was the first thing that came to mind but the comrades seemed to think it a huge joke. A titter swept up the line. The next thing, Warder Hannetjie whipped out a knobkerrie and gave Brille several blows about the head. What surprised his comrades was the speed with which Brille had removed his glasses or else they would have been smashed to pieces on the ground.

16   That evening in the cell Brille was very apologetic. "I'm sorry, comrades," he said. "I've put you into a hell of a mess."

17   "Never mind, brother," they said. "What happens to one of us happens to all."

18   "I'll try to make up for it, comrades," he said. "I'll steal something so that you don't go hungry."

19   Privately, Brille was very philosophical about his head wounds. It was the first time an act of violence had been perpetrated against him but he had long been a witness of extreme, almost unbelievable human brutality. He had

twelve children and his mind traveled back that evening through the sixteen years of bedlam in which he had lived. It had all happened in a small drab little three-bedroom house in a small drab little street in the Eastern Cape and the children kept coming year after year because neither he nor Martha managed the contraceptives the right way and a teacher's salary never allowed moving to a bigger house and he was always taking exams to improve this salary only to have it all eaten up by hungry mouths. Everything was pretty horrible, especially the way the children fought. They'd get hold of each other's heads and give them a good bashing against the wall. Martha gave up somewhere along the line, so they worked out a thing between them. The bashings, biting, and blood were to operate in full swing until he came home. He was to be the bogeyman and when it worked he never failed to have a sense of godhead at the way in which his presence could change savages into fairly reasonable human beings.

20   Yet somehow it was this chaos and mismanagement at the center of his life that drove him into politics. It was really an ordered beautiful world with just a few basic slogans to learn along with the rights of mankind. At one stage, before things became very bad, there were conferences to attend, all very far away from home.

21   "Let's face it," he thought ruefully. "I'm only learning right now what it means to be a politician. All this while I've been running away from Martha and the kids."

22   And the pain in his head brought a hard lump to his throat. That was what the children did to each other daily and Martha wasn't managing and if Warder Hannetjie had not interrupted him that morning he would have sent the following message: "Be good comrades, my children. Cooperate, then life will run smoothly."

23   The next day Warder Hannetjie caught this old man with twelve children stealing grapes from the farm shed. They were an enormous quantity of grapes in a ten-gallon tin and for this misdeed the old man spent a week in the isolation cell. In fact, Span One as a whole was in constant trouble. Warder Hannetjie seemed to have eyes at the back of his head. He uncovered the trick about the cabbages, how they were split in two with the spade and immediately covered with earth and then unearthed again and eaten with split-second timing. He found out how tobacco smoke was beaten into the ground and he found out how conversations were whispered down the wind.

24   For about two weeks Span One lived in acute misery. The cabbages, tobacco, and conversations had been the pivot of jail life to them. Then one evening they noticed that their good old comrade who wore the glasses was looking rather pleased with himself. He pulled out a four-ounce packet of tobacco by way of explanation and the comrades fell upon it with great greed. Brille merely smiled. After all, he was the father of many children. But when the last shred had disappeared, it occurred to the comrades that they ought to be puzzled.

25   Someone said: "I say, brother. We're watched like hawks these days. Where did you get the tobacco?"

26   "Hannetjie gave it to me," said Brille.

27   There was a long silence. Into it dropped a quiet bombshell. "I saw Hannetjie in the shed today"—and the failing eyesight blinked rapidly. "I caught him in the act of stealing five bags of fertilizer and he bribed me to keep my mouth shut."

28   There was another long silence.

29   "Prison is an evil life," Brille continued, apparently discussing some irrelevant matter. "It makes a man contemplate all kinds of evil deeds."

30   He held out his hand and closed it. "You know, comrades," he said. "I've got Hannetjie. I'll betray him tomorrow."

31   Everyone began talking at once.

32   "Forget it, brother. You'll get shot."

33   Brille laughed.

34   "I won't," he said. "That is what I mean about evil. I am a father of children and I saw today that Hannetjie is just a child and stupidly truthful. I'm going to punish him severely because we need a good warder."

35   The following day, with Brille as witness, Hannetjie confessed to the theft of the fertilizer and was fined a large sum of money. From then on, Span One did very much as they pleased while Warder Hannetjie stood by and said nothing. But it was Brille who carried this to extremes.

36   One day, at the close of work Warder Hannetjie said: "Brille, pick up my jacket and carry it back to the camp."

37   "But nothing in the regulations says I'm your servant, Hannetjie," Brille replied coolly.

38   "I've told you not to call me Hannetjie. You must say, Baas," but Warder Hannetjie's voice lacked conviction.

39   In turn, Brille squinted up at him. "I'll tell you something about this Baas business, Hannetjie," he said. "One of these days we are going to run the country. You are going to clean my car. Now, I have a fifteen-year-old son and I'd die of shame if you had to tell him that I ever called you Baas."

40   Warder Hannetjie went red in the face and picked up his coat.

41   On another occasion Brille was seen to be walking about the prison yard, openly smoking tobacco. On being taken before the prison commander, he claimed to have received the tobacco from Warder Hannetjie. All throughout the tirade from his chief, Warder Hannetjie failed to defend himself, but his nerve broke completely.

42   He called Brille to one side. "Brille," he said. "This thing between you and me must end. You may not know it but I have a wife and children and you're driving me to suicide."

43   "Why, don't you like your own medicine, Hannetjie?" Brille asked quietly.

44   "I can give you anything you want," Warder Hannetjie said in desperation.

45   "It's not only me but the whole of Span One," said Brille cunningly. "The whole of Span One wants something from you."

46   Warder Hannetjie brightened with relief. "I tink I can manage if it's tobacco you want," he said.

47   Brille looked at him, for the first time struck with pity and guilt. He wondered if he had carried the whole business too far. The man was really a child.

48   "It's not tobacco we want, but you," he said. "We want you on our side. We want a good warder because without a good warder we won't be able to manage the long stretch ahead."

49   Warder Hannetjie interpreted this request in his own fashion and his interpretation of what was good and human often left the prisoners of Span One speechless with surprise. He had a way of slipping off his revolver and picking up a spade and digging alongside Span One. He had a way of producing unheard-of luxuries like boiled eggs from his farm nearby and things like cigarettes, and Span One responded nobly and got the reputation of being the best work detail in the camp. And it wasn't only take from their side. They were awfully good at stealing certain commodities like fertilizer which were needed on the farm of Warder Hannetjie.

—1973

READING QUESTIONS

1. Is there any significance to the fact that Brille wears glasses?
2. Why did Brille get into politics?
3. What was Brille's home life like?
4. Why won't the prison authorities allow black warders to guard the political prisoners?
5. How does Brille get Hannetjie to help the prisoners?
6. Why won't Brille call Hannetjie *Baas*?
7. What is the arrangement Brille and Hannetjie eventually agree on?

WRITING TOPICS

1. Keeping in mind that the prisoners in Span One are political prisoners—men jailed for their beliefs—explain why the story's ending is disturbing.
2. Hannetjie, it can be said, represents an oppressive and racist government. Brille and the other prisoners represent the oppressed freedom seekers. What does the end of the story suggest about cooperation?

GROUP ACTIVITIES

1. Brille is described as very clever and cunning. As a group, note some of the passages in the story that suggest Brille may not be as clever as he thinks.
2. In the last paragraph we are told that Span One becomes "the best work detail in the camp." The members of Span One are political prisoners. Have each member of the group list the reasons why they should not be the best workers.

RESEARCH TOPICS

1. The setting for this story is South Africa, during the time of Apartheid. Research the topic of Apartheid. Why was it considered one of the worst policies in the world?
2. Under the policy of Apartheid, how were political prisoners treated?

Alabanza: In Praise of Local 100

by Martín Espada

Martín Espada is a poet whose latest collection of poetry is A Mayan Astronomer in Hell's Kitchen: Poems *(W. W. Norton, 2001). He has received the PEN/Voelker Award for Poetry and the Paterson Poetry Prize. Martín Espada is an associate professor of English at the University of Massachusetts–Amherst and lives with his wife and son in Amherst, Massachusetts. This poem was written shortly after the September 11 attack on the World Trade Center.*

PREREADING QUESTIONS

1. When most people think of the people who were killed in the September 11 attacks, they usually think of the firemen, rescue workers, and professional businesspeople in the offices. What other people might have been working in the building?

2. The Spanish word *alabanza* means "praise" or "song of praise." In what kind of building do we expect to hear praises sung? As you read, notice any other references that could be applied to a church.

For the 43 members of Hotel Employees and Restaurant Employees Local 100, working at the Windows on the World restaurant, who lost their lives in the attack on the World Trade Center.

Alabanza. Praise the cook with a shaven head
and a tattoo on his shoulder that said *Oye*,
a blue-eyed Puerto Rican with people from Fajardo,
the harbor of pirates centuries ago.
Praise the lighthouse in Fajardo, candle
glimmering white to worship the dark saint of the sea.
Alabanza. Praise the cook's yellow Pirates cap
worn in the name of Roberto Clemente, his plane
that flamed into the ocean loaded with cans for Nicaragua,
for all the mouths chewing the ash of earthquakes.
Alabanza. Praise the kitchen radio, dial clicked
even before the dial on the oven, so that music and Spanish
rose before bread. Praise the bread. *Alabanza.*

Praise Manhattan from a hundred and seven flights up,
like Atlantis glimpsed through the windows of an ancient aquarium.
Praise the great windows where immigrants from the kitchen
could squint and almost see their world, hear the chant of nations:

Ecuador, México, República Dominicana,
Haiti, Yemen, Ghana, Bangladesh.
Alabanza. Praise the kitchen in the morning,
where the gas burned blue on every stove
and exhaust fans fired their diminutive propellers,
hands cracked eggs with quick thumbs
or sliced open cartons to build an altar of cans.
Alabanza. Praise the busboy's music, the *chime-chime*
of his dishes and silverware in the tub.
Alabanza. Praise the dish-dog, the dishwasher
who worked that morning because another dishwasher
could not stop coughing, or because he needed overtime
to pile the sacks of rice and beans for a family
floating away on some Caribbean island plagued by frogs.
Alabanza. Praise the waitress who heard the radio in the kitchen
and sang to herself about a man gone. *Alabanza.*

After the thunder wilder than thunder,
after the shudder deep in the glass of the great windows,
after the radio stopped singing like a tree full of terrified frogs,
after night burst the dam of day and flooded the kitchen,
for a time the stoves glowed in darkness like the lighthouse in Fajardo,
like a cook's soul. Soul I say, even if the dead cannot tell us
about the bristles of God's beard because God has no face,
soul I say, to name the smoke-beings flung in constellations
across the night sky of this city and cities to come.
Alabanza I say, even if God has no face.

Alabanza. When the war began, from Manhattan and Kabul
two constellations of smoke rose and drifted to each other,
mingling in icy air, and one said with an Afghan tongue:
Teach me to dance. We have no music here.
And the other said with a Spanish tongue:
I will teach you. Music is all we have.

READING QUESTIONS

1. What do we learn about the lives of each of these characters: the cook, the dishwasher, the waitress? What details make them seem like real people?

2. The name of the restaurant where they worked was "Windows on the World." Why do you think a restaurant on top of the world's tallest building had that name? What other meaning for the name is suggested in the second stanza?

3. What things are mentioned in the poem that could be found in a church? Why does the poet compare the restaurant kitchen to a church?

4. The first three stanzas tell us about the restaurant just before the attack. Which stanza describes the attack? What do we see in that stanza that we have seen in the first part of the poem?

5. In the last stanza, what does the poet imagine happening after the attack? How is this related to the name of the restaurant? How is it related to the idea of a church? What else does this stanza make you think about?

6. Why does the soul of the Afghan say, "We have no music here"? Why does the other say, "Music is all we have"?

7. What do you think is the main point of this poem?

WRITING TOPICS

1. Write an essay explaining the comparison between the restaurant and the church. Tell your reader why the poet makes this comparison, and show where it happens.

2. Why does the poet praise the people who worked in the restaurant kitchen? Write an essay explaining why these workers were or were not worthy of being praised.

GROUP ACTIVITIES

1. Each member of the group should pick one character. Find the details that describe your character, and think of one sentence that could summarize your character. As a group, try to write a sentence or paragraph that summarizes all the characters.

2. As a group, make a list of the things that the poet compares to other things. Also, look for comparisons that are only suggested, not clearly stated. What is the point of each comparison?

RESEARCH TOPICS

1. Make a list of all the proper names in the poem. Try searching online to find out who or what each refers to.

2. What do you know about the immigrants from other countries who live and work in your area? Using either local newspapers or interviews, find out what parts of the world people come from and what work they do in your area.

3. Where did your own family come from before moving to the United States? When did they come here? Interview family members to find out.

Media

Exploring the Theme

■ What do we mean by media? What are some different kinds of media that you encounter daily?

■ Who controls different types of media? Why do they invest their time, energy, and money in these different forms of communication?

■ Can we always be sure that what we see, hear, or read in the media is true? Why or why not?

■ How has the media changed in the last fifty years? How has it changed in the last ten years?

■ How can people ensure that they are not deceived by media?

The Media's Image of Arabs

by Jack G. Shaheen

Arabs make up more than 100 million of the world's population. Most live in Saudi Arabia, Jordan, Qatar, Kuwait, Oman, the United Arab Emirates, Bahrain, Yemen, Iraq, Egypt, Syria, Israel, Lebanon, Libya, Algeria, Morocco, the Sudan, Tunisia, and Turkey, although Arabs also live in the Americas. Shaheen, a first-generation Lebanese-American, has written The TV Arab *and* The Hollywood Arab. *The essay that appears here was first published in* Newsweek *in 1988.*

PREREADING QUESTION

Make a list of Arabs you have seen in the media (on the news, in movies, on television). How would you characterize each?

1 America's bogeyman is the Arab. Until the nightly news brought us TV pictures of Palestinian boys being punched and beaten, almost all portraits of Arabs seen in America were dangerously threatening. Arabs were either billionaires or bombers—rarely victims. They were hardly ever seen as ordinary people practicing law, driving taxis, singing lullabies or healing the sick. Though TV news may portray them more sympathetically now, the absence of positive media images nurtures suspicion and stereotype. As an Arab-American, I have found that ugly caricatures have had an enduring impact on my family.

2 I was sheltered from prejudicial portraits at first. My parents came from Lebanon in the 1920s; they met and married in America. Our home in the steel city of Clairton, Pa., was a center for ethnic sharing—black, white, Jew

and gentile. There was only one major source of media images then, at the State movie theater where I was lucky enough to get a part-time job as an usher. But in the late 1940s, Westerns and war movies were popular, not Middle Eastern dramas. Memories of World War II were fresh, and the screen heavies were the Japanese and the Germans. True to the cliché of the times, the only good Indian was a dead Indian. But when I mimicked or mocked the bad guys, my mother cautioned me. She explained that stereotypes blur our vision and corrupt the imagination. "Have compassion for all people, Jackie," she said. "This way, you'll learn to experience the joy of accepting people as they are, and not as they appear in films. Stereotypes hurt."

3   Mother was right. I can remember the Saturday afternoon when my son, Michael, who was seven, and my daughter, Michele, six, suddenly called out: "Daddy, Daddy, they've got some bad Arabs on TV!" They were watching that great American morality play, TV wrestling. Akbar the Great, who liked to hear the cracking of bones, and Abdullah the Butcher, a dirty fighter who liked to inflict pain, were pinning their foes with "camel locks." From that day on, I knew I had to try to neutralize the media caricatures.

4   It hasn't been easy. With my children, I have watched animated heroes Heckle and Jeckle pull the rug from under "Ali Boo-Boo, the Desert Rat," and Laverne and Shirley stop "Sheik Ha-Mean-le" from conquering "the U.S. and the world." I have read comic books like the "Fantastic Four" and "G.I. Combat" whose characters have sketched Arabs as "lowlifes" and "human hyenas." Negative stereotypes were everywhere. A dictionary informed my youngsters that an Arab is a "vagabond, drifter, hobo and vagrant." Whatever happened, my wife wondered, to Aladdin's good genie?

5   To a child, the world is simple: good versus evil. But my children and others with Arab roots grew up without ever having seen a humane Arab on the silver screen, someone to pattern their lives after. Is it easier for a camel to go through the eye of a needle than for a screen Arab to appear as a genuine human being?

6   Hollywood producers must have an instant Ali Baba kit that contains scimitars, veils, sunglasses and such Arab clothing as *chadors* and *kafiyahs*. In the mythical "Ay-rabland," oil wells, tents, mosques, goats and shepherds prevail. Between the sand dunes, the camera focuses on a mock-up of a palace from "Arabian Nights"—or a military air base. Recent movies suggest that Americans are at war with Arabs, forgetting the fact that out of 21 Arab nations, America is friendly with 19 of them. And in "Wanted Dead or Alive," a movie that starred Gene Simmons, the leader of the rock group Kiss, the war comes home when an Arab terrorist comes to the United States dressed as a rabbi and, among other things, conspires with Arab-Americans to poison the people of Los Angeles. The movie was released last year.

7   **Racial slurs:** The Arab remains American culture's favorite whipping boy. In his memoirs, Terrel Bell, Ronald Reagan's first secretary of education, writes about an "apparent bias among mid-level, right-wing staffers at the White House" who dismissed Arabs as "sand niggers." Sadly, the racial slurs continue. At a recent teacher's conference, I met a woman from Sioux Falls, S.D., who told me about the persistence of discrimination. She was in the process of

adopting a baby when an agency staffer warned her that the infant had a problem. When she asked whether the child was mentally ill, or physically handicapped, there was silence. Finally, the worker said: "The baby is Jordanian."

8   To me, the Arab demon of today is much like the Jewish demon of yesterday. We deplore the false portrait of Jews as a swarthy menace. Yet a similar portrait has been accepted and transferred to another group of Semites—the Arabs. Print and broadcast journalists have started to challenge this stereotype. They are now revealing more humane images of Palestinian Arabs, a people who traditionally suffered from the myth that Palestinian equals terrorist. Others could follow that lead and retire the stereotypical Arab to a media Valhalla.

9   It would be a step in the right direction if movie and TV producers developed characters modeled after real-life Arab-Americans. We could then see a White House correspondent like Helen Thomas, whose father came from Lebanon, in "The Golden Girls," a heart surgeon patterned after Dr. Michael DeBakey on "St. Elsewhere," or a Syrian-American playing tournament chess like Yasser Seirawan, the Seattle grandmaster.

10   Politicians, too, should speak out against the cardboard caricatures. They should refer to Arabs as friends, not just as moderates. And religious leaders could state that Islam like Christianity and Judaism maintains that all mankind is one family in the care of God. When all imagemakers rightfully begin to treat Arabs and all other minorities with respect and dignity, we may begin to unlearn our prejudices.

READING QUESTION

According to Shaheen, how are Arabs depicted in the media? What is objectionable to him about these depictions? What effects does he attribute to these depictions?

WRITING TOPICS

1. Shaheen writes that Arabs are portrayed negatively in the media. Write an essay in which you describe another group of people who are depicted stereotypically in the media.

2. Shaheen writes that people's attitudes toward Arabs are affected by the stereotypes they see in media. Do you think that people's behavior is affected by what they see or hear in the media?

GROUP ACTIVITY

Have each member of the group make a list of news events that focused on Arabs. Explain whether your impression was positive or negative. What in the media's portrayal led you to your positive or negative perception? How many positive portrayals were recorded in your group? How many negative?

RESEARCH TOPICS

1. Research one or all of the events and people mentioned in this article. Share your findings with your class in discussion or a brief written summary.

2. Search for recent articles and cartoons on topics related to Arabic countries, such as oil, Middle East peace agreements, etc. Do these recent articles reflect the biases that Shaheen discusses?

3. Search for more information about contributions of Americans of Arabic descent, either in the nation or in your own locality. Report on those findings to your class.

The Bias of Language, The Bias of Pictures

by Neil Postman and Steve Powers

Neil Postman has written many books and articles on education and the media, including Building a Bridge to the Eighteenth Century: How the Past Can Improve Our Future. *He is professor of communication arts and sciences at New York University. Steve Powers is a reporter. In this article, they examine the ways that we think about television news coverage.*

PREREADING QUESTIONS

1. What is the most recent event that has been reported on TV news? How much of that did you watch? What other events can you remember receiving national attention on television?

2. Have you ever seen two different reports of the same event? Were they similar or different?

1 When a television news show distorts the truth by altering or manufacturing facts (through re-creations), a television viewer is defenseless even if a re-creation is properly labeled. Viewers are still vulnerable to misinformation since they will not know (at least in the case of docudramas) what parts are fiction and what parts are not. But the problems of verisimilitude posed by re-creations pale to insignificance when compared to the problems viewers face when encountering a straight (no-monkey-business) show. All news shows, in a sense, are re-creations in that what we hear and see on them are attempts to represent actual events, and are not the events themselves. Perhaps, to avoid ambiguity, we might call all news shows "re-presentations" instead of "re-creations." These re-presentations come to us in two forms: language and pictures. The question then arises: what do viewers have to know about language and pictures in order to be properly armed to defend themselves against the seductions of eloquence (to use Bertrand Russell's apt phrase)? . . .

2 [Let us look at] the problem of pictures. It is often said that a picture is worth a thousand words. Maybe so. But it is probably equally true that one word is worth a thousand pictures, at least sometimes—for example, when it comes to understanding the world we live in. Indeed, the whole problem with news on television comes down to this: all the words uttered in an hour of

news coverage could be printed on one page of a newspaper. And the world cannot be understood in one page. Of course, there is a compensation: television offers pictures, and the pictures move. Moving pictures are a kind of language in themselves, but the language of pictures differs radically from oral and written language, and the differences are crucial for understanding television news.

3   To begin with, pictures, especially single pictures, speak only in particularities. Their vocabulary is limited to concrete representation. Unlike words and sentences, a picture does not present to us an idea or concept about the world, except as we use language itself to convert the image to idea. By itself, a picture cannot deal with the unseen, the remote, the internal, the abstract. It does not speak of "man," only of *a* man; not of "tree," only of *a* tree. You cannot produce an image of "nature," any more than an image of "the sea." You can only show a particular fragment of the here-and-now—a cliff of a certain terrain, in a certain condition of light; a wave at a moment in time, from a particular point of view. And just as "nature" and "the sea" cannot be photographed, such larger abstractions as truth, honor, love, and falsehood cannot be talked about in the lexicon of individual pictures. For "showing of" and "talking about" are two very different kinds of processes: individual pictures give us the world as object; language, the world as idea. There is no such thing in nature as "man" or "tree." The universe offers no such categories or simplifications; only flux and infinite variety. The picture documents and celebrates the particularities of the universe's infinite variety. Language makes them comprehensible.

4   Of course, moving pictures, video with sound, may bridge the gap by juxtaposing images, symbols, sound, and music. Such images can present emotions and rudimentary ideas. They can suggest the panorama of nature and the joys and miseries of humankind.

5   Picture—smoke pouring from the window, cut to people coughing, an ambulance racing to a hospital, a tombstone in a cemetery.

6   Picture—jet planes firing rockets, explosions, lines of foreign soldiers surrendering, the American flag waving in the wind.

7   Nonetheless, keep in mind that when terrorists want to prove to the world that their kidnap victims are still alive, they photograph them holding a copy of a recent newspaper. The dateline on the newspaper provides the proof that the photograph was taken on or after that date. Without the help of the written word, film and videotape cannot portray temporal dimensions with any precision. Consider a film clip showing an aircraft carrier at sea. One might be able to identify the ship as Soviet or American, but there would be no way of telling where in the world the carrier was, where it was headed, or when the pictures were taken. It is only through language—words spoken over the pictures or reproduced in them—that the image of the aircraft carrier takes on specific meaning.

8   Still, it is possible to enjoy the image of the carrier for its own sake. One might find the hugeness of the vessel interesting; it signifies military power on the move. There is a certain drama in watching the planes come in at high speeds and skid to a stop on the deck. Suppose the ship were burning: that would be even more interesting. This leads to an important point about the

language of pictures. Moving pictures favor images that change. That is why violence and dynamic destruction find their way onto television so often. When something is destroyed violently it is altered in a highly visible way; hence the entrancing power of fire. Fire gives visual form to the ideas of consumption, disappearance, death—the thing that burned is actually taken away by fire. It is at this very basic level that fires make a good subject for television news. Something was here, now it's gone, and the change is recorded on film.

9   Earthquakes and typhoons have the same power. Before the viewer's eyes the world is taken apart. If a television viewer has relatives in Mexico City and an earthquake occurs there, then he or she may take a special interest in the images of destruction as a report from a specific place and time; that is, one may look at television pictures for information about an important event. But film of an earthquake can be interesting even if the viewer cares nothing about the event itself. Which is only to say, as we noted earlier, that there is another way of participating in the news—as a spectator who desires to be entertained. Actually to see buildings topple is exciting, no matter where the buildings are. The world turns to dust before our eyes.

10   Those who produce television news in America know that their medium favors images that move. That is why they are wary of "talking heads," people who simply appear in front of a camera and speak. When talking heads appear on television, there is nothing to record or document, no change in process. In the cinema the situation is somewhat different. On a movie screen, closeups of a good actor speaking dramatically can sometimes be interesting to watch. When Clint Eastwood narrows his eyes and challenges his rival to shoot first, the spectator sees the cool rage of the Eastwood character take visual form, and the narrowing of the eyes is dramatic. But much of the effect of this small movement depends on the size of the movie screen and the darkness of the theater, which make Eastwood and his every action "larger than life."

11   The television screen is smaller than life. It occupies about 15 percent of the viewer's visual field (compared to about 70 percent for the movie screen). It is not set in a darkened theater closed off from the world but in the viewer's ordinary living space. This means that visual changes must be more extreme and more dramatic to be interesting on television. A narrowing of the eyes will not do. A car crash, an earthquake, a burning factory are much better.

12   With these principles in mind, let us examine more closely the structure of a typical newscast, and here we will include in the discussion not only the pictures but all the nonlinguistic symbols that make up a television news show. For example, in America, almost all news shows begin with music, the tone of which suggests important events about to unfold. The music is very important, for it equates the news with various forms of drama and ritual— the opera, for example, or a wedding procession—in which musical themes underscore the meaning of the event. Music takes us immediately into the realm of the symbolic, a world that is not to be taken literally. After all, when events unfold in the real world, they do so without musical accompaniment. More symbolism follows. The sound of teletype machines can be heard in the studio, not because it is impossible to screen this noise out, but because the sound is a kind of music in itself. It tells us that data are pouring in from all

corners of the globe, a sensation reinforced by the world map in the background (or clocks noting the time on different continents). The fact is that teletype machines are rarely used in TV news rooms, having been replaced by silent computer terminals. When seen, they have only a symbolic function.

13   Already, then, before a single news item is introduced, a great deal has been communicated. We know that we are in the presence of a symbolic event, a form of theater in which the day's events are to be dramatized. This theater takes the entire globe as its subject, although it may look at the world from the perspective of a single nation. A certain tension is present, like the atmosphere in a theater just before the curtain goes up. The tension is represented by the music, the staccato beat of the teletype machines, and often the sight of news workers scurrying around typing reports and answering phones. As a technical matter, it would be no problem to build a set in which the newsroom staff remained off camera, invisible to the viewer, but an important theatrical effect would be lost. By being busy on camera, the workers help communicate urgency about the events at hand, which suggests that situations are changing so rapidly that constant revision of the news is necessary.

14   The staff in the background also helps signal the importance of the person in the center, the anchor, "in command" of both the staff and the news. The anchor plays the role of host. He or she welcomes us to the newscast and welcomes us back from the different locations we visit during the filmed reports.

15   Many features of the newscast help the anchor to establish the impression of control. These are usually equated with production values in broadcasting. They include such things as graphics that tell the viewer what is being shown, or maps and charts that suddenly appear on the screen and disappear on cue, or the orderly progression from story to story. They also include the absence of gaps, or "dead time," during the broadcast, even the simple fact that the news starts and ends at a certain hour. These common features are thought of as purely technical matters, which a professional crew handles as a matter of course. But they are also symbols of a dominant theme of television news: the imposition of an orderly world—called "the news"—upon the disorderly flow of events.

16   While the form of a news broadcast emphasizes tidiness and control, its content can best be described as fragmented. Because time is so precious on television, because the nature of the medium favors dynamic visual images, and because the pressures of a commercial structure require the news to hold its audience above all else, there is rarely any attempt to explain issues in depth or place events in their proper context. The news moves nervously from a warehouse fire to a court decision, from a guerrilla war to a World Cup match, the quality of the film most often determining the length of the story. Certain stories show up only because they offer dramatic pictures. Bleachers collapse in South America: hundreds of people are crushed—a perfect television news story, for the cameras can record the face of disaster in all its anguish. Back in Washington, a new budget is approved by Congress. Here there is nothing to photograph because a budget is not a physical event; it is a document full of language and numbers. So the producers of the news will show a photo of the document itself, focusing on the cover where it says "Budget of the United

States of America." Or sometimes they will send a camera crew to the government printing plant where copies of the budget are produced. That evening, while the contents of the budget are summarized by a voice-over, the viewer sees stacks of documents being loaded into boxes at the government printing plant. Then a few of the budget's more important provisions will be flashed on the screen in written form, but this is such a time-consuming process—using television as a printed page—that the producers keep it to a minimum. In short, the budget is not televisable, and for that reason its time on the news must be brief. The bleacher collapse will get more time that evening.

17   While appearing somewhat chaotic, these disparate stories are not just dropped in the news program helter-skelter. The appearance of a scattershot story order is really orchestrated to draw the audience from one story to the next—from one section to the next—through the commercial breaks to the end of the show. The story order is constructed to hold and build the viewership rather than place events in context or explain issues in depth.

18   Of course, it is a tendency of journalism in general to concentrate on the surface of events rather than underlying conditions; this is as true for the newspaper as it is for the newscast. But several features of television undermine whatever efforts journalists may make to give sense to the world. One is that a television broadcast is a series of events that occur in sequence, and the sequence is the same for all viewers. This is not true for a newspaper page, which displays many items simultaneously, allowing readers to choose the order in which they read them. If newspaper readers want only a summary of the latest tax bill, they can read the headline and the first paragraph of an article, and if they want more, they can keep reading. In a sense, then, everyone reads a different newspaper, for no two readers will read (or ignore) the same items.

19   But all television viewers see the same broadcast. They have no choices. A report is either in the broadcast or out, which means that anything which is of narrow interest is unlikely to be included. As NBC News executive Reuven Frank once explained.

> A newspaper, for example, can easily afford to print an item of conceivable interest to only a fraction of its readers. A television news program must be put together with the assumption that each item will be of some interest to everyone that watches. Every time a newspaper includes a feature which will attract a specialized group it can assume it is adding at least a little bit to its circulation. To the degree a television news program includes an item of this sort . . . it must assume that its audience will diminish.

20   The need to "include everyone," an identifying feature of commercial television in all forms, prevents journalists from offering lengthy or complex explanations, or from tracing the sequence of events leading up to today's headlines. One of the ironies of political life in modern democracies is that many problems which concern the "general welfare" are of interest only to specialized groups. Arms control, for example, is an issue that literally concerns everyone in the world. And yet the language of arms control and the complexity of this subject are so daunting that only a minority of people can actually follow the issue from week to week and month to month. If it wants to act responsibly, a

newspaper can at least make available more information about arms control than most people want. Commercial television cannot afford to do so.

21   But even if commercial television could afford to do so, it wouldn't. The fact that television news is principally made up of moving pictures prevents it from offering lengthy, coherent explanations of events. A television news show reveals the world as a series of unrelated, fragmentary moments. It does not—and cannot be expected to—offer a sense of coherence or meaning. What does this suggest to a TV viewer? That the viewer must come with a prepared mind—information, opinions, a sense of proportion, an articulate value system. To the TV viewer lacking such mental equipment, a news program is only a kind of rousing light show. Here a falling building, there a five-alarm fire, everything the world as an object, much without meaning, connections, or continuity.

READING QUESTIONS

1. The vocabulary in some parts of this reading will be challenging. Try to read without stopping to look up words, but underline or circle the ones you don't know. Then look them up and reread the essay.

2. Why are pictures different from words, according to Postman and Powers? What point do they make when they mention that kidnappers sometimes show pictures of their victims? Why are violence and destruction such good topics for moving pictures?

3. How does the size of the TV screen affect the kinds of pictures that are shown?

4. What are "nonlinguistic symbols"? What does music, for example, communicate without using words? Why do newscasts often show the staff, the cameras, and so on?

5. What is the news anchor? How is that person's image of control established? Why is that important?

6. Why is it important that newscasts show many short images with little explanation? Why does that happen?

7. How are the different stories arranged? How is that different from the way that a newspaper is arranged? What is the effect on the viewer or reader?

8. What do the authors suggest that viewers do to make better sense of the news?

WRITING TOPIC

1. Watch a news broadcast, and find examples of the techniques that Postman and Powers describe. Write an essay applying their ideas to the program you watched.

2. Using one of the following group activities or research topics, write an essay. Be sure to use Postman and Powers's ideas as well as the information that you find.

GROUP ACTIVITIES

1. Record a news program. As a group, watch the program; assign each member of the group one aspect of the coverage to observe (picture selection, nonlinguistic symbols, order of giving the different topics, etc.).

2. Each member of the group should watch a different news program and report back to the group on the topics covered and what he or she remembers about them. How similar or how different were the broadcasts?

RESEARCH TOPICS

1. Watch news coverage of one story, and take notes on the pictures shown, the music used, the time devoted to it, and what stories came before and after it. Finally, make note of what you remember about the story and what your opinion is. Then find a newspaper story covering the same event. Note the pictures used, where it is located on the page, and finally, what information you are given and your reaction to the event. Compare the coverage of the two.

2. Find a newsmagazine that gives even more coverage of the event you observed in question 1. What do you notice about how it is presented and what information you are given? Does that affect your opinion?

The Myth of the Latin Woman: I Just Met a Girl Named María*

by Judith Ortiz Cofer

Judith Ortiz Cofer came to mainland United States from Puerto Rico with her family when she was a young child. She is the author of many essays, poetry, short stories, and other fiction, and she has published several collections of poems and essays. She recounts growing up in New York as a child of two cultures in Silent Dancing: A Partial Remembrance of a Puerto Rican Childhood, *a collection of essays with some of her poetry. Her novel* The Line of the Sun *develops the lives and domestic relationships of Puerto Ricans living on the mainland. Judith Ortiz Cofer's work is recognized for its challenging and consciousness-raising discussions of identity and heritage. "The Myth of the Latin Woman" shows how stereotyping can arise from misunderstandings about cultural codes of dress and conduct and the media.*

PREREADING QUESTION

Do you think certain groups of people are stereotyped? What do you think is the basis of the stereotyping? Does the media, especially entertainment media such as film or TV, present minorities fairly, as complex individuals?

1   On a bus trip to London from Oxford University where I was earning some graduate credits one summer, a young man, obviously fresh from a pub, spotted me and as if struck by inspiration went down on his knees in the aisle. With both hands over his heart he broke into an Irish tenor's rendition of "María" from *West Side Story*. My politely amused fellow passengers gave his lovely voice the round of gentle applause it deserved. Though I was not quite as amused, I managed my version of an English smile: no show of teeth, no extreme contortions of the facial muscles—I was at this time of my life practicing reserve and cool. Oh, that British control, how I coveted it. But María had followed me to London, reminding me of a prime fact of my life: you can leave the Island, master the English language, and travel as far as you can, but if you are a Latina, especially one like me who so obviously belongs to Rita Moreno's gene pool, the Island travels with you.

2   This is sometimes a very good thing—it may win you that extra minute of someone's attention. But with some people, the same things can make *you* an island—not so much a tropical paradise as an Alcatraz, a place nobody wants to visit. As a Puerto Rican girl growing up in the United States and wanting like most children to "belong," I resented the stereotype that my Hispanic appearance called forth from many people I met.

3   Our family lived in a large urban center in New Jersey during the sixties, where life was designed as a microcosm of my parents' casas on the island. We spoke in Spanish, we ate Puerto Rican food bought at the bodega, and we practiced strict Catholicism complete with Saturday confession and Sunday mass at a church where our parents were accommodated into a one-hour Spanish mass slot, performed by a Chinese priest trained as a missionary for Latin America.

4   As a girl I was kept under strict surveillance, since virtue and modesty were, by cultural equation, the same as family honor. As a teenager I was instructed on how to behave as a proper señorita. But it was a conflicting message girls got, since the Puerto Rican mothers also encouraged their daughters to look and act like women and to dress in clothes our Anglo friends and their mothers found too "mature" for our age. It was, and is, cultural, yet I often felt humiliated when I appeared at an American friend's party wearing a dress more suitable to a semiformal than to a playroom birthday celebration. At Puerto Rican festivities, neither the music nor the colors we wore could be too loud. I still experience a vague sense of letdown when I'm invited to a "party" and it turns out to be a marathon conversation in hushed tones rather than a fiesta with salsa, laughter, and dancing—the kind of celebration I remember from my childhood.

5   I remember Career Day in our high school, when teachers told us to come dressed as if for a job interview. It quickly became obvious that to the barrio girls, "dressing up" sometimes meant wearing ornate jewelry and clothing

that would be more appropriate (by mainstream standards) for the company Christmas party than as daily office attire. That morning I had agonized in front of my closet, trying to figure out what a "career girl" would wear because, essentially, except for Marlo Thomas on TV, I had no models on which to base my decision. I knew how to dress for school: at the Catholic school I attended we all wore uniforms; I knew how to dress for Sunday mass, and I knew what dresses to wear for parties at my relatives' homes. Though I do not recall the precise details of my Career Day outfit, it must have been a composite of the above choices. But I remember a comment my friend (an Italian-American) made in later years that coalesced my impressions of that day. She said that at the business school she was attending the Puerto Rican girls always stood out for wearing "everything at once." She meant, of course, too much jewelry, too many accessories. On that day at school, we were simply made the negative models by the nuns who were themselves not credible fashion experts to any of us. But it was painfully obvious to me that to the others, in their tailored skirts and silk blouses, we must have seemed "hopeless" and "vulgar." Though I now know that most adolescents feel out of step much of the time, I also know that for the Puerto Rican girls of my generation that sense was intensified. The way our teachers and classmates looked at us that day in school was just a taste of the culture clash that awaited us in the real world, where prospective employers and men on the street would often misinterpret our tight skirts and jingling bracelets as a come-on.

6   Mixed cultural signals have perpetuated certain stereotypes—for example, that of the Hispanic woman as the "Hot Tamale" or sexual firebrand. It is a one-dimensional view that the media have found easy to promote. In their special vocabulary, advertisers have designated "sizzling" and "smoldering" as the adjectives of choice for describing not only the foods but also the women of Latin America. From conversations in my house I recall hearing about the harassment that Puerto Rican women endured in factories where the "boss men" talked to them as if sexual innuendo was all they understood and, worse, often gave them the choice of submitting to advances or being fired.

7   It is custom, however, not chromosomes, that leads us to choose scarlet over pale pink. As young girls, we were influenced in our decisions about clothes and colors by the women—older sisters and mothers who had grown up on a tropical island where the natural environment was a riot of primary colors, where showing your skin was one way to keep cool as well as to look sexy. Most important of all, on the island, women perhaps felt freer to dress and move more provocatively, since, in most cases, they were protected by the traditions, mores, and laws of a Spanish/Catholic system of morality and machismo whose main rule was: *You may look at my sister, but if you touch her I will kill you.* The extended family and church structure could provide a young woman with a circle of safety in her small pueblo on the island; if a man "wronged" a girl, everyone would close in to save her family honor.

8   This is what I have gleaned from my discussions as an adult with older Puerto Rican women. They have told me about dressing in their best party clothes on Saturday nights and going to the town's plaza to promenade with their girlfriends in front of the boys they liked. The males were thus given an

opportunity to admire the women and to express their admiration in the form of *piropos:* erotically charged street poems they composed on the spot. I have been subjected to a few piropos while visiting the Island, and they can be outrageous, although custom dictates that they must never cross into obscenity. This ritual, as I understand it, also entails a show of studied indifference on the woman's part; if she is "decent," she must not acknowledge the man's impassioned words. So I do understand how things can be lost in translation. When a Puerto Rican girl dressed in her idea of what is attractive meets a man from the mainstream culture who has been trained to react to certain types of clothing as a sexual signal, a clash is likely to take place. The line I first heard based on the aspect of the myth happened when the boy who took me to my first formal dance leaned over to plant a sloppy overeager kiss painfully on my mouth, and when I didn't respond with sufficient passion said in a resentful tone: "I thought you Latin girls were supposed to mature early"—my first instance of being thought of as a fruit or vegetable—I was supposed to *ripen,* not just grow into womanhood like other girls.

9   It is surprising to some of my professional friends that some people, including those who should know better, still put others "in their place." Though rarer, these incidents are still commonplace in my life. It happened to me most recently during a stay at a very classy metropolitan hotel favored by young professional couples for their weddings. Late one evening after the theater, as I walked toward my room with my colleague (a woman with whom I was coordinating an arts program), a middle-aged man in a tuxedo, a young girl in satin and lace on his arm, stepped directly into our path. With his champagne glass extended toward me, he exclaimed, "Evita!"

10   Our way blocked, my companion and I listened as the man half-recited, half-bellowed "Don't Cry for Me, Argentina." When he finished, the young girl said: "How about a round of applause for my daddy?" We complied, hoping this would bring the silly spectacle to a close. I was becoming aware that our little group was attracting the attention of the other guests. "Daddy" must have perceived this too, and he once more barred the way as we tried to walk past him. He began to shout-sing a ditty to the tune of "La Bamba"—except the lyrics were about a girl named María whose exploits all rhymed with her name and gonorrhea. The girl kept saying "Oh, Daddy" and looking at me with pleading eyes. She wanted me to laugh along with the others. My companion and I stood silently waiting for the man to end his offensive song. When he finished, I looked not at him but at his daughter. I advised her calmly never to ask her father what he had done in the army. Then I walked between them and to my room. My friend complimented me on my cool handling of the situation. I confessed to her that I really had wanted to push the jerk into the swimming pool. I knew that this same man—probably a corporate executive, well educated, even worldly by most standards—would not have been likely to regale a white woman with a dirty song in public. He would perhaps have checked his impulse by assuming that she could be somebody's wife or mother, or at least *somebody* who might take offense. But to him, I was just an Evita or a María: merely a character in his cartoon-populated universe.

11   Because of my education and my proficiency with the English language, I have acquired many mechanisms for dealing with the anger I experience. This was not true for my parents, nor is it true for the many Latin women working at menial jobs who must put up with stereotypes about our ethnic group such as: "They make good domestics." This is another facet of the myth of the Latin woman in the United States. Its origin is simple to deduce. Work as domestics, waitressing, and factory jobs are all that's available to women with little English and few skills. The myth of the Hispanic menial has been sustained by the same media phenomenon that made "Mammy" from *Gone with the Wind* America's idea of the black woman for generations; María, the housemaid or counter girl, is now indelibly etched into the national psyche. The big and the little screens have presented us with the picture of the funny Hispanic maid, mispronouncing words and cooking up a spicy storm in a shiny California kitchen.

12   This media-engendered image of the Latina in the United States has been documented by feminist Hispanic scholars, who claim that such portrayals are partially responsible for the denial of opportunities for upward mobility among Latinas in the professions. I have a Chicana friend working on a Ph.D. in philosophy at a major university. She says her doctor still shakes his head in puzzled amazement at all the "big words" she used. Since I do not wear my diplomas around my neck for all to see, I too have on occasion been sent to that "kitchen," where some think I obviously belong.

13   One such incident that has stayed with me, though I recognize it as a minor offense, happened on the day of my first public poetry reading. It took place in Miami in a boat-restaurant where we were having lunch before the event. I was nervous and excited as I walked in with my notebook in my hand. An older woman motioned me to her table. Thinking (foolish me) that she wanted me to autograph a copy of my brand new slender volume of verse, I went over. She ordered a cup of coffee from me, assuming that I was the waitress. Easy enough to mistake my poems for menus, I suppose. I know that it wasn't an intentional act of cruelty, yet of all the good things that happened that day, I remember that scene most clearly, because it reminded me of what I had to overcome before anyone would take me seriously. In retrospect I understand that my anger gave my reading fire, that I have almost always taken doubts in my abilities as a challenge—and that the result is, most times, a feeling of satisfaction at having won a convert when I see the cold, appraising eyes warm to my words, the body language change, the smile that indicates that I have opened some avenue for communication. That day I read to that woman and her lowered eyes told me that she was embarrassed at her little faux pas, and when I willed her to look up at me, it was my victory, and she graciously allowed me to punish her with my full attention. We shook hands at the end of the reading, and I never saw her again. She has probably forgotten the whole thing but maybe not.

14   Yet I am one of the lucky ones. My parents made it possible for me to acquire a stronger footing in the mainstream culture by giving me the chance at an education. And books and art have saved me from the harsher forms of

ethnic and racial prejudice that many of my Hispanic *compañeras* have had to endure. I travel a lot around the United States, reading from my books of poetry and my novel, and the reception I most often receive is one of positive interest by people who want to know more about my culture. There are, however, thousands of Latinas without the privilege of an education or the entrée into society that I have. For them life is a struggle against the misconceptions perpetuated by the myth of the Latina as whore, domestic, or criminal. We cannot change this by legislating the way people look at us. The transformation, as I see it, has to occur at a much more individual level. My personal goal in my public life is to try to replace the old pervasive stereotypes and myths about Latinas with a much more interesting set of realities. Every time I give a reading, I hope the stories I tell, the dreams and fears I examine in my work, can achieve some universal truth which will get my audience past the particulars of my skin color, my accent, or my clothes.

15   I once wrote a poem in which I called us Latinas "God's brown daughters." This poem is really a prayer of sorts, offered upward, but also, through the human-to-human channel of art, outward. It is a prayer for communication and for respect. In it, Latin women pray "in Spanish to an Anglo God / with a Jewish heritage," and they are "fervently hoping / that if not omnipotent, / at least He be bilingual."

READING QUESTIONS

1. What is suggested by the title of Cofer's essay?
2. In what two ways does Cofer's Hispanic appearance affect how she is treated by others?
3. Where did Cofer grow up? What was her neighborhood like?
4. How did Cofer's experiences growing up reflect her Puerto Rican heritage?
5. Why was Career Day such an embarrassing experience for Cofer?
6. Describe the rules determining the behavior of young Puerto Rican men and women. Why can it be misinterpreted?
7. What does Cofer mean when she says that to the man who sang a vulgar song rhyming "María" with "gonorrhea" she is "merely a character in his cartoon-populated universe" (paragraph 10)?
8. In addition to being stereotyped as passionate and emotional, Cofer describes how she has also been "sent to [the] 'kitchen'" (paragraph 12). What example illustrates this point?
9. What point is Cofer making when she refers to her poem about "God's brown daughters" (paragraph 15)?

WRITING TOPICS

1. Do you agree with Cofer that the media plays a significant role in stereotyping? Why or why not?

2. How can cross-cultural differences lead to misconceptions?

3. Do you think people are judged by their appearance? Why or why not?

GROUP ACTIVITIES

1. Watch a variety of TV stations and programs to see how different groups of people are portrayed. Which groups have the most variety in terms of jobs, clothing style, and accent? Compare your results with your classmates and present your findings to the rest of the class.

2. Look at the front page of the most popular daily newspaper for one week. Classify the people in the front page photographs into categories by race, ethnicity, gender, and age. How many pictures are there of different groups? What can you infer from these results?

RESEARCH TOPICS

1. Look up the winners of special awards for films, such as the Oscars or Golden Globes. What films and which actors won the most awards? Compare these findings with a list of currently playing films in your area. How are different groups represented in current films? How represented are they by the awards process?

2. Research immigration patterns in the United States. What groups of peoples came when? What cultures and languages did they bring? How have language patterns changed?

3. Stereotyping has been linked to discrimination. Sociolinguists, sociologists, and anthropologists have pointed out that speakers with non-mainstream accents or non-Anglo names are treated differently. For example, research shows that résumés of applicants with names like Jane receive more responses than résumés of applicants with names like Kwanika. What research can you find that supports or refutes the notion that stereotyping can be linked to discrimination?

Morality

Exploring the Theme

■ How do groups of people (families, teams, organizations, societies) let individual members know the standards of acceptable behavior? How do they enforce and encourage this behavior?

■ How did you learn right from wrong? Who were your teachers? What rewards and/or punishments did you receive for right and wrong behavior?

Money for Morality

by Mary Arguelles

Mary Arguelles is a freelance writer whose articles are often published in magazines for parents. This essay first appeared in Newsweek's *"My Turn" column in October 1991.*

PREREADING QUESTIONS

1. How did your parents reward you when you did what you were supposed to do as a child? If you are a parent, how do you reward your children?

2. What is the point in doing what is right? What do you expect to get out of doing the right thing?

1   I recently read a newspaper article about an 8-year-old boy who found an envelope containing more than $600 and returned it to the bank whose name appeared on the envelope. The bank traced the money to its rightful owner and returned it to him. God's in his heaven and all's right with the world. Right? Wrong.

2   As a reward, the man who lost the money gave the boy $3. Not a lot, but a token of his appreciation nonetheless and not mandatory. After all, returning the money should not be considered extraordinary. A simple "thank you" is adequate. But some of the teachers at the boy's school felt a reward was not only appropriate, but required. Outraged at the apparent stinginess of the person who lost the cash, these teachers took up a collection for the boy. About a week or so later, they presented the good Samaritan with a $150 savings bond, explaining they felt his honesty should be recognized. Evidently the virtues of honesty and kindness have become commodities that, like everything else, have succumbed to inflation. I can't help but wonder what dollar amount these teachers would have deemed a sufficient reward. Certainly they didn't expect the individual who lost the money to give the child $150. Would $25 have been respectable? How about $10? Suppose that lost money had to cover mortgage, utilities and food for the week. In light of that, perhaps $3 was generous. A reward is a gift; any gift should at least be met with the presumption of genuine gratitude on the part of the giver.

3   What does this episode say about our society? It seems the role models our children look up to these days—in this case, teachers—are more confused and misguided about values than their young charges. A young boy, obviously well guided by his parents, finds money that does not belong to him and he returns it. He did the right thing. Yet doing the right thing seems to be insufficient motivation for action in our materialistic world. The legacy of the '80s has left us with the ubiquitous question: what's in it for me? The promise of the golden rule—that someone might do a good turn for you—has become worthless collateral for the social interactions of the mercenary and fast-paced '90s. It is in fact this fast pace that is, in part, a source of the prob-

lem. Modern communication has catapulted us into an instant world. Television makes history of events before any of us had a chance to absorb them in the first place. An ad for major-league baseball entices viewers with the reassurance that "the memories are waiting"; an event that has yet to occur has already been packaged as the past. With the world racing by us, we have no patience for a rain check on good deeds.

4   Misplaced virtues are running rampant through our culture. I don't know how many times my 13-year-old son has told me about classmates who received $10 for each A they receive on their report cards—hinting that I should do the same for him should he ever receive an A (or maybe he was working on $5 for a B). Whenever he approaches me on this subject, I give him the same reply: "Doing well is its own reward. The A just confirms that." In other words, forget it! This is not to say that I would never praise my son for doing well in school. But my praise is not meant to reward or elicit future achievements, but rather to express my genuine delight in the satisfaction he feels at having done his best. Throwing $10 at that sends out the message that the feeling alone isn't good enough.

5   *Kowtowing to ice cream*   As a society, we seem to be losing a grip on our internal control—the ethical thermostat that guides our actions and feelings toward ourselves, others, and the world around us. Instead, we rely on external "stuff" as a measure of our worth. We pass this message to our children. We offer them money for honesty and good grades. Pizza is given as a reward for reading. In fact, in one national reading program, a pizza party awaits the entire class if each child reads a certain amount of books within a four-month period. We call these things incentives, telling ourselves that if we can just reel them in and get them hooked, then the built-in rewards will follow. I recently saw a television program where unmarried, teenaged mothers were featured as the participants in a parenting program that offers $10 a week "incentive" if these young women don't get pregnant again. Isn't the daily struggle of being a single, teenaged mother enough of a deterrent? No, it isn't, because we as a society won't allow it to be. Nothing is permitted to succeed or fail on its own merits anymore.

6   I remember when I was pregnant with my son I read countless child-care books that offered the same advice: don't bribe your child with ice cream to get him to eat spinach; it makes the spinach look bad. While some may say spinach doesn't need any help looking bad, I submit it's from years of kowtowing to ice cream. Similarly, our moral taste buds have been dulled by an endless onslaught of artificial sweeteners. A steady diet of candy bars and banana splits makes an ordinary apple or orange seem sour. So too does an endless parade of incentives make us incapable of feeling a genuine sense of inner peace (or inner turmoil).

7   The simple virtues of honesty, kindness and integrity suffer from an image problem and are in desperate need of a makeover. One way to do this is by example. If my son sees me feeling happy after I've helped out a friend, then he may do likewise. If my daughter sees me spending a rainy afternoon curled up with a book instead of spending money at the mall, she may get the message that there are some simple pleasures that don't require a purchase. I fear that in our so-called upwardly mobile world we are on a downward spiral toward

moral bankruptcy. Like pre–World War II Germany, where the basket holding the money was more valuable than the money itself, we too may render ourselves internally worthless while desperately clinging to a shell of appearances.

READING QUESTIONS

1. Why were the teachers "outraged" that the boy who returned the $600 received only $3 as a reward? Why does Arguelles think that these teachers are "confused and misguided about values" (paragraph 3)?

2. How does Arguelles feel about paying children for making good grades? Why? What is the connection between this example and her opening example?

3. What other payments to children does Arguelles object to?

4. What point is Arguelles illustrating with the example of ice cream and spinach (paragraph 6)? How does this example relate to the point she has made so far in the essay?

5. According to Arguelles, how can we give "the simple virtues of honesty, kindness, and integrity" a "makeover" (paragraph 7)?

6. What other values does Arguelles praise in this essay?

WRITING TOPICS

1. Arguelles implies that virtue is its own reward and that rewarding children for doing the right thing teaches them to value the reward rather than the behavior itself. Should people be rewarded for doing what is right?

2. Arguelles writes that "as a society, we seem to be losing a grip on our internal control" and that "instead we rely on external 'stuff' as measure of our worth." Do you agree with Arguelles that we seem to find our self-worth outside ourselves instead of within?

3. According to Arguelles, the golden rule no longer motivates us because our fast-paced lives have caused us to expect an immediate payoff for our deeds. Do you agree that we are impatient when it comes to seeing results of our actions? Why or why not?

GROUP ACTIVITIES

1. Plan a debate in which you address the major issue brought up in Arguelles's first examples: should children be financially rewarded for honesty or hard work? Assign one half of your group to each side of the issue and have each half explain as clearly as possible the arguments that support that side.

2. Arguelles says that "the role models our children look up to these days— in this case, teachers—are more confused and misguided about values than their young charges" (paragraph 3). List specific role models your group is familiar with that children look up to. In each case, what values does the role model present to children? Are these values positive or negative examples for children?

RESEARCH TOPICS

1. Survey parents of school-age children, asking them whether they reward their children for good grades. Also ask how well the children do in school. Can you draw any conclusions from the presence or absence of a reward and the child's school success?

2. Arguelles lists a variety of programs that offer children incentives to behave in certain ways to participate in certain activities. Find other programs that offer such incentives and look for evidence of their effectiveness. Write a report in which you present your findings. Do they support Arguelles's argument or provide evidence against it?

On Restoring the Moral Voice: Virtue and Community Pressure

by Amatai Etzioni

Amatai Etzioni, a sociologist, calls himself a communitarian, a person who believes in a balance between individual rights and group responsibilities. This article was first published in 1994 in Current.

PREREADING QUESTIONS

1. Would you tell a friend that the person they are dating has a drinking problem? Would you tell your mother not to use her employer's photocopier to reproduce the annual family newsletter?

2. Do you often act on impulse, or do you sometimes defer your actions until you have had time to think about the consequences? Describe one time when you acted on impulse and another time when you waited to act. How were the situations similar or different?

1 Audiences that are quite enthusiastic about the communitarian message, which I carry these days to all who will listen, cringe when I turn to discuss the moral voice. One of my best friends took me aside and gently advised me to speak of "concern" rather than morality, warning that otherwise I would "sound like the Moral Majority." During most call-in radio shows in which I participate, sooner or later some caller exclaims that "nobody should tell us what to do." *Time* magazine, in an otherwise highly favorable cover story on communitarian thinking, warned against busybodies "humorlessly imposing on others arbitrary (meaning their own) standards of behavior, health and thought." Studies of an American suburb by sociologist M. P. Baumgartner found a disturbing unwillingness of people to make moral claims on one another. Most people did not feel it was their place to express their convictions when someone did something that was wrong.

2   At the same time, the overwhelming majority of Americans, public opinion polls show, recognize that our moral fabric has worn rather thin. A typical finding is that while school teachers in the forties listed as their top problems talking out of turn, making noise, cutting line, and littering, they now list drug abuse, alcohol abuse, pregnancy, and suicide. Wanton taking of life, often for a few bucks to buy a vial of crack or to gain a pair of sneakers, is much more common than it is in other civilized societies or than it used to be in America. Countless teenagers bring infants into the world to satisfy their ego needs, with little attention to the long term consequences for the children, themselves, or society.

How We Lost Our Moral Voice

3   How can people recognize the enormous moral deficit we face and at the same time be so reluctant to lay moral claims on one another? One reason is that they see immorality not in their friends and neighborhoods but practically everyplace else. (In the same vein, they find members of Congress in general to be corrupt but often re-elect "their" representative because he or she is "O.K.," just as they complain frequently about physicians but find their doctors above reproach.) This phenomenon may be referred to as moral myopia; a phenomenon for which there seems to be no ready cure.

4   In addition, many Americans seem to have internalized the writings of Dale Carnegie on how to win friends and influence people: you are supposed to work hard at flattering the other person and never chastise anyone. Otherwise, generations of Americans have been told by their parents, you may lose a "friend" and set back your "networking." A study found that when college coeds were asked whether or not they would tell their best friend if, in their eyes, the person the friend had chosen to wed was utterly unsuitable, most said they would refrain. They would rather she go ahead and hurt herself rather than endanger the friendship. Also, Daniel Patrick Moynihan has argued convincingly in his recent article in the *American Scholar*, "Defining Deviancy Down," that people have been so bombarded with evidence of social ills that they have developed moral calluses, which make them relatively inured to immorality.

5   When Americans do contemplate moral reform, many are rather asociological: they believe that our problem is primarily one of individual conscience. If youngsters could be taught again to tell right from wrong by their families and schools, if churches could reach them again, our moral and social order would be on the mend. They focus on what is only one, albeit important, component of the moral equation: the inner voice.

6   In the process many Americans disregard the crucial role of the community in reinforcing the individual's moral commitments. To document the importance of the community, I must turn to the question: what constitutes a moral person?

7   I build here on the writings of Harry Frankfurt, Albert Hirschman, and others who have argued that humans differ from animals in that, while both species experience impulses, humans have the capacity to pass judgments on their impulses. I choose my words carefully: It is not suggested that humans

can "control" their impulses, but that they can defer responding to them long enough to evaluate the behavior toward which they feel inclined. Once this evaluation takes place, sometimes the judgments win, sometimes the impulses. If the judgments always took precedence, we would be saintly; if the impulses always won, we would be psychopaths or animals. The human fate is a constant struggle between the noble and the debased parts of human nature. While I reach this conclusion from social science findings and observations, I am often challenged by those who exclaim "Why, this is what religion taught us!" or as one heckler cried out "What about the rest of the catechism?" As I see it, while some may find it surprising that religions contain social truths, I see no reason to doubt that the distillation of centuries of human experience by those entrusted historically with moral education, has resulted in some empirically solid, sociologically valid observations.

8   It is to the struggle between judgments and impulses that the moral voice of the community speaks. The never-ending struggle within the human soul over which course to follow is not limited to intra-individual dialogues between impulses that tempt us to disregard our marital vows, to be deceitful, or to be selfish, and the values we previously internalized, which warn us against yielding to these temptations. In making our moral choices (to be precise, our choices between moral and immoral conduct rather than among moral claims), we are influenced by the approbation and censure of others, especially of those with whom we have close relations—family members, friends, neighbors; in short, our communities. It may not flatter our view of ourselves, but human nature is such that if these community voices speak in unison and with clarity (without being shrill), we are much more likely to follow our inner judgments than if these voices are silent, conflicted, or speak too softly. Hence, the pivotal importance of community voices in raising the moral level of their members.

The Critics

9 I need to respond to various challenges to this line of argumentation, beyond the general unarticulated uneasiness it seems to evoke in a generation that has largely lost its moral voice. Some argue that the reliance on community points to conformism, to "other-directed" individuals who merely seek to satisfy whatever pleases their community. This is not the vision evoked here. The community voice as depicted here is not the only voice that lays claims on individuals as to the course they ought to follow, but rather is a voice that speaks in addition to the inner one. When the community's voice and the inner voice are in harmony, this is not a case of conformism, of one "party" yielding to the other, but one of two tributaries flowing into the same channel (e.g., if I firmly believe that it is wrong to leave my children unattended and so do my neighbors, and I stay home, this is hardly an instance of conformism). If these two voices conflict, I must pass judgment not only vis-a-vis my impulses (should I yield or follow the dictates of my conscience?) but also pass judgment on whether or not I shall heed my fellow community members, or follow my own lead. In short, the very existence of a community moral

voice does not necessarily spell conformism. Conformism occurs only if and when one automatically or routinely sets aside personal judgements to grant supremacy to the community. That happens when personal voices are weak— far from a necessary condition for the existence of a community voice. To put it differently, while conformism is a danger so is the absence of the reinforcing effects of the communal voice. The antidote to conformism is not to undermine the community's voice but to seek to ensure that the personal one is also firmly instilled.

Pluralism

10   Above all, it must be noted that while the moral voice urges and counsels us, it is unable to force us. Whatever friends, neighbors, ministers, or community leaders say, the ultimate judgment call is up to the individual. (True, in some limited situations, as when a community ostracizes or hounds someone, the pressure can be quite intense, but this rarely happens to modern-day communities because individuals are able to move to other communities when they are unduly pressured, and because they often are members of two or more communities—say of residence and of work—and hence are able to psychologically draw on one community to ward off excessive pressure from the other.)

11   Others argue that the community voice is largely lost because of American pluralism. Individuals are subject to the voices of numerous communities, each pulling in a different direction and thus neutralizing the others. Or the cacophony is so high that no clear voice can be heard. The notion that no community is right and all claims have equal standing, championed by multiculturalists, further diminishes the claim of the moral voice. The fact is that there is no way to return to the days of simple, homogeneous communities. In any case, these communities were often rather oppressive. The contemporary solution, if not salvation, lies in seeking and developing an evolving framework of shared values—one which all subcultures will be expected to endorse and support without losing their distinct identities. Thus, Muslim-Americans can be free to follow the dictates of their religion, cherish their music and cuisine, and be proud of select parts of their history (no group should be encouraged to embrace all of its history). But at the same time they (and all other communities that make up the American society) need to accept the dignity of the individual, the basic value of liberty, the democratic form of government, and other such core values. On these matters we should expect and encourage all communities to speak in one voice.

12   Other critics argue that the essence of individual freedom is every person following his own course and social institutions leaving us alone. (More technically, economists write about the primacy of our preferences and scoff at intellectuals and ideologues who want to impose their "tastes" on others.) In honoring this pivotal value of free society one must be careful not to confuse allusions to freedom from the state's coercion and controls with freedom from the moral urgings of our fellow community members. One can be as opposed to state intervention and regulation as a diehard libertarian and still see a great deal of merit in people encouraging one another to do what is right.

(Technically speaking, the reference here is not to frustrating people and preventing them from acting on their preferences, which is what the coercive state does, but rather appealing to their better selves to change or reorder their preferences.)

13   Indeed, a strong case can be made that it is precisely the bonding together of community members that enables us to remain independent of the state. The anchoring of individuals in viable families, webs of friendships, communities of faith, and neighborhoods—in short, in communities—best sustains their ability to resist the pressures of the state. The absence of these social foundations opens isolated individuals to totalitarian pressures. (This, of course, is a point Tocqueville makes in *Democracy in America.*)

Getting Our Voice Back

14   In my discussions with students and others about the moral voice, I have borrowed a leaf from Joel Feinberg's seminal work *Offense to Others.* In this book, Feinberg provides a list of activities others may engage in that he believes we will find offensive. He asks us to imagine we are riding on a full bus, which we cannot readily leave. He then presents a series of hypothetical scenes which would cause offense, such as playing loud music, scratching a metallic surface, handling what looks like a real grenade, engaging in sexual behavior, and so on.

15   I am interested not so much in the question of what members of the community find tolerable versus unbearable, but what will make them speak up. Hence I asked students and colleagues "imagine you are in a supermarket and a mother beats the daylights out of a three year old child—would you speak up?" (I say "mother" because I learned that if I just say "someone" most of my respondents state that they would not react because they would fear that the other person might clobber them.) Practically everyone I asked responded that they would not speak up. They would at most try to "distract" the mother, "find out what the child really did," and so on. However, when I asked "imagine you are resting on the shore of a pristine lake; a picnicking family, about to depart, leaves behind a trail of trash—would you suggest they clean up after themselves?" Here again, many demurred but a fair number were willing to consider saying something.

Environment

16   Possibly, my informal sample is skewed. However, it seems to me something else is at work: we had a consensus-building grand dialogue about the environment. While there are still sharp disagreements about numerous details (for instance, about the relative standing of spotted owls vs. loggers), there is a basic consensus that we must be mindful of the environment and cannot trash it. However, we have had neither a grand dialogue nor a new consensus about the way to treat children. This would suggest one more reason our moral voice is so feeble and reluctant: too many of us, too often, are no longer sure what to state.

17   A return to a firm moral voice thus will require a major town hall meeting of sorts, the kind we have when Americans spend billions of hours in bowling alleys, next to water coolers, and on call-in shows, to form a new consensus, the kind we had about the environment, civil rights, and excessive general regulation, and are now beginning to have about gay rights. This time we need to agree with one another that the common good requires that we speak up and enunciate the values for which we speak. To reiterate, heeding such consensus should never be automatic; we need to examine the values the community urges upon us to determine whether or not they square with our conscience and the basic values we sense no person or community has a right to violate. However, here the focus is on the other side of the coin; it is not enough individually to be able to tell right from wrong, as crucial as that is. We must also be willing to encourage others to attend to values we as a community share.

READING QUESTIONS

1. What is "moral myopia"? Do you agree that individuals fail to notice the moral shortcomings of those who are closest to them? Why or why not?

2. What "constant struggle" does Etzioni identify? Do you agree that humans are in a state of inner conflict?

3. Etzioni identifies a second opposition, one between the inner voice and community voices. How is this opposition sometimes in conflict and sometimes in harmony?

4. Etzioni discusses a connection between pluralism and the community moral voice. According to Etzioni, what should this connection be? What other possible connections does he reject? Why?

5. Etzioni writes that "a strong case can be made that it is precisely the bonding together of community members that enables us to remain independent of the state" (paragraph 13). What point is he trying to make? How well is this idea developed? Is he convincing?

WRITING TOPICS

1. Etzioni identifies a conflict between acting on impulse and acting on judgment. He suggests that it is always more appropriate to act on judgment. Do you agree? Why or why not?

2. What connection does Etzioni note between social science observations and religion? Do you find this connection surprising? Why or why not?

3. Etzioni contrasts the role of "the inner voice" with "community voices" (paragraphs 5, 8). Do you agree with his claim that "the never-ending struggle within the human soul . . . is not limited to intra-individual dialogues between impulses to tempt us . . . and the values we previously internalized" (paragraph 8)? Why or why not?

4. Etzioni writes that "while the moral voice [of the community] urges and counsels us, it is unable to force us" (paragraph 10). Do you agree that individuals have that much choice in making decisions? That is, can they follow their inner voice instead of conforming to pressure from the "moral voice" of the community?

GROUP ACTIVITIES

1. In paragraph 5, Etzioni identifies a shortcoming in addressing the problems resulting from poor moral decisions by youth. In a small group, make a list of specific, concrete programs that he is criticizing. Do you think these programs make a difference? Why or why not?

2. Do the activities described in paragraphs 14 and 15 (the bus and the child in the supermarket). Compare your responses with those of others in your group. Write some of your own "moral voice" activities. What issues are being explored by each activity?

3. Etzioni suggests that America has already formed a new consensus on "the environment, civil rights, and excessive general regulation," and that one of gay rights is beginning. What are areas of disagreement in America? In your state or local community? Why did you list these areas? What are the differing positions on these issues? Do you think it is possible to begin to have a dialogue that will lead to a new consensus? Why or why not?

RESEARCH TOPICS

1. What is the Moral Majority? Who are its leaders? What are its goals? Who are libertarians? What are their goals?

2. Etzioni says "Wanton taking of life . . . is much more common than it is in other civilized societies or than it used to be in America. Countless teenagers bring infants into the world to satisfy their ego needs, . . ." (paragraph 2). Are there statistics to back up his claims? Are violent crime and teenage pregnancy really increasing?

3. Who is Dale Carnegie? What is he famous—and rich—for?

4. Who is Daniel Patrick Moynihan? Etzioni cites him as an authority on moral judgment. Is he an appropriate authority figure? Why or why not?

5. What is multiculturalism? What is pluralism? How are they the same? How are they different?

6. Etzioni refers to the work of other writers. These include Harry Frankfurt, Albert Hirschman, Tocqueville, Joel Feinberg. Find out more about these people. What do you think about their ideas?

Why Nothing is "Wrong" Anymore
by Meg Greenfield

Meg Greenfield (1931–1999) was the editorial page editor for The Washington Post *and won a Pulitzer Prize in 1978. She also wrote a regular column in* Newsweek, *where this column appeared on July 28, 1986.*

PREREADING QUESTIONS

1. Define right and wrong. How do you know the difference?
2. Do public figures such as politicians and celebrities accept responsibility for their actions? How do you know?

1   There has been an awful lot of talk about sin, crime, and plain old antisocial behavior this summer—drugs and pornography at home, terror and brutality abroad. Maybe it's just the heat; or maybe these categories of conduct (sin, crime, etc.) are really on the rise. What strikes me is our curiously deficient, not to say defective, way of talking about them. We don't seem to have a word anymore for "wrong" in the moral sense, as in, for example, "theft is wrong."

2   Let me quickly qualify. There is surely no shortage of people condemning other people on such grounds, especially their political opponents or characters they just don't care for. Name-calling is still very much in vogue. But where the concept of wrong is really important—as a guide to one's own behavior or that of one's own side in some dispute—it is missing; and this is as true of those on the religious right who are going around pronouncing great masses of us sinners as it is of their principal antagonists, those on the secular left who can forgive or "understand" just about anything so long as it has not been perpetrated by a right-winger.

3   There is a fairly awesome literature that attempts to explain how we have changed as a people with the advent of psychiatry, the weakening of religious institutions and so forth, but you don't need to address these matters to take note of a simple fact. As a guide and a standard to live by, you don't hear so much about "right and wrong" these days. The very notion is considered politically, not to say personally, embarrassing, since it has such a repressive, Neanderthal ring to it. So we have developed a broad range of alternatives to "right and wrong." I'll name a few.

4   **Right and stupid:** This is the one you use when your candidate gets caught stealing, or, for that matter, when anyone on your side does something reprehensible. "It was really so dumb of him"—head must shake here—"I just can't understand it." Bad is dumb, breathtakingly dumb and therefore unfathomable; so, conveniently enough, the effort to fathom it might just as well be called off. This one had a big play during Watergate and has had mini-revivals ever since whenever congressmen and senators investigating administration crimes turn out to be guilty of something similar themselves.

5 **Right and not necessarily unconstitutional:** I don't know at quite what point along the way we came to this one, the avoidance of admitting that something is wrong by pointing out that it is not specifically or even inferentially prohibited by the Constitution or, for that matter, mentioned by name in the criminal code or the Ten Commandments. The various parties that prevail in civil-liberty and civil-rights disputes before the Supreme Court have gotten quite good at making this spurious connection: it is legally permissible, therefore it is morally acceptable, possibly even good. But both as individuals and as a society we do things every day that we know to be wrong even though they may not fall within the class of legally punishable acts or tickets to eternal damnation.

6 **Right and sick:** Crime or lesser wrongdoing defined as physical and/or psychological disorder—this one has been around for ages now and as long ago as 1957 was made the butt of a great joke in the "Gee Officer Krupke!" song in "West Side Story." Still, I think no one could have foreseen the degree to which an originally reasonable and humane assumption (that some of what once was regarded as wrongdoing is committed by people acting out of ailment rather than moral choice) would be seized upon and exploited to exonerate every kind of misfeasance. This route is a particular favorite of caught-out officeholders who, when there is at last no other recourse, hold a press conference, announce that they are "sick" in some wise and throw themselves and their generally stunned families on our mercy. At which point it becomes gross to pick on them; instead we are exhorted to admire them for their "courage."

7 **Right and only to be expected:** You could call this the tit-for-tat school; it is related to the argument that holds moral wrongdoing to be evidence of sickness, but it is much more pervasive and insidious these days. In fact it is probably the most popular dodge, being used to justify, or at least avoid owning up to, every kind of lapse: the other guy, or sometimes just plain circumstance, "asked for it." For instance, I think most of us could agree that setting fire to live people, no matter what their political offense, is—dare I say it?—wrong. Yet if it is done by those for whom we have sympathy in a conflict, there is a tendency to extenuate or disbelieve it, receiving it less as evidence of wrongdoing on our side than as evidence of the severity of the provocation or as enemy-supplied disinformation. Thus the hesitation of many in the antiapartheid movement to confront the brutality of so-called "necklacing," and thus the immediate leap of Sen. Jesse Helms to the defense of the Chilean government after the horrifying incineration of protesters there.

8 **Right and complex:** This one hardly takes a moment to describe; you know it well. "Complex" is the new "controversial," a word used as "controversial" was for so long to flag trouble of some unspecified,

dismaying sort that the speaker doesn't want to have to step up to. "Well, you know, it's very complex. . . ." I still can't get this one out of my own vocabulary.

9   In addition to these various sophistries, we also have created a rash of "ethics committees" in our government, of course, whose function seems to be to dither around writing rules that allow people who have clearly done wrong—and should have known it and probably did—to get away because the rules don't cover their offense (see Right and not necessarily unconstitutional). But we don't need any more committees or artful dodges for that matter. As I listen to the moral arguments swirling about us this summer I become ever more persuaded that our real problem is this: the "still, small voice" of conscience has become far too small—and utterly still.

READING QUESTIONS

1. Summarize Greenfield's argument.
2. Explain each of the alternatives to "right and wrong" that Greenfield describes. Why does Greenfield refer to each of these as "sophistries"?
3. Greenfield ends her essay by stating that there is a deeper problem than these excuses used in public life. What is this problem?

WRITING TOPICS

1. Greenfield claims, "As a guide and a standard to live by, you don't hear so much about 'right and wrong' these days" (paragraph 3). Agree or disagree with her argument.
2. Choose one of Greenfield's alternatives to "right and wrong." Does the alternative represent a justifiable defense of a person's actions? Explain your answer.

GROUP ACTIVITIES

1. Greenfield draws her examples almost exclusively from politics, not from society in general. With a small group, brainstorm examples from the workplace, families, schools, and other areas of public interaction that support her observations (or that contradict them).
2. With a small group, brainstorm other alternatives for "right and wrong" to add to Greenfield's list. Be sure to describe the alternative, and give examples of when it is used.

RESEARCH TOPICS

1. In paragraph 7, Greenfield mentions "the brutality of so-called 'necklacing.'" What is necklacing? When and where was it done? Why?
2. What is an "ethics committee"? What are some of the issues or events that have prompted the creation of an ethics committee?
3. What was Watergate? Why does Greenfield use it as an example of the excuse of "right and stupid"?

Answers for Chapter 19

BAS EXERCISE 1

The story of the Heike <u>is</u> a very sad story from Japanese history. The emperor (whose family <u>was called</u> the Heike) <u>was fighting</u> his enemies, who <u>chased</u> him until finally he <u>boarded</u> a ship with his family and followers. A nurse <u>carried</u> the baby, the son of the emperor. When the enemies <u>captured</u> the ship, she <u>took</u> the baby emperor to the prow of the ship and <u>jumped</u> into the water where she and the baby <u>drowned</u>, but <u>escaped</u> their enemy in death. All the family and soldiers of the Heike <u>were killed</u> and their bodies at <u>were lost</u> at sea. Now the crabs who <u>are caught</u> in that part of the ocean <u>have</u> strange markings on their shells. Local people <u>call</u> them the faces of the Heike.

BAS EXERCISE 2

A very old <u>story</u> from the Middle East <u>is called</u> *Gilgamesh*. <u>Gilgamesh</u> <u>was</u> the ruler of his country, and <u>he</u> <u>was</u> very strong and handsome. Another <u>man</u> in that country <u>was called</u> Enkidu. Enkidu <u>lived</u> in the forest and <u>had</u> only animals for friends. <u>Gilgamesh</u> <u>sent</u> a woman to Enkidu, and when the <u>animals</u> <u>saw</u> him with another human, <u>they</u> <u>became</u> afraid of him. <u>Enkidu</u> <u>left</u> the forest. <u>He</u> and <u>Gilgamesh</u> <u>fought</u> each other, but finally <u>became</u> good friends. The <u>importance</u> of friendship <u>is</u> a theme of the story.

BAS EXERCISE 3

From an ancient African county in Mali <u>comes</u> the story of Son-Jara, who <u>was born</u> a prince. His mother <u>was</u> one of the king's wives, but another of the king's wives <u>hated</u> her. (Being jealous) <u>was</u> a common problem among the king's wives in those days. This woman <u>cursed</u> Son-Jara so that he <u>was</u> unable to walk when he was a child. (To be) a king's mother <u>was</u> his mother's ambition, so she <u>wanted</u> him (to be) stronger than other men, but instead he <u>was</u> weaker. His mother's hopes for her son <u>seemed</u> impossible, but she <u>went</u> (to ask) help from a Djinn, a supernatural creature. (Following) the Djinn's instructions <u>was</u> difficult, but she <u>obeyed</u>. She <u>sent</u> her son on a Haj, which <u>is</u> a pilgrimage to Mecca. Finally the curse <u>was destroyed</u>, and Son-Jara <u>became</u> a great king.

BAS EXERCISE 4

<u>Do</u> all <u>people</u> <u>have</u> the same idea about how the <u>world</u> <u>was created</u>? <u>People</u> in different parts of the world <u>can</u> sometimes <u>have</u> very different ideas. Many <u>cultures</u> <u>have asked</u> these questions: Where <u>do</u> <u>we</u> <u>come</u> from? How <u>were</u> <u>we</u> <u>made</u>? The <u>question</u> <u>is</u> often <u>answered</u> by a story. The Mayan <u>people</u> of ancient Guatemala long ago <u>told</u> the story of creation, <u>which</u>, according to the stories <u>they</u> <u>told</u>, <u>had been accomplished</u> by a group of gods. These <u>gods</u> <u>were called</u> Bearer, Begetter, Maker, and Modeler (also called Plumed Serpent). <u>They</u> <u>used</u> many grains, fruits, and vegetables to create the first people.

BAS EXERCISE 5   Many (of the stories) we find (in one country) are also found (in the tales) (from other countries.) (For example,) the story (of a great flood) that destroys the earth is found (in many stories) (from all over the world). (In ancient China,) (in Babylon,) (in Israel,) (in South America,) and probably (in many other lands) as well, we can read or hear (of one man) who survives the flood (with his family) and starts the world again. The story (of the flood) appears (in the Bible) and (in the Koran.) One man suggested a theory (about these universal stories.) (In his book *Man and His Symbols*,) Carl Jung called these stories *archetypes* and reminded us that people (in all parts) (of the world) tell similar stories, and also dream similar dreams.

BND EXERCISE 1   A writer of many plays and poems. William Shakespeare is considered to be one of the greatest writers in the English language. We usually think of Shakespeare as the writer of tragic plays. Plays about murder and unfortunate deaths. However, Shakespeare also wrote plays referred to as the histories and the romances. Also, twelve plays which are called the comedies. His plays were very popular in his own time. Performed at the Old Globe theater. Today, his plays are perhaps most often seen in movie theaters. Some film directors will update the play and set it in modern times. Rewriting the play's original language so it is more accessible for today's audiences. These directors may also film the play outdoors. Instead of indoors on the stage.

Revision for BND 1: (answers may vary, but all sentences should be complete):
A writer of many plays and poems, **W**illiam Shakespeare is considered to be one of the greatest writers in the English language. We usually think of Shakespeare as the writer of tragic plays, **p**lays about murder and unfortunate deaths. However, Shakespeare also wrote plays referred to as the histories and the romances, **as well as** twelve plays which are called the comedies. His plays were very popular in his own time **and were p**erformed at the Old Globe theater. Today, his plays are perhaps most often seen in movie theaters. Some film directors will update the play and set it in modern times, **r**ewriting the play's original language so it is more accessible for today's audiences. These directors may also film the play outdoors, **i**nstead of indoors on the stage.

BND EXERCISE 2   William Shakespeare, who wrote the play *Hamlet*. Was born in England in 1564. The town of his birth was Stratford-on-Avon, and after his death, he was buried there. Little is known about his father, who some biographers say was a merchant. However, Shakespeare's father may also have been a mayor. Although it is not known for certain. It is believed that Shakespeare attended grammar school where he learned to read and write. At the age of eighteen he became a husband. When he married Anne Hathaway. We think of Shakespeare as a playwright, but he was also known for his acting. While most people have heard of *Hamlet* and *Romeo and Juliet*. Many of us don't realize that he wrote more than thirty other plays. In addition, he was an accomplished poet. Who wrote some of the greatest sonnets in the English language. Because he wrote plays that are still popular today and wrote poems that are still models for aspiring poets. He is considered one of the greatest writers who ever lived.

Revision for BND 2 (answers may vary, but all sentences should be complete):

William Shakespeare, who wrote the play *Hamlet*, was born in England in 1564. The town of his birth was Stratford-on-Avon, and after his death, he was buried there. Little is known about his father, who some biographers say was a merchant. However, Shakespeare's father may also have been a mayor although it is not known for certain. It is believed that Shakespeare attended grammar school where he learned to read and write. At the age of eighteen he became a husband when he married Anne Hathaway. We think of Shakespeare as a playwright, but he was also known for his acting. While most people have heard of *Hamlet* and *Romeo and Juliet*, many of us don't realize that he wrote more than thirty other plays. In addition, he was an accomplished poet, who wrote some of the greatest sonnets in the English language. Because he wrote plays that are still popular today and wrote poems that are still models for aspiring poets, he is considered one of the greatest writers who ever lived.

BND EXERCISE 3   One of Shakespeare's outstanding works is *Hamlet*. <u>Which is about a young prince trying to avenge his father's death.</u> The play begins with the ghost of Hamlet's father appearing to Horatio and the sentries on duty. They tell Hamlet about their experience. That night, Hamlet also sees the ghost of his father. <u>Who was the former king of Denmark. The experience that young Hamlet has.</u> <u>Deeply disturbs him.</u> Hamlet discovers that his father was murdered by Hamlet's uncle, Claudius. <u>Who is now the king of Denmark and who has married Hamlet's widowed mother.</u> Hamlet is commanded by his father's ghost to kill Claudius. Although Hamlet seems to know that he must take revenge, he delays. <u>Which leads to the deaths of other characters in the play.</u> It can even be argued that Hamlet's inability to carry out the act of revenge leads to the death of Ophelia. <u>Who was Hamlet's true love. That the play ends on a tragic note.</u> <u>Is a vast understatement.</u> In the final scene, there are four dead bodies sprawled across the stage.

Revision for BND 3 (answers may vary, but all sentences should be complete):

One of Shakespeare's outstanding works is *Hamlet*, which is about a young prince trying to avenge his father's death. The play begins with the ghost of Hamlet's father appearing to Horatio and the sentries on duty. They tell Hamlet about their experience. That night Hamlet sees the ghost of his father who was the former king of Denmark. The experience that young Hamlet has deeply disturbs him. Hamlet discovers that his father was murdered by Hamlet's uncle, Claudius, who is now the king of Denmark and who has married Hamlet's widowed mother. Hamlet is commanded by his father's ghost to kill Claudius. Although Hamlet seems to know that he must take revenge, he delays, which leads to the deaths of other characters in the play. It can even be argued that Hamlet's inability to carry out the act of revenge leads to the death of Ophelia, who was Hamlet's true love. That the play ends on a tragic note is a vast understatement. In the final scene, there are four dead bodies sprawled across the stage.

BND EXERCISE 4   <u>Because this play has so many problems.</u> Readers have always argued about Hamlet's character. They can decide whether he is a brave and cautious man. <u>Or just can't make up his mind. A really indecisive character!</u> Why should we care about a fictional character? Some readers see themselves reflected in characters like Hamlet. <u>Who may seem to have unusual problems, but is very human all the same.</u>

Revision for BND 4 (answers may vary, but all sentences should be complete):

Because this play has so many problems, **r**eaders have always argued about Hamlet's character. They can decide whether he is a brave and cautious man **or** just can't make up his mind. He is a really indecisive character! Why should we care about a fictional character? Some readers see themselves reflected in characters like Hamlet, **w**ho may seem to have unusual problems but is very human all the same.

BND EXERCISE 5   One of the most interesting characters in the play *Hamlet* is Ophelia, who is Hamlet's love interest. She is often portrayed as a weak-willed person \ she is dominated by her father Polonius. In the beginning of the play, Ophelia tells her father that Prince Hamlet has been expressing his love to her. Polonius tells her that she should ignore Hamlet's vows of love, \ Ophelia obeys him \ she doesn't even protest. Even though she loves Hamlet and wants to see him, she follows her father's orders. Later in the play when Polonius and the king want to spy on Hamlet, she allows herself to be used \ she talks to Hamlet while Polonius and the king hide behind the curtains and listen. After this scene, Hamlet never sees her alive again, \ she is later found dead in a stream. It is said that Hamlet couldn't decide what to do \ Ophelia couldn't stand up for what she wanted.

BND EXERCISE 6   An often overlooked character in the play *Hamlet* is Fortinbras, \ however, he is very important. Hamlet and Fortinbras are in the same situation, \ they have both lost their fathers. At the beginning of the play, we learn that Fortinbras has raised an army and is demanding that Denmark return the lands his father lost. This is Fortinbras' way of avenging his father's death \ Fortinbras is a man of action. Hamlet, like Fortinbras, formulates plans to take revenge for his father's murder \ he delays \ he doesn't act. In the middle of the play, Fortinbras' army is allowed to cross Denmark on its way to do battle with the Poles. Again we see that Fortinbras craves action \ Hamlet, at this point in the play, is being shipped off to England \ he still hasn't taken action against Claudius, his father's murderer. Fortinbras only appears in the play once. In the very last scene, Fortinbras arrives at the castle \ he finds Hamlet dead. The man of action has survived, \ the man of thought has perished.

Revision for BND 6 (answers may vary, but all should be correct sentences):

An often overlooked character in the play *Hamlet* is Fortinbras; however, he is very important. Hamlet and Fortinbras are in the same situation **since** they have both lost their fathers. At the beginning of the play, we learn that Fortinbras has raised an army and is demanding that Denmark return the lands his father lost. This is Fortinbras' way of avenging his father's death. **F**ortinbras is a man of action. Hamlet, like Fortinbras, formulates plans to take revenge for his father's murder, **but** he delays **and** he doesn't act. In the middle of the play, Fortinbras' army is allowed to cross Denmark on its way to do battle with the Poles. Again we see that Fortinbras craves action. Hamlet, at this point in the play, is being shipped off to England **although** he still hasn't taken action against Claudius, his father's murderer. Fortinbras only appears in the play once. In the very last scene, **when** Fortinbras arrives at the castle, he finds Hamlet dead. The man of action has survived; the man of thought has perished.

BND EXERCISE 7   Hamlet believes that his mother, Gertrude, has betrayed his father's memory. After the death of King Hamlet, Gertrude marries <u>Claudius. Who</u> is King Hamlet's <u>brother this</u> infuriates Hamlet. Hamlet sees his father as a <u>god, he</u> sees Claudius as a satyr, a creature half goat. Hamlet cannot understand how his mother could so quickly forget his godlike <u>father, therefore</u> he concludes that women are faithless. In addition to feeling betrayed by his mother, Hamlet also feels that Ophelia has betrayed him. At her father's command, Ophelia rejects Hamlet and she returns the letters and gifts he has given her. This sends Hamlet into a <u>rage, it</u> confirms his belief that women are weak and unfaithful.

Revision for BND 7 (answers may vary, but all sentences should be correctly punctuated):

Hamlet believes that his mother, Gertrude, has betrayed his father's memory. After the death of King Hamlet, Gertrude marries Claudius, **w**ho is King Hamlet's brother. This infuriates Hamlet. Hamlet sees his father as a god, **but** he sees Claudius as a satyr, a creature that is half goat. Hamlet cannot understand how his mother could so quickly forget his godlike father; therefore, he concludes that women are faithless. In addition to feeling betrayed by his mother, Hamlet also feels that Ophelia has betrayed him. At her father's command, Ophelia rejects Hamlet and she returns the letters and gifts he has given her. This sends Hamlet into a rage. **I**t confirms his belief that women are weak and unfaithful.

BND EXERCISE 8   Although *Hamlet* is one of Shakespeare's tragedies, it has moments of humor. One of the most humorous scenes takes place in a <u>graveyard, Hamlet</u> has a dialogue with a gravedigger who won't give Hamlet a straight answer. When Hamlet and his friend Horatio enter, they find the gravedigger in the act of digging a grave. Hamlet asks to whom the grave <u>belongs, the gravedigger</u> responds that it is his own grave. Hamlet wants to know who will be buried in <u>the grave, however</u>, the gravedigger's logic is that the one who makes the grave owns the grave. This gravedigger is fond <u>of wordplay he is</u> also fond of riddles. Prior to the arrival of Hamlet and Horatio, the gravedigger has asked his fellow worker who builds stronger than a mason, a shipwright, or a carpenter. His co-worker's answer <u>is good he says</u> a gallows-maker. After all, the man who makes the gallows lives longer than those who find themselves on the gallows. The gravedigger, however, has a <u>better answer. Which he</u> gives to his co-worker. The gravedigger says that a grave maker builds stronger than a mason, a shipwright, or a carpenter, his logic is twisted but sound. The grave you are buried in lasts longer than the house a mason might <u>build, therefore,</u> the grave maker builds the strongest.

Revision for Exercise 8 (answers may vary, but all should be correct sentences):
Although *Hamlet* is one of Shakespeare's tragedies, it has moments of humor. One of the most humorous scenes takes place in a graveyard **where** Hamlet has a dialogue with a gravedigger who won't give Hamlet a straight answer. When Hamlet and his friend Horatio enter, they find the gravedigger in the act of digging a grave. **When** Hamlet asks to whom the grave belongs, the gravedigger responds that it is his own grave. Hamlet wants to know who will be buried in the grave; however, the gravedigger's logic is that the one who makes the grave owns the grave. This gravedigger is fond of wordplay, **and** he is also fond of riddles. Prior to the arrival of Hamlet and Horatio, the gravedigger has asked his fellow worker who builds stronger than a mason, a shipwright, or a carpenter. His co-worker's answer is good; he says a gallows-maker. After all, the man who makes the gallows lives longer than those who find themselves on the gallows. The gravedigger, however, has a better answer, which he gives to his co-worker. The gravedigger says that a grave maker builds stronger than a mason, a shipwright, or a carpenter. His logic is twisted but sound. The grave you are buried in lasts longer than the house a mason might build; therefore, the grave maker builds the strongest.

BND EXERCISE 9 Hamlet's negative view of life is in part the result of the betrayals he has <u>experienced. Which</u> leave him with few people to trust. His mother betrayed both King Hamlet and Hamlet <u>by quickly marrying Claudius Ophelia betrayed Hamlet</u> by rejecting his affections. In addition to these betrayals, Hamlet is also betrayed by Rosencrantz and <u>Guildenstern. Who</u> are friends of Hamlet's. Although Hamlet doesn't know it, his two friends are really <u>spying</u> on him for Claudius. Hamlet finds out they are spying <u>on him, therefore,</u> he decides to toy with them. He asks Guildenstern to play <u>a recorder. Which is a wooden</u> flute. Guildenstern says that he doesn't <u>know how to play the instrument, then Hamlet tells</u> his two friends what he thinks of them. Hamlet says that they think they can play him more easily than one can play a flute. This is not however the end of their betrayal. The King has Hamlet sent to England so he can have Hamlet executed. Rosencrantz and Guildenstern <u>accompany Hamlet they are carrying</u> a letter which requests that Hamlet be killed immediately upon his arrival in England. Hamlet <u>changes the letter now it says that Rosencrantz and Guildenster</u> should be killed immediately. Rosencrantz and Guildenstern pay dearly for the betrayal of their friend.

Revision for Exercise 9 (answers may vary, but all sentences should be correctly punctuated):
Hamlet's negative view of life is in part the result of the betrayals he has experienced which leave him with few people to trust. His mother betrayed both King Hamlet and Hamlet by quickly marrying Claudius, and Ophelia betrayed Hamlet by rejecting his affections. In addition to these betrayals, Hamlet is also betrayed by Rosencrantz and Guildenstern, who are friends of Hamlet's. Although Hamlet doesn't know it, his two friends are really spying on him for

Claudius. Hamlet finds out they are spying on him; therefore, he decides to toy with them. He asks Guildenstern to play a recorder, which is a wooden flute. Guildenstern says that he doesn't know how to play the instrument. Then Hamlet tells his two friends what he thinks of them. Hamlet says that they think they can play him more easily than one can play a flute. This is not however the end of their betrayal. The King has Hamlet sent to England so he can have Hamlet executed. Rosencrantz and Guildenstern accompany Hamlet. They are carrying a letter which requests that Hamlet be killed immediately upon his arrival in England. Hamlet changes the letter **so that** now it says that Rosencrantz and Guildenstern should be killed immediately. Rosencrantz and Guildenstern pay dearly for the betrayal of their friend.

END EXERCISE 1

Many single <u>mothers</u> who work have too many responsibili**ties**—they can't find enough <u>hours</u> in one day to do all the <u>jobs</u> that must be done. Their children need lunch for school, the <u>dish**es**</u> need washing, the car needs gas—all at the same time. No magic will give those <u>mothers</u> the five extra <u>minutes</u> in each hour, but some <u>tricks</u> will help them. <u>Mothers</u> with too many <u>chores</u> can try this: set a timer for fifteen minute**s** after each meal, and each member of the family must spend those <u>minutes</u> putting away <u>objects</u> that are out of place. Keep a table or a shelf by the door, and put on it all the <u>books</u>, <u>coats</u>, <u>lunches,</u> keys, and other <u>things</u> that need to be taken when the family leaves.

END EXERCISE 2

Another problem for single (mothers') families is keeping the (children's) rooms neat. When a (child's) toys are scattered everywhere, children fight about them more often. Is the truck in the living room (Renita's) or (Robert's) truck? Is that (Lara's) paintbrush or her (brother's)? If the children know each (toy's) place, they will be more likely to put (their) toys away.

END EXERCISE 3

Keeping <u>children**'s**</u> clothes clean is yet another problem for single <u>mothers'</u> families. If the laundry is just the <u>mother's</u> job, then she will be washing her <u>family's</u> clothes all day. Each child must learn to be responsible for clothes. If <u>Tara's</u> shirt is dirty, or if her <u>brother's</u> sheets need washing, the children themselves must be sure to put them in the hamper. Each <u>child's</u> room should have a hamper, and it should also be the <u>children's</u> job to put towels in the bathroom hamper.

END EXERCISE 4

What are the most important foods to eat? Whether (it's) dieters' waistlines or <u>athletes'</u> muscles, many people are trying to change (their) bodies, but (they) need to know (their) bodies' needs. (Everybody) should eat some foods with protein, some with carbohydrates, some with fats. (Your) muscles' strength comes from protein—(it's) found in meats, soybeans, and dairy products. Carbohydrates give (us) quick energy for the <u>day's</u> work. Carbohydrates are found in bread, candy, alcohol, potatoes, rice, and cereal. Fats store energy to meet (your) body's needs at any time. Be sure to give (your) body enough to meet (its) needs. Without any fats, (we'd) be like bunnies without batteries, but (we) only need a few batteries at a time.

END EXERCISE 5   A student's future may not totally depend on her grad**es**, but grades will help when she looks for jo**bs**, so a course in study ski**lls** might make a difference in a student's life. Studen**ts** sometimes don't want to take these cours**es**, because the credits aren't required for degre**es**, but they don't realize that what's most important is having a good GPA. When cred**its** are analyzed at graduation time, a course's grade might be just as important as its cred**its**.

END EXERCISE 6   When Lisa <u>plants</u>ᴾ a garden, she always <u>uses</u>ᴾ lots of fertilizer, just as her mother did when she <u>was</u> a little girl. Her mother <u>told</u> her how to plant, and now Lisa <u>follows</u>ᴾ that advice. Lisa sometimes <u>buys</u>ᴾ fertilizer at a discount store but she also <u>gets</u>ᴾ compost from the city. Last fall the city <u>took</u> all the leaves people <u>had</u> <u>raked</u> and <u>ground</u> them up. Now the compost <u>is</u>ᴾ ready to use. Each weekend, Lisa <u>spreads</u>ᴾ the compost on her garden and <u>digs</u>ᴾ it in. Then she <u>rakes</u>ᴾ it smooth.

END EXERCISE 7   Sean always <u>takes</u> care of his car. He <u>cleans</u> it every weekend, he <u>changes</u> the oil every three thousand miles, and he <u>takes</u> it for a tune-up every thirty thousand miles. The tires <u>take</u> some of his attention, too, because they <u>need</u> to be rotated often so that they <u>wear</u> evenly. Sean's brother <u>Charles takes care</u> of the tires for him, but he <u>charges</u> Sean a small amount. Rotating the tires <u>takes</u> time and tools, Charles <u>says</u>. Time and tools cost him money, so he <u>wants</u> Sean to pay.

END EXERCISE 8   Computers <u>do</u> exactly what we <u>tell</u> them to do. If we <u>tell</u> a computer to type a letter, the computer <u>types</u> a letter. If we <u>tell</u> a computer to sing a song, it <u>will sing</u> a song. Sometimes when I <u>write</u>, I <u>look</u> back and <u>see</u> that what I <u>have written</u> <u>looks</u> really strange. It <u>looks</u> strange because I <u>told</u> the computer to write in capital letters or italics. Of course the computer <u>did</u> exactly what I <u>told</u> it to do. Sometimes my hands <u>write</u> words that my brain <u>knows</u>, and other times my hands <u>seem</u> to write on their own. It <u>takes</u> time to go back and correct these mistakes, but it <u>saves</u> more time, since I just <u>type</u> the corrections, not the whole paper.

END EXERCISE 9   Trying to lose weight <u>has</u> <u>been</u> really confusing. (It also <u>takes</u> a lot of willpower, of course.) Some experts <u>were</u> <u>saying</u> that bread <u>makes</u> you fat and others <u>have</u> <u>said</u> that butter and cheese <u>make</u> you fat. My friend <u>was</u> <u>reading</u> a book that <u>says</u> exercise <u>works</u> best. My friends Marla and Rene <u>were</u> <u>trying</u> to run a mile every day, and Mike <u>went</u> with them. Mike <u>has been</u> <u>losing</u> weight by not eating any dessert, because he <u>had</u> <u>heard</u> that sugar <u>makes</u> you fat.

END EXERCISE 10   We sometimes wonder what would have happened if things in history had been different. For example, things might have been safer for everyone if the nuclear bomb had never been invented. Maybe scientists should think more carefully about what will happen to their inventions. An inventor who make**s** a new way to run cars may think she will help the world, but she may really fin**d** that the new invention can kill many people.

END EXERCISE 11   We'd like to think that the invention of medicine was one way to impro**ve** the world. It is certainly better that no child has to catch polio and that no one even has to get a smallpox vaccination anymore. But now that fewer people die from infectious diseases, there is not enough room for all of us to li**ve** well. We are going to become even more crowded every year. So even the miraculous inventions of a vaccine to cure a terrible disease can turn out to be a problem no one knows how to sol**ve**.

END EXERCISE 12   Sometimes a <u>person</u> <u>wants</u> (to go) on a trip but <u>doesn't</u> know how (to get) to her destination. Now there <u>is</u> a <u>site</u> on the Internet that <u>tells</u> you how (to get) from one place to another. The <u>traveler</u> <u>has</u> (to type) in the city <u>she</u> <u>is</u> leaving from and the place where <u>she</u> <u>wants</u> (to go). Then the <u>computer</u> <u>tells</u> her what route (to take) and also <u>warns</u> her (to avoid) any delays.

END EXERCISE 13   Yesterday Alicia <u>want**ed**</u> some ice cream, so she <u>borrow**ed**</u> her sister's car. Then she <u>remember**ed**</u> that she also <u>need**ed**</u> some money, so she <u>ask**ed**</u> her sister for money. Her sister <u>laugh**ed**</u>. She <u>want**ed**</u> some ice cream, too, so she <u>call**ed**</u> to Alicia: "When you get to the store, please buy two cones! I want chocolate!" Alicia <u>us**ed**</u> the money for the cones of ice cream. She and her sister <u>lick**ed**</u> the cones while they <u>watch**ed**</u> TV yesterday evening.

END EXERCISE 14   If you <u>have</u> ever <u>us**ed**</u> a car with a manual shift, you must <u>have</u> <u>notic**ed**</u> the clutch. In most cars, clutches <u>are</u> <u>locat**ed**</u> on the floor to the left of the brake pedal. When the clutch <u>is</u> <u>push**ed**</u> in, the driver <u>is</u> able to change gears with the right hand, using a gearshift on the floor. Drivers who <u>are</u> <u>us**ed**</u> to this arrangement <u>are</u> sometimes <u>confus**ed**</u> when they <u>change</u> to an automatic transmission. In these cars, there <u>is</u> no clutch, and the gears <u>are</u> <u>chang**ed**</u> by a gear shift that <u>is</u> <u>locat**ed**</u> on the steering column.

END EXERCISE 15   (Did) the weather seem warmer this year? <u>Has</u> it <u>rain**ed**</u> as much as it usually (does?) If you <u>aren't</u> <u>worr**ied**</u> about the icebergs melting, maybe you (don't) <u>worry</u> about the ocean rising near the beach, either. When the temperature of the water <u>has</u> <u>been</u> <u>rais**ed**</u> only a few degrees, the level of the water <u>will have been</u> <u>rais**ed**</u> by a few feet. That<u>'s</u> not much, but it (doesn't) <u>take</u> much to make a difference if you <u>live</u> in Miami or Charleston or Boston.

END EXERCISE 16   Have you ever <u>been</u> <u>charg**ed**</u> a lot for medicine? People who (would) <u>pay</u> $50 to see a basketball game <u>will</u> not <u>pay</u> $50 for medicine, <u>will</u> they? Most people <u>say</u> they (would) <u>think</u> about whether they (could) <u>find</u> cheaper medicine, and then they (might) <u>try</u> to wait a few days. If they <u>had</u> <u>learn**ed**</u> about another medicine that they (could) buy, they (would) buy it. If they hadn't asked their doctor for cheaper medicine, they (might) call the office and ask the nurse.

END EXERCISE 17   Why do athletes receive so much money? When a major league pitcher has ~~brung~~ brought in as much money as Greg Maddux, the fans have ~~gave~~ given him their respect. But other athletes haven't ~~came~~ come as far as he has, and they don't deserve the salary he makes.

AGR EXERCISE 1   One ~~of the biggest problems for students~~ is finding time to keep ~~in shape. In the morning,~~ a student could get up early to run if it is the time ~~of year~~ when mornings are lighted, but ~~in the winter~~ the light ~~of the sun~~ doesn't appear ~~until almost seven.~~ A woman ~~by herself in the darkness~~ has to be a little more careful than usual. ~~After school,~~ a student could go ~~to the gym,~~ but a student ~~with expenses~~ must work. ~~At night,~~ a student ~~with a family~~ makes dinner for them, and a student ~~without a family~~ tries to have a little time to be ~~with her friends.~~ Nevertheless, most ~~of the students~~ I know have found some time to get the exercise they need.

AGR EXERCISE 2   If you want to be healthy, eating and exercising **are** very important subjects to understand. Being a healthy vegetarian requires a little knowledge about the foods your body and your health need. Protein and iron **are** nutrients you must be sure to have. A milk product and a bean dish usually provide enough protein, but iron is more difficult. A vegetarian often must take an iron supplement.

AGR EXERCISE 3   My friends think that getting in shape means getting smaller, period. They don't realize that muscles are healthy and also attractive, even on a woman. Diets and pills **are** a bad way to lose weight, but eating well and exercising are good ways. Even weightlifting can be healthy for a woman. If she **doesn't** want big muscles, small weights help her to be strong. Muscles and bones benefit from weightlifting, because the pressure of the weights makes bones tougher.

AGR EXERCISE 4   Traveling in the summer can be very unpleasant. It can make you want to stay at home forever. Travelers sometimes forget their manners. You have to expect the worst from an airline trip. They can take twice as long as scheduled. When the traveler comes home, he calls the airline to complain, but they don't offer him a refund.

Revision for AGR Exercise 4:

Traveling in the summer can be very unpleasant. That experience can make travelers want to stay at home forever. Travelers sometimes forget their manners. They have to expect the worst from an airline trip. It can take twice as long as scheduled. When travelers come home, they call the airline to complain, but the airline doesn't offer them a refund.

CLR EXERCISE 1   Mathabane was embarrassed because his father insisted on wearing tribal ~~cloths~~ clothes and his friends referred to him as Tarzan. He wanted to live a modern life like his friends did instead of the traditional ~~weigh~~ **way** of life his father ~~wonted~~ **wanted** him ~~too~~ **to**. My parents always ~~wonted~~ **wanted** me to dress like a nice young man but the ~~cloths~~ **clothes** that were in style when I was a teenager were those jeans with ~~wholes~~ **holes** in the knees. Even though I ~~new~~ **knew** that my parents thought that I looked like a hood in those pants, I would change into my favorite jeans the minute I left the house so I would be dressed the way my friends ~~where~~ **were** when I got to school.

CLR EXERCISE 2
When my brother and I would play basketball, I would always ~~loose~~ **lose** because I was shorter ~~then~~ **than** him and he used to block every shot I tried to make. In fact, he would tease me ~~sense~~ **since** he could just stand ~~their~~ **there** and still reach higher than me even when I jumped as high as I could. But now that I'm taller ~~then~~ **than** he is, I'm the one ~~whose~~ **who's** winning every game. ~~Its~~ **It's** nice to get him back for all those games I ~~loss~~ **lost**.

CLR EXERCISE 3
1. S   V
    (By me working very hard) was able to pull up my grade in math.
    By working very hard, I was able to pull up my grade in math.
2. S
    (With them taking care of my children) helped me to have time to study.
    Their taking care of my children helped me to have time to study.
3. S   V
    (In the textbook for my math class) says that calculators are sometimes necessary.
    The textbook for my math class says that calculators are sometimes necessary.
4. S   V
    (With two children at home,) I can't always have time for myself.
5. S   V
    (By knowing about my problems) helped my teacher understand how to help me.
    Knowing about my problems helped my teacher understand how to help me.

CLR EXERCISE 4
Gus said that he'd like to go to the mountains. (answers may vary)

CLR EXERCISE 5
Lara asked Gus when he would be ready to go.

CLR EXERCISE 6
Pollution is everywhere: <u>out in the country,</u> <u>in the city,</u>and <u>also found in our homes.</u> Pollution is caused <u>by manufacturing processeses</u> and <u>we drive cars,</u> as well as <u>to waste many products.</u> For example, when consumers buy broccoli at the store, the vegetable <u>has a wire around it</u> and <u>in a plastic bag, then puts it in a bigger bag with other vegetables.</u> This makes three different wrappings for the broccoli when one would be enough.

Revision for CLR Exercise 6:

Pollution is everywhere: out in the country, in the city, and in our homes. Pollution is caused by manufacturing processes, driving cars, and wasting many products. For example, when consumers buy broccoli at the store, the vegetable has a wire around it, is in a plastic bag, and is also in a bigger bag with other vegetables. This makes three different wrappings for the broccoli when one would be enough.

PUNC EXERCISE 1 On my way home, I passed a group of older women. Since I could see that they were walking slowly, I felt that I should ask if they needed any assistance. One of them thanked me and said she was able to walk but just not very quickly. Although I worried about them, I felt that I needed to get to my destination. When I came back, I saw the same ladies. They had walked just one more block while I had walked five.

PUNC EXERCISE 2 When a single parent is a man, he may have more problems, however, than a woman. My brother, the parent of a three-year-old, has to work and arrange for child care. With these problems, he's just a like a single mother. In the evening, though, it's hard for him to find another single father to share child care or to trade babysitting jobs. Surprisingly, he doesn't know any other single fathers. He knows single women who have children, but they live far away from him.

PUNC EXERCISE 3 The best rituals in my family were those around holidays, birthdays, and vacations. Those were the times when we cooked special food, visited family, and went on trips. We might visit our cousins, they might visit us, or we might all go to the beach together. When we went to the beach with my older cousin, her favorite rituals were singing silly songs in the car, telling ghost stories, and playing card games in the middle of the night.

PUNC EXERCISE 4 We all react differently to feelings of guilt. Orwell and the prison officials may have felt guilty about hanging the man, but they denied their feelings and hid from them by drinking and joking. Other people may use these same ways to hide from guilt, or they may get angry at the person they have hurt. Admitting that you feel guilty is a difficult thing to do, and many people never can take that step. Thinking about your feelings and your reactions is difficult but necessary.

PUNC EXERCISE 5 The interview with the new governor was really boring, wasn't it? First a reporter asked him if he planned any changes in the next year. He said that he would wait and see what happened. Then another reporter asked, "Will you approve a bill to raise taxes?" The governor replied, "Didn't I just answer that?" Would you listen to an interview as boring as that? Why do the sponsors want to pay for boring news? I just don't get it.

PUNC EXERCISE 6 I found a number of good sources for my paper. I'm going to use a novel called The Scarlet Letter, a story entitled "Where I'm Calling From," and a poem called "My Papa's Waltz." The best book I read was The Firm, but I don't think I'll use that. I might also discuss the movie How Green Was My Valley, or another movie, American Beauty. My little sister used the movie Beauty and The Beast for her project.

PUNC EXERCISE 7 Marla went to visit her aunt in Buffalo, New York. Aunt Mary told her, "Don't expect it to be as warm here as it is in California," but Marla thought it would be warm anywhere by Easter. She took her tee shirts and plenty of Levis. Her cousins laughed at her idea of warm clothes, and told her, "You need to go to the mall to get some **really warm clothes**."

PUNC EXERCISE 8 The capital of the United States is Washington, D.C., and the capital of China is Beijing (Sims 156). Beijing is like Washington in some ways and different in others. Beijing once had emperors who "lived in the center of Beijing in a great palace called the Forbidden City" **(Sims 156)**. Washington has the White House and our president lives there now, but the leader of China does not live in the Forbidden City, which is now open to all of the people of China (Sims 156). Washington and Beijing both have many museums and restaurants, and in both you might find exotic ethnic foods, elegant cuisine, and streets where "Pizza Hut competes with McDonald's" (Sims 156).

PUNC EXERCISE 9 (Answers will vary. Students should use quotations and paraphrases from the selection and should punctuate them correctly.)

PUNC EXERCISE 10 A natural disaster in the United States occurred recently when "Mt. St. Helens erupted with ashes." We don't expect volcanoes to erupt so suddenly, because they look so peaceful, "like kindly white-haired grandparents." However, we should be afraid of volcanoes, which can "spew tons of suffocating ashes."

PUNC EXERCISE 11 1. Some results of volcano eruptions include "suffocating ashes, . . . hot mud, or . . . rivers of lava."

2. Three volcanoes that have erupted recently are "Mt. St. Helens . . . in the United States; Mt. Pinatubo in the Philippines and Mt. Fako in Cameroon. . . ."

PUNC EXERCISE 12 1. People who live near a volcano should be concerned because the "eruptions [could] destroy all life in the path of the outpouring."

2. Anyone who was climbing a volcano and thought that it was peaceful should have realized that "this [was] deceptive."

ESL EXERCISE 1 Even though **the** United States is one country with **an** official language which is called English, many people speak **a** dialect which means that they use language differently from people in other parts of **the** country. **A** person who lives in **the** North Carolina mountains might not understand **a** person who lives in **a** northern city like New York. Sometimes **the** misunderstanding is funny, but sometimes **a** big problem can result.

ESL EXERCISE 2 When Adam first arrived **at** this college, he insisted **on** buy**ing** new books. He worried **about** having the books because he hoped **for** a good grade in his classes. When he went **to** the bookstore, he looked **at** many books. He didn't want to leave out any of his courses. He listened **to** the salesman explain **about** new books and used books, and finally Adam decided **on** the ones he needed to buy. While he stood in line, he met a friend who introduced him **to** another student who wanted to sell his used books.

ESL EXERCISE 3 Many people have difficulty living **in** a climate that is different from their home.

They may complain **about** the cold or the heat. If they become ill, they blame their illnesses **on** the climate. They fool **with** the thermostat in their homes. After living in a new climate for several years, they may get used **to** the new climate, and may no longer ask **for** changes in the temperature **of** the office.

ESL EXERCISE 4   Tomorrow we will **be** going to our new apartment. We **own** too much furniture, so we **will hire** a van to help us move. We will **have** worked all day packing things when the van arrives. Last time we were moving, we **tried** to do all the work ourselves. We **have** better judgment this time, even though it **will cost** us more money. However, we **will save** money if the dishes are not **broken** and the chairs **are** not **lost**.

ESL EXERCISE 5   Lee **must hope** to make a high salary, because he will **be** majoring in computer science. He thinks he **ought to** (or **should**) **start** at a salary as high as many people make with several years' experience because he **is going to study** many new aspects of computers. He will be very disappointed if he **receives** a lower salary. He **can** (or **could**) make more than his friends who study art, but they **might enjoy** their work, even if their salaries **are** low.

ESL EXERCISE 6   I **own** a car now, and it **can be** a big responsibility. I **must worry** about gasoline, repairs, and insurance. Because my car **is painted** white, it **gets** dirty very easily. My brother **is teaching** me how to take care of the car. He **drives** to work every day, and he **must park** in a garage, which also **costs** him more money. One day I was driving my car and I **could** hear a terrible sound. I was very worried, but then I saw that the door was open and the seat belt **was dragging** on the road.

Glossary

Abstract—referring to something that cannot be seen, touched, or directly experienced. The opposite is **concrete.** For example, *bicycle* is concrete; *transportation* is abstract.

Academic reading/writing—work done for college classes or other scholarly purposes.

Action words—words in a prompt that indicate what the student has to do to successfully complete the assignment. Also called **key action words.**

Active reading—reading in which the reader pays close attention to the ideas, evidence, tone, and strategies an author uses as well as to his or her own thoughts and emotional reactions to the written piece.

Active voice—verb in which the subject does the action of the verb. For example, in the sentence *I broke the window,* the verb *broke* is active voice, since the subject *I* did the action.

Annotation—notes made in the margin of a reading.

APA—documentation style issued by the American Psychological Association, used primarily in the social sciences such as psychology, sociology, and linguistics.

Argument—reasons and evidence presented to support a position but without intending the audience to change its actions or attitudes. Similar to persuasion.

Argumentative writing—writing that presents reasons and evidence to support a position but without intending the audience to change its actions or attitudes. Similar to **persuasive writing.**

Article—word used to specify a noun (*a, an, the*).

Audience—the readers of a piece of writing.

Auxiliary verb—the word in a verb phrase that may affect tense, aspect, or voice. For example, in the verb *will learn*, the auxiliary verb is *will*. Also called a **helping verb.**

Bibliography—a list of detailed information about a source of words or ideas.

Body—the middle portion of an essay, between the **introduction** and **conclusion,** that contains the main ideas and support for the thesis.

Body paragraph—a paragraph in an essay that contains a main idea and development (examples and explanations) that support the thesis.

Cause and effect—organization in which the writer discusses the reasons for or the results of an event.

Character—a person in a work of literature, and what the reader knows about that the person.

Chronological organization—organization in which the order is based on a time sequence.

Citation—information about a source of words or ideas used in a piece of writing. This information allows others to find it or judge its reliability.

Classification—organizing information into groups and categories to show the relationships, differences, connections, and associations among them.

Cluster map—a visual depiction of ideas in which related ideas are joined by circles or lines.

Clustering—making a cluster map.

Collaboration—working with others.

Collocations—words that are customarily used with other words; synonyms for the words cannot be substituted into the phrase. For example, *pay the bill* cannot be changed to *spend the bill*, even though *pay* and *spend* have very similar meanings.

Colloquial communication—communication intended for an audience the speaker or writer knows well and who does not expect formality or correctness in the communication. An example of colloquial communication is a letter to a friend.

Collusion—accepting or providing help on a piece of writing that incorporates the ideas or words of the helper without proper documentation.

Comma splice—grammatical error in which two complete sentences are joined by a comma.

Compare and contrast—to explore the similarities and differences among related items.

Comprehension—understanding what one is reading.

Conclusion—the last section of an essay that typically summarizes the main idea of the essay.

Concrete—refers to a thing or event that can be directly experienced (seen or touched). The opposite of concrete is **abstract.**

Connecting word—coordinating conjunction or word that connects the previous part of the sentence to the next part of the sentence (*and*, *but*, *or*, *nor*, *for*, *yet*). For example, in the sentence *I told you when I left*, the word *when* is a connecting word.

Connotation—the emotional meaning of a word that goes beyond the dictionary definition; ideas or feelings associated with a word. For example, the dictionary may list *strong-willed* and *stubborn* as having the same definitions, but *stubborn* has the connotation of being negative, while *strong-willed* is positive.

Context—the parts of a reading that surround a word, phrase, or sentence and can make the meaning of that word, phrase, or sentence clearer.

Count noun—name of things that can be counted.

Critical reading—reading analytically. This type of reading includes separating emotional reactions from intellectual ones, understanding ideas presented in a reading, applying these ideas to other situations, recognizing the techniques used by the writer, and evaluating the writer's logic.

Critical thinking—thinking analytically. This type of thinking includes separating emotional reactions from intellectual ones, understanding new ideas, applying ideas to different situations, recognizing the techniques used to present the ideas, and evaluating logic.

Critique—(v) to discuss what a writer attempts to do and how well he or she does it; (n) discussion of what a writer attempts to do and how well he or she does it.

Definite article—the article *the*; it specifies the noun that follows. For example, *the dog* means only one specific dog.

Denotation—the dictionary definition of a word.

Descriptive writing—writing that puts into words how something looks, appears, or acts.

Determiner—like an article; specifies a particular noun or a general one.

Development—clarifying ideas with examples and explanations.

Direct quote—words spoken or written by another repeated exactly as they were originally used.

Documentation—the identification of words or ideas used by a writer or speaker and the source where the words or ideas were found.

Draft—version of a written document.

Drafting—step in the writing process in which the writer produces the first version of a written document.

Editing—a step in the writing process in which the writer makes the writing correct, ensuring that it follows the rules of written English. Editing usually includes making changes in grammar and usage, punctuation, and spelling.

Editing log—a written record of grammar, punctuation, and spelling errors kept by a writer to help him or her learn to recognize, correct, and prevent the errors he or she most commonly makes.

Elements of fiction—the different aspects of a story or novel, including **plot, character, setting,** and **point of view.**

End notes—notes published at the end of a piece of writing to identify a source of information or provide additional information.

ESL—English as a Second Language.

Essay—a format for writing characterized by an introduction that contains a thesis (or point the writer is trying to make) supported by main ideas presented and supported in separate paragraphs and a conclusion.

Evaluate—determine whether a reading is well-written or appropriate for some purpose.

Evocative description—description which emphasizes the emotional aspects of the subject to create a vivid impression.

Example—a specific thing presented to demonstrate what is true about other similar things.

Exemplification—writing that uses extended examples as its major form of development.

Explanation—information given to make an idea or example clear and understandable.

Explication—an essay that explains the meaning of the different parts of a literary text.

Flat characters—simple characters, often minor ones, about whom the reader knows only a few things.

Flowchart—a diagram that shows steps that should be taken to complete a process.

Focused freewriting—type of prewriting in which the writer focuses on one idea and records whatever comes to mind about that idea without regard for correctness.

Focus words—words in a prompt that point you to specific ideas or issues you are to write about; also called **key focus words.**

Footnote—notes published at the bottom of a page to identify a source or provide additional information.

Formal writing/communication—writing intended for an audience who expects standard forms and correctness. Job résumés and research papers are examples.

Format—the placement and presentation of an essay on paper. Format may include line spacing, margins, page numbering, and running headers.

Fragment—part of a sentence punctuated as if it were a whole sentence; also called a **sentence fragment.**

Fragment word—word used to join two sentences that causes a sentence fragment if the two sentences are not joined. These words are also called **subordinating conjunctions** or **relative pronouns.**

Freewriting—type of prewriting in which the writer records whatever comes to mind without regard for relevance or correctness.

Fused sentence—grammar error in which two sentences are written as though they are one with no punctuation mark separating them. Also known as a **run-on sentence.**

Grammar—the rules that govern how sentences can correctly be constructed.

Grammar checker—program in a word processor that indicates possible grammar problems and suggests corrections.

Hanging indent—a group of lines of text in which the first line is flush with the margin and each additional line is indented. (The entries in this glossary are all formatted with hanging indents.)

Helping verb—the word in a verb that may show tense, aspect, or voice, but that does not carry the meaning of the verb. For example, in the verb *will learn*, the helping verb is *will*. Also called an **auxiliary verb.**

Hypothetical example—example that is made up by the author and clearly presented as fiction.

Idea tree—a diagram that shows a hierarchy of ideas (like an outline).

Idiom—a group of words that has a meaning that is different from the meanings of the individual words. For example, the phrase *to throw light on* means to make the meaning clearer, not to physically toss light.

Indefinite article—*a* or *an*; this type of article does not refer to a specific person, place, or thing. For example, *a dog* could be any dog.

Indirect quote—quote that uses some of the original words but paraphrases other words.

Infinitive—the word "to" followed by a verb; for example, *to learn*. It does not have tense.

Informal communication—communication intended for an audience that expects standard form and some amount of correctness but not formality. An example is a newsletter.

Interpretation—a reader's understanding of a reading.

Introduction—the first section of an essay in which the writer makes clear the subject of the essay as well as the ideas he or she will address.

Irony—Basically, irony is a difference between what is said and what is meant. In literature it can be a difference between what the reader knows is true and what the characters think, or a difference between what the reader or characters expect to happen and what really does happen.

Justification—spacing words of type so that the ends of printed lines are even. Left justification means lining up the left sides of lines of print; full justification means spacing words so the left and right sides of each line are even. In academic essays, left justification is preferable.

Key action words—words in a prompt that indicate what the student has to do to successfully complete the assignment. Also called **action words**.

Key focus words—words in a prompt that point you to specific ideas or issues you are to write about; also called **focus words.**

Keyword—an identifying word or phrase used in indexes or to tell a search engine what to look for.

Ladder of abstraction—metaphor describing the relationship of increasingly general or increasingly specific ideas.

Lead-in—the first part of an essay that introduces the topic of the essay and captures the reader's interest.

Listing—prewriting method in which the writer jots down words and phrases quickly to generate as many ideas as possible.

Literary analysis—an essay or discussion that examines different parts of a literary text (such as elements of fiction) and their relation to the meaning of the text.

Main verb—the word that carries the meaning of a verb that consists of more than one word. For example, if the verb is *will learn*, the main verb is *learn*.

Map—a diagram or drawing that lets you visualize the connections between ideas, either in a reading or as a prewriting exercise.

Mapping—type of prewriting in which the writer diagrams the connections between ideas.

Mechanics—refers to spelling, apostrophes, capitalization, underlining and italics, abbreviations, and other details.

MLA—documentation style issued by the Modern Language Association, used primarily in the discipline of English.

Mode—a standard way of organizing written material.

Model—(n) an example you try to imitate; (v) to use an example for imitation.

Narration/narrative writing—writing that describes a series of events or actions.

Narrator—a chartacter who tells the story. The narrator may or may not appear in the story.

Non-count noun—a noun that cannot be counted. For example, *dirt* is a non-count noun; it cannot be counted.

Noun—a word that refers to a person, place, thing, or idea.

Organization—the order in which a writer presents his or her ideas.

Outline—list of ideas found in a piece of writing which shows how smaller, more specific ideas and details are related to larger, more general ones.

Overview—summary; a brief statement that repeats the major ideas included in a longer work.

Paragraph—a group of sentences that are closely related to each other and address a common idea.

Paraphrase—(v) to restate an author's ideas using different words. (n) The author's ideas restated in different words.

Passive voice—verb in which the subject is acted upon. For example, in the sentence, *The window is broken,* the verb *is broken* is passive voice, since the subject *window* did not do the action of the verb.

Peer editing—process in which people who are equals (such as fellow students) help each other improve their writing.

Personal writing—writing produced only for the writer. Examples are journals, prewriting, shopping lists.

Persuade/persuasion—to convince someone through your writing to believe in a certain way or take a certain action.

Plagiarism—using someone else's ideas, facts, or words as if they were your own.

Plan of development—list of ideas sometimes included in a thesis to indicate what will be covered in the body of an essay.

Plot—the events of the story, usually involving some form of conflict, which start at a certain point, are developed, reach some type of climax, and are resolved or settled.

Point—idea a writer is trying to get across to an audience.

Point of view—perspective from which a narrative is told. This perspective can be first-person (using I) or third-person (using he or she).

Portfolio—collection of writing that represents a writer's work.

Portfolio assessment—a method of evaluating a writer's work by judging a group of pieces rather than a single piece of writing.

Prefix—syllable added to the beginning of a word that changes the meaning of the original word. For example, adding the prefix *anti-* to the word *inflammatory* creates a different word, *anti-inflammatory*, which has a different meaning.

Preposition—a word that connects a noun or pronoun to a noun or pronoun that appears earlier in the sentence. Most prepositions will make sense when inserted into the blank in the following sentence: *The airplane flew _____ the cloud.*

Prepositional phrase—a group of words that includes a preposition, the noun or pronoun after the preposition, and any words that come in between the preposition and noun or pronoun.

Prewriting—writing used to generate ideas, may include freewriting, listing, mapping, and questioning as well as research.

Primary research—research in which the researcher collects data and interprets it; also called field research—for example, the experiment a scientist conducts is primary research.

Primary source—information that is studied directly by a researcher. For example, if a student is analyzing an essay by Mark Mathabane, this essay is the primary source, since the student is reading and studying it.

Professional reading—reading done to keep up with new developments in a career field.

Prompt—a statement or question that directs you to write an essay.

Pronoun—a word that takes the place of a noun.

Proofreading—the final step in the writing process in which the writer corrects misspelled words, omitted words, punctuation errors, or typographical errors.

Purpose—reason for producing a piece of writing.

Question word—word used to indicate the beginning of a question. For example, in the sentence *When did you leave?* the question word is *when.*

Questioning—type of prewriting in which the writer asks and answers questions about the topic in an attempt to find deeper and more complicated meanings.

Quote—(v) to use words that someone else has already spoken or written. (n) the use of words that someone else has already spoken or written.

Revision—step in the writing process in which the writer makes big changes to improve thesis, ideas, organization, examples, or explanations.

Rhetorical analysis—an analysis in which the writer identifies and explains the strategies or techniques used in a piece of writing to get a point across or create an effect in a reader.

Rogerian argument—method of structuring an argument in which the writer states the audience's position, shows where he or she finds the position to be valid, explains where the position is not valid, presents his or her own position, and describes the advantages of this position.

Root—the central part of a word that contains the basic meaning.

Rough draft—a version of an essay that is not ready to be submitted.

Round characters—characters that are complex; often they are major characters who change in some way during the story.

Run-on sentence—two or more sentences joined together without the correct punctuation. Also called a **comma splice** or **fused sentence.**

Search engine—computerized research tool that finds resources related to specified words or fitting specified criteria.

Secondary research—research in which the researcher uses someone else's primary research and analyzes it. For example, the newspaper reporter who summarizes the data a scientist collected in an experiment is conducting secondary research.

Secondary source—source that contains a report and analysis of someone else's primary research. For example, if you were writing about Mark Mathabane's essay "My Father's Tribal Rule," this essay would be your primary source and J. P. Myers's essay analyzing Mathabane's essay would be a secondary source.

Sentence boundaries—the beginning and end of a sentence.

Sentence fragment—part of a sentence punctuated as if it is a sentence. Also called a **fragment.**

Sentence-level editing—editing that focuses on the correctness of sentences, including fragments, comma splices, fused sentences, word choice, spelling, subject-verb agreement, and so on.

Skim—to read very quickly, not attempting to read every word but to pick up important words, main ideas, and the organization of a reading.

Simple verb—a one-word verb.

Source—place or person where information and ideas used in a piece of writing originated.

Spatial organization—organization that is based on physical or geographical layout. For example, a paragraph describing a room could be organized from left to right or ceiling to floor.

Spell checker—program within a word processor that indicates words that may be misspelled and suggests alternatives.

Standard English—dialect of English most commonly accepted in workplace and school settings.

Standard written English—dialect of written English most commonly accepted in workplace and school settings.

Story line—the events presented in a narrative, usually in chronological order (that is, the order in which the events happened).

Subject—the word that tells who or what performed the action of the verb.

Subject-verb agreement—the match of number (singular or plural) between a subject and verb.

Subordinating word—word used to join two sentences that causes a sentence fragment if the two sentences are not joined. These words are also called **fragment words** or **relative pronouns.**

Suffix—a syllable added to the end of a word that changes the meaning or part of speech of a word. For example, adding the suffix *-less* to the word *home*

creates a new word, *homeless*, which has a different meaning.

Summary—a short statement that contains the main ideas of the original.

Support—information offered as proof of an idea. Support may be an example, an explanation, a fact, or a quote.

Survey—to look at the overall content, organization, and form of a reading.

Symbol—an object or action that stands for an idea, concept, or feeling.

Technical description—description that provides pictorial data in an orderly manner that reveals the purpose, function, or appearance of the subject. This type of description is most often found in instructional materials and manuals.

Tense—form or part of a verb that indicates the time of an action or condition.

Theme—the central or main idea that lies behind a work of literature; it may not be clearly stated.

Thesis—main idea of a piece of writing.

Tone—the attitude of the writer toward the subject and reader as revealed in a piece of writing.

Topic sentence—sentence in a paragraph that announces the specific subject and focus of a paragraph; also called a **main idea.**

Transition—word, phrase, sentence, or paragraph that connects new information that follows to old information that has already been presented.

Transitional word—word that provides information about the relationship between the ideas that come before and after it.

Usage—the way a word is used; *good usage* refers to using words in generally accepted ways.

Verb—a word that shows action or state of being. Verbs are the part of the sentence that changes when the time of the sentence is changed.

Verb phrase—a verb containing more than one word (the main verb and at least one helping or auxiliary verb). For example, in the sentence *I would have ridden my bicycle yesterday*, the verb phrase is *would have ridden.*

Works Cited page—list of articles, essays, and books used in an essay; included at the end of the essay.

Text and Photo Credits

Index